GEORGE WALLACE

Also by Stephan Lesher

Inside the Warren Court, 1953–1969
with Bernard Schwartz

Media Unbound

Vested Interest
with Charles Lipsen

A Coronary Event
with Michael Halberstam, M.D.

GEORGE WALLACE

American Populist

Stephan Lesher

A WILLIAM PATRICK BOOK

ADDISON-WESLEY PUBLISHING COMPANY
Reading, Massachusetts   Menlo Park, California   New York
Don Mills, Ontario   Wokingham, England   Amsterdam   Bonn
Sydney   Singapore   Tokyo   Madrid   San Juan
Paris   Seoul   Milan   Mexico City   Taipei

Library of Congress Cataloging-in-Publication Data

Lesher, Stephan.
    George Wallace : American populist / Stephan Lesher.
        p.   cm.
    "A William Patrick book."
    Includes bibliographical references and index.
    ISBN 0-201-62210-6
    1. Wallace, George C. (George Corley), 1919–   2. Governors—Alabama—
Biography.   3. Alabama—Politics and government—1951–   I. Title.
    F330.3.C3L47   1994
    976.106092—dc20
    [B]   93-40384
                                          CIP

Jacket design by Lawrence Ratzkin
Text design by Karen Savary
Copy edited by Sharon Sharp
Set in 11-point Baskerville by Pagesetters Inc.

1 2 3 4 5 6 7 8 9-MA-96959493
First printing, December 1993

*To the memory of my best pal and biggest fan,
Jack McDonald, who stands before kings.*

*Who calls me villain? breaks my pate? Plucks
off my beard and blows it in my face?*

HAMLET

*The fault, dear Brutus, is not in our stars,
But in ourselves . . .*

JULIUS CAESAR

Contents

Prologue
The Wallace Evolution

I*NSIDE HIS DARK GREEN*, air-conditioned Dodge sedan, Jesse Jackson was sheltered from the crushing Alabama heat radiating from the asphalt of Zelda Avenue. The car motored beyond Gatsby Street and Malone Court, turned onto Fitzgerald Road, and rolled to a stop at one of the substantial new homes in the fashionable yet aridly treeless Montgomery neighborhood.

It was singularly Southern that a modern suburb would memorialize a past steeped in tragedy—Montgomery's beauteous, gifted, and mentally shattered Zelda Sayre Fitzgerald; her brilliant, successful, and emotionally broken husband, Scott; and several of the glittering, talented, and finally dissolute characters from his jazz age stories. The exercise poignantly evoked the South's insistent inclination to eulogize those who, in fact or fancy, quixotically pursued Lost Causes. And the pursuit of lost causes seemed ironically appropriate to the meeting about to take place in July 1987—a meeting in which the leading black spokesman of the time would try to further his presidential ambitions by courting the consummate icon to the separation of the races, George Corley Wallace.

When Jackson—tall, smiling, confident, and cool despite his dark suit and tightly knotted necktie—emerged from the car, a clutch of waiting reporters and photographers engulfed him. He stuck out his hands, touching everyone around him and intermittently waving to neighbors, some excited, others merely curious. Security guards wedged a path through the enveloping journalists and onlookers who crowded Wallace's lawn, permitting Jackson, one of his aides, two local black ministers, and Wallace's son (Alabama Treasurer George C. Wallace, Jr.) to reach the front door, beyond which the former governor was making ready to meet his guests.[1]

The elder Wallace was looking forward to the meeting, perhaps as a turning point in what had been, until then, a particularly cruel 1987. Having decided some months earlier not to seek reelection to the office he had controlled or dominated since 1963, he had lapsed, in the words of an intimate, Elvin Stanton, into "a depression . . . a sense of dislocation" in the weeks following the inauguration of his successor.[2] Shortly after Wallace announced his retirement from politics, his third wife, the onetime country singer Lisa Taylor, thirty years his junior, filed for divorce after six years of marriage. That "was hard on the governor. He felt very, very lonely," Stanton said.[3] The loneliness was compounded by the relative emptiness of the days after he moved from the governor's mansion and no longer was at the center of the state's affairs. Perhaps even more devastating was the deep and incessant pain that Wallace had borne since being gunned down in Laurel, Maryland, during his 1972 campaign for the Democratic presidential nomination. "The Lord has been good to me," Wallace said, "to allow me to be successful in the secular sense. But, at the same time, the shots I got in Maryland have made life miserable for me ever since."[4]

It was a mark of the times that it did not seem unusual for Jackson, surely the most visible among those laying claim to Martin Luther King, Jr.'s mantle, to be greeted as a political celebrity in a white neighborhood in the city that had nurtured both the Confederacy and the bus boycott. Nonetheless, that Jackson was making this *particular* campaign stop in his quest for the presidency was a breathtaking reminder of the sweeping, constructive changes of which American democracy is capable. Jackson had come to call on the man who, for a quarter of a century, had symbolized the South's harsh politics of defiance—the man who some twenty-five years earlier had stood in the schoolhouse door to symbolize Southern intransigence toward U.S. Supreme Court rulings on, and federal enforcement of, racial equality.

But Wallace and the circumstances had changed. And, as the next hour of conversation between Wallace and Jackson would make clear, Wallace had come to symbolize much more than racial intolerance. He had also come to be regarded as a champion of those whom he had once characterized as "the poor, the lame, and the halt." He was an abiding critic of a big, faceless government that had lost touch with "ordinary folks: taxi drivers, beauticians, construction workers"—and, in this, Wallace had struck a chord of commonality with Jackson's ambition to develop a "rainbow coalition" among blacks, whites, and Hispanics with similar economic needs and educational yearnings.

Jackson neither expected nor received Wallace's endorsement, but the former governor offered him more than mere pleasantries. He approved of Jackson's ideas to "stir up the economy," to seek more than just a service economy. And he admired Jackson's "charisma" and speech-making ability: "If anyone can bridge the gap [between black and white], you can," Wallace said. Jackson, in return, recalled Wallace's "message about challenging the rich and the powerful to be fair" and asserted, "The extremes of wealth and poverty . . . have become a real threat to our stability now." Wallace nodded agreement. But the political kinship between the two men had its limits. Wallace may have denounced the "superrich," but he also was a caustic foe of what he deemed the intellectual elitism of "ultraliberal" academicians, politicians, and bureaucrats. Wallace's insistent messages—anti-Communist, antiliberal, antigovernment, antibureaucracy, antitaxes, antiwaste, antihandouts, anticrime, antibusing—forged a new, xenophobic political consensus among Americans who chauvinistically venerated their nation while fearing and resenting the institutions governing it.

But depending on how Wallace's views were developed and emphasized by various campaigners, he could be described as the political godfather to an odd assortment of bedfellows, ranging from Jesse Jackson to Jesse Helms—and including Jimmy Carter, Ronald Reagan, George Bush, and Bill Clinton. Indeed, every successful presidential campaign from 1968 through 1992 was founded on popular issues and rhetoric first identified and articulated by Wallace. When, in his later years, Wallace would say, "They all saying today what I was saying back then," he wasn't whistling "Dixie."[5] That's why George Corley Wallace was the most influential loser in modern American politics.

■　　■　　■

From his politically insignificant base in Alabama, Wallace thrust himself into the national consciousness in 1963 and, in little more than a decade, turned the face of America around. Almost single-handedly, he moved most Americans away from an open willingness to follow and even make sacrifices for an ever-expanding government toward an overriding determination to shrink government wholesale (except for defense) by shrinking its taxes and nearly all social programs, such as welfare, from which they did not benefit themselves. Wallace also kindled a sense of self-worth in millions of middle-class people who felt used and abused by remote, often arrogant "liberal" politicians, judges, and bureaucrats seemingly concerned only with the very rich or the very poor.

Wallace pulled enough usually Democratic votes away from Hubert Humphrey in several key states to assure Richard Nixon, who had shrewdly co-opted Wallace's "law-and-order" issue, the 1968 presidential victory.[6] And Wallace provided the model for Jimmy Carter's campaign for governor of Georgia, where Carter emphasized his opponent's moderation on segregation, and for president, where the Georgian glorified his antiestablishment credentials ("I'm not a lawyer and I'm not from Washington").[7] The so-called Reagan revolution, in its fierce commitment to free enterprise, military might, anticommunism, and government shrinkage, was in many ways (though not in its tilt toward the rich) a Wallace evolution.[8] George Bush's 1988 campaign, from its first superpatriotic pledge of allegiance to its last racially flecked, scare-tactic TV commercial, seemed more suited to an Alabama country boy politician than to a Greenwich Country Day School patrician.[9] In 1992, starting with the primaries, every presidential candidate of both major political parties professed a special kinship with middle-class Americans, berated the Washington establishment (their condemnation joined, even from that establishment's pinnacle, by President Bush), and responded to race-triggered riots in Los Angeles with calls for law and order. And the broadly supported independent candidacy of Ross Perot, bought and paid for with $60 million of his personal fortune, nonetheless reverberated with echoes of down-home populism—"putting the hay down where the goats can get at it," according to Wallace.

■　　■　　■

Like the imagined indelible bloodstains on Lady Macbeth's hands, the stains of racism on Wallace's reputation will never be washed away. But his success did not derive from any one issue—certainly not from race baiting. Rather, Wallace became the dominant and most important issue maker of his time because of his political instincts, his sense of theater, his overpowering energy and magnetism, and his single-minded dedication to vote getting. Indeed, governance and personal concerns held far less interest for him than pressing the flesh. For George Wallace, the *act* of campaigning was life itself.

When Wallace moved through crowds or took the podium, as the columnist David Broder observed, "there was no more vital or compelling political figure in America."[10] The journalist Marshall Frady, reaching for an explanation, saw Wallace as "a simple primitive natural phenomenon, like weeds or heat lightning. He is a mixture of innocence and malevolence, humor and horror." One person told Frady, "He's simply more alive than all the others."[11]

The narrator in William Kennedy's novel *Legs*, defining the deeply hated, feared, loved, and admired title character, Legs Diamond, might have been describing Wallace:

> Here was a singular being in a singular land, a fusion of the individual life flux with the clear and violent light of American reality. . . . [He was] a moving glob of electricity . . . conveying it to you, generating himself into yourself whether you wanted to receive him or not. You felt something had descended upon him, tongues of fire maybe or his phlogiston itself, burning its way into your own spirit. I liked it.[12]

And, God help me, so did I. He was a man who, for me, symbolized the Mr. Hyde of America's Jekyll-and-Hyde personality. He was the icon of racial segregation, and I had been scorched by segregation in the 1950s—forced from jobs as a reporter in Montgomery, Alabama, and Columbus, Georgia, because of my open support of integration and my involvement with biracial groups. Yet, despite my experiences and personal instincts, I was drawn to this magnetic, enigmatic, thoroughly irrepressible man.

Our paths first crossed in 1956 when I was covering the Montgomery, Alabama, bus boycott for the *Montgomery Advertiser* and he was a garrulous critic of civil rights who, like a young starling flapping furiously for its mother's attention, was trying to gain political notice from his judicial perch in his native Barbour County. I then covered his unsuccessful 1958 campaign for governor, the 1970 gubernatorial run for his political life, and the personal triumphs and tragedy of his 1972 campaign in the presidential primaries.

As he passed from state politics to the national political scene, concomitantly stifling his earlier racial rhetoric (as had many other Southern politicians, from Hugo Black to Lyndon Johnson), I grudgingly began to note qualities in him that, frankly, I respected. I admired his effrontery to reporters during campaign swings by his refusal to play the role of travel agent and tour guide—a role pursued vigorously by other national candidates that ostensibly facilitated coverage but smacked of the subtle seduction that inexorably draws journalists closer to the candidates they are covering. The Wallace campaign had no daily press releases, no printed schedules, no collection of the press's luggage in hotel lobbies prior to departure, no press bus, no press plane, no hotel reservations made by campaign aides to accommodate reporters at the next stop. Journalists were mightily inconvenienced, but there was something refreshingly honest in a candidate who went about his business and left it to the press to take care of itself.

After a Wallace rally one night in Miami during the 1972 Florida Democratic primary campaign, we reporters were told the governor would be attending a fair in Palatka, Florida, the following morning. Once we located Palatka on a map, we determined that it was not possible, via commercial flight and rental car, to arrive there in time to attend the event. Having been assigned to the Wallace campaign by *Newsweek,* I decided to inform Wallace, somewhat testily, that his inept press arrangements virtually assured that his day of campaigning would attract little, if any, national publicity. He looked at me with his half-smile, half-sneer and said, "If y'all want to *be* in Palatka, you'll figure out a way to *get* to Palatka." In fact, we did (working through half the night to establish an ad hoc consortium of publications and networks to charter a plane for the rest of the campaign), just as we found overnight accommodations in a college dormitory in Fort Wayne, Indiana, when our hotel reservations were somehow "lost" and our rooms given over to campaign cronies invited to accompany Wallace on the trip to the Midwest.

At the same time, Wallace, unlike many national candidates, was almost always accessible to reporters. It was a rare day during a state or national campaign when I could not see or talk to him if I expressed urgency. His 1970 campaign for governor, for instance, was a do-or-die contest: if he won, he would regain the political springboard to national politics that he had lost when his first wife, Lurleen, died in 1968 halfway through her term as stand-in governor (Wallace had been prohibited by law in 1966 from succeeding himself); if he lost the 1970 race, his national career likely would be over. Yet, Wallace invited me and four other reporters to join him at his home on the night of the critical Democratic primary vote to watch the returns with him. (He won, of course—but in a breathlessly close contest.)

And he could be funny. "I doubt," wrote David Broder, "that there has been a politician since Huey Long with Wallace's gift for ridicule."[13]

During the 1972 campaign, Wallace, annoyed with barbed editorials aimed at him by a Montgomery, Alabama, newspaper, joked that when he became president he would provide a fitting reward to the offending editorial page editor, Ray Jenkins: an ambassadorship to Chad. Next day, as I was rushing alongside Wallace and his entourage in the lobby of Miami Beach's Fontainebleu Hotel, I mischievously asked the governor whether he had any postelection plans for *me.* He stopped dead in his tracks, looked at my thick, black beard, and said; "I tell you what we'll do with *you.* We'll dress you up in khakis, put you in one of those Barnum and Bailey circus cages, and haul it down Pennsylvania Avenue during the inaugural parade. And when it comes by the reviewing stand, I'll say, 'Looky here, the Wallace administration's done brung back *Castro!*' "

■   ■   ■

Finally, there was the perverse pleasure in seeing him play the contrarian, attacking the smug, superior, self-satisfied posturings of those among the Washington power brokers or liberal cognoscenti whose practices rarely matched their preachings. When he denounced the "highpocrisy" of federal officials (including Earl Warren and George McGovern) who demanded integration in the South but sent their own children to nearly all white private or suburban schools rather than the predominantly black District of Columbia public schools, civil rights supporters were reduced to stuttering explanations about "special circumstances" or "the difficulties of celebrity." When he said there wasn't "a dime's worth of difference" between the major political candidates on key economic and foreign policy questions, the candidates, unable to answer effectively, dodged by saying they wouldn't dignify Wallace's criticism. When he talked about "pointy-headed pseudo-intellectuals who can't park their bicycles straight" or bureaucrats complicating the lives of old people and "taxing hard-working folks to death," he scored heavily with elderly people trying to survive on Social Security payments and with their struggling middle-class children. When he condemned anti-Vietnam demonstrators who shouted down speakers they did not like or agree with (whether Wallace himself or Hubert Humphrey), he posed a conundrum for those who opposed U.S. participation in Vietnam but who cringed at the degradation of free speech and good manners. When he denounced the growing incidence of "crime in the streets" and what he described a breakdown in "law and order," millions of urbanites of all economic strata applauded. To those critics who accused him of using crime and a call for law and order as "code words" to ignite racial antipathy, he had a ready answer. "Code words?" Wallace asked rhetorically. "Well, let me ask *you*: Would *you* walk on the streets of New York at night? Or on the streets of Detroit? No. You're afraid. Everybody's afraid. People in big cities put locks and chains and bolts on their doors and windows. But reporters tell me *they* say they're 'code words.' *They* say . . . *they* say. Who're *they*?"[14]

"They" surely were not the millions who voted for Wallace or for those who carried his message on crime (Richard Nixon, 1968), or who echoed his antagonism to the federal establishment (Jimmy Carter, 1976; Ronald Reagan, 1980), or who articulated the concern that traditional values in America had eroded and needed restoring (Carter, 1976 and 1980; Reagan, 1980 and 1984; George Bush *and* Michael Dukakis, 1988), or that the Supreme Court must return to judicial conservatism (Nixon, Reagan, and Bush), or that the federal government must start paying attention to a beleaguered middle class, balance the budget, reduce waste, and reform welfare (*all* the candidates in 1992).

■ ■ ■

In articles for *Newsweek* and the *New York Times Magazine* in 1972, I conveyed my belief that Wallace's importance to America's changing political climate was greatly underestimated. Despite his anger with me over other observations (such as my insistence that he had indeed practiced racism by any reasonable definition of the word, and that he frequently played fast and loose with facts concerning civil rights legislation), my views on his political significance apparently led him to cooperate fully with me in the preparation of this book. He believed that I would treat him fairly and respectfully. And, evidently, he agreed that a biography by someone whom he had considered something of an adversary would carry greater credibility. He provided more than sixty hours of interviews and recollections, as well as access to his papers. He maintains a guileless belief that anyone hearing him out will accept him at face value.

"They rehabilitated Lyndon Johnson," Wallace once told me, "and he filibustered against civil rights. They rehabilitated Sam Ervin, and he said integration laws were unconstitutional. They rehabilitated Hugo Black, and when he ran for the Senate [in 1926], he had signs saying, Keep Alabama White—Vote Black. Why won't they rehabilitate me?"[15] Wallace asked the question earnestly and often in his final years as governor—years in which he tried as hard to overcome his self-inflicted reputation as a racist as he did the assassin-inflicted pain wracking his body.

My purpose, I explained, was neither to apologize for Wallace nor to lay his tempestuous past to rest, but rather to demonstrate that, despite the dark aspect of his message that attracted the votes of the hard-core haters in America, he can by no means be dismissed as a transient rabble-rouser who hollered "nigger" and then faded away as the nation returned to the mainstream.

The reality is that Wallace *became* the mainstream, moving national campaign rhetoric (and, to a large extent, presidential governance) sharply to the right for the rest of the twentieth century and perhaps beyond. His brilliant 1972 campaign slogan was Send Them a Message—and he became the lightning rod for Americans to shout their "message" (or, more accurately, their "messages") loudly enough to be heard and heeded for the first time in decades.

Wallace offered most Americans an outlet for their pent-up resentments: they were troubled by a faraway war claiming more and more lives and treasure, but galled by the excesses of antiwar demonstrators who seemed to them privileged, pampered, and unpatriotic; they were stunned by incendiary urban riots and stupefied that the government seemed to placate the looters and arsonists; they sensed that the country was losing its moral compass, that drugs and crime and teenage pregnancies and abortion and pornography and strictures on public prayer were symptoms of a society coming apart at the seams.

Yet, there is no doubt that, for many whites, as the historian Dan Carter put it, "moving always beneath the surface was the fear that blacks were moving beyond their safely encapsulated ghettos into 'our' streets, 'our' schools, 'our' neighborhoods."[16] However, if race had been the only factor in the Wallace phenomenon, or even the principal one, then his influence would have declined along with his demagogy after a crazed gunman truncated his national political career in 1972. But long after Wallace had become, in the words of the journalist Roy Reed, "the darling of the Alabama NAACP,"[17] Americans were still sending to the White House men who espoused (during campaigns, at least) his rallying cries to get government off their backs, put welfare loafers to work, help the middle class, and put America first.

Until he was struck by a would-be assassin, Wallace drew consistently larger crowds on the campaign trail than any of his opponents. His supporters at rallies often were transported into quasi-religious (some say near-sexual) rapture. His campaigns were financed by tens of thousands of small donations, making them closer to authentic "people's crusades" than anything in previous political history; he alone among serious presidential candidates was wholly independent of special interests. One of his most far-reaching (and universally overlooked) campaign proposals was to tax foundations and churches while rigidly controlling the explosion of tax-free organizations—an idea that, if implemented in the 1990s, would have been worth an estimated $50 billion a year in new federal taxes.[18] Anyone with the sense to look past Wallace's racist origins— among them the political analyst Kevin Phillips, who perceived in 1968 an emerging Republican majority based on Wallace's propositions—could see that his support extended far beyond the rednecks, yahoos, or freckle-bellies whom the major parties condescendingly conceded to him.

Yet not even Wallace himself, except in fleeting fantasy, believed he could be elected president. Implicit in his rueful hope to be "rehabilitated" was the instinctive recognition that while Americans may grudgingly accept a few pockmarks on their heroes (and sometimes even make moral mountains into molehills, as in the peccadillos of John F. Kennedy or Martin Luther King, Jr.), they prefer their villains intact. The absolute villain enables people to identify a clear dichotomy between the bad guys and the good guys, between "them" and "us." Projecting all evil onto a play's single character makes all the other personae appear relatively honorable. If Iago, Medea, and Richard III are absolute villains, the superficial spectator is free to disregard or minimize Othello's monstrous jealousy, Jason's insensitive self-indulgence, or Buckingham's bloodless ambition. Similarly, if Wallace and his followers are America's bêtes noires in the struggle for racial equality, other citizens can overlook or discount their own complicity in racial discrimination—opposition to school busing, not because of race but to protect the health and safety of children; opposition to affirmative action, not because of race but to avoid inherent unfairness to more experienced workers; opposition to integrating neighborhoods, not because of race but to preserve their ethnic identity and America's vaunted diversity. When "respectable" candidates embraced Wallace's proposals and slogans, they allowed voters to have it both ways—to vote for what Wallace advocated without voting for Wallace. Voters could rationalize their support for law and order, greater local authority, a less activist federal judiciary and bureaucracy, welfare reform, and improved benefits for the (mostly white) middle class without questioning their underlying motives.

■   ■   ■

This story explores the origins of George Wallace's racism, his relentless dedication to his own political advancement, the impact of his ambition on his personal life, and, most important, the influence of his public life on the nation.

But the penumbra shadowing Wallace's story tells us as much about ourselves as it does about Wallace—that while we try to persuade ourselves that America is, in the words of New York's first black mayor, David Dinkins, a "gorgeous mosaic," it often reveals itself as a fire-breathing chimera. Wallace's extraordinary political legacy is often ignored or dismissed precisely because it is too painful to consider. More than any other modern politician, Wallace, in bone-jarring rhetoric shorn of political niceties, forced us to look into an abyss of our own making: the reality that many, if not most, whites did not want to accept blacks as neighbors or schoolmates, whether in Boston or Birmingham, Los Angeles or Little Rock; that most Americans were not willing to put up with urban violence, whatever the underlying economic or social causes; that most Americans really did believe they were being "taxed to death" for frivolous enterprises, mostly involving the poor.

Accepting George Wallace as America's political guru of the final quarter of the twentieth century requires a validation of his assertions. But most of those who set the nation's intellectual and informational agenda have been unwilling even to consider that possibility. In place of honest self-searching that could lead to racial reconciliation (as, ironically, has been occurring in many areas of the South), we are experiencing what the literary historian Alfred Kazin described as "the breakdown of intellectual authority that gives every sexual and ethnic faction the brief authority of anger."[19]

We made George Wallace, not the other way around. As the heavyweight champion Joe Louis said when advised that a challenger, Billy Conn, would use his speed to dodge Louis's powerful blows, "He can run, but he can't hide." Neither can we.

1

"The Good White Families"

MORE THAN MOST people, George Wallace was a creature of his time and place, and his ideas, ideals, and actions reflected his roots in the rural American South and in the loamy soil of Barbour County, Alabama. The land in which he was born on August 25, 1919, was hardscrabble poor, and by age ten, he had been plunged into the unremitting destitution of the Great Depression. His earliest memories reflect the deeply embedded sense of tribulation, victimization, isolation, and poverty to which the South and its people had been heir since the Civil War. "The two things that had the greatest impact on my life," Wallace recalled, "were Reconstruction and the Depression."[1] And the stormy political tradition of Wallace's native Barbour County, where he participated in election campaigns before he was a teenager, confirmed his instinctive knowledge that the path to a better life for himself and his community lay in the acquisition of political power.

Americans, by and large, are not noted for a sense of history. But if any people in the United States may lay claim to being blessed (or cursed) with a concept of their past, it is the people of the South, welded together by a wholly distinctive and fascinating American experience that was at once graceful and violent, creative and deca-

1

dent, pious and evil. The overwhelming Southern experiences, of course, were slavery, war, defeat, occupation, segregation, and black liberation. But through it all, Southerners, black and white, stubbornly dug in their heels against surrendering the perception (idealized, perhaps) of their region's ambience. Like the Renaissance Italian poet Matteo Boiardo, the Southerner "knows that chivalry is an outmoded system, but he wants to keep something of its value, its respect for grace and noble behavior, even while he relinquishes its forms and structures. . . . [He] wants to check the urge to dissolution [that] time seems inevitably to embody . . . [and] recapture the sense of control of oneself . . . that marked life under the old system. He wants to be able to praise something other than the giddy, headlong rush."[2]

For George Wallace, as for most Southerners after the Civil War, his only acquaintance with grace and nobility in a world of want and subsistence was through antebellum history; his only intuition of roots was through an identification with and celebration of his region, his land, his South. Indeed, Wallace, who speaks reverently of people from "old" or "good" families (meaning, invariably, those that reach back to antebellum days), knows little of his own family origins beyond his grandparents.

■   ■   ■

Genealogical material developed by some of Wallace's distant relatives traces his forebears to Scottish Protestants who were encouraged to populate Northern Ireland after William III quelled Catholic uprisings there with a victory at the Battle of the Boyne in 1690.[3] Over the ensuing three hundred years, generations of Wallaces would prosper largely at the expense of subjugated peoples—Irish Catholics, American Indians, and African slaves.

Wallace's first-known ancestor to arrive in America was the adventurous James Huey, a cabinetmaker, who at age seventeen sailed from Antrim County in Northern Ireland to seek his fortune. He landed in Charleston, South Carolina, shortly before the outbreak of the Revolution, joined the brigade of Gen. Thomas Sumter at the outset of the war, and was wounded in a 1780 battle.[4]

After the war, Huey married his childhood sweetheart, Jane Walker, whose family also had emigrated from Antrim County. Their eldest sons, Alexander and Robert, married sisters—Elizabeth and Eleanor McCain—and they moved south to Harris County, Georgia.

The three families—the Hueys, the Walkers, and the McCains—all had emigrated from Antrim County and remained close: they intermarried, named children for each other, and witnessed one another's wills.[5]

Eleanor's first cousin, Richard M. Johnson, became the vice-president under Martin Van Buren in 1837. But as a colonel in the Kentucky volunteers in 1813, Johnson led the charge at the historic Battle of the Thames, in which the most powerful and charismatic Indian leader of the era, the Shawnee leader Tecumseh, was slain.[6] In one of those odd turns of history, Tecumseh's death at the hands of George Wallace's distant kinsman led directly to an opening of the Alabama territory to widespread settlement by whites, including Wallace's forebears.

Tecumseh had organized the tribes of the Mississippi Valley to try to check the inroads of whites into Indian territory.[7] In October 1812, he rode into Alabama to enlist the mighty Creek nation to his anti-American cause.[8] By January, the Creek were attacking white settlements in full force, prompting a corps under the command of Andrew Jackson to move in from Tennessee and attack the warring tribes.[9] In August 1814, following nine months of furious fighting, the surviving hostile Creek were driven into Spanish-held Florida. The tribes that had stayed out of the fighting were nonetheless forced to sign away their homelands.[10]

In 1817 the Alabama Territory was created with William Wyatt Bibb as governor. Heavy migration started almost immediately. One traveler that year encountered Carolinians and Georgians streaming to Alabama—three thousand whites and slaves in "carts, gigs, coaches, and wagons, accompanied by pigs and cattle." "The result," the historian Page Smith notes, "was wild speculation in Alabama lands," with town sites often selling for three hundred dollars an acre or more.[11] On December 14, 1819, Alabama, with a population of 128,000, was admitted to the Union.

In 1836, Robert Huey, then forty-four and a gunsmith, was killed when a gun he was repairing discharged; his widow, Eleanor McCain Huey, forty-one, was left with five sons and five daughters. She decided to leave Georgia for Alabama, where a number of her relatives and other Antrim County families had already settled. The McCains, who had extensive landholdings in South Carolina and a number of slaves, were able to help Eleanor's family.[12] And in 1836, with that old Indian fighter Andrew Jackson in the White House, the government began forcibly transferring Alabama's remaining Indians to reservations in the West. The effect in Alabama was to open up more land for white settlers at more affordable prices; by 1840, the state's population had quadrupled to half a million.[13] Eleanor Huey found a homestead in Barbour County, a large, sparsely populated area bounded by the Pea and Chattahoochee rivers in southeastern Alabama. One of her daughters, also named Eleanor, would marry Allen Wallace, a young man whose family, also originally from Antrim County, had moved from North Carolina to Alabama.[14] While little is known about Allen's apparently unremarkable life, his and Eleanor's progeny would make an indelible impact on Barbour County, on Alabama, and on the United States.

■   ■   ■

Three years after Andrew Jackson had overwhelmed the Creek nation in Alabama, cotton and greed attracted ambitious and adventurous settlers to Barbour County—people whose frequently confrontational and occasionally rapacious behavior established a pattern from which no progeny of Barbour, like George Wallace, could escape entirely. Until the 1820s, the whites of Barbour County posed no threat to the remaining Indians. By 1827, however, the settlers, often using violence, usurped some Indian lands; the chiefs, angered and feeling betrayed, appealed to the federal government for protection.[15]

President John Quincy Adams sympathized with the Indians' plight. He responded to their pleadings by ordering troops into Barbour County to force white settlers off Creek lands, an action that engendered among Alabamians a lasting fear and loathing of federal power. The dispossessed white settlers branded the episode "The Intruders' War," and it fairly described an attitude toward the federal government that Alabamians, George Wallace prominent among them, would hold and nurture for a century and a half.[16]

Whites, however, rationalized their intrusion into Indian lands with arguments such as the "rights" belonging to the "superior" white race, their desire to civilize and Christianize the "savages," and their inherent "expansionist spirit," or what would later be called Manifest Destiny.[17] But despite their antipathy to federal authority, white Alabamians were not averse to asking the government in Washington to arrange a treaty allowing settlers to purchase, rather than pillage, lands from the Indians. The resulting agreement, however, did little to enrich the Indians. They soon found themselves working as hired hands alongside slaves planting cotton and peanuts on land that once had been their hunting grounds. Unlike the slaves, who had been imported in growing numbers, the Indians were paid for their labor. But pay was low and work was hard, and bloody fights frequently erupted between them and the new landowners.[18] Eventually, the federal government invoked the Indian Intercourse Act of 1834 and forced the remaining Creek and other tribe members in Alabama to move west to Indian Territory. By the fall of 1836, all Indians had been removed from Barbour County.[19]

Barbour County had been made safe for those who had moved to the southeastern corner of Alabama like the McCains, the Hueys, and the Wallaces—"the good white families," as another Wallace would say 70 years later (see chapter 2). But the area retained an undercurrent of violence. A local historian wrote of frequent fights "with knives, sticks, straight razors, and guns," perhaps resulting "from the reckless individualism of the Scotch-Irish" who populated the county.[20] George Wallace remembered being told often that his county had a history of "hot-blooded" men.[21] On the more genteel side, the stream of settlers to Barbour County included investors who grew rich as interstate commerce flourished; they built the mansions and established the plantations that created the antebellum Southern legend of widespread wealth and graciousness.[22] Barbour County typified the prewar South in its volatile mix of aristocratic pretensions, rough-hewn individualism, a rapidly growing economy, acute political awareness, and, above all, virulent antagonism to the North.

Barbour County's growing wealth was based primarily on land and slaves; in 1858, the county's 12,000 slaves (of the state's 435,000) were valued at $8 million and outnumbered whites two to one.[23] At the time, the average Southern white male was nearly twice as wealthy as his Northern counterpart; but, with most of that Southern wealth invested in land and slaves, there was relatively little capital to develop industries in the region.[24] One Alabama newspaper pointed out, "[While Northerners] abuse and denounce slavery and slaveholders, we purchase all our luxuries and necessaries from the North."[25] But most Southerners didn't mind; one Alabamian of the time, representing a general view, wrote, "We are willing . . . that the North does our trading and manufacturing. . . . Ours is an agricultural people, and God grant that we may continue so. It is the freest, happiest, most independent, and with us, the most powerful condition on earth."[26] *Us* excluded slaves, of course, but also most whites. Of Alabama's 565,000 white people, fewer than 6 percent were slaveholders, accounting for perhaps one in five or six families. Only thirty-four planters in the entire state owned two hundred or more slaves each. "Cotton brought the major influx of settlers to the state," one chronicler of Alabama history observed, "and set the pattern of its social and economic system. Cotton built railroads, steamboats, and fine mansions. Cotton stratified society, enabling the wealthier planters to live with a grace and leisure seldom equaled in history, keeping the small farmers in hopeless poverty and ignorance."[27]

Twice the percentage of Southern workers as Northern workers were employed in agriculture, but nearly twice the percentage of Northern youth attended school. The two-to-one Northern advantage also held among men distinguished in literature, art, medicine, and education; the ratio was three to one in business, and six to one among engineers. The overriding Southern reaction to this disparity was to dismiss it as inconsequential; typical was a Georgia lawyer and planter who maintained, "[Northerners and Southerners] have been so entirely separated by climate, by morals, by religion, and by . . . all that constitutes honor, truth, and manliness, that they cannot longer exist under the same government."[28]

Those virtues revealed themselves in the South both in the inhabitants' Jeffersonian attachment to the land and in their high regard for the military; even before the Civil War, the proportion of Southerners holding military commissions was twice that of Northerners.[29] Few Southerners doubted their own superior fighting ability. One Alabama member of Walker's Brigade believed that, if it came to it, his unit alone could "whip twenty-five thousand Yankees." And, he boasted, "I think I can whip twenty-five myself."[30]

Inevitably, the institution of slavery tore the Union apart. Describing itself proudly as "the hot bed of the Confederacy,"[31] Barbour County strongly supported secession. Its representative in Congress, Col. James L. Pugh, a Barbour County native, articulated the anti-Northern sentiment of his constituents during a House debate in January 1860, when, according to the Washington correspondent of the *Philadelphia Press*, "he sneeringly reviled the psalm-singing to the Union which takes place in the North, and said it was but the tail of the anaconda." Pugh defended slavery and urged the creation of a separate and united South.[32]

Alabama's fiery politician William Lowndes Yancey advocated reopening the African slave trade, talked of forming committees to "precipitate the cotton states into a revolution," and led the Southern walkout from the 1860 Democratic National Convention when supporters of Stephen A. Douglas opposed a platform pledging a federal slave code for the territories.[33] Within three months of Abraham Lincoln's election, the Confederate States of America "organized itself, drafted a constitution, and set up shop in Montgomery, Alabama."[34] On February 9, 1861, the Confederacy's Provisional Government, in convention in Montgomery, elected Jefferson Davis of Mississippi its president. Davis reached Montgomery on Sunday night, February 17, and was driven by carriage along crowded, festive, torch-lit avenues to the steps of the old Exchange Hotel where Yancey, to wild cheers amid the strains of "Dixie," introduced him: "The man and the hour," he said, "have met."[35]

While Davis and Lincoln, trying to avoid war, exchanged diplomatic parries over who should control Fort Sumter in South Carolina, spokesmen for Alabama were among the most vociferous advocates of going to war. An editor in Wetumpka said the South could not wait for an "overt act" by Lincoln; a Mobile editorial condemned Davis's "do-nothing policy." Col. James L. Pugh, fearing that inaction would strengthen abolitionist sentiment, urged "taking Fort Sumter at any cost." He told an aide to Davis, "Sir, unless you sprinkle blood in the face of the people of Alabama, they will be back in the old Union in less than ten days."[36]

To shore up flagging spirits among nonslaveholders, who composed the large majority of white Southerners, leaders throughout the South drummed a tattoo of white supremacist messages proclaiming that slavery was in everyone's best interest, white and black—messages that would stick in Southerners' minds for more than a century. Georgia's governor, Joseph E. Brown, announced in 1861, "Slavery is the poor man's best government. Among us, the poor white laborer . . . does not belong to the menial class. The negro is in no sense his equal. . . . He belongs to the only true aristocracy, the race of *white* men." Cutting to the heart of the matter, Brown warned that "in the event of the abolition of slavery, they [yeoman farmers] would be greater sufferers than the rich, who would be able to defend themselves."[37]

Barbour County's political consciousness was manifested by its two county courthouses in Eufaula and Clayton—two because "despite its being barely populous enough to justify even one courthouse . . . [one] simply wasn't enough to satisfy its appetite and energies for politicking."[38] Its residents' response to the election of Lincoln and his "Black Republicans" was to hang and burn him in effigy from a gallows erected in a Eufaula square, and to organize numerous military companies, among them the Eufaula Rifles, Eufaula Light Infantry, Pioneer Guards, Clayton Grays, and Louisville Blues.[39] Soon, Alabama, where the Confederacy was born, would send its boys and men to war.

Some, like Adm. Raphael Semmes and Gen. Henry Clayton, proved to be genuine heroes. Semmes terrorized the Northern merchant fleet by capturing or destroying eighty-two ships before his own vessel was sunk.[40] Clayton, who came from the Barbour County town bearing his family's name, commanded Alabama's infantry units in some of the bloodiest battles of the war; he was severely wounded at Stones River near Murfreesboro, Tennessee, and barely escaped death at Chickamauga. In 1866, he was elected judge of Alabama's Third Judicial Circuit and attracted some national notice for his efforts to calm postwar racial and regional antagonism.[41] Eighty-six years later, George Wallace would be elected to that same judicial seat and would gain some national attention for *exacerbating* racial and regional antagonism. The difference, Wallace would maintain in later years, resulted, in effect, from how the North had responded to Clayton's conciliatory pleas: not with forbearance and compassion, but with military occupation and Reconstruction.

■   ■   ■

Deep animosity between Southerners and Northerners was more than understandable. In 1862, at the battle that Northerners called Antietam and Southerners, Sharpsburg, the casualties were four times the total suffered by Americans on the beaches at Normandy on June 6, 1944; more than twice as many Americans died on that one day in 1862 as were killed in the War of 1812, the Mexican War, and the Spanish-American War combined. And the most bracing statistic of all is that more Americans died in the Civil War than the combined total of those lost in *all* other wars the country has fought, including both world wars, Korea, and Vietnam. In all, 620,000 soldiers— 360,000 from the North and at least 260,000 from the South—died in the four-year struggle; there are no figures on how many Southern civilians died as a result of the fighting.[42]

Making matters worse, Southern soldiers returned to a land laid waste by war. In Alabama, farm property valued at nearly a quarter of a billion dollars when the war began now was worth about thirty-five cents on the dollar. Small landowners found it almost impossible to borrow money on their depreciated property, and many had to sell part of their holdings for operating expenses. Many others sacrificed everything they possessed so they could feed their families.[43] Adding insult to injury was the conquerors' treatment of the South's leaders. Jefferson Davis was arrested, imprisoned, and humiliated by being placed in chains. Northern tax collectors seized the Arlington home of Robert E. Lee, and although he had taken a loyalty oath to the Union just two months after Appomattox, Lee's citizenship was never restored and he died disfranchised.[44]

On the whole, however, magnanimity had been the basis of Lincoln's reconstruction policy; to the surprise of Republicans in Congress, his successor, Andrew Johnson, embraced the concept of leniency as well. In the final six months of 1865, with Congress in recess, Johnson allowed the defeated Confederates to form their own state governments if they pledged to obey national laws and deal fairly with former slaves. Johnson also restored to the former white owners lands that had been abandoned in the face of the Union invaders; Congress had directed that the land be redistributed among freedmen.

But the unyielding attitude of former Confederates toward former slaves all but guaranteed reprisals from a vengeful Congress. Andrew Johnson urged, but did not require, enfranchisement of educated and propertied Negroes. In response, the Southern states denied the vote to former slaves and based legislative representation solely on the white population.[45] And enactment of so-called black codes by nearly all Southern legislatures made abundantly clear the South's belief, as one historian put it, "that the black man's preparation for freedom, after two hundred years of bondage, should include an indefinite interlude of peonage."[46] In Alabama and South Carolina, blacks, unlike whites, could engage in no trade or business, except farming, without a license—and licenses, costing up to one hundred dollars, could be withdrawn on complaint. Mississippi's blacks could own property only within towns and cities. In Florida, whippings were authorized as punishment for "misbehaving" freedmen. In Louisiana, black farm laborers were required to enter into year-long contracts that, among other things, imposed fines for refusing to obey any "proper" order.[47]

Southerners vigorously defended black codes as "desperately needed" for "the ending of idleness and crime and the return of freedmen to the fields." In the account of Reconstruction that

George Wallace and his contemporaries studied when they were in high school in the mid-1930s, the writer Claude G. Bowers maintained that "the intent of the Black Codes of the South [was] for the most part a conscientious and straightforward attempt to bring some order out of the social and economic chaos," and that the laws were "faithful on the whole to the actual conditions with which they had to deal."[48] Wallace, who remembered the book vividly and regarded it highly (though conceding "it might be a little extreme"), also remembered being taught, quite correctly, that at the very moment Radical Republicans in Congress were denouncing the black codes in the South, a number of Northern states (including Connecticut, Illinois, Maine, New York, and Ohio) maintained restrictive laws directed at blacks, some of them as harsh as those in the South.[49]

Perhaps, as W. E. B. Du Bois suggested in his *Black Reconstruction in America*, a single Southern legislature's extension of the franchise to literate and propertied blacks would have led Radical leaders to modify their harsh policies in the face of Southern intransigence.[50] As it happened, the black codes were the last straw—or the final excuse—for the Radicals to move against the South with what Southerners regarded as a terrible, swift sword. Over President Johnson's veto, the Republicans passed the Civil Rights Bill of 1866 and sent the Fourteenth Amendment to the states for ratification. When Southern legislatures refused to ratify the amendment, Congress placed Southern states under the yoke of military rule. The military authorities required the occupied territories to adopt new state constitutions that, among other things, granted former slaves the franchise and, for the most part, barred former Confederates from holding office.[51] Congress thus ushered in a decade in which the dispirited Southern states became the "Solid South, more firmly united in defeat than it had been during the brief span when it claimed independence."[52]

Most Southerners of the time—and their progeny, including George Wallace—viewed the period of military occupation as cruelly harsh. In reality, as one chronicler wrote, "the administrations of even the worst of the military governors were more high-handed and pettily autocratic than brutal." Nonetheless, for Southerners, "the unforgivable reality was not that military rule was unbearably strict or unreasonably long but that it had been imposed at all; what mattered was that the bayonets had glittered among a people who had complied, whatever their reluctance or misgivings, with the Lincoln program for Reconstruction, only to find that the rules had changed as the political balance shifted."[53]

Military rule (but not military occupation) ended in most states in 1868. By then, however, the federal Reconstruction Acts had placed the South's political structure firmly under the control of Radicals who, in practice if not in law, hand picked governors, legislators, judges, tax collectors, and postmasters. Many of the jobs were lucrative political plums that lent themselves to graft and payoffs.[54] Legislators were bribed to sell railroad holdings to speculators for next to nothing. An Alabama editor of the time complained that "inside the state capitol and outside of it, bribes were offered and accepted at noonday and without hesitation or shame," which helped "to drive capital from the state, paralyze industry, demoralize labor, and force [the] best citizens to flee Alabama as a pestilence, seeking relief and repose in the wilds of the distant West."[55]

Bribes and frauds notwithstanding, Reconstruction's greatest dollar cost to the South came from enormous (and frequently wasteful) legislative spending on new programs fostered by the novel and, for the time, somewhat extraordinary notion that social responsibility was a function of government. These programs involved not only the establishment of free public school systems for white and black children but also the construction of insane asylums, hospitals, roads, and bridges.[56] Despite extravagances and often misused funds, America's first integrated governments—legislatures comprising blacks, carpetbaggers, and scalawags—were experimenting with social programs that state governments in the North had never before financed. But these largely noble experiments were undertaken at the expense—financially and psychologically—of Southern white landowners, who saw the American republic's traditional rights and values being overturned by what seemed to them a motley collection of blacks, Northern usurpers, and Southern traitors.[57]

■   ■   ■

To the world, the end of the Civil War marked a new unity "best defined," as one writer observed, "by the change in number of a simple verb. In formal as in common speech . . . 'the United States *are*' became 'the United States *is*.' "[58] But to Southerners, the end of the war—the War between the States, as most Southerners would refer to it for at least the next 125 years—meant encroaching federalism and government involvement in theretofore private sectors.

Thenceforth, at least well into the heyday of George Wallace, Alabamians would distrust and often detest the federal government, or at best, view it with deep misgivings.

In Barbour County, the defeated whites told their children and grandchildren horror stories of Reconstruction that would burn into their memories: black constables "paraded the streets," administering "powers of sovereignty" over whites; federal troops carried off or killed farm animals, burned cotton, and plundered stores and homes; once-wealthy families were reduced to penury; local leaders were arrested on trumped-up charges; most whites were prohibited from voting in local and state elections while blacks, induced by threats, money, or liquor, were permitted to vote two or three times each for candidates sympathetic to the Radicals.[59]

"My father used to tell me," George Wallace recalled in a 1986 interview, "that poverty and illiteracy in the South resulted from the way we were treated after the war when they burned the schools down, burned the railroads, just desecrated the South. We are just now overcoming the effects of that tyranny and of the iniquitous Thaddeus Stevens [the Radical Republican leader in Congress], who wanted nothing but vengeance."[60]

Retaliation was not long in coming. In 1869, the Ku Klux Klan, which three ex-Confederates had formed in 1866 in Pulaski, Tennessee, made its appearance in Barbour County, terrorizing blacks who supported Radical officeholders; the Klan's guerrilla-like night rides, which enjoyed widespread community support, made its control by federal troops virtually impossible.[61] Alabamians even temporarily defeated Radicalism in 1870 by electing a Democratic governor, Robert Lindsay. But his administration proved even more corrupt than those of his postwar predecessors, and the disgusted citizenry allowed the Radicals to win back the State House in 1872.[62] In 1874, however, largely because of an outburst of deadly violence in Barbour County, Alabama effectively rid itself of federal intrusion for the next eighty years.

At the center of the storm was Elias M. Kiels, a shrewd Barbour County politician who, after the war, acquired property and wealth by working closely with the occupying forces. In 1870, Kiels became judge of the Third Judicial Circuit. He endorsed lenient voter registration procedures, thus helping to expand black suffrage.[63]

Kiels was branded a scalawag by his white townsmen, and resentment against him was fanned by Barbour County's White Man's party.[64] What was called Barbour County fever raged out of control on election day in 1874. As crowds of blacks and whites grew at the polling places, so did tensions.[65] At the Eufaula precinct, someone fired a shot, and general rioting erupted. As many as one hundred blacks died and many more were wounded; some whites were wounded as well, but none was killed.[66] Ignorant of the carnage, Kiels was supervising the vote counting at a precinct eighteen miles away. A gang of vigilantes from the Eufaula riot broke into the precinct and started shooting. When the smoke cleared, Kiel's 15-year-old son lay dead. Kiels, whose life was spared when he agreed to forfeit his house and property, was put aboard a train to Texas the next day without being permitted to attend his son's funeral. A few months after the election, in which the Democrats swept state offices, charges against the boy's murderers were dropped.[67]

Throughout the South, Redeemers, "with systematic use of terror . . . intimidated black voters and forced the restoration of white supremacist rule. . . . [T]he North backed away from a commitment to equal protection under the law, and the federal government failed to contain the violence."[68]

Before long, a black Southerner named Henry Adams would lament, "The whole South—every state in the South—had got into the hands of the very men that held us slaves."[69] After four years of war and a decade of occupation, Alabama had regained its political autonomy. But it was entering a period of unremitting poverty and hardship for most of its people, white as well as black.

Planters needed to replace slave labor but had no money for wages, so blacks and dispossessed whites agreed to work the land for a share of the crops they produced.[70] Banks and other lenders who viewed cotton as a sure cash crop discouraged landowners from diversifying. As a result, most Southern landowners remained almost totally reliant on cotton. A surfeit in the world's cotton supply wiped out many landowners and sharecroppers alike.[71]

The farmers' plight started a domino effect that impinged on small merchants and small banks throughout the South and Midwest.[72] And the South not only had endured conquest and occupation but now was being pillaged by an all-powerful Wall Street. Thus "began the forging of a new class structure to replace the shattered world of slavery—an economic transformation that would culminate, long after the end of Reconstruction, in the consolidation of a rural proletariat composed of the descendants of former slaves and white yeomen, and of a new owning class of planters and merchants, itself subordinate to Northern financiers and industrialists."[73] From his earliest days, George Wallace felt himself as one with the South's "rural proletariat." And as Wallace grew, so did his driving desire to rid the region of what he considered a Northern-imposed inferiority.

"After the war," an eminent Alabama historian has observed, "the South was in the same position that an underdeveloped country is. It needed capital to develop [and] had to turn outside the South for that capital. When you do that, you lose some degree of control over your destiny."[74] An example of outside control that particularly rankled was the railroads' establishment of discriminatory freight rates; goods shipped from Mobile to Chicago, for example, would carry a shipping charge nearly twice that of goods shipped from Chicago to Mobile. Later, when Northern industrialists gained control of the nascent steel industry in Birmingham, they instituted a pricing plan in which Birmingham steel, though cheaper to produce, cost Southern customers the same as Pittsburgh steel, plus a freight charge as if the steel had been shipped from Pittsburgh. "Pittsburgh Plus," as it was called, meant higher profits for the Northern owners while diminishing Southerners' economic benefits from a nearby source of steel.[75] (Discriminatory freight rates would remain in force into the 1950s and were regularly attacked at Democratic Party conventions and in the Alabama legislature by the young state Rep. George Wallace.)[76]

Planters and merchants, buttressed by the growing influx of corporation executives and lawyers, formed a so-called Bourbon dynasty that controlled most Southern states until late in the century. The Bourbons "were mannerly aristocrats or pretenders to aristocracy who had proved their mettle in war and Reconstruction."[77] But, as a class, they callously enriched themselves at the expense of the impoverished white majority. As an example, railroad lobbyists, powerful under Radical leaders, proved equally at home with Bourbon Redeemers. In Alabama, railroad speculators who had received extravagant state aid from the Radicals continued to benefit from advantageous financing under the first Redeemer governor, George S. Houston.[78]

Poor white Southerners, numbed by invasion, defeat, occupation, and the specter of blacks' equality, remained in an unnatural political alliance with Democratic Bourbons for two decades. By the 1890s, however, the mass of farmers in the rural white South had joined the agrarian political movement that was sweeping large segments of the country.[79] For one brief, shining moment, in the early part of the decade, Populists in the South, typified by Georgia's Tom

Watson, succeeded in welding the farmers, rural poor, and urban workers of both races into an unstoppable political force capable of wresting control from the Bourbons so that the masses could enjoy civil liberties and economic security. But the Bourbon leadership struck back at men like Watson by stoking inherent embers of racial fear and hatred among whites until most Populist spokesmen were politically and financially ruined.[80] Impelled by ambition (or, in Watson's case, perhaps madness), Southern Populists regained political success only when most of them turned to a fierce racism. When Watson died in 1922, he was described as "a tough old champion of the working man and of the oppressed everywhere, so long as they were not black or Catholic or Jewish."[81]

Watson set the pattern for political success in the South: populism for the whites; effective disfranchisement, economic servitude, and social separation for the blacks. It was an established and accepted pattern in Barbour County when George Wallace was born just three years before Tom Watson's death. And not long before he died, Watson, writing of his failure as a national candidate, could have been talking of Wallace half a century later:

> Consider the advantage of position that [William Jennings] Bryan had over me. His field of work was the plastic, restless, and growing West; mine was the hidebound, rock-ribbed, Bourbon South. Besides, Bryan had no everlasting and overshadowing Negro Question to hamper and handicap his progress; I had.[82]

2

"A True Blue Southerner"

I N *1 8 9 1,* just as Alabama and other Deep South states were imposing rigid and repressive segregation on blacks whose interests had been abandoned by the federal government,[1] George Oscar Wallace, just twenty-three years old and freshly graduated from a two-year medical college, decided to seek his fortune in the tiny Barbour County town of Clio.[2]

Actually, Clio was more of a settlement than a town: established as a trading post a decade earlier, Clio in 1891 comprised thirteen families with only one school-age child, six wooden stores, a cotton gin, and no physician. Settled by railroad crews and, later, by blacksmiths and cotton warehousemen, it was a promising place for a young, inexperienced, minimally trained doctor to set up shop, settle down, and raise a family that, twenty-eight years later, would include his first grandson, George Corley Wallace.[3]

Although Clio was only a few miles from the place where he had been born in neighboring Pike County, George Oscar Wallace had, figuratively, journeyed leagues to get there. His grandparents, Allen and Eleanor Huey Wallace, had farmed just south of Barbour County. Their only son, George H. Wallace, married and acquired some land in the Buckhorn community of Pike County. George Oscar—or

Oscar, as he came to be called—was born there in 1868. When Oscar was only fourteen months old, his father died, and the baby and his widowed mother were forced from their farm. Though family members sustained them as best they could in impoverished postwar Alabama, mother and son lived hand to mouth. Oscar's mother, a deeply religious woman, assured him that God would provide. Oscar, who accepted his mother's faith, also believed strongly in the delivering power of hard work. As would his grandson George, in similar circumstances half a century later, Oscar financed his own education—first, by working his way through State Normal College in nearby Troy, from which he received a teaching certificate, and then, after teaching for a year and scrupulously husbanding his earnings, by working weekends to finance his two years at Alabama Medical College in Mobile.[4] Clio, rather than the more populated, more competitive, more gentrified Eufaula, seemed right for a pious, penniless, but enterprising young doctor.

Though barely forty miles due west of Eufaula, Clio at that time represented a new kind of South—at least to those trying to create, from the ashes of war, a South less dependent on class than on individual industry. Eufaula had been a quintessential antebellum town of Bourbons, plantations, and slaves. Clio, on the other hand, was created *after* the war—and then, by landless laborers prepared to live by thrift and their own sweat. Eufaula, sitting on a bluff overlooking a broad bend of the Chattahoochee River, clung to its memories of grandeur. Clio, perched on the less prepossessing, more prosaically named Pea River, evoked dreams of a populist yeomanry.

Eufaula's residents, who celebrated graceful mansions and exquisite manners, were considered worthy enough to warrant the town's inclusion on Jefferson Davis's triumphal and emotion-laden tour in April 1886 to commemorate the silver anniversary of Sumter. Despite the economically depressed times, Davis's visit occasioned formal balls and seated dinners.[5] Clio, on the other hand, was a town whose people (including its postmaster) did not wear shoes in the summer and pursued such favorite pastimes as playing dominoes, doing "heavy courting," and getting drunk on Saturday afternoons. Not until November 1973 did Clio celebrate the "largest and most colorful gathering of people in the town's history"—a homecoming honoring its favorite son, Gov. George Wallace; the festivities featured a fish fry and a chicken dinner at $2.50 a plate.[6]

As Clio grew (there were 326 residents by 1900), farmers with small holdings that surrounded the town hauled in their cotton for ginning. White townsfolk lived in relative affluence in Clio's center. Most blacks resided in bottom land on the outskirts of the town, renting three- and four-room clapboard, metal-roofed houses built in clusters so that their occupants could share communal wells.[7]

Clio was the sort of postwar community whose people believed that "the much heralded breakup of the plantation system . . . [would] produce the yeoman farmer,"[8] the sort mythologized by the poet and onetime Alabama schoolteacher Sidney Lanier: "Small farming means . . . meat and bread for which there are no notes in the bank; pigs fed with homemade corn . . . yarn spun, stockings knit, butter made and sold (instead of bought); eggs, chickens . . . products of natural animal growth, and grass at nothing a ton."[9]

Lanier's was "an inspired vision," the historian C. Vann Woodward commented, representing "everything that the Southern farmer was *not* and *had not*." "But," Woodward continued, "the vision was made of the tough stuff of myths and was destined to endure. The new myth fulfilled the old Jeffersonian dream of an independent yeomanry, self-sufficient lords of a few acres."[10]

Oscar Wallace embraced the myth with a vengeance. Deprived of land in his youth because of the premature death of his father, he believed deeply that land would provide him with ultimate security and freedom. From that perspective, he viewed his profession as a means to an end—the acquisition of land. He set up a medical practice and a pharmacy in a wooden building at one corner of a lot on which he eventually built his residence—a large white frame house in downtown Clio that would later become the home of his eldest son, George Corley Wallace, Sr., the future governor's father. As his medical practice grew, Oscar earned enough to buy "considerable acreage," which he devoted to cotton and to the first commercial pecan orchards in Barbour County.[11]

He hired sharecroppers to work the land, thus unwittingly helping to create, as one historian put it, "a new peasant class of tenant farmers under the crop lien system."[12] Indeed, Oscar's tenants were among the nearly 60 percent of Alabama's farmers who did not own the land they worked, most of them "poor whites . . . in bondage along with Negroes."[13]

But larger economic forces were not what Oscar had in mind as he established himself as a doctor and landowner; he simply was building security to benefit the family he intended to start one day. That day came in 1896, after five years in which his medical practice and gentleman farming consumed all his time and consideration. Indeed, he took his first "vacation" that year—a trip to New Orleans for what he described as a "postgraduate course" at New Orleans Polytechnic Institute, though in what discipline remains unclear. Then, at age twenty-eight, he married a childhood acquaintance, Mary McEachern. A year later, she gave birth to George, the first of their seven children.[14]

In 1906, Oscar's health failed, and he relocated to the mountains of North Carolina for several months, leaving his family behind. Whatever his problem, he returned in 1907 to resume practicing medicine and doing business in the growing Clio community.[15] By then, there were several churches, a few establishments built of brick, a factory for mixing and bagging guano, a nascent telephone company, a hotel opposite the depot, and a school with more than a hundred children and four teachers, one of whom taught music.[16] Oscar predicted continued progress for his town:

> There is nothing that makes a permanent fixture [so much] as to be surrounded by a good agricultural soil, cultivated in small tracts by thrifty, energetic people. . . . We live in the white part of the county of Barbour, and the good white families are finding good homes among clever, neighborly people; hence, our population is always increasing.[17]

Mary McEachern Wallace died in childbirth in 1915 after bearing her seventh child and fourth daughter. Her grief-stricken husband decided to leave the big white house he had built for himself and Mary, and was lured to the nearby town of Bakerhill.[18] Its residents, desperate for a physician, made Wallace an irresistible offer: the option to buy a house with a number of luxuries absent from his Clio home, including a generator for electric lights, indoor running water, and the only private telephone in the community.[19] Dr. Wallace had a telephone installed in his Clio office, too, but had difficulty persuading patients to use the newfangled device, despite its potential value in saving lives.

■ ■ ■

Oscar's eldest son, George, went off to Methodist Southern College in Greensboro, North Carolina, for two years and became one of the few people in Clio with any formal education beyond high school.[20] At Methodist Southern, he had his first brush with politics, a passion he later would pass on to his children. It came when he was named a national representative of Sigma Alpha Epsilon fraternity, a position requiring his participation in the fraternity's national convention and election of officers in New York City. (A photograph of him in tie and tails attending the fraternity's formal banquet at the Waldorf Astoria Hotel remained a lifelong cherished possession of his son George C. Wallace.)[21] It may have been the high point in the life of a man who would be, as one writer put it, "totally absorbed in a ceaseless, savage, losing cat fight with life . . . a frail man, outrageously harried by sickness and failure."[22]

Sickness for George C. Wallace, Sr., had started when he was an infant; due to a bout with pneumonia, doctors had decided to remove a lung. By the time he was an adult, as a son would recall, "one side of his chest was caved way in. He also had this terrible sinus trouble. They finally had to carry him to Montgomery and cut out a piece of his skull right above his eyes. . . . It left a real bad looking place there . . . a dent in his forehead. . . . He suffered so much from it, it affected his heart. When I was old enough to drive, I'd take him up to Montgomery every time his head swelled up again."[23]

George C. Wallace, Sr.'s sickliness excluded him from conscription in World War I; in 1917, when twenty-seven other Clionians (ten of them black) went off to war, George left college and returned to Clio. He moved into the house that his father, now living in Bakerhill, had built more than twenty years earlier, and he assumed responsibility for the family's farm holdings.[24] He also struck up a correspondence with a pretty, trim girl he had met in a railroad terminal a few months earlier. She was Mozelle Smith, a Florida native who, on the early death of her father, moved to Mobile to live with an aunt and attend a female academy that emphasized music and manners for young ladies.[25] After completing high school and taking some secretarial training, she decided to move to Barbour County and enter into a formal courtship with George.[26] As the doctor's son, George could offer Mozelle property and relative security, but by most accounts, he was an irritable and often feisty man—likely because of his almost constant physical discomfort. Still, in 1918, they married. Years later, their second son, Gerald, would recall that Mozelle "was thrown into a totally different environment when she came to marry my father. There was some dissension over drinking; my mother couldn't stand drinking, and my father was known to get his share."[27]

The next year, on August 25, 1919, their first son, George Corley

Wallace—or George C., as he would be called from then on in his home county—was born. His brothers, Gerald and Jack, followed about two years apart; a sister, Marianne, was born ten years after Jack.

Also in 1919, Oscar Wallace married a Kentucky schoolteacher, May Wyatt, whom he had met while indulging his love of owning and training show horses, an extravagance he apparently developed after his first wife's death.[28] Mother May, as she would be known to her stepgrandchildren, was a warm, good-humored woman—a moderating balance to the doctor's pious Methodism, regular Bible reading, and (unlike his eldest son) repugnance toward tobacco, whisky, and politics.[29] Oscar needed May's comforting cheer on more than one occasion, such as when he bought a mare that, he had been told, had been bred to a Tennessee walking horse. "I don't believe I ever saw him so excited in all the time I knew him," Mother May recalled. She continued:

> After the mare foaled, Doctor Wallace would go out every
> evening when he was through with his duties just to look at it
> for a while, and then come back in the house and talk all
> through supper about how he couldn't wait for [it] to get
> grown. Even after a few people began to remark how the colt's
> ears seemed to be growing unnaturally fast, seemed to be
> awfully long already, he kept on talking a little more and a
> little faster about it. Finally, one evening a close friend of his
> came by [and] told him, "Doctor, I don't believe I've ever
> seen a Tennessee Walking Horse with ears quite like that."
> And Doctor Wallace said, real quiet, "No." His friend said,
> "Doctor, I believe that is actually a mule out there." And
> Doctor Wallace said, "Yes, I suppose it is." He had finally
> admitted it, and he was sick for months afterward.[30]

Dr. Wallace remained a notoriously easy mark. His daughter Eleanor recalled her brothers remonstrating with their father for "lend[ing] money to the sorriest people in the county" without charging interest and for failing to press patients for unpaid bills. His grandson, George C., said the doctor "gave all his money away to anybody who would go to be a minister. People beat him out of his money, saying they would be setting up a ministry, and really didn't."[31]

Nor was he parsimonious with his affections, especially with his eldest grandchild. Perhaps he was consciously filling a void that he had helped to create by saddling his son George with responsibility for the heavily mortgaged farms. From sunup to sundown, George supervised tenants and, when he was not ill, worked the land hard himself. George C.'s earliest recollection of his father was watching him plow behind a mule. "I was sitting on the ground in a hot sun," he said, " . . . watching him walk away from me, following that mule, going away so far, so far, and I didn't think he was ever coming back."[32]

The special bond between Oscar and George C. was forged when Gerald was born. George C., then two years old, was staying with his grandparents and refused to go home. "Dr. Wallace tried to take him back," Mother May remembered, "and then an hour or so later returned, driving up the street with George still sitting there beside him. It sort of stayed like that ever after. George stayed with us more than . . . the others. He liked to crawl into bed with his granddaddy in the mornings, and he'd ride around with him on his calls to Bakerhill and everywhere."[33]

The house calls, made in his grandfather's Model T Ford, gave George C. an early picture of the poverty and suffering beyond his relatively affluent early years. Most often the doctor and his grandson visited tenant farmers' houses, which were shutterless, windowless, and sometimes, partially roofless. "I can see him now," George C. recalled of his grandfather, "giving morphine shots to people with cancer."

> He would take a spoon of bucket water from the well and light
> a kitchen match and hold it under the spoon until the water
> began to bubble and then it became distilled. Then he would
> put a morphine tablet into the water and it would dissolve.
> Then he took the syringe and sucked it up into the syringe
> and gave the patient a shot.[34]

■   ■   ■

Home and childhood in Barbour County for George C. and his brothers suggest comparisons with Tom Sawyer, a boy equally at home in the respectable, rural, small-town milieu of his Aunt Polly as he was in the parentless, self-reliant world of Huck Finn.

George C.'s mother played the piano at Clio's Methodist church and insisted on regular attendance by her husband and children at

Sunday services. But it was Oscar who drilled his grandchildren in religion. Whenever they stayed with him (which, in George C.'s case, was most of every summer and many weekends during the school year), he followed a daily routine of reading biblical passages, commenting on them, and listening to each of the boys recite Bible verses from memory. George C., unprepared one morning, quickly thought of an old Sunday school dodge: he said he knew the shortest verse in the Bible and triumphantly quoted John 11:35—"Jesus wept." His grandfather nodded warily, accepting the ploy—and then sternly informed George C. that it was a one-time evasion. From then on, Oscar would assign George C. a daily verse to memorize.[35]

From his youngest days, George C. would test his limits. At age three, while riding in his grandfather's Model T, he crawled to the floorboard and pressed the accelerator to the floor with his hands. Oscar managed to yank George C. away and stop the car just before it careered off the road. At five, he insisted on fishing in the collected rainwater of an unused dipping vat built during a statewide effort to rid cattle of an infestation of ticks. Oscar forbade his grandson to climb up on the vat's lip, from which he could fall and drown; he assured George C. there were no fish in the vat, anyway. "But I didn't believe that," George C. said. ". . . So I got me a string, and bent a pin to make it look like a fishhook and dug some worms up for bait, and I slipped off . . . and went fishing in the dipping vat." A tenant spotted George C. and reported him to Oscar, who rushing to the scene, pulled his grandson to safety, and gave him "a real good spanking"— enough that George C. "didn't fish in the dipping vat anymore."[36]

When he reached school age, George C., like most other rural boys whose parents' days were filled with farm chores, was left to roam freely. He and his friends—black and white—swam, hunted snakes, and played games with balls patched with tape. They climbed pecan trees and leaped from the branches into soft, freshly turned earth. They built tree houses from which they suspended ropes so they would swing two and three at a time. In ginning season, George C. and his brothers helped pack raw cotton into a wagon by jumping up and down on it as it was tossed up by tenants. In the fall, Carlton McInnis, a black handyman who did odd jobs for the Wallaces, took the boys hunting for squirrel and rabbit.[37]

In third grade, George C. first entered the political arena. A classmate named Louise Sconyers nominated him to be class president (Wallace never forgot her name—nor would he forget the name of any of his political supporters for any office). It was only the third

grade, but Wallace also remembered that he "ran without opposition—which is the best way to run."[38]

Jack Wallace recalled those early years "as the most fun I ever
had."[39] George C., on the other hand, remembered those days as,
alternately, "a great time" or "boresome" and "monotonous."[40]
Two events, however, would make the rest of his life anything but
"boresome:" his participation, at age nine, in his grandfather's campaign for probate judge, and his exposure, at age ten, to the turbulence and hardships of what would come to be called the Great
Depression.

■   ■   ■

As the United States plunged into the economic abyss of the 1930s,
George Wallace, Sr., despite his relatively privileged status in Barbour
County as "the doctor's son," lost whatever hope he may have harbored of presiding as a gentleman farmer of sorts over a conglomer-
ate of thriving cotton plantations. Although loans from the Federal
Land Bank enabled him to retain three tenant farms of about 150
acres each, his creditors, themselves failing and desperate, foreclosed
on most of the heavily mortgaged land his father had ceded to his
care.[41]

In addition, the house his father had built some thirty-five years
earlier, into which George, Sr., and Mozelle had moved after their
marriage, was falling into disrepair. Its wood shingles were rotting,
the front porch sagged, the roof leaked badly, and much of the
wallpaper had come loose. The high ceilings helped keep the house
cool in summer but increased its draftiness in winter; with no heating
system of any kind, the family had to huddle around fireplaces to
keep warm. Until 1927, when the town installed a cold water pipe
directly to the house's kitchen, where the Wallaces installed their only
indoor spigot, family members took turns drawing water from the
well and carrying the buckets into the house.[42]

Indeed, the town itself seemed to be taking on the haggard,
shorn look borne of hard times. In the late 1920s, a wood-planing
mill had been established south of Clio, providing jobs and an infu-
sion of relative prosperity into the local economy. In order to sate the
mill's ravenous appetite for raw material, however, the graceful for-
ests surrounding Clio were stripped bare in an indiscriminate quest
for lumber. Acres of felled trees were stacked to dry for finishing at
the planing mill. In what appeared to be an ill omen of the era, the

mountains of wood sweepings and sawdust that soon surrounded the mill like slag heaps around a Welsh coal-mining town caught fire spontaneously in 1930. As one longtime resident recalled, "The smoke from the smoldering mass pervaded the atmosphere of the town, particularly when the winds blew from the south and east." Fifteen years later, coincidental with the end of World War II, the fire finally burned itself out.[43]

In 1930, the number of Alabama sharecroppers had grown to about 100,000; only just over 40,000 farmers in the state, including George, Sr., owned the land they worked.[44] The writer James Agee described the life of Alabama's tenant farmers, black and white, as "a relentless cycle of work, debt, and more work."[45]

With foreclosures rampant, scores of people in Clio lost their farms and homes—and when the Clio bank failed, many lost their savings as well. Merchants and others who faced destitution often resorted to arson to collect insurance; local sympathies usually assured that those who were caught were punished lightly, if at all. Even the authorities generally winked at bootlegging, unless it spawned mayhem and murder, as it did on occasion in Clio. At least four people were killed in Clio in internecine warfare among bootleggers. Although those responsible were never apprehended, violent incidents invariably prompted local authorities to raid some stills or make a public show of destroying kegs of illegal whisky.

The elder George Wallace's determination to retain some of the family's land, even though it meant piling debt on top of debt, afforded some short-term benefits. He owned enough farm animals to provide the family with a steady supply of meat, milk, and eggs. Mozelle's large garden, plus the fruit trees on the Wallace property, assured a cornucopia of vegetables and fruit which, when canned, would last through the year.[46] Also, George, Sr., with the help of politically connected friends whom he had cultivated over the years, got part-time state jobs as an agricultural consultant. The pay, though low, was enough to keep the family afloat during the Depression.[47]

The relative good fortune in which the Wallaces found themselves did not, of course, obviate day-to-day hardships. George, Sr.'s response to daily difficulties contrasted sharply with his wife's. Mozelle's premarital picture of a secure, upwardly mobile life had been shattered by the Depression, but her quiet stoicism and resourcefulness masked her disappointment. She put her musical training to profitable use by teaching piano at fifty cents a lesson to those few children whose parents could afford to pay. She found countless ways to economize, such as fashioning shirts for her sons from inexpensive cloth. And she saw to it that her children contributed to the household by doing farm chores, gathering and selling pecans, collecting discarded soda pop bottles for a nickel a case, and collecting cottonseed from surrounding farms and delivering it to the railroad siding for a commission of fifty cents a ton.[48]

George, Sr., on the other hand, grew more and more bitter. He tended increasingly to blame the North for his own problems and the problems of a South devastated by the boll weevil and the Great Depression. "My father was a true blue Southerner," George C. recalled. "My daddy told me that Southerners couldn't be elected to national office because [Northerners] looked down on us." More than that, George, Sr., passionately condemned the North for overtly impoverishing the South with discriminatory regulations like Pittsburgh Plus; the result, he maintained, was the South's inability to educate its people, dooming the region to continued destitution. "I was about ten or eleven years old," George C. said. "He talked to me until he died about those kinds of things."[49]

He also talked about how state and local political power could influence national politicians and then, perhaps, make things better for everyone. The elder Wallace's plunge into politics started in 1926 when he supported the gubernatorial campaign of Bibb Graves; seven-year-old George C. helped hand out pro-Graves leaflets.[50] In 1928, George, Sr., persuaded his father, then sixty, to run for the influential office of probate judge in Barbour County. Oscar did not want to run, especially against the incumbent, a distant relative named Huey Lee. And, his daughter Merle said, he "didn't like politics. It was too crooked."[51]

But George, Sr., was adamant. He argued that if Oscar was elected probate judge, his resulting political stature would improve business and job opportunities for the whole family. In addition, George, Sr., asserted, Huey Lee had taken to drinking and occasionally would browbeat citizens.[52]

Ultimately, Oscar agreed to run but refused to campaign personally; becoming directly involved in the process, he said, might sully his reputation for honesty. George, Sr., willingly assumed responsibility for the campaign, which he knew would involve extensive vote-buying by each candidate's supporters—a time-honored Barbour County practice that would continue even through George C.'s run for the state legislature in 1946.[53] On election night in 1928, nine-year-old George C. was permitted to view the official vote tabulation in the clerk's office at the Clayton courthouse, and he later described that as "the most exciting night of [his] life, being with the grown-ups and politicians till almost midnight." It was doubly exciting because his grandfather won.

After the victory Dr. Wallace publicly boasted, "See, you can run for probate judge without putting out money to buy the office." George, Sr., who had worked hard for his father's victory and apparently resented his naïveté, decided to set him straight. "That's absurd," he told Dr. Wallace. "There was plenty of money on both sides." The older man was shocked. He said he could not accept a position that had been obtained illegally and he proposed resigning the office immediately after the swearing-in ceremony. "Papa," George, Sr., said patiently, "you're doing a bad thing, talking like that. Now, quit talking about no money being in the race, because there was and always will be as long as people are as poor as they are." Oscar backed down, saying that he would accept the post after all. He would atone for the vote buying in his behalf—"repay the people," as he put it—by being a good, attentive, and hardworking judge. But, he pledged, he would refuse to run again when his six-year term expired in 1934. Indeed, he did not, even though he probably would have run unopposed. This time, George, Sr., failed to persuade him to change his mind; Oscar even backed Huey Lee's unsuccessful attempt to recapture the office.[54]

George, Sr.'s financial circumstances, if not his deteriorating health, improved somewhat after his father's election, because Oscar's position helped him secure a part-time state job. And in 1930, the death of an eighty-five-year-old uncle brought an unexpected boon. Will McEachern, the brother of Oscar's deceased first wife, had amassed an estate of thirty-five thousand dollars—a small fortune for the day—as a traveling salesman for a Montgomery hardware manufacturer. McEachern died without leaving a will, so the money was distributed equally among his only blood relations— the seven Wallace children to whom his late sister had given birth.[55]

The five thousand dollars that George, Sr., received as his share fulfilled a modest dream. He told the family, "We're going to build us a house that don't leak, pay some of the bills around here, and go back to trying to sweat it out somehow—but I'm going to live in a house that don't leak before I die, and one with inside plumbing fixtures." He tore down the house his father had built, salvaged as many of the original timbers as he could, and bought bricks for $8 a thousand. He then hired an out-of-work contractor who charged him

$700 to construct a small brick-veneer house. In all, it cost $3,500. George, Sr., used the rest of his inheritance to pay off some of his accumulated bills and even make a small payment to the Federal Land Bank.[56]

In 1931, George, Sr., was named to a delegation to call on Gov. Franklin Delano Roosevelt at his office in Albany, New York, to discuss the formation of delegate slates in Alabama in support of FDR's presidential aspirations. For weeks before the visit, the excitement in the Wallace household was palpable. George, Sr., with a loan from his father, bought a three-piece suit for the occasion.[57]

When George, Sr., returned from New York, he was ecstatic. "Son," he told George C., "I think things are going to start to change quite a bit. . . . It's not going to be done in just a few years, but it can and will be done."[58] The enthusiasm for FDR was infectious. The prospect of his election, George C. recalled, "electrified everybody, especially the children. Things were so bad, the children could never hope for a toy or good clothes—just something to eat."[59]

Mozelle tried to assuage her own children's concerns. "We are not poor," she would say. "We have plenty to eat, and we have screen doors." But George C. was not convinced. Not only were his clothes ragged, but when he was ten, his mother could not afford to order from the Sears Roebuck catalogue a cowboy suit that George C. had wanted desperately for Christmas. "She couldn't get the $1.27," he remembered. "We didn't have the money, and she said, 'Maybe Santa Clause can bring it.' But Santa came and went and didn't leave the suit; he left a note saying he had given out of cowboy suits and maybe he could bring me one next Christmas." But he never did.[60]

George C. may have believed (along with most others of his generation) that FDR could produce results that Santa could not. In any event, he eagerly participated in the 1932 campaign, helping his father to gather signatures and contributions for the Dollar for Roosevelt Club. On election day, the Barbour County vote for FDR fell about a hundred votes short of being unanimous. "Now," George C. said, "our confidence increased. . . . And in school—right there in the middle of the Old South—we all learned to sing 'The Sidewalks of New York.' "[61]

Ironically, while the early agricultural programs of FDR's New Deal helped to undermine the harsh sharecropping system, they also inflicted still greater hardship on those who lived off the land. The historian E. Culpepper Clark wrote that "the crop-lien peasants began a great outmigration from the lands they had farmed. The agribusiness policies of the New Deal made it abundantly clear that farming was not to be an enterprise of the simple folk but an entrepreneurial venture in capitalism."[62] By paying farmers to plow under 35 percent to 40 percent of the cotton crop to raise prices, the government, "in confronting the paradox of want in the midst of plenty . . . did away with the plenty."[63]

Still, there was the sense that "the poor people in the South didn't feel it as bad in the country as they did in the cities because they could raise something to eat. As George C. remembered, "In our little town, people always had a garden, a cow, and a hog to eat. But if you lived in a city in the tenement section, there was no place to get food unless you stole it. . . . But we didn't have any money, and it was hard to do anything that cost money."[64]

In the poor, rural South, boys came early to what the writer Marshall Frady called "the implacable realities of life." When he was twelve, George C. experienced the death of two of his chums—a baseball teammate named Easterling whose neck was broken when he was thrown from a truck on the way to market with a load of peanuts; and the painful death from sunstroke of his constant playmate and next-door neighbor, Terrell Douglas Rush. The boys had been swimming and playing throughout a hot summer day in 1931; when they returned home, Terrell Douglas collapsed, went into convulsions, fell into a coma, and died.[65]

In Clio, as in the rest of the rural South, families bathed and dressed their dead for burial. Clio's barber shaved dead men and prettied the hair of dead women. Bodies were laid out in plain pine boxes and were "buried quickly," George C. recalled, "especially in the summertime because decomposition set in very fast." "One funeral I went to," he said, "the smell [of the corpse] was evident throughout the church, and it made many people sick."[66]

If young George C. was neither oblivious to nor spared by the hard realities of life, he nonetheless rode through them with a single-minded determination to make the most of his youth. Despite his small stature, he participated aggressively in physically challenging sports; despite his size and occasional imperiousness, he was popular and sought after by girls. And in almost everything he did, he seemed naturally to assume the role of organizer, leader, and chief activist.

At thirteen, he organized a baseball league among youngsters in four Barbour County towns—Clio, Clayton, Louisville, and Brundidge—that were separated by distances ranging from seven to seventeen miles. Whenever the Clio team played away from home,

George C. would persuade some Clio resident to lend him a car so he could drive the entire team to the game. He was too young for a driver's license, but he drove "very slowly"—not only to avoid a wreck but also to conserve the gasoline, which the boys could not afford to buy. George C. acquired the necessary fuel on Sundays when the filling stations were closed and the pumps were unattended. He would go from station to station, draining into a can the small amounts of gasoline that remained in each hose.[67]

Although he weighed only 120 pounds, George C. quarterbacked the Barbour County High School Yellow Jackets. In George C.'s senior year, the team won eight of its nine games and would have been undefeated if, in the final game, a penalty had not nullified a touchdown. George C. was elected team captain in that year.[68]

■　■　■

But even more revealing of the man to come—the willingness to expose himself to risk in the pursuit of personal achievement; a combination of confrontational scrappiness with a frank recognition of his own limitations; and a shrewd ability to assess an opponent's strengths and weaknesses—was George C.'s devotion to boxing, a pursuit that brought him Alabama's Golden Gloves bantamweight championships in 1936 and 1937.

Wallace was a fighter from his earliest years and, as his brother Jack recalled, "had as hard a lick as a little man could hit."[69] Jack would know; George C. and his brothers scrapped frequently. "Daddy got tired of us fighting each other all the time, so he bought us gloves."[70] They may have softened the blows, but they did not stop the fights—fights that George C., at age seven, would go to great lengths to stage. He arranged with John Horne, a seventeen-year-old part-time night telephone operator, to peer into the Wallaces' house from a top-floor room at the nearby telephone exchange. "There in the wide front hall," Wallace recalled, "we kids would have a boxing match. The telephone was hanging on the wall, and we would go at it until John rang the telephone, signaling the end of a two-minute round. Then, after one minute of rest, he would ring it again and we would go back to boxing. We'd keep it up until we were so exhausted that we had to quit."[71]

George C. whipped himself into shape, running at least two miles a day; he rigged a punching bag by filling a burlap sack with sand and suspending it from the limb of a chinaberry tree outside his house.[72] In junior high school, he persuaded the basketball coach to allow him and a friend, Wilbur Knight, "to slug it out with each other in a three-round fight there on the basketball court during the half." The coach ended the half-time bouts after a few fights because "the players would not go sit down and rest and listen to the coach; they wanted to see the boxing match."[73]

At fifteen, George C. was the youngest entrant in the 115-pound division of a statewide tournament, his first taste of organized boxing. George C. easily defeated his first opponent, a sixteen-year-old, then outlasted the favorite, a nineteen-year-old named Tommy Dinton, to earn the right to fight for the state title in Birmingham. In the championship fight against Aaron Franklin of Tuscaloosa, a high school senior, George C. battled gamely and lost a close decision, despite having broken his thumb in the first round. The injury and subsequent surgery did not stop George C. from playing football the following fall, or from entering the Golden Gloves boxing tournament in January 1936. He won the Alabama championship in the 115-pound class that year and followed it the next year by winning the crown in the 120-pound division. In both years, George C. lost close decisions in the Southern regional Golden Gloves contests.[74]

George C. nonetheless pursued his amateur boxing career into college and even the army during World War II. In his last fight in organized competition, he won the title in his weight division at the Air Corps' Lowery Field in Denver in 1943.[75]

Even in fighting, politics was not far from George C.'s mind. In college, when he was a candidate for president of the University of Alabama's prestigious Cotillion Club, he worried about being knocked out. If that occurred, he fretted, "it would hurt me politically. I could see the headlines: 'Alabama's Hard-Hitting Wallace Knocked Cold.' "[76]

Boxing provided an obvious release for George C.'s seemingly limitless energy. It also offered reassurance not only that he could be knocked down and still bounce back but also that, as in the Southern myth, glory could arise in defeat. But fighting also illuminated a darker side of George C., a side edged with the violence that lurked as an almost breathing presence behind the mannerly veneer of the South in general and of Barbour County in particular.

Not all of George C.'s fighting was done in the ring, and some of his brawls were ferocious. Once during his university days, he was at a nightclub when someone came up behind him and pushed his face into the table, apparently to settle some old score. George C. "came up and caught him around the waist, pinned his arms to his back, and knocked him through a screen door." Later, his attacker and a group of friends tracked George C. to a café and stormed in. "I grabbed a butcher knife," Wallace remembered, "and jumped over the table and said I was going to cut his throat if he came any further." When the police arrived, the melee ended.[77]

While he was a member of the state legislature, George C. mixed it up with a drunk, off-duty Alabama state trooper at a picnic near Montgomery. George C., intervening when the trooper slapped a woman, grabbed the trooper's tie and tightened it against his throat, then beat him to the ground. When onlookers intervened, they took some blows; during the wrangling, George C. fell awkwardly and broke his right arm. The combatants were persuaded to seek treatment at a nearby clinic, but the fight broke out again when the bloodied state trooper cursed at George C. His right arm immobilized in a cast, George C. nonetheless leaped to his feet and landed a crushing left hook that knocked the trooper down a flight of stairs.[78]

Other fights occurred during George C.'s often-tempestuous youth, fights he claimed were unavoidable; they indeed seemed inevitable in the hard-drinking, apparently violence-prone company he kept. Even his fighting style revealed George C.'s propensity for calculation. Against bigger men, he would burrow low, protecting his head, and pummel opponents in the stomach. Then he would pin their arms and push them backward until they fell to the ground with him on top. "That was about the only way I could fight a bigger fellow," he said. "Otherwise, a big fellow could break my neck with one punch." As a nondrinker, he also knew that he held an advantage over challengers who had consumed one too many, whatever their size.[79]

But if fighting for George Wallace was a metaphor for the bare-knuckled realities of life, life itself could be mastered only through politics—the only sure route to power and respect for himself and his region.

As George, Sr.'s health worsened and his business ventures grew more precarious, and as George C. realized as a teenager that anything he gained in life would be wrought through his own unceasing exertions, George C.'s interests became more and more focused: he would find out how politics was played, and he would become its master.

■   ■   ■

George C.'s official entry into the real world of politics came early and, unsurprisingly, at the instigation of his father. George, Sr., arranged for a political ally to nominate George C. to become a page in the Alabama Senate for the term starting in January 1935, when the boy would be seven months shy of his sixteenth birthday.[80]

Becoming one of the senate's four pages, however, required election by the senate itself on the opening day of its term. Since paging was a full-time job, a page had to miss a semester of school and subsequently take extra classes. But paging paid two dollars a day in the midst of the Depression, so dozens of politically connected young people eagerly sought the positions. Few of the candidates, as it turned out, were as active or as eager as George C., who had more in mind than the money. Unlike most of his competitors, he viewed the post as a means to acquire future political connections, and that was where he gained his competitive edge.

His father drove him to Montgomery two nights before the opening session, booked a room at the historic Exchange Hotel (where Jefferson Davis, seventy-four years earlier, had been greeted by adoring throngs on the eve of his inauguration), stayed overnight with his son, and, after wishing him good luck, returned to Clio.[81] But George C. took to the game as if the rules had been written for him. While most of the other candidates were content to rely on their senate sponsors to campaign in their behalf, Wallace's father had instructed him to seek face-to-face meetings with the senators. Wallace persuaded a desk clerk to give him a list of senators staying in the hotel; the night before the vote, Wallace went from room to room canvassing his electorate. Early the next morning, he rushed to the capitol to try to find those whom he had missed the night before or who were not staying at the Exchange.[82] In all, he located 27 of the 35 senators; he received commitments from 23 and "probables" from 2 others. To win, a candidate required an absolute majority, or 18 votes; if more than four candidates won a majority, victory would go to those receiving the most votes. As it was likely that there would be several no-shows among the senators, 20 to 25 votes surely would make Wallace a shoo-in.[83]

He scurried to the visitors' gallery as the vote was about to begin, and his heart sank. Surveying the floor, he observed that several of the senators who had pledged to support him were not present. When his name was called, he kept a careful tally. Before long, he realized it would be close. One of his "probables" had come through, but so far, 2 who had committed to him had voted nay. In addition, he was pretty sure that 3 of those who had pledged their votes to him were absent. Now there were only 4 more senators to be polled, and Wallace counted 16 ayes. Of the 4 remaining, 1 was a commitment and 1 a "probable." The committed senator came through; that made 17. Then came the "probable," Sen. Vernon St. John. Almost offhandedly, he responded, "Aye." Wallace did all he could to restrain himself. "It was one of the happiest moments of my young life," he recalled.[84]

Nonetheless, shortly after being sworn in as a page, Wallace braced those senators who, after having pledged their votes to him, had voted nay. To a man, they blamed their errant votes on memory lapses; there had been so many candidates, they had forgotten the name of the boy to whom they had made the commitment. Wallace accepted the explanations but filed the information away in the same political memory bank with the name of the girl who had nominated him for class president in the third grade. Twenty-seven years later, in Wallace's first campaign for governor of Alabama, he reminded those same surviving senators that they now had an opportunity to make up for their unfulfilled commitments; he recalled, "Some of those that did not vote for me [for page] turned out to be my strongest supporters when I ran for governor." And even when he ran in his last campaign twenty years after that, in 1982, Wallace remained well aware that among the senate nay-sayers of 1935, "the one still living [had] supported" him.[85]

Wallace moved out of the Exchange Hotel and into a decaying boardinghouse owned by the widowed mother of a boy who had been selected by the Alabama Senate to be one of its two messengers during the 1935 session. The house was infested with roaches, and Wallace usually had to share his room with an itinerant worker, or someone "down and out who was hunting a job [or] an old drunk who carried on." But room and board was eighty-seven cents a day, and that left him enough of his daily salary of two dollars to open a savings account at the First National Bank.[86]

Wallace learned the legislative process—how the committee system worked, how many readings were required before a bill could be acted on, how a bill was enrolled or engrossed, how many days it took to pass a bill.[87] But most of all, he learned politics—which committees were most powerful, which senators were independent, which were in the governor's pocket, which were influenced by vested interests. He provided extra service to his home-county representative, Chauncey Sparks, and that service would pay off years later when Sparks became governor.[88]

On key issues such as prohibition, he learned the importance of counting votes and identifying who was voting which way. After repeal of the Eighteenth Amendment, Alabama voters had decided nonetheless to retain prohibition in their state. Gov. Bibb Graves's administration, responding to pressure from big-city businessmen, tried to push through a controversial local option bill allowing individual cities and counties to permit whisky consumption. On the day of the vote, an important "wet," Sen. Shelby Fletcher, was nowhere to be found, so Lt. Gov. Tom Knight, seeking to ensure an administration victory, directed Wallace to search for Fletcher in downtown Montgomery.

Wallace looked everywhere he could think of—restaurants, private clubs where the knowledgeable could down an illegal snort, hotel lobbies—but without success. At the Exchange Hotel, he encountered Sen. Dave Waldon. "Senator," Wallace said breathlessly, "they're getting ready to vote on the local option bill, and Governor Knight sent me to find Senator Fletcher. Do you know where he is?" "No, son, I don't," Senator Waldon replied. "But I need to get up to the capitol right away myself so *I* can vote." The local option bill was approved by a narrow margin—but, as it turned out, no thanks to Wallace. Knight called Wallace on the carpet, informing him hotly that Waldon was a "dry." Not only had Wallace failed to deliver the vote the administration wanted, but he inadvertently had added a vote to the opposition. Young Wallace learned his lesson and remained a careful nose counter ever after.[89]

But Wallace's upbringing, personal experiences, and instincts already had taught him *another* important lesson—the lesson of survival through hard work and opportunism. Ignoring his mother's advice to find a tutor in Montgomery who could keep him current with his high school class, Wallace instead found someone to teach him typing and shorthand; he quickly capitalized on his investment by selling his services to three senators. He pulled in extra money from tips he received for running special errands for senators, concentrating on the more open-handed members. During one legislative recess, Wallace hired on as a chauffeur to an aging senator-cum-physician, driving him to his home district to visit constituents and patients—a task that Wallace had performed more than once for his own grandfather.[90]

Through high school and college, Wallace—wiry and trim, with the dark, surly, heavy-lidded good looks of an Elvis Presley—dated a parade of girls he remembered as beautiful and flirtatious. Many of them he "followed throughout the years," a predilection that likely contributed to strains between him and his first wife, Lurleen, early in their marriage, and that figured in a messy divorce from his second wife, Cornelia (see chapter 6 and Epilogue).[91]

His personal appeal, powers of huckstering, and ease in almost any setting were more apparent when, during summer breaks from school, he traveled widely selling magazine subscriptions. In May 1937, after graduating from high school, Wallace landed his sales job through the good offices of Elton B. Stephens, a former Clionian in his mid-twenties who had become an early proponent, and subsequent beneficiary, of the idea that competing magazines could nonetheless profit from cooperative efforts to sign up new subscribers.[92] Wallace and five other young men ranged through Kentucky and North Carolina in a Model A Ford selling magazines as diverse as the *Saturday Evening Post*, the *Ladies' Home Journal*, and the *Delineator*, a monthly collection of sewing designs. Wallace made $150 and won a prize as the operation's "rookie of the year."[93] Little wonder. In eastern North Carolina, he helped tobacco farmers tie and hang racks of tobacco leaves in their curing bins, an arduous and dirty job; farmers usually showed their appreciation by taking at least one subscription. When cashing a check in central Kentucky, Wallace aroused the suspicions of a bank teller to whom the name George Wallace meant the proprietor of the local hardware store; George C., after properly identifying himself, went directly to look up his namesake, laughed over the mix-up, sold him a subscription, and started a correspondence that continued until the older man's death some years later.[94]

The following summer, Wallace was placed in charge of a crew of his own and was assigned an expanded territory ranging from North Carolina and Kentucky into Tennessee and parts of the Midwest. It was a major challenge, and he encountered some problems: he was bitten by a dog in Benton Harbor, Michigan; lost his wallet containing forty-two dollars in a movie theater in Paducah, Kentucky; and came down with intestinal flu in a town near the Cumberland Gap. But he and his crew rarely went hungry: he bartered subscriptions for laying hens, and scavenged plums and berries from bushes growing near the roadsides; one of his crew occasionally acted crippled to beg for money or food. For the most part, however, the team survived through sheer salesmanship, though its techniques would not always have withstood scrutiny by the Better Business Bureau. They sold subscriptions to barely literate country people by claiming they represented a government agency—"the Bureau of Recapitulation and Matriculation"—that required every American to read something in addition to the Bible and the *Progressive Farmer.* Wallace did double duty by working as a waiter at a dinner party in return for the hostess's purchase of a five-year subscription to the *Ladies' Home Journal;* he then shamelessly proceeded to sell subscriptions to the *Saturday Evening Post* to two of the dinner guests. Once, a woman not fully recovered from a recent childbirth passed out on her doorstep under the barrage of Wallace's persistent pitch. When Wallace helped to carry her into the house and to revive her, a grateful husband bought a subscription to the *Ladies' Home Journal.* Perhaps his pièce de résistance was selling a subscription to a blind woman. She was the doyenne of a small estate in Kentucky who agreed to subscribe if Wallace could guess her age. He confessed that her maid already had mentioned that her mistress was ninety. "But, ma'am," he said, "you don't look but sixty." "I'm not *that* blind," she laughed—but she could not resist the flattery. "You've earned your sale," she said. And, for the summer, despite dog bites, a lost wallet, and flu, he cleared $250.[95]

From the day in 1937 when Wallace packed his few belongings (including a single sport coat and one pair of dress trousers) into a cardboard case and, with eleven dollars in his pocket, hitchhiked from Clio to a Tuscaloosa boardinghouse at 627 Tenth Street, Wallace knew what he wanted: that essential ticket to a political career—a law degree. And he wanted it in a hurry. So he signed up for the University of Alabama's prelaw program, which required only two years of undergraduate study before permitting entrance into the three-year college of law.[96]

With his father's failing health and growing inability to make ends meet, Wallace needed every dollar as well as his family's political connections. One family friend, Charlie McDowell, whose brother's gubernatorial campaign had been supported by the Wallaces, used his leverage as a member of the University of Alabama's board of trustees to secure a National Youth Administration job for Wallace in the university registrar's office; this New Deal job (which would cover the tuition during his two undergraduate years), was waiting for him when he started school. He still needed money for books, room, board, and an occasional night out, so he took an additional job as a waiter in a Tuscaloosa boardinghouse in return for room and board. Jobs, classes, and freshman boxing made for a full schedule: waking at 4:00 A.M. to run three miles; waiting tables from 6:00 A.M. to 8:00 A.M.; attending classes until 11:00 A.M.; waiting tables from noon until 2:00 P.M.; returning to classes until 4:00 P.M.; working at the registrar's office until 5:30 P.M.; waiting tables from 6:00 P.M. until 8:00 P.M.; studying until 11:00 P.M. The schedule did not leave much free time or facilitate intense studying, but he managed to maintain a grade point average midway between a B and C.[97]

■   ■   ■

George C. had been at college barely two months when his father collapsed with a high fever caused, some thought, by a form of typhus transmitted by lice or fleas. Whatever the cause, George, Sr.'s chronic problems with his heart, lungs, and sinuses rendered him too weak to cope. George C. was called at the Tuscaloosa campus and told to hurry home "if [he] wanted to see him alive again." He borrowed money from a friend for bus fare, but by the time he arrived in Clio, his father had suffered a massive stroke and had lapsed into a coma. Surrounded by his family, he died the next afternoon.

During the funeral, George C. tried to generate thoughts of deep filial devotion; what he remembered most was his father's perorations about the South's mistreatment by the North and the salvation that politics could bring. It was a far more enduring legacy than anything else his father left behind. George, Sr., had died broke, the land that Oscar had placed in his care hopelessly mortgaged. At the cemetery, several neighbors approached Mozelle with offers to work the land for the Wallaces if she could manage to keep the farm together, but with a son in college and three children still at home, she knew that hanging on to the farm was wholly unrealistic. All the land, except a small piece surrounding the house, was reclaimed by the Federal Land Bank. And even to maintain the house, Mozelle had to take a job as a supervisor of a sewing room established by the National Youth Administration.[98]

"After his father's funeral," Mozelle recalled, "George said he wanted to stay home. But I told him to go on back to school. I could get along without him. I was probably right cruel about it, but I told him I could make out."[99] Four years later, with all three sons serving in the military during World War II and only her daughter still living at home, Mozelle decided to put Clio and its memories of hardship and sickness behind her. She moved to Montgomery, living rent-free with a friend while learning typing and stenography. Then, through still-viable political links, she was hired as a secretary in Montgomery's Office of Price Administration, the wartime inflation-fighting agency. Toward the end of the war, she became a secretary in the Alabama Department of Public Health and remained there until she retired twenty-five years later, after having seen her son become governor and run for president. Over the years, she frequently saw her children and their families, but she discouraged regular visits to avoid any thought on their part that they were "obligated" to her.[100]

She lived almost another twenty years, watching the rise and fall of her son's dynasty, remaining resolutely on the sidelines and, until her death at ninety, completely self-supporting and fiercely independent. If George C. had inherited his father's desire for respectability and thirst for political power, he had acquired his mother's self-reliance and determination to cope.

■ ■ ■

The gregariousness that had enabled George Wallace to flourish as a magazine salesman put him at ease with what must have seemed to a raw country boy like an exotic olio of housemates and boxing teammates at the University of Alabama—Michael Gnowskie and Johnny Kurek, both from the Midwest and both in the engineering school; Gene Cocoa of Buffalo, New York, also planning to be a lawyer; another boy named George Wallace from Hazelton, Pennsylvania, who wanted to be a teacher; Salvatore Cusimano of Chicago, who became a labor organizer; and Marco DeBarodina from Texas, who would later study medicine. He would maintain contact with many of them and many other classmates over the years, and several would form the core of widely dispersed early support groups a quarter of a century later when he cast his political gaze beyond Alabama.[101]

But Wallace's bedrock friends were enterprising rural Alabamians like himself—boys who would become integral parts of Wallace's later life. They included Glen Curlee, barely taller than Wallace but beefier, whose affable, off-the-wall humor would later make him one of Wallace's most valuable traveling companions during national campaigns; Bill Jones, articulate and well-read, characteristics that made him an obvious choice for press secretary when Wallace became governor; Ralph Adams, mild-mannered and gentle, whose unswerving loyalty and support would be rewarded in later years with a sinecure as a college president.

This group also included Frank Johnson, a gangly and studious youth from Jasper, a northern Alabama town that had remained loyal to the North during the Civil War and most of whose citizens had since remained that rarest of breeds in pre-1970 Alabama, Republicans (see chapter 7). That distinction virtually guaranteed that, in 1955, when President Dwight D. Eisenhower was trying to fill a federal court vacancy in Alabama, he would choose Johnson, a highly regarded lawyer who actually professed membership in the Grand Old Party. Barely a year later, Johnson would gain national notoriety when, in a case arising out of the Montgomery bus boycott, he cast the deciding vote on a special three-judge panel to declare segregation in municipal transportation to be unconstitutional.[102] (See chapter 5.) Johnson's belief that the judiciary had the responsibility of rushing in to impose justice where governors and legislatures refused to tread would set him on a rancorous collision course with his one-time college intimate George Wallace.

Among Wallace's inner circle, Adams had borrowed enough money from relatives to make a down payment on a boardinghouse of his own.[103] If he could keep the house filled with boarders at seventeen dollars a month for meals and another ten for those who roomed there as well, he could pay his way through school and then some. Wallace struck a deal to lessen the risk of Adam's investment and, at the same time, to benefit himself. Wallace would work the tables and wash dishes at Adam's place in return for free meals; in addition, if Wallace could attract ten boarders to Adam's house, he would get his room free also. It worked so well that Bill Jones soon opened up his own house, and to compensate for not having an energetic huckster like Wallace to rake in boarders, Jones undercut the competition by charging fifteen dollars a month for meals and eight for a room. Wallace worked at Adam's boardinghouse six hours a day during four school years for room and board. In his fifth and final year, after Adams had closed his house, Wallace moved in with Jones; by then, however, he had saved enough to forego the work and pay his fifteen dollars a month for meals. Jones let his friend have a room gratis.[104]

Ever alert to an opportunity, Wallace dropped his summer magazine job in the summer of 1939 when the Alabama legislature, trying to throttle a rabies epidemic among farm animals, enacted a law requiring all dogs in the state to be inoculated each year with anti-rabies vaccine. Wallace, with his continuing contacts among Barbour County's elected officials, succeeded in talking his way into a summer job as the official inoculator in the western half of his home county (a real veterinarian, J. M. Luke of Eufaula, was awarded the eastern half).

Wallace was permitted to charge fifty cents a shot the first year and a dollar a shot in the summer of 1940. But he had to purchase his own medicine and pay all his expenses, including the cost of advertisements and signs calling on people to bring their dogs to an inoculation "clinic" at a particular store or crossroads. Some people who could not afford the fifty cents or dollar a shot paid Wallace with fresh vegetables or sweet potatoes from their gardens or farms.[105] Occasionally, Wallace called in the law to force recalcitrant owners to have their dogs inoculated. A typical clinic would attract fifty dog owners with seventy-five dogs, plus a dozen or more young men and women for whom the occasion provided a morning's entertainment and an opportunity to socialize.[106]

Like nearly everything else in which he was involved from his teen years onward, Wallace saw to it that his years as a rabies inoculator paid political dividends. "When I came back from service [in World War II] to run for the legislature, I had so many people tell me, 'Son, you made us a good dog man, so I'm going to vote for you—and if you're as good a legislator as you were a dog catcher, I'll be pleased.' So the old adage about not voting for someone for dog catcher was turned around; people voted for a good dog catcher to be promoted to the legislature."[107]

■   ■   ■

It is no exaggeration to say that George Wallace arrived at the University of Alabama running for office. Though the large fraternities and sororities formed the campus political machine, Wallace was prevented by regulations governing his NYA job from joining a fraternity, even if he could have afforded membership. But he promptly started organizing his own supporters among his newly and quickly acquired circle of friends and acquaintances.[108] Only about 150 students were in the College of Arts and Sciences, and before the fraternities and sororities even settled on their candidates for the college's freshman class president, Wallace, purely on pumping hands and asserting his powerful personality, had sewn up a clear majority. But the victory put the machine on notice; except for his election to the honor court as a law school freshman, Wallace never again won political office at the university.[109]

Nonetheless, Wallace examined the political ramifications of his nearly every act in college—his performance in the ring (being kayoed might cost him votes), his membership in clubs (belonging to a fraternity might seem elitist), and even his relationships with girls (good-looking dates helped attract votes; beautiful and rich girls, however, might cause problems). Wallace protested, "I always had an inferiority complex around beautiful women because I was only five-feet-eight . . . and I was not an overly handsome man at all—but not nondescript." Still, he was always dating campus beauties. One—a well-to-do girl from the Northeast who, despite having a regular boyfriend, "fell totally in love" with Wallace—drove a convertible in which Wallace refused to accompany her on their dates. "I was afraid students would see me driving in a modern convertible and it might hurt me politically," he said. One day, she drove to his boarding-house, and when he refused to climb in, she drove off in a rage, found her other boyfriend, and raced across the Mississippi line for a quickie marriage. Realizing her mistake as the two headed back to Alabama, the girl put her new husband out of the car and drove straight back to Wallace's boardinghouse, where she and Wallace spent her wedding night (in separate rooms, Wallace said), before Wallace helped her secure an annulment the next day.[110]

During Wallace's years at the University of Alabama, money was always a problem. On a trip to an Alabama–Tennessee football game in Knoxville, Wallace was so low on cash that he persuaded local jailers to put him and his friends up for a night in empty cells.[111] And ten days before his last day of school, Wallace was flat broke but could not do any part-time work because he needed to prepare for final exams. Dan Gurney, a friend from upstate New York, worked in a café about a block from Wallace's room. Between the noon and evening meals, when the boss ran errands, Gurney would let Wallace slip into the kitchen and eat leftovers. "For ten days," he remembered, "I existed on asparagus and Irish potatoes. There'd be no leftover meat, and I started to get weak."[112]

At last, graduation day came in May 1942. Wallace owed the college forty-nine dollars in overdue fees, so he was handed a blank sheet of paper instead of a law degree. He would receive his degree when he ponied up the money. Broke and hungry, Wallace relied on his wits and turned to his friends. (as he would do so often in future political and personal crises). One friend, Paul Bailey, operated a "side hole" restaurant—a room-sized eatery. He allowed Wallace two meals on credit at a quarter apiece. Meanwhile, Ralph Adams had bought an apartment complex in which he housed students who could afford something more commodious than a boardinghouse room. With school out and the students gone, he allowed Wallace to live in one of the apartments in return for keeping an eye on the property during the summer.

Wallace scavenged all the apartments for wire coat hangers that, due to wartime demands for metal, were in short supply. He found a hundred that had been abandoned by the recent occupants and lugged them to a nearby dry cleaning establishment whose proprietor bought them for fifty cents. Returning home, Wallace gathered all his clothing, except a single winter suit, two shirts, two pairs of trousers, and some underclothing. He bundled his belongings and piled them into a taxi that, for twenty-five cents, took him to a store specializing in the sale of old clothes. There, Wallace was paid $4.50 for his wardrobe. With a quarter left over from the sale of the coat hangers, Wallace had $4.75. He walked back to Bailey's side hole eatery; paid "Mr. Paul," as he called him, the fifty cents he owed for the two meals on credit; and purchased a $4.00 meal ticket that would carry him through the next week. With his last quarter, he bought a city bus ticket that allowed him to ride the bus to the end of the line. Alighting, he walked across a cotton field to an Alabama Highway Department encampment whose district engineer had advertised for truck drivers. Wallace had never driven a truck, but certain he could learn quickly, he asserted he was a qualified driver and was hired on the spot at thirty cents an hour. He was told to pick up a truck in the camp and drive it to nearby Elberta City, where the department was widening a section of the highway to four lanes. "There was a black man near the truck," Wallace said, "a prison trusty who worked on the highways. I told him I'd give him a quarter on payday if he'd show me how to drive the dump truck. He said there was nothing to it; he showed me how to crank it up, work the hydraulic pump, release the load, use the different gears—and I took off right then and drove it to Elberta City."[113]

Wallace quickly became the leading driver in the crew. "They had old men, illiterates, and folks who couldn't find a job, and one or two right out of the penitentiary," Wallace said. One of his jobs was driving the squad truck loaded with black prisoners assigned to work on the road gangs. Wallace believed that "the convicts liked this kind of work because of the different scenery; it was like a free day for them." Still, they did not like prison, and they looked to Wallace for help. "They called me 'Lawyer,' " Wallace said. "All of them asked me to help get them a parole or pardon, but I didn't know how."[114]

The truck driving was hard, hot work. Wallace, stripped to the waist and bronzed by the broiling Alabama summer sun, wore a wide-brimmed hat and chomped two-for-a-nickel King Edward cigars as he worked eleven and a half hours a day for take-home pay of just over sixteen dollars a week. But what caught Wallace's state-employed superiors' attention even more than his production on the job was his education and political ties. His gum-chewing foreman, Ed Sealy, offered Wallace an easier job—as a timekeeper or a flagman—on the grounds that Wallace was a law school graduate and should not be driving a truck. In passing, Sealy suggested that Wallace, who had worked earlier that year in the successful gubernatorial primary campaign of Barbour County's Chauncey Sparks, put in a good word for him with the next governor. Wallace replied that he wasn't sure his recommendation would do any good; in any event, he opted to stay on the truck.[115]

■   ■   ■

About every other week between May and September, Wallace drove the truck to an Army Air Corps induction station in Tuscaloosa. It was less than six months after Pearl Harbor, and Wallace "had to be a cadet and a flyer." "But," he recalled, "when I went to enlist, they told me my pulse was too fast and I should come back. But each time, my pulse was still too fast and they wouldn't accept me." One afternoon in July, after Wallace had been turned down once again by the Air Corps, he stopped at Kresge's five-and-dime store for a sandwich. When he passed the cosmetics counter, he noticed a pretty, slender clerk with large, luminous eyes. Wallace, nearly twenty-five years old, stopped and introduced himself to Lurleen Burns, sixteen, and ordered a bottle of hair oil.[116]

Lurleen, an only child, lived with her parents outside of Tuscaloosa. She had completed high school in two and a half years by taking several summer courses and had then taken a job at Kresge's. "I remember liking George from the start," Lurleen told an interviewer in 1964. "He had the prettiest dark eyes, and the way he'd cut up!" When he visited the Burns's home, "he ate quite a lot. . . . Even then, he was talking about politics all the time. That's what seemed to be really occupying his mind. He was already talking about running for governor." Most of the talk was with Lurleen's father, a barge worker on the Warrior River; politics was not a subject that particularly interested Lurleen. "Politics," she once explained, "was something Daddy discussed at our house with other people—not with me."[117]

But Wallace had Lurleen on his mind as well as politics. At every opportunity, he would drive his dump truck into town, pull up in front of Kresge's, leave the motor running (the battery was so weak, Wallace was afraid the truck would not restart if he switched off the ignition), "run in and say hello to her, and run back and get in the truck and drive back out to the job."[118] "She was all I could think about," Wallace explained. "There she was, olive complexioned, with auburn hair that was brown with a little tinge of reddish in it. She wanted to get married—and I did, too. But we knew I'd be going into the service as a private and wouldn't be able to send her much money."[119]

Actually, they did not *know* that Wallace would be a private, although they thought that might happen if he continued to fail his physical for the Air Corps cadet program. He was eager to resolve the question. "While we were dating," Lurleen said, "people wanted to know why he wasn't already in the service, and this bothered him. He was nervous about that. It worried him a lot."[120]

The end of summer brought the new college semester, and the waves of returning students forced Wallace to relinquish his free lodgings at Ralph Adams's apartments. But his other chum, Glen Curlee, allowed Wallace to share his tiny garage apartment—as long as Wallace was willing to sleep on a couple of blankets laid out in a corner. (After two weeks, Curlee reluctantly agreed to give up the apartment's one easy chair to make room for an old bed and mattress on which Wallace could get a good night's sleep.) Then, in mid-September, while operating a dump truck, Wallace was struck on the elbow by a flying chunk of asphalt. The bruise became infected, and the arm swelled to twice its normal circumference; the doctor lanced the infected area and put the arm in a sling. Unable to drive, Wallace was forced off the job. Although Wallace was not entitled to severance benefits, his boss handed him a full week's pay. Wallace was grateful—but not enough to turn down a better job that came along about the time he recovered the use of his arm.[121]

■　　■　　■

The new job, which paid fifty cents an hour, required him to check out tools at a wartime training center for airplane mechanics. About the same time, the recruiting sergeant Wallace had been seeing regularly since the spring decided to accept him into the cadet pilot program. He knew that Wallace, in trying to reach the minimum weight required, would drink as much water as he could hold just before stepping on the scale. "Son," he told Wallace, "you look pregnant. If you want to get in that bad, I'll go ahead and pass you. You were a truck driver, so there can't be anything wrong with you except a little nervousness." The sergeant's confidence was borne out when Wallace passed his induction physical with flying colors. On October 20, 1942, Wallace was sworn in to the Army Air Corps as an aviation cadet and was told to await his orders."[122] When the orders arrived at the garage apartment in January 1943, having been forwarded from Mozelle Wallace's new home in Montgomery, Curlee rushed them to the training center where Wallace was working. Wallace blanched when he saw that he was to have reported to the Madison Hotel in Miami Beach, Florida, three days earlier. Thinking he would be arrested at any moment by the military police, George sped home, bathed, put on his only suit, and telephoned Lurleen to ask her to meet him at the depot. When he arrived, the train had pulled out, but George and Lurleen hailed a taxi, in which they raced along a road parallel to the tracks. They caught up with the train at a boarding junction eight miles south of Tuscaloosa. George leaped out of the taxi, flagged the train down, kissed Lurleen, and hopped on a passenger car.[123] He waved goodbye to Lurleen—and to his youth.

3

The Desperate Hours

WALLACE, AFTER LEAVING TUSCALOOSA, changed trains twice and arrived in Miami Beach the next day with nothing but the clothes on his back and a change of underwear. The Madison Hotel, where he was billeted, had been expediently converted into military quarters through the removal of anything that might suggest comfort: beds had been replaced by GI cots; carpets had been ripped up to expose the bare concrete floors; lamps had been removed, leaving only naked lightbulbs in the ceilings. Rifles and training manuals were issued to the recruits, but uniforms did not arrive for ten days. As the boys were marched up and down the steamy streets of Miami Beach, Wallace's wool trousers, perfect for the January chill in Tuscaloosa, clung to his legs like towels in a Turkish bath. Each night, he washed his only shirt and hung it out to dry in the breeze blowing from Biscayne Bay. And when, at last, he was issued a uniform, the pants and shirtsleeves were too long, disguising his taut body and emphasizing his short stature; he looked for all the world like an adolescent boy playing soldier.[1]

The next stop was Arkadelphia, Arkansas, for five months of academic courses required before pilot training. Wallace disliked the school from the start; he thought the courses were far too elementary for college graduates and, for the most part, irrelevant to aspiring pilots. Most of all, he detested the overheated classrooms from which he would emerge, moist with sweat, into Arkadelphia's February chill. Before long, Wallace developed sniffles and a cough. Two days later, he woke up with an overwhelming, radiating headache and a stiff neck; nauseated, he crawled to a toilet, where he vomited and passed out. Help was summoned and Wallace, burning with fever, was carried to the infirmary; the staff doctor tapped Wallace's spine for a fluid sample and correctly diagnosed the illness as meningitis, a highly contagious inflammation of the membranes covering the brain. Semiconscious, Wallace was trundled into an ambulance that raced to the Army-Navy Hospital in Hot Springs. Doctors there placed him in isolation and pumped antibiotics into his veins to quell the infection. Thrashing in his delirium over the next six days, Wallace was wrestled back to his bed and frequently pinned by orderlies working round the clock. Wallace remembered the moments of emerging into consciousness: "I thought that if I didn't get up out of the bed, I would die. So I fought with as much strength as I could, but I was unable to get up because they would hold me down."

Wallace's fever broke on the seventh day; doctors pronounced Wallace out of danger from a disease that, in the 1940s, killed nearly 90 percent of its victims. But Wallace developed an allergy to the sulfa drugs he was receiving; his rash-covered body itched unbearably. "I was swollen all over and itching all over. I'd lie on my stomach so I could rub my itching face and body against the sheets while using my fingers and toes to get at whatever else I could. I told one of the officers, 'If y'all can't help me with this itch, I'm going to jump out of that window. I can't stand it any longer.' " The doctors treated Wallace with a form of adrenaline to speed the blood coursing through his system and, thereby, temporarily reduce the itching; because of the drug's strain on the heart, however, the physicians were forced to limit Wallace to no more than one shot an hour. "They'd give me a dose and my itching stopped for forty minutes. Then there was twenty minutes of terror again before I could take another shot. Finally, after six shots, the swelling started to go down and the itching stopped."

Now recovering, Wallace was placed in quarantine for three weeks, then allowed to convalesce through April 1943. Wallace was discharged at the end of the month and given a thirty-day furlough.[2] "My mother lived in Montgomery and worked for the OPA and didn't have room for me; she hadn't bought her house yet and lived in a one-bedroom apartment with my little sister. So there was no

place for me to go but back to Tuscaloosa to the same apartment."
Still "haggard and worn" from his ordeal, weak from weight loss he
could hardly afford, Wallace also was "so very lonesome."

■ ■ ■

Being young and lonesome, and being near the fresh and pretty
Lurleen, George found himself thinking more and more about marriage.[3] The day he and Lurleen chose was Saturday, May 22, 1943. By
then, the war was beginning to turn in favor of the Allies. Three
months earlier, the Germans had surrendered in Stalingrad, and the
Japanese had evacuated Guadalcanal; ten days before, about a quarter of a million Axis troops had surrendered to the Americans, the
British, and the Free French in North Africa. George, despite his
illness, was sure he would soon be in the thick of the fighting, so the
young lovers decided not to wait any longer. The couple sought out
Adolph Forester, whom George knew as "a crippled Jewish justice of
the peace—a fine friend" of his. "I wanted him to marry me and
make the little fee because he made his living that way," Wallace
explained later. Judge Forester's office was above the H&W Drug
Store in downtown Tuscaloosa. Lurleen's father was working a barge
on the Black Warrior River, so her mother had to sign a form permitting the underage Lurleen to marry. Judge Forester performed the
ceremony; George paid him all he could afford—a dollar—but he
invited the judge to accompany Lurleen's mother and the newlyweds
to a café downstairs for a wedding meal of chicken salad sandwiches
and Cokes. George and Lurleen then walked to the depot and
boarded a train for Montgomery, where they broke the news to
Mozelle. "My mother was shocked and surprised at me being married," Wallace remembered. "We had gotten married without informing her; it was so hurried and I had so little money that I didn't
want to make any phone calls." Lurleen was sixteen and seven
months.[4]

George and Lurleen spent their wedding night in a Montgomery
boardinghouse in a room described as having "a linoleum floor, a
large iron frame bed, and a naked light bulb dangling from a cord in
the center of the ceiling." The next day, on Sunday, they caught a bus to
Clio, where they spent the night with Roy and Sue Reynolds, friends
who had rented the old Wallace house from the realtors who had purchased it from Mozelle. On Monday, George and Lurleen were driven
to nearby Brundidge to see his maiden aunt, Hadley McEachern,

who fawned over the young people; Aunt Hadley died shortly thereafter and bequeathed George a thousand dollars, which would finance his first legislative campaign after the war (see chapter 4).[5]

After their three-day honeymoon, George and Lurleen boarded a bus to Montgomery, visited Mozelle once more, then continued to Mobile, where Lurleen's father had moved to take a wartime job as a crane operator at Brookley Field, an Air Corps training center. Lurleen would live in Mobile until George could send for her.[6]

■   ■   ■

Shortly after George returned to Arkadelphia, his air cadet detachment was sent to San Antonio, Texas, for training as pilots, navigators, or bombardiers. Within a week, he realized that if he continued in the air cadet program, he might not see Lurleen for months. The discipline rankled as well. "I did not want to live that strict life of a cadet," Wallace said. "You have to eat by the numbers—and there was no way to see your wife." George made up his mind: he wanted out, and he tried to use his meningitis as the lever. But the officer in charge of his squadron told George meningitis was no barrier to becoming a pilot. George insisted that it would bother him constantly; he said he might have a headache at a critical moment or, worse, a fit. Although skeptical, the officer agreed to wash George out of the unit if he really wanted that. "But you can be sure you won't get some easy job," the officer warned, "and you'll just be an enlisted man. That won't pay much for your wife, and you won't have much chance for advancement." George said he understood, and he was promptly sent to Amarillo to await reassignment—a stroke of personal luck, as it turned out, because the military virtually ignored George's detachment for more than a year. Amarillo became home to the Wallaces until, as the Americans were making their final push against the Japanese, George and the others who had washed out of cadet training were assigned for training in the relentless air attacks of the Japanese homeland.[7]

George's superiors proved right about what he would encounter as an enlisted man. For nearly half a year, he and the others, all college graduates, did little more than police the grounds, picking up paper, cigarette butts, and other debris. No quarters existed for married enlisted men and their wives, but George ingratiated himself to his first sergeant, a man named Duncan, by helping him with clerical duties such as morning reports and payroll duties. As a reward, Duncan allowed George to live off base. For five dollars a week, George rented the attic in the home of an elderly widow named Theidens, and he sent for Lurleen. It wouldn't be easy for George: to get to the base by six each morning, he would have to wake at four; he paid a quarter a day to a sergeant, who also lived in town, to drive him to the base. And it wouldn't be easy for Lurleen: the door of her new attic home was a drapery hung from the attic entranceway; her cooking range was a hot plate on which she would frequently boil potatoes when the couple was too low on cash to afford a regular meal. She found a job in a five-and-dime store for twelve dollars a week. But, as always, when it came to scraping by, George proved resourceful. He mowed his landlady's lawn for a dollar a week. On his weekly day off, as well as one or two nights a week, he worked at an Amarillo ordnance plant unloading bomb casings from railroad cars and stacking TNT, earning as much as twenty dollars a week. When the sergeant wanted to find an apartment in town for himself, he instructed George to find him one—and issued him a two-week pass in which to accomplish the task. George found a suitable place for Sergeant Duncan within two days and used the remaining time to work at the ordnance plant every day for seven-fifty a day. As hard as he tried to earn enough to keep Lurleen with him, George ran short of cash; for ten dollars, he hocked the wristwatch that Lurleen had saved six months to buy as George's first wedding anniversary gift (he would redeem it a few months later).[8]

Sergeant Duncan's friendship soon came in handy in another matter regarding money. George was in charge of the payroll register that soldiers in the squadron were required to sign on payday before picking up their money. If they missed the deadline for signing, they would have to wait until the following month to get their pay. George, as a favor to a number of his buddies, made it a practice to forge their signatures and later give them their cash personally. Eventually, the adjutant general got wind of what George was doing, and George was accused of pocketing some of the cash for which he was signing other soldiers' names. But George—with Sergeant Duncan's support— explained that his actions, though technically improper, were taken to help fellow soldiers who needed their money but did not have time to go to the orderly's office. As to embezzlement, he asked if anyone had complained about not getting their pay; the answer was no. The authorities backed down and did not file any charges.[9]

With both of them working days and George working many evenings, the young lovers did not have much time together, and

George's long and frequent absences set a pattern for the rest of their marriage—a pattern that was at the root of later friction and at least one discussion of divorce. Still, despite his neglect of Lurleen, George believed he fervently loved her and could not live without her. And their trystlike nights behind the curtained entrance to their attic apartment resulted in Lurleen's first pregnancy in the cold Amarillo winter of 1944. In the spring, George's unit of college-educated, air cadet washouts was designated as a flight-engineering detachment. After a three-day stint in Lincoln, Nebraska, for preliminary training, the detachment returned to Amarillo and learned how to keep four-engine bombers in the air. By the summer, when Lurleen was six months pregnant, she thought it best for her to relocate in Mobile, because her parents had moved there.[10]

In September, the unit was ordered to Denver for an introduction to the B-29 Superfortress. Since the Allied occupation of the Mariana Islands in the summer of 1944, this new U.S. long-range bomber had enabled the Allies to attack the Japanese home islands 1,300 miles from the principal air base in Tinian. In October, George received a telegram from Lurleen: their daughter, Bobbi Jo, had been born at the base hospital in Mobile. They would be ready to join Wallace as soon as he was transferred to a town where the three of them could find housing.[11]

George couldn't wait. As soon as he was ordered to the Alamagordo, New Mexico, air base in December 1944, for crew training, he called Lurleen and told her to pack her bags, dress the baby, board a train, and head west. In a borrowed car, he met them at the train station, where he first saw his daughter. But he was forced to confess to a distressed Lurleen that he had not had time to find a place to stay. Looking for shelter, they drove all day but had no luck. When it grew dark and they were about an hour's drive from the base, they found a family willing to let the three sleep on their screened porch for a couple of nights. Two days later, the Wallaces located a permanent rental—in a converted chicken coop.[12]

■ ■ ■

Even in these scabrous circumstances, Wallace still found time for politics. While in Amarillo, Wallace had asked a friend to send him the Barbour County voting list. Then he ordered stacks of Christmas cards, which were furnished free by Bell Telephone to GIs—enough to send to nearly every family in the county, plus the current state legislators. "And," he remembered, "it didn't cost any postage to send them. All you had to do was put your return address on it that showed you were a soldier. The boys from my barracks [in Amarillo in 1943 and Alamagordo in 1944] helped me by putting my address in the upper left-hand corner of the envelope while I signed a Christmas card, and they would stuff them for me, and we would carry them by the stack to the post office." This was an early manifestation of Wallace's genius at organizing people and somehow persuading them it was important to devote their time to further his goals.[13]

In Alamagordo, Wallace was one of a crew of eleven that was either in a classroom, at a hangar, or up in a B-29 with experienced counterparts undergoing rigorous combat preparation. In the spring, the crew was ordered back to Denver for a final checkout on B-29s. The men would get a brief leave and then would meet in Topeka, Kansas, for assignment to their own plane. He bid another tearful goodbye to his wife and daughter, and, before leaving for Denver, dropped by his neighborhood grocer to promise that he would pay off his eight-dollar debt as soon as possible—a promise he kept a few weeks later. Wallace left Alamagordo in June 1945. He would return as a presidential nominee twenty-three years later and be introduced at a political rally by that same grocer, who said, "I know this man will tell the truth and pay his debts—at least, the little ones, anyway."[14]

Although Wallace had a keen memory for people who had helped him along the way, his eye for history was not as sharp. In later years, when he recalled leaving Alamagordo in June 1945, he was unaware that barely a month later, the air base at which he had trained in a bleak region appropriately called Jornada del Muerto ("Journey of Death") would be the site for secret testing of a very special bomb, code named Fat Man. A second bomb, code named Little Boy, would catch up to Wallace and his crew on Tinian the next month.[15]

■　■　■

Through the spring of 1945, the air attacks on the Japanese home islands were intensifying. With Germany's surrender in May, Wallace, now a sergeant, was certain that when he returned from his brief leave, he would be joining in the dangerous bombardment of Japan.

A sense of doom overwhelmed him on his last day of leave in Mobile. During training, he had seen B-29s lose power on takeoff and crash, setting their fuel tanks ablaze. He had heard that some kamikaze pilots were ramming U.S. bombers, sacrificing themselves in defense of their homeland. "I really thought I would never get back alive," he recalled.[16]

He and Lurleen were staying in her parents' home. In an upstairs bedroom, Wallace packed his flight bag; as he went downstairs, he saw Lurleen waiting for him. "I grabbed her and broke down and cried again." They took the baby and strolled through the sun-drenched Bienville Square, then turned into a corner drugstore and ordered a couple of Cokes. "I would look at her and she would look at me, and I thought my heart would break."[17]

Wallace and his fellow crew members met in Topeka to pick up their plane; they christened it *Sentimental Journey*. Unexpectedly, the men were granted another three-day pass, and Wallace made straight for the phone to call Lurleen. He told her to leave the baby with her folks and take the earliest train to Memphis, roughly halfway between Mobile and Topeka; he said he would phone his friend Ralph Adams, now an army major back in Alabama after a tour in Europe, and ask him to make the arrangements for Lurleen. Allowing for round-trip travel time, George and Lurleen would have little more than a day together. He packed an overnight bag, hopped a bus, and asked the driver to let him out at the depot. "Which one?" the driver asked. Unfamiliar with Topeka, Wallace was uncertain. "Whichever is the closest," he said. To his chagrin, that depot turned out to be the wrong one. Wallace rushed to the street and looked around feverishly for a taxicab, but there was none in sight. "I saw a man there in a car, and I told him that I was going overseas and that I would have just one day in Memphis with my wife and that if I missed the train, I might never see her again. He graciously gave me a ride and drove hurriedly to the other station and I just did make it."[18]

After spending two nights and a day together in Memphis, the couple separated for what George thought might be the last time. He took a train back to Topeka, and the crew headed to Sacramento the next day for final briefings before going overseas. Among other administrative requirements, the men were asked to make out their wills. "We went through a line waiting for lawyers from the adjutant general's office to make out our wills. I willed everything I had— which was nothing—to Lurleen. One boy in our crew, Johnny Petroff from Pennsylvania, the left gunner, was only nineteen, the youngest man in the crew. He was told that he had to be twenty-one to make a will. And he said, "Sergeant, what if something happens to me?" And the sergeant said, "Boy, if something happens to you, they'll grieve for a while, but they'll get it straight. Don't you worry about that. Now, move on." The crew then left the American mainland and headed for the Mariana Islands.

■   ■   ■

The crewmen spent a night in Saipan, where they experienced warlike conditions for the first time. "We were in a tent with mud everywhere," Wallace remembered. "Boards were laid down so we could get to our beds without bogging down." The next morning, they flew over to Tinian; to their dismay, a more experienced crew was given the newer *Sentimental Journey*. Wallace's crew was given an older B-29 with the unlikely name of the *Little Yutz*.[19]

Commanding the Marianas-based B-29s was Gen. Curtis LeMay (who in 1968 would become Wallace's running mate on the American Independent party's national ticket; see chapter 14). For more than a year, LeMay had been advocating strategic bombing to shorten the war. Despite initial resistance from the high command, LeMay was authorized in mid-1944 to proceed with his plan to inflict wholesale destruction on enemy homelands through long-range bombing. He was assigned to the Pacific theater after commanding a heavy bomber group in the campaign against Germany. He believed that Japan's war-making ability should be destroyed by raining fire on Japanese cities—a bombing technique that resulted in an enormous number of deaths and immense suffering among Japan's civilians. "I think it's more immoral to use less force than it is to use more," he later wrote. He compared the use of "less force" with a well-meaning man who cut off his dog's tail an inch at a time "so that it wouldn't hurt so much."[20]

Through June, July, and early August of 1945, Wallace participated in turning many of Japan's cities—including Tokyo, Atsuta, Yokohama, Oita, Otaki, Kochi, Toyama, Sakai, and Nagoya—into massive infernos. Tinian, slightly smaller than Manhattan Island, had become the world's largest air base. At times, nearly a thousand B-29s would take off in fifteen-second intervals from six 10-lane runways to bomb targets in Japan. In eleven missions over Japan, the *Little Yutz* crew dropped napalm, clusters of oil containers, and magnesium thermite bombs on military targets; but the intense fires that ran through the streets of the cities inevitably extracted a mind-numbing toll. By mid-August, nearly half the aggregate area of sixty-six cities—178 square miles—had been razed.

Like nearly every other bomber crew in combat, the men of the *Little Yutz* experienced their share of close calls. On their first combat mission, Capt. Robert Ray instructed Wallace not to use cruise control en route to the target. "We'll make a little faster time without it," he said. Wallace, whose principal job was to manage fuel consumption for the eighteen-hour round-trip flights, warned that the *Little Yutz*, unlike the newer *Sentimental Journey*, did not have fuel-injected engines, which used fuel more efficiently. Sure enough, during the return to Tinian, the aircraft's engines began sputtering. Wallace called for an emergency straight-in approach, and they made it without incident. From then on, however, they used cruise control.[21]

On a subsequent night flight, a Japanese suicide plane flew barely ten yards below the *Little Yutz*; its pilot had somehow failed to spot Wallace's bomber. Another time, the *Little Yutz*, flying at an altitude of nine thousand feet, was caught in a powerful thermal updraft, heaved to nineteen thousand feet, and nearly overturned. "It tore things loose from the walls," Wallace said, "and water jugs, papers, and navigator instruments were thrown about. And my helmet, which was not buckled, was torn off and smashed into the glass files in front of me." The pilot called back that they had lost two engines, and Wallace suggested replacing the voltage regulator so the engines would surge back to full use. But he cautioned Captain Ray to maintain the throttles in their present position, because if the captain tried to regain power by pushing forward on the throttles, the excess power resulting from engagement of the new voltage regulator might cause a "runaway" propeller. Ray concurred; the engines coughed and then roared, and the craft headed back to the safety of Tinian.[22]

■   ■   ■

On August 1, 1945, the *Little Yutz* was approaching the coast of Japan on a bright, moonlit night when Wallace noticed on his gauge that the number-three engine was losing power. "I think we blew a piston," he told the pilot. Ray called back, "There's an oil fire starting up on the top of the cowling!" He feathered the engine and ordered Wallace to foam the engine. Wallace turned off the ignition, cut the fuel supply to number three, put the mixture control forward, and then foamed the engine as ordered. As Ray notified the crew to prepare to bail out, the bombardier, Lt. George Harbinson, emptied his load of bombs over the sea, and the radio operator, Richard Zind, notified the other aircraft on the mission that they might be ditching. The gunners George Leahy, Arthur Feiner, and Johnny Petroff searched the skies for enemy aircraft; the navigator Thomas Lamb reminded them jokingly that once before, they had reported seeing the blinking light of a Japanese fighter—but that it had turned out to be the planet Venus.

Everyone checked his bailout gear. There was an oxygen bottle strapped to the leg with an attached hose that ran to the mouth; it would provide oxygen until the jumper reached an altitude of five to seven thousand feet, at which it would be comfortable to breathe in the atmosphere. There was the front button that, when pushed as the feet hit the water, would release the safety latch and loosen all the buckles so the chute would blow off and not pull the jumper underwater. There was the self-inflating one-man life raft and the C-1 vest with fishing tackle, fishhooks, a mirror, a can of water, rations, shark repellent, and dye markers. And, of course, there was the Mae West life preserver. But no one was sanguine about jumping—and not only because they feared the wrath of any Japanese civilians who might find them. On one mission, the *Little Yutz* crew had seen several airmen jump from a crippled bomber; only one parachute had opened—and it had caught fire and collapsed when hit by tracer bullets from the ground. Another time, a crew from their own barracks had been forced to ditch near a friendly convoy; despite rescue parties coming promptly to their aid, two nineteen-year-old airmen had drowned. The survivors had graphically described the scene to Wallace and the others in the barracks. "Both drowned even though they had on life preservers," Wallace remembered. "They drowned because they became so wretchedly sick and vomited and had swallowed so much water. Strong men from the crew swam to them to bring them together to wait for a rescue launch from a nearby vessel, but they fought them off. Finally, they had to swim back or they might have drowned themselves and the boys drifted off and died."

It was that grisly picture that Wallace had in mind as they prepared to ditch the *Little Yutz*. Captain Ray put the plane in a dive, and as it gained speed, Wallace noticed that the combination of the fire-retardant foam and the induced rush of air had extinguished the flames. "Captain," Wallace called, "the fire's gone out and the other engines are operating okay." Ray asked him what the chances were of getting back to Tinian on three engines. Wallace said he was sure they had enough fuel and power to make it to Iwo Jima, but he thought that reaching Tinian would be a close call. Ray did not hesitate. He knew that aircraft in worse shape than his—many with casualties aboard—would not have a prayer to make it beyond Iwo Jima and would be stacked up there. He ordered the bombardier to salvo remaining bombs to lighten their load, maintained the fuel-economizing air speed of 210 miles per hour, and headed for home base. Wallace monitored the fuel supply carefully, and they made it safely to their own barracks bunks before midnight.[23]

■   ■   ■

The crewmen of the *Little Yutz* did not know that they would have only one more combat mission. Less than a week before the crew's brush with catastrophe, the USS *Indianapolis*, a heavy cruiser, had dropped anchor a thousand yards off Tinian Harbor and unloaded a top secret cargo—a lead cylinder only eighteen inches in diameter but weighing three hundred pounds. It was the U-235 core of an atomic bomb, itself weighing about a hundred pounds; the rest of the weight was lead insulation. The uranium had been delivered earlier. The *Indianapolis* promptly weighed anchor and headed to sea; four days later, it was torpedoed by a Japanese submarine. It sank in twelve minutes, claiming the lives of all but 315 of its 1,200-man crew.[24]

Following the crew's close call on August 1, four B-29s crashed and burned on takeoff from Tinian on August 4. The *Little Yutz* was scheduled for its next mission on August 5—a long night flight to the west coast of Japan. The mission went without incident; the weather was clear, and the plane dropped its incendiary bombs on target and returned home. When they arrived shortly after 11:00 A.M. on August 6, the base was buzzing with scuttlebutt about some superbomb that had been dropped on Japan some three hours earlier. But Wallace and his buddies were almost too tired to care. By the time they filed their afterflight reports, each had been awake nearly twenty-four hours. They hit the sack around 2:00 P.M., a few minutes after a plane named *Enola Gay* had returned from its historic mission.[25]

At nearly 7:00 P.M., the crew of the *Little Yutz* was awakened and told to report to the briefing room. The crew was ordered back to California, where its members were to undergo training for lead crew in daylight missions over Japan. Wallace knew that lead crews frequently were the primary targets for kamikaze suicide planes. More-over, better visibility during daylight missions would make them much more vulnerable to treacherous antiaircraft fire. When they returned to their barracks, they heard all about the bomb that had been dropped by the *Enola Gay* crew and the devastation it had wreaked at Hiroshima. The next day, the *Little Yutz* took off for Hawaii, and en route, its crew heard Wallace suddenly declare that he had flown his last; to all intents and purposes, he said, the war was over—but even if the war continued, he would accept some other combat assignment—but one that would keep him on the ground.[26]

■   ■   ■

When they reached Los Angeles, they were granted leave. But Wal-lace, whose apprehension had turned into a genuine fear of flying, squandered much of his furlough by spurning a seat aboard a mili-tary air transport heading toward Mobile. Instead, he took a train that required three days and two nights of travel in each direction. While traveling to see his family, he heard that a second atomic bomb had been dropped on Japan, this one on Nagasaki.[27]

The air war over Japan continued for a few days after Wallace reached Mobile. Wallace grew progressively tense and anxious; he ate irregularly and started losing weight. When, on August 14, Japan agreed to surrender unconditionally, he even declined to join the thousands of people in Mobile who swarmed to Bienville Square, for fear he might somehow be injured seriously. "Aren't you going down and celebrate?" Lurleen's father asked George. "Mr. Burns," he replied, "I was just over Japan on a bombing mission a few days ago. We got caught in the searchlights from the ground, but the anti-aircraft flak missed us and we made it out all right. Now, suppose I go down there to the square and somebody who's been drinking gets all carried away and throws a beer bottle that hits me? I came out unscathed after eleven B-29 missions—and I'm not going to get knocked in the head by some drunk who's never even heard of Tinian!"[28]

Wallace returned by train to California in late August. The trip had been hot and uncomfortable; for two nights, he stretched out between the aisles and used his duffel bag as a mattress. He arrived unshaved, rumpled, and edgy. When he learned that, despite the war's end, his crew still was assigned to fly practice missions, his nerves broke. He braced Captain Ray: "Captain, I've flown my last. I did my duty." He said he had never tried to get out of a mission and had, in fact, once flown an extra mission for which he had volunteered. "George," Ray said, "there is nothing I can do about it. You'll have to see the colonel."[29]

Neither Wallace's memory nor available records yielded the name of the officer whom he confronted, but in reconstructing the exchange, Wallace remembers affirming that he was not a shirker, that he could have avoided overseas duty from the start because he was underweight and, later, had suffered from meningitis. "I'm tired and I'm afraid of flying," he recalls saying, "especially in these big bombers that catch fire mighty easy—and the war's over."

Not surprisingly, the colonel resisted, but Wallace continued to make his case. He had volunteered to fight the Germans and the Japanese, but now the war was over. The colonel repeated his order that Wallace must fly.

"Colonel, sir," Wallace replied, "I do respect discipline, and I do respect you. But if there is any way to respectfully disobey a colonel, I respectfully disobey your order. I shall not fly."

Wallace recalled that the colonel rose from his chair, pointed a finger at him, and said incredulously, "You are a sick man. You are *sick*! You get over to the hospital right away. You go straight there—and don't you stop for anything because if you do, I'll have you court martialed and throw the book at you and you'll wind up in Leavenworth. Now get over there and don't stop. You're sick!"[30]

Wallace was admitted to the base hospital where, he remembered, "they let me sleep quite a bit, gave me [vitamin] B_1 shots, a lot of milk, a lot of good food, and I got straightened out pretty good. I was haggard and worn; the colonel really didn't want to do anything to harm me because he knew I was in no condition to fly. The bomber crew went ahead and flew the lead-crew training without me; they got a replacement engineer. They all took bets on whether or not I'd fly again—and the ones who bet that I would not certainly won their money. My condition was listed as 'anxiety severe,' which, you might say, was battle fatigue."[31] (Wallace's flying phobia has persisted throughout his life, even after logging tens of thousands of miles on campaign flights, much of it in aircraft of questionable soundness. Every takeoff and landing was, to him, literally a white-knuckle episode. But his passion for campaigning overwhelmed his dread.)

Wallace's official records describe him as having been in a "severe anxiety state (chronic), manifested by tension states, anxiety attacks and anorexia and loss of weight."[32]

Wallace remained in the hospital for nearly two months; he remembers "having a good time eating and reading." After his release, he moved to the barracks with his crew. At the end of November, discharge papers came through for everyone.[33]

■   ■   ■

Sgt. George C. Wallace was honorably discharged from the Army Air Corps in El Paso, Texas, on December 8, 1945, with the Air Medal, Pacific Theater Medal, and the Good Conduct Medal. He headed back to Alabama, reading and rereading a two-year-old letter from Gov. Chauncey Sparks of Barbour County, promising his young supporter that, if the Sparks administration remained in office when Wallace returned from the war, a job would be waiting for him in the state capital.[34]

The war's tribulations left Wallace with some permanent scars. His progressive deafness could be attributed to his meningitis, likely compounded by his hundreds of hours in a B-29. His emotional anxiety persisted for an entire decade, according to the Veterans Administration. In December 1946, the Veterans Administration ruled that Wallace should be granted a 10 percent service-connected psychological disability, which carried a monthly payment of twenty dollars. When he was reexamined by the Veterans Administration in November 1956, to determine whether the payments should be continued, his examiners wrote that Wallace "was tense, restless, and ill at ease, frequently drummed the desk with his fingers, changed position frequently, sighed occasionally and showed a tendency to stammer," resulting in the diagnosis of "anxiety reaction." Although that diagnosis might well fit nearly any active, hard-driving man in his late thirties—much less an impatient George Wallace, who already had launched his campaign in the 1958 governor's race—the 10 percent disability rating was continued. Wallace, hard up for cash, was loath to challenge that decision.[35]

None of these events likely would have been remembered, however, had not someone in the Pentagon or the Veterans Administration, hoping to embarrass and weaken Wallace during the Birmingham crisis in the fall of 1963 (see chapter 8), leaked Wallace's confidential military hospitalization records to Sen. Wayne Morse of Oregon. In a Senate speech designed to suggest that a madman was running the state of Alabama, Morse gleefully disclosed Wallace's diagnosed "psychoneurosis" and proposed that "it would seem appropriate for him to volunteer to be examined at this time."

Far from being abashed by the disclosure, Wallace responded briefly and cuttingly: "I receive 10 percent disability for a nervous condition caused by being shot at by Japanese airplanes and anti-aircraft guns in combat missions during World War II. To what does Senator Morse attribute *his* condition?"[36]

4

Onto the Playing Field

DISCHARGED FROM THE SERVICE in El Paso, Texas, on Friday, December 8, 1945, Wallace met his wife at the Mobile train station late Sunday afternoon. And on Monday morning, he donned his uniform (sporting the yellow emblem, irreverently called the "ruptured duck," signifying a discharged serviceman) and hitch-hiked to Montgomery. Reaching the capitol shortly after lunch, Wallace went directly to the governor's office. Chauncey Sparks promptly admitted his young home-county supporter and, after inquiring into George's health and war experiences, asked how he could be of service. Wallace produced Sparks's letter. "It was about to fall apart," he recalled, "because I had shown it to so many people . . . and they held that letter from the governor in awe because most of the folks in my outfit had never even seen a letter from a governor, much less got a letter from one."[1]

Sparks remembered both the letter and his promise. He instructed Wallace to go directly to the office of Billy McQueen, whom Sparks had appointed attorney general when the elected office-holder, Arch Carmichael, had entered the service. "Billy has an opening for an assistant attorney general that pays $175 a month," Sparks said. "Tell him I said to put you to work."[2]

Wallace hastened to see McQueen and explained that the governor had sent him down to talk about a position of assistant attorney general. McQueen, apparently believing that Sparks simply wanted to rid himself gently of a job-seeker, greeted Wallace's declaration politely but unenthusiastically. "I'll be glad to take your application, Sergeant," he said, "if you'll go ahead and fill out the papers." He started to summon his secretary when Wallace stopped him. "Let me go back and talk to the governor first," he said, "just to make sure I understood him correctly." McQueen smiled and nodded, and Wallace sped back to Sparks's office. "Governor," he reported, "Mr. McQueen said he was just going to take my application and would consider me, but that was all." Sparks picked up the phone and asked to be connected to McQueen. "Billy," he said. "That young soldier I sent down. I don't want this fella filling out an application. This is not one to be *considered*. This is one to have a *job*. I want you to put him to work." He replaced the receiver, smiled at Wallace, and told him to try again. Wallace was on the payroll before the day was out.[3]

He was elated, but not exactly wealthy. His annual $2,100 salary would equate, in buying power, with about $11,000 a year in 1990—below the federal government's poverty level for a small family. George, Lurleen, and Bobbi Jo lived in a boardinghouse room, ate sparingly, foreswore new clothes, and rarely went out in the evenings. It was the beginning of years of penury and boredom for Lurleen, Bobbi Jo, and the children to come. But for George, it was the electricity of life itself—*his* life; he had consciously, if humbly, set out on his single-minded ambition to become a political power in Alabama.

■　■　■

Governor Sparks's generosity was prompted by more than the services rendered to Sparks when he was a state legislator and Wallace a page, or by Wallace's hard work as Sparks's gubernatorial campaign chairman in Tuscaloosa in 1942. Reinforcing Sparks's good opinion of Wallace was an endorsement from Billy Watson, the governor's longtime friend and adviser who was a well-to-do Barbour County businessman, landowner, prankster, and putative political sage. Since early childhood, Wallace had known Watson and had called him "Uncle Billy"; later, Wallace more or less adopted Watson, who was twenty-five years older, as a substitute father. Watson was seen frequently at Sparks's side at the capitol and was a regular member of the entourage when the governor traveled. He would be as much in demand by Sparks's successor, James E.

Folsom, during Folsom's two terms as governor. And, in Wallace's statewide campaigns and forays outside Alabama, Watson was a virtual fixture until his death in 1967.

"He went with me all over the country," Wallace said of Watson, "and he'd ride with me when I was running for governor and speaking at different places. I would go to DeKalb County, and he would ride with me. I'd go to Marengo County, and he'd go with me. He traveled with me all the time and had a lot of influence on my life. In fact, Billy played a bigger part in my life, maybe, than anybody with the exception of my own folks." Watson's special genius was in knowing and sizing up all the political players in the state and acting as a sounding board for Wallace's ideas. The journalist Marshall Frady once aptly compared Watson to V. K. Ratliff, William Faulkner's ubiquitous sewing machine salesman in Yoknapatawpha County, a shrewd and perceptive observer who knew practically everyone but preferred the role of spectator to that of participant.[4] Watson was the first of several men—Ralph Adams, Glen Curlee, Oscar Harper, and Dave Silverman among them—who would serve Wallace as cronies in the literal sense: people who would spend *time* with Wallace, listening, chatting, joking—but, above all, just *being* there for a man to whom solitude was almost unbearable. In the words of Joe Azbell, who would be Wallace's chief wordsmith in national campaigns, Wallace "was the most love-starved man I ever saw in politics."[5]

Both Wallace and Governor Sparks knew that the position in the attorney general's office was merely a stepping-stone. With his family installed in a Montgomery boardinghouse, Wallace spent most of his time over the next few weeks renewing his acquaintance with politicians in the capital, some of whom he had known since his days as a page in the legislature. He sounded out nearly everyone he met about his plans to run that spring in the Democratic primary for the legislative seat from Barbour County. He had set his sights on the legislature when he was just sixteen; at the time, a Clayton businessman, Frank Childre, had advised George, "Finish high school, go to college, then come back and run for the legislature. I can tell you'd be a good one." (In later years, Wallace would repay Childre for his prescience by appointing one of his sons to the state accounting board.) In 1940, the year Wallace had turned twenty-one, he had tried to qualify to run for the Alabama House of Representatives from Tuscaloosa County, but he had missed the filing deadline by a day. (The experience taught Wallace to school himself thoroughly in the qualification rules for any ballot position, rules that varied from

county to county and from state to state; this predilection for knowledge of such idiosyncratic rules would pay spectacular dividends in
1968; see chapter 14.)[6] By the end of February 1946, Wallace took a
leave of absence from his state position and moved back to Barbour
County to run for the legislature. Through his state connections, he
obtained a job for Lurleen as a clerk in the Alabama Agricultural
Department's extension office in Clayton. A widow rented them a
room with a shower and allowed them kitchen privileges.[7]

The family subsisted on Lurleen's meager salary; George campaigned on the bequest of $1,000 (reduced to $900 by probate costs
and legal fees) from Hadley McEachern, his great aunt (see chapter
3). George husbanded the money for his three-month campaign and
spent it on advertising in the two county newspapers, campaign cards
for distribution, and gasoline for the 1938 Chevrolet borrowed from
his grandfather. At seventy-eight, Oscar was finding it more and more
difficult to drive himself; George, after chauffeuring him to his two or
three destinations a day, would use the car to swing through the
county to meet voters and seek their support.[8]

Wallace drove from farm to farm and house to house. He went
to school plays and church meetings, always introducing himself as a
candidate for the legislature who was interested in helping farmers,
the elderly, and the schools. He would greet workers at the gate of the
cotton mill near Eufaula and tell them of his interest in the working
man. At night, Lurleen, still too young to vote, would come home
from work, feed the baby, cook George's dinner, and then write a
dozen or more campaign letters for George's signature; on weekends
and on lunch breaks during the week, she would hand out campaign
cards. Many people remembered the Christmas cards George had
sent them during the war; others recalled his work inoculating dogs
during the rabies epidemic. His earlier activities all served him well;
he carried every precinct in the county, even the precinct in Clayton
in which his principal opponent lived. A second opponent, who had
been a major during the war, made the mistake of campaigning in his
uniform. Wallace, displaying his ability to bond with common folk
against the haughty, suggested to the county's large contingent of
veterans, nearly all of whom had been privates or noncommissioned
officers, that a fellow enlisted man would know and understand their
needs much better than a former officer "with those fancy pants."
The voters agreed overwhelmingly; the former major received only
200 votes of a total of about 5,000 cast. In all, Wallace polled more
than 2,800 votes, some 600 more than his two opponents combined.[9]

Wallace's appeal went beyond his inexhaustible energy and instinctive knack for politicking. He also was riding a resurgent wave of Southern populism stirred by another south Alabamian—James E. "Big Jim" Folsom, a lumbering giant of a man (six-eight, 275 pounds). Folsom campaigned for governor in 1946 against "the big mules"—the political cliques encompassing bankers, industrialists, Black Belt plantation owners, and country club gentility who collectively controlled much of Alabama's political structure—all of whom were anathema to Wallace's inherent political ideology as well. Folsom swept the state by a two-to-one margin. But Wallace, who early on established his own vote-getting prowess, ran ahead of Folsom in Barbour County by 579 votes: while Folsom led the county in the governor's contest by winning 44 percent of the ballots cast, Wallace amassed 56 percent of the votes in the legislative race.[10]

■   ■   ■

Wallace, however, had no time to savor his heady victory. It would be nearly eight months before he would take his house seat and become, at twenty-seven, the state's youngest legislator. Having exhausted Aunt Hadley's bequest, he was forced to rush back to Montgomery to reactivate his state job and salary. So the day after winning the Democratic nomination (which, in those days in Alabama and much of the South, equated to election), he returned his grandfather's old Chevy and hitchhiked his way to the capital. The driver, on learning that his passenger had just been elected to the legislature, asked why he was hitchhiking. "I just don't have the money," Wallace said. "I'm sorry. I hope you're not embarrassed that your legislator has to hitchhike." On the contrary, the man said, "if you're going to mind the state's money like you mind your own, you'll make a fine legislator."[11]

Wallace, who never would accumulate much money, couldn't care less about material goods. He ate sparingly, lived wherever he had to, and wore whatever clothes he could afford. But his indigence continued to impose a burden on his wife and daughter. When Lurleen and Bobbi Jo joined George in Montgomery a few days after he had resumed his state job, the three lived in a boardinghouse room "just large enough to put in a baby carriage and a double bed." As the legislative session approached, the family moved to a somewhat larger room in another boardinghouse—the one where George and Lurleen had spent their wedding night three years earlier. Nothing had changed; all the other residents were, as they had been then, grizzled, hard-drinking railroad workers who slept much of the day. Now, however, the Wallaces had a baby, and the landlady was concerned that her other residents might be disturbed by Bobbi Jo's occasional crying; the couple promised to move as soon as they could find suitable accommodations elsewhere.

"Suitable," to the gregarious and ambitious Wallace, meant a location, like the present one, near the Jefferson Davis Hotel (or "Jeff Davis," as the locals called it), a central gathering place for politicians.[12] The imposing, relatively new Jeff Davis anchored an area of hotels, eating places, and watering holes surrounding Court Square, an open commercial and transportation hub at the west end of the wide expanse of Dexter Avenue, just a few blocks from Alabama's graceful capitol, which overlooked Dexter from its east end. When the legislature was in session, the eateries within walking distance of the hotels were alive with midday debate and intrigue. Morrison's Cafeteria, because of its good, cheap food, attracted the younger, less well heeled members like Wallace. The Young China Restaurant, with its fully enclosed booths, was the perfect spot for deal making and vote trading. And the Elite Café (pronounced EE-light) was an afterhours dining and tippling favorite among legislators, lobbyists, and reporters.

The Jeff Davis—and, more specifically, its Mirror Lounge adorned by a portrait of the Confederacy's president and (for no discernible reason) a collection of African spears and shields—was headquarters to the "Folsom Chosen," a group that would help shape and enact the incoming governor's legislative program. Wallace was eager to become part of this new power structure. The nearby, tradition-drenched Exchange Hotel, where Jefferson Davis had spoken on the eve of his inauguration, housed, among others, the leaders of the outgoing Sparks administration—a group with which Wallace was more familiar and more at home. But Billy Watson, who floated between the two groups, introduced Wallace to political mainstays of both crowds—bosses like Shorty Millsap of Monroeville and Bert Boswell of Montgomery, plus well-to-do entrepreneurs (like himself and Oscar Harper of Montgomery and Marshall Johnson of Selma) for whom politics was a profitable and pleasurable pastime. Watson also helped Wallace learn to look the part of a legislator; he had regularly chided Wallace about wearing suits a size or two too large (an attempt at masking Wallace's diminutive if wiry build, but succeeding only in making him look downright runty and scrawny). So Watson introduced Wallace to several downtown haberdashers willing (and able) to give legislators deep discounts.[13]

Wallace also emulated Folsom by cultivating friendships in Montgomery's small but financially secure (and, in terms of political contributions, generous) Jewish community. Alabama's Jews felt comfortable with Folsom's relatively liberal ideology; not only were his racial policies quite progressive for the time, but so were his attitudes toward issues ranging from capital punishment to women's rights. It was not that Alabama's Jews personally, much less publicly, supported social change; on the contrary, most Montgomery Jews in those years advocated preservation of racial separation. Indeed, some, like financier Les Weinstein, were among the first to join the White Citizens Council when it was organized in 1956 as a somehow respectable, prosegregationist alternative to the Ku Klux Klan.[14] Nonetheless, the Jews in Montgomery and Alabama—and, probably, in most of the South—felt instinctively uneasy with those politicians who fanned racism or washed their hands of its fruits; they sensed the wisdom of those who, like the Atlanta editor Ralph McGill, warned ominously that hatred, once unleashed, cannot neatly be channeled toward one group in particular.

With Folsom, however, it was more than his benign racial views that endeared him to Jews; it was also his supremely warm and personal style, his overt reaching out to Jews and others who felt themselves on the social or economic fringes of Alabama's white power structure in the 1940s and 1950s. It was not unusual, for example, to see Folsom striding alone through the streets of Montgomery (or any other town he was visiting), stopping passersby to chat, holding forth on street corners, and greeting store proprietors and customers. Once, on a lovely spring day in Montgomery during Folsom's second term as governor, he burst into Golson's Drug Store near Court Square, heartily pumped the hand of the surprised but pleased druggist, and draped a huge arm around the druggist's shoulders. "Dr. Harold," he drawled, "whur's that beautiful wife of yours?" Then, spotting her standing just a few feet away, he disengaged himself from her husband, loped over to her, reached out, and planted a kiss on her hand as gallantly as his large, ill-coordinated, and well-liquored frame would allow. "Miz-rez Golson," he intoned, "you look as fresh as a spring blossom." Then he disengaged from the delightedly flushed woman and pointed a long, bony finger at her. "Now, it's gettin' to be Passover time, right?" he asked, pronouncing it "Pay-sover." Then, with mock gravity, he added: "So I better be gettin' some of that geh-filty fish, y'hear? It shore was good last time." Then he was back on the street, the entire encounter lasting no more than a minute.[15]

Wallace, with his innate sociability, curiosity, and essentially progressive political views, was cut from the same cloth as Folsom, and politically active Jews responded to him much as they did to Folsom. Wallace sought them out at Willie's Sports Center, a combination New York–style deli and poolroom, where the daily lunch crowd invariably included Jewish real estate entrepreneurs like Hilliard and Aaron Aronov, investors like Les Weinstein, physicians like Harry Glazer, and jewelers like Dave Silverman. They would become the nucleus of Wallace's later statewide campaigns, and some, like Silverman, would become close, lifelong confidantes.[16]

■   ■   ■

As the 1947 legislative session opened, the Wallaces settled into a relatively comfortable routine. They found an apartment in the same building in which his mother lived; Wallace's legislative pay was a comparatively bounteous twenty dollars a day, more than twice the rate of his state salary; and, through George's political contacts, Lurleen obtained a job as an enrolling clerk in the legislature, keeping a low profile to avoid charges of nepotism.[17] Despite his freshman status, Wallace walked into the state's house brimming with confidence that bordered on cockiness (he even allowed someone to suggest to Folsom that he might make a good speaker of the house, a position unheard of for one so young and of seeming inexperience). But Wallace, having spent part of his boyhood as a page, knew his way around the capitol at least as effectively as many members considerably senior to him, and he was determined to make his mark early.

Setting a goal that would have been difficult for even a seasoned legislator to attain, he aimed first at nothing less than realizing his father's long-held dream—the creation of a group of technical and vocational schools in Alabama. The hurdles were challenging: the idea of state-supported, nonuniversity, postsecondary schools was both novel for the time (even "radical," as Wallace once characterized it) and relatively costly; and, being a concept that smacked of Folsom's brand of antiestablishment populism, it was found suspect by a large, well-organized anti-Folsom bloc of self-styled traditionalists who feared losing their power to the new governor and his "galumphing galoots." So Wallace consciously adopted a noncontroversial demeanor: "I did not jump up and speak on every bill that came along because I didn't want to make a lot of enemies; I wanted to get my first bill passed in the legislature. . . . I kept everybody friendly with me by not taking a big part in opposing other people's bills; if I was against something, I just voted that way but didn't make a speech." The young lawmaker appealed to Southerners' pride by replaying his father's oft-intoned belief that Northerners' post–Civil War vindictiveness had sapped the South's brain power, and that trade schools would offer economic hope to thousands of young people and, ultimately, to the entire region.[18]

Though he held his tongue on most issues, Wallace decided he would be unremittingly resolute and even irritating, if necessary, on his trade schools proposal. Toward the end of the session, as the bill was nearing a crucial vote, one legislator, only half in jest, maintained that "Wallace was in my bathroom this morning trying to pass the trade school bill while I was doing my ablutions—so I can say that he is, at least, very persistent."[19]

Wallace spoke passionately of Alabama's need to improve its standard of living. Echoing his father's sentiments, he bitterly accused the North of trying to keep the South in economic peonage with such ploys as discriminatory freight rates; indeed, one of Wallace's earliest acts as a legislator was to introduce a resolution to equalize freight rates, a goal ultimately achieved through a 1949 decision of the U.S. Supreme Court. Wallace argued, "If we are going to build an industrial economy, we must have people trained in tool and die machines and as lathe operators. . . . Many young men don't want to go to college or to law school, but they want to learn a trade or a craft—brick masons, welders, auto mechanics. . . . Trade schools require just as much intelligence as going to college, and it's just as important to become a good welder as to get a degree in psychology."[20]

The bill received a major boost when the highly respected Rep. Rankin Fite of Marion County, a former speaker of the Alabama House and a member of the Alabama Board of Higher Education, joined Wallace in his quest. Fite advised Wallace to propose a sales tax on liquor to pay for the construction of the eight schools his bill authorized; that ploy proved brilliant. One could hardly oppose educational opportunities for the tens of thousands of returning veterans who faced uncertain job prospects, as long as the state could cover the cost. And, in the Bible Belt, one could hardly oppose a sin tax to finance the building of trade schools that would help put to work many of those courageous young men. Fite and Wallace guessed correctly that the legislature would not agree to a sales tax on liquor. Alabama's state-controlled system of liquor sales allowed extensive patronage for legislators and the governor (a system that would not be reformed until well into Wallace's governorship). A tax might cut into liquor sales; that, in turn, might reduce the commissions that liquor companies paid their Alabama "sales representatives"—men recommended to the companies by politicians, and who, for generous commissions, did little more than occasionally tour the certified liquor outlets throughout Alabama to ensure that those were carrying the "right" brands. The system made wealthy a number of politically well connected men (including Billy Watson and Oscar Harper), so a sales tax was unacceptable. But the beneficiaries of the clearly corrupt kickback system knew better than to risk a debate that might well require an extensive examination of their open but dirty secret.[21]

Wallace understood that fully, so he suggested that the money could be found elsewhere. Liquor companies paid a premium to a trust fund for the privilege of doing business in Alabama, and the fund's balance then stood at $15 million—enough to finance almost twice the number of schools proposed in Wallace's bill. Could not trust fund monies be appropriated to pay for the trade schools? Liquor interests agreed; but legislative leaders, including Fite, thought it imprudent to use more than a third of the trust fund, which meant $5 million. At an estimated construction cost of $1 million per school, Wallace would be required to compromise by settling for five schools instead of eight. He promptly agreed—and the legislature passed the trade school bill on the final day of the 1947 session. Three schools (in Dothan, Mobile, and Decatur) would be for whites and two schools (in Winona and Gadsden) for blacks. A few months later, the Alabama Board of Higher Education approved a resolution (introduced by Fite) naming one of the institutions (the one planned for Dothan) in memory of the man who many years earlier had planted the trade school idea in his young son's mind: it would be called the George C. Wallace, Sr., Technical School—a monument far grander and more permanent than the elder Wallace could have ever hoped for during his brief, difficult life.[22]

■   ■   ■

The legislature would not meet again until 1949, so Wallace faced the prospect of finding a new source of income in the intervening year and a half. Practicing law was the not-so-obvious answer. For one thing, Wallace's political future required him to return to Barbour County, which seemed to have plenty of lawyers for the population. And for another, in the practice of law, as opposed to the making of law, Wallace had precious little experience.

He had, however, participated in two cases while still in law school. His first case had involved the cook in Bill Jones's Tuscaloosa boardinghouse. The cook, Reuben Cobb, returning by bus from his day off in Birmingham, had been found with a suitcase filled with pints of whisky—an amount well over the legal limit permitted at the time for intercounty transport.[23] Cobb telephoned Jones from the county jail to say he had been locked up. Jones, in turn, called Wallace and asked him, as someone more familiar with the law than he, to help get Cobb out of jail. "We'll have to see the judge, and I don't have a coat to wear," Wallace said. "I'll go if I can borrow a coat from you." Jones obliged, but by the time they reached the courthouse, Cobb already had been fined fifty dollars, plus six-fifty in court costs, and locked up. Wallace told Jones there was nothing to do but pay the fine. Jones took out his checkbook, but the clerk raised his hand and said, . . . "Cash only." Jones did not have the cash, and the banks were closed because it was the weekend. Cobb would have to stay in jail until past nine Monday morning.

Wallace asked to see the judge. "Judge," he said, "now Reuben is a fine boy[24] and one of the best boardinghouse cooks in town. You know he just aimed to drink that whisky himself and never sell it to anyone. And Mr. Jones here is an upstanding student and runs that boardinghouse where Dr. Foster and many fine folks come in to eat now and then. See, if you don't take Mr. Jones's check, then there's no way Reuben'll get back in time to cook breakfast on Monday, and you'll have a whole bunch of students maybe failing some test because they're so hungry and can't think straight, and maybe that could ruin their whole career." Whether he was persuaded or simply had heard more than he wanted to, the judge agreed to accept Jones's check for $56.50.[25]

Another case had allowed young Wallace to use histrionics, if not legal knowledge, in an attempt to sway a jury. A Tuscaloosa lawyer, John Rufus Beale, had been appointed by the court to defend a man suspected of murdering his wife. The defendant had supposedly planted thirty sticks of dynamite beneath the room of the house in which his wife had been sleeping, ignited a half-hour fuse, then driven to a beer joint some fifteen miles away. As Wallace recalled, "When the dynamite went off, it blew the house almost away and blew her through the roof, and she fell down a mass of meat. That's a cruel way to describe it, but that's the way it was."[26]

By the time the husband had returned, authorities had been given an earful by neighbors about how he had abused his wife and had regularly threatened to kill her. They had immediately charged him with murder. Beale asked around for a hardworking law student to assist him in the case and found Wallace, who handled the clerical work, researched the case, interviewed witnesses, and, best of all, was given permission by the judge to appear in court, examine witnesses, and, if Beale wished, address the jury. It seemed an open-and-shut case; the defendant had confessed at one point that he had killed his wife because of her constant nagging, but Beale was able to cast some doubt on the confession by suggesting his client had been distraught and had since recanted. Since the only evidence was circumstantial, both Beale and Wallace tried in cross-examination to provide alternatives: yes, the defendant had purchased dynamite a few weeks before the murder, but might he not have been planning to use it to dislodge some boulders from his property? Yes, the defendant had threatened his wife frequently but had he not also taken her to church occasionally? This admittedly weak approach was all they had. At one point, Beale asked the prosecutor, Gordon Davis, to accept a guilty plea with life imprisonment; Davis turned him down and said he would ask for the death penalty.[27]

One morning before court opened, just as Beale and Wallace thought all was lost, a relative brought the defendant's son to see his father. "He was about ten or eleven," Wallace remembered, "but he looked younger than that. He was a sallow-looking boy, like he had hookworms, and he ran over to his daddy when he came into the courthouse and hugged him and kissed him." Wallace, who witnessed the scene, told Beale they could use the boy to try to whip up some sympathy among the jurors. Beale agreed; the two took the boy into a room, and Wallace asked him if he understood what was going on. "Do you understand that people in that courtroom are asking that your daddy be electrocuted? That they want to do away with him? Do you understand that?" And Wallace said that every time he would mention it, the boy would break down and cry. So Wallace sat the boy right behind the defendant's table. "Every time Attorney Beale was asking questions of a witness," Wallace said, "I would lean over and whisper to this young boy, 'Son, they're trying to kill your daddy.' He would immediately break down in sobs, and the judge would have to recess the court."

After the testimony concluded, Beale addressed the jury on the circumstantial nature of the state's evidence; then he asked Wallace to make a final statement for the defense. "I pinned it all on the boy," Wallace recalled. "I put my arms around him and I said, 'Now listen, this fellow here has nobody left in the world but his father. His father is no good, he's no account—but his son still loves him; you saw that in the courtroom. So I am pleading with you for this boy. Save his daddy's life so he'll have somebody in the world who loves him, even though he's in prison." The prosecutor had asked for the death penalty, Wallace told the jury. "He said, 'If anybody deserves the electric chair, this man deserves it.' If we were trying this man on whether he is a sorry, no-good individual, I would agree: he's no good; he's no account; he's killed his wife for no good reason. But I ask you to let this man live so the son will still have a father." Wallace then brought the boy to the jury box and said: "Gentlemen, think of this child when you are making that decision. He comes from a poor family. He has not had many good things in life. But he still loves his daddy, whether or not he has committed this horrible crime. I plead with you for this little boy." After the judge's charge, Wallace and Beale went to a café, but they had barely finished a cup of coffee when the bailiff rushed over and told them the jury was coming back in. "We find the defendant guilty," the foreman said, "and we fix his punishment at life in prison." Wallace was elated—so much so that he refused the hundred-dollar fee that Beale offered him. "I would have given you a hundred dollars for the experience this gave me," he told Beale.[28]

■　　■　　■

Wallace decided to open his law practice in Barbour County. His political ambition dictated that he should be in his home county rather than seek employment with a law firm in a large city like Montgomery, Birmingham, or Mobile. And, though he might have done better financially by tying in with an established firm in Clayton, he wanted the freedom to come and go as he thought politically beneficial.

Wallace hung out a shingle in an office above Rufus Little's drugstore in Clayton; his rent was $7.50 a month. Except for handling a few deeds and wills and an occasional case of a moonshiner or drunk driver, George did not have much business, so Lurleen went back to work at the local office of the Alabama Agriculture Department. She again endured the multiple hardships of working full-time, trying to raise a child with little help from her husband, and living on a paltry income. They moved into the attic of an old, three-story house that its owner, indebted to George for a legislative favor, let the Wallaces have for twenty dollars a month. The attic was a large room divided into a bedroom, a kitchen, and a bathroom, all heated by a coal grate. Rain or a strong wind would whip coal soot into the room; to prevent the grime from covering their possessions, the Wallaces would spread old newspapers on their bed, chairs, and tables at the earliest hint of inclement weather. On cold days, they would huddle around the coal-burning fireplace and endure the irritating coal dust. They also endured the rats that visited their kitchen most winter nights seeking food and warmth; each morning, they would find at least one crushed in the rat traps they had baited the night before.[29]

George bought a few sticks of furniture, for which he paid twenty dollars down and fifteen dollars a month over the next several years. In those days, such an expenditure was a serious financial obligation for the Wallaces. But providing Lurleen with her own things was at least an attempt to make her happy—and George did precious little else in that department.

Wallace's thoughtless dismissal of his wife and baby was yet another display of his dark side—the part of him that surfaced during youth as violent outbursts in the ring and in bars, and that would surface again during his flush political years as pernicious racism. It was all of a piece—his inner anger and total self-absorption. Wallace never cared about himself in the sense that he lusted after money, possessions, or personal comforts. He cared only about the quest for power: confronting, striking out at, and, if possible, besting those who had demeaned and impoverished him, his people, and his region—to Wallace, the whites-only South. Nothing—not personal safety, his family, or interracial tranquility—was as important.

Between his meager law practice and ceaseless wandering among his constituents, George rarely was home. Even on weekends, George, with the only car available to the family (his grandfather's), often stranded Lurleen and Bobbi Jo while he drove around the county, stopping at town squares to corral passersby, calling on farmers to pass the time, asking people what was on their minds, and always offering to be of some service. And should he pause from his obsessive need to shake a hand, slap a back, or bend an ear, he would find recreation that kept him from home until time to sleep. He frequently spent what little leisure time he had with his card-playing buddies. Lurleen once borrowed a car, drove to a farm where George and his pals were in the midst of a poker game, and stormed in, carrying the baby. She thrust the child at her husband and snapped, "You leave me with the baby and without a car and no way to go anywhere. Okay, *you* look after her, and I think you'll come home pretty quick." This did not work; George gave fifty cents to a kibitzer to show Bobbi Jo the cows, mules, and other farm animals. "She stayed pretty interested in that for a while," Wallace recalled. Hours later, Lurleen drove out in another borrowed car. "Let's go home," she pleaded. "You've played enough for today. The baby is tired and wants to go to bed." George maintained that he did not *really* want to be away from the family; he *had* to play poker, he said, because they were poor and he was trying to make money. He conceded in later years, however, that he rarely had won and that, in fact, he had broken even most of the time.[30]

In 1952, when running for a circuit judgeship, Wallace stopped playing, but not for his wife. Some voters thought it unseemly for a judge to gamble, and Wallace agreed: "I'm not going to play anymore," he said. "I promise you that. Don't be against me for the judgeship. I'm not going to be playing poker as a judge." He never played another hand.[31]

■ ■ ■

Early in 1948, President Harry S. Truman proposed a strong civil rights program, lending impetus to the growing campaign for racial equality in education and public facilities. Southerners felt as if they had lost one of their own.

Southerners had been in the vanguard of those who, in 1944, had advocated that President Franklin D. Roosevelt dump his liberal vice-president, Henry A. Wallace, and replace him with Missouri's Senator Truman. At the 1944 Democratic National Convention, after FDR had selected Truman as his running mate, Alabama's Gov. Chauncey Sparks said, "The South has won a substantial victory. . . . In the matter of race relations, Senator Truman told me he is the son of an unreconstructed rebel mother." Indeed, Martha Truman often remarked, "I thought it was a good thing that Lincoln was shot." And on her first visit to the White House, she warned, "If Harry tries to put me in Lincoln's bed, I'll sleep on the floor." Truman himself had acquired an abiding belief in white supremacy; at the age of twenty-seven, he wrote his childhood sweetheart, Bess Wallace: "I think one man is as good as another so long as he's honest and decent and not a nigger or a Chinaman." But Truman, genuinely shocked at a series of violent outrages directed at black Southerners in 1946, named a committee to investigate the state of civil rights; when its historic report, "To Secure These Rights," was issued late in 1947, Truman supported it fully.[32]

But Truman had fallen out of favor with much of the electorate outside the South, as well. Despite the successes of the Truman Doctrine, the Marshall Plan, and the dramatic Berlin Airlift, a majority of Americans characterized the president as inadequate, at best. According to a Gallup poll in March 1948, only 36 percent of Americans thought Truman was doing a good job; the poll also indicated that Truman would lose in November to Dewey, Taft, Vandenberg, or nearly any respectable Republican. "Dump Truman" was the conventional political wisdom among Democrats concerned about losing the White House in the 1948 presidential election.[33]

On the left, Henry Wallace announced a third-party candidacy. On the right, Gov. Strom Thurmond of South Carolina declared that he and at least five fellow Southern governors were prepared to secede from the Democratic party and back a Southerner for president. Mainstream Democrats who vowed to block a Truman nomination included FDR's sons, James and Elliott Roosevelt; Ed Flynn of New York, a former Democratic National Committee chairman; Sen. Claude Pepper of Florida; Walter Reuther, the United Auto Workers leader; and Hubert Humphrey, the young mayor of Minneapolis. Alabama's two senators, Lister Hill and John Sparkman, were among the leaders of a Democrats-for-Eisenhower movement. But Dwight D. Eisenhower, a World War II hero (who, unknown to most Democrats, regarded himself as a conservative Republican), refused to be considered; he announced, "I would refuse to accept the nomination under any conditions, terms, or premises." Truman—who twice unsuccessfully had importuned Eisenhower to accept the Democratic nomination for president (offering to stand as Ike's vice-presidential running mate)—obviously was not sanguine either about his chances for reelection.[34]

Given the circumstances, it was no surprise that Wallace, a state representative still too young in service to Alabama's Democratic party to be chosen as a delegate to the forthcoming Democratic National Convention in Philadelphia, filed for election as an alternate. His campaign advertisement in Barbour County's weekly newspaper came right to the politically correct point: "Unalterably opposed," it read, "to nominating Harry S. Truman and the so-called civil rights program." Wallace was elected without opposition; like the other alternates, he did not expect to go to Philadelphia. But dumb luck was on Wallace's side; the delegate for whom Wallace was standing in took ill, and Wallace excitedly headed for what he knew would be an opportunity for broad exposure. Philadelphia was soggy and sweltering when he arrived on the afternoon of July 12, and despite the Associated Press reporter's observation that "the Democrats act as though they have accepted an invitation to a funeral," Wallace was ebullient.[35]

Senator Hill, the senior member of the Alabama delegation, convened a caucus on July 13. (Governor Folsom, an unabashed admirer of the unpopular president, earlier had refused to join Thurmond's call for secession; now, he adopted the politically wise course of finding himself unable to attend the convention because of personal obligations.) Hill tried to persuade the delegation not to walk out of the convention if a strong civil rights plank was approved. Hill pointed out that the plank's principal advocates were younger men on the fringes of party power—Humphrey and the Democratic nominees for, respectively, senator and governor in Illinois, Paul Douglas and Adlai Stevenson. Hill said that even President Truman had made it known that he preferred to keep civil rights out of the Democratic platform, since the Republicans, meeting three weeks earlier in the same hall, had left it out of theirs. (Truman privately called Humphrey and his followers "crackpots" whom he believed were overtly trying to drive the South out of the Democratic party.)[36] A member of the delegation accused Hill of "secretly being for Truman." Hill, who had been among those Democrats calling for a draft of Eisenhower, went red but remained calm and dignified. Quietly, he said: "The gentleman does me a grave injustice. I am as unalterably opposed to the nomination of Harry Truman as any man in this room." However, most of the delegates made it plain that they intended to walk out, but they failed to persuade Hill—or Wallace—to join them.[37]

During the boisterous debate over civil rights, the behavior of one of the Alabama delegates struck one sympathetic observer as that of "a lovable clown whose antics were winning but grotesque at such a time." He was Eugene "Bull" Connor, the Birmingham politician who, fifteen years later, as the city's police commissioner, would engage in anti–civil rights tactics that would shock the nation (see chapter 8). On this occasion, Connor amused his racially insensitive colleagues by masquerading in a feathered headdress and performing his grotesque version of a rain dance up and down the aisles. From time to time, he stopped and "roared that [the delegates] should stop worrying about the colored man's lot and do something about the disgracefully cast off and downtrodden American Indian."[38]

The pro–civil rights forces barely carried the day by 69 votes of more than 1,200 cast. Southerners were outraged and bitter. The Dixiecrats—so named some weeks earlier by a headline writer for the *Charlotte Observer*—were led from the floor by Alabama's Handy Ellis, who cried out, "We bid you goodbye!"[39] The editor of the *Montgomery Advertiser*, Grover C. Hall, who had accompanied the delegates to Philadelphia, wrote:

> The South asked the Democratic Convention for understanding and forbearance, and received a savage blow on its face in return. The Convention dealt Alabama and the South a brutal and contemptuous blow. . . . It is clear that we of the South are alone, quite alone, with our oppressive and gathering problem. We stand alone somewhat as England did in 1940.[40]

Wallace was among a few Alabamians who stayed behind with Hill; he did so, he would explain later, because he had promised his constituents to represent them by casting his vote to nominate for president Sen. Richard Russell of Georgia. But Wallace's refusal to walk served other purposes as well: it helped Wallace maintain close ties to the principal elected leaders of Alabama's Democratic party, the state's two senators and its governor; and it gave him an opportunity for national publicity, since Senator Hill saw to it that Wallace would be among those to second Senator Russell's nomination. Given the times and the attitudes of most Southerners and of many other Americans, it was almost incidental that Wallace was effectively launching his national career by denouncing civil rights legislation. Shedding his suit jacket in the steaming hall, his shirt opened at the neck, his patterned tie pulled down a couple of inches below his collar, Wallace told the assemblage, "[Russell] will see that the South is not crucified on the cross of the so-called civil rights program." This was another of those losing causes that Wallace and the South seemed to cherish, but it gave the young legislator his first taste of national politics—including a helping of how he could generate passions with his opposition to civil rights. It was just a taste, but as he said later, he knew that he would someday want the entire meal.[41]

■　■　■

When George and Lurleen moved back to Montgomery for the 1949 legislative session, he was determined to expand the popularity he had gained with his notoriety at the convention. While Lurleen went back to work as a legislative clerk, George tore into ideas that he sensed would firmly establish his reputation as a man of the people. His first involved a bill to provide free college tuition to widows and orphans of Alabamians killed in World War II, as well as to Alabama GIs (and their dependents) who sustained war-related disabilities certified at 40 percent or more. The bill sailed through the house, and under the presumptive sponsorship of Sen. Preston Clayton (see chapter 5), the state senate passed it as well. Some thirty-six years later, during his final term as governor, Wallace was presented a special plaque endorsed by various state service organizations, including the American Legion, the Veterans of Foreign Wars, and the Disabled American Veterans. By then, the citation read, more than thirty thousand Alabamians—a third of them black—had received postsecondary education under the provisions of the Alabama GI Dependents Act of 1949.[42]

This bill was the first manifestation of the extraordinary racial schizophrenia that would envelop Wallace's public life: his vigorous determination to promulgate populist ideas and legislation—all of which would benefit both races—overshadowed by his uncompromising support for, and intensification of, the legal repression of blacks. The seeming discrepancy is understandable only by grasping Wallace's consuming hunger to become governor; all else was subordinated to that singular objective.

The emergence of the benign half of Wallace's split political personality was evident in his legislative efforts, successful or otherwise, that would help blacks as well as whites. His bill to provide scholarships to medical students who agreed to practice in rural areas never got out of committee; a proposal to waive the poll tax for GIs was dismissed as an initial wedge to kill the poll tax altogether; an idea to require literacy tests for voters was ignored because, ironically, it might weaken an existing Alabama requirement (meant to minimize blacks' suffrage) that prospective voters be able to interpret selected portions of the Constitution.[43]

Wallace's devotion to educational and populist causes, his advocacy of the bills that would give them life, his instinct for effective politics, and his growing popularity among his colleagues and the press—all these drew him inexorably closer to Governor Folsom, who earlier had endeared himself to Wallace through strong support of the State Vocational and Trade School Act and the naming of the George C. Wallace, Sr., school. Now, the governor agreed to Wallace's request to be appointed to the board of trustees of Tuskegee Institute, the historic college for blacks—founded in 1881 by Booker T. Washington and further made famous by George Washington Carver—for which Wallace had pushed for additional funds. It was a shrewd, farsighted request—one that recognized the need for an advocate of segregated education who could point to his support for improving black schools and colleges. Wallace, who also supported the Folsom administration's programs for improving highways and supplementing teachers' salaries, quickly became identified as a leading Folsomite—a label Wallace tried to denigrate because he already was attracting many of Folsom's friends but did not want to inherit Folsom's enemies.

The anti-Folsom bloc in the legislature tried to enlist Wallace's support, but he put them off. "Listen," he told one of the bloc's leaders, "I don't know whether I want to join with you or not because I don't know what his program is going to be. I mean, some of what he said when he was running was not bad at all—things on education, health, welfare, old-age pensions, farm-to-market roads, higher teacher salaries. I'm just not going to take the attitude that I'm against everything that Jim Folsom is for." Wallace said he would examine Folsom-sponsored legislation the way he would all other proposals—on their individual merits. In fact, he voted against Folsom about 50 percent of the time, but it was the other 50 percent—relating to social, educational, and public works proposals that tended to be somewhat ahead of their time—that attracted most public attention. And, despite his public protestations to the contrary, Wallace reinforced his Folsomite image by quietly agreeing to become an active part of Folsom's campaign for governor should

Folsom run again in 1954, the next time he would be permitted to seek the office under the state constitution.[44] But Wallace was aware even then that the two might part company over their essential difference—Folsom's discomfort with Southern intransigence to integration, and Wallace's refusal to risk his future on deviating from the accepted system of white domination.

■   ■   ■

For the immediate future, however, Wallace had other plans. He did not have to worry about his own seat; he was unopposed in his bid for renomination and reelection in 1950. However, Wallace actively supported his old mentor, Chauncey Sparks, who wanted to return to the Governor's Mansion. But, after four years of Folsom, the "big mules" desperately wanted one of their own—a more traditional, more conservative team member. They did not fully trust Sparks any longer because of his south Alabama roots, since that area had spawned neopopulists like Folsom and Wallace. So the entrenched interests with whom both Folsom and Wallace were at odds—banks, power companies, railroads, and the like—threw in with Gordon Persons, an experienced political leader whose gentlemanly mien was as far from Folsom's raucous, backslapping, hard-drinking style as his politics. Persons won handily, and in the 1951 legislative session, Wallace for the first time found himself in opposition to the administration. And, in sharp contrast to his earlier, low-profile approach, Wallace came out swinging against the Persons crowd, a group that included Sen. Preston Clayton as an administration floor leader who, the following year, would regret his ties with Persons when he took on Wallace in a race for circuit judge.[45] (See chapter 5.)

A secret file on legislators maintained by Governor Persons supposedly described Wallace as "energetic, ambitious, liberal, smart, [and] probably . . . hostile" in the future. It allegedly added that Wallace was "for appropriations, against taxes." The Alabama Chamber of Commerce, staunchly anti-Folsom and pro-Persons, was rumored to have described Wallace as a "radical."[46] Wallace did little to dispel those notions that, at the time, bore no relationship to a Southern politician's racial views. He attacked Alabama's hundreds of small loan companies, whose powerful lobby counterattacked through a house committee that issued a report calling Wallace's proposed Small Loan Act "a subterfuge, a deceit, a fraud," because it had proposed a small loan limit of 3 percent per month on loans up to $300.[47] In fact, small loan companies at the time were charging up to 1,000 percent annual interest. Wallace testified that once, as a student, he had borrowed $25 with a car worth about $250 as collateral. He paid off the loan nine months later, after having paid $36 (or nearly 200 percent) in interest. He said, "The man told me, 'You owe us 4 more dollars for this month's interest.' I said, 'Well, sir, I done paid you $36 for a $25 loan guaranteed by an automobile worth more than the loan, and I've just paid you all I'm going to pay. I'm going to give you the $25 here and that's the end of it.' He said, 'Well, you still owe us $4.' And I said, 'Well, you just keep it on the books and sue me sometime.' So I got very upset with loan sharks in Alabama." Wallace did not succeed in changing the law at the time, but Alabama newspapers described him that year as "a champion of legislation to put small loan operators in a tighter harness."[48]

When Persons proposed a $25 million bond issue for highway construction, Folsom rallied his troops, including Wallace, in opposition. The former governor, starting early on his 1954 campaign, told a southwestern Alabama gathering that he had paved more roads than any three administrations—and had done so without a bond issue. "If you expect to get any more help down here in Coffeeville, you're going to have send someone up to Montgomery to steal it for you. They sure ain't going to turn it loose." Wallace, in the legislature, maintained that the state was paying $800,000 a year in interest on old bond issues, and that Governor Persons wanted "to borrow $25 million more from fancy-pants bankers."[49] The legislature approved the bond issue, but the people voted it down in November. Wallace played a major role in spoiling a $500,000 fund that Persons planned to use for "special hiring" of additional personnel in an "emergency"—jobs neither subject to civil service requirements nor limited in number to those authorized by the budget. A Persons floor leader described the proposal as "just a little bill that the governor wanted passed" so he could get "a little money for clerks in the governor's office."

But Wallace, joined by George Hawkins of Etowah County, and his old ally, Rankin Fite, denounced the measure as "a pork-barrel bill" permitting the governor "to hire his friends to draw a check for doing nothing." (Ironically, that was a reasonably fair description of Wallace's own state job following World War II.) In this case, however, Wallace called the proposal "the biggest slush fund [he had] ever seen." Fite, however, did more than anyone else to torpedo the bill by delivering a speech dripping with sarcasm:

I'm *for* this bill. And I'll tell you why I am for it. I believe in the spoils system. I believe that a man, when he is elected governor of Alabama, ought to have an unlimited amount of money to pay off his friends with jobs. I'm not like those who think we ought to have everything under civil service. I believe my friend from Barbour and my friend from Etowah are mistaken in the idea that a governor should not have an open-ended appropriation . . . to give out hundreds of jobs to those who worked for him to elect him governor of Alabama. I believe in the spoils system, and, therefore, I am for the bill.

The bill lost in a close vote.[50]

In one of his most spectacular efforts, Wallace led a filibuster in an attempt to defeat an increase in the state sales tax from 2 percent to 3 percent. He argued that a regressive sales tax would penalize "the lathe operators, the brick masons, the welders, the tool and die workers"—part of a Wallace litany that he would hone over the years. "We are opposing the taxing of the little man," he said, "and we should tax those more able to pay." Wallace, to prolong the inevitable, had drawn seventy-two proposed amendments to the bill. Schooled in the legislative rules from his teenage years, he knew that the rules required immediate action on any amendment that was hand-carried to the well, placed on the table, and accepted by the clerk. So he carried all the amendments to the clerk's desk at once and asked the speaker of the house for permission to introduce them all at once to "save the time" of Wallace's proposing of an amendment while legislators were speaking. The speaker, thinking that introducing the amendments en masse would mean they could be voted on as a package, readily agreed. Wallace then informed him that each of the amendments would be debated individually—and reminded him that each supporter was allotted five minutes to discuss each amendment.

The amendments were a complex combination of proposals, each seeking to permit a sales tax increase—but only by a small increment of the proposed 1 percent raise—and allotting a percentage of whatever increase was approved to raise teachers' salaries. One outraged legislator, Rep. Pelham Merrill of Cleburne County, leaped to his feet during the filibuster and stormed at Wallace:

In my limited House experience, I have never seen such an effort to make us look like nincompoops. Seventy-two pending amendments have been offered by the man who has been

doing most of the talking. . . . One of the seventy-two, for
example, says that 'seventy-five percent of one-third of the
total proceeds shall go to classroom teachers.' The next,
'seventy-seven percent,' and so on, to ninety-nine percent.
How can a man consistently say he's sincere when he resorts to
such tactics? Has he come here with clean hands? There are
enough amendments pending to keep us tied up indefinitely.

Wallace and his supporters, clearly in a minority by a three-to-one
margin, finally agreed to back down after two weeks. But they exacted
a price: they succeeded in getting a bigger pay raise for what one pro-
Persons reporter snidely called "the school marms of Alabama."[51]

Wallace did not spend the session entirely in negativism, however. He pushed through a bill permitting cities to reach beyond
municipal borders to form gas districts so areas could join forces
and issue bonds for construction of natural gas lines. The idea of
financing municipal needs through bonds gave birth to Wallace's
greatest legislative contribution to Alabama's economy—the
Wallace-Cater Municipal Bonding Act. The state constitution prevented cities from awarding value to corporations, so Wallace,
prompted by Ed Reid, the executive director of the Alabama
League of Municipalities, looked for an alternative method through
which cities could attract industry to their locales. He found it in
Mississippi, where an industrial bonding act had been adopted. It
allowed cities to float bonds to finance new industrial facilities; the
industries would repay the cities through rentals and would be
exempted from taxes during the repayment period. In all, this
arrangement was a sweet deal for the industries (Congress, pressed
by organized labor in the North, eventually placed an annual cap of
$150 per capita on the total value of the bonds that any state could
issue). When Wallace introduced the idea in Alabama, some legislators branded it a form of socialism because municipalities would be
involved in the financing of private industry.

One skeptic was Wallace Malone, George Wallace's distant
cousin. During the debate, Malone asked, "Does my friend from
Barbour admit that this is a bit like socialism?" Wallace knew that
Malone had actively supported the 1948 Dixiecrat presidential ticket
(comprising South Carolina's governor, Strom Thurmond, and as his
running mate, Mississippi's speaker of the house, Walter Sillers).
"Cousin Wallace," George responded, "I don't see how in the world

you can call it socialism because the man who gave me this bill, the man who sponsored it in the Mississippi legislature, was the man you gave five thousand dollars to so he could be vice-president of the United States. So if that's socialism, then you voted for a Socialist for vice-president." Malone threw up his hands and pleaded, "That's enough, that's enough! If Walter Sillers was for it, then it must be all right." The bill passed and, over the ensuing years, attracted a variety of industries to Alabama—among them, General Motors, Chrysler, Proctor & Gamble, Sony, Michelin, U.S. Steel, Boeing, Monsanto, Kerr-McGhee, and Mitsubishi.

In interviews, Wallace often spoke of that achievement more than any other in his career, save for his presidential forays. He maintained that industry came to the state "not for cheap labor like some people would say, but they came for the climate and the work ethic." And, he said, "usually the company bonds sold themselves because they were used for well-known industries like General Motors . . . and they were tax-exempt. Now, if it were some unknown industry that had no rating in Dun & Bradstreet, of course the bonds wouldn't sell. . . . The last time I ran for governor, labor endorsed me because they knew I always listened to them and my policies had brought them jobs. And, of course, the Chamber of Commerce said that a labor endorsement raised a red flag about my attitude toward business. They had never been my friends because they thought I was too rude and too crude and too much a redneck. Well, I pointed out to them that every one of the industries they represented were built under the Wallace-Cater Act, and you cannot say that you don't have a good business attitude when you've been responsible for bringing in more business to Alabama than any other person in the history of the state."[52]

Wallace's contributions did not go unnoticed by the Alabama League of Municipalities. In its publication in April 1951, the league asserted, "[Wallace is] one of the youngest, yet one of the ablest members of the legislature . . . the champion of the local governments, the veterans, and the trade school program [who] makes dozens of speeches every month all over Alabama to luncheon, veterans, and education groups." Ed Reid would be a lifelong supporter of Wallace—and that, in turn, would bring most of the state's mayors, especially those of the medium-sized and small towns, firmly into the Wallace camp. The considerable statewide publicity that Wallace had generated in five years in the legislature, however, was a clear signal to him for moving ahead. He thought about Congress, but his district's seat was occupied by the popular George Andrews. So he cast his eye instead on a circuit judgeship—a post that not only would pay better and afford Wallace even more time for statewide travel, but that, with the increasing involvement of the judiciary in the turmoil over segregation, might provide him with a platform from which he could spring into contention for governor.[53]

5

Here Comes the Judge

J. *S . W I L L I A M S,* the long-time judge of Alabama's Third Judicial District, which encompassed Barbour, Bullock, and Dale counties, had announced his retirement early in 1952, possibly because he had learned that young Rep. George Wallace wanted the job.[1] But the other contender for the vacancy was one of Wallace's colleagues in the legislature, Sen. Preston Clayton.

The two men represented mirror images of Southern leadership of the time. Clayton's family was considered Southern aristocracy; Wallace's people were farmers and professionals. Clayton's grandfather, Gen. Henry Clayton, was a Civil War hero who himself had been the judge of the Third Judicial Circuit (see chapter 1); Wallace's grandfather was a widely respected country doctor who had been a probate judge. Clayton lived in a small but gracious home that had been occupied by Claytons for more than a century; Wallace, whose family home had been sold years earlier, was paying twenty-five dollars a month to rent a garage apartment. Clayton had been a lieutenant colonel during World War II; Wallace had been a sergeant. Clayton had been a member of the relatively genteel Alabama senate for sixteen years; Wallace had been part of the more raucously political Alabama house for six years.

This was a contest between the Southern Bourbons and the neopopulists—but it was really no contest at all. In the wake of the war, with its international dangers and domestic opportunities, Southerners wanted vigorous leaders who they believed would protect America's freedom and carve a piece of the future for the "average" person (the average *white* person, of course; black suffrage was expanding but remained far from pivotal). Wallace knew from instinct and experience how to respond to populist yearnings, and with folksy campaigning he stressed not only his own strong record in behalf of "the little man" but also found Clayton's major vulnerability—a seeming upper-class remoteness.

Although Wallace's campaign tactics were tame compared to later assaults he would launch on his political foes, Clayton long retained sour memories of the 1952 judgeship race. Wallace, he recalled, "went all over saying, 'Now, all you officers vote for Clayton, and all you privates vote for me.' He'd tell those country men that I was living out here in a mansion while he was living in a little house and paying twenty dollars a month rent, that I didn't *need* to be circuit judge. He even talked about my [owning] horses. He had all those rednecks."[2] Not quite all, but almost: Wallace swept the three-county district, receiving nearly 6,700 votes to less than 2,400 for Clayton.[3]

But if Clayton was wounded by the extent of Wallace's victory, he nonetheless claimed to have turned his defeat to financial advantage. Wallace said that Clayton told him "a year or so after I defeated him that I had done him the best favor in the world because he made more money practicing law in a month than a judge did all year."[4]

That may have been true, but to Wallace, the take-home pay of $600 a month (equivalent to about $3,000 a month in 1990) was a kingly sum. And he would receive it month in and month out, not as in the legislature when he was paid on a per diem basis only during legislative sessions. He needed the extra money because there were now two additional mouths to feed: Peggy Sue, born in 1950, and George, Jr., born the year after that. Also, the additional income (plus the freedom to schedule court dates at his own convenience), allowed him to devote more time to traveling throughout Alabama in pursuit of his dream of one day becoming governor. Indeed, his pay was even enough money to allow him to promise Lurleen that, within a year, they likely would have put enough aside to be able to make a down payment on a home of their own.

Despite Lurleen's continued virtual imprisonment with the three children in the family's garage apartment, and her strong dislike of George's frequent out-of-town speaking engagements, the promise of better times encouraged Lurleen to suppress her discontent. She even volunteered to spend most of her evenings as George's unpaid secretary, writing a raft of thank-you notes to the people (and prospective future voters) whom he had met in his informal campaign travels. She also undertook the tedious task of combing through hundreds of pages of legal materials from which she developed a card file that George could refer to when sitting on the bench trying cases. The indexed file was a security blanket for Wallace, who was professionally uncomfortable in his new role as judge. Neither his years as a lawmaker nor his election to the bench altered the reality that he remained a legal novice; he certainly was in uncharted waters when it came to presiding over the variety of criminal and civil cases that confronted him in court.

Wallace sought and received help from the state's preeminent trial judge of the day, Walter B. Jones of Montgomery. Jones sent Wallace dozens of his decisions and charges to juries in cases ranging from simple trespass to murder, and from petty theft to grand larceny. Lurleen dutifully spent hours each evening excerpting the material and adding it to the file.[5] Wallace also regularly received advice and suggestions from J. Ed Livingston, one of his former law school professors whose breadth of legal knowledge Wallace admired (Livingston would become the chief justice of the Alabama Supreme Court in the late 1950s), and whose disregard of convention Wallace found refreshing (Livingston would, on occasion, wear bib overalls while lecturing his students; he would continue the practice on the supreme court, although his overalls would be covered by his judicial robe).

■ ■ ■

If Wallace faced his new duties with some trepidation, he did not show it publicly. At 9:00 A.M. on February 2, 1953, Wallace climbed onto the bench at the Bullock County courthouse in Union Springs, called on the pastor of the Union Springs Methodist Church to offer a prayer (an innovation), qualified and charged a county grand jury, and disposed of several civil cases (either by granting continuances or approving pretrial settlements)—all within ninety minutes. Just before adjourning the court at 10:30 A.M., Wallace introduced to the public his new employee—a full-time official court reporter, the first to work in the circuit in a decade. Indulging what would be his lifelong proclivity to elevate the status of those surrounding him, Wallace contended that the reporter was "nationally famous for taking, single-handed, several million words of testimony in a long and complicated federal case in Kansas. His notes on that occasion, before he transcribed them, were piled from the floor to the ceiling." Wallace lit a cigar; granted an interview to a reporter from a daily newspaper in nearby Columbus, Georgia; and then, with the cigar clamped at a rakish angle, went off to an early lunch with two local lawyers—one of them the brother of U.S. Representative George Andrews and the other the son of Bullock County's probate judge. Wallace, as would ever be his wont, wasted neither time nor opportunity.[6]

Wallace's demeanor on the bench remained folksy, and his disposition of cases involving essentially petty crimes has been described as "usually genial and casual."[7] But he tended to be tough on juvenile offenders. "When I was fifteen, I was just as knowledgeable as someone who was twenty-one," he maintained. "When I was fifteen years old, if I had committed a murder, I would have known exactly what I had done and why I did it and that I deserved no juvenile status, because a man fifteen years old is knowledgeable enough in the world to know that killing somebody is wrong and murder is wrong. . . . So, when I was a judge, I had a case or two of so-called juveniles who committed a heinous crime. I never would remand them to juvenile court because I remembered myself at fifteen—and I knew right from wrong. . . . I never had much sympathy in the matter of young people who have been bound over as juveniles when they had killed somebody or raped somebody."[8] However, he was respectful and fair to those who came before him, including, to an unusual degree for the time, blacks. In a case involving an urban renewal project in Barbour County, about fifty blacks displaced from their homes thought they had been underpaid for their property. Wallace tried all fifty cases in a week, impaneling alternate juries: one would hear a case, visit the property site, and start making a judgment; meanwhile a second jury would have begun hearing the next case. In every case, the juries, following Wallace's recommendations, awarded more money to the plaintiffs than had been offered by the housing authority—and in some cases, more than the plaintiffs had requested. The young black lawyer representing the plaintiffs, Fred Gray (who would become prominent in December 1955, when he would defend a Montgomery, Alabama, seamstress named Rosa Parks for refusing to give up her seat on a bus to a white man), was mightily impressed by Wallace. Certain that the decisions in Wallace's court would be biased in favor of the government, Gray had filed a series of motions in preparation for appellate proceedings. But when the last case had been tried and adjudicated, he rose in court and thanked Wallace:

> Your honor, I have practiced in many courts, but I have never been treated more fairly by a judge, by the jurors, by the officers of the court, than I have here. We are not going to appeal a single one of these cases, and we are appreciative that you saw our side of the matter.[9]

In another case, the husband of an eighteen-year-old Dale County black girl had been killed in an accident while being transported to work by a company truck. The dead man, however, had not been covered by workers' compensation provisions, and his employer, a well-to-do white man, was not insured. When sued for damages, the employer dropped in on Wallace and reminded him that he had been among the judge's biggest supporters. Wallace recalled having treated the man cordially but having ruled against him in court. The Alabama Supreme Court upheld Wallace's ruling, and the young girl was awarded damages.[10]

Poor whites, as well as blacks, benefited from Wallace's tendency to sympathize with "working folks." An example was when a Bullock County justice of the peace sentenced a young man to thirty days in jail for reckless driving because the youth's father had angered the magistrate by using abusive language. The case was appealed to Wallace, who heard it without a jury; after ten minutes, he stopped the proceedings, vacated the jail sentence, and fined the driver twenty-five dollars. He said the sentence had been unduly harsh and, in any event, had been meted out to "a poor boy whose daddy didn't know any better."[11] Wallace even dug into his own pocket to assure the comfort of those hauled before his court; he regularly handed his bailiff a dollar or two, then instructed him to drop by a nearby diner to buy bags of hamburgers for the prisoners, white or black, who were required to wait for trial past the lunch hour.[12]

Wallace's acts of kindness and his dispensation of justice to black litigants and defendants were especially notable in the context of his own racial positions. The roots of his beneficence lay at least partially in the widespread and often-articulated belief among white, middle-class Southerners that Northerners "love the Negro race" but despise its individual members, whereas Southerners feel just the opposite. The "love" that Southern whites believed they felt for individual blacks was, of course, paternalistic at best and was dependent on blacks remaining subordinate. But even on that basis, there were tens of thousands of relationships between blacks and whites in the South; they talked to one another and had a sense, however incomplete or illusory, of how the other lived—and that may well have provided a foundation for eventual racial progress in the South.

Still, Wallace's evenhandedness seemed particularly out of character, given his political ambition and white Alabamians' strong, widespread opposition to compliance with desegregation directives. In 1952 the U. S. Supreme Court had ordered state universities to desegregate; although blacks had been admitted to a number of state universities in the South, including some in Arkansas, Tennessee, Texas, and Virginia, stout resistance continued in Alabama. In early 1956, in fact, a mob prevented a young black woman, Autherine J. Lucy, from entering the University of Alabama (as discussed later in this chapter). The 1954 *Brown v. Board of Education* decision, in which the Supreme Court declared unconstitutional the separate-but-equal doctrine in the South's primary and secondary schools, met with massive resistance in Alabama; indeed, by the end of 1956 Alabama was among eight Southern states that had no desegregation at all.[13] And in Montgomery, a boycott of city buses had begun in December 1955 in response to Rosa Parks's conviction for refusal to relinquish her bus seat (she was fined ten dollars, plus four dollars in court costs). The boycott generated widespread recriminations among Alabama's blacks and whites, spurred the growth of the relatively new White Citizens Council organizations (considered so respectable compared to the Ku Klux Klan that Montgomery's police commissioner publicly announced that he had become a member), and triggered sporadic racial violence. The boycott also catapulted a young black minister, Martin Luther King, Jr., into the national spotlight and ultimately led to a federal court ruling in June 1956 (later upheld by the U.S. Supreme Court) that ended intrastate segregation on buses and other modes of public transportation. The ruling was written by Frank Johnson, one of Wallace's law-school buddies (see chapters 2 and 7).

In day-to-day court dealings with blacks, however, Wallace seemed unaffected by the racial turmoil beginning to sweep his state. When a jury exonerated a white man charged with stealing peanuts from a local warehouse, Wallace promptly released the man's three hired accomplices, all black men who could not afford to hire a defense lawyer.[14]

One of the more remarkable testaments to Wallace's insistence on racial fairness in his court came years later in a book by a black civil rights activist who had condemned Wallace as "a dangerous and unprincipled opportunist, willing to destroy Alabama to promote himself." J. L. Chestnut, Jr. (who would become an important figure in the civil rights movement in the mid-1960s), was, at age twenty-eight, the only black lawyer in Selma, Alabama, in late 1958. He was assisting another black lawyer, Peter Hall, in representing a group of poor black cotton farmers who claimed they had been cheated by one of the South's largest cotton oil–processing companies. The case ended up before Wallace in his Barbour County courtroom, and Chestnut wrote:

> The company brought several smooth big city lawyers down from Birmingham who were not only eager to use subtle racist ridicule on us and our clients but sought to overwhelm us with the technicalities of the law. One of the Birmingham lawyers had a particularly disgusting and scornful way of referring to our black clients as "these people." Every time he used that phrase, Wallace got red in the face and looked with some sympathy toward our clients and us. Finally, he told the lawyer, "Please refer to Mister Hall's and Mister Chestnut's clients as 'the plaintiffs' or don't refer to them at all." His voice was ice cold. We won every case. Wallace was sitting as judge and jury, and he awarded our clients more money than we had asked for. George Wallace was for the little man, no doubt about it. . . . George Wallace was the first judge to call me "mister" in a courtroom.[15]

But as Chestnut observed (and as Wallace himself frequently conceded), "What [Wallace] wanted more than anything else was to be governor"[16]—and Wallace found ways to use his circuit court bench as a rostrum to dramatize the South's bitter opposition to federally imposed racial integration.

In 1953, Wallace was the first judge in the South to enjoin local officials (who, of course, hardly required his entreaties) from removing railroad-station signs that denoted "white" and "colored" facilities.[17] In 1956, when federal officials demanded to see judicial records in a Georgia county near Atlanta to determine whether blacks had been systematically excluded from grand juries there, Wallace, from his Alabama perch some two hundred miles away, proclaimed that if federal agents tried to probe records in *his* jurisdiction, he would "invoke [his] full power and authority" and "issue an order for [their] arrest."[18] And, as would become his modus operandi, he used a local incident to dramatize a broader issue; in this instance, he denounced the investigations as a "direct insult to the people of Cobb County, Georgia, and to state sovereignty." He said that recent decisions by the U. S. Supreme Court and rulings by the Interstate Commerce Commission to facilitate integration had led to "deterioration in the fine race relations" that had until then "existed in the South." Continuing, Wallace contended, "We represent both races, [and] laws of this state are and should be enforced without discrimination. We can preserve our segregated way of life without violence and within the law and to the satisfaction of a majority of our people, both black and white."[19]

Wallace somehow sensed that, as improbable as it might seem for a circuit judge in Alabama to condemn a federal action in another state, his self-righteous outburst would gain respect and attention. He was right. On his home turf, a grand jury in Union Springs (orchestrated by the judge) pledged to Wallace its "full support to the utmost in whatever action he takes if it is necessary to protect the integrity of this circuit and its grand jury." The grand jurors also endorsed Wallace's recommendation to urge law enforcement officers to continue upholding segregation laws.[20] And, incredibly, the Georgia legislature summoned the young judge to address a joint session, and the *Montgomery Advertiser* noted that Wallace's actions typified "the spirit and skill which Wallace [had] demonstrated in resisting federal intrusions."[21] In the summer of 1956, Wallace represented Alabama on the platform committee at the Democratic National Convention in Chicago; working "as the right hand" of Gov. James P. Coleman of Mississippi, he was credited with having watered down the party's civil rights plank by preventing endorsement of the *Brown* decision and the creation of a Fair Employment Practices Commission. He was "so effective," the *Advertiser* editor Grover C. Hall crowed in a subsequent editorial, "that the National Association for the Advancement of Colored People [NAACP] and Walter Reuther [of the United Auto Workers, or UAW] left Chicago in wrath, publicly accusing the Wallace committee of locking them out of their meeting place in the Conrad Hilton Hotel."[22]

■   ■   ■

In 1957, demonstrating ever-increasing brashness, Wallace, through the good offices of his friend and congressman, George Andrews, managed to have himself summoned as a witness to the House Judiciary Committee's hearings on civil rights legislation. In his testimony, Wallace articulated the intense, if unoriginal, Southern imprecations against racial integration, based on the usual insupportable and often contradictory assertions popular among Southern whites: First, Southern blacks would not be "ready" for integration until they had received more and better education; their schools were, nonetheless, equal in every sense to those attended by whites; still, on the off-chance that some schools for blacks were *not*, in fact, equal to those for whites, Southern states as a group were spending lots of money to improve the schools for blacks. Next, black and white Southerners alike actually preferred separation; however, in those instances where Southern blacks had demonstrated (both figuratively and literally) a desire for integration—as with the fifty-thousand blacks in Montgomery, Alabama, who had refused to ride segregated buses for a year—the protesters probably had been encouraged to do so by "outsiders" like Martin Luther King, Jr. (who was from Atlanta, Georgia, just a few miles from Cobb County, into whose affairs Wallace had unhesitatingly injected himself). And last, organizations that supported integration, such as the NAACP, were communist inspired; and congressmen who supported integration, like House Judiciary Committee Chairman Emanuel Celler of New York, were dupes. Wallace's testimony lacked the more memorable, if somewhat indelicate, rhetoric of his later stump speeches, but his overt, face-to-face challenging of the formidable Celler was, to many Southerners, exhilarating; Wallace's "collision with [Celler], that New York holy roller . . . attracted wide notice to the earnestness of Alabama's opposition to race mixing," a *Montgomery Advertiser* editorial said.[23]

Over time, Wallace honed his spiel and calibrated his arguments to sound less offensive to many racially sensitive ears in both the North and South, so his celebrity as a "sensible" representative of his region grew. His widening reputation prompted an invitation from Christopher King, a radio personality who moderated a weekly discussion program, "Sounding Board," for the Mutual Broadcasting System. The program's discussion, "Is the Southern Plan Sensible?" was broadcast from the Broadmoor Hotel in Colorado Springs; Wallace not only held his own against Jack Foster, the editor of the *Rocky*

Mountain News of nearby Denver, but he drew his share of cheers and applause from an enthusiastic audience.[24] Foster argued, "Segregation in the schools is un-American and impractical," and he maintained that desegregation was working in parts of Oklahoma and Texas and in Washington, D.C. "There has been a gradual evolution of the equality of the races, and the Supreme Court decision is the climax according to the American way of life," Foster claimed; and he asked rhetorically, "How can we appear honest before the communist world when there is segregation in our own country?"[25]

Wallace was a paragon of sweet reasonableness as he enunciated positions that he would repeat, with variations, for years to come:

> The South holds the United States Supreme Court in esteem,
> but the South will lawfully resist the Court's decision of
> desegregation. . . . The Southern policy is not based on hatred
> because the whites and the Negroes in the South actually love
> each other. After all, the people of the South are Christians. . . .
> The South has one objective and that is to raise the economic
> level of all its people. In the South, we do not proclaim one
> principle and practice another as is done in so many of the
> Northern and Midwestern states. Segregation is sensible,
> sane, and unhypocritical.

Wallace maintained that if segregation were abolished, Alabama's eighty-five hundred black teachers would likely find themselves out of work because, he implied, they were not as well prepared as their white counterparts. (That suggestion, further indicating an admission of inequality between schools for whites and blacks, went unquestioned.) The goal of segregation, he argued fatuously, was "a cooperative ambition [among blacks and whites] to raise the economic and cultural level of all people." Wallace pointed out that starting with *Plessy v. Ferguson* in 1896, the Supreme Court had issued five rulings upholding the separate-but-equal doctrine. "Does this, Mr. Foster, mean that the Court has been wrong five times and right only once?" "They were right the *last* time," Foster snapped. Wallace held that "to appease a few communist soreheads, we are tearing down our own American traditions. . . . The Supreme Court decision was founded on socialism and surveys which were unreliable."[26]

■ ■ ■

Still, Wallace clung to the populist views that Jim Folsom epitomized in Alabama politics. By 1954, as Folsom moved to win control of state government back from the "big mules," Wallace, as he had promised, was at his side. Wallace, with two legislators, Rankin Fite and Charlie Pinkston, ran Folsom's campaign; Folsom referred to the three as his "committee to take politics out of politics." Wallace wrote the speech Folsom used to launch his 1954 campaign formally. The delivery was disappointing, according to Wallace, who noted, "but the people were already for him anyway, and he was going to be elected regardless of what his platform was. . . . The main thing is that he went on record for what he stood for. . . . You might say he was ahead of his time. He had the right emphasis on education, health, welfare, and old-age pensions. . . . I reckon I got some of my political bringing up with Jim Folsom."[27]

And Folsom, who won that year without a runoff, was an endless source of amusement to Wallace, as well as a powerful political ally. The two, who frequently traveled together on the governor's official trips, complemented one another: both enjoyed raucous humor, both drew strength from admiring crowds, both believed in politics as the road to salvation for "the little man," both grew up with a patina of Jacksonian egalitarianism in their souls and a film of red clay covering their clothes—sometimes literally. On one jaunt to Nashville, where Folsom was to speak in support of the Tennessee Valley Authority, Folsom, Wallace, and Ed Reid of the Alabama League of Municipalities checked into the Hermitage Hotel. Folsom, deep into his bourbon, fell into bed fully clothed. He slept for about an hour, then bolted upright. "What hotel is this?" he roared. When he learned it was the Hermitage, he ordered Wallace and Reid to pack up. "We're going to the Jackson Hotel," he explained. "I want to stay in a place named for Andy Jackson." "Governor," Wallace said, "the Hermitage is the place where Jackson lived. There's no reason to move to another hotel because this hotel stands for President Jackson." Folsom thought a moment, then agreed. "Well, that's fine," he said. "We'll stay here then." Then he fell back asleep.[28] Two days later, as they were boarding their train to return to Montgomery, Folsom persuaded the conductor to allow him to call out the train's departure. When the time came, the conductor pointed to Folsom, and the governor of Alabama bellowed, "All aboard! All aboard!" Then he called out, "And all who can't get a board—get a plank!" The conductor quickly helped him to his seat, where he slept through most of the journey home.[29]

But even as Folsom's drinking assumed calamitous proportions (one story had it that he consumed a fifth of bourbon each morning with breakfast and then started drinking seriously the rest of the day), the teetotaler Wallace remained drawn to the bristling excitement and "fun" that surrounded the governor.[30] Many years later, Wallace, in characterizing Terry Sanford, a former governor of North Carolina and Wallace's opponent in North Carolina's 1972 Democratic presidential primary, perhaps unwittingly explained the underlying reason for his own attraction to Folsom: "He's a fine, high-type gentleman," Wallace said of Sanford, "but he'll bore your ass off."[31] The opposite may have been said of Folsom, whose legendary drinking habits, depending on one's perspective and political proclivities, were viewed with either good ole boy amusement or embarrassed disdain. But the booze clearly took its toll.

The writer Marshall Frady relates a story from Billy Watson (probably apocryphal) about a visit to the Governor's Mansion by the British ambassador, Lord Halifax, during which Watson asked Halifax to observe Alabama "custom" by removing his shoes and socks before dining with the governor. Halifax gamely complied and did his best to maintain his dignity even when he realized the governor, though drunk, was not similarly barefoot. Folsom, his head drooping with an abundance of liquor, had little to say during the first course. Halfway through the entree, Folsom, looking ill, muttered, "Aw, shit!"—then teetered backward in his chair until it toppled, his feet upending the table and sending meat and gravy in all directions. He was helped from the room while Halifax, dabbing bits of food from his clothes and pulling on his socks and shoes, pronounced Folsom "probably the most interesting man I have ever met in my life."[32] (Wallace maintains that the visit from Lord Halifax occurred during Chauncey Sparks's administration, and it was Watson, not the governor, who was in his cups. Even in this version, however, Watson, to Governor Sparks's chagrin, persuaded Lord Halifax to remove his shoes and socks as a gesture of respect, an indication of the highly distinctive nature of Alabama politicians of the time.)[33]

As Folsom was about to take office for his second term in 1955, before drink, scandal, and racial liberalism wrecked his career, Wallace's close association with the governor-elect catapulted the thirty-five-year-old judge into public consciousness as a political force in his own right. An Associated Press story that ran on front pages throughout Alabama described Wallace as a "newly risen unofficial cabinet member" who would "carry more weight" with Folsom than most other official advisers. The story emphasized Wallace's close contacts with reporters throughout the state.[34] Several months into the administration, Wallace was being touted as a leading contender for governor by the erudite, anti-Folsom Grover C. Hall. In an editorial that Wallace saved in one of his scrapbooks, Hall wrote that Wallace, "one of the foremost Folsom campaigners and counselors," was, nonetheless "quite likeable, energetic, and not without admirable qualities." Hall continued: "In fact, we've often wondered how Wallace can operate right in the middle of it all without gagging. But he evidently hopes to run as a Folsom candidate. Indeed, he couldn't run any other way."[35]

Despite Folsom's overindulgence and boorishness, he was deified for a time by the poor, the economically marginal, and the neopopulists who gloried in his socially conscious agenda. But his luster dimmed even in their eyes as many grew frankly wary of Folsom's unabashed liberalism on sensitive issues. He was, for example, vociferously opposed to Sunday blue laws; when a group of legislators proposed culling libraries of books by so-called Communist sympathizers, Folsom denounced the suggestion as "book burning."[36] But what made Folsom most vulnerable to abandonment by even those deeply committed to his social programs was his demonstrative concern about the plight of Alabama's blacks. He freely pardoned and paroled black convicts, believing they had been wrongly jailed or punished excessively because of their race.[37] He harbored deep misgivings about the death penalty, especially in Alabama because use of the electric chair seemed reserved almost exclusively for blacks. In 1956, at a time of growing racial tension in the state, two black men were scheduled to die in Kilby Prison's electric chair on the same night, one for murdering his wife and the other for raping a white woman. Folsom commuted the murderer's sentence to life in prison, but he allowed the young rapist (who had been nineteen at the time of the crime) to die and said that he "just couldn't" commute the sentence of a black man convicted of raping a white woman. "I'd never get anything done for the rest of my term if I did that," he said. "Hell, things are getting so bad, they're even trying to take Black & White Scotch off the shelves." (It was true. The government of Alabama, which controlled the sale of liquor in the state, seriously considered barring that brand of Scotch whisky because of the name and because its label showed two

Scottish terriers—one white and one black—joyfully playing to-gether.)[38]

Given the unpopularity of Folsom's strong inclination to uphold federal court decisions and his obvious distaste for segregation (as early as 1949, he had warned Alabamians, "If blacks are held down by deprivation and lack of opportunity, all the other people will be held down alongside them"), he was unable politically to surmount his larger-than-life personal foibles.[39] Expenses at the Governor's Mansion often ran to four hundred dollars a day, mostly for food and liquor (much of it allegedly purchased from a tiny crossroads general store owned by Folsom's cousin in Cullman, Alabama).[40] He was accused of siring children outside his marriage. He acquired a state yacht and named it after his striking young wife, Jamelle.[41] Whatever Folsom was accused of—much of it seemingly true—he responded with a plea of guilty. "Ain't no use denying it if they're accusing you of something," he once said. "Always enlarge on it, especially if it ain't so. You go to denying something, they'll say, hell, he's guilty."[42]

An incident in late 1955 convinced Wallace (and many others politically identified with Folsom) that he had to make a clean break if he were to aspire to the governorship in the near future. In October, Folsom sent his Cadillac to Montgomery's airport to meet Rep. Adam Clayton Powell, the flamboyant black congressman from New York. Powell was driven around town by the governor's chauffeur and then taken to the mansion, where the two were photographed sipping drinks. What Folsom naïvely had thought might be viewed broad-mindedly as a demonstration of old-fashioned Southern hospitality proved instead, given the growing racial intemperance among Alabama's whites, to be a public relations disaster.

■   ■   ■

There followed a series of race-related incidents that served to effectively destroy any vestige of Folsom's ability to lead, though he tried mightily to inject thoughtfulness into the rancorous arguments over desegregation. On February 6, 1956, a white mob kept Autherine J. Lucy from entering the University of Alabama's school of education. (In later years, Wallace blamed the mob violence that day on Folsom's shortsightedness in not keeping troublemakers far from the campus, a step that Wallace said he took to avert violence in 1963 when two black students were admitted to the University of Alabama [see chapter 9].)[43] Folsom immediately denounced the violence and said he would not tolerate mob rule. At the same time, he refused to sign an interposition bill passed by the legislature, saying that it would be struck down by the courts. Then, on February 10, he was accused of opposing the White Citizens Council, a meeting of which filled Montgomery's coliseum for a keynote address by Sen. James O. Eastland of Mississippi. Folsom was asked why he had not invited Eastland to the Governor's Mansion when he had previously invited a black congressman. Folsom replied that Powell had requested a meeting and Eastland had not. In any event, Folsom left Montgomery on the day of the council's huge rally to attend a meeting in Birmingham of the Alabama Mental Health Society. While there, he issued a statement denying—after a fashion—his opposition to the White Citizens Council:

> I'm not opposed to the White Citizens Council, the Red
> Citizens Council, the Yellow Citizens Council, or the Brown
> Citizens Council, if there are such things. All I have ever said is
> that nothing based on hate can exist for any length of time in
> a Christian democracy. And I hope the Citizens Council
> doesn't have an existence based on hate.[44]

Folsom invited editors throughout Alabama to the state capitol and pleaded with them to endorse his call for a biracial commission:

> The race problem demands the prayerful attention of all men
> of good will, both white and Negro. It is written in the pages of
> history that no problem can be solved, nor can any good be
> produced, by emotional mob violence. Violence breeds
> violence. All our citizens, therefore, must face today's
> problems with calmness and in a spirit of determination based
> firmly on law and justice to all.

The biracial commission won the enthusiastic support of only one editor at the statewide meeting, Buford Boone of the *Tuscaloosa News.* "I was there," he told his colleagues. "I saw the hate. You don't know how ugly it can get. We must try this biracial commission."[45] Even Grover Hall tried to overcome his dislike of Folsom and offered lukewarm support in the *Montgomery Advertiser.* "A biracial commission is, if nothing more, a symbol of reason. And reason is the thing in Alabama which is today in short supply." Still, Folsom had "systematically and sometimes sportively refused to join the resistance to the holy-rolling of the reckless, pietistical abolitionists of the North." But Folsom could not win for losing. When he tried to recapture a shred of credibility among his prosegregation constituents by denouncing the NAACP and other "outside agitators," and reassuring whites that they would not go to school with blacks in Alabama "any time in the near future—in fact, in a long time," critics continued to badger him. Hall wrote:

> Here had been the only governor in the Southern states with a dissenting race viewpoint. He was indeed . . . the only major demagogue in Southern history, with the short-time exception of Tom Watson in Georgia, who ever successfully yoked the woolhat and the Negro. But public opinion has so hardened in the teeth of the outside assault upon Alabama custom that Folsom has been forced to switch about.[46]

Racially related incidents began mounting too quickly for Folsom either to control them or to dodge them. Lucy was suspended from the university, ostensibly because her presence would provoke violence. Ordered reinstated by a federal district court in Birmingham, she was expelled by the university's trustees for accusing them of trying to evade the law; the court refused to overturn this expulsion.[47] The strain of the case was becoming unbearable for Lucy; in New York for medical treatment, she was besieged by reporters. "Please, somebody" she pleaded, near tears, "get me out of here!" She dropped her efforts to return to the university.[48] At the same time, the Montgomery bus boycott was gaining national attention, and though the boycott was aimed at pressuring the local government and was unrelated to state law, many whites took it as yet another indication that Folsom's soft line on segregation was encouraging blacks' aspirations and contributing to racial unrest. Then on March 1, the Alabama Senate unanimously passed a resolution asking Congress for money to move the entire black population out of the state—an obviously empty ploy but, nonetheless, as one reporter wrote, "shocking evidence of the mounting racial tensions in the state."[49]

The tension—and its concomitant portents of danger—drew calls for moderation from unexpected sources. U.S. District Court Judge J. Skelly Wright, in ruling against segregation in Louisiana's public schools, included in his opinion a plea for patience:

> The problems attendant on segregation in the Deep South are considerably more serious than generally appreciated in some

sections of the country. The problems of changing a people's mores, particularly those with an emotional overlay, is not to be taken lightly. It is a problem which will require the utmost patience, understanding, generosity, and forbearance from all of us of whatever race.[50]

Robert Bird, a thoughtful and soft-spoken reporter for the *New York Herald-Tribune*, spent a month in Alabama preparing a series of articles on racial problems in the state and concluded:

A social system, whatever ills may be imbedded in it, cannot be struck down overnight without a kind of chaos that must be avoided. . . . If it is folly for the South to talk of "mongrel-ization," it is wrong for the North to speak of using "the Army, the Navy, and the FBI." The NAACP, having won much and confident of winning more, can set an example of restraint.

And the *New York Times* commented, "Obviously, New Yorkers could more consistently argue for the rights of minority groups elsewhere if such rights were more completely secure here."[51]

The moderate comments from the North suggested to Grover Hall "a hint of spring in the air," but he noted cautiously, "These few swallows don't make a summer." And, in a remarkable yet defiant recognition of just how isolated the South had become, Hall listed the "consequential 'agitators' of the race problem:

- The Democratic Party and its platforms.
- The Republican Party, likewise.
- The executive branch of government as represented by the President now sitting and all presidents to come.
- The judicial branch of government.
- The legislative branch.
- A majority of the governors and their legislatures and attorneys general.
- A majority of the citizens of the United States, who have little contact with the problem.
- A majority of newspapers, magazines, and television stations.
- The churches.
- A majority of nations of the United Nations.
- A majority of people in the world, two-thirds of whom are colored one hue or the other."

Then, in the almost-contemptuous, bunker-mentality language that had helped drive the South into a disastrous war nearly a century earlier, Hall concluded: "You've got to recognize your adversary before you can make skillful resistance."[52]

Given white Southerners' growing sense of hopelessness about preserving segregation and the desperation even of supposedly learned, broad-minded Southern leaders like Hall, anyone closely associated with Folsom—even had he been sober and strait-laced, rather than drunk and scandal-tainted—could kiss his political future good-bye. Within weeks of Folsom's hospitality to Powell at the Governor's Mansion, Wallace publicly denounced the federal probe of discriminatory practices in grand jury selection in Cobb County, Georgia. But he knew that confining his differences with Folsom to racial issues would be viewed as rank political expediency. So he mounted a well-publicized effort to establish that he was not now— nor had he *ever* been—a Folsomite. He showed reporters copies of articles from his legislative days showing that he had voted with Folsom only about half the time during the governor's first term and that, while Folsom was between terms, he had repeatedly denied being a Folsomite.

Most important was a public break with Folsom, ostensibly over cabinet appointments and the failure to name Billy Watson to a lucrative vacancy on the Barbour County Board of Revenue, appointing instead a long-time Wallace opponent. Wallace said, "Some of [Folsom's] cabinet members opposed me. I had no alternative but to leave his camp. Many of these members were men that Big Jim had told me would not be appointed to the cabinet, and I knew I would be compromised politically if I remained. He made it clear that he did not need me or want me around."[53] Although Folsom's cabinet appointments may have been as much an excuse for Wallace to break with the governor as they were politically troubling to him, Wallace seemed truly angered when Folsom passed over Watson. Folsom was using the appointment to trade votes in the legislature on a reapportionment bill. "I thought he should talk to me about it since I was one of his campaign managers," Wallace recalled, "but he went to the legislators." Wallace said that, in retrospect, he understood Folsom's position, and admitted the Watson appointment was a rather "petty" reason for a falling out.[54] At the time, however, Wallace was—or pretended to be—angry enough to drive to Montgomery and storm up and down the halls of the capitol and the Jeff Davis Hotel announcing that he was through with Folsom. "Why, he appointed a man who's *fought* me down there," he reportedly told some legislators.[55]

But the protestations were just part of Wallace's Machiavellian scheme to establish a credible reason for breaking with Folsom. And he did all he could to widen the breach, including efforts in 1956 to weaken the Democratic party's civil rights plank and offering testimony in Washington the next year against the civil rights bill. Wallace correctly anticipated the growing polarization in the South on segregation in general and especially in the schools—and he simply could not risk being identified with Folsom's views. Wallace wanted to be governor, and ties to Folsom might drag him down. As far as he was concerned, past allegiances notwithstanding, there was nothing further to consider.

■   ■   ■

Throughout the South, white citizens' angry and sometimes violent opposition to school integration signaled politicians that there could be no middle ground on the race issue. A growing legion of reporters was assigned to cover racial incidents throughout the South, and the journalists jocularly awarded themselves "battle stars" where they thought the "campaigns" merited them: Clinton, Tennessee; Mansfield, Texas; Clay and Sturgis, Kentucky.

Then, in the fall of 1957, a colorless and virtually unknown governor sparked "the first on-site media extravaganza of the television era and the most severe test of the Constitution since the Civil War,"[56] and the situation's denouement would further scar the politics of Wallace and the South for the next decade. Orval Faubus, facing an uphill fight for reelection to a third, two-year term as governor of Arkansas, injected himself into the plans—until then, proceeding peacefully—to integrate Central High School in Little Rock. Declaring, without a shred of supporting evidence, that violence was about to erupt over the planned integration, Faubus ordered the National Guard to prevent the enrollment of nine black students.[57] The first day, most teachers and students "behaved with scrupulous rectitude."[58] But with each passing day, the mob of whites outside the school grew larger and angrier. A federal judge, supplied with a five-hundred-page FBI report concluding that the peace in Little Rock was not being threatened by integration or anything else, ordered Faubus to show cause why he should not be enjoined from interfering further with the local school board's integration program.

Faubus started cracking under the increasing pressure. He claimed in a wire to President Eisenhower that his phone was being tapped and that a federal scheme was afoot to take him "into custody, by force." Eisenhower replied that he would uphold the Constitution "by every legal means at [his] command."[59] Ten days into the crisis, Eisenhower agreed to meet with Faubus; the White House's impression was that Faubus was confused over what to do but that he intended to be cooperative. However, Faubus took no action and tensions mounted. A week later, when the judge made it clear that Faubus would be found in contempt if he continued to block integration, the governor indicated to the White House that the mission of the National Guard would switch from preventing the black students from entering the school to protecting them from the white mob. In fact, Faubus merely removed the guard; seventy Little Rock policemen replaced them but were unable—and, in some cases, unwilling—to prevent the mob from beating up several white and black news reporters. The violence, Faubus claimed, far from being self-fulfilling, "vindicates my good judgment."[60]

When violence erupted again the next day, Eisenhower reluctantly decided to send troops to Little Rock to quell the unrest and uphold the court orders. The president had sympathized with those resisting the Supreme Court's school integration decision in *Brown v. Board of Education,* commenting that it was "cutting into established customs and traditions" and that "you cannot change the hearts of people by law."[61] But now persuaded that the nation was facing an insurrection and not an integration problem, Eisenhower ordered the army's chief of staff, Gen. Maxwell Taylor, to move quickly and strongly by nationalizing the Arkansas National Guard and sending in crack troops of the 101st Airborne Division to take control. Taylor put a thousand soldiers into Little Rock by nightfall.[62] For the first time in eighty years, federal troops forced white Southerners to back down on their racial intransigence and accept the law of the land. Ten days later, Faubus and the race issue were, for a time, wiped from the front pages and television screens when the Soviet Union launched the space satellite *Sputnik.* But the emotional and political ramifications of Little Rock spread widely throughout the South—and Southern politicians responded accordingly.

The widely respected Sen. Richard Russell of Georgia accused Eisenhower of "applying tactics that must have been copied from the manual issued to the officers of Hitler's storm troopers." Other Southern officeholders vied with one another in heaping invective on the president. Even Folsom announced that he would disband Alabama's National Guard before he would allow it to be federalized by any president.[63] And the message to would-be officeholders in the South was that, despite Faubus's ineffectual posturing, his outright lies, and the international ridicule that his actions had brought down on his state, he had become virtually unbeatable in Arkansas.[64] That reality—plus Congress's creation (only a week before Little Rock) of a six-member Civil Rights Commission to investigate the denial of blacks' voting rights in the South—set Wallace on a path to political defeat, transient humiliation, and ultimate resurrection.

6

Striking Out

AS WALLACE PREPARED for a statewide political campaign and continued to distance himself from Folsom, he knew that
severing himself from his one-time mentor involved some political
risks. For one thing, Wallace feared that diehard populists might
construe such a severing as a rejection of Folsom's antiestablishment
stance, not merely his racial views. If that happened, someone else in
what promised to be a crowded field of gubernatorial candidates
might outmaneuver Wallace for the so-called woolhat vote. Wallace
also recognized that, because his break with Folsom had to be total to
be believed by the voters, he could not afford to enlist the services of
Folsom's advisers and benefactors, many of whom would have supported Wallace's candidacy with their aggregate knowledge of statewide politics as well as with their money.

So in 1956, Wallace started assembling a team that would be
distinctly his own—a team that, insofar as possible, would infuse his
candidacy with ideas and cash, yet remain unsullied in the public
mind by Folsom's unpopular racial views, scandalous conduct, and
profligate, if not downright corrupt, practices. Wallace's first priority
was to raise enough money to underwrite an "informal" campaign—enough to fuel his political forays until an official campaign
(and, consequently, official fund-raising activities) might begin early
in 1958. He turned first to his early docent, Billy Watson, the one

man of political prominence in Alabama whose wit and protean nature allowed him to escape political pigeonholing (he was considered a friend by a succession of governors with diverse views and diverse cliques—Sparks, Folsom, and Persons, as well as Wallace). At Wallace's prompting, Watson organized a committee of five Barbour County patrons—Watson, Sparks, Mayor Marvin Edwards of Eufaula, State Rep. Sim Thomas of Barbour County, and Clayton businessman Marshall Williams—to finance Wallace's travels through Alabama and occasional out-of-state jaunts to burnish his budding national image. For nearly two years starting in 1956, the five men each contributed $50 a month (equal to about $225 a month in 1990) to a Wallace campaign fund.

As a brain trust, Wallace relied on two men—Seymore Trammel, the solicitor (or state's attorney) in Wallace's judicial circuit, and Grover Hall of the *Montgomery Advertiser*. Trammell (until his conviction in 1970 for tax evasion) would remain Wallace's principal campaign and political strategist; Hall (until his death in 1973) would provide intellectual guidance to Wallace on critical state and national issues.

The most immediate issue confronting Wallace—and the one most resistant to thoughtful resolution in the Southern political context—was race. Hall, who loathed Folsom's crudeness and misdeeds (he maintained that Folsom, in his 1954 campaign, had "*repeatedly* slobbered: 'Shore I stole—that was the only way you could get [money] from them fellas in Montgomery' "), still found himself grudgingly agreeing with most of Folsom's racially moderate views.[1] Despite that, and despite having been reared in an atmosphere of tolerance (his father, as the editor of the *Advertiser*, had won a 1928 Pulitzer Prize for editorials attacking the Ku Klux Klan), Hall agreed with Wallace that reality demanded forceful, if not shrill, establishment of one's segregationist credentials. That required Wallace to portray unswerving allegiance to segregation; his only concession to rationality could be an announced opposition to violence as a means of preventing or retarding integration. Hall made it clear that breaking with Folsom was Wallace's first order of business—partly because of the scandals surrounding the administration, but mostly because of Folsom's racial attitudes. In early 1956, Hall concluded, "Folsom is shattered." Voicing views he shared with Wallace, Hall wrote in a letter to Justice Hugo Black:

It is a combination of [Folsom's] daily debauches, his spending
an average of nine thousand, five hundred dollars a month on
mansion expenses alone, his new taxes, and—above all—his
race views (the Scotch and soda episode with Adam C. Powell,
etc.). He and his gang are stealing the state blind.[2]

And what struck Hall as the paradigm of Southern polarization
and insensitivity over the race issue was the Montgomery bus boycott.
In January 1956, when the boycott was barely six weeks old, Hall
wrote Black:

[Negroes] are not asking for desegregation but a "first-come,
first-serve" seating arrangement. It could have been handled
in the beginning, but poor leadership let the concrete get set.
The white community is afraid to "lose face" lest it open the
dike. . . . Never in my nine years as editor have I seen
Montgomery as inflamed as now. Trying to be moderate, I
have taken quite a mauling. Facts and reason are nothing to
[white leaders]: you are either for the white folks or against
'em.[3]

Hall said he was "pilloried" for opposing the arrest of Martin
Luther King, Jr., and other bus boycott leaders for violating a
nineteenth-century Alabama statute prohibiting boycotts. It would
make as much sense, Hall wrote in an editorial, to arrest Montgomery's police commissioner, Clyde Sellers, for having publicly
joined the White Citizens Council, which had been advocating cutting off from blacks identified as antisegregation activists all credit,
supplies, sales, and other economic sustenance—that, too, was a
boycott. Hall said that the leader of the White Citizens Council in
Selma, Alabama, Alston Keith, had assured Hall, "We can put them
niggers back on the buses if only we'd fire the niggers." As Hall
observed, "The result of firing thirty thousand blacks [gave] him no
pause." In the end, however, Hall remained captive to a deeply
ingrained Southern white paternalism rooted in the belief that
blacks, childlike and inexperienced, could not chart their own destiny:

Despite my contempt for the feeble-minded emotionalism of
the mass mind, I must say in candor that I'm uneasy over
letting the ignorant, easily-led blacks prevail in this bus
boycott. The white mass, with all its centuries of experience
and training, readily becomes an incompetent mob. The

blacks are even more primitive and can be led about as easily now as they were when the carpetbaggers sold them the "painted sticks." Several years ago I wrote, without challenge, that no longer could an Alabama politician be elected by bawling "nigger." I was right—then. It is otherwise now. Not for a long time to come is any politician going to be elected who fails to make himself clear.[4]

Hall's intrinsic, if relatively indulgent, racial prejudices ultimately persuaded him that Wallace could succeed only by explicitly declaring his segregationist sympathies. Hall's most significant impact on Wallace's later racial discourses, however, was in pressing home the view that race was a national, not a regional, problem. Hall documented his thesis in a series of special reports in the *Advertiser* entitled "Tell it not in Gath, publish it not in the streets of Askelon"—King David's biblical proscription against publicly discussing painful truths.[5] The articles, some written by Hall and others by staff reporters, depicted incidents of racial segregation in the North that were often as not ignored or distorted by the Northern press: a whites-only housing policy enforced in Dearborn, Michigan; an Atlantic City, New Jersey, racial clash reported only as "a teen-age disturbance"; adoption of a no-blacks faculty policy at several Northern colleges; and (Hall's favorite) the *New York Times*'s systematic exclusion from its society pages of photographs of black brides-to-be or newlyweds—while the *Advertiser* and many other Southern newspapers regularly ran blacks' engagement and wedding photos (albeit separately from whites) in weekly black news sections.[6] Hall contended—as Wallace would later, to much acclaim—"The sorrowful but evident fact, not yet adequately grasped or reported by the press, [is] that wherever the Negro migrates in significant numbers, he encounters rejection—overtly and legally in the South, covertly and illegally in the North." In a 1958 speech in Chicago, Hall maintained, "There is more residential segregation in Chicago than in Montgomery."[7]

■   ■   ■

If the Northern press failed to recognize in 1956 that racial problems were not confined to the South, the same could be said for many Northern politicians—especially those with national ambitions. When, at the 1956 Democratic National Convention in Chicago,

Adlai Stevenson decided to allow the delegates to choose his vice-presidential running mate, John F. Kennedy openly sought—and received—Southern support for the nomination with the argument that he, unlike his opponents, had not articulated a strong civil rights position.[8] (Indeed, shortly after Robert Kennedy became the attorney general of the United States four and a half years later, he stated his own belief in racial integration; but he added, "Other people have grown up with totally different backgrounds and mores, which we can't change overnight.")[9] John Kennedy, dispersing his sizable family in the quest for delegate votes, assigned his sister, Eunice Shriver, to address the Alabama delegation. Wallace was selected to escort her to the meeting. By prearrangement, Wallace met Senator Kennedy and Mrs. Shriver on the mezzanine of the Blackstone Hotel. Kennedy, apologizing that a conflicting engagement prevented his own appearance before the Alabamians, asked Wallace to introduce Shriver. The Alabama delegation was more than receptive; indeed, it gave her a standing ovation. And, unlike the Democratic party sachems, the Alabamians were unperturbed by Kennedy's Catholicism.[10]

Both Harry Truman and Jim Farley, the former Democratic party chairman, had warned Stevenson, "America is not ready for a Catholic yet," and Sam Rayburn, the long-time speaker of the House of Representatives, told the nominee, "If we have to have a Catholic, I hope we don't have to take that little piss-ant Kennedy."[11] But when a television reporter on the convention floor asked Alabama delegates whether Southerners would reject a Democratic ticket with a Catholic on it, Wallace lectured him on how the South had been virtually alone in supporting Al Smith in 1928. "I told him," Wallace recalled, "that he and others had things all mixed up. Southern folks—the majority of them—would not refuse to vote the Democratic ticket because there was a Catholic on it. The reason our states get smeared around so much is a preconception of what goes on down here by people who don't know what they're talking about." The Alabama delegation gave Kennedy all but three of its votes.[12]

Kennedy nurtured his Alabama support, accepting an invitation to address the Alabama League of Municipalities early in 1957. He thanked Wallace, who met him at the Birmingham airport, for his support at the convention, but added, "If I had been nominated, it might have been the end of my career." A year later, during his campaign for governor, Wallace received a letter from Kennedy:

I have been told by my friend, Ed Reid [the executive director of the Alabama League of Municipalities], that you are going to win the nomination for governor of Alabama in the Democratic primary. After you win and take a much-needed rest, if you are in Washington I hope you will come by to see me at the office. I would like to talk with you.[13]

Wallace, who maintained that he "loved Senator Kennedy" (perhaps distinguishing Kennedy as a senator from Kennedy as the president), lost the election that year.[14] But the winner, John Patterson, also had been wooed by the Kennedys; not only was he a leading Kennedy supporter at the Democratic National Convention in 1960, but Robert Kennedy once described Patterson as the Kennedys' "great pal in the South."[15] Barely a year after John Kennedy became president, he learned that with friends like Patterson and Wallace, he did not need any enemies. Alabama, under Governors Patterson and Wallace, would be the scene of two of the most critical civil rights confrontations during the Kennedy administration—the Freedom Riders during Patterson's tenure (see chapter 7) and Wallace's "stand in the schoolhouse door" at the University of Alabama (see chapter 10).

■　■　■

Wallace opened his first campaign for governor on January 20, 1958, by renewing his pledge to protect his court's records from civil rights investigators. On February 14, speaking in Ozark, Alabama, Wallace carefully set out his racial views—his opposition to violence and his plea for time:

> We shall continue to maintain segregation in Alabama completely and absolutely without violence or ill-will. . . . I advocate hatred of no man because hate will only compound the problems facing the South. . . . We ask for patience and tolerance and make an earnest request that we be allowed to handle state and local affairs without outside interference.

But in mid-March, he made certain that voters knew he stood foursquare with them and against "outside interference." He maintained that segregation represented the "sensible and non-hypocritical manner by which the races [had] lived in peace and harmony for many years." He reacted promptly to a report of racial violence in a New York City school: "I am sick and tired of bad-faith demagogues from other sections of the country spouting off about our social order in the South for purely partisan political reasons when they can't control a bunch of hoodlums in their own school system."[16]

During the campaign, the editor of *The Opelika News* asserted, "Segregation is the dominant issue in this campaign . . . [but] there are other important issues." Wallace staked out his program on nearly all of them. He proposed improving public school education, building additional trade schools, attracting industries to Alabama, increasing old-age pensions, building highways, and restoring honesty and integrity to government. With the obviously stark exception of the race issue, Wallace's was a classic liberal, Democratic program with which many of his party's candidates for major office in Northern states would have felt entirely comfortable. In April, observers agreed, "the Wallace campaign had caught fire" and "Wallace was the odds-on favorite."[17]

■　■　■

But the single-minded intensity with which Wallace pursued his personal Golden Fleece was not making him a favorite with his family. "I was traveling from one end of the state to the other, speaking to twenty-five to fifty to a hundred people, then coming home at court time to try the cases I had." His time available to Lurleen and his children was reduced further by his efforts to earn more income by practicing law; he received some relief, in that regard, when his youngest brother, Jack, completed law school and joined him as a partner. Jack effectively was responsible for the day-to-day business, while George's primary duty was to expand their clientele through his political connections.[18] Nonetheless, most of Wallace's income, in addition to the campaign money from his financial angels, "was spent on barely living and traveling over the state." As he recalled, "I spent my money driving all the way to north Alabama to speak to fifteen people at a small club, all the way back that afternoon to Dothan to speak to a tuberculosis society meeting, spend the night somewhere, and then the next day drive all the way to western Alabama to speak to a Rotary club, and then coming home—getting home at one or two o'clock in the morning."[19]

George's uncompromising commitment to his statewide campaign troubled Lurleen even more than his compulsive press-the-flesh jaunts and poker games during his legislative career. For one thing, she worried about all those miles of driving. A few years earlier, in the spring of 1952, she and George had had a near-fatal accident while driving during a rainstorm. A small bridge had been washed out in the storm. George, racing at about sixty miles per hour, had careered around a curve and, with a shock, realized that the bridge was gone and that he was about to plunge into a swollen creek below. He had braked hard, causing the car to skid and spin with such force that both he and Lurleen had been thrown through her door and into the surging water. Both had barely missed being struck by large limbs that had been torn from trees and were being swept downstream. They had escaped injury and, in fact, later waved off two other vehicles about to crash into the stream.[20]

Of more immediate concern to Lurleen was her suspicion that George was philandering (an allegation he denied consistently to all interviewers, although Lurleen, as well as George's second wife, Cornelia, certainly believed it).[21] In the main, however, George's domestic problems derived simply from the question of whether family or power was more important in his life; for him, there was really no contest:

> I wanted to be governor. I pursued it to the extent that I don't believe anybody ever pursued a campaign. . . . I think it was worth it, but I did miss being with my children when they were at such a young age, and I wish I could have been with them more. . . . I remember my wife at times had differences about my being gone so long and so many times, and I tried to explain—but it was really not explainable: how much time I had to invest in trying to run for governor, which was my life's ambition for me and my family, which, of course, included her. . . . Lurleen and I did have problems the last few years before I was elected, because I kept going, going, and going. . . . She wanted a divorce.[22]

The Wallaces managed to buy a house in Clayton—one with a large yard, a front porch, three bedrooms, a den, a dining room, an eat-in kitchen, and a wide hallway—and they could even afford to hire a black woman to help clean it; but the changes were not enough to assuage Lurleen's disappointment in the marriage. She retreated more and more into the children. Her son, George, Jr., remembered it as a lonely and painful time:

> Sometimes I would wonder why [Dad] couldn't spend more time with me, or at least stay home more. I used to nag him about coming out and playing more with me. . . . And yet I can't recall my dad ever explaining why he couldn't spend more time with me. Because of his frequent absences, I think I relied more on my mother for company. She and I were very close. I believe she tried to fill the gap that was caused by his being gone so much.

Even so, George, Jr., recalled poignantly, "I never heard Mother complain about my father's increasing absences from home. It was not in her nature to reveal such feelings, but the loneliness must have been there."[23]

George was wholly consumed by his own agenda. Lurleen liked to fish, but George never accompanied her; George, Jr., loved to swim in the town pool in the summer, but he and Peggy were escorted by their father only when Lurleen insisted on it. George's interest in the children was little more than perfunctory. "When Dad went to the pool," George, Jr., said, "he seldom went in swimming with us. But when I'd say, 'Watch me dive!' he always obliged. 'That's great!' he'd say—and then he'd resume talking with the other fathers. Thinking back, I can see how politically ambitious he was even then."[24]

George remained curiously disengaged from the family even on Christmas Day. Lurleen barely slept on Christmas Eve because she was getting everything ready and putting the children's presents under the tree. Before dawn she started preparing a traditional Christmas dinner of turkey and dressing, mashed potatoes, peas, sweet potato pie, and coconut pie. She was on hand at 5:30 A.M. when the children rushed downstairs, as George, Jr., remembered, "because she liked to see our expressions when we opened our gifts, and take pictures of us." By contrast, George "lounged around in bed until seven-thirty or eight. Every time we'd open a present, we'd run in to see him and say, 'Look at this! Look at this!' . . . Eventually, he'd get up and join us."[25]

Attempting to counter this indifference, Lurleen insisted that George take the children on some of his jaunts. Then the candidate decided to kill two birds with one stone; he incorporated George, Jr., into the basic campaign speech. Occasionally falling asleep on stage because of the long travel and the late hours, six-year-old George, Jr., would be awakened to walk to center stage and ask support for his father—ending, invariably to tumultuous applause, "With God's help, my daddy will make you a good governor." Wallace recalled that at political rallies, "they'd always keep George, Jr., for last because he'd help hold the crowd there."[26]

■ ■ ■

In his political quest, Wallace ran as part of an unusually large pack of fourteen candidates seeking the Democratic nomination for governor. That number reflected the depth of Folsom's failure; even those with relatively modest political stature and limited access to money thought they could command a reasonable following based on the extent to which they had opposed Folsom or, in one or two instances, supported Folsom's populism, if not his racial moderation. The field extended from the ridiculous to the sublime. The former category was perhaps best represented by Shorty Price, a state legislator whose real first name, if actually known, never was used. He stood five feet, three inches tall, chomped a cigar nearly as big as he was, and unabashedly admired Folsom's excesses as well as his programs. One of Price's campaign photographs, showing him standing arm-in-arm with the governor, was captioned, "The Long and the Short of It." The self-styled "clown prince" of Alabama politics, Shorty often called attention to himself clamorously, as in drunken revelry during the annual football game between arch-rivals the University of Alabama and Auburn University (for which he invariably was arrested), or for urinating on a fire hydrant one night outside the Jeff Davis Hotel. Sobering up in a jail cell to which he had been removed following that incident, Shorty complained indignantly that his arrest for relieving himself on a hydrant demonstrated that he did not "have as many rights as a damn common dog."[27]

At the other end of the respectability spectrum was the ostensible front-runner at the start of the campaign, Jimmy Faulkner. Faulkner, the publisher of a newspaper in Bay Minette, a small town some twenty miles northeast of Mobile, was both well financed and well admired as Alabama's "boy wonder" state senator. He had run a distant second to Folsom four years earlier, but over the years, runners-up in gubernatorial races (where incumbents were not permitted to succeed themselves) frequently won their second time out. But Faulkner suffered from an uninspired campaign ("Pocket Dollars for Alabama" was his slogan) and a style that made him seem aloof and inaccessible.[28]

By contrast, Wallace dominated the early days of the campaign through his feisty rhetoric (he ran as "The Fighting Little Judge" who had stood up—hypothetically and from a safe distance, to be sure—to the federal behemoth), his folksiness, and his unmistakable magnetism. No group was too small, no prospective voter too obscure to escape Wallace's attention. And no detail that might tarnish Wallace's populist persona was overlooked. An example was the Cadillac in which Oscar Harper, the entrepreneurial huckster who had attached himself to Wallace (see chapter 4), drove the candidate to many of his campaign stops. Harper once recounted that when they would stop for gas, Wallace would "hurry right over to the station attendant to let him know that Cadillac wasn't his" and that "he didn't have nothing but an old six-cylinder 1952 Ford." Then, said Harper, "he'd look at my Cadillac like he'd never seen one before. . . . You'd of thought him and that Cadillac just happened to coincide from separate directions at that filling station accidentally at the same time."[29]

But another candidate—a true dark horse who never before had run in a contested political race—was slowly and unobtrusively gathering strength. He was Alabama's attorney general, John Patterson—a likable, soft-spoken young man with a reserved, thin-lipped, unexciting demeanor that, in other circumstances, might have made him virtually invisible to a majority of the state's voters. But these were not "other circumstances"; Patterson held a very special place in Alabamians' hearts.

He had become the fair-haired boy of Alabama politics through a wholly unexpected and tragic turn of events four years earlier. His father, Albert Patterson, with whom John practiced law, decided to run for attorney general in 1954 on a pledge to "clean up" his hometown of Phenix City, a squalid river-town stepchild of Columbus, Georgia, which was across the Chattahoochee River. Columbus, with six times Phenix City's population of twenty-five thousand, not including the thousands of soldiers based at nearby Fort Benning, was the business, industrial, and (such as it was) cultural hub of west-central Georgia and east-central Alabama. Phenix City, overshadowed by Columbus and underdeveloped through years of neglect by important business and industry, nonetheless provided a fat living to a minority of crooks, wheeler-dealers, and shysters through gambling, bordellos, and illicit saloons. As John recalled years later, casinos and brothels were operating openly; local officials were being paid off; Phenix City's representatives in Montgomery were controlled by the racketeers and saw to it that Phenix City's "problems" were considered "a local matter."

Albert was opposed by the full political and financial weight of the mob, but he squeaked through to a six-hundred-vote victory in the attorney general's race. Seventeen days later, he was gunned down in an alley outside his law offices.[30] The furor and public outrage at the assassination led to a series of indictments and convictions that swept corrupt officials and their mob-affiliated masters from the Phenix City scene. Meanwhile, voters and opinion leaders throughout Alabama implored a reluctant John to take his father's place as the state's chief law enforcement officer. "I really had no interest in politics," Patterson remembered. "There was something inconsistent about practicing law and politics." But the public pressure fed his own desire to somehow help avenge his father's death, and John agreed to become a candidate in a special election called by the Democratic party—an election in which no other aspirant even bothered to qualify.[31]

Thus, John Patterson was catapulted into high state office—and into the life and career of George Wallace. Though he had eschewed politics earlier, Patterson, once in office, took to it as easily as slipping into a comfortable pair of slippers after a hard day in court. During his first year as attorney general in 1955, Patterson concentrated on establishing his credentials as a crime fighter, cut from the same cloth as his father.[32] He maintained a regular presence in Phenix City during the months of investigations and trials provoked by his father's murder; his office instigated local and state laws providing harsher penalties for illicit gambling; he made numerous public appearances denouncing official corruption (directing most of his ire at the Folsom administration, an easy target), and making certain to exempt current or prospective political allies from any such taint.

But with the onset of the Montgomery bus boycott in December 1955, Patterson turned his attention to the race issue. In 1956 he supported the University of Alabama trustees' suspension and, later, expulsion of Autherine J. Lucy (even before she had enrolled [see chapter 5]). He applauded the mass indictments of black organizers and supporters of the bus boycott, and he pledged his backing to local prosecutors who decided to press the case in a show trial of the boycott's principal leader, Martin Luther King, Jr. And, in the dumfounding ignorance of black affairs that characterized white Southern officialdom, Patterson identified the National Association for the Advancement of Colored People as the real power behind the bus boycott. Patterson was not alone in this vacuity; most of Montgomery's white residents held the NAACP responsible for the boycott, and no less a journalistic personage than Alastair Cooke of the *Manchester Guardian* described King as "the cat's paw of the NAACP." The truth, however, was far different: the NAACP had scorned the bus boycott as a wildcat movement; even during King's trial for violating Alabama's old antiboycott law, the NAACP issued an aloof statement suggesting that the effectiveness of passive resistance techniques would not be known until the final outcome of the bus boycott.[33]

Still, the NAACP specter provided Patterson with an opportunity for a personal political breakthrough. On June 1, 1956, on the strength of his assertion that the NAACP had been "organizing, supporting, and financing an illegal boycott by black residents of Montgomery," he obtained a court order banning NAACP activities—including fund raising, collection of dues, and soliciting of new members—across Alabama. When the NAACP resisted an order to surrender its membership and contribution rolls to Patterson, an Alabama court imposed a contempt fine of $100,000. The ensuing case was tied up in litigation for eight years, during which the NAACP effectively ceased to exist in Alabama, until the federal courts overruled the Patterson-inspired state rulings. As other Southern states tried to follow Alabama's example, a number of NAACP-sponsored school integration lawsuits languished.[34] Patterson had scored heavily among white voters, and that would pay off in the 1958 primaries for governor.

■   ■   ■

Two weeks before the May 6 primary, Wallace clearly sensed the dangers ahead. At a Birmingham hotel 250 of his top campaign workers from around the state gathered to pump themselves up for the homestretch run and to report on their candidate's apparent strength. As each worker delivered an estimate, it became clear that Wallace held a comfortable lead over Faulkner and the rest of the field—but for one opponent. Patterson seemed to have at least as much strength as Wallace, and the support was as widely dispersed as Wallace's. Wallace concluded that his only chance to stop Patterson's obvious momentum was to establish himself as a crime fighter, the image that Patterson had crafted for himself over the previous four years. In his speeches, Wallace emphasized his legislative sponsorship of an antilottery bill. "I didn't start fighting crime when it became popular to fight it," he said at a Clayton rally in a direct cut at Patterson. "I've been fighting crime all my life."

But then Wallace became more strident than ever about segregation, criticizing Patterson for not having done enough to prevent the bus boycott and the court-ordered entry of Lucy into the University of Alabama; and in a speech in Selma, he issued his first threat to close any public school ordered to integrate. "If the federal courts try to integrate the schools . . . they're going to be pointing bayonets at empty school houses."[35] Wallace could sense the race issue beginning to work for him, and Patterson feared that Wallace was making inroads. Patterson retaliated with innuendoes: he told north Alabama audiences that Wallace preferred south Alabama, and vice versa; he accused Wallace of routinely going easy on black defendants in his court, including a seventeen-year-old black traffic offender whom Wallace had put on probation instead of sending to jail; he maintained that Wallace's espousal of segregation with "fair play for all" suggested a diluted, mixed message on the issue that Folsom himself would embrace wholeheartedly.[36]

By primary day, Patterson held the clear edge. Despite Wallace's colorful, antifederal posturing regarding segregation, he remained a small-town judge, while Patterson used a statewide platform to defy advocates of integration. Despite Wallace's efforts to dissociate himself from Folsom, Patterson succeeded in reminding voters of the long-time connection—and he managed to cast doubt on Wallace's commitment to retaining segregation. And Patterson had seen to it that voters retained a vivid memory of the extraordinary story of his role in vindicating his martyred father's death. Patterson received nearly 200,000 votes, almost a third of the total in the crowded field, and about 35,000 votes more than the second-place Wallace. Faulkner, with just over 90,000 votes, ran a distant third. Because Patterson had failed to win a majority, Wallace was entitled to request a runoff election between the top two candidates. Having trailed Patterson in the first primary by five and a half percentage points, simple mathematics suggested Wallace's prospects were grim. Of the some quarter million votes that had been cast for candidates other than the two leaders, Wallace would need 57 percent to overcome Patterson's lead.

Over the next forty-eight hours, Wallace pondered his chances. The bad news was the enormous amount of ground he would have to make up to catch Patterson. Although the profile of most Faulkner supporters suggested they might prefer Wallace to Patterson, Wallace would need them all—plus another 55,000—to surpass Patterson; Wallace's campaign staff often used the words *bleak* and *hopeless*.[37] On the other hand, Wallace was not about to give up his dream if the slightest chance remained; more important, even if Patterson won, he would be prevented by law from running the next time—leaving as Wallace's early principal opponents in 1962 the twice-beaten Faulkner and the defamed, vilified Folsom. Wallace decided to run.

At a hastily organized meeting of supporters, Wallace tried to muster their confidence. "I was trying for the runoff and I've made it," he said. "I hope none of you are concerned about my coming in second. We've come a long way from the beginning and we are going to win because there are elements in this state who are going to support me."[38] Privately, Wallace conceded, "I knew I wasn't going to win when the thing started, but I was not going to get out of it, because I knew I'd run second. Then the next time I knew the newspapers would support me because they knew I could beat Folsom in 1962."[39]

However slim Wallace's chances may have been at the start of the month-long runoff campaign, they soon evaporated entirely. For one thing, Patterson's campaign manager, Charles Meriwether, a Birmingham business executive characterized as a "political genius" even by his opponents, made certain that Patterson would not dissipate his lead through errant remarks or slips of the tongue.[40] According to a Wallace campaign aide, Meriwether "ordered Patterson to keep his mouth shut—to say nothing on his hand-shaking rounds." For another thing, Patterson's celebrity paid dividends: he was invited to Hollywood for the filming of a "This Is Your Life" installment that celebrated his achievements; such veneration through this nationally telecast, widely popular television show was a major plus during the campaign.[41]

On a more sinister level, Meriwether, a one-time associate of a zealous racist proselytizer named John Crommelin, sought the Ku Klux Klan's support.[42] To every suggestion that the Klan was backing Patterson, Meriwether and the candidate refused comment—"but they were careful never to *deny* Klan support," as Joe Azbell recalled. And Meriwether never denied that he was the person who anonymously mailed to Grover Hall a copy of a letter from Alabama's Grand Wizard to his Klan membership urging support for Patterson. Hall published the letter on the front page of the *Advertiser* alongside an editorial condemning the Klan and urging Patterson to publicly eschew its support. Then, swallowing the bait, Hall persuaded Ed Reid, who, in turn, persuaded Wallace, to make the Patterson–Klan link central to the runoff campaign. In speech after speech, Wallace excoriated the Klan and all who either supported it or accepted its support. Then, in a thirty-minute speech televised throughout the state, Wallace asserted that however much Alabamians were determined to maintain racial segregation, the vast majority, as people of goodwill, found the Klan and its preachings anathema. The tactic proved disastrous, even though the Klan was not popular. Indeed, Alabama had enacted a generally effective antimasking law directed at the Klan some thirty years earlier. But in the heated racial environment of the time, many whites felt that open opposition to the Klan showed Wallace's devotion to separation of the races to be weaker than Patterson's. Worse, the Alabama NAACP, facing extinction at the hands of Patterson and heartened by Wallace's strong anti-Klan statements, foolishly issued a public endorsement of Wallace, a politically naïve act guaranteed to drain even more white support from Wallace.[43]

And when Wallace tried to recover by condemning Hugo Black, an associate justice of the Supreme Court, as a "traitor" and a "turncoat," he only made matters worse; he did not win back many segregationists, and he lost the small but potentially pivotal white moderate vote that had been his for the asking. A representative reaction came from Virginia Durr of Montgomery, Black's sister-in-law and a trenchant observer of her times, who wrote Black: "I might have voted for Wallace as the lesser of two evils, but after his attack on you, I simply could not vote for either one."[44] "He tried to run a progressive campaign," a long-time commentator on Alabama politics, Ray Jenkins, believed. "And he got the black vote, such as it was."[45] It wasn't much. Of the 565,000 votes cast in the second primary on June 3, 1958, Patterson polled more than 315,000—56 percent.

Both candidates agreed that the key issue was segregation, although Wallace thought he still might have defeated Patterson had it not been for the sympathy engendered by Albert Patterson's assassination four years earlier.[46] Patterson did not dispute the likelihood of a so-called sympathy vote, but was persuaded that the difference hinged on the public's perception of the candidates' racial stances. In an apologia nearly thirty years later, Patterson said:

Within a matter of weeks after the campaign started, it turned out that the main thing people were interested in was the segregation question. I would have preferred it otherwise, but that's the way it was. [Wallace] probably feels the same way about it. If you happened to be a politician or somebody running for public office and you were perceived by the white majority to be weak on the black question, then you wouldn't be elected. If what the public wants is different from what you want, are you going to be a martyr, say what's going to defeat you and go on about your business? The human animal ain't made that way, and if the fellow wants to be elected governor, he has got to articulate the issues the public is interested in.[47]

Patterson's awareness of the importance of the race issue had grown so intense that, in an election-eve interview with me, then a reporter for Georgia's *Columbus Ledger,* which had substantial circulation in Phenix City and some neighboring areas of eastern Alabama, he continued to avoid denouncing the Klan. When asked if he accepted the Klan's support he would reply that organizations did not vote for candidates: individual Alabamians did—and he did not reject anyone's vote. When I persisted, he hesitated a moment, and then asked, "What time does your paper come out?" "People won't see it till they get home from work," I replied. As the polls would be closing at six o'clock, Patterson understood that anything he might be quoted as saying in a newspaper of modest circulation could hardly result in any serious damage to his campaign. Still, he framed an answer cautiously and told me that, as attorney general, he opposed violence and those who advocated violence; but he added that the Klan's membership numbered "many fine peace-loving individuals who merely" wanted to preserve white Southerners' "way of life."[48]

Two days after the election, Virginia Durr wrote that "life in the Confederacy may be interesting but hardly rewarding." Virginia, who had been reared as a Southern belle in a financially secure household, and her husband, Clifford, a one-time official in FDR's New Deal administration, were among the few courageous whites who openly opposed continued segregation. They paid for it with public opprobrium and with progressively diminishing income from Clifford's law practice. Still, Clifford retained a heartfelt belief, typical of most Southern gentry, that the South would find its way through the reefs of racial hatred and reach a safe and shining harbor. Virginia held some doubts. After Clifford returned from delivering lectures at Princeton University and Sarah Lawrence College, Virginia wrote to her brother-in-law, Justice Black, to say, "Cliff . . . said once again that he thought there was more life and hope here than anywhere else." She added:

> I think this is an expression of faith, not reason, but this is where he wants to stay and so this is where we will stay. And at least it is not boring. But after this election, it may get too hot for comfort or even safety. These poor, benighted people— how can you blame them when they never hear anything else? Their frustration is so deep, they have to have some outlet for it—but such a foolish and pitiful way to relieve themselves.[49]

Ultimately, Clifford's optimism about the ability of Southern whites and blacks to reach a peaceful and constructive accommodation would prove justified—but not before Virginia's admonition that comfort and even safety might well be casualties of the heated rhetoric to which the elected Southern leaders of the time had abandoned themselves. Patterson would preside over what would be some of Alabama's meanest and most dangerous days. But before Wallace ceded center stage in Alabama politics to Patterson, he found a way to parade himself before the footlights once again—and, in so doing, he laid the groundwork for his ultimate rise to un-challenged power in Alabama and an extraordinary impact on the nation.

7

Stand and Deliver

BY SOME ACCOUNTS, Wallace was devastated by his loss to Patterson. His long-time national publicist, Joe Azbell, recalled that after midnight on election night, as the results of the second primary became painfully clear, Wallace, who "ran himself ragged" and looked "tired and worn" as if he were "waiting for the undertaker to come," climbed on a table to speak to his supporters gathered at the Exchange Hotel in Montgomery. "I let you down," Azbell remembered Wallace saying. "I apologize for not doing more—for not being a winner. You worked so hard. I wish I could make you all winners. And you're all winners in my book. What we've done we've done decent, honest, straightforward. It's been a lot of work and we've done it without money. All I've got to say is, I apologize. I let you down."[1]

The writer Marshall Frady, in his scantly documented biography of Wallace, quotes an unnamed observer who described the postelection Wallace as having looked like "a hermit who had just come out of the woods. His eyes were dilated, and he had this wild stare. He was talking wild—he was just pitiful."[2] Frady asserts that Wallace "dropped out of sight for a brief while," reappeared a month later in "a smoky and clamorous room full of other politicians" at the Jeff Davis Hotel, and announced "in a flat and heartless voice, 'John Patterson out-nigguhed me. And boys, I'm not goin' to be out-nigguhed again.' "[3] That harsh, cynical line, in one form or another, clung to Wallace like a sweat-soaked shirt throughout his career. Despite the inability of any other reporter to find a single credible source who could or would say that he heard Wallace make the remark, it was repeated so often in articles about Wallace that it took on the coloration of gospel truth. After the statement first appeared in the Frady book, Joseph B. Cumming, then the chief of *Newsweek*'s Atlanta bureau, could not confirm that Wallace had ever uttered it. (Wallace said that Patterson himself was the source of the expression in 1962 to explain Wallace's harsher, more blatant defense of segregation in his second campaign for governor. "I was as strong a segregationist as he was," Wallace said, "and we were sincere about it.")[4] Cumming did, however, report that some people (also unnamed) remembered that Wallace said he would never be "outsegged" again.[5] Wallace always denied having said anything remotely like being out-niggered or out-segged. He maintained that using the word *nigger* was uncharacteristic for him (in public, at any rate); and of the second term, he said, "The phrase they use is not even a Southern phrase—'out-segged me.' I have never heard of that expression before. I never said anything like that in my life."[6]

In running for governor, Wallace had been forced to give up his judgeship. Though it was some consolation that his brother Jack had been elected overwhelmingly to succeed him, Wallace faced the prospect of four years of political desolation. Despite anguishing over his loss, he bounced back with his usual resilience and determination. And, as he had managed so often before—and would again and again in the course of his public career—he found an innovative and controversial way to thrust himself back into the public consciousness. In this instance, Wallace, for the first (but hardly the last) time, would force a face-off between states' righters and federal authorities—and, perhaps inadvertently, he started a rancorous twenty-year confrontation between himself, embodying state prerogatives, and his old law-school chum, Frank Johnson, symbolizing the preeminence of the United States.

The Wallace-versus-Johnson struggle was rooted in the Civil War and in the geographical accident of the birthplaces of both men— Wallace from the rabidly pro-Confederate Barbour County, and Johnson from the staunchly pro-Unionist Winston County in the small pocket of northwestern Alabama that had opposed secession. On July 4, 1861, a convention of three thousand residents had voted to take Winston out of the Confederacy; one of the citizens had complained that a county with fewer than two dozen blacks was being asked by planters "to fight for their infernal Negroes," adding, "and after you do their fightin' you may kiss their hind parts for all they care." Johnson's great-grandfather had been a Reconstruction-era sheriff in Winston County. In the 1874 election that had returned the Democrats to power in Alabama and had ended Reconstruction in the state, Winston had been the only predominantly white county to produce a Republican majority; in contrast, Barbour had exploded in violence to keep its black majority from the polls, then had ousted scalawag officeholders and elected Democrats.[7]

In the main, Winston County residents, Johnson among them, had retained their Republicanism even though they knew that their future in statewide Alabama politics almost certainly would be forfeit. Nonetheless, Johnson, like his forebears (his father was for years a probate judge in Winston County), exulted in politics—and he took the craft seriously. As a young man, he had once become enraged at a political opponent of his father for uttering what he branded slanderous remarks; in defense of his father's honor, Johnson had slugged the offender and subsequently had been arrested and fined.[8] Given his fiery love of politics, Johnson had naturally been drawn to the clique headed by George Wallace and Glen Curlee during law school (see chapter 2). The three men and their dates had regularly attended dances, parties, university functions, and football games as a group. But despite their friendship, an unspoken tension between Johnson and Wallace had remained. Both were politically ambitious, but only one had a serious chance to succeed. "I just wanted to be governor," Wallace recalled. "But Frank was a Republican, and he thought he'd never have a political career; and he, frankly, was a little jealous to begin with."[9]

■   ■   ■

Although electoral politics in Alabama was effectively closed to Johnson, his participation in Republican party activities—he was a member of the Republican State Executive Committee and headed Alabama Veterans for Eisenhower in 1952—would pay dividends. With the election of Eisenhower, the door was opened through which he would attain governmental advancement.[10] With Johnson's distinguished service during World War II (he was wounded twice during combat in Normandy, across France, and into Germany), with his seven years of legal experience as a partner in an Alabama law firm, and with his impeccable Republican credentials, he was a natural choice for the Eisenhower administration in 1953 to fill the position of U.S. Attorney for the Northern District of Alabama.

Less than two years later, Johnson let it be known that he was interested in being elevated to fill a vacancy as a federal judge for the Middle District of Alabama, based in Montgomery. Eisenhower sent Johnson's name to the Senate late in 1954, but Alabama's Democratic senators, John Sparkman and Lister Hill, delayed the Senate's consideration; they were responding to lawyers in central Alabama who believed that one of their own, rather than someone from the northern part of the state, should get the plum. Eisenhower's attorney general, Herbert Brownell, sympathized. But the Montgomery bar could not find a Republican in their region even remotely qualified for the job. Late in the spring of 1955, Sparkman and Hill relented, and the Senate confirmed Johnson's nomination without dissent.

About a year later, on June 4, 1956, Johnson became a national figure (and hero to civil libertarians) as part of a special three-judge court that declared Montgomery's bus segregation illegal, a decision the Supreme Court would affirm later that year. Johnson had joined Richard Rives of the U.S. Court of Appeals for the Fifth Circuit in a two-to-one decision to assert that the principles enunciated in *Brown v. Board of Education* would apply to segregation on buses as well as in schools. The dissenting judge, Seybourn Lynne of the federal bench for Alabama's Northern District, sharply disagreed and, using an earlier Rives opinion as a guide, found it "pernicious" to rule that *Brown* applied to anything other than schools.[11]

Plunged into the miasma of segregation almost from the inception of his appointment, Johnson developed a reputation as a judicial activist in his consistent extension of civil rights—for mental patients and prisoners as well as for blacks. But, at least during his early days on the bench, he hesitated in diverging from precedent. In a celebrated 1958 decision in *Gomillion v. Lightfoot,* Johnson upheld the gerrymandering of Tuskegee, Alabama, which fenced off black voters from municipal elections. Johnson relied on a 1946 Supreme Court decision, *Colegrove v. Green,* that warned courts "not to enter [the] political thicket" of legislative apportionment. But the Supreme Court, in an opinion written by Justice Felix Frankfurter (who also had written *Colegrove*), reversed Johnson on grounds that *Gomillion* was an exception to the *Colegrove* rule. Frankfurter wrote that Tuskegee's shape had been changed from a square to "an uncouth twenty-eight-sided figure," removing nearly all the black voters from town but none of the white voters. He determined that, although the statute may have appeared to deal narrowly with redistricting, "actually and demonstrably from objective manifestations, it is a function of separating black from white."[12]

At about the time that Johnson was considering the *Gomillion* case, he found himself face-to-face with another, unexpected challenge—this one from George Wallace, in the waning days of Wallace's judgeship. This fateful challenge would demean both men—Johnson, by permitting personal distaste for Wallace's posturing to become a reason for infusing spite into a judicial ruling; Wallace, by carrying the encounter shamelessly beyond good taste, even for politics, by denouncing Johnson with stinging malevolence. Yet, curiously, the skirmish also proved to be a turning point that elevated both in the eyes of admirers—Johnson, into a symbol of lone courage against legalized discrimination; Wallace, into a symbol of defiance of federal overreaching.

■   ■   ■

When the battle between Johnson and Wallace began, it was inevitable that journalists would characterize it as a clash between the Big Judge (Johnson: tall, rangy, and a federal jurist) and the Little Judge (Wallace: short, scrappy, and a state court trial judge). Their struggle started in September 1958, when the year-old U.S. Civil Rights Commission announced an investigation into allegations that registrars in Alabama and several other Southern states were deterring blacks from voting. The commission's office of complaints requested access to voting records in six Alabama counties, including Barbour and Bullock, which fell under the jurisdiction of both judges. But Alabama's attorney general and governor-to-be, John Patterson, advised county officials that the records were not public records and, therefore, not subject to scrutiny by the commission. In response, the commission announced that it would conduct public hearings in Montgomery in December at which it would compel, through its subpoena powers, disclosure of the voter registration records. But Wallace, who had won some notoriety two years earlier by challenging a federal investigation into the exclusion of blacks from juries in a Georgia county, determined to launch a deterrent strike.[13]

The previous summer, after Wallace had returned to the bench following his defeat for governor, he had dismissed as baseless a challenge to a local election in which the losing candidate claimed his opponent had engineered the improper registration of blacks. Now, however, Wallace perceived an opportunity arising from that old case. In late October, he asked a friend, a one-time prosecutor in Barbour County, to file a petition requesting seizure of the county's voting records on grounds that unqualified people had been registered to vote because of misrepresentation to the board of registrars. Three weeks later, an official in Bullock County did the same thing. On the basis of the petitions, Wallace impounded the voting records, holding them, he said, for a future grand jury investigation of the allegations. On Wednesday, December 3, he announced that the investigation would "be in the interest of law enforcement and [would] be more important than any civil rights investigation."[14]

The next day, Wallace was served with a subpoena from the Civil Rights Commission ordering him to produce the Barbour and Bullock voting records the following Monday at the hearing in Montgomery. Wallace asserted that he would ignore the subpoena; he denounced the commission's action as illegitimate trespassing by the executive branch into judicial matters and declared, "They are not going to get the records." And echoing his 1956 threat to jail FBI agents who might try to seize records from his court, he said, "If any agent of the Civil Rights Commission comes to get [the records], they will be locked up."[15]

The Civil Rights Commission convened in a small, fourth-floor courtroom in Montgomery's federal building. Patterson and his advisers turned up prepared to offer legal guidance for the eight Alabama registrars and five probate judges who responded to their subpoenas; Wallace was not among them. Instead, Wallace issued a statement reiterating his position that the commission's demand for his records was an unjust incursion by the executive branch into the judicial arm of government. At the hearing, five of the eight registrars, taking Patterson's advice, refused to be sworn in as witnesses, a sixth declined to testify for reasons similar to Wallace's, and two cooperated with the commission. The probate judges, as mere custodians of lists of certified voters, could not shed light on whether any prospective voters were victims of discrimination.[16]

The commission turned to the federal court, asking for and receiving from Johnson an order for Wallace and the six recalcitrant registrars to produce the subpoenaed records and furnish appropriate testimony. Patterson responded with motions to quash the order by questioning the constitutionality of the 1957 Civil Rights Act and Johnson's jurisdiction over the records in Wallace's possession. Johnson scheduled a hearing for the first Monday of the new year, but that morning, lawyers for the Justice Department and the defendants assembled in Johnson's chambers to forge a compromise. They agreed to forgo personal testimony and production of the records in Montgomery; instead, Johnson instructed commission agents "to inspect official voter registration records in Barbour, Bullock, and Macon" counties to the extent "relevant to the commission's inquiry." He ordered commission agents to conduct on-site inspections at a mutually acceptable time and in a manner "not to interfere with the proper judicial processes of the State of Alabama." Wallace's lawyers, Patterson and Preston Clayton (both of whom, ironically, had opposed Wallace in election campaigns [see chapters 4 and 6]), supported the compromise. Patterson recalled that Johnson "got a little rough" with government lawyers, instructing them to complete their inspections expeditiously. Johnson, as Patterson remembered, snapped, "Now, I want you to get in there and I want you to photostat what you want and I want you to get out."[17]

Macon County officials complied promptly, but Wallace, whose circuit included Barbour and Bullock counties, had other ideas. When investigators first drove to Clayton on January 7, two days after the compromise was worked out, Wallace (employing a tactic he would use more than once during his career) made himself impossible to find. But the persistent commission investigators returned the next day. Wallace reluctantly agreed to see them, but he required them to itemize the records they wanted and to identify the complainants. The investigators did as they were told; when they returned their lists, Wallace suspended the meeting, supposedly to consult with his brother, Jack, and his circuit prosecutor, Seymore Trammell. Inconveniencing the federal representatives further, Wallace waited until 7:15 P.M. to reconvene the session. Then he permitted the federal representatives to see only the specific records they had requested. The following day, the investigators complained to Johnson, who summoned Clayton to explain his client's failure to cooperate. Johnson rejected Clayton's assertion that, because the court's order was vague about which records were relevant, Wallace had submitted only those that he believed were germane to the commission's proceedings. On Friday, January 9, Johnson directed Wallace to make available immediately after the weekend "all the voting and registration records" in his custody. Wallace issued a peevish statement complaining of "Roman holiday investigations" and a "circus atmosphere with . . . newsreel cameras and hired publicity agents." But privately he was becoming uneasy over the consequences of his conduct.[18]

On Sunday, the day before Wallace was required to make the Barbour and Bullock records available for inspection, Glen Curlee drove from his home in the town of Wetumpka, near Montgomery, to see Wallace in the town of Clayton. Curlee, who had embarked on what would be a thirty-year term as a district attorney, told Wallace that in a showdown, Johnson held all the cards. "I said, 'The judge could put you in jail for contempt of court for a long time. What the hell difference does it make about the records?"[19] He suggested they see Johnson right away to try to work something out. Curlee drove back to Johnson's home on Haardt Drive in Montgomery, but the Johnsons and their son, Johnny, were out for dinner. When they returned at about seven-thirty, Johnson recalled in an interview with his biographer, Tinsley Yarbrough, that

> Curlee was waiting there at the house in his automobile and came in and chewed around on his cigar a while and finally told me that little George—that's what we called him—wanted to talk to me. I told him I'd talk with him. So he called me back on the telephone fifteen minutes after he left the house and said George is on his way. He's having to drive up from Clayton. So I sat around and read, and Mrs. Johnson went on to bed. I guess he got to the house about eleven-thirty. The doorbell rang and I went to the door. First statement he made—and my wife heard this because the doorbell woke her up—he says, "Judge, my ass is in a crack." I invited him on in and we went in the kitchen and sat. He asked if I could give him just a ten- or fifteen-day sentence, and that would help him politically. And I told him, no, that if he defied that order, I was going to give him a longer sentence. And he said he didn't think his wife would care much, but a longer sentence would kill his mama, and he just couldn't stand to be incarcerated. I told him that the option was his, that I didn't have any options; he would have to comply with the order. Finally, he asks, "Well, if I get them [the records] to them [the commissioners] indirectly, will that be all right?" I said, "If you get them to them by the deadline, I don't care if you go by the moon."[20]

Wallace maintained that Curlee telephoned to convey Johnson's invitation to conduct an informal meeting (Curlee did not remember it that way). Wallace said that Ruth Johnson, not the judge, greeted him and Curlee at the door (Curlee's recollection supports that) and said, "Come in, Cousin George. Brother Frank is going to elect you governor in spite of everything he can do." (Curlee could not recall her words one way or another, but said Johnson's subsequent actions "sure helped elect him.") Wallace remembered, "Frank made threats, and he said if we didn't get those records to Montgomery like the Civil Rights Commission wanted and which he had ordered, he was going to put me in jail until past the next running time for the governor's race, which would have been four years. And I said, 'You mean, Frank, you're prejudging this case without listening to the law in this matter?' And he said, 'I sure am because I know what the law is in this matter.' He said I asked him to put me in jail for three or four days as it would help me politically. Not only is he wrong and inaccurate, but—I hate to say he lied—but what he said was not correct or true at all, and he knows it. So I left the house about twelve o'clock that night, drove the eighty miles to Clayton, and got home about two o'clock in the morning.[21]

Before starting on his drive to Clayton, Wallace climbed into Curlee's car to discuss what had transpired. Curlee was not present for the conversation, but Wallace told him about Johnson's intention to slap him behind bars "past the next running time." Curlee said, "You're going to have to outfox him." He suggested that Wallace, who was holding the voting records for the ostensible grand jury investigation into improprieties in registering blacks, promptly deliver the records to the grand juries for whatever disposition they chose to make. "Then," Curlee said, "you can't be held in contempt because you're not the custodian of the records, and you haven't given them over to the federals. The grand juries can turn them over, and everybody wins." Upon reaching home, Wallace telephoned Trammell and told him to round up the grand juries by eight in the morning—two hours before he was to start producing the records. "This is a grave matter," Wallace told the jurors who had been roused from sleep and directed to assemble at the courthouse in Clayton. "Today, I am turning the records over to you. I have kept them intact and inviolate. When I turn the records over to you, I realize I no longer have control over them. The grand jury is the supreme inquisitional body of the county. The records are yours to do with as you see fit. I am willing to accept whatever consequences there are for my action in impounding the voting records and in turning them over to you."[22]

The ploy worked. Over the next three days, commission agents and Justice Department attorneys acknowledged that they had obtained all the records they sought—and, by all accounts, they did not look at many. But Wallace's public posturing that the independent grand juries, not he, had turned over the records and that he had preserved the constitutional gulf between executive and judicial authority rankled federal agents and Johnson. The illusion of Wallace's victory (on January 13, the *Alabama Journal* in Montgomery described Wallace as "still defiant and still free") troubled Johnson and the Justice Department as much as the reality that the records indeed had been made available.[23] In fact, a spokesman for the Civil Rights Commission in Washington contended that "the dispute is between Wallace and the federal court, and that under the order, the commission has no authority to seek to examine the records when they are in the possession of anyone other than Wallace."[24]

On Thursday, January 15, a Justice Department attorney reported to Johnson that "although the agents were harassed by dilatory tactics and questionable and rather childish conduct on the part of persons who were ordered to cooperate and to produce the records," that, in fact, "the purpose of this court's order was effectuated in that all of the records were produced for inspection finally, if in jumbled up form, and there was inspection permitted." A spot check of the records proved sufficient, the report said, and no additional inspection time was required; the government, therefore, requested dismissal of its suit against Wallace. Johnson agreed, but he did not want to let Wallace off the hook. He said that Wallace "possibly" had "failed and refused to technically comply with the order of this court." On that flimsy possibility of a technical violation, Johnson ordered Wallace hauled before him to show cause why he should not be cited for criminal contempt.[25] The citation said, "[Wallace's actions] in persistently refusing to make the described records available for inspection in accordance with this court's order in spite of repeated demands . . . and the actions . . . in delivering the described records to the grand juries . . . which he had hastily called into session . . . constitute a disobedience and defiance of this court amounting to criminal contempt."[26] Once again, Wallace quickly saw the benefits—as well as the risks—of theatrics. Nationally, he was the object of editorial shock and dismay; the *Washington Star* complained that the country had reached "a deplorable pass . . . when a state judge, in effect, challenges a federal judge to send him to jail." In Alabama, committees to raise money for Wallace's defense sprang up in several cities.[27]

On Monday, January 26, two weeks after Wallace had turned the records over to the grand juries and the inspection had commenced, the Little Judge walked into the Big Judge's courtroom in Montgomery. In a written answer to the show cause order, he pleaded guilty "to failing to deliver the voter registration records to agents of the Civil Rights Commission," but not guilty of contempt because his duties as a judge "prevented his compliance with the order of the court." The government, on the other hand, sought to show that Wallace had only feigned defiance of the order while, in reality, complying with it to the letter.[28]

It was as if the courtroom had been turned into a hall of mirrors. Johnson, obviously miffed that Wallace had been making political hay by shrewdly manipulating the judicial process, accused Wallace of contempt—not because he had defied the court's order, but because he would not admit his cooperation. Wallace, for his part, though eager to avoid a jail sentence, nonetheless wanted to be found guilty. The antagonists were both playing politics. But it was Johnson, angry at his powerlessness to prevent Wallace from using the court to political advantage, who allowed the proceedings to degenerate into burlesque.

The testimony of the government's probers described the difficulties they had encountered before Johnson had ordered Wallace to produce the records; however, the agents testified that after Johnson's order had been issued, they had been notified by Wallace that they could see the records if they requested them from the grand juries. The foreman of the Bullock County grand jury acknowledged he had telephoned the investigators to tell them the records would be available to them.[29] Thus, the government's case was dedicated to suggesting the probability that Wallace had directed the grand juries to surrender the records and that the commission's agents had not, in any formal way, requested the records from the grand juries. The intention of the trial—to prove criminal contempt—seemed beside the point. No testimony or statement from either side suggested that Wallace had obstructed the court's order. The only point that the government tried to drive home was that, contrary to Wallace's public posturings, he was personally responsible for making the voting records available to the commission.

When the testimony concluded late in the morning, Johnson

recessed court until after lunch; he then returned with his verdict of not guilty. The crowd of courtroom spectators burst into cheers, prompting Wallace to smile and Johnson to curtly demand order. Then Johnson continued with an opinion singular for its judicial intemperance and, because he had assured Wallace that he would agree to an "indirect" method of obtaining the records, personally disingenuous as well:

> Even though it was accomplished through a means of subterfuge, George C. Wallace did comply with the order of this court. . . . As to why the devious methods were used, this court will not now judicially determine. In this connection, the court feels it sufficient to observe that if these devious means were in good faith considered by Wallace to be essential to the proper exercise of his state judicial functions, then this court will not and should not comment upon these methods. However, if these devious means were for political purposes, then this court refuses to allow its authority and dignity to be bent or swayed by such politically generated whirlwinds.[30]

Wallace strutted from the courtroom, lit a cigar, and—accompanied by his wife and an entourage of about twenty other people, including supporters wearing "Win with Wallace" buttons, reporters, and lawyers—strolled to the Jeff Davis Hotel. There, about ninety minutes later, before a bank of television lights, he read a prepared statement that neatly encapsulated the Wallace style. He declared victory: "I turned the voter registration records over to the grand jury to do with as they saw fit; all testimony of the hearing verifies this. . . . I plead guilty to failing to deliver the voter registration records to the Civil Rights Commission. . . . No witness testified otherwise." He dramatized his role while enlarging the issue: "I was willing to risk my freedom to test . . . a grave constitutional question." Wallace affirmed the doctrine of states' rights that, for all its identification with racism, was a deeply rooted concept in American politics, dating to the 1790s when Jefferson and Madison raised it in opposition to federal Alien and Sedition Laws. Wallace said that he "respect[ed] the dignity and integrity" of Johnson's court, "as this is a government of laws and not of men," but that his submission would have meant the "state courts would have been plowed under by judicial edict." He demonized the federal enemy and extolled the politics of defiance: "These characters from the evil Civil Rights Commission and Justice Department were backed to the wall; they were defied and backed down." And he rhetorically waved the Confederate flag: "This 1959 attempt to have a second Sherman's march to the sea has been stopped in the cradle of the Confederacy."[31]

Wallace received widespread editorial support. The *Montgomery Advertiser* astutely noted that whether or not Wallace acted for political reasons, "Johnson likewise made his ruling upon the basis of political considerations and so proclaimed"; the *Birmingham News*, pointing out that the "fundamental issue"—whether a state judge must yield to a federal agency in such cases—was unresolved, observed hopefully, "It may be for the good of all concerned that the solution to this question is, simply, left hanging." Wallace added a self-aggrandizing postscript by submitting a proposed "final report" that the Barbour County grand jury certified and filed officially. With shameless conceit, Wallace commended himself for "courageous action" in "risking his very freedom" in carrying out his duties, and he described his "foresight and determination" as a beginning in filling "the great need of the South" at that time.[32]

But Wallace's most consequential use of the confrontation with his old college comrade would come a few years later in his second run for governor of Alabama. During that campaign, in establishing his intention to "stand up for Alabama" from courthouses to schoolhouses, Wallace recalled his encounter by denouncing Johnson as "an integrating, carpet-bagging, scalawagging, race-mixing, bald-faced liar." Needless to say, the venerable triumvirate of Curlee, Wallace, and Johnson was never the same again.

■　■　■

The Big Judge–versus–Little Judge encounter secured Wallace's already growing reputation—earned fairly or inadvertently, depending on whose story one accepted—as a man who would stand up for Alabama, whatever the personal consequences. Wallace consciously promoted that image through a spate of public appearances where he peppered his audiences with tough talk on his unwillingness to yield to "unconstitutional" federal pressure. Before long, the perception of Wallace as the "Fighting Judge" was branded indelibly into the political consciousness of Alabamians. Building on that foundation, and with the objectives of cornering the market on early financial contributions while limiting serious opposition, Wallace launched a campaign to install himself as the prohibitive favorite for governor in 1962.

He embarked on his new quest—or, more accurately, merely extended the old one—back in his home county of Barbour, where he insisted on maintaining his residence even though he had become a titular partner with his brother Gerald in a Montgomery-based law firm. "Staying home" was of surpassing importance in Wallace's political doctrine; he embraced unreservedly his father's oft-repeated injunction that all politics is local—that to be successful in electoral politics on statewide or even national levels, aspirants must stay close to their roots, listen to and understand the "home folks," and be well liked on their own turf. The fatherly advice was not lost on the son.

After his defeat for governor in 1958, Wallace returned to his home in Clayton, where he and Lurleen spent hours every night producing hundreds of handwritten thank-you notes to supporters in the losing campaign—he between excursions into Clayton or Eufaula to mingle with the good ole boys at the courthouses, and she after a long day's work followed by attending to her domestic responsibilities.[33] Early in 1959, shortly after declaring victory in his clash with federal authorities over voter registration rolls, Wallace set out on a grueling, nonstop statewide excursion. As a team of reporters from the *Montgomery Advertiser* put it:

> Wherever a group of potential voters gathered, there was a chance Wallace would show up. From the red clay hills of Barbour County to the governmental whitewash of Montgomery to the pine-studded shores of Lake Guntersville, Wallace scoured the state, ensuring that no hand would go unshaken, no pair of eyes unmet, no minds unfilled with the Wallace name.[34]

MacDonald Gallion, elected in 1958 to succeed Patterson as the attorney general after a campaign as racially strident as Patterson's campaign for governor had been, said of Wallace, "After he lost [to Patterson], he hit the ground running. It was like he never quit running. . . . The all-important thing was he was completely organized. . . . He had contacts and he maintained them."[35]

In the 1958 campaign, Wallace not only developed and solidified political contacts, but he broadened his knowledge and honed his campaigning techniques. One thing he learned was that each community, over the years, had developed singular customs relating to when and where nearly all its residents would leave field and hearth to congregate at the center of town for marketing, trading,

or socializing. There were good Saturday "day" towns in Alabama—
Athens, Russellville, Geneva, Oxford, Anniston—when the square
and surrounding commercial establishments teemed with people
buying groceries, getting haircuts, picking up feed, refitting ax handles, and replenishing salt blocks. There were "lottery" towns where
food markets gave away a free lottery ticket for every dollar's worth of
groceries a customer purchased; the holder of the winning ticket
would win a twenty-five-dollar prize at a 2:00 P.M. drawing. Wallace
rallies in lottery towns, therefore, invariably would begin at 2:15—
just as the excited crowd started to disperse. There were the "night"
towns—Selma, Monroeville, Greenville, Gadsden, Tuscaloosa,
Florence—"where you had so many people you could hardly see the
end of them," Wallace recalled, and people were in a party mood and
receptive to rallies that featured country music. There were "first
Monday" towns like Scottsboro where, on the first Monday of every
month—trade day, it was called—the entire population of surrounding Jackson County would congregate to trade pocket knives, 'coon
dogs, and setting hens. Over the years, the wares may have changed,
but the tradition remained. A longtime Wallace aide, Elvin Stanton,
explained, "In Jackson County, you campaigned on first Monday; any
other time, *you'd* be there, but the people would be somewhere else."

Conversely, Wallace learned where he and his brand of politics
were met with such disdain that it was not worth his campaign time to
try to change even a single mind. One place he *never* campaigned in
all his public years, for example, was in the posh Birmingham suburb
of Mountain Brook; its relatively urbane residents were repelled by
both Wallace's unpolished, often earthy attacks on federal demons
and the raw, revival-meeting intensity of his rallies. But he turned to
his advantage the existence of such hostile enclaves. "Instead of
going to Mountain Brook," Stanton said, "he would campaign in the
nearby community of Roebuck where the factory workers were. And
he'd say, 'I wouldn't make a speech in Mountain Brook if they paid
me, 'cause they too busy riding around in limousines and going to
the country clubs to care about the working people of Alabama.' "36

Wallace's decision to continue his inexorable quest for the governorship placed additional strains on his marriage. Lurleen was
raising their three small children with only sporadic help from her
husband; her job with the Alabama Agricultural Extension Service
accounted for the family's only steady income (the money Wallace
received from Billy Watson and his other key supporters was consumed by campaign activities). Not only was she tired and ignored,

but she feared the specter of another loss in 1962; if that were to happen, she warned, it would be as if George were just starting out professionally—some twenty years behind his contemporaries. There were, Wallace later conceded, "serious repercussions" in the marriage—heated arguments and threats of divorce.

■   ■   ■

Meanwhile, racial tensions were building throughout the South as blacks pressed more and more demonstratively for voting rights and school integration. Southern blacks' efforts to gain access to the ballot box were mired, for the most part, in slow-moving legal suits and a slow-moving Congress. And several states—Alabama among them—succeeded in avoiding widespread school integration through pupil-placement and school-option plans; the Supreme Court ruled that such laws, though constitutional on their face, might be overturned if proof arose that their principal purpose was to maintain racial segregation. The words and intentions were brave, but they had little practical impact on determined and defiant white Southern resistance; even a decade after *Brown*, barely more than 2 percent of all black Southern children attended desegregated schools.[37]

Nowhere—not in Mississippi nor in South Carolina—was a group more defiant of integration orders than the white people of Alabama. And no state had a governor more shrewdly determined to block integration. Even before he took office, John Patterson had effectively banished the NAACP from Alabama, and the organization had to fight for eight years to win the legal battle that allowed it to return. In the months between his election and his inauguration, Patterson helped his defeated political rival, George Wallace, face down—in appearances, at least—the federal government's demand for voter registration records. And in his first year as governor, Patterson demonstrated further that his racist campaign had been built on more than mere rhetoric.

It may be, as one observer put it, that "Patterson's style was somewhat more subtle than Wallace's or that of . . . Faubus and . . . other unreconstructed contemporaries in Southern statehouses," but he consciously, insidiously—and rather smugly, to boot—pounded on the race issue throughout his administration. To be sure, as he explained in a 1980 statement, it was necessary to use the issue to get votes even though he "knew that there was no way by which we could ultimately prevail constitutionally." Speaking of the campaign focus on the race issue, he added, somewhat unctuously:

> [It] was not any of my making. . . . It was political suicide to offer any moderate approach. . . . Alabamians are gullible for that kind of thing. . . . Give the people something to dislike and hate, create a straw man for them to fight. They'd rather be against something than for something. As long as our people are of that frame of mind and like their politics with that brand, then we're going to have people to take advantage of that kind of situation.[38]

Obviously, Patterson was one of those people—and perhaps one of the most opportunistic in the state's history to that time. Indeed, Marshall Frady ascribes to Patterson, rather than to Wallace, responsibility for changing the nature of Alabama's political preoccupation with blacks from generally "tacit and sometimes modestly charitable" to "volatile, unabashed, brutal irascibility."[39] This profound transformation spread beyond Alabama's borders and created a tone so harsh and unyielding that it was bound to spiral out of control and spawn violence—even well before its iniquitous legacy was inherited and extended by Wallace.

Patterson could not take refuge in the rationalization that his harsh racial attitudes were required by political necessity. The fact was that Alabama's constitution proscribed him from succeeding himself. In fact, he initiated actions and struck poses that seemed openly designed to exacerbate racial animosity.

At a time when Martin Luther King, Jr., was neither engaged in any civil rights demonstrations in Alabama nor, indeed, even living in the state any longer (he had moved his home and his movement's headquarters from Montgomery to Atlanta), Patterson nonetheless demanded King's extradition from Georgia on charges that he had perjured himself in signing his state income tax returns for 1956 and 1958. The charges grew out of Alabama's refusal to allow King to deduct donations he had received in those years for the Montgomery Improvement Association and the Southern Christian Leadership Conference (SCLC); the state auditors suggested that the donations were, in reality, personal income. Rather than fight the allegations, particularly during the moving of his family and his newly formed SCLC to Atlanta, King sent the state a check for more than $1,600 to settle the matter. Now, however, Patterson alleged that, technically,

King had committed perjury by signing the two tax returns that failed to declare these contributions as personal income. The implication, of course, was that King took money destined for the movement and used it for himself. Although tax matters of the kind and size involving King were usually settled through payment of principal and interest or, at worst, resulted in misdemeanor charges, King was the first person in Alabama history to be prosecuted for felony tax evasion. The allegations stunned King and the civil rights community; Patterson added to their outrage when he quipped, while signing papers requesting King's extradition from Georgia, "If you dance, you must pay the fiddler." Even more shocking, perhaps—but in an unexpectedly hopeful way—was an all-white jury's decision a few months later in Montgomery to find King not guilty of the charges.[40]

By spitefully prosecuting King, Patterson unwittingly spawned a landmark Supreme Court decision, *New York Times v. Sullivan*, which broadened press freedom. To raise money for King's defense, the social activist Bayard Rustin and the entertainer Harry Belafonte drafted an appeal for funds that ran as a full-page advertisement in the *New York Times*. The ad contained brief descriptions of events in Montgomery in which authorities allegedly had harassed blacks who had been seeking access to public places reserved for whites. Prompted by Patterson, Montgomery's police commissioner, Lester B. Sullivan, filed a $500,000 suit, claiming that he had been libeled by the ad. The newspaper published a retraction to all assertions made in the ad that may have offended Alabama officials. Sullivan sued anyway—and the Court ultimately ruled that public officials could not recover damages for libel unless the accused publications and reporters had demonstrated actual malice or reckless disregard for the facts.[41] Later decisions extended to all public figures the burden of demonstrating that a libel was committed with "actual malice."

In Greensboro, North Carolina, on February 2, 1960, blacks began sit-ins at eating facilities reserved for whites. Such sit-ins reached Alabama later that month with a relative whimper, but Patterson's stern reprisals suggested that the challenge was thunderous. In February thirty-five students from the all-black Alabama State College chose a public target, walked into the basement cafeteria of the capitol in Montgomery, asked for food service, were refused, and walked out again. Some white patrons stared angrily at the students, but no confrontation occurred. Yet, Patterson summoned the college's president, H. Council Trenholm, ordered him to expel all the students who had requested service at the white cafeteria, and issued a statement asserting that Alabama's citizens (presumably including black citizens) "do not intend to spend their tax money to educate law violators and race agitators." He said he told Trenholm, "If you do not put a stop to it, you might well find yourself out of public funds." A large crowd turned out at a rally to protest the governor's demand (which Trenholm had meekly obeyed), but the protest came to naught. Despite rumors of planned sit-in actions throughout Montgomery, none materialized. Unfortunately, the rumors were enough to spur white toughs to accost some black shoppers; in the worst episode, a woman was bludgeoned with a baseball bat. A photograph of the incident was published in the *Montgomery Advertiser* and the attacker was identified. The reporter and the photographer at the scene (both white) said that local police had witnessed the attack but had not responded. The governor blandly said that he would leave the investigation to Montgomery's police commissioner, Sullivan; Sullivan, in turn, denounced black students for inciting the incident and the Montgomery newspaper for publishing the photograph, and claimed the attacker's identity could not be determined with enough certainty to warrant an arrest and prosecution. Grover Hall, the *Advertiser* editor, blamed the violence on both "rash, misled young Negroes" and "white thugs," and he characterized Sullivan's problem as "not a photographer with a camera" but "a white man with a baseball bat."[42]

■   ■   ■

Patterson's coldly methodical success in fending off blacks' challenges to voting rights barriers and to segregation in public accommodations went largely unnoticed in the national media or by his pals in the Kennedy White House. But his open contempt for the safety and well-being of a small, courageous band of civil rights activists calling themselves Freedom Riders would change all that.

In December 1960, the Supreme Court had outlawed segregation on buses, trains, and terminals used in interstate transportation. The following spring, seven black people and six whites decided to test the court's ruling by taking an interstate bus trip through the segregated South. The trip went without incident (and without much public notice) until the Freedom Riders reached Rock Hill, South Carolina, where some white youths punched and bloodied three of them. But local authorities quickly broke up the fracas and gave full support to the travelers, who went through the rest of South Carolina and then through Georgia without any further violent episodes—certainly due to heavy police protection. But danger loomed in Alabama: Klansmen and other thugs, alerted to the Freedom Riders by growing publicity and tacitly encouraged by authorities, were planning an ugly welcome.[43]

The Freedom Riders, aboard two buses—one a Greyhound bus and the other a Trailways—crossed into northern Alabama on Sunday, May 14, Mother's Day. As the Greyhound pulled into the terminal at Anniston, thirty miles west of the Georgia line, a large, frenzied crowd of white men beat on the bus with clubs, bricks, and iron pipes and slashed at its tires until the driver restarted the engine and made a hasty getaway. But the slashed tires went flat a few miles out of town, and the vigilantes, who had been in hot pursuit in about fifty cars, smashed and burned the bus and then assaulted the escaping passengers, nearly all of whom—Freedom Riders as well as a few ordinary travelers—required hospitalization. The Trailways bus, running about an hour behind the Greyhound, was boarded by Anniston policemen when it pulled into the terminal; when the Freedom Riders refused orders to segregate themselves, the police vanished. In moments, eight white men rushed aboard, brutally beat the civil rights activists, and dragged them to their racially "acceptable" places on the bus. The policemen reboarded, pronounced the seating arrangement acceptable, and directed the bus to continue to Birmingham.[44]

Martin Luther King, Jr., once described Birmingham as the Johannesburg of the American South—the psychological citadel of segregation. And the journalist Howell Raines, who grew up in Birmingham, considered his hometown "the most violent and regimented expression" of segregation in the South—"segregation maintained through the nighttime maraudings of white thugs, segregation sanctioned by absentee landlords from the United States Steel Corporation, segregation enforced by a pervasively corrupt police department."[45] That same police department had made a deal with the Ku Klux Klan that when the Freedom Riders pulled into Birmingham, a Klan-sponsored mob could have fifteen minutes to "greet" the travelers before the police would step in. An FBI informant within the Klan, Gary Thomas Rowe, told his handlers in Washington of the plot; they, in turn, conveyed the information to the police (without, of course, disclosing their source)—sometimes, ironically, to the very officers who were collaborating with the Klan.

In another ironic twist, when a policeman telephoned Klan head-quarters to advise the plotters that a bus was heading for the Trailways terminal, the man who took the call was Gary Thomas Rowe (see chapters 10 and 12).

Armed with the information—as well as with bats, pipe lengths, and chains—the Klan-led mob pummeled the arriving Freedom Riders. As Rowe would write many years later, "Everybody who got off the bus was clubbed, kicked, or beaten. . . . When people looked up, I couldn't see their faces for blood. . . . I observed several FBI men . . . taking movies of the beatings." None of the attackers were arrested. Governor Patterson said that he could not "guarantee protection for this bunch of rabble-rousers." Birmingham's police commissioner, Eugene "Bull" Connor, said the beatings occurred because Mother's Day vacations had left the department shorthanded. He maintained, "The people of Birmingham are a peaceful people, and we never have any trouble here unless some people come into our city looking for trouble." Even the *Birmingham News*, a staunch defender of seg-regation, acknowledged the absurdity of Connor's excuse and dis-puted his depiction of the city's pacific nature; "fear and hatred," the *News* editorialized, "did stalk Birmingham's streets."[46]

Startling as it seemed in retrospect, neither the attorney general nor the president paid much, if any, heed to the Freedom Riders' undertaking before the events in Anniston and Birmingham. Robert Kennedy maintained that he "never knew they were traveling down there" until the bus burning in Anniston. For his part, the president, in the midst of preparing for European meetings with Charles de Gaulle and Nikita Khrushchev, was frankly unsupportive of the en-deavor. When his civil rights aide, Harris Wofford, initially told him of the Freedom Riders, President Kennedy said he thought they were unduly militant and snapped, "Tell them to call it off." But Wofford replied, "I don't think anybody's going to stop them right now."[47] Wofford was correct: even after most of the bloodied group of Free-dom Riders agreed to fly to their ultimate destination of New Or-leans rather than continue aboard a bus to Montgomery, other riders—including some new recruits en route to Birmingham from Nashville—were determined not to be bullied by Connor and Klan-organized vigilantes.

Confronted by the Freedom Riders' stubborn courage, the Ken-nedy administration developed plans to organize, under the com-mand of the deputy attorney general, Byron White, a civilian force of U.S. marshals, border patrolmen, Treasury Department agents, and even prison guards for possible dispatch to Alabama. The Kennedys hoped that their old ally, John Patterson, could be persuaded to vouch for the safety of the Freedom Riders. They knew that Patterson faced a political dilemma: assuring protection to the interracial travelers might be viewed in Alabama as kowtowing to Washington; conversely, maintaining a hands-off attitude in the face of local inability (or refusal) to safeguard the Freedom Riders might provoke federal intervention. Neither option appealed to Patterson, and White House advisers tried to be sensitive to the political realities; indeed, they invented an idea that Patterson could declare that he was protecting the state's highways rather than the Freedom Riders.

Although the Kennedys anticipated some difficulties in dealing with Patterson, they did not expect that, when the president tried to telephone him in Montgomery to discuss the crisis personally, the Alabama governor would decline to take the call; he instructed his secretary to say that he was on a fishing boat somewhere in the Gulf of Mexico. The president tried a second time, after Connor had ordered the arrest of those Freedom Riders who had boarded a bus for Montgomery; this time, Patterson refused the call without even concocting a far-fetched excuse. News of the governor's rude disrespect leaked to the press, provoking embarrassing headlines and infuriating Robert Kennedy. The attorney general telephoned Patterson's aides and angrily threatened federal intervention unless the governor agreed to discuss the issue of protecting the Freedom Riders. Patterson, seated nearby, picked up the phone and traded hostile accusations: Patterson charged Kennedy with trying to run roughshod over a governor upholding his oath of office; Kennedy chastised Patterson for delivering political speeches over the telephone. In the end, Patterson insisted on a face-to-face meeting with someone representing the president.

The Justice Department assigned the job to John Seigenthaler, a Tennesseean already in Alabama to handhold the Freedom Riders. Patterson expressed pleasure at hearing Seigenthaler's Southern accent, and then fulminated—presumably for the benefit of state legislative leaders at the meeting—"There's nobody in the whole country that's got the spine to stand up to the goddamned niggers except me." And he declared that people throughout the country had congratulated him on his stand against Martin Luther King, Jr., and the "rabble-rousers." Then he warned ominously, "By God, I'm telling you if federal marshals come into Alabama, there'll be blood in the streets." Nonetheless, he concluded with words that were music to Seigenthaler: "The state of Alabama has the will, the force, the men, and the equipment to give full protection to everyone in Alabama on the highways and elsewhere." Furthermore, Patterson said he neither needed nor expected federal assistance.[48]

Alabama's public safety director, Floyd Mann, assured Robert Kennedy personally that his state troopers would keep the peace by protecting the bus on the highways. On Saturday morning, May 20, six days after the Mother's Day attacks, a Greyhound bus carrying nineteen weary Freedom Riders at last was ready to leave Birmingham for Montgomery. But an unexpected hitch developed, frustrating the Freedom Riders, the attorney general, and even the Birmingham police, who were eager to see the last of the civil rights activists. Just as the bus was scheduled to depart, its driver, Joe Caverno, told reporters, "I have but one life to give, and I don't intend to give it to CORE [the Congress of Racial Equality] or the NAACP." With that, Caverno walked away from the bus and slipped into the locker room for drivers. No one seemed to know what to do next. When someone informed Robert Kennedy, the exasperated attorney general telephoned Greyhound's superintendent in Birmingham, George Cruit. Presumably for his own protection and unknown to Kennedy, Cruit recorded the conversation:

> CRUIT (responding to Kennedy's demand for an explanation): Drivers refuse to drive.
>
> KENNEDY: Do *you* know how to drive a bus?
>
> CRUIT: No.
>
> KENNEDY: Well, surely somebody in the damn bus company can drive a bus, can't they? . . . I think you should—had better be getting in touch with Mr. Greyhound or whoever Greyhound is and somebody better give us an answer to this question. I am—the government is—going to be very much upset if this group does not get to continue their trip. . . . We have gone to a lot of trouble to see that they get to continue this trip and I am most concerned to see that it is accomplished. . . . Under the law, they are entitled to transportation provided by Greyhound. . . . Somebody better get in the damn bus and get it going and get these people on their way. Mr. Cruit, I think that if some of your people would just sit down and think for a few minutes that somebody would be able to drive a bus eighty or ninety miles.[49]

In fact, Caverno was persuaded to return to his post and pilot the bus, accompanied by Mann's troopers, to Montgomery. Fourteen miles from the city, Mann, under instructions from Patterson not to interfere with local law enforcement operations, radioed Montgomery's police commissioner, Sullivan, to be ready for the arrival of the bus. But Sullivan's minions were nowhere in sight; there was no one to protect the riders from a large, menacing crowd armed with chains and ax handles. John Doar, the Justice Department attorney who was in Alabama to investigate civil rights violations, viewed the ensuing bloodletting from an office window in the federal building overlooking the bus terminal; he breathlessly described what he saw to the attorney general's office in Washington via telephone:

> The passengers are coming off. Oh, there are fists, punching.
> A bunch of men led by a guy with a bleeding face are beating
> them. There are no cops. It's terrible. It's terrible. There's not
> a cop in sight. People are yelling, 'There those niggers are. Get
> 'em, get 'em.' It's awful.[50]

Mann, contravening the governor's orders, pushed into the melee and drew his pistol to save at least one rider from a savage beating. Seigenthaler was circling the terminal in a car when he tried to rescue a young woman who was being beaten over the head by a woman swinging a heavy purse and a man jabbing his fists in her face. He jumped from his car, and as he was trying to push the attacked girl into the front seat, someone clubbed him unconscious. He was found twenty minutes later when police finally arrived at the scene. He came to just long enough to identify himself and then passed out again. Meanwhile, at Governor Patterson's direction, Alabama Attorney General Gallion had obtained a state court order declaring the Freedom Riders to be guilty of breaching the peace; he arrived on the scene and, while standing over some of the prostrate and bleeding men and women, read the injunction aloud and ordered their arrests. Robert Kennedy, "possessed by an enormous anger," as the Washington journalist Peter Maas recalled, telephoned Seigenthaler in the hospital and told him he was ordering five hundred marshals into Alabama the next day. Seigenthaler, attempting humor, offered some advice: "Never run for governor of Alabama. You couldn't get elected."[51]

That was an understatement. Kennedy already had become abominated in the South when his conversation with Cruit—including statements construed as indicating government complicity with the Freedom Riders—was leaked. Not only did Kennedy send federal marshals to protect the Freedom Riders, but he demanded that Patterson use the Alabama National Guard to protect Martin Luther King, Jr., who was flying to Montgomery. Patterson told Kennedy that the guard's commanding officer, Brig. Gen. Henry Graham, could not guarantee King's safety. Kennedy shot back: "I don't believe that. Have General Graham call me. I want to hear a general of the United States Army say he can't protect Martin Luther King." To play it safe, Kennedy directed that a contingent of marshals meet King. Patterson, clearly disgusted, said later, "Fifty marshals met King at the airport and escorted him through town . . . just like he was the president of the United States."

King went to Ralph Abernathy's First Baptist Church, where fifteen hundred people gathered to support the Freedom Riders, many of whom—some with fresh bandages over their wounds—were present. But so was a large, surly crowd of whites who threatened to overrun the church. Patterson declared martial law, but Graham initially declined to move in and get the people in the church safely home. The marshals, dressed in business suits but armed with pistols, clubs, and tear gas canisters, managed to keep the mob from getting in but could not protect anyone wanting to leave. Mann, already operating outside his governor's mandate, consulted with White about providing "reserves" to help protect the people in the church. Throughout the tense night, Patterson and Kennedy talked over the telephone several times, usually acrimoniously. Patterson later complained, "[Kennedy] showed no knowledge whatsoever of the problem, and he ran the whole affair from his command post at the Justice Department, and making telephone calls at two or three o'clock here in the morning, telling us we didn't have enough policemen on a certain corner. . . . He didn't understand who these people were. . . . They were known Communists, some of them." Patterson also accused Kennedy of fomenting the violence by abetting the Freedom Riders' efforts and then by invading the state. "Who's invading you, John?" Kennedy asked. "You know better than that. . . . You can say that on television. You can tell that to the people of Alabama, but don't tell me that. Don't tell me that, John."[52]

Inside the church, where the crowd heard that the mob was preparing a final push to break in and set it afire, King telephoned Kennedy with his own harsh criticism of the government's handling of the crisis. Kennedy replied in terms similar to those he had used to fend off Patterson: "Now, Reverend, don't tell me that. You know just as well as I do that if it hadn't been for the United States marshals, you'd be dead as Kelsey's nuts right now."[53]

At last, as dawn neared, a Justice Department lawyer representing Byron White persuaded General Graham to order his troops to disperse the threatening crowd and escort the people safely from the church. Graham, who, according to the federal official, had been "just outright hostile," mellowed after he saw to it that the Freedom Riders were safely aboard their bus to Jackson, Mississippi. "This may be a hazardous journey," he told the riders in obvious admiration of their mettle. "We have taken every precaution to protect you. And I sincerely wish you all a safe journey." It was safe—largely due to the intercession of an unlikely benefactor, Sen. James O. Eastland of Mississippi. As the bus pulled out of Montgomery on Sunday, May 21, there was good reason for apprehension: the former governor of Mississippi, James P. Coleman, had warned the Justice Department that his successor, Ross Barnett, could not be relied on to keep the peace and that the Freedom Riders would be killed before reaching Jackson. But when Kennedy turned to Eastland, the senator assured Kennedy he would keep the lid on. "He always kept his word," Kennedy said later of Eastland. "He always told me exactly where he stood and what he could do and what he couldn't do. He also told me who I could trust and who I shouldn't trust. . . . I think Jim Eastland really took a responsibility for it. . . . I said to him that my primary interest was that they weren't beaten up."[54]

What Eastland arranged, with Kennedy's tacit agreement, was that the Freedom Riders would be arrested when they reached Jackson. With that as a trade-off, he was able to assure full protection to the bus and its occupants by state authorities. The safe exodus of the Freedom Riders from Montgomery and their uneventful arrival in Jackson signaled the effective end to the specter of violence surrounding integrated interstate travel. Kennedy himself called for a "cooling off" period. He was growing exasperated with continued rides, telling Harris Wofford, "I wonder if they have the best interest of their country at heart. Do you know that one of them is against the atom bomb?" Nonetheless, Kennedy pressed the Interstate Commerce Commission to issue regulations requiring an end to segregation at all railroad depots, bus terminals, and airports, thus abolishing overt racism in interstate travel. His Justice Department also began supporting voter registration efforts by blacks throughout the South.[55]

■ ■ ■

Through the turmoil, Wallace, just short of a year before the 1962 Alabama Democratic gubernatorial primary, wisely maintained a low profile. But the lessons of the Freedom Riders for an Alabama politician were not lost on him. To start with, he compared Patterson's reluctance to interfere with local authorities to Folsom's dilatory response to threats against Autherine J. Lucy at the University of Alabama five years earlier. In Lucy's case, Wallace thought "it was terrible" and that Folsom had "let it get out of hand." The Freedom Riders "came to put on a show and stir things up," Wallace thought, "and just a few thugs attacked the people. But they should have been protected more. . . . It was a blot on our state." Indeed, Patterson was criticized in the *Montgomery Advertiser* for allowing Alabama to be the only state to experience a "problem" with the Freedom Riders. So here was yet another twist to the ensnarling dilemma of race: Wallace, who would champion local control and states' rights in Alabama and over the nation, would involve the state in racial matters if the locals seemed unable or unwilling to handle them the way he saw fit. (Sometimes, as described later, the actions of Wallace and other state authorities, though hardly faultless, would diminish violence. At other times, Wallace's intervention would disrupt plans for peaceful school integration.)

The second lesson Wallace learned from events under Patterson was that federal intervention could provide residual benefits to a Southern governor: it shifted responsibility to Washington to protect civil rights demonstrators, and it precipitated considerable sympathy both within and outside the South. The day after the Freedom Riders left Alabama, Patterson displayed to reporters piles of telegrams running seventy-five to one supporting his opposition to both federal interference and the Freedom Riders "provocation." Backing included a congratulatory wire from a group of Princeton students and succor from as far away as California and Canada. Lastly, Wallace learned that segregation was doomed. He said later: "I was carrying out my commitment [to fight desegregation]. People realized it was a promise that couldn't be kept. I knew that was the end of it, but I could say at least I tried, because in my platform . . . it says I will do all I can to keep schools segregated within the law and without violence." The lessons of the Freedom Riders would shape Wallace's campaign over the next year and his strategy in meeting racial crises during his stormy first term. But the strategy also displayed again his priorities. Even though he knew segregation was, in his word, "doomed," he nonetheless chose to defend it with unparalleled energy rather than risk being a one-term governor by trying to lead his people down a more benevolent path.[56]

■   ■   ■

As Wallace's campaign for governor began formally in late January 1962, Wallace and his key supporters and advisers—Billy Watson, Oscar Harper, and Seymore Trammell—determined that their principal opponent would be Wallace's old mentor, Jim Folsom, who wanted to make Alabama history by being the first person elected governor three times. Accordingly, they decided to hit Folsom where he was most vulnerable—on the issues of race and drinking. Additionally, Wallace resolved that the temper of the times demanded that he express his racial views more stridently than ever before, especially with other candidates in the contest—including Attorney General Gallion, Lt. Gov. Albert Boutwell, and Birmingham's notorious Bull Connor—who sought to outdo one another in pledging their allegiance to continued segregation.[57]

As it turned out, Folsom played into Wallace's strategy. Far from muting his progressive views on segregation, Folsom emphasized them. "The Civil War is over," he said in one speech, even ignoring the accepted Southern appellation, the War between the States. "Let us join the people together again. Let us furnish leadership for our colored people. You were raised amongst them. Go down in the Black Belt and the white folks talk more like the Negroes than the Negroes do." The specter of the Freedom Rides, he said, had "turned our bad face to the world. They took pictures of mobs running in the streets of Birmingham." He even exaggerated the extent of the violence there by adding, "They was taking people out at night, flogging them and mutilating and castrating. Let us have peace in the valley."[58]

And, by emphasizing his own avoidance of alcohol, Wallace subtly reminded voters of Folsom's overindulgence. At a rally near Folsom's hometown of Cullman, Wallace pledged there would be no liquor in the Governor's Mansion as long as he was governor, and he vowed to end the state's liquor-agent system in which cronies of incumbent governors would collect thousands of dollars a year. He also preached temperance to high school students, telling them, "You don't have to drink to be a man or a lady."[59]

With less than two months to go before the May 1 Democratic primary, Wallace was the odds-on favorite. Nonetheless, he suddenly was gripped by a curious foreboding—a sense that, somehow, the financial support for his campaign would evaporate. "Wallace could get pretty glum at times," recalled Bill Jones, the newspaper editor and old college friend who would become Wallace's first press secretary (see chapter 8). "When he thought things weren't going well, something like that could happen." The "something" in this case was Wallace's strange inability to remember the names of even his close friends. Oscar Harper told a story that Wallace was spirited secretly to a hospital where, after only a day or two, supporters showed up with a satchel of cash contributions totaling some twenty thousand dollars. Upon seeing the cash, the story goes, Wallace, without a word, sprang from his bed, dressed, bolted from the room, and acted as ebullient and gregarious as ever.[60]

The next night, Wallace electrified a packed city auditorium in Montgomery with a pledge to "stand in the schoolhouse door" if necessary to block any effort to integrate the schools in Alabama—a pledge that would catapult Wallace into the national consciousness little more than a year later. It was also at that March 10 rally in Montgomery that Wallace unveiled his frontal attack on the federal courts by characterizing Frank Johnson with a series of deprecations: "an integrating, carpet-bagging, scalawagging, race-mixing, bald-faced liar." Later, Wallace audiences would wait for and then chant along with the candidate's litany, always punctuating the line with stomping feet and roars of approval, even in Johnson's hometown of Jasper.

On the stump, Wallace underscored his family values by featuring George, Jr., and the newest Wallace addition, year-old Lee, at most rallies. Nor did he ignore his ingrained populist beliefs—increasing school funding even if it meant new taxes; expanding the trade school system and establishing a network of junior colleges; increasing old-age pensions; encouraging private housing for the elderly; and starting "remedial programs" of health care for the aged, the handicapped, and the infirm. "Those were threaded throughout his campaign," Jones said, "and he went on to do them. But . . . where he got the applause and where he got the news coverage was always on the segregation and on cussing out the federal judges. Everything else got very little play."[61]

Wallace thundered his racial policies throughout the state, conducting rallies to crowds in growing numbers in all sixty-seven counties in just over seven weeks. In one typical rally—in the north-central town of Hartselle—he told a throng:

I will continue to fight for segregation in Alabama because it is based on our firm conviction of right, and because it serves the best interests of all our people. I shall react vigorously to outside meddling. We shall fight the federals in the arena of an increasingly sympathetic national public opinion. We shall fight them in the arena of our courts by interposing constitutional questions involving the sovereignty of this state and the constitutional prerogatives of its chief executive. I pledge to stand between you and those who would impose on you doctrines foreign to our way of life and disruptive of the peace and tranquility of our citizens. I will face our enemies face-to-face, hip-to-hip, toe-to-toe—and never surrender your governor's office to these [modern-day] carpetbaggers, scalawags, and polliwogs [*sic*]. Right will prevail if we fight. We can have peace and progress in Alabama if we stand firm. There is no other way.[62]

That kind of oratory—punchy, powerful, pointed, but carefully framed within legal and, presumably, nonviolent boundaries—overwhelmed his less articulate opponents. Unable to attract sufficient contributions, Gallion and Connor fell by the way early in the race. Boutwell proved ineffective on the stump and pulled out, nudging much of his support to a young, handsome dark horse—a state senator from an old and wealthy Alabama family, Ryan de-Graffenried. On the eve of the first primary, even though nearly all political observers believed Wallace would win, Folsom's camp remained confident that their man might win or, at worst, run a reasonably close second.[63]

But the night before the balloting, Folsom arrived at a studio for a live, statewide telecast calamitously drunk. Aides were unable to dissuade him from going on, and once in front of the cameras, Folsom's performance would have been funny had it not been so sorrowful. When he started to introduce his children, he could not remember their names. "Let's see," he slurred, "which one are you?" Next, he reached out with his great paw of a hand and fondly tousled his wife's hair. Then he gazed into the camera with a vacuous smile and started making incoherent cooing sounds. For years after that disastrous television program, Folsom claimed that someone had "dropped a pill in [his] steak" or otherwise drugged him. At last, when he finally and fully recognized that his political sun in Alabama had long since set, he recalled that fateful and fatal night with melancholy: "I don't know *what* happened. It don't make any difference now. I'm way the hell out of the picture, anyway."[64]

Despite the catastrophe, Folsom's residual vote-getting potency was such that he finished just a thousand votes, or two-tenths of one percent, behind the second-place finisher, deGraffenried. But by law, only the top two vote getters were permitted to compete in a second primary for the nomination that, in one-party Alabama, would name the next governor. Folsom's political career was over. The winner of the first primary, as expected, was Wallace; with 39 percent of the vote, he led deGraffenried by nine percentage points and forty-six thousand votes. Wallace had been hoping to face Folsom in the run-off election scheduled for May 29; he believed that whatever strength Folsom could muster would have peaked in the first primary. De-Graffenried, on the other hand, was described by Wallace as a "clean-cut, good-looking young fellow . . . who also was a very able young man." But when Folsom endorsed deGraffenried, who already was viewed as a racial moderate in comparison to Wallace, de-Graffenried's campaign unraveled. Pro-Wallace editorializers labeled him "Big Jim deGraffenried," suggesting that his election would mean a continuation of "Folsomism," implying corruption, intemperance, and racial moderation.[65]

Wallace wasted little time pinning deGraffenried in a corner by drumming for his own brand of segregation. He denounced "judicial dictatorship and judicial tyranny." He decried the Supreme Court ruling regarding prayer in the public schools, giving it his own special twist that characterized Alabama as a righteous, God-fearing victim: "The Supreme Court has made it against the law to read the Bible in public schools. Certain Northern newspapers and magazines, in an effort to be derogatory against Alabama, said, 'Alabama is in the Bible Belt.' What's so wrong about being for the Bible?"

DeGraffenried was put in the position of assuring voters that he, too, embraced the Bible, and he tried to establish that he also strongly favored segregation. But just as Wallace, four years earlier, was perceived as not being for segregation with the same committed fervor as his opponent, so deGraffenried could not overcome Wallace's overheated oratory on this most crucial of issues. A typical Wallace speech involving segregation came just ten days before the second primary vote—and it played on all the hopes and fears of white Southerners, linking integration to a loss of jobs and an increase in crime. With supreme irony, he chose as a model for Alabama the state of Mississippi, which, just four months later, would be enmeshed in a racial crisis every bit as frightening as the one involving the Freedom Riders:

> Mississippi in the last five years has obtained more new industries than any other state in the South except Florida. Mississippi has conducted its racial affairs on a sound and tranquil basis with peace and dignity for both the white and Negro races. Georgia, on the other hand, recently changed its racial policy to admit racial integration, and what did they get? They got sit-ins, shoot-ins, fall-ins, and all sorts of other racial disturbances and crimes. I say that I choose to follow Mississippi's example and not the example set by Georgia.[66]

Actually, the city of Atlanta, not the state of Georgia, had permitted limited integration at lunch counters and many public accommodations. Indeed, segregation persisted throughout most of the state in schools, courthouses, and restaurants; and discrimination continued statewide in voter registration.[67] But those were fine points that Wallace chose to ignore. And he achieved much of his mileage by pointing to racial disturbances outside of Alabama, especially in the North: "All over America, people are now realizing what we in the South and Alabama have been talking about. The people of Newburgh know. The people of New Rochelle know. They know that we have been fighting for the principle of local government."[68]

Wallace was referring to two towns in New York whose residents were enmeshed in bitter racial strife, one over a public housing project and the other over the reassignment of black students from an all-black school. He also cited black–white flares of violence in such diverse places as Brooklyn, Harlem, Chicago, and Alameda. And he vowed that he could hold back the tide of integration, knowing full well that he lacked the power to stop the waves:

> I pled guilty to refusing to obey this federal court order, and what did they do? This Washington crowd and the federal judge backed down. . . . I can say tonight in no uncertain terms that this state is not going to be big enough for me as the elected sovereign of this state and a bunch of Supreme Court yes-men appointed for life trying to run Alabama's school system. One of us is going to have to go. . . . I shall ask the legislature to give me the right to assign pupils to schools in cases where they are threatened by integration. As your

governor, I shall refuse to abide by any illegal federal court order even to the point of standing at the schoolhouse door in person. . . . And if your governor and your officials stand as we will stand, there will be millions of Americans who will say, "This was Alabama's finest hour."[69]

During the run-off campaign, faint whiffs of Klan involvement with Wallace arose. The Alabama Klan's wizard, Kenneth Adams, told a reporter, "You saw what happened to George Wallace last time when he denounced the Klan. Well, he's not going to make the same mistake this time, and we're going to put him in. You'll see."[70] Six days before the voting, Folsom claimed that the Klan was "in the Wallace camp" and that his one-time protégé had waged an "outlaw" campaign. This time, as he had in 1958, Wallace did not denounce the Klan, but left the job to Grover Hall and other anti-Folsom editors. Hall wrote that it was "unbearable to Folsom" when his "former understudy" took "the branchhead vote away from him." It was that "vengeful motive," Hall wrote, that prompted "Folsom's wrathful attack."[71]

DeGraffenried tried to strike back by belittling what he called Wallace's "blustering defiance" with "foolish warfare against the United States." "A farmer downstate told me long ago," he said, "that a cow that moos the loudest and eats the most gives the least milk." And, excoriating Wallace as a "loud-mouthed demagogue," deGraffenried asserted, "We need a man in the governor's chair— and not in a jail cell—to aid our people."[72]

In the end, it was no contest: Wallace carried 56 of the state's 67 counties, establishing a new record by amassing more than 340,000 votes, or 56 percent of the total.[73] After the victory, Wallace immediately became the focus of a debate among Alabamians who wondered if he meant what he had said during the campaign. "Wallace was stuck with his campaign promise to fight," the Southern journalist Joseph Cumming observed. "Yet, he knew he would be ruined if he surrendered to the lead-pipe boys. He attempted to steer the near-impossible course between resistance and violence. It was obviously a fraud . . . a shoddy fraud. But he had an anti-Kennedy sentiment working for him . . . and [was] able to reconstruct history as he did with his so-called defiance of Frank Johnson."[74] U.S. Representative Tom Bevill of Alabama, who was a state representative under Patterson and during Wallace's first administration, said that Wallace "knew that it was wrong" to pledge shrilly that segregation would continue.[75] Another Southern journalist, Ray Jenkins, recalled that Wallace either believed, or had convinced himself, that blacks were inferior and dangerous. He described one conversation with Wallace as "real *Birth of a Nation* stuff. It was that mentality. It wasn't Ku Klux Klan, but it was close. He sold himself to it."[76] For his part, Wallace insisted that he believed that segregation would benefit both races: "Of course, you couldn't be otherwise and be elected, but I was for it. I took it for granted. It had been here for all those years and we took it as a matter of course. Just like in India, the British would take something as normal until later on when things began to change. So, no, I didn't do it for political reasons. I believed it." But he denied believing blacks were inferior and said, "In the days of segregation, I wasn't going to be patronizing. The blacks were not as capable because of a lack of education."[77]

■   ■   ■

Whatever he believed in retrospect, Wallace drew around him a team of advisers comprising several unbending racists. These men—who included two long-time associates from Barbour County, Seymore Trammell and Albert Lingo, and a tall, somewhat tattered patrician lawyer from Montgomery, John Peter Kohn—held Wallace's ear during the nearly eight months between his nomination and his inauguration and in the first months of his administration.[78]

Kohn, whom the press secretary–designate, Bill Jones, described as "a mean-spirited racist," would for a time displace Grover Hall as Wallace's chief idea man outside the official cabinet. Wallace shifted away from sole reliance on Hall, Jones recalled, principally because Kohn's severe racial attitudes were "fairly representative of the general populace," and, secondarily, because Kohn's lawyerly familiarity with the federal courts helped Wallace gather ammunition with which to keep heaping disdain on them. And because their own views closely coincided with Kohn's, both homeboys—Trammell, who would serve as finance director, and Lingo, selected as public safety director—consistently pointed Wallace in Kohn's direction.[79] Kohn did not, however, return the admiration with which he was regarded by many of Wallace's aides. "Hangers-on," "jerks," and "rats" were some of Kohn's terms for many Wallace advisers. But if he faulted some Wallace aides as bootlickers and tail-waggers, he himself was not without nearly unbridled adulation for the governor-elect. From the earliest days of Wallace's suzerainty in Alabama, Kohn asserted, "If this country is going to be saved, it will take a man like Wallace to save it. He's the Andrew Jackson of today—the closest thing to Jackson that's ever come along. He's permeated with the spirit of the Confederacy. . . . He would have ridden with Forrest or Jeb Stuart."[80]

Kohn, however, in a remarkably candid 1966 interview where he openly acknowledged his personal hatreds and discussed his views of the barely contained hatreds of millions of other Americans, exempted Wallace from the racism that he, himself, practiced. "Now, George Wallace," Kohn said, "is not a racist. I am." His distinction was that a racist like himself believes deeply that blacks cannot do much more than to "jump up and down and eat each other." He said that Wallace and his ilk, on the other hand, possessed far higher regard for blacks but had "enough practical political sense to know cussing Negroes was popular." "The mass of people," Kohn continued, "were looking subconsciously for someone, and now [in Wallace] they have him. He created a devil and then slew him. Hitler used the Jews the same way; Jacob Javits did the same thing with the South. Hitler, of course, was a paranoid. The Germans are either at your ass or at your throat. But this country's full of little Hitlers—people with animosity toward everybody."[81]

Wallace was no little Hitler. There was no philosophy blaming blacks for the South's troubles, as Hitler had blamed Jews for Germany's; on the contrary, he believed that most Southern blacks and whites were victims of Northern repression and that he had worked to expand opportunities for both races. The devil he created, if any, was the federal government and Northern liberals, not Southern blacks. Even in his dedication to segregation, Wallace followed no *conscious* formula for oppressing blacks by hurting them educationally or economically. Yet, the distinction that Kohn and Wallace tried to draw between a racist and a segregationist meant little in the practical effect on Southern blacks: they were demeaned, kept from competing with whites for most jobs, and denied all access to political power. The only difference, perhaps—and a critical one—is that the hater may be unable or unwilling to change, while the manipulative opportunist is both capable of change and inclined to adapt.

In 1982, when Wallace openly courted black support, an aging Kohn denounced Wallace and would have nothing more to do with him.[82] But in the months following Wallace's nomination in 1962, Kohn, supported by Trammell and Lingo, persuaded Wallace to align himself with last-ditch segregationist governors in Georgia and

Mississippi, and to embrace rhetoric in his inaugural address—
"Segregation now! Segregation tomorrow! Segregation forever!"—
that would thereafter define him as the embodiment of Southern
resistance to equality for blacks (see chapter 8). Wallace, brimming
with his new power and certain he could parlay it into persuading the
legislature to grant him a second term, embraced their advice fully
and with almost no thought of the consequences. This was a decision
that would contribute to great pain in Alabama over the next few
years—one that Wallace would later regret but that indelibly marked
the course of his early years as governor.

8

The Fire This Time

WALLACE DIDN'T WAIT for the November election, much less for his inauguration, to embroil himself in racial controversy. He injected himself into Georgia's 1962 gubernatorial campaign by appearing at a rally for Marvin Griffin, a former governor seeking election against an opponent supposedly more moderate on segregation.[1] Wallace assured the crowd, "Marvin Griffin and I are in complete agreement on . . . what is needed to save Georgia, Alabama, and the nation. The time has come when we've either got to put up or shut up about a return to constitutional government. In the next four years in Alabama, we are going to put up."[2]

More ominously, Wallace vociferously supported Mississippi's Gov. Ross Barnett in the massive and ultimately tragic confrontation between state and federal authority over the admission of a black student, James Meredith, to Ole Miss. For weeks, Robert Kennedy had engaged Barnett in the sort of political gamesmanship that much of the electorate finds cynical, if not corrupt—but which is essential to minimize confrontations in a heterogeneous democracy. Kennedy had tried to reach an accommodation with Barnett on how Meredith might be enrolled—perhaps by quietly slipping him onto the Oxford, Mississippi, campus on a Sunday—while the governor made a show of storming and fuming about federal tyranny. But Barnett kept vacillating, leading Kennedy to believe at one point that the governor was "genuinely loony," but later to conclude that he was "an agreeable rogue—[but] weak." That coincided with the historian William Manchester's assessment of Barnett as

> charming, ignorant, friendly, suspicious, blindly loyal to the lost Confederacy, appalled by the present and frightened of the future. . . . Under great pressure he would look for a way out, a deal. His tragedy, which became Mississippi's, was that he just didn't know how to find or make one. . . . The governor didn't know how to strike a bargain. He knew he would have to sacrifice something to make peace, but he couldn't decide how much he would give up, how much resistance he could show for the sake of appearances and still remain below the flash point of violence. . . . If he had been as able a politician as George Wallace, the crisis might have been resolved. . . . But he wasn't able. His sense of timing . . . was wrong."[3]

Wallace's timing did not seem much better. Even before his formal election, much less his inauguration, he injected himself needlessly into the Mississippi crisis by dispatching his adviser Albert Lingo to Oxford as an "observer," and simultaneously issuing a powerful statement championing Barnett:

> I wholeheartedly endorse and agree with Ross Barnett in his stand. Millions of Americans are grateful that at least one governor, Governor Barnett, has the guts to stand fast. I, like Governor Barnett, am tired of being pushed around by the Justice Department and the irresponsible, lousy federal courts. I am going to stand up against those who would try to take over our school system.

And then, presaging his essential role in political history, he added: "I'm not going to tell you I'm going to win, but I'm going to wake the country up. I believe that's the destiny of the people of this state."[4]

What Lingo observed in Oxford was the abrupt and foolhardy withdrawal of state troopers from the campus, allowing it to be invaded and overrun by well over a thousand rioters—students and out-of-state troublemakers alike—searching for Meredith while screaming epithets at the federal marshals. Many in the mob were armed with guns, bottles, rocks, and chains. The marshals, under orders not to return gunfire except to defend Meredith's life, protected themselves by lobbing tear gas canisters into the ever-surging mob. But the determined horde—urged on by a frenzied Edwin A. Walker, a retired major general who decided he had been "on the wrong side" five years earlier when he had coordinated troop movements to support integration in Little Rock—continued to shoot at, pelt, and injure the thinning lines of marshals. The administration's key troubleshooter at the scene, Deputy Attorney General Nicholas Katzenbach, feared that some of his people would be killed; but even after his boss reluctantly authorized returning fire if absolutely essential, the courageous marshals never drew their weapons. In the end, 160 marshals were wounded, 28 by gunfire. By the time the long-delayed federalized National Guardsmen and regular army units arrived, two people—a French journalist and a local curiosity seeker—had been killed. Forty of the soldiers were injured. Most of the attackers, many of whom were students, vanished after the night-long siege. More than 200 people, including Walker, were arrested.[5]

Lingo, a big, burly man in his early fifties, came back from the Oxford experience in full agreement with Wallace that state troopers should be employed vigorously to quell public disturbances and maintain order, if not peace. To be sure, the "troublemakers" whom Lingo and his troopers would repel with electrified cattle prods, shotguns, or whatever it took, would, more often than not, be those protesting against segregation rather than those seeking to retain it.[6] And the helmeted, jackbooted troopers would be used regularly at Wallace's direction to try to preserve the status quo rather than to enforce court orders. But both Lingo and Wallace believed that the reluctance to use state forces in racial disorders—as happened in both the Freedom Riders and Ole Miss crises—ultimately worsened the melees, underlined the states' inability to preserve calm, and increased criticism from Southerners as well as from the public at large. From Lingo's and Wallace's perspectives, the Oxford experience also demonstrated that racial trouble often was exacerbated by outsiders, white or black, whether they were seeking justice or trying to pervert it. As a result, Wallace would strive to pose as the public proxy for those who might otherwise take matters into their own, violent hands.[7]

"It was a ploy," Wallace insisted. "Groups would come see me and want to help keep segregation—meaning they wanted to be vigilantes. And I would tell them, 'Thanks, boys, but I can handle it— and if I need your help, I'll call y'all.' That was the best way to keep out violence."[8] Replaying the tunes that he would sing over and over in his later years, Wallace continued:

Barnett wasn't a bad man. He didn't expect all those kooks to come down there. I learned from Ole Miss. I learned to expect neo-Nazis, the Socialist Workers Party, Minutemen. I told them to stay away. I stirred the people up about the court system, not against black folks. I said the good white and black people of Alabama can work these problems out themselves. We don't need the Justice Department to tell us everything to do and what time frame to use. We can do that ourselves in Alabama.[9]

Wallace's first press secretary, Bill Jones, also believed that Wallace "felt that if he could inject himself, he could minimize violence." Jones, three years Wallace's junior, was considered "moderate" on the segregation issue (he had worked for a progressive Alabama congressman, Carl Elliott), and was described by a national journalist covering Wallace's administration as "a balding, possum-shaped little fellow who always seemed to maintain his cool and integrity." Jones said that Wallace "knew that integration was coming. . . . He felt that the way to keep violence down and prepare the people to accept what they were going to have to accept was to say repeatedly— repeatedly: 'Let me do it, let me stand for you'—not only in the schoolhouse door, but in every way, such as in the courts and everything. He realized that he could be a catalyst for getting the thing accepted finally that he knew was going to be forced down the South's throat, whether they wanted it or not."[10] Jones may have overstated the case; Wallace, after all, was always aware of the impact of his dramatic confrontations with federal authority. But in becoming the apotheosis of the Southern ideal of fighting the good fight, Wallace undoubtedly clarified the inevitability of integration while psychologically easing the people's sense of defeat.

The Oxford tragedy also taught Wallace that the Kennedys would be willing to strike a deal in which a governor could make a show of resistance while, in reality, bowing to the inevitable. But, at the same time, he developed a deep mistrust of Robert Kennedy, whom he believed, mistakenly, had been the one, rather than Barnett, who had waffled on making and keeping agreements.[11]

That mistrust was trumped in spades by John Peter Kohn, who considered John Kennedy "the most dangerous man in the history of our country" and who, just a year after Ole Miss, would dance a jig along Dexter Avenue in Montgomery to celebrate the president's assassination.[12] Antipathy toward the Kennedys was shared by Lingo and Trammell: the former would become Wallace's villain-in-chief in the vain effort to hold back integration; the latter would become Wallace's single most influential adviser until Wallace began suspecting Trammell's honesty during the 1968 presidential campaign.[13] (See chapter 14.) Trammell also grew to be known as Wallace's hatchet man. He played the role of "bad cop" in punishing, often ham-handedly, those legislators who refused to support Wallace's programs—often those in which Trammell himself had a personal interest. One such occasion involved a scheme that would have given the governor authority to appoint lawyers to handle property condemnation cases arising from state highway construction. An intrigue ripe for kickbacks, the scheme would have become law had not Trammell overplayed his hand. When he threatened four of the bill's opponents with loss of road projects in their counties, the legislators went public and the plan fell apart.[14]

Trammell and Lingo strongly supported Kohn in his advocacy of resistance to integration. Lingo's views would manifest themselves through the billy clubs of his troopers, even though he insisted lamely, "I am not a Negro hater. I've played with them, I've eaten with them, and I've worked with them—but I still believe in segregation. You can say that some of my best friends are Negroes."[15] Trammell's outlook on segregation was more direct. In a speech to a White Citizens Council rally in Selma, Alabama, shortly before Wallace's inauguration, Trammell urged a throng of thirty-five hundred whites to socially ostracize any judges in Alabama who might rule against segregation. Wallace often defended Lingo and Trammell by pointing out that Trammell once prosecuted a white man accused of killing a black; Lingo, the foreman of the jury, tried, unsuccessfully, to persuade fellow jurors to impose the death sentence.[16] That kind of simplistic notion of what constituted fair play toward blacks characterized Wallace's attitudes throughout most of his career; but he believed—or said he did—that his was an even-handed approach shorn of Northern hypocrisy. The irony of the Wallace camp's suspicion of the Kennedys was that, until the Barnetts and Wallaces chose the road of extremism, the Kennedys were their intellectual allies in their sentiments toward the South. In *Profiles in Courage*, John Kennedy described the Reconstruction-era, anti-Southern congressman Thaddeus Stevens as "the crippled, fanatical personification of the extremes of the Radical Republican movement."[17] He believed, as Arthur Schlesinger recalled, that "Reconstruction was a matter of Southern whites rescuing their states from ignorant and incompetent ex-slaves."[18] But after reading the

Mississippi legislature's defense of the Oxford events—blaming Meredith and the federal government—the president said, "They can say these things . . . and believe it. They must have been doing the same things a hundred years ago. . . . I'm coming to believe that Thaddeus Stevens was right."[19]

Meanwhile, Wallace advisers like Grover Hall and Bill Jones, segregationists of a tamer stripe, were all but ignored in the early part of Wallace's administration. They tried to dissuade Wallace from identifying with racial diehards like Griffin and Barnett. They held that segregation should be dismantled gradually in the interests of order, and that Wallace would be ill advised to wave a red flag in the federal government's face. They were, however, thoroughly overridden by the hard-liners in Wallace's coterie and by the governor-elect's conviction that his campaign pledges bound him to establish himself as the premier defender of the white Southern "way of life."

The calamitous tumult at Oxford provoked an outpouring of petitions and speeches from people whom Wallace dismissed as leaders of the so-called power structure—upper-income business and professional people, leaders in academia, several editors, absentee managers of major corporations and federal facilities, and others removed from the day-to-day realities of integration. They wanted Wallace's assurances that nothing resembling the violence and disruption at Ole Miss would happen in Alabama. Many of the pleas reflected common sense and common decency—virtues in greater supply in Alabama than widely believed at the time.

One Anniston woman who wrote to Wallace implored, "Law and order . . . should be uppermost in your mind. . . . One Ross Barnett is more than the South can afford. Much of the tragedy was due to his poor leadership. . . . Please remember [to] conduct yourself with dignity and to back the decent and law-abiding citizens in their desire to comply with federal laws. It is also your responsibility to behave as an American first and as an Alabamian second." Another constituent praised Wallace for his postnomination trips around the country seeking industry for Alabama and for his "sympathetic understanding of the aid-to-dependent-children problem [and] fair-minded appraisal of the right-to-work law." But the constituent, who admired Wallace's "hustling approach" to issues, was distressed by his "extreme stand" and "incendiary sentiments" regarding desegregation.[20]

A Methodist minister in Gadsden, Alabama, who had supported Wallace because of his "Christian character and sound common sense" wrote, "Fight for segregation if you will, but please do so through the courts and not by inflammatory statements and defiance." Numerous letters pleading for restraint and nonviolence poured in from church groups and ministers. One Huntsville pastor, speaking of a campaign visit, reminded Wallace, "You and our neighbor, Doctor [Werner] von Braun, engaged in some lighthearted joking about making so many campaign promises that you would not be able to keep them all. American voters understand well the psychology of such promises. We do not expect jot-and-tittle keeping of promises nearly as much as we expect responsible leadership." And a Fort Payne woman also embraced pragmatism, though at a somewhat different level: "If we are going to let Hindus, Chinese, and other internationals into our universities, then I think the American Negro has a right to go also."[21]

But calls for reason were outweighed in both numbers and vehemence by demands for Wallace to stand his ground. A Birmingham man "implored" Wallace to adhere to his promises despite the campaign for the governor-to-be to accept integration. A man in Rockford wrote that he and a majority in Coosa County "voted for you because of your firm stand." He added, "I believe you have as much courage as Ross Barnett." A lawyer, concerned that businessmen in Tuscaloosa had petitioned Wallace to back down on his campaign pledges, appealed to Wallace to "fight to preserve our way of life in Alabama." There were the expected missives dripping with hate for blacks, Jews, Catholics, the Kennedys, Hugo Black, and many others; but the argument that fully captured Wallace's inclination was reflected in a letter from C. E. Hornsby, Jr., the chairman of the Alabama Association of Citizens Councils:

> Don't be dissuaded by those of carpetbagging and
> scalawagging nature who . . . believe that the issue is between
> law and order . . . and lawlessness. The issues are the same now
> as ever: segregation versus integration; states rights versus
> federal usurpation; and constitutional government versus
> judicial and executive fiat. Naturally, we hope violence and
> bloodshed can be avoided. However, if it comes, the blame will
> rest squarely on the shoulders of the NAACP and the federal
> government.[22]

Alabamians and the nation, in the months ahead, would hear that argument from Wallace time and again during racial crises; invariably, he would express regret and even outrage at violence, but would place the responsibility for any violence on federals, outsiders, Martin Luther King, Jr., and almost anyone except Bull Connor and Al Lingo.

And even though Wallace knew he would eventually lose the struggle to maintain segregation, he also knew that a firm attitude against the federal government's intrusions would stand him in good stead. Hornsby's letter even provided Wallace with the justification for defeat, so essential to Southern culture:

> [It is] a tribute to the people of Mississippi that it took . . .
> thirty thousand U.S. troops and hundreds of marshals to put
> the unwanted person in the University of Mississippi. . . . Ole
> Miss was not integrated, for she never submitted. It can
> only be said that she has been subjected to integration by
> overwhelming and unlawful force. Thus, Ole Miss's honor is
> still intact.[23]

That kind of thinking—a direct throwback to the "glorious Lost Cause" mentality that distorted Southern politics for a century— powered Wallace's response to the dangerous events that confronted him.

■　　■　　■

After his formal election in November, Wallace threw a symbolic glove in the face of his critics when he told the Alabama Chamber of Commerce that he was unmoved by appeals for concessions on segregation:

> My position is unchanged from what I stated during the
> campaign. I am going to resist and my resistance will gain
> respect from over the rest of the country. We are going to have
> some trying days but, again, I say I believe in peace. Any
> breakdown in law and order in Alabama will come from
> outsiders and people like Martin Luther King. I appreciate the
> people saying to me, 'let's have peace,' but you should direct
> such resolutions to the Kennedys and the Martin Luther
> Kings. We are going to keep peace in Alabama and, also, we
> are going to keep our social and educational order if we have
> the insides to do it. . . . Those who charge Alabama and the
> South with discrimination are the same hypocrites who for so
> long discriminated against the South in an economic way.

Those people who want to destroy our educational and social order are the same people who want to destroy the free enterprise system in America.[24]

Wallace's unyielding polemics assured his short-run popularity with the vast majority of whites, but it opened the entire moderate flank to any politician willing to risk his future by rushing into the minefield of racial temperance. Two men decided to gamble that, because of the inescapable onrush of history, staking out the moderate position now would set the stage for a successful gubernatorial run four years hence. One was Ryan deGraffenried; the other was the newly elected attorney general, Richmond Flowers, who, like Wallace, was a former Folsomite from southern Alabama. During his own campaign in 1962, Flowers had frequently followed Wallace's campaign trail, dogging his footsteps and jumping up on platforms as soon as Wallace had vacated them. He had cashed in on the sizable crowds Wallace invariably attracted, and he had regularly identified with Wallace's positions. After he was safely nominated for attorney general, however, Flowers perceived in the Ole Miss eruption an opportunity to establish his own persona and serve as a counterpoint to Wallace. He decided to broach racial moderation—gingerly, to be sure—before the inauguration. He criticized Wallace, but was not yet audacious enough to abandon segregation fully:

> Certain top political figures in Alabama have concerned themselves over Mississippi's problems for the purpose of fattening their own stature rather than interesting themselves in the stabilization of Alabama's position as a segregated state. . . . To advise our sister states while preannouncing our plans of defiance of any federal court is worse than waving a red flag in a bull's face. This completely disrobes us of legal defenses and delaying maneuvers. . . . I will tolerate no violence. That applies to all race agitators, both white and Negro, and on all demonstrators and curiosity-seeking mob-makers. State's rights is a matter of deep principle with me, but I will use the full powers of the attorney general's office to preserve law and order.[25]

■   ■   ■

Amid the growing political maelstrom, the preinaugural days also held anticipation, froth, and frippery, as well as everyday necessities.

George Wallace, Sr., cradles his son George C. at their Clio home. Son, like his father, learned to be a "true blue Southerner."

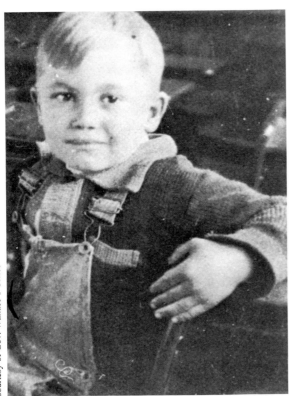

George C. bravely tries to smile for the camera on his first day of school in Clio.

Wallace's scrappiness, willingness to take risks, and ability to assess an opponent's weaknesses brought him two Alabama Golden Gloves championships.

Wallace, with University of Alabama boxing teammate Bart Tatmio in 1941, sports a mouse under his left eye after he won a hard-fought match against rival Louisiana State University in Baton Rouge.

Wallace, not yet sixteen, was elected one of four pages to the Alabama Senate in 1935. The job paid two dollars a day and enabled Wallace to learn about the legislature.

College chum Glen Curlee joined Wallace in 1946 to help him in his first campaign for the Alabama House of Representatives.

Convalescing from meningitis in an Army hospital in Hot Springs, Arkansas, Wallace had been through a week of high fever, delirium, and a severe reaction to sulfa before being declared out of danger of death.

George, Lurleen, and Bobbi Jo in 1944 at their rented "home" in Alamagordo, New Mexico—a converted chicken coop. It was the only housing they could afford.

Flight engineer Wallace (kneeling, third from left) with the crew of **Sentimental Journey,** *commanded by Captain Robert Ray (standing, left) in Topeka. Later, in combat, the crew flew an older B-29,* **Little Yutz.**

The Montgomery bus boycott launched the modern civil rights movement, and its successful conclusion late in 1956 was commemorated by the Rev. Ralph Abernathy (left) and the Rev. Martin Luther King, Jr. (second from left), among others, by riding in the front of a once-segregated bus.

This 1963 photograph taken during antisegregation demonstrations in Birmingham shocked the nation. President Kennedy urged Martin Luther King, Jr., to keep children out of the marches, but he realized why King was growing impatient.

By order of Birmingham's police commissioner, Bull Connor, black protesters were subjected to attacks by powerful fire hoses as well as by police dogs. Wallace publicly supported Connor but ultimately sent in state troopers to restore order through less extreme means.

Governor Wallace briefly blocked Deputy Attorney General Nicholas Katzenbach, shown wiping away perspiration in the broiling sun, from escorting two black students into the University of Alabama. His symbolic stand against federal power gained Wallace national notoriety and new adherents.

Rescue workers, neighbors, and authorities mill around the rubble of Birmingham's Sixteenth Street Baptist Church, where four young black girls attending Bible classes were blown apart by a powerful dynamite bomb. The resulting universal horror caused Wallace to mute his racist rhetoric.

An interracial march from Selma to Montgomery in March, 1965, dramatized demands of Southern blacks for voting rights. The one-legged Jim Letherer of Saginaw, Michigan, covered the entire fifty miles on his crutches.

Twenty-five thousand civil right proponents massed at Alabama's state capitol, climaxing the historic march from Selma. Wallace watched from an aide's window as King delivered his classic "How long? Not long!" speech.

Bobbi Jo, at eighteen, was dating and wondered about bringing her current beau to the inaugural ball (she would). Lurleen started preparations for moving to the mansion and looked at the neighborhood schools to which Peggy Sue and George, Jr., twelve and eleven respectively, would be expected to transfer. Not yet able to afford a maid, Lurleen carried toddler Lee, not yet two, everywhere with her.[26] Lurleen also had to settle the family's accounts. Since moving her family to Montgomery in mid-September, Lurleen had charged her food purchases at the Cloverland Red and White grocery store, running up a bill totaling $414.77. The proprietor, Ed Spencer, figured that Wallace, having been nominated the previous June, was a good risk. Spencer's faith was justified when, ten days after he became governor, Lurleen paid the bill in full.[27]

She was also busy making out her invitation list for the ball—and she did not forget old friends such as "Mom" Sanders, who had befriended the young soldier and his bride in Arkadelphia, Arkansas, and from whom they had rented a room. Sorely anxious about being "properly clad" for the inaugural ball, she wrote Lurleen two weeks prior to the event that, while she owned a "very nice short formal" gown, she did not have a long one, so she wanted to know the gown length George's and Lurleen's mothers would wear. "I've saved my Christmas money and will buy a long formal if the elder women will be dressed that way," she said.[28] Lurleen was just as concerned with her own attire and that of her children. She playfully typed out her own "press release" entitled "Inaugural Ball Fashions" in which she described her outfit as "a beautiful gown of candlelight silk brocade . . . especially designed for the inauguration by Larrabe of New York" and made from "Hong Kong silk in a muted white-on-white design." She described in detail the design of the neck, bodice, and skirt and of the matching coat. She wrote that Bobbi Jo would wear "a silver and white brocade gown gathered full at the waist" set off by "a white fox shrug which was her Christmas present this past year." Daughter Peggy would wear "a floor length gown of silver metallic brocade . . . wrist-length white kid gloves, pearls, and silver brocade slippers." She did not mention that George, Jr., would be decked out in a cutaway and top hat, a scaled-down version of his father's outfit. But she did note that "Baby Lee Wallace [would] not appear at the inaugural ball" because she would be tucked away in her crib at the mansion wearing cozy knit sleepers in a washing machine shade of pink."[29]

■　　■　　■

The inaugural day was bitterly cold, but it didn't daunt the thousands of Wallace supporters and state dignitaries huddled on and near the gleaming steps of the Alabama capitol. Standing near the spot where Jefferson Davis had been inaugurated, Wallace spewed a litany of racism worthy of the Ku Klux Klan pamphleteer who, retained by Kohn, had, in fact, written most of it.[30]

> Today I have stood where Jefferson Davis stood and took an oath to my people. It is very appropriate then that from this Cradle of the Confederacy, this very heart of the great Anglo-Saxon Southland, that today we sound the drum for freedom. . . . Let us rise to the call of freedom-loving blood that is in us and send our answer to the tyranny that clanks its chains upon the South. In the name of the greatest people that ever trod this earth, I draw the line in the dust and toss the gauntlet before the feet of tyranny, and I say: segregation now, segregation tomorrow, segregation forever.

He cautioned national politicians against relying on "insipid bloc voters" rather than on the South's "race of honor." He charged that "government has become our God. It is a system that is the very opposite of Christ." He said, "the international racism of the liberals seeks to persecute the international white minority to the whim of the international colored so that we are footballed about according to the favor of the Afro-Asian bloc." In classic racist terms, he argued that if the races "amalgamate into the one unit as advocated by the Communist philosopher, then . . . we become . . . a mongrel unit of one under a single, all-powerful government. . . . We invite the Negro citizen of Alabama to work with us from his separate racial station . . . to grow in individual freedom and enrichment." He closed on an ominous note:

> But we warn those of any group who would follow the false doctrines of communistic amalgamation that we will not surrender our system of government, our freedom of race and religion [that] was won at a hard price; and if it requires a hard price to retain it, we are able—and quite willing—to pay it.[31]

The heated, overripe, racially allusive rhetoric was guaranteed to secure Wallace's base of support in Alabama and the Deep South. But at the same time, it was certain to set off alarm bells in Washington signaling that Wallace's Alabama would ignite more than a few racial firestorms.

For his part, Richmond Flowers decided to establish himself as a relative moderate, a stance he thought would be politically acceptable in Alabama by 1966. If not, he might ingratiate himself with Washington and be in line for a federal judgeship.[32] On inauguration day, Flowers issued a statement concurring with Wallace's position that state officials must "stand up" for the people. But then he drew the line:

> The people of this state must discern and distinguish between a fighting chance and a chance to fight. . . . To defy the same federal arm that speaks for America to Castro, Khrushchev, and Mao Tse-tung, to preannounce that any decision concerning us that is contrary to our likes will not be heeded, is only a chance to fight and can bring nothing but disgrace to our state, military law upon our people, and political demagoguery to the leaders responsible.[33]

A call for common sense in the heated atmosphere of the time would have gone unheeded in any circumstances. On the day of the inaugural, however, it was thoroughly overwhelmed by Wallace's extraordinary oratory.

After the speech, the Wallaces barely noticed the cold during the huge parade that followed—a six-hour spectacle involving thousands of people and dozens of bands and floats. It seemed to George that the years of friction between him and Lurleen—discord resulting from his obsessive campaigning and neglect of her and the children—melted away amidst the splendor of public adulation for the new governor. "She stood there," George said of Lurleen, "and waved to the crowd that was packed in front and behind her as far as you could see. She leaned over and put her arm around me and kissed me and said, 'Honey, I now know that it was worth it all.' She came to a complete understanding of what I had gone through."[34]

Wallace may have overstated reality, but there is no doubt, judging by how thoroughly Lurleen had thrown herself into the celebration, that she was, at the least, somewhat mollified. For his part, the long and arduous activities of the day generated in Wallace an uncharacteristically premature fatigue. During the inaugural ball at the mansion, Wallace milled through the crowd for barely more than an hour before asking Lurleen to make his excuses. "Tell them I said just to go ahead with everything, but to excuse me." He went upstairs and was asleep by nine-thirty.[35] It would be one of the few wholly tranquil slumbers that he would enjoy in the next twelve months.

■ ■ ■

Not long after the inauguration, proceedings began in federal court in Birmingham to enroll two or three blacks in the University of Alabama.[36] As the case was before Judge Hobart Grooms, the plaintiffs did not hold out much hope for an early victory; just two days after Wallace's swearing-in ceremonies, Grooms pronounced sentence on six men who confessed to charges of mayhem and assault in destroying a bus carrying Freedom Riders in Anniston: the judge placed five of the six on a year's probation and allowed the sixth to serve time concurrently with a prior sentence for burglary. Not one of them served a day in jail.[37]

Whites committing crimes against those challenging segregation in Alabama rarely had cause to worry about the law or justice, but whites opposing the status quo were not as fortunate. The plight of John Robert Zellner, a twenty-three-year-old white Alabamian who was a field-worker for the Student Nonviolent Coordinating Committee (SNCC), is a case in point. A week before Wallace's inauguration, an overzealous Albert Lingo, outraged that Zellner had been helping register blacks to vote in several Alabama counties, decided to arrest him for the unheard-of "crime" of "conspiracy against the State of Alabama." The allegation was so preposterous that Floyd Mann, whom Lingo would replace in a few days, refused to honor the arrest; even outgoing Governor Patterson backed up Mann's decision. Undaunted, Lingo persuaded Selma police to charge Zellner with vagrancy; they told Zellner the charges would be dropped if he left town.

Zellner apparently moved around for a few weeks to avoid arrest, but when Lingo took over the Department of Public Safety following Wallace's inauguration, he resumed the harassment of Zellner, who had become something of an obsession to Lingo. When Lingo heard that Zellner's grandmother was dying in a Mobile nursing home, he ordered his troopers to stake out the home; when she died two days later, Alabama State Patrol cars surrounded the residence in Loxley, Alabama, during her wake, and later were conspicuous at the cemetery during the burial.[38] Zellner, a SNCC veteran (he had already been jailed for protesting segregation in Mississippi and Albany,

Georgia), was not intimidated—and he would clash with Lingo again three months later.[39]

Meanwhile, racial relations in Birmingham—which Martin Luther King, Jr., had called "the most segregated city in the United States," a description that Birmingham's notorious police commissioner, Bull Connor, often quoted with pride—were reaching a flash point.[40] The previous September, the fiery civil rights leader, Fred Shuttlesworth, had announced he would organize demonstrations to protest segregated lunch counters in, and discriminatory hiring practices by, Birmingham's retail stores. The merchants urged patience; although they were loath to challenge Connor by openly defying segregation ordinances, they agreed to a trial step—removal of signs designating restrooms and water fountains for "colored" and "white." Within days, building inspectors threatened to close stores for alleged infractions of the building and safety codes. They ordered numerous repairs and upgrades costing proprietors thousands of dollars. A number of white customers canceled charge accounts. The merchants backed down—but they pledged to work hard for passage of a November referendum to replace the three-commissioner system of city government, which gave Connor enormous power, with a city council of nine members plus a mayor.[41]

The referendum carried, but Connor decided to run for mayor in a March 5 election; he and Albert Boutwell, the lieutenant governor under Folsom and a relative racial moderate (though castigated by Shuttlesworth as little more than a "dignified Connor"), were the top two vote getters and would face each other in a runoff the following month. Although King had joined forces with Shuttlesworth in plans to lead major protests in Birmingham, they decided that, to avoid helping Connor's campaign, they would delay any demonstrations until after the runoff vote on April 2. Because Connor had infuriated merchants with his heavy-handed and sometimes costly enforcement of segregation, an unlikely alliance of the Chamber of Commerce and the civil rights movement overwhelmed him and elected Boutwell. But Connor, desperate to retain power, announced that the newly elected city officials could not legally take office until the commissioners' terms expired some two years later.

Boutwell and the new city council members were sworn in, but Connor and his cohorts remained in day-to-day control. Boutwell initiated a court fight and urged black leaders to back off on their plans to challenge the segregation laws in the streets. But King and Shuttlesworth were determined to go forward. Even before Connor made clear his intentions to seek to retain authority, black demonstrators took to the streets, and Connor met them by arresting twenty—a disappointingly small number to protest leaders. But most merchants had devised a simple yet ingenious plan of defense. As soon as black patrons took seats at lunch counters, the counters would close—in effect, refusing service to everyone, black and white. But marches and picketing continued, and the number of arrests—including those of King and Ralph Abernathy on Good Friday (as discussed later in this chapter)—grew daily. By the end of April, nearly a thousand people had been arrested; that—and especially King's confinement—was beginning to attract national attention.[42]

But a few hopeful signs of change appeared. For one thing, police were firm but civil in their treatment of the demonstrators. Vincent Harding, a black professor at Atlanta's Spelman College who had been assisting in negotiations between black protesters and white merchants in Birmingham, reported that several sit-in demonstrators had been encouraged by whites to press their demands. He said a Birmingham police lieutenant had shared a sandwich with a black protester on a picket line, and that several white churches "actually welcomed" blacks who sought to integrate them.[43]

Wallace, seemingly unimpressed (or, more likely, unaware) of a small but growing inclination among middle-class whites to accept integration, publicly supported Connor, though he "privately cussed him," his press secretary, Bill Jones, said. Wallace, Jones said, "never thought much of Bull Connor's way of doing things."[44] But Wallace did not try to dissuade Connor from his intransigence, partly because he believed that affluent whites were insulated from integration and, therefore, that their views did not count for much—especially when assessing the potential for violence between the races.[45] Additionally, Wallace could not very well interfere in the Birmingham dispute without compromising his loudly broadcast views on local control. Finally, just when the Birmingham demonstrations started, his attentions were diverted from that crisis by some public officials in Huntsville, Mobile, and Tuskegee who indicated they might comply with desegregation directives. He was angered particularly at Mobile's district attorney, Vernol Jansen, who declared that Wallace's "segregation-or-jail position" was untenable. Worse, in Wallace's eyes, Jansen, a federal appointee, had persuaded Mobile's city officials to accept his view. On the very day that blacks started demonstrating in the streets of Birmingham, Wallace issued a statement directed to Jansen and any others opposing segregation:

It behooves any local or state official to use all his ingenuity and ability to prevent integration rather than bring it about. Any official who by overt acts encourages efforts to integrate any school system in Alabama and then, at the same time, says he wants to maintain law and order is, in effect, taking action which is not conducive to law and order. In the campaign for governor, I spelled out definitely what I would do if there were any attempts to integrate any schools in Alabama. My stand, now that I am governor, is still the same. . . . I am going to take the action I promised. Therefore, all should be governed accordingly.[46]

The next day, Wallace fired off a telegram to Alabama's U.S. senators complaining that Jansen had made a financial contribution at a rally to support black voter registration and that "such acts prejudice the district attorney in pending suits."[47]

Amid the Birmingham protests and indications that some Alabama school officials might break ranks from Wallace's segregation-or-jail stand, the governor was blindsided by an unlikely source—a white Baltimore postal worker with a passion for civil rights. William Moore, regarded by his co-workers as "a likable screwball" and as "a kook" by leaders of the Congress of Racial Equality (CORE), decided to use his ten-day vacation to stage a "freedom walk" from Chattanooga to his native Mississippi to personally deliver a civil rights plea to Gov. Ross Barnett. Moore, a thirty-five-year-old former U.S. Marine who had been diagnosed as a schizophrenic and had been confined to a New York mental institution for more than a year, had asked CORE, of which he was a member, to sponsor his walk; CORE had refused. Moore also was rebuffed by the White House, where a letter to President Kennedy was ignored and unanswered; in it, he offered to deliver any messages the president cared to send to the South, and he urged Kennedy to oppose "Cuban war hawks" and avoid involvement in Vietnam. Wearing signboards reading "End Segregation in America" and "Equal Rights for All Men," and pushing a two-wheeled postal cart containing extra clothes and toiletries, Moore set off on his trek.

Neither Alabama nor Wallace was his focus—he had added "Mississippi or Bust" to one of his signs—but he would have to cross through Alabama to reach his goal. He never would. Though he had drawn angry epithets and a few tossed rocks from roadside hecklers, Moore did not seem worried.[48] On the afternoon of April 23, in an interview with a radio reporter near Gadsden, Alabama, seventy-five miles southwest of Chattanooga, he discounted shouted threats that he would never make it alive. "I don't believe the people in the South are that way," he said. Later that day, only about a mile from where the reporter had left Moore, a passing motorist discovered the body. Lying face up in the grass, still wearing his signs, his meager belongings and money (fifty-one dollars) still intact, Moore had been shot twice through the head at close range.[49]

Both Kennedy and Wallace denounced the slaying, with Wallace offering a reward for information leading to the murderer's apprehension. Within days, a white grocer from Attala, Alabama, F. E. Simpson, was arrested and charged with murder. Held without bail, Simpson was freed in September when a grand jury declined to indict him.[50] Now, the outcry against Wallace swelled. A Herblock cartoon in the *Washington Post* depicted Wallace, while decrying the murder, handing a loaded shotgun to a Neanderthal redneck.[51] The *Chicago Sun-Times* blamed the murder on "all who have condoned violence . . . and who create the atmosphere of brutality."[52] A Denver editor more directly assessed blame: "Governor Wallace surely did not kill Moore, but Moore's blood is on the governor's hands—and on the hands of all those who encourage the people of the South to defy the laws that guarantee basic American rights to the Negroes."[53] Even before the killing, Wallace's friend Grover Hall, concerned about the undue influence on the governor by the likes of Kohn, Trammell, and Lingo, had published a warning that went unheeded: "Alabama and its governor are going to sup sorrow unless the governor makes it clear there isn't going to be any violence or mob rule [but] the governor has evaded any opportunities to make himself plain on violence."[54]

Belatedly and somewhat shamefacedly, CORE, in conjunction with SNCC, at last took up Moore's freedom walk, dispatching volunteers to follow Moore's intended route from Chattanooga to Jackson. The path took about a dozen marchers thirty-five miles from Chattanooga through the extreme northwestern corner of Georgia to the Alabama line. As they crossed into the state on May 3 and approached the town of Sulphur Springs, ten miles down U.S. Highway 11, white onlookers lined the road and pelted the marchers with rocks and eggs. Then the marchers were confronted by Alabama state troopers, under the command of Albert Lingo, who ordered the freedom walkers to retreat to Georgia or disperse. When several of the marchers lay down on the highway rather than disband, Lingo directed the troopers to use electric cattle prods to force the marchers to their feet. They were then arrested on a charge of breaching the peace.[55]

The transparently racist posture struck by Wallace and his state troopers in the face of Moore's murder persuaded black leaders in Birmingham that negotiating with anyone in authority would be useless. They resolved to step up their demonstrations; King even decided to permit children under fourteen to march, even if they were arrested and jailed—a decision that many black leaders denounced, but one that would help convince a recalcitrant federal government to become directly involved in the Birmingham battle.[56]

■　■　■

On April 25, just two days after Moore's killing, and in the midst of the expanding Birmingham crisis, Attorney General Robert Kennedy arrived in Montgomery to meet with Governor Wallace. Kennedy's reason for seeing the governor, however, was coincidental to the two ongoing difficulties in Alabama. The meeting had stemmed from Kennedy's concern, with Ole Miss still fresh in his mind, over what he knew would be an eventual federal-state confrontation over the admission of blacks to the University of Alabama. He did not want another Oxford; neither did Wallace. Even before taking office, Wallace had asked Sen. John Sparkman to tell the White House to "please give Alabama as much breathing time as possible," making it clear that he understood integration was inevitable.[57] Hearing the governor-elect's request, the president told his brother, "Perhaps if we put this off until next September, we might . . . get a favorable solution."[58] But the case was progressing through the federal courts, and it was doubtful there would be that much time.

Trying to arrange a meeting, Robert Kennedy phoned Wallace, but the governor refused his calls. Wallace's chum Ralph Adams was at the governor's mansion one evening when the attorney general called; at Wallace's direction, Adams told Kennedy the governor was unavailable. Adams recalled that "Kennedy kept saying, 'I don't see why he won't talk to me,' and Wallace—he was standing just a few feet away from me—kept whispering, 'Adams, just tell him I plain don't want to talk to him.' "[59] Finally, Kennedy called Ed Reid of the Alabama League of Municipalities, a reliable supporter of both the president and Wallace, to set up the meeting. After arriving, Kennedy went out of his way in meetings with the press and public to compliment Alabama, its people, and its leaders—including Wallace—and repeatedly asserted his belief in the principle of local people handling local problems, as long as they obey court orders. He said Martin Luther King, Jr.'s violation of a state court injunction against demonstrating in Birmingham involved constitutional questions in which the protesters might eventually be vindicated; meanwhile, however, King and his supporters violated court directives "at their own peril"—meaning they risked jail terms. As he approached the state capitol, he was greeted by hundreds of friendly white people, many of whom shook his hand and welcomed him to the state; he even signed autographs for a number of children. And when an Alabama reporter asked him what he thought of paying a courtesy visit to a governor who had called Kennedy "a pugnacious sapling," Kennedy replied, to the laughter of journalists, "I think he's entitled to his opinion."[60]

Reid ushered Kennedy and Assistant Attorney General Burke Marshall into the governor's office, where, after Wallace said he was taping their conversation to avoid misunderstandings, they engaged in a few minutes of strained small talk about flags and the charm of the state capitol. Wallace then asked Seymore Trammell to join them, and Kennedy quietly suggested, "We might discuss the problem we are perhaps facing here in the state in connection with the integration . . ." "I don't hear good," Wallace interrupted. Kennedy raised his voice slightly and repeated his proposal to discuss the likely integration of the university. "You want to discuss that?" Wallace asked disingenuously. Kennedy said he hoped the matter would be handled at the local level "without any outside influences." Wallace replied he had pledged to resist integration through legal means because "you just can't have any peace in Alabama with an integrated school system." With that, Kennedy's voice hardened:

> KENNEDY: You think it would be so horrifying to have a Negro attend the University of Alabama, Governor?
>
> WALLACE: Well, I think it's horrifying for the federal courts and the central government to rewrite all the law and force upon the people that which they don't want. . . . For a hundred years we operated under what the Supreme Court said was legal. . . . I will never submit myself voluntarily to any integration in a school system in Alabama. . . . There is no time in my judgment when we would be ready for it in my lifetime.

Wallace said that, unlike Gov. Ernest Hollings in South Carolina, he would not allow integration without putting up a fight. Kennedy said if everyone disobeyed court orders he did not like, it would result in "complete havoc and lawlessness." Wallace replied irrelevantly that there was more law and order in Alabama "in one minute than you have an entire year up in Washington, D.C." Kennedy agreed there were racial problems everywhere, but that court orders had to be obeyed. "When you were a judge," he said, "did you care . . . if your orders were not obeyed?" Wallace stammered that "it's not an analogous situation," but Kennedy shot back, "But don't you think it's fundamental?"

Wallace redirected the discussion by asking Kennedy to use his influence with black leaders to call off demonstrations and voter registration drives, and Trammell chimed in with a request for "some time—maybe in a year, maybe in five years, maybe ten years." Kennedy was astounded. "Would you keep a Negro college professor from registering to vote in an election for five years?" Wallace extricated Trammell by stating that the governor and the attorney general understood one another and would likely "wind up in court." Kennedy said, "That's all I ask. . . . I just don't want it to get into the streets. I don't want to have another Oxford." "I don't want another Mississippi myself," Wallace said, "but you folks are the ones that will control the matter—because you have control of the troops." Then Kennedy fell into a trap:

> **KENNEDY:** We have a responsibility to ensure that the orders of the court are followed, and all the force behind the federal government must be used for that purpose.
>
> **WALLACE:** I know that. . . . In fact, what you're telling me today is that if necessary, you're going to bring troops into Alabama.
>
> **KENNEDY:** No, I didn't say that, Governor.
>
> **WALLACE:** You didn't? Well, you said all the force of the federal government.
>
> **KENNEDY:** To make sure that the orders of the court are obeyed.
>
> **WALLACE:** But "all the force" includes troops, doesn't it?

They sallied back and forth, Wallace trying to pin Kennedy to a plan to use troops, Kennedy trying to evade the question by saying he hoped the matter would stay in the courts and be litigated. "Maybe somebody wants to use troops," Kennedy said, "but we're not anxious to." Then Wallace said, "I can assure you I do not want to use troops. I can assure you there's no effort on my part to make a show of resistance and be overcome. . . . I mean to stand . . . because I believe we've got to wake the people of this country up to the fact that this business of the central government, every time you turn around, moving in with troops and bayonets. I believe the people don't like it—I believe all over this nation . . . We get thousands of letters from Michigan and former Southerners in California, in Michigan— automobile workers—who say, 'We gonna stand with you people in the South.'" Kennedy said, "I don't blame people for not liking it, Governor. I don't like it myself."

Both realized they were talking across each other, so Wallace rapidly concluded the meeting by repeating his proposal for the Justice Department to persuade blacks to "be patient and hold off and let things evolve. He continued, "I've been trying to get some new industry—we've gotten one hundred and fifty million dollars worth of it in the past five or six months. . . . That's the most important thing you can do for the Negro people, is enhance their standard of living. . . . We're trying to do some real things for them, but all this agitation and all this business of Martin Luther King—who's a phony and a fraud, marching and going to jail and all that; they're just living high on the hog." Kennedy said, "Well, I appreciate your seeing me, Governor." Wallace replied that he appreciated Kennedy's visit. The two parted and issued vague, general statements that neither had changed his views but that they had frankly discussed pending problems.[61]

Kennedy had no idea what Wallace intended to do. His press aide, Ed Guthman, said, "Bob was dumbfounded by Wallace's attitude. It was the closest I ever saw him come to throwing up his hands in despair." The White House, in a move that the attorney general later apologized for, ordered that photographs be made of the University of Alabama campus in overflights by the same reconnaissance planes that had been used over Cuba. Later, however, officers at the Pentagon used the photographs to map campus maneuvers.[62]

For his part, Wallace knew he would make some sort of stand to bar the likely entrance of black students to the university. He also planned to force his own arrest, if necessary, to dramatize his determination to prevent integration. He was convinced there would be no violence. After all, as he had told Kennedy, "we have safety and peace and goodwill [in Alabama], and there's no place in Montgomery or Birmingham that you cannot walk at night, white or colored section. . . . But you can't do that in Washington. You can't do that in Chicago or Philadelphia."[63] Just a week after he made that boast to the attorney general, however, Wallace would no longer be quite as sure of his premise. Explosive events in Birmingham would begin tempering his self-deceptive mythologizing about racial harmony in the South, and the fallacious conviction that he could fan the defiance without it bursting into flames.

■   ■   ■

When Bull Connor's police force arrested Martin Luther King, Jr., and Ralph Abernathy for demonstrating on Good Friday in violation of a prohibitive court order, Birmingham's white business leaders belatedly realized that their city's racial crisis, exacerbated by its divided government, could literally blow up without some intervention—even if unofficial. Tentatively and fearfully, white and black leaders began a series of secret meetings to search for a peaceful solution. The meetings were understandably strained; in Alabama's racially stratified society, whites were unused to dealing with blacks on an equal and businesslike footing, and black representatives chafed when their white counterparts addressed them, as was often the case, by first name. But the sessions were further hampered by the white businessmen's resistance to putting themselves at public risk without the support of an established city government. Connor, who retained day-to-day governmental control while the newly elected Boutwell regime was mounting a legal challenge to his legitimacy, earlier had harassed businessmen who displayed any inclination to compromise with blacks on integration demands. As a result, all the whites involved in the discussions (with the single exception of the realtor Sidney Smyer) refused even to acknowledge that any discussions were being conducted, much less that they were participating.

Nonetheless, most black leaders, including King and Abernathy, who were bailed out from jail after serving eight days, were heartened by the tentative but hopeful interracial contacts. Still, they were forced to agree with the steel-willed Fred Shuttlesworth, the fiery integration leader in Birmingham, that blacks must press on with the street demonstrations if they hoped to persuade the city's power structure to accept desegregation proposals. And a movement veteran, James Bevel, prevailed on King to further heighten the national impact of the Birmingham movement by allowing children to march in the next big demonstration, planned for May 2.[64] King, usually more cautious than Shuttlesworth and Bevel, nonetheless concurred that the secret meetings were moving at a snail's pace; he also accepted Bevel's notion that children's participation in the marches would strengthen the pride of young people in their blackness and give them a "sense of their own stake in freedom and justice." Many black community leaders, like the financier and real estate owner A. G. Gaston (who believed street demonstrations of any kind would sabotage the delicate interracial negotiations), became more apprehensive when he heard about King's intention to use children, whom he feared might be injured seriously on the streets or beaten after their arrests. Even militants like Malcolm X, usually a critic of King as a puppet to white interests, objected from afar to King's decision, commenting that "real men don't put their children on the firing line."[65] But, on May 2, march they did—by the thousands. Nearly a thousand protesters were arrested, joining a like number already in custody from participation in earlier demonstrations; when the police ran out of paddy wagons and patrol cars to haul the young people to jail, they called in school buses to transport the demonstrators, most of them high school students, to waiting cells.

The next day, aware that already bulging jail cells (into which as many as seventy-five youngsters had been crammed) made further arrests impractical, Connor devised a new strategy. He directed the fire department to place hoses, capable of spewing water at a high pressure, into position at the demonstrators' mustering point at Kelly Ingram Park. More ominously, eight German shepherds and their police handlers—called K-9 units—were arrayed around the park to prevent demonstrators from breaking through the police cordons and entering the downtown area. Connor had two objectives in mind: First, with the jails overflowing, the police needed to drive off as many demonstrators as possible to minimize arrests. Second, Connor wanted to help maintain the fiction, promulgated by the Chamber of Commerce and the editors of the *Birmingham News* (who virtually blacked out local coverage of the demonstrations), that if black protesters were not seen at the city's major department stores (although black boycotts of those stores were effectively disrupting commerce), or that if their activities were not publicized locally (though they received wide press and television attention throughout the rest of the world), the movement would somehow vanish.[66]

At about noon on May 3, the first group of some fifty young demonstrators stepped off while hundreds of onlookers, many of them anxious parents, watched nervously from the park. Hoses were aimed at the demonstrators as the police ordered them to disperse; they did not. A reporter for radio station WSGN, Elvin Stanton, who was on scene and broadcasting live from a telephone booth at Seventeenth Street and Fifth Avenue North, said hoses were turned on "full blast," so that many of the people were "knocked down." Stanton continued, "You can probably hear the water and the screams. . . . They have turned the hose full force on the Negroes, washing them into the streets." He said police were directing firemen, telling them where to aim the hose. Streams of water were then directed toward the crowd of bystanders, who were "all just soaked, literally soaked, and some of them were knocked down by the force of the water," which was "standing eight inches deep" in some places. Although some of the young people reacted by frolicking through the streams and puddles, thereby content to taunt their assailers benignly, others, according to Stanton, were "becoming very angry." They started chucking rocks and bricks toward the authorities.[67]

Many of Birmingham's usually conservative black leaders, seeing young people drenched and bowled over by high-powered fire hoses, were shocked into the realization that their city's white power structure would not willingly yield to the movement's demand for equal treatment. Some, like Gaston, after witnessing Connor's men discharge their hoses at a young black girl, tossing and rolling her along the black-topped roadway like a rag doll, reconsidered his previous opposition to King's tactics. And when Connor loosed his snarling dogs on the demonstrators, masses of whom panicked and ran stumbling and screaming in terror as they tried to flee, King's efforts won the sympathy of a majority of Americans, including those who earlier had viewed civil disobedience as unnecessarily provocative. An Associated Press photograph of a dog ripping at the sweater of a well-dressed black youth sickened and jolted even those Americans—including the president—who continued to urge King to call off his demonstrations and, especially, his use of children. The president commented, "I can well understand why the Negroes of Birmingham are tired of being asked to be patient."[68]

Still, Robert Kennedy publicly opposed using schoolchildren in the demonstrations as "a dangerous business" that raised the specter of "an injured, maimed, or dead child." King rejected what one writer described as "a white man's belated tender solicitude for Negro children," but he welcomed the attorney general's decision to dispatch Burke Marshall to the scene in an effort to revivify the

stalled negotiations among white and black leaders. Marshall faced a
seemingly impossible task because positions had hardened. Predictably, white leaders—including presumed moderates such as Albert
Boutwell, the mayor-elect, and Talbot Ellis, a juvenile court judge—
joined federal officials in condemning King for exposing children to
danger. And a number of white leaders even wanted to ask Governor
Wallace to declare martial law to restore order and "suppress this
whole business." Marshall quietly dissuaded them from taking that
drastic step.[69]

Over the next couple of days, Marshall shuttled between increasingly tense leaders as demonstrations intensified. On May 5, Wallace
said that most Birmingham residents of both races were "fed up"
with demonstrations, which he blamed on "left-wing groups." On
May 6, a thousand black protesters, 40 percent of whom were juveniles, were arrested. Among them was a woman who was photographed being pinned to the ground by two policemen, one of whom
was pressing a knee into her neck. And on May 7, an estimated three
thousand blacks, about half of whom were unconnected to the movement and its formal training in nonviolence, pushed their way
through police barricades and raced into the theretofore inviolable
downtown area. Bricks and bottles flew at policemen and firemen,
who used hoses and dogs more indiscriminately than ever. Shuttlesworth was banged against a building by a fire hose until he
collapsed and was rushed to an emergency room. Hundreds of protesters swarmed into several downtown stores, collapsed on the
floors, and sang freedom songs. With the jails literally overflowing,
hundreds of young people were confined in the jail yards.

Coincidentally, the regular session of the Alabama legislature
opened the same day; and Wallace, in his first state of the state
message, remained every bit as contentious as he had been less than
four months earlier in his notorious inaugural address. Indeed, he
quoted from the inaugural, repeating some of his more audacious
references to blacks ("insipid bloc voters") and whites ("a race of
honor"). He vowed to "fight agitators, meddlers, and enemies of
constitutional government," and contended, "So-called clergymen
and their communist, left-wing-inspired followers have set out to
destroy the freedom and liberty of Americans everywhere. It's tragic
to me that in Washington, we have weaklings who are afraid to
expose the reds wherever they may be." With his broader political
ambitions forming embryonically, he asserted, "The national parties
are beginning to realize that the South may well control next year's

presidential election. . . . I read in newspapers from all sections of the country that both parties are beginning to pay more attention to the South and to its bloc of votes . . . and I am pleased to tell you that there is increasing sympathetic public opinion for our stand." And signaling his intention to dramatize his position by a literal "stand" against integration, Wallace said, "I will meet our enemies face to face. I will not surrender."

Before the day ended, "to preserve law and order," the governor dispatched to Birmingham 800 law enforcement officers—250 state troopers buttressed by a mélange of sheriff's deputies, Alabama Conservation Department officers, Alcoholic Beverage Control Board agents, and individual National Guardsmen deputized as special state officers. Wallace officially retained personal command, but the state forces were under Albert Lingo's de facto command. Amazingly, considering the extent of confrontations in Birmingham, there were few injuries, none of them serious. Indeed, despite the chaos and inherent danger in the demonstrations, a carnival air imbued many of the subsequent encounters. The civil rights movement lieutenant Wyatt Walker complained that the demonstrators had lost dignity and turned the events into a "Roman holiday." The *Newsweek* correspondent Joseph B. Cumming recalled that, "ironically, the level of true brutality was not high. Nobody got bitten by a dog that didn't want to be. Almost the same thing with the fire hoses, although some bystanders got soaked. Mostly it was a big lark. Yet the pictures of the dog biting the kid and the policeman wrestling the Negro woman on the ground, stirred the nation's conscience."[70]

The urgency of events prodded white and black negotiators to reach the broad outlines of an agreement on May 8: desegregation in stores would come in stages over a sixty-day period, starting with dressing rooms and culminating with lunch counters; hiring practices, monitored by a biracial committee, would be reformed and upgraded; federal officials—specifically, Robert Kennedy—would use his influence with contacts as diverse as the entertainer Harry Belafonte and the United Auto Workers president, Walter Reuther, to raise $200,000 to bail out the thousand-plus demonstrators still incarcerated.[71]

Marshall promptly notified Robert Kennedy, who, in turn, passed the good news along to his brother with the suggestion that the president announce the settlement at his news conference that day. On the strength of the tentative agreement, Marshall then persuaded King to suspend demonstrations temporarily. Shuttlesworth was still in the hospital when he learned of King's unilateral decision; offended that King had not consulted him first, Shuttlesworth rushed to movement headquarters to confront King. "I'll be damned if you'll have it like this," he shrieked at King. "You're Mister Big, but you're going to be Mister S-H-I-T!" He threatened to derail the agreement by leading his supporters back on the streets, but King, who maintained a cool demeanor throughout Shuttleworth's verbal assault, took him into a back room and calmed him. When they emerged, they were smiling; at a press conference, Shuttlesworth himself announced the truce he had condemned only a half hour before. Less than an hour later, President Kennedy told the nation at his televised news conference that within a day, Birmingham's business leaders would disclose "substantial steps" to meet blacks' "justifiable" demands. Wallace and his aides watched the news conference on a portable television set placed atop a filing cabinet in his inner office in the capitol, after which they quickly patched together a statement rejecting Kennedy's implication that "the people of Birmingham have inflicted abuses on the Negroes."[72]

Wallace, in fact, maintained, "The white people of Birmingham should have been commended for their restraint during the present demonstrations. White people have not been involved—only lawless Negroes." These "lawless Negro mobs," he said, had injured ten policemen, violated court injunctions and municipal ordinances against demonstrations, and thrown in with "Martin Luther King and his group of pro-communists who have instigated these demonstrations." He disavowed knowledge of negotiations among black leaders and white businessmen; but even if there were such meetings, he said, he would refuse to be a party to them if they meant "compromise on the issues of segregation." He commended Bull Connor "and his forces."[73]

Predictably, the rival city governments both denounced the agreement. Although the newly elected Mayor Boutwell had participated in the negotiations, he did not dare to recognize or support them—at least, not until his election and that of the new city council was legitimized in Alabama's courts. Nonetheless, the fragile truce held—for a few tense days, at least.[74]

In that time, epithets flew across the Mason-Dixon line from Northern congressmen, mayors, and governors, including a wire to Wallace from Connecticut's Gov. John N. Dempsey expressing "deep dismay" over Birmingham's racial difficulties and urging the Alabama governor to step in and ease the crisis. Wallace fired off a telegram telling Dempsey, "Mind your own affairs. . . . I assume that the state of Connecticut has ample problems to occupy your interests and talents."[75] Wallace's tactic of deflecting criticism of segregation by pointing to discrimination in the North was, in the case of Connecticut, at least, well aimed. The 1961 report of Connecticut's Advisory Commission on Civil Rights had reported that public schools in the state were "almost wholly" segregated, that there were only two black students among the seventeen hundred graduates from the University of Connecticut in 1960, and that blacks occupied "probably no more than one percent . . . of the thousands and thousands of privately financed housing units built in Connecticut."[76] And the May 9 issue of the *Hartford Courant* reported that the Real Estate Board of Greater Hartford, fearing adverse reactions from potential home sellers in all-white neighborhoods, had rejected an application for membership from a black real estate agent.[77]

Wallace's sharp reply to Dempsey provoked an outpouring of mail from Northerners sympathetic to his plight, if not his cause. A Kensington, Connecticut, man apologized for his governor's "ill-bred wire."[78] The editor of Connecticut's *Farmers Journal* wrote that the "vast majority" of his acquaintances "believe the able men of the South can handle the problem if left alone."[79] Others from Connecticut complained hyperbolically that "vandals" and "thugs" roamed the streets, and that "murder, rape, lust, robbery and every sort of violence is legally condoned [by] our feeble-minded governor." New Yorkers commended Wallace: "More power to you," said one; "Plenty of Northerners agree with you and understand your problems," said another. Similar sentiments were expressed in letters from California, Hawaii, Iowa, Missouri, Rhode Island, Texas, and Washington.[80] To be sure, there were some letters—a decided minority—who defended Dempsey and his concerns, often with literary allusions. A North Carolina woman, quoting the tortured ghost of Jacob Marley in Dickens's *Christmas Carol,* insisted that suffering *anywhere* was, indeed, Governor Dempsey's (and everyone's) business; a Californian quoted the suggestion in Genesis that we *are* our brother's keeper; a Connecticut doctor quoted John Donne's assertion that "no man is an island" and that "any man's death diminishes" all of us.[81] But the hundreds of favorable letters, many of them pleading for Wallace's candidacy for president, demonstrated that the Alabama governor had, depending on one's view, struck a vein filled with political gold or opened a vein spilling moral blood.

While Wallace was basking in his newfound national spotlight—

a light reflecting much more popular favor than the political establishment and the media seemed either aware of or willing to concede—the Birmingham crisis appeared to be winding down. Hundreds of young blacks and their adult leaders who had been herded into Birmingham's jails were being released, most of them on bond totaling hundreds of thousands of dollars raised by personalities in government, labor, and the entertainment community.[82] Juvenile prisoners were released to their parents after brief court hearings, one of which produced a remarkable and revealing encounter between a black youth of fifteen and Talbot Ellis, the kindly white juvenile court judge. The occasion poignantly and graphically depicted the enormous gulf of understanding between the races (and, among blacks, between the generations) that existed at the time and would remain virtually unchanged for decades to come. The teenager, accompanied by his mother to his court appearance, bore the unusual name of Grosbeck Preer Parham; he had been incarcerated for five days. The judge told the teenager he would be released—but, as it turned out, only after a mild lecture:

> Now, Grosbeck, you know violence in the streets is not the answer to this. Just the other day, Attorney General Kennedy said this problem won't be solved in the streets. And I often think of what one of the founding fathers said: "There is no freedom without restraint." Now, I want you to go home and back to school. Will you do that?

The boy stood silently and sullenly. The judge leaned forward:

JUDGE ELLIS: Are you mad at me, son?

GROSBECK: Can I say something?

JUDGE ELLIS: Anything you like.

GROSBECK: Well, you can say that about freedom because you've got your freedom. The Constitution says we're all equal, but Negroes aren't equal.

JUDGE ELLIS: But your people have made great gains and they still are. It takes time.

GROSBECK: We've been waiting over a hundred years.

Judge Ellis described how, at professional conferences, white and black lawyers and judges treated one another equally "not because the Constitution says so, but because we are equal in our profession." Then Aileen Parham, Grosbeck's mother, asked to be heard:

> **MRS. PARHAM:** I don't approve of street violence either. But after a civil rights meeting, we did try to get in touch with city officials and they wouldn't see us. And I know this, Judge; these younger people are not going to take what we took. . . . If I'm going to spend my money in the stores, I think I should have the right to sit down and eat a sandwich in them.
>
> **JUDGE ELLIS:** Mrs. Parham, what do you think of Booker T. Washington?
>
> **MRS. PARHAM:** I think he was a fine man—but his day is past. The younger people won't take what we did. . . .
>
> **JUDGE ELLIS:** Well, I expect we could talk all day about these things. I want you to go now, and I still hope you'll go back to school.
>
> **MRS. PARHAM:** Thank you, Judge.
>
> **GROSBECK** (*sotto voce*): Thanks for nothing.[83]

Grosbeck's parting shot exposed a sullen anger that had been building in Birmingham's black populace—a simmering fury that would erupt in the late hours of Saturday, May 11. Their wrath was ignited by four dynamite explosions—two at the home of the Reverend A. D. King, Martin Luther King, Jr.'s younger brother; and two at the black-owned and -patronized Gaston Motel—that shattered the city's tenuous peace. A day earlier, an anonymous threat had been received at the motel, which also served as an unofficial headquarters for the leaders of Birmingham's civil rights movement. The caller said the motel would be bombed after a Ku Klux Klan rally in Bessemer, a working-class factory town on the outskirts of Birmingham. Authorities were notified; they said the motel was under police surveillance. But the terrorists struck first at 10:45 P.M. at King's modest brick home. After the first blast blew a hole in King's front yard, the minister and his wife wakened their five children and were ushering them out the back door when a second, more violent explosion, ripped the house, crumbling a corner of the home, shaving off a third of the roof, and blowing out the living-room wall where Mrs. King had been sitting. "It's brick," Mr. King said later. "That's the only thing that saved us." A crowd of angered black residents gathered near the house at about the same time policemen and firefighters arrived.

Some from the crowd slashed tires on police and fire vehicles while the authorities inspected the ruins.

A little more than an hour later, four white men sped by the Gaston Motel and, from their car, tossed two bombs out the window. One exploded next to the motel's office, just downstairs from the room that Martin Luther King, Jr., had occupied before leaving Birmingham for a weekend at his Atlanta home. The other explosive, apparently missing its mark, demolished a house trailer in a lot next to the motel. Diners and waitresses in the motel restaurant started screaming and rushing into the street. By the time police arrived in numbers, crowds of black people filled the streets and started hurling rocks, bricks, and bottles. Rioters overturned a cab and set it afire; one policeman was stabbed twice in the back; fires were set in two white-owned grocery stores near the motel, and the blaze spread to several nearby homes and apartment dwellings. "Let the whole fucking city burn," someone shouted. "This'll show the white motherfuckers," someone else screamed. "Kill 'em, kill 'em," someone shouted as more police rolled up in squad cars to the scene.[84]

A.D. King and other black leaders plunged into the crowds, urging people to go home; some people threw rocks at them, too. "They started it," someone shouted to justify the violence. A six-wheeled, armored riot car roared up, and the hated dogs arrived, too—but this time the animals were reined in tightly by their handlers. Police made numerous forays in attempts to drive off rock throwers, but for the most part, they and firefighters were forced to retreat and conduct holding actions to keep the riots from spreading. Before long, Lingo and his troopers arrived. Not only did he command his 250 state troopers and hundreds of additional state law enforcement officers, but he had impressed into service a volunteer posse headed by Jim Clark, the tough, beefy sheriff of Dallas County, which embraced the racially tense city of Selma. Jamie Moore, Birmingham's police chief, vainly sought to persuade Lingo and his heavily armed forces to pull back. "Will you please leave," he pleaded. "We don't need any guns down here. You all might get somebody killed." "You're damned right it'll kill somebody," Lingo snapped. Lingo's troops and his irregulars then charged into the crowds of blacks, using gun butts and nightsticks to club those bunched near the motel area. They then sealed off a twenty-eight-block area around the motel.[85]

As the riots continued into the early Sunday morning hours,

Martin Luther King, Jr., rushed back to Birmingham and quickly got in touch with the Justice Department in Washington; though he did not ask for federal intervention, he vividly depicted the critical nature of the situation; he was especially worried that the effort to cement the agreement among the white businessmen and the black leaders might come unstuck. President Kennedy decided that a show of federal force was needed to keep the agreement intact.[86] He dispatched troops to military bases in Alabama and took preparatory steps to federalize the Alabama National Guard. By then, the state forces had all but quelled the disturbances through rough tactics, but the president's actions weighed heavily in buoying hopes of both the black leaders and the white businessmen that the agreement—and ultimate racial progress—would withstand the harsh opposition of official white Alabama.

■   ■   ■

The president stepped before the press and television cameras on Sunday night to announce his actions and to pledge the government's commitment "to uphold the law of the land." "I am certain," he announced, "that the vast majority of the citizens of Birmingham, both white and Negro—particularly those who labored so hard to achieve the peaceful, constructive settlement of last week—can feel nothing but dismay at the efforts of those who would replace conciliation and good will with violence and hate." The agreement, he said, "recognized the fundamental right of all citizens to be accorded equal treatment and opportunity. It was a tribute to the process of peaceful negotiations and to the good faith of both parties. The federal government will not permit it to be sabotaged by a few extremists of either side who think they can defy both the law and the wishes of responsible citizens by inciting or inviting violence." Off camera and off the record, government officials blamed Wallace and Lingo while exculpating local authorities. They said that the state police made matters worse with their heavy-handed tactics.[87]

Although Wallace's minions may have overreacted, they succeeded in capping the violence with no further serious injuries to whites or blacks. And the governor was plainly flustered by the uprising. "I didn't quite know how to feel," Wallace said years later. "We hadn't had anything like that in Alabama. I thought it would blow over, but it didn't. I sent the troopers to protect property. My good friend Bull Connor was a little too abrasive about the matter . . . I'm sorry it happened that way, and the sheriff [Mel Bailey of Jefferson County, which encompasses Birmingham] could have handled it better than Connor. Connor didn't realize the effect his actions would have."[88] Wallace was far from alone in his shock at the uprising in Birmingham. A later study of the riot by two Southern political scientists found that nothing like the black insurgence had happened in the postbellum South. "The passivity and nonviolence of American Negroes could never again be taken for granted," the study concluded. "The 'rules of the game' in race relations were permanently changed in Birmingham."[89] Still, the compact between the white businessmen and the black leaders held together. Despite his public statements to the contrary, Wallace disingenuously maintained later that he "had no objection to the agreement reached between business leaders and blacks. Of course," he said, illuminating the essential hypocrisy of integration agreements entered into by upper-income Southern whites, "the businessmen of Mountain Brook [a wealthy Birmingham suburb] could avoid all this [eating with black patrons at lunch counters], but the steelworkers and the working [white] people couldn't."[90] Pointing to the "highpocrisy" of integrationists would become a Wallace trademark.

Wallace's public reaction to the riots offered little comfort to those who sought racial moderation. In a thousand-word statement issued in the wake of the riots, he barely mentioned the bombings, except to suggest that the perpetrators might have been agents of the civil rights movement and the Communist party. In the bulk of his message he denounced street violence by blacks and "the so-called biracial group of appeasers who have . . . played right into the hands of Martin Luther King and his cohorts who had failed to bring strife and turmoil to the extent they desired."[91] But the most vituperative critic of the Kennedys was not Wallace but Arthur Hanes, one of the three members of Birmingham's deposed city commission; Hanes had the title of mayor and, like fellow commissioner Bull Connor, retained his office while litigation continued over determining the city's rightful government. When riots followed the bombings, Hanes placed the onus on King, whom he described as "a revolutionary," and on the Kennedys. "The nigger King ought to be investigated by the attorney general," Hanes spewed. "This nigger has got the blessing of the attorney general and the White House. I hope that every drop of blood that's spilled, [Robert Kennedy] tastes in his throat—and I hope he chokes on it."[92]

Fortunately, Birmingham's mayor-in-waiting, Albert Boutwell, despite his fear of being branded a supporter of integration, used the occasion to begin to assert some control. Though his government was not yet legally in power, Boutwell moved swiftly to effectively block action by Connor. He called into conference Police Chief Moore, Sheriff Bailey, and representatives of the FBI. He requested "that every investigative power be put immediately into action to identify and apprehend the perpetrators of these outrages . . . especially the dastardly hit-and-run bombers who wreak vengeance without regard for life and property."[93] Still, Boutwell joined Connor and Wallace in deploring the presence of federal troops in the state; Wallace pledged a legal battle to force the president to remove the troops.[94]

In the days and weeks that followed, the tension in Birmingham gradually subsided. White businessmen moved ahead with plans for gradual integration of their stores; black residents refrained from further demonstrations; the benign presence of federal troops seemed to have a calming effect on both the populace and on state police who continued to patrol the city's streets; the churlish action by the Connor-controlled board of education in expelling more than a thousand black students for participating in the protests was reversed by a federal court; and, perhaps most important, the Alabama Supreme Court ruled on May 23 that the Boutwell government must take office immediately.[95]

In a typical manner, Wallace declared victory (taking personal credit for restoring peace to Birmingham) and moved on to the next encounter. Wallace was far too clever (as neither Orval Faubus nor Ross Barnett were) to keep pouring salt into an open wound. Birmingham was quiet, and he knew that continued bombastic criticism of the modest integration agreements might inflame still-smoldering embers. He knew when to quit. The weight of the post-riot outrage that swept from Alabama around the world, bringing cries of shame on the head of its governor, persuaded Wallace there was no more upside to prolonging a confrontation there. For one thing, it was costing money; where it usually cost the state $9,000 a month to support Lingo's Department of Public Safety, it was now costing $28,000 a month to finance the continued occupation of Birmingham by the state troopers and the "irregulars" supporting them. In addition, Lingo's use of irregulars to buttress the state police was causing other problems: prison authorities feared that with so many of their guards in Birmingham, they might not be able to adequately control an inmate uprising, should one occur; and the number of conservation officers supporting Lingo's troopers left too few available to enforce conservation laws—encouraging a "widespread outbreak of hunting and fishing violations" and causing increased "destruction of [Alabama's] fish and wildlife resources."[96]

Wallace also realized that the fires of Birmingham, with their accompanying negative publicity, could drive off the industrial investment in Alabama that he so desperately sought to improve the state's economy. He received, for example, a letter from the manager of Northrop Space Laboratories in Huntsville, Alabama, complaining that the state's racial problems were making it difficult to lure experienced engineers to Huntsville from Northrop's California operations. The manager, J. A. Barclay, wrote that "two engineers with graduate degrees who had agreed to move to Huntsville changed their minds with the explanation that they didn't want to get into a racial mess." He warned that continued similar defections would impede the task of "building sizable operations in Huntsville."[97] And William J. Rielly of the Cincinnati-based Velva-Sheen Manufacturing Company, which bought a quarter of a million dollars worth of Alabama textiles every year, wrote Wallace: "The recent race riots . . . and the backward, unyielding position that your government is taking are causing us, both as Christians and as businessmen, to reexamine our entire purchasing program concerning Alabama goods." He asserted, "If it was wrong to buy goods from the slave-labor communist countries behind the Iron Curtain, how long can we continue to buy cotton goods behind your cotton curtain?"[98]

Wallace, reading the handwriting on the wall, wanted to divert attention from Birmingham—and he was helped immeasurably by racial conflicts elsewhere in the nation. In the months following the Birmingham riots, demonstrations in seventy-five Southern cities resulted in nearly fourteen thousand arrests. The North encountered its share of racial protest and tension, too: in Philadelphia, white and black construction workers clashed with each other and with police over alleged discriminatory hiring practices; in Englewood, New Jersey, blacks conducted a sit-in at a predominantly white school to protest de facto segregation in the public schools; demonstrations alleging various forms of segregation and police brutality were staged, sometimes sparking violence, in Cleveland, New York, Chicago, Detroit, and elsewhere. In all, the Justice Department counted more than 750 demonstrations in the ten weeks following the Birmingham truce.[99]

Although he welcomed diversion of the press's spotlight from Birmingham, Wallace by no means was content for the spotlight to shift from him personally. Despite the harsh words that he and President Kennedy had exchanged publicly over the Birmingham crisis and the president's decision to move troops into the state, the governor lunged at the opportunity to be on hand when the president came to Alabama a few days after the riots to commemorate the thirtieth anniversary of the Tennessee Valley Authority (TVA). Kennedy first spoke on the Tennessee side of the valley, where he upbraided Wallace for his defiance of school integration; Kennedy said that "for one man to defy a law or court order he does not like is to invite others to defy those which they do not like, leading to a breakdown of all justice and all order."[100] But when he arrived in Muscle Shoals, Alabama, where Wallace was on hand to meet him, he wanted to talk about Birmingham. After a perfunctory speech praising TVA, Kennedy invited Wallace to join him on the presidential helicopter for a flight along the Tennessee River valley to Huntsville. Kennedy's press secretary, Pierre Salinger, recalled the president observing that the very people who objected to black employees in downtown stores employed blacks to serve tables in their homes. According to Salinger, Wallace replied that the real problem in Birmingham was the "faker" Martin Luther King, Jr.; in fact, Salinger noted Wallace saying, King and Shuttlesworth vied with one another over "who could go to bed with the most nigger women, and white and red women, too."[101] Wallace vigorously denied he ever said anything of the sort—and it stretches credulity to believe he would have gratuitously laid himself open to a foe by using the word *nigger* and referring to the stereotyped sexual appetites of black men, ministers or no. Salinger's recollection also was at odds with the deference, bordering on obsequiousness, with which Wallace comported himself in the presence of people of high rank. Wallace did remember Kennedy's reference to employing blacks; he replied, he said, by saying that government shouldn't be able to tell a businessman whom to hire.[102]

Whichever version was true, neither President nor Attorney General Kennedy, following their face-to-face meetings with the governor of Alabama, was able to size him up or discern how he might behave in future racial confrontations. Burke Marshall told the cabinet that he believed Wallace meant personally to prevent the entry of two black students ordered by the court to enter the University of

Alabama. "He has intended to require his own arrest or removal by force, and to require the federal government to use troops to enforce the court order."[103] Robert Kennedy said, "The great question for us was not having to arrest the governor, not having to charge him with contempt, and not having to send troops into the state of Alabama— and yet getting the students [Vivian Malone and James Hood] into the university."[104]

9

The Defining Moment

FROM THEIR MEETING in late April 1963, all through their long-distance jousting during the Birmingham crisis, George Wallace and Robert Kennedy viewed one another with chilly suspicion, if not downright contempt. But, as their confrontation at the schoolhouse door neared, the antagonists agreed on at least two things: neither wanted violence, and neither wanted Wallace to go to jail.

"I don't think that he wanted to go to jail," Kennedy said of Wallace, "and . . . we didn't want to go through the same thing that we went through at the University of Mississippi."[1] Wallace thought it was "fantastic in [that] day and time to even to be trying to handle a governor of a sovereign state just like a common lawbreaker." But he vowed that, when he sought to bar two blacks from registering for classes at the University of Alabama, there would be "not one rock . . . thrown, not one brickbat, not one overt act of violence."[2]

His desire to stay out of jail and keep the peace notwithstanding, Wallace was not about to allow the federal establishment to rob him of his momentous opportunity—the chance to fulfill his campaign pledge to "stand up for Alabama" (specifically, to block school integration) while, simultaneously, capturing a national audience. So when Attorney General Kennedy sought to legally restrain the governor from interfering with the students, Wallace started a cat-and-mouse game to avoid being served with a subpoena. On Friday, May

24, two federal marshals arrived in the governor's outer office with papers ordering Wallace to appear for a June 3 hearing in the U.S. district court in Birmingham. The litigants would argue Kennedy's petition enjoining the governor from barring the students' entry into the university. But after the marshals cooled their heels for four hours, they eagerly pressed the subpoena into the hands of the first man who emerged from Wallace's office; unfortunately for them, it was Earl Morgan, Wallace's executive secretary. Over the weekend, Wallace confined himself to the governor's mansion, remaining out of the marshals' reach.

He emerged on Monday morning, surrounded by sixteen helmeted state troopers. When a motorcade of six cars roared out of the driveway, the marshals, who watched from their nearby car, sped to the capitol. They formulated a plan to serve the papers without risking a physical encounter with the troopers. They intended to hide on either side of a narrow doorway that Wallace was certain to pass through; the troopers would be forced to peel away, and as Wallace walked through alone, the marshals would surprise him and quickly depart. But the plan was defeated before it was ever tried. Instead of going from the executive mansion to the capitol, Wallace and his entourage headed to the Jefferson Davis Hotel. The governor, intent on evading the marshals, rode the service elevator to a fourth-floor suite, where he met with the so-called State Sovereignty Committee, specially created to arm Wallace with arguments supporting states' rights; its members, at Wallace's behest, were appointed by the Alabama Bar Association to add a patina of legality to the unsupportable challenge to federal supremacy.

Meanwhile, the U.S. marshals, after waiting an hour at the capitol for Wallace and his motorcade, finally asked the governor's secretary where he was; she obligingly directed them to the hotel where, she knew, Wallace would by now be safely ensconced. Indeed, when the marshals showed up there and approached the meeting room, troopers guarding the hotel door again frustrated them in their attempt to serve the papers. Discreetly, they retreated, concluding there was no way to reach Wallace without risking a serious confrontation with troopers. They returned to the executive mansion, where they handed the papers to a black servant, Martha Davis, who answered the door. "Now, you be sure the governor gets this," one of them told her. In an ironic twist, the woman receiving the court's papers from the federal lawmen was a trusty serving time at Alabama's state prison for women; it was an Alabama tradition for black convicts of both sexes, selected on the basis of good behavior, to compose the governor's household and grounds staff. Whether or not Davis actually passed the papers along to the governor is not known; if so, Wallace ignored them.[3]

In another action to enhance the appearance of legality in his impending stand at the university, Wallace directed his legislative leaders to ensure a resolution of support. He ran into surprising resistance from a pair of state senators. A longtime political foe, George Hawkins, condemned the resolution as "a call to arms to every hoodlum in the state." James E. Horton, Jr., from the politically contrary northwestern corner of Alabama, cried that Wallace's stand would "create an atmosphere so potentially dangerous that the slightest spark would engender a holocaust." He warned that Wallace's presence at the university would "attract a mob" that would "make Oxford seem like a Sunday-school picnic." Horton allowed that he favored Wallace's prosegregation position, but that the effort to retain segregation must rely on "subtler approaches." Horton led a filibuster until nearly midnight on May 29, when he agreed to a resolution supporting Wallace but containing an amendment calling for "law and order" and urging the citizenry to stay home and "leave the matter in the hands of the governor."[4] Wallace picked up on the "let-George-do-it" theme when he addressed the influential Alabama Road Builders Association on May 31. "I don't want you to stand with me," he told the cheering audience of contractors. "I'm going to stand *for* you. I won't need any help. [The black students] will be met with dignity, not violence." And he was by no means unaware of the political potential of his actions. He predicted that the South would trigger "a political revolution" in the 1964 elections and that his stand would help ignite the Dixie rebellion. "These people who are pushing integration," he said, "are the same ones who are attempting to destroy private enterprise."[5]

Wallace scheduled two television appearances to implore people to stay away from the campus on June 11, the date for the scheduled enrollment of Malone and Hood. Additionally, "messages were sent through various channels to groups most likely to stir up trouble."[6] Key among those groups, obviously, was the Ku Klux Klan—and Wallace, overcoming his strong repugnance for the organization, decided that keeping the peace at the university required him to strike a note of camaraderie with the Klan's imperial wizard, Robert M. Shelton, the man who had openly supported Wallace's opponent, John Patterson, in the 1958 gubernatorial campaign (see chapter 6).

Through intermediaries, Wallace told Shelton that disruptions at the campus would jeopardize the effort to maintain segregation in Alabama for as long as possible—something that both of them wanted. Shelton, flattered by this official recognition, announced in Tuscaloosa that his organization would stay away from the campus on June 11. Sounding as if he were reading from a script prepared by Wallace, Shelton said, "We have a sovereign leader here in Alabama. The governor has taken on his shoulders the fight of every citizen of Alabama." As a result, the Klan "has no intention of bringing about any form of violence on the campus."[7] Though Wallace denied any quid pro quo, Shelton later gained employment as a modestly paid contractor for the Alabama Highway Department, and, more than a year later, the Wallace-appointed State Parole Board granted a parole to a Klansman convicted of emasculating a black man.[8]

However lofty his stated motives, Wallace's decision to cozy up to the Klan and like-minded groups branded him as a hatemonger in the minds of millions. His image was not helped by the frequently intemperate (and often ungrammatical) responses to the voluminous correspondence his highly publicized defiance was generating around the country—and Wallace insisted that every letter be answered. Most of the replies were ghostwritten by staffers who signed Wallace's name; most don't even sound like Wallace—but they were written and signed with the governor's permission and, presumably, with his broad support of the sentiments expressed.[9] One typical letter referred to "statistics of our courts [and] public health departments" demonstrating "that a vast majority of the crime committed in this area has been committed by members of the Negro race." The letter continued:

> This crime includes the most atrocious acts of humanity, such as rape, assaults, and murder. Their health records record the fact that a vast percentage of people who are infected with venereal diseases are people of the Negro race. Statistics from the health department also reveal the fact that an exceedingly high percentage of illegitimate children in this state and surrounding states are of the Negro race. We find that Negroes are not aggressive in the respect of making progress and their own ability to live even among themselves. I do want to emphasize that whenever and wherever a member of the Negro race has the ability to work and a desire to learn, an

opportunity is awaiting him for a job and an opportunity to grow.[10]

These fatuous and unsubstantiated assertions were repeated in letter after letter that streamed from Wallace's office—an estimated 300,000 replies that he made in his first year as governor. Invariably, Wallace or his ghostwriters would assert that blacks enjoyed greater opportunities in the South than elsewhere in the country, and that blacks "who have made a success on their own initiative . . . are not in agreement of [*sic*] the so-called 'rabble-rousers' who want everything for nothing."[11] The letter said further:

> It is our firm belief that when God in Heaven made the Negro black, he meant for him to stay that way. Likewise, when he made the white race white, He meant for them to be a pure race. It is our further belief that when the two races mix and mingle in schools, from the first grade through college, this mixing will result in the races mixing socially, which fact will bring about intermarriages of the races, and eventually our race will be deteriated [*sic*] to that of the mongrel complexity.[12]

Most of the letters from the governor's office that year were written by volunteers, who were instructed by Wallace or his top staffers to harp on several points: that Wallace's principal concern was not racial integration but the "constitutional crisis in this country"; that Wallace's central goal—to halt or slow federal encroachment on state and individual rights—was obfuscated by the "news media, outside agitators, and the Kennedy administration"; and that the Birmingham riots were not interracial outbreaks as had occurred in recent months outside the South, but mob violence and lawlessness perpetrated by blacks "against police who were attempting to only maintain law and order."[13] The repeated suggestions that blacks were inferior, the incessant tone of self-righteousness and pomposity, the unrelieved know-nothingism, the misuse of language, the misspellings, the grammatical errors, and the frequent claims that he was a victim of "a nationwide campaign of character assassination,"[14] were more than enough to stigmatize Wallace as a dedicated racist and, worse, as an ignorant and irrational man. He was neither—but the perception dogged Wallace throughout his national political career. That perception would limit Wallace's personal vote-getting potential in national campaigns (though not his influence on the electorate), and, with the exceptions of Jimmy Carter in 1976 and Bill Clinton in 1992, would cause Democrats with presidential ambitions (though not Republicans) to dismiss the message as well as the man.

The missives from the Wallace ghostwriters were received less critically, as might be expected, by like-minded correspondents. When the Wallace staff lauded the head of Atlanta's Henry Grady Hotel for "standing strong in the face of continuing federal usurpation" (meaning that he had refused to join Atlanta's other hostelers in a plan for gradual, partial integration), he replied, "I felt like I had been decorated by the commander-in-chief."[15] Henry L. Lyon, Jr., the pastor of Montgomery's Highland Avenue Baptist Church, basked in the governor's praise for his campaign to ensure "that our churches be rescued from the hands of preachers who are brainwashing the people with their messages of racial integration."[16] And a Boston housewife who condemned the Kennedys for meddling in racial matters received an invitation from Wallace to visit his offices, should she be in Alabama. Four years later, the woman—Louise Day Hicks—would become a popular figure and, later, a congresswoman, on the strength of her stand against proposals to redress racial imbalances in Boston's schools.[17]

But the cumulative effect of the tens of thousands of letters spewing racist myths made Wallace appear a "pigheaded, vainglorious, politically motivated [person whose] bizarre course of action was doomed to futility from the start."[18] Even worse, the *Richmond News Leader* in segregated Virginia said Wallace was "absurd." The editorial continued:

> He is not impressive; he is ludicrous. He does not arouse the respect that may be claimed by a hard fighter in an hour of defeat; he arouses no more than the head-wagging incredulity reserved for the fool. By his inane conduct, the governor strips the Southern position of high tragedy; Birmingham becomes a pratfall and the play a low burlesque. The South cannot survive as the butt end of ridicule. . . . Sound reason supports the South's position [against] compulsory racial integration . . . but Mr. Wallace has forfeited his chance to engage in reasoned discourse. He cannot effectively challenge the legality of the president's actions. He cannot soberly speak to the country of Negro gains in the South. He has become a

clown, a buffoon, a petty little Napoleon, hand in shirt, who struts and postures to an inattentive throng.[19]

Or so it might seem from reading the words of Wallace (or the words of those empowered to correspond in Wallace's name). Wallace, however, was never a man of the written word. In his long career, his only memorable prepared speech—his 1963 inaugural—was written by someone else; and Wallace, in later years, bitterly regretted mouthing its harsh language. His strength, his popularity, his influence emerged not from his words but from his actions, his presence, his magnetism, his physicality. At the very time his language and written views were being derided by many Alabamians and Southern editors, as well as by opinion molders in the rest of the nation, he was planning the action that he sensed would sear his image indelibly on the national consciousness as the people's Saint George with the courage to stand up to the federal dragon. He did not know exactly what he would do at the University of Alabama on June 11, and he did not know precisely what would happen or what he would say; but he knew that through his very presence, the world would be watching—and would remember what he did there, not what he said.

■   ■   ■

Wallace prepared for his big day by doing what he did best—playing to his personal strengths by conducting one-on-one interviews with national print journalists and appearing on televised news-panel programs. In the relaxed, informal atmosphere of an hour-long interview, like the one he granted to *Newsweek*'s Joseph Cumming two weeks before his "stand" at the university, Wallace occasionally would slip into the racial and political conspiracy theories that were de rigueur among most white Southerners and many Northern conservatives of the time: that racial unrest was inspired largely by Communists, that Martin Luther King, Jr., was a Communist pawn, that the press regularly was duped by Communists, and that American black leaders supported a clandestine plan for blacks to take over the nations of black Africa. "When they [blacks] are in the majority," Wallace said, "they want to take over. When they are in the minority, they want to integrate."[20] But for the most part, Wallace kept his conversation tightly focused on what he contended was the constitutional battle he was waging against Washington—and he did so with disarming directness and casualness. "I am the highest constitu-tional officer in this state, elected by the people of this state," he told Cumming. "And when I go to stand in the door, it is to raise dramatically the question of sovereignty of the state. It is raising a constitutional question. . . . Does the state of Alabama run its school system, or does the federal court and the Justice Department? If I was an individual standing in the door, it wouldn't be legal. But I'm the governor of a state. If Martin Luther King, in order to test the trespass laws of a state, can break the law when he is only an individual, why can't the governor of a state, elected by the people, test the laws?" He marshaled a panoply of presidential greats—Jefferson, Jackson, Lincoln, and FDR—to support his contention that the Supreme Court was like "a thief in the night" intruding on congressional prerogatives. "It's a matter of constitutional process. The Supreme Court says things are moving too slowly, so they're going to write laws and dictate what must be done. They're not going to let Congress write the laws. Then the president can't accept the fact that Congress wouldn't pass an anti-discrimination-in-housing law, so he issued an executive order. They have cruelly emasculated the orderly processes of government. People have been bullied by the power of the federal courts until sometimes they are depressed. But they haven't changed their attitude and you're going to see something happen next year when they walk to the polls that's going to surprise you." Then Wallace leaned back, propped his feet on his desk, lit a cigar, and smiled. "Isn't it good somebody has some spirit?" he said.[21]

Then Wallace, in the biggest public relations coup of his six months in office, was invited to appear on the June 2 edition of NBC's "Meet the Press," the most prestigious televised news inter-view program of the time. The network, for vague reasons of security never explained, decided to originate the program from New York rather than Washington; someone—it is not clear who—thought it best if Wallace traveled under an assumed name. (The subterfuge did not fool federal marshals, who finally were able to serve Wallace, traveling as Jack Bailey, with a summons to appear in federal court; a U.S. marshal tossed the papers at the governor's feet during his commercial flight to New York.)[22]

Wallace faced a panel of tough, knowledgeable, unsympathetic reporters—Lawrence Spivak, the program's host; Frank McGee of NBC (who had been the head of news at a Montgomery TV station during the bus boycott), Anthony Lewis of the *New York Times*, and

Vermont Royster of the *Wall Street Journal.* It was a panel, an aide later opined, "out to demolish him." But Wallace, through instinct or guile, responded to the questions (and the cameras) directly and succinctly, hammering on the themes he perceived would have wide appeal (nonviolence and federal encroachment) and avoiding racist pseudo-science or stereotypes that had peppered his earlier speeches and press interviews. In a characteristic exchange, Lewis posed this challenge:

> LEWIS: Governor, you have just said several times that you want to get these constitutional questions adjudicated in the courts. As a lawyer and former judge, you must know that the question of the supremacy of the federal constitution has been in the courts and been adjudicated dozens of times since the country was founded and the supremacy of the constitution has always prevailed, most recently in Little Rock, Arkansas, and Oxford, Mississippi. In light of that, what is your real purpose in what you are doing? Are you there as a political gesture to try to arouse violence, or what is your purpose?
>
> WALLACE: Mr. Lewis, in the first place, let me tell you that I am not there to arouse violence because my attitude and the action I took in the Birmingham matter indicates that I am against violence. . . . *Plessy versus Ferguson* many years ago was decided in favor of the separate-but-equal-facility doctrine, but constant efforts by those who opposed this interpretation resulted in the *Brown* case, so I see no reason why we should not continue to raise questions, and the court might decide to change its mind as it did in the *Brown* case.

When McGee asked if Wallace was "hoping to have [himself] arrested," Wallace said he was not; he continued "[I] made a commitment in the campaign for governor that I would do this, and I feel this is a good and dramatic way." Wallace then underscored his goal of maximizing attention through drama when McGee asked:

> McGEE: Could it be done any other way?
>
> WALLACE: It may be done in some other ways. I am not sure about that. But I think it is a dramatic way to impress upon the American people this omnipotent march of centralized government that is going to destroy the rights and freedom and liberty of the people of this country if it continues, and we in Alabama intend to resist this centralized control, where they

now tell us whom you can eat with and whom you can sit down with and swim with and whom you can sell your house to. This is the great constitutional principle upon which we stand in Alabama.

Then Wallace came as close as he had before (or would in the ensuing week) to tipping off the White House and Justice Department on what they could expect during the confrontation on campus:

> McGEE: Sir, if it comes to it, and you are told by some representative of the federal government that you are under arrest, will you accept this and go peacefully?
>
> WALLACE: Of course, if I am ever arrested by the federal government, I will go peacefully. There has never been any intention to resist and fight the federal forces with force. The people of this country have been victimized by the press. I have never made any statement or indicated at all that I intended to fight with bottles and rocks and guns. I am against that as much as you or anyone else.

McGee then tossed the proverbial journalistic softball:

> McGEE: Sir, have you in any way, through issuing public statements or in press conferences, let the people of Alabama know that you do not want them present in Tuscaloosa that day—that you would like them to stay at home?
>
> WALLACE: . . . I made a speech the other day—I made several statements in which I have asked the people to stay away from the university campus. I do not want them there. I am going to stand for them because I represent them. . . . We are not going to have violence at the University of Alabama.[23]

The response to Wallace's appearance was overwhelming. Mail, which had been pouring in at the rate of a couple of hundred pieces a week, increased to a thousand or more a week. And the tone of the correspondence became much more positive. While some editorializers, like those in Richmond, Virginia, sneered at Wallace, others—from the *Winona Leader* in Kansas to the *Montgomery Advertiser* (which had grown wary of Wallace's rhetoric during the Birmingham crisis)—were considerably kinder. The Kansas newspaper did not wish "to become embroiled in a local controversy over the merits or shortcomings of segregation," which supposedly was "no problem" in Winona and was "consequently none of [their] business." But the paper's editorializer continued:

> It becomes our business, however, when we see the federal government using [segregation] as an excuse to abandon its policy of gradual encroachment into state, local, and private affairs in favor of a policy of outright autocracy. By playing upon the emotions of the well-meaning but hopelessly confused proponents of universal brotherhood, the government and the minority groups manage to convince a large share of the public that any means which would result in the desired goal is legally and morally right. Thus, the very people who have the greatest stake in preserving the constitution are doing the most to destroy it.[24]

The *Montgomery Advertiser*'s Grover Hall, who earlier had grieved over Wallace's seeming refusal to eschew violence, gloried in the governor's performance on *Meet the Press*:

> Wallace was sought by the network . . . that it might show the famous mob leader from Alabama in the land of lynch. But they moved the show from Washington to New York because [they] thought Wallace might not be safe in Kennedy's city. Nevertheless, [Robert] Kennedy was safe enough in the Alabama of Wallace. . . . Wallace has earned the gratitude of his fellow Alabamians for the excellence with which he represented them before the United States. . . . As for Americans everywhere, they saw a Wallace that much belied the one that has been presented in the national magazines and the abolitionist press.[25]

The next day, a brief hearing was conducted in federal court on the Justice Department's request for an injunction to prevent Wallace from barring the enrollment of black students at the university. Wallace did not appear, but the federal judge, Seybourn Lynne, simply ignored the governor's absence rather than make an issue of it. Two days later, he issued the injunction. "Thoughtful people," he wrote, "if they can free themselves from tensions produced by established principles with which they violently disagree, must concede that the governor of a sovereign state has no authority to obstruct or prevent the execution of the lawful orders of a court of the United States." Judge Lynne, who some five and a half years earlier had been the dissenter in the two-to-one federal court decision to strike down bus segregation (see chapter 7), now gently but firmly lectured the governor on the established legal supremacy of federal authority:

> In the final analysis, the concept of law and order, the very essence of a republican form of government, embodies the notion that when the judicial process of a state or federal court, acting within the sphere of its competence, has been exhausted and has resulted in a final judgment, all persons affected thereby are obliged to obey it. . . . Too well settled in the law to admit of persuasive arguments to the contrary are the twin propositions that the courts of the United States have statutory authority . . . as well as inherent power to enter such orders as may be necessary to effectuate their lawful decrees and to prevent interference with, or obstruction to, their implementation, and that the United States has standing to seek the injunctive relief for which it prays. . . . May it be forgiven if this court makes use of the personal pronoun for the first time in a written opinion. I love the people of Alabama. I know that many of both races are troubled and, like Jonah of old, are "angry even unto death" as the result of distortions of affairs within this state, practiced in the name of sensationalism. My prayer is that all of our people, in keeping with our finest traditions, will join in the resolution that law and order will be maintained.[26]

Lynne's attempt to mollify Wallace through mild language fell on deaf ears. The governor focused on the bald words of the injunction, which prohibited him or anyone associated with him from "preventing, blocking, or interfering with, by physically interposing his body or that of any other persons under his direction or control" the students' admission. But Wallace was not barred from being on the campus on June 11, nor from making statements while there, and he immediately reiterated his intention to stand in the door. Clearly, he risked arrest and imprisonment, although deep down he felt that the Kennedys would try at all costs to avoid that possibility; not only would an arrest make a martyr of Wallace, but it would raise serious constitutional questions as well. And, as far as he was concerned, Lynne's decree, in the words of Wallace's press secretary, "started the destruction of segregated schools in Alabama, the fiftieth state to fall under the federal heel, and was to grind state control of schools into nothingness within two years."[27]

Wallace instructed Albert Lingo to post enough troopers on the university campus to assure that it would be "the safest place in America to be" on the day of the confrontation.[28] Lingo pulled together many of the same irregulars that he had used in Birmingham—deputy sheriffs, game wardens, prison guards, and even some liquor agents—to join a contingent of his state troopers. There were seven hundred in all.[29] And, in an action he called "an abundance of caution," the governor ordered the Alabama National Guard to activate five hundred troops and to quarter them in armories near the university campus in Tuscaloosa. He wired President Kennedy that the troops were to be used "only to prevent violence"—implying that Wallace would not use troops to forestall the black students from enrolling.[30] The suggestion was clear: Wallace would personally bar the way.

Meanwhile, the U.S. Army, stung by earlier criticism that it had been slow to respond to the Ole Miss crisis because of communications foul-ups, set up a sophisticated communications command post. It would allow on-scene federal authorities to provide Washington with minute-to-minute updates—and, if necessary, receive prompt military support should they summon troops to the campus in a face-off with Alabama forces. The command post was established in the U.S. Army Reserve Center housing the Seventy-fifth Field Hospital unit. When Deputy Attorney General Nicholas Katzenbach, whom the Kennedys had designated as their point man in Tuscaloosa as he had been in Oxford, arrived in Alabama on Sunday afternoon to prepare for the Tuesday encounter, he was somewhat taken aback by the elaborate telephone installation in his headquarters. "They put in communications that must have cost a half-million dollars," Katzenbach recalled. "Red phones, yellow phones. I could pick up the phone and talk to Berlin. It was a military network, completely bypassing the phone system—just in case someone cut the telephone lines . . . [and] all because they had been embarrassed at Ole Miss."[31]

The army's deeper interest in communications may well have been to fend off criticism of the kind it had received in the wake of Ole Miss, but in actuality, no one—neither Katzenbach nor the Kennedys nor anyone else in Washington (nor perhaps even Wallace himself)— knew what the governor would do, nor the true level of danger that the participants would be facing. As Katzenbach said later:

> He [Wallace] kept saying he didn't want any violence, and I'm sure that was sincere on his part, but it didn't make us feel all that much better. When you create all the conditions which

have a potential for violence, and then say you don't want any violence—even if you're very sincere about it—it doesn't mean there's not going to be any. . . . That was what made us nervous. He got the feelings up so high that he might be unable to control them. That was what worried us.[32]

Indeed, communications—or the lack thereof—would be a persistent problem among all the major players on all sides of the issue, starting with the weekend before the students were to enroll. On Saturday, June 8, the day before Katzenbach departed for Alabama, the attorney general tried to find out what Wallace planned to do: would he step aside for the students or for Katzenbach or the U.S. marshals who would accompany him? Or would the president be forced to summon U.S. troops or federalize Alabama guardsmen other than those whom Wallace had placed on active duty? And would Wallace then stand aside? Late Saturday afternoon, Robert Kennedy tried telephoning Wallace, but Cecil Jackson intercepted the call at Wallace's direction. Jackson said that Wallace was "not available" (he was actually listening in). Jackson added, "We have some question as to whether or not it would be proper for you to talk with him since you . . . have filed suit against him."

Jackson then said he wanted to put John Kohn, whom he described as "one of the governor's leading counsel," on the line. Kennedy said he would talk to Kohn—but interjected that his purpose in calling was to find out what the governor would "do on Tuesday" so the White House could make "other plans and the possible chance of having a couple of coordinators there." When Kohn picked up the extension, Kennedy repeated his hope that a coordinated plan could be worked out between the adversaries. But Kohn, who was enthusiastically promoting the confrontation, was not interested in any stage-managed diminution of the drama:

> **KENNEDY:** I wanted to find out from the governor what he is going to do on Tuesday. . . .
>
> **KOHN:** Well, Mr. Kennedy, I think that's a prerogative exclusively within the governor's mind. . . .
>
> **KENNEDY:** Well, that is just what I wanted to find out . . . specifically what he was going to do. Obviously, he doesn't want to tell me and there is no way I can force that.
>
> **KOHN:** Well, first, for the record, this call was not initiated down here. It was initiated by yourself. . . . and I don't think

any human being can tell what . . . in all reasonable probability is going to happen. That will just be a matter of events as they unfold. . . .

KENNEDY: Looks as though I can't find out. Is that right?

KOHN: That would be my answer.

Kennedy asked that Jackson return to the line.

KENNEDY: I thought we were going to handle it as civilized people and gentlemen. . . .

JACKSON: Well, now, Mr. Kennedy, I think you know that we are civilized people. . . . But let me say this: we feel that we have a proposition here where you have instituted suit against the governor.

KENNEDY: I don't blame . . . I don't mind that, not being able to talk to him. I am not going to raise any question about that. All I am saying is that I think difficulty and misunderstanding can't arise if everybody understands exactly what the other party is going to do, and I would be glad to discuss that.

JACKSON: . . . I think the governor would be willing to talk to you if you are interested in discussing ways and means by which these . . . Negroes withdraw their efforts to go to the University of Alabama. Other than that, we don't feel that it would be proper [or] that there is anything else that could be negotiated about it.

KENNEDY: There is nothing to be negotiated. But they are going to be attending the University of Alabama—no question about that. Just a question of how they are going. . . .

JACKSON: Well, of course, I don't know that I would agree with you there. We feel that the proposition here is not a question of integration or segregation or whether Negroes go to the University of Alabama, but that we have this overall proposition of whether or not there will be any state sovereignty whatsoever, whether or not the constitution of the United States will be preserved.

"Okay, thank you, Mr. Jackson," Kennedy said, unable (or unwilling) to disguise his disdain and frustration. With that, he hung up the phone.[33]

Wallace and his people chose not to communicate with the

Kennedys for three reasons: first, Wallace believed that if he agreed to a planned scenario to avert violence, the attorney general would leak Wallace's connivance to the press and embarrass him as he mistakenly thought Robert Kennedy had done when dealing with Ross Barnett; and second, Wallace, knowing that integration was inevitable, wanted to insulate himself from political recriminations by forcing the president to use federal troops.[34] "I can't fight bayonets with my bare hands," he would say later, explaining why he could not be blamed for backing down.[35]

There was a third reason: Wallace really did not know himself what he intended to do. He knew he wanted to stand in the door to keep his campaign pledge and symbolically turn back the federal government; he knew he wanted publicity; and—having been bombarded by letters and phone calls from businessmen over the state to avoid a repeat of the Ole Miss disaster—he knew he wanted the encounter to proceed without violence. His strategy boiled down to three Ps—the pledge, the press, and peace. It was an uncertain parlay at best, given internal as well as external communications problems.[36]

Lingo, for instance, almost sabotaged Wallace's grand plan for national publicity. At about the time Jackson and Kohn were stonewalling Robert Kennedy, Lingo led a second Wallace contingent to the university to set up security measures and select the doorway at Foster Auditorium where the governor would prevent the two black students from entering and registering for the summer session. But in his zeal for sealing off the campus from possible troublemakers, Lingo decreed that all reporters would be barred from the campus except for the handful that regularly covered state politics. Bill Jones, the press secretary, was furious with Lingo for his capricious and unilateral pronouncement, taken in large measure, Jones believed, because Lingo simply did not like reporters. Jones knew, of course, that the governor wanted to milk the national media for all it was worth, and as Jones later said, "It was necessary for me to change many of the rules [Lingo] had arbitrarily established. . . . I was assigned to look after Wallace's PR policies, and I felt that what Lingo was doing was harmful to them. . . . Lingo misunderstood the governor's plan to dramatize his position to the nation."

In an effort to mollify Lingo's fervent insistence on security, Jones directed a university maintenance crew to paint a white line near the lectern from which Wallace would read a proclamation denying entrance to the black students. The reporters would be required to stand behind the line, but with a clear view of events. The workers, eager to please the governor's staff, went beyond their instructions: they painted several lines—one for the reporters, one for Wallace's lectern, one where federal officials were supposed to stop and go no farther. The lines appeared to some reporters and to Katzenbach himself to resemble "stage instructions, showing everyone where to stand in the production." When Katzenbach heard about the lines, he telephoned the university president, Frank Rose. " 'What the hell is this?' " Katzenbach recalled saying, "and he said, 'Well, the governor wanted that.' I said, 'Get rid of those damn things.' They couldn't get rid of all of them, but they didn't finish them. I walked beyond where he wanted me to, anyway."[37]

Katzenbach's imperious tone in addressing Rose illustrated the tough spot in which the university president had been placed. He was trying to serve two masters in hopes that he could contribute to a calm resolution of the crisis. On one side, the governor's staff and state troopers, to all intents and purposes, had made it clear to Rose that he was, after all, just another state employee expected to carry out the governor's wishes. On the other side, the Justice Department enlisted Rose as its principal ally in trying to persuade Wallace to avoid the dangers inherent in a confrontation. The trouble was, Rose had no influence with the governor or with any of his key aides; but unlike his counterpart at the University of Mississippi the previous fall, Rose was willing to risk his position to preserve order. Weeks before the court's decision to admit Vivian Malone and James Hood to the university, Rose had called in student leaders and demanded their help in maintaining campus decorum; he let it be known that any student demonstrators would be severely disciplined. Rose played a role in rallying more than two hundred Tuscaloosa business and professional leaders to sign a petition to the governor to "respectfully urge" him not to act on his "announced intention of personally and physically interfering with the order of the United States Court." Rose ordered maintenance crews to manicure the campus to rid it of loose rocks and sticks. He replaced bottled soft drink vending machines with ones that dispensed paper cups. And, at his request, a contractor building a wall behind a sorority house carted off a load of bricks before the weekend.

Also working for Rose (and against the likelihood of a campus flare-up) was that the summer student body was only half the size of the regular school year enrollment and included a large proportion of graduate students, schoolteachers, and those taking makeup courses needed for graduation—in short, students whose greater maturity and concentration on their studies made them less likely to cause trouble.[38] But Wallace was growing impatient with Rose; he commended the responsible efforts to minimize the possibility of violence, but he thought Rose's involvement with the Justice Department and support of the petition from local business leaders bordered on insubordination. Wallace also resented how the national media invariably described Rose in positive terms ("tall and energetic," said *Newsweek*; "an able educator and a moderate," said *Time*) while casting Wallace as the villain.

Wallace was determined to pull Rose and the university board of trustees back into line. He scheduled an emergency meeting with Rose and the trustees for Monday, the day before the showdown; he made it clear he expected them to express solid support of his actions. On Sunday, just before Wallace went on statewide television to reassure Alabamians that he would handle the situation in their behalf and to ask that they stay at home and remain calm, Rose issued a brief and perfunctory statement of contrition: "It is necessary for the governor to be here"—no ringing endorsement, to be sure, but sufficient grounds for Wallace's pretext that he needed to assume personal control of the campus.[39]

Then, over the next two days, cadres of opposing forces—one led by the Kennedys and the other by Wallace—engaged in a riveting, if sometimes histrionic, skirmish of wits after which both sides not only claimed, but actually achieved, victory.

■   ■   ■

On Monday morning, the dramatis personae were spread among four cities. The governor and most of his top aides were in Montgomery for last-minute strategy sessions before leaving for Tuscaloosa. The Kennedys were in Washington, where they would make the crucial decisions about how to conduct the confrontation with Wallace, whether to use troops, and whether the president should use the occasion to advocate a civil rights bill, for which little support in Congress existed. Katzenbach and Gen. Creighton Abrams were in Tuscaloosa to appraise the situation firsthand. And, in Birmingham, the principals—Vivian Malone and James Hood— would spend the day being advised by black leaders and the Justice Department's John Doar on what to expect and how to conduct themselves.

Malone and Hood, attractive and articulate twenty-year-olds, were good students at black colleges in Alabama. Both wanted to attend the university because it offered courses unavailable at their respective colleges. Both were understandably nervous, but not frightened. "Once the governor took his stand [to keep the university segregated], I recognized that I needed help," Malone said later. "I had in mind the situation at Ole Miss. I sort of expected things might be worse.... I think Hood and I both convinced ourselves that we were not afraid. You can get so frozen with fear about what's going to happen that there's no way you would go through it." Hood helped to lighten the mood. During a break in a mock press conference, Hood entertained Malone by pretending to be his own questioner: "What do you want to do most in life?" he asked himself, playing reporter. He replied with sham gravity, "Become the governor of Alabama." A twitter from Malone encouraged Hood to amplify: "I heard a man the other day say, 'You give the Negroes an inch, they'll take a mile.' So, you let me in your university—I'll become your governor." That moved Malone to peals of laughter. But it was a rare moment of levity. The two were peppered with information, instructions, and advice until nearly midnight; no detail was unimportant. Doar even advised them on what to wear: "You should dress as if you were going to church, for example—modestly, neatly. And you should remember it's a pretty dignified, orderly procedure." The last was by way of assuring the students that all would go smoothly—more confidence than conviction because, at the time, Doar was not privy to the details of President Kennedy's plan. But Doar told Malone and Hood that if Wallace turned them back, they would face no danger; they would simply withdraw and try again sometime later.[40]

There was, in fact, no such certainty of dignity and order. Both sides recognized the possibility that the worst could happen, though both were determined to avoid it. The continuing danger lay in neither side knowing how the other was going to behave.

■   ■   ■

Monday started serenely enough both for Robert Kennedy, who would emerge as the real general of the Washington operation, and for Wallace. At his gracious manor outside Washington, Kennedy telephoned his brother at the White House to propose a meeting at five-thirty to plan their strategy "in view of Wallace's statement now that he's going to stand in the door in any case." Then, with three of his children in tow, he headed for his Justice Department office.

Some nine hundred miles to the south in Montgomery, Wallace took several Northern reporters on a quick tour of the mansion before setting out for his office at the capitol. He pointed to a portrait of the Alabama firebrand William Lowndes Yancey (see chapter 1). "You know," he said, "he made a profound statement I was thinking about: 'To live is not all of life and to die is not all of death. I'd rather live a short life of standing for principle than live a long life of compromise.' " With a hint of contempt for the reporters, he added, "Of course, that might not mean much to you folks." He gestured to the portraits of Civil War heroes lining the walls of a large receiving room: "I think it does us good to reflect and draw on the courage of people who fight and stand for what they believe in, and there were brave folks on both sides of that combat." Then he paused, smiled, and said, "There was just a lot more of them than there were of us." The intended relevance to the forthcoming battle of Tuscaloosa was not lost on the listeners.[41]

En route to the capitol, Wallace was asked to justify the morality of segregation. "A moral issue," he said, "comes from your heart in the first place. If I thought it was sinful and irreligious and immoral to separate myself socially and educationally from Negro citizens, then I would commit a sin when I did so, I suppose. But I believe that separation is good for the Negro citizen and the white citizen." "In their best interests," Cecil Jackson interjected. "And in their best interests," Wallace echoed. "And if I do something that my heart tells me is good for both groups, there's not anything that runs counter to any religion or any law of morality, and it's not sinful." (Years later, Vivian Malone would observe, "Wallace would say he wanted the best for both black and white—but he certainly didn't want the best for *me*.")[42]

In his office, Wallace was surrounded by aides as he stood at his desk studying photographs of the university areas where the action would occur the next day (their *own* set of pictures; no one thought to ask Washington for a set of the shots made from the U-2 a few weeks earlier). "It's a beautiful university," he said. "It's peaceful and serene." His tone hardened slightly when he added, "And it's gonna be peaceful and serene on Tuesday." He looked around the table and at the reporters present and issued his marching orders (and his public relations message): "I just want you all to be sure that . . . not one rock is thrown, not one brickbat, nor one overt act of violence in any manner Tuesday or any day thereafter. We're not going to let any-body desecrate this university, 'cause you've got agitators and pro-vocateurs who come from . . . outside this state who themselves will want to stir up some violence in order to hurt our cause." "And to further *their* cause," Jackson inserted. "And to further *their* cause," Wallace repeated, "because they thrive and raise money on disorder. So, people working under me, I just want you to know—that's my orders. We're gonna keep the peace." As he left for the airport, he was surrounded by well-wishers visiting the capitol; they told him they were proud of him and they loved him.[43]

At the Justice Department, Kennedy called in Marshall, and the two, in consultation with Katzenbach, decided to recommend to the president that he nationalize the Alabama National Guard. Rose made it clear to Kennedy that Wallace would not step aside for federal marshals, but that he might do so for the military, and they reasoned that soldiers from Alabama would be less likely to inflame passions than imported federal troops. Marshall checked with Abrams, who informed him that the 101st Airborne was on alert at Fort McClellan, 120 miles east of Tuscaloosa. And if and when the president federalized the National Guard, a contingent of one hun-dred guardsmen under the command of Lt. Gen. Henry Graham[44] would be dispatched to the campus from their domiciles at the Tuscaloosa armories; the remainder would be held in reserve and used if needed. The attorney general worried that a hundred men might not be enough; even using all five hundred would still mean that Wallace's forces outnumbered them.

Kennedy did not want a repeat of the Ole Miss problem. As Katzenbach commented later, "At the University of Mississippi . . . there were a lot of people from outside, not just university students by any means, who had guns. And a riot started and we ended up having to bring in federal troops to quell the riot. That was a failure on the part of the federal government; we were determined not to let that happen again." Still, Abrams was convinced that a hundred would be sufficient, and in an emergency, they could bring in the remaining four hundred guardsmen in Tuscaloosa. Finally, there were several hundred additional Alabama guardsmen participating in annual training exercises at Fort McClellan; as soon as they were federalized, Abrams would have them moved to Tuscaloosa as reinforcements. Kennedy wanted to be reassured that the guardsmen would be on the campus no more than four hours from the time the president feder-alized them. He worried that the longer the delay, the greater the chance that the tension might trigger an incident among one or more of the twelve hundred armed men at or near Foster Auditorium. "We could have a big battle," he said, "even before we get on the campus. . . . I just want to make sure nothing happens." Abrams said it would be done. Kennedy then suggested that Graham, a Birmingham real-estate agent when not on active duty, be whisked immediately to Tuscaloosa by helicopter so he would be ready to lead the troops.[45]

Wallace arrived in Tuscaloosa before noon, toured the tightly secured campus, visited the National Guard troops at one of the armories, checked into the Stafford Hotel, and met with the board of trustees. Wallace persuaded the trustees to adopt a resolution asserting that his presence on the campus was needed to preserve order; they agreed reluctantly. Many of them believed that Wallace's presence was more likely to spark disorder than prevent it. But they agreed to words that amounted to a lukewarm endorsement, stating that his continued presence was "desirable under the circumstances to preserve peace and order." The reason, they added at Wallace's insistence, was "the apparent willingness of unauthorized persons to abide by [his] request . . . to stay away from the campus" so long as he was there representing their interests.[46] Wallace returned to his hotel room, convinced he had done all in his power to preserve peace, yet make his point. "I wanted to raise an issue: who could set the timetable of integrating the university—the trustees or the courts?"[47]

But Robert Kennedy was not as comfortable as Wallace apparently was—principally because he did not know when or in what circumstances Wallace would yield his ground and permit the students to register. He telephoned Abrams in Tuscaloosa: "Hey, General, I thought we would try to develop a plan about what's going to happen when General Graham gets there." There had been some discussion of forcing their way past Wallace, but Kennedy clearly wanted an alternative. "Now," he said to Abrams, "I'm not very much in favor of picking the governor up and moving him out of the way. I think it'd be much better if we could develop some system, if you had enough people, just to push him aside or something. I don't want to pick the governor up very much."[48] Abrams said he would talk to Katzenbach and Graham and try to come up with some ideas.

Late Monday afternoon, the attorney general went to the White House to meet with the president and his key advisers. In addition to the immediate concern over Tuscaloosa, there was the related, pressing question of whether to publicly support civil rights legislation. At the White House meeting on Monday, the president was cool to the

idea of delivering a televised civil rights appeal, unless trouble occurred at the university. Robert Kennedy unhesitatingly disagreed: "I
think it'd be helpful. I think [Tuscaloosa] is a reason to do it. . . . Do
it for fifteen minutes. I think it would alleviate a lot of problems . . .
that we're having at the present time." Larry O'Brien and Kenny
O'Donnell, the president's closest political advisers, opposed the
idea of making a plea, which they thought would hurt the president's
entire program in Congress. Robert Kennedy replied that they could
make the situation clear to Congress: "We're going to have some
problems during the summer [and] we hope that [because] we're
making this kind of effort at the federal level . . . Negroes would
understand their responsibilities." O'Brien argued they should wait
until after they pushed through other important legislation, saying,
"That's when you may want to do this." Robert Kennedy differed
again. If they waited for other legislation to clear, he said, that could
be as late as November, "and I don't think you can get by now without
saying [something] direct on television."[49]

The attorney general knew firsthand the vehemence of many
black Americans on the segregation issue. Ten days earlier, in a
meeting with several black academicians and artists in his New York
apartment, Kennedy, despite his aggressive actions to quell disturbances in Birmingham, was rudely upbraided by a young civil rights
worker named Jerome Smith, brought to the meeting by the writer
James Baldwin. Smith said he was nauseated to be in the same room
with Kennedy, that he did not know how long he could remain
nonviolent and refrain from shooting whites, and that he would
never consider fighting for his country. Kennedy, already reddening
at the personal insult and the suggestion of racial violence, was
shocked at what he considered a near-treasonous statement. Kenneth
Clark, the social psychologist, said later, "We were shocked that he
was shocked. . . . It became really one of the most violent, emotional
verbal assaults . . . that I had ever witnessed." The singer Lena Horne
explained that Smith "just put it like it was. He communicated the
plain, basic suffering of being a Negro." The playwright Lorraine
Hansberry told Kennedy, "Look, if you can't understand what this
young man is saying, then we are without any hope at all because you
and your brother are representatives of the best that a white America
can offer—and if you are insensitive to this, then there's no alternative except our going in the streets." She even talked about arming
blacks so they could start killing whites. Later, when the entertainer
Harry Belafonte told Kennedy privately that the attorney general

"had done more for civil rights than anyone else," Kennedy demanded to know why Belafonte had not made that statement in front of the others who had attacked him for the better part of three hours. Belafonte replied that if he had sided with Kennedy, he would have risked his position of influence among the others and his chance to be a moderating influence. Clark walked away from the meeting convinced that the whole thing was hopeless. . . . [Kennedy] just didn't seem to get it." Upon his return to Washington, Kennedy told Arthur Schlesinger, the historian and a White House aide, that the meeting "was all emotion, hysteria." Schlesinger feared that Kennedy's reaction "would be a sense of the futility rather than of the urgency of trying to bridge the gap." But though Kennedy "resented the experience," Schlesinger wrote, "it pierced him all the same. . . . It was another stage in his education." Clearly, ten days later at the White House, Robert Kennedy's sense of urgency was obvious.[50]

The president, bending to his brother's insistence, said, "I guess we ought to get something ready anyway, because we may use it tomorrow." Robert Kennedy glanced at the speechwriter Ted Sorenson and, without missing a beat, replied, "Well, we've got a draft which is . . . something to work with. And there are some pretty good sentiments and paragraphs." The president again agreed to have a speech ready that he might use. Then he wanted to know the plan for the next day. The attorney general said the strategy was to get around jailing Governor Wallace and yet avoid backing down in the face of his defiance.[51]

The first step, Robert Kennedy said, would allow the governor to sidestep disobeying the court order; Katzenbach would confront Wallace while leaving the two students in a nearby parked car. That way, Wallace would not technically be barring the students from entering.[52] "Then if he still refuses," Kennedy continued, "Nick Katzenbach will say that we've got this court order and we have to go through on a legal basis; he's made the test [and] this matter should be determined in the courts—it shouldn't be determined out here. He's had this opportunity and should let them go through, or otherwise we're going to have to take other steps, because these students are going to attend the University of Alabama. And then if he still doesn't move, then we'll try to get by him." The president looked skeptical. "Pushing?" he asked. "By pushing a little bit," Robert Kennedy said. There was a long silence.

Just as the attorney general was concerned about the idea of lifting Wallace and carrying him out of the way, the president was troubled by the thought of any physical contact. "Try to walk around him," he said firmly. Robert Kennedy suggested that perhaps they could go through one of the two doors flanking the one the governor was intending to obstruct. "Anyway," he added, "that's going to be up to Nick Katzenbach as to how far we can go on that." Realizing the president's continuing apprehension, Robert Kennedy backed away from any thought of laying hands on Wallace. "If he's able to keep the doors locked and actually keep them out," he said, "and it would require knocking him down or some real forceful action, then they will pull away. What we think, then, is that they'll go to their dormitories and we'll work out the registration sometime else." Someone suggested returning with the students the next day. Burke Marshall did not like that scheme. He said retreating and waiting twenty-four hours would be "an embarrassment." "It's just twenty-four hours," the president said. Marshall persisted. "I think our being turned back by the governor and letting that situation be seen throughout the country and the world for over twenty-four hours . . ." "All right," the president said. "Let's go with the [National] Guard."[53]

Attorney General Kennedy pointed out that the negative political impact might be alleviated if troops had to be called out because of Wallace's refusal to abide by the court order. The president warned that calling out the guard prematurely might allow Wallace to disavow responsibility for keeping the peace. But he added that, after all, Wallace had summoned the guard to meet what he called a "critical situation." "So to meet my responsibility," noted the president, "I federalized the Guard." Still, President Kennedy thought it best to wait twenty-four hours; he said he would go on television to urge calm and avoidance of violence. Robert Kennedy had won; he had persuaded his brother to make a national appeal for civil rights legislation. Now he wanted to win his other proposal—to get the students registered without a day's delay. He picked up a phone in the Oval Office and called Secretary of the Army Cyrus Vance to assure the president that if Wallace turned Katzenbach away at 10:30 A.M., federalized troops could be on the campus no later than 4:00 P.M. "We'll go with that," John Kennedy said. But, in fact, the fluidity and uncertainty of the circumstances dictated that no decision could be engraved in stone. As late as the morning of the confrontation, no one was completely sure of when or whether the guard would be federalized, or, if they were, when they would set foot on the campus.[54]

■   ■   ■

In Washington on Tuesday morning, Robert Kennedy, again with some of his kids in tow, was at his office along with Burke Marshall at 7:00 A.M. As Kennedy paced the floor, Marshall telephoned Katzenbach in his makeshift office at the U.S. Army Reserve Center in Tuscaloosa. "We're still considering what we ought to do this morning," Marshall said, "and whether or not we should call up the Guard and have them already there—go in with you. What do you think?" Katzenbach, who had been receiving some alarming reports, replied that Wallace "won't step aside under [the court order] in the first place." Kennedy did not agree; on "Meet the Press," he said, Wallace had asserted that he would not fight federal force with force. "Well," Katzenbach replied, "I have every indication he's not going to step aside up there. And I have every indication he will dramatize to that group of reporters and that crowd the fact that he has been forcibly removed." Marshall said he did not see a third alternative to escorting the students with the marshals or with the guard. "Well," Katzenbach said, "the third alternative is the one that I indicated, Burke. Everybody else can see it. That is simply that we just reduce the going through that door to nothing, and they start attending classes. Now, the governor cannot block all those classes."

Kennedy, who had picked up an extension, interjected, "You mean, and not bring the National Guard out at all?" Marshall rejected the idea. "He [Wallace] won't put up with it," he said. "It won't work." Katzenbach reconsidered and said, "The only danger with that plan that I see, and it's one that ought to be weighed, is that the governor's resentment at being made a fool of will be such that he will move way over to the segregationists' side and make life much more difficult and more dangerous in the future. Of course, he might do that, anyhow." No one spoke for a few moments. Then Kennedy said, "No. The governor's got to have his show. Otherwise, there may be a lot of violence." Kennedy then asked what Katzenbach thought about going in alone, being turned back, and returning later with a federalized guard unit. "You want to think about that for a few minutes?"[55]

Katzenbach replaced the receiver and then looked up at Abrams, Abrams's two aides, and U.S. Marshal Peyton Norville. He related Washington's proposal, but then had a better idea: rather than retreating from Wallace, even for the few hours it would take for the guard to arrive, Katzenbach proposed they leave the administration building—but escort the two students to their dormitories. It was a surprise move; all attention would be focused on the registration effort. And it would be a de facto demonstration that the students were part of the university even before Wallace permitted their formal enrollment.

Katzenbach called Kennedy back. He told the attorney general that he and Abrams liked the plan because "it makes clear the basis of calling in the Guard."

"Let's plan that," Kennedy said, thereby settling on their scheme. "What do you think first?" Katzenbach said, "I'll take the students in. I will leave them in the car, and they will go to their dormitories thereafter." "And then," Kennedy interjected, "the students will come back and register in the afternoon? Nick, now what are you going to say to him again, now? I know you're going to have to play it a little bit by ear, but I wouldn't take him too seriously; I mean, almost dismiss him as being rather a second-rate figure for you. I mean, he's wasting your time and he's wasting the students' time, and he's caused a big scene up there—you know. I'd have that sort of tone of voice, don't you think? All right," he said evenly, "good luck. You'll do well. It'll work well." Katzenbach nodded, hung up, phoned Doar, and suggested they meet at ten o'clock on the highway outside Tuscaloosa; then the two of them and the two students would proceed to the campus behind a car carrying Norville and a U.S. attorney.[56]

On Tuesday morning, Wallace slept soundly until shortly past eight, then even before he had brushed his teeth, called his press secretary, Bill Jones, and told him to bring to his suite two hometown reporters—Bob Ingram of the *Montgomery Advertiser* and Rex Thomas, the Montgomery bureau chief of the Associated Press. A few minutes later, as the reporters were walking down the hotel corridor toward the governor's room, Wallace stuck his head out the door and shouted, "Bob, you and Rex come on in." He had not yet combed his hair, but he clenched in his teeth the stub of the previous night's cigar. As the reporters followed Wallace into the sitting room, the governor pulled off his pajama top, scratched his somewhat softening middle, and said jokingly, "Boys, I feel a little sick this morning; I think I'll stay in bed today." He walked into the bathroom, lathered his face, and continued to chat over his shoulder while shaving; he told the reporters he had received hundreds of telegrams, mostly favorable. He pushed the door almost closed as he stepped into the shower, but bellowed above the water that he did not anticipate any violence. With only a towel drawn around his middle, he stepped out of the bathroom just as NBC television correspondent Bob Abernethy joined them. As Wallace dressed in the adjoining bedroom, he repeated for Abernethy what he had just told Ingram and Thomas;

he asked Abernethy if he knew whether "they" intended to federalize the National Guard or bring in troops "or what," but Abernethy said he did not know.

Wallace emerged from the bedroom wearing a dark suit, striped tie, and blue shirt; "getting ready for the TV cameras," Thomas said. As friends and aides streamed in and out of the room, a bellman arrived with Wallace's breakfast—two eggs over light, sausage, toast, sweet rolls, milk, and coffee. As he prepared to depart, Wallace's race relations éminence grise, Kohn, walked over to him and said solemnly, "You have divine blessing today. There is absolute peace here. It is a great tribute to this city and to the state. The people have shown great dignity." Then the tall, somewhat formidable Kohn reached down, draped his arm around Wallace's shoulders, and added, "Good luck and may God bless you."[57]

■   ■   ■

Wallace arrived at Foster Auditorium at 9:53 A.M. He climbed out of his limousine and walked alone down the asphalt path lined with state troopers in riot gear—helmets, pistols, gas canisters, and truncheons. Wallace nodded to some of his 150 state patrolmen who were ringing Foster Auditorium and made a special effort to greet many of the 400 reporters who crowded behind the specially drawn white line. Everyone was perspiring in the already broiling sun. But then Wallace went inside an air-conditioned office, stripped off his jacket, and sat down to read that morning's copy of the *Montgomery Advertiser*. Katzenbach was late. He showed up at 10:48 A.M. Jones rushed inside to summon the governor, who donned his suit coat, walked briskly to a lectern set up in front of the entrance to Foster Auditorium, set his speech before him, and allowed Jones to loop a microphone around his neck.

As Katzenbach emerged from an official car, Malone and Hood remained nervously behind. "That was the only time I was really apprehensive," Malone recalled later. "I had in mind the situation at Ole Miss. I sort of expected things might be worse." Katzenbach, flanked by a marshal and a U.S. attorney, approached Wallace, who abruptly raised his left hand in the manner of a traffic cop. Katzenbach and the others stopped. The deputy attorney general identified himself and said, "I have a proclamation from the president of the United States ordering you to cease and desist from unlawful obstructions." Then, crossing his arms across his chest and beginning to sweat in the direct sun, Katzenbach leaned toward the governor and said, "And I've come here to ask you for an unequivocal assurance that you will permit these students who, after all, merely want an education at a great university . . ." Wallace cut him off in midsentence. "Well," Wallace said, his voice flat and hard, "you make this statement, but we don't need for you to make a speech. You make your statement." Katzenbach grew increasingly uncomfortable.[58]

"I wasn't concerned about safety," he said later. "I was nervous because of the public attention and you know that the president's looking." But he responded to Wallace as firmly as his physical and personal uneasiness permitted. "I'll make my statement, Governor," he said. "I was in the process of making my statement. I'm asking from you an unequivocal assurance that you will not bar entry to these students, to Vivian Malone or to James Hood, and that you will step aside peacefully and do your constitutional duty as governor."[59]

Wallace simply ignored Katzenbach's request and said, "I have a statement to read." Wallace then launched into a thousand-word statement and proclamation that kept Katzenbach and the others sweltering for nearly fifteen minutes. He began by saying that as the governor and chief magistrate, he was representing "the rights and sovereignty" of Alabamians. He continued:

> The unwelcome, unwanted, unwarranted, and force-induced
> intrusion upon the campus of the University of Alabama
> today of the might of the central government offers a
> frightful example of oppression of the rights, privileges,
> and sovereignty of this state by officers of the federal govern-
> ment. This intrusion results solely from force, undignified
> by any reasonable application of the principle of law,
> reason, and justice.[60]

After casting himself as the aggrieved party, Wallace maintained, "While some few may applaud these acts, millions of Americans will gaze in sorrow upon the situation." He then recited, in arduous detail, his version of the history of the U.S. Constitution regarding state sovereignty, and repeated several times that he was representing "thousands of other Alabamians" who would have confronted Katzenbach had it not been for the governor's intervention. And he maintained that his action was not "defiance for defiance sake, but for the purpose of raising basic and fundamental constitutional questions." Years later, Katzenbach said he was thinking that Wallace's "was a ridiculous course. All this business about wanting to make a constitutional point; he had no constitutional point that hadn't been made before. . . . Wallace was making the same argument that had been made a hundred years before." More than anything, however, Katzenbach wanted it to be over. Then, finally, it was. Wallace looked up from his text and said, "I hereby denounce and forbid this illegal and unwarranted action by the central government." He stepped back sharply as if to punctuate his closing assertion.[61]

It took a moment for Katzenbach to realize that Wallace had finished. With his arms still folded across his chest, he said, "Governor Wallace, I take it from that statement that you are going to stand in that door and that you are not going to carry out the orders of this court and you are going to resist us from doing so. Is that correct?" "I stand upon this statement," Wallace said. A disdainful smile crossed Katzenbach's lips. "You stand upon that statement," he repeated. "Governor, I'm not interested in a show. I don't know what the purpose of the show is. I am interested in the orders of this court being enforced. That is my only responsibility here. I ask you once more. The choice is yours. There is no choice that the United States government has in this but to see that the lawful orders of this court are enforced." Wallace stood mute, his jaw jutting belligerently. Twice more, Katzenbach asked Wallace to remove himself, but the governor, standing rigidly, stared past him.

At last, Katzenbach leaned forward and said sharply, that the students "will register today to go to school tomorrow and go to school this summer." Then he mumbled, "Very well," turned abruptly, and, trailed by the marshal and the U.S. attorney, walked back to the car. He said he would escort Malone to her dormitory, and he directed Doar to take Hood to the dormitory to which he had been assigned. In Robert Kennedy's office in Washington, the attorney general and several aides and secretaries stood listening to a radio commentator provide a running account of events in Tuscaloosa. When the reporter announced that the students, having been refused entrance to Foster Auditorium, had nonetheless entered their dormitories, Kennedy smiled broadly and the others joined in a collective sigh of relief. But they knew the greatest potential for disruption lay ahead.[62]

Doar and Hood entered the men's dormitory without incident; in fact, it appeared to Doar as if the white students were consciously ignoring them. Katzenbach, however, remained wary of possible hostile, if not violent, behavior as he approached Malone's dormitory building. "I had to go right through that line of forest rangers to get to her dormitory," Katzenbach said later, referring to the green-uniformed Alabama game wardens recruited for special campus duty. "We got into the dormitory, and the housemother was there where everybody was waiting." The housemother, whom Katzenbach recalled as "exactly what you'd expect"—white hair, grandmotherly dress, gentle face—found herself surrounded by dozens of serious-looking white men and one lone, slim, pretty young black woman; the older woman approached Malone and made perhaps the most self-evident observation since Stanley met Livingstone: "Ah," she said, "you must be Vivian."[63]

Katzenbach suggested that Malone go to her room and then come back down and eat lunch in the dormitory cafeteria. As she neared her room, Malone recalled, "some girls were sitting on the floor of the lounge to greet me. They asked me about playing bridge with them. . . . Some girls came by the room and said they were glad I could come there—that they thought they would profit by it personally." To be sure, there would be loneliness and some slights and very little opportunity to socialize, but "this happening the very first day, you know—it was very encouraging; it gave me a kind of added stimulus,"[64] she recalled. After freshening up, Malone went to the cafeteria and entered alone. Rose had strongly cautioned Katzenbach to discourage Malone from dining with the white girls, at least until a few days had passed, but Katzenbach was adamant that she assert her equality as soon as possible. "I'm not putting that off one minute," he recalled telling Rose. "That's what's going to happen in the future, and it's going to happen right now." Watching from the cafeteria entrance, Katzenbach said that Malone "took a tray and went over and sat down at an empty table—and in thirty seconds, half a dozen girls had gotten up and gone over. It was really very, very moving."[65]

In Washington, Marshall phoned Katzenbach's Tuscaloosa headquarters. He asked a marshal to raise the deputy attorney general on the car radio so that Kennedy could get a final report before asking his brother to nationalize the guard. Katzenbach's driver summoned him from the dormitory to the car. Over the radio, the marshal transmitted Marshall's question: Did Katzenbach expect any trouble? Katzenbach replied, somewhat vaguely, "I do not presently expect any problem, but they're probably thinking." "Ten-four," the marshal said, and relayed the comment, with some unintended alterations, to Washington. Marshall, looking puzzled, said into the mouthpiece, " 'He is not expecting any trouble but the people here think he is?' That's a garbled answer." He looked up at Kennedy. "Can we get Nick on the phone? Why don't we just go ahead and do it?" "Because," Kennedy said firmly, "I want to find out what the governor says."[66]

Katzenbach returned to his office to advise Kennedy to nationalize the guard; he said that anything could happen, but that judging by Wallace's earlier behavior, he did not expect violence. Kennedy then called the White House and told the president to sign the executive order federalizing the Alabama National Guard. General Abrams was assigned the task of ordering Lt. Gen. Henry Graham to active duty. Abrams, dressed in mufti, as he had been throughout the Tuscaloosa crisis ("he was the least 'general' general I've ever seen," Katzenbach recalled), was about to leave for the National Guard armory when his aide stopped him and asked, "General, I assume this will be in uniform?" Abrams shook his head and said, "Aw, no. Henry knows who I am."[67]

During the time the black students were checking into their dormitory rooms and Katzenbach was setting the wheels in motion for the president to federalize the guard, Wallace was holding forth in his makeshift Foster Auditorium office, to which he had returned after Katzenbach's departure. Wallace was relieved and jubilant. "I think we got the better of that, don't you?" he asked his smiling friends and assistants. No one contradicted him. "You made good on your promise," one said. "You stood in the schoolhouse door." They heard that the guard was being federalized. Wallace turned to two of his military aides. "I guess you've gone from my side to their side," he said with a cackle. Then Wallace summoned the *Montgomery Advertiser* reporter Bob Ingram; he wanted Ingram to explain to the national press the reasons for his stand. "I hope they understand," he said, "I am not against any person, white or black. I only seek to raise constitutional questions and to take some action which might call the nation's attention to the encroachments of the federal government."

Shortly before 3:00 P.M., Albert Lingo rushed into the room to tell Wallace that a hundred federalized troops were only minutes away. Wallace donned his suit coat and walked back outside. This time, Katzenbach remained out of sight. Graham, accompanied by four armed enlisted men, stepped vigorously along the path. Graham—tall, straight-backed, dressed in combat drab with the Confederate flag of the Thirty-first Division (called the Dixie Division) stitched to his breast pocket—stopped three feet in front of Wallace, saluted, and said, "Sir, it is my sad duty to ask you to step aside under orders from the president of the United States." After a moment's hesitation, Wallace snappily returned the salute and said, "General, I want to make a statement." "Certainly, sir," Graham replied, and moved to one side. Glancing at notes scribbled on a calendar pad, Wallace characterized the federalization of the guard as an "unwarranted . . . bitter pill" for Alabama guardsmen to swallow and called on Alabamians to remain "calm and restrained." He concluded by maintaining, "Alabama is winning this fight against federal interference because we are awakening the people to the trend toward military dictatorship in this country. We shall now return to Montgomery to continue this constitutional fight." He turned and walked quickly to an awaiting state patrol car.[68]

In Robert Kennedy's office, there were sighs of relief all around as the radio reporter announced that Wallace had stepped aside. A reporter shoved a microphone at Wallace, now seated in the rear of the patrol car. Wallace said firmly, "We're winning." Listening in Washington, Kennedy allowed himself a small smile. Wallace continued to speak to reporters: "I just hope that you'll come back to see us in Alabama. . . . The South next year will decide who the next president is. Whoever the South votes for will be the next president, because you can't win without the South. And you're going to see that the South is going to be against some folks." As the car started rolling past the huge crowd of students and townspeople who had been kept far from the scene of the confrontation, an enormous roar of approval filled Wallace's ears. He felt a surge of triumph, but he revealed a hint of bitterness when he said, "We had peace, but we got troops. No telling what we'd get if we had a little disorder. Might get the United Nations down on top of us." As Wallace was leaving, Hood and Malone entered the auditorium separately and registered. Both would be accompanied by bodyguards throughout the summer term. A contingent of guardsmen remained on active duty for the rest of the year.[69]

Hood left the university after the summer semester and transferred to Wayne State University, where he completed his undergraduate studies. He did graduate work at Michigan State University and Cambridge in England, entered law enforcement in Michigan, and switched to public education in Wisconsin. A quarter of a century after his historic enrollment, Hood said he would not have done it over again: "I was not prepared for what I experienced, in terms of of having the mind-set to endure the isolation. That was stifling for me." In addition, Hood was troubled that his unwanted presence "negatively affected . . . a lot of people." He reflected, "I was more concerned about 'me' than I was about the impact I had on others." Interestingly, Hood grew to admire Wallace as "one of the most astute Southern politicians that this country will ever know." Although he did not agree with Wallace's attempt to deny him entry to the University of Alabama, Hood maintained that Wallace's position "had nothing to do with race" but, rather, with constitutional questions, just as Wallace asserted. Hood even called Wallace's act "courageous" and "very noble" because the governor had been ready to risk being jailed to keep his promise to his constituents and raise the issue of states' rights. And Hood did not think Wallace was a racist. "I think all of us are racists, if you really want to be honest. I think the problem of racism is an ingrained idea that people have and are willing to deny another whatever is justly theirs simply because of color. I don't think George Wallace did that." Malone, on the other hand, believed that Wallace's stance was all about race. But, unlike Hood, she persevered at the university and, two years after her admittance, became its first black graduate. She married and had children, and among other professional positions she undertook, she became the executive director of the Voter Education Project, which was responsible for registering millions of Southern blacks as voters.[70]

■   ■   ■

President Kennedy's assessment of the issue was very clear. The president used the occasion to deliver one of the most eloquent and moving speeches in America's history. In a firm yet gentle tone, devoid of preaching, Kennedy looked into a television camera the night of Wallace's stand and asked that every American "stop and examine his conscience":

> This nation was founded by men of many nations and
> backgrounds. It was founded on the principle that all men are
> created equal and the rights of every man are diminished
> when the rights of one man are threatened. We are confronted
> primarily with a moral issue. It is as old as the Scriptures and
> as clear as the American constitution. The heart of the

question is whether all Americans are to be afforded equal rights and equal opportunities, whether we are going to treat our fellow Americans as we want to be treated. If an American, because his skin is dark, cannot enjoy the full and free life which all of us want, then who among us would be content to have the color of his skin changed and stand in his place? Who among us would then be content with the counsel of patience and delay? A hundred years of delay have passed since President Lincoln freed the slaves, yet their heirs—their grandsons—are not fully freed. They are not yet freed from the bonds of injustice. They are not yet freed from social and economic oppression. And this nation—for all its hopes and all its boasts—will not be fully free until all its citizens are free. We face, therefore, a moral crisis as a country and a people. It is time to act—in the Congress, in your state and local legislative body, but, most of all, in all our daily lives.[71]

"It was by far the strongest speech [on civil rights] that ever had been made by any president," Katzenbach declared. "I think it's a very proud moment in our history." To all outward appearances, Wallace had been beaten. As the historian and Kennedy family friend William Manchester observed, "The Kennedys thought [Wallace] had been made to look ludicrous, and the country would see his posturing for the absurdity it was. Millions of Americans agreed, and since more than three hundred blacks enrolled in the university after Hood and Malone without incident—indeed, without a word or even a glance from the statehouse—it appeared that the governor had been outwitted." But years later, Robert Kennedy came to understand that Wallace "did not fear defeat as a political pitfall. . . . In the past, defeat had been imposed upon Alabama, and in a way, [the] good fight and a noble defeat . . . had a redemptive quality." As Marshall Frady observed shrewdly, it was clear that Wallace "had discovered a dark, silent, brooding mass of people whom no one— the newspapers, the political leaders, the intellectuals—no one but Wallace had suspected were there."[72]

Without question, Wallace sniffed the rich, heady aroma of potential national political power. He had faced down the federal dragon, retreating only before the threat of military force—and he had accomplished his mission without the hint of violence. He was on a roll.

But he did not know when to quit. As summer turned to fall, he persisted in resisting school integration, using troopers and bold rhetoric to delay temporarily his preordained defeats—but maintaining always that resistance to federal force really meant victory. What he did not count on was that his calls for peace would sound progressively emptier, more like persiflage than serious statements—the kind of language needed to show good intentions to the outside world while surreptitiously winking and giving his friends a gentle poke in the ribs. In a few months, he would learn the bitter lesson that the language and actions of defiance are difficult, if not impossible, to contain.

10

The Turning Point

A *QUARTER OF A CENTURY* after his stand in the school-house door, George Wallace lamented, "It will probably be my legacy that this sensational thing we pulled at the University of Alabama will probably obliterate all the good we've done since those days." He insisted frequently that his action was predicated on states' rights and that the state of Alabama would have allowed the university to be integrated the following year. Additionally, Wallace wanted it remembered that he had preserved the peace; in the only potentially fractious incident in connection with the confrontation, a car carrying armed people (whom Wallace described as "Minutemen from California" who were "tools of the Communist party") was detained by state troopers. Its occupants were jailed, their weapons were confiscated, and they were ordered to leave the state—"And," Wallace said, "I don't think they ever did come back." He even ordered round-the-clock surveillance of Vivian Malone's dormitory to guard against "anybody that threw a firecracker or made an obscene remark or made any noise or racial slur or anything." After the surveillance detail had hidden behind bushes and hedges for four days and nights, its leader phoned Wallace, "saying nobody was going to do any of those things [Wallace] was afraid they might do . . . and they wanted to come home; they were being eaten up by mosquitos." At Wallace's urging, they remained one more day and night. All the same, Wallace said he came to regret the action: "I made a very bad mistake in saying 'segregation forever'—[and] that day at the University of Alabama, carried nationwide [on radio and television], gave me a bad image and was not good for the state's image. . . . If I had it to do over, I would not have stood in the schoolhouse door at all; I would have prevented violence on the campus in some other manner."[1]

Wallace's sentiments in his later years had been less a reflection of an intellectual or political judgment than of a powerful, emotional desire to be "rehabilitated" by history.[2] In the three days following his highly publicized attempt to defy federal authority, Wallace's office was inundated with more than forty thousand letters and telegrams, the vast majority of which were supportive. Even more remarkable was that more than half the communications came from areas outside the South.[3] In addition, Wallace received hundreds of speaking invitations, many from illustrious universities including Stamford, Northwestern, and Princeton, handing him a prestigious national platform that otherwise would have been denied him.[4] Indeed, the widespread favorable national reaction to the stand buoyed Wallace's spirits so much that he began thinking the unthinkable—that a man who had been the governor of a small Southern state for less than six months might one day soon make a serious presidential run. He laid the groundwork by asking the state legislature to amend the state constitution so he could succeed himself. He reasoned that if he wanted to make a full-blown run at the presidency in 1968, he would need his incumbency to build on.[5] And before 1963 was out, he was proclaiming publicly that he might even run in the following year's Democratic presidential primaries.[6]

Wallace's nationally televised performance allowed him to boast that he had "stood eyeball to eyeball" with federal authorities who had been "turned back." Much of the public accepted Wallace's version of events because his statement of defiance and Katzenbach's departure were seen by millions on television but the subsequent registration of the two students, portraying ultimate victory for the government, occurred off camera. Additionally, the absence of violence and disorder lent credence to Wallace's claim that he had been raising a constitutional, not a racial challenge.[7] But then everything changed.

The night of Wallace's "stand" and President Kennedy's civil rights speech, Medgar Evers, the NAACP field secretary in Mississippi, was shot in the back by a sniper lying in wait near Evers's home.[8] Evers's murder occurred during a national eruption of civil rights demonstrations and militant black demands in hundreds of communities; the wide-ranging racial traumas helped to dilute antagonism toward a single state or its governor. Between early May and late July, protests were mounted in cities as diverse and scattered as Tallahassee, Philadelphia, and San Francisco. In the South, street fighting broke out between those protesting segregated restaurants and white hecklers. A white man was killed in Lexington, North Carolina, during riots triggered by antisegregation demonstrations. The National Guard was sent into Cambridge, Maryland, to quell racial unrest that had simmered for months. Clashes between police and antisegregation marchers in Danville, Virginia, resulted in injuries to more than forty people and hundreds of arrests. In Selma, Alabama, Sheriff Jim Clark, who had led his cadres to Birmingham and other Alabama trouble spots to defend segregation, ruthlessly suppressed black voter registration efforts.

Welling emotions at Evers's funeral in Jackson nearly erupted into what might have been the bloodiest episode of all. A hundred black youths, backed up by thousands of other black mourners, defied a court order against demonstrations by marching downtown and spontaneously breaking into freedom songs. They came nose to nose with a phalanx of policemen armed with shotguns and backed up by dogs and fire hoses. When some of the young black protesters started throwing rocks, several were clubbed to the ground and about thirty were dragged away and arrested. A full-scale riot seemed inevitable when the Justice Department's John Doar, who had worked with Evers and considered him a friend, walked into the midst of the angry crowd and, in a singular act of courage, attempted to calm mounting passions. With bricks and bottles crashing around him, Doar shouted and spelled his name, and said, "Anybody around here knows that I stand for what's right." He walked into the crowd, assuring one and all that local black leaders whom he knew wanted them to disperse and go home. To the amazement of the police and reporters on the scene, they did.[9]

Racial protest and tension were as prevalent outside the South as within it—and that fact provided fuel for Wallace's assertion that race was a national problem, not a sectional one. Job discrimination allegations provoked clashes between police and protesters in Philadelphia; making similar allegations in Brooklyn, New York, black protesters chained themselves together to prevent workers from entering building sites. Demonstrations against de facto school segregation were mounted in Englewood and Jersey City, New Jersey, and in

New York, Cleveland, and Chicago. (In the fall, 225,000 students boycotted Chicago's public schools and, in October, 10,000 people marched to the offices of the city's board of education to demand racial equity. After blacks demonstrated in front of the White House, members of the American Nazi party—wearing jackboots and swastika armbands—staged a counterdemonstration. In Harlem, grocery stores carrying Sealtest dairy products were picketed because of the company's alleged discriminatory hiring practices. And in Los Angeles, the actor Marlon Brando joined in a protest march against a segregated housing development.[10] And just three days after he had masterminded the government's success in enrolling the black students at the University of Alabama, Robert Kennedy was confronted by angry civil rights demonstrators who maintained that the Justice Department itself was guilty of employment discrimination.[11]

The climax of the summer's demonstrations came on August 28 when more than 200,000 people, the largest crowd to assemble in Washington to that time, gathered on the mall stretching from the Lincoln Memorial to the Capitol to display their commitment to civil rights; the most memorable moment came when Martin Luther King, Jr., enthralled the multitude with his moving "I have a dream" speech.[12]

Wallace profited from the jackhammer of civil rights news by veiling his own dramatic action with the wispy mists of memory. People remembered a cocky, strong-voiced governor standing up to a big, hulking man representing a big, hulking government and forcing both to back away, albeit for only a few hours. And most people either did not know or did not care about the irony of ironies—that within a year, Wallace's Alabama was integrating at a rate as fast as or faster than most other states in the Union, much less the South. As the respected Southern journalist Pat Watters observed:

> In the basics of desegregation, things were little or no better—
> indeed, could be worse—under moderate governors than
> under ultra-racist ones. . . . George Wallace, when he was
> governor, was [an] example *par excellence* of the recalcitrant
> segregationist who, by forcing the federal government to act,
> did more to advance the Negro cause than the most fervent
> of civil rights advocates. . . . Alabama was the first state to
> go under an all-inclusive federal court order that said
> integration's meaning included white children going to

formerly all-Negro schools—real abolishment of the dual
system. Sadly, what became most clear during the little time of
transition when moderates seemed in ascendancy in the South
was that all the federal forces . . . wanted from the states was
mere lip service to that ideal [of] enforcing the sweeping
social law to pry Southern society open [and] an absence of
publicity-creating confrontations of state and federal power.
Thus, if holding on to as much as possible of the old system of
segregation was the main purpose of Southern racist voters,
they were better served by men who caused Washington no
trouble—who, in effect, conformed to national hypocritical
standards on race, mouthing equality but doing virtually
nothing to achieve it [and] allowing ghastly conditions to
fester on unseen.[13]

Just two days after the suspense and histrionics of Tuscaloosa,
David McGlathery, a black mathematician at the U.S. Space Flight
Center in Huntsville, enrolled for a night course at the University of
Alabama extension there. Except for a few policemen who stationed
themselves at a discreet distance from the school offices, there was
no state or local presence. McGlathery walked in alone, registered,
and began attending classes the following week without incident.[14]
Thousands would follow Malone, Hood, and McGlathery—all without incident and in numbers significantly exceeding the national
average.

■   ■   ■

Wallace was not seriously troubled by the reality of integration; over
the years, he conceded time and again that he knew segregation was
doomed—and that he had known it even at the moment he was
vowing there would be "segregation forever." His authentic concern
was for the political capital he could earn in the South by attacking
integration (even if it meant hastening its arrival by forcing federal
action in Alabama) and the prominence he could attract throughout
America by turning the issue away from race and toward Big Brother
incursions on the states—them versus us.

His opening post-Tuscaloosa publicity gambit was vintage Wallace, allowing him to revile integration and its supporters in the
harshest terms while diverting attention to a seeming federal folly. It
came during Senate hearings on the civil rights bill that President

Kennedy had announced on the fateful Tuscaloosa night. The president had proposed the bill at his brother's urging and over the objections of several advisers who feared that the fiery controversy it was bound to ignite would sink the rest of the administration's legislative program. But Robert Kennedy was convinced, as Arthur Schlesinger, Jr., wrote, that "Bull Connor and George Wallace had at last made civil rights a legislative possibility."[15] The bill provided equal access to places of public accommodation, contained voting rights proposals, authorized the attorney general to sue for school desegregation, and barred the use of federal funds in discriminatory state or local activities. Despite major omissions from the bill—notably, a fair employment practices provision—it was at the time, as the White House adviser Joseph Rauh said, "the most comprehensive civil rights bill ever to receive serious consideration from the Congress of the United States."[16]

For his Washington forum, Wallace could choose between two Senate committees conducting hearings on the civil rights bill—the friendly confines of the Senate Judiciary Committee, chaired by Mississippi's Sen. James O. Eastland, or the less hospitable Senate Commerce Committee, led by Washington's Sen. Warren Magnuson. The Senate Judiciary Committee hearings were receiving most of the media's attention, especially the jousts between the attorney general and his chief inquisitors, the venerable Southern senators Sam Ervin of North Carolina and Richard B. Russell of Georgia. Not only did Wallace not want to risk being upstaged by the folksy Ervin or the revered Russell, but the Commerce Committee was where the real action was: all Washington knew that Eastland's committee, which never had allowed a civil rights measure to reach the full Senate for a vote, was not about to approve the president's proposals. So Wallace chose Magnuson's committee, which was much less hostile both to Robert Kennedy and to the administration bill. But Wallace was not without his allies on the committee, most notably Sen. Strom Thurmond of South Carolina, who had run for president in 1948 on the so-called Dixiecrat ticket. While he was preparing his testimony, Wallace spoke to Thurmond about strategy. With his unerring instinct for news, Wallace thought the two Southerners could grab a headline. He was right. His testimony, which came barely a month after his stand in the schoolhouse door, returned him to front pages across the nation—including the top of page one in the *New York Times*.[17]

He opened his testimony by accusing the federal government of misusing blacks "for selfish political reasons," going "to ridiculous extremes and [taking] unheard-of actions to appease the minority bloc-vote leaders of this country."

> I was appalled and amazed to read of recent statements by Pentagon officials [using] the threat of withdrawal of military bases to accomplish political purposes. . . . The Air Force is encouraging its personnel to engage in street demonstrations with rioting mobs and is even offering training credits as an inducement. Perhaps we will now see Purple Hearts awarded for street brawling.

To be sure, Wallace was engaging in some hyperbole. The U.S. Air Force had directed its commands in the United States to permit participation in demonstrations by servicemen, provided they were off duty, wearing civilian clothes, and facing no danger of injuring themselves or damaging any government property. Still, Magnuson seemed surprised by Wallace's allegations; when he demanded to know who had issued such an order, Thurmond produced two instructions issued by the commanding officer of an air force installation in South Carolina. The first prohibited members of his command from participating in demonstrations: the second—issued less than three weeks later—retracted the first on orders from the Pentagon that had been issued just after the president's nationally televised address on civil rights. The air force order, however, "permitted" rather than "encouraged" participation, and did not offer any training credits. But those details did nothing to discourage Wallace or diminish the press coverage.

On the civil rights bill itself, Wallace condemned it in terms that would become familiar in succeeding years as he intensified his national political roadshow:

> These so-called demonstrators break laws, destroy property, injure innocent people, and create civil strife and disorder of major proportions. Yet, they receive sympathy and approval of the leaders of our federal government. . . . I resent the fawning and pawing over such people as Martin Luther King and his pro-communist friends and associates. . . . [This bill] places upon all businessmen and professional people the yoke of involuntary servitude. . . . The lawyer, doctor, hairdresser or barber, plumber, public secretary–stenographer, etcetera, would no longer be free to choose their clientele. . . . this

legislation . . . invited the Negro to come North to a land of milk and honey . . . and instead of finding this Utopia, they have found unemployment. They have been stacked in ghettos on top of one another. . . . [T]his gross hypocrisy has brought guerrilla warfare and insurrection to every large city in the United States, endangering the lives of millions of our citizens. Because of this hypocritical spectacle, [the Negro] no longer wants mere equal treatment; he expects, and apparently intends, to bludgeon the majority of this country's citizens into giving him preferential treatment. . . . If you intend to pass this bill, you should make preparations to withdraw all our troops from Berlin, Vietnam, and the rest of the world because they will be needed to police America.[18]

Wallace never expected to change anyone's position on the civil rights bill—least of all, that of Northern senators, whether Democrats or Republicans. But he had achieved his objectives—gaining more national publicity and highlighting yet another indicator of federal duplicity and intrusiveness. And his triumph was completed a few days later when Secretary of Defense Robert S. McNamara issued a memorandum reversing the air force edict and acknowledging that the policy had been a mistake:

While the Congress is considering legislation to end the injustices which originated these demonstrations and this department is implementing the recommendations of the president's committee on equal opportunity in the Armed Forces relating to off-base discrimination, it is highly inappropriate and unnecessary for military personnel, with their special obligations of citizenship, to participate in these activities. I urge every man and woman in uniform to conduct himself accordingly.[19]

■   ■   ■

Back in Montgomery, Wallace had no intention of leaving well enough alone by allowing justice to take its arduously slow path toward token integration in the public schools. He believed he had an obligation to pursue at the public school level the schoolhouse-stand strategy that he had initiated at the university; it had not prevented integration, but it certainly had spawned widespread publicity and revealed surprisingly broad political support for Wallace's defiance of federal authority. So he and his anti-integration team of Kohn, Trammell, and Lingo laid plans for the inevitable federal court order requiring integration of Alabama's public schools.[20] They were certain that Judge Frank Johnson would find Alabama's pupil-placement law constitutionally wanting, even though a three-judge federal court panel earlier had refused to toss it out as unconstitutional on its face, and the panel's ruling had been subsequently upheld by the Supreme Court.[21] On August 13, Johnson met Wallace's expectations. He ruled that "an honest and fair application" of the placement law would "result in the immediate admission of a number of qualified Negro students" to currently all-white schools in Macon County, Alabama, whose seat was Tuskegee. Johnson ordered the Macon County school board to start desegregating the schools when the fall term opened the following month, and to submit a general desegregation plan before Christmas.[22]

To Wallace's surprise, the school board chose not to appeal. Macon County's white power structure seemingly had been wearied by an effective two-year boycott of white-owned businesses mounted in retaliation for voting rights discrimination. The overwhelmingly black population in the county (blacks outnumbered whites 22,000 to 5,000) had succeeded in shutting down sixteen establishments, and a score more were in trouble. So the school board agreed to accept 13 of 48 black applicants to join the 570 white students at Tuskegee High School. And in the wake of Johnson's ruling, federal judges elsewhere in the state ordered the immediate desegregation of public schools in Birmingham and Mobile; the Huntsville school board, meanwhile, announced that it would begin desegregation voluntarily. But Wallace was not having any such compliance; he claimed that violence was imminent. Years later he said, "A group came to see me from Bessemer [on the outskirts of Birmingham] volunteering to help maintain order. I thanked them and told them they were not needed now—but if I needed them, I'd call. 'Don't do anything 'til I call,' I said. They trusted me. Now, if I would not have stood in the door, I couldn't have kept those people out—and some of them were mean folks. I could not have kept the peace."[23]

But when school opened on Monday, September 2, no public official in Tuskegee either expected trouble or thought it necessary to prepare for any. They were thus astonished when they learned that more than one hundred blue-helmeted state troopers, under Lingo's command, had descended on Tuskegee at 6:25 A.M. and ringed the high school. Five minutes later, the Tuskegee police chief, O. L.

Hodnett, was awakened by a caller who asked, "Did you know the patrol was in town?" Hodnett, who had not known, notified Mayor Howard Rutherford of the seemingly manufactured crisis; both rushed to the school, where Lingo handed each a copy of Wallace's executive order closing the school for a week to keep "the peace and tranquility of this state." When troopers refused entrance to a dozen students, including the student council president, Rutherford said acerbically, "I've heard about states' rights—but I wonder if there are any cities' rights?" At Wallace's request, Huntsville officials agreed to delay from Tuesday until Friday the opening of schools scheduled to be desegregated. He struck a similar deal with Mobile school leaders: the two blacks assigned to all-white schools would be permitted to register at city school board offices, but as in Huntsville, the schools would remain closed until Friday. Wallace's thinly veiled objective was to provoke the president into using federal troops or deputies to force any public school integration; that way, he could continue to claim that he yielded only in the face of overwhelming strength.[24]

On Tuesday, Lingo ordered a token force of twenty-five troopers to maintain segregation at Tuskegee High. Meanwhile, he assembled another 450 troopers in Birmingham, where Wallace had ordered him to prevent five black children from integrating three public schools scheduled to open the next day. But late Tuesday afternoon, Birmingham's city council urged in a formal resolution that Wallace keep his troopers out: "We have confidence in the ability of our local law enforcement agencies to protect the lives and property of our people and to maintain law and order."[25]

Chastised two days running for interfering in local affairs, Wallace reluctantly instructed Lingo to keep his men in their hotels when the schools opened on Wednesday morning. Wallace was not pleased, especially considering that the presence of state troopers in Birmingham was much easier for him to justify than at Tuskegee, Huntsville, or Mobile. Not only had Birmingham's civil rights activists endured ferocious attacks during the Freedom Rides and sit-ins of the previous two years, but the homes and churches of middle-class blacks had been the targets of two dozen unsolved bombings over the past seven years; the hardest-hit area was nicknamed, with gallows humor, "Dynamite Hill."[26] Violence in Birmingham over school integration could reasonably be expected. But the harried Birmingham mayor, Albert Boutwell, was convinced that the best hope for peace was to keep outsiders away—and that meant not just troops sent in by Washington but those ordered in by Montgomery. Boutwell's refusal to honor the governor's request to delay the school openings angered Wallace, who was livid when he learned of the city council's public rebuff. He snapped that Boutwell was "weak" (a view, interestingly, shared by Martin Luther King, Jr.) and that without the state troopers, he would "reap the whirlwind." In the end, Boutwell lost his nerve and sought a last-minute court-ordered delay of the school opening; his plea for the court to consider new evidence of "inherent differences in the races" was, predictably, turned down.

Just as predictably, the school openings did not go smoothly. Noisy knots of demonstrators scared off the three black students due at two high schools, but the two elementary school students— brothers who lived near the all-white school—slipped in a side door and were registered. That night, however, despite carloads of black volunteers patrolling Dynamite Hill, night riders tossed a bomb into the front yard of a black lawyer, Arthur Shores, whose home was still being repaired from a bomb attack two weeks earlier. Shores was unhurt, but his wife suffered a concussion when a light fixture fell on her head. Worse, the explosion triggered an outpouring of blacks running angrily through the streets, throwing rocks and glass at police and white passersby. Most police—but not all—responded by firing shotguns and rifles into the air. When the disturbances were quelled, one black man lay dead and twenty-one other blacks were hurt and wounded. After an all-night exchange of telephone calls with Wallace, Boutwell agreed to close the affected schools "temporarily" and to allow Lingo's troopers to seal them the next day.[27]

On Thursday, Wallace arrived at his capitol office wearing dark glasses to cover eyes red and puffed from a sleepless night. Although he had succeeded in persuading Boutwell to close the three Birmingham schools that were to be integrated, he failed with the school boards in Huntsville and Mobile, both of which refused to extend their earlier concessions. So Wallace instructed Lingo to continue the state patrol's "strike, occupy, and move" strategy; just as Lingo had left a token force in Tuskegee to surround the high school while moving a massive force to Birmingham, he now left 50 troopers at the three Birmingham schools while relocating 400 men to Huntsville and Mobile. In addition, Wallace directed aides to confer with lawyers to develop a battery of suits that might further delay integration.[28]

Wallace was tired. He was frustrated at the Huntsville and Mobile school officials' recalcitrance toward his demands that they close the schools scheduled for integration. Weariness and anger combined to make his mood more combative and more apocalyptic than usual. He paced back and forth, telling a reporter, "The society is coming apart at the seams. What good is it doing to force these situations when white people nowhere in the South want integration? [Federal officials] should recognize reality instead of letting theorists decide these things." Then he made a remark that he would come to regret in the days ahead, even though he meant it only as a warning of voter rebellion. "What this country needs," he said, "is a few first-class funerals, and some political funerals, too." And, later, after a news conference at which he firmly abhorred the violence in Birmingham, he told reporters that whites who physically resist racial integration "are not thugs; they are good working people who get mad when they see something like this happen." And then, as if whites and not blacks had been victimized by aggressive police tactics, Wallace added, "It takes courage to stand up to tear gas and bayonets."[29]

When the troopers arrived in Mobile, school officials there eased away from their resistance to Wallace; they agreed to a weekend "cooling-off" period through an agreement in which schools would open on Friday, troopers would stay away, and the black enrollees-to-be would remain home. But in Huntsville, officials stood fast, and troopers ringed the four schools scheduled for integration. Some white parents bearded the troopers; a mother, speaking for fifty children and parents lined up behind her, told a trooper, "I want to go in. Will you hurt us if we try?" The trooper, Lt. Maurice Chambers, replied respectfully, "No, ma'am," and he stepped aside as the group filed in. Then he called for additional troopers, whose presence discouraged anyone else—including the blacks—from attempting to enter.[30] Newspaper editorials throughout the state and most of the rest of the South expressed puzzlement, chagrin, or outrage. The *Knoxville News-Sentinel* said that Wallace "continues to bring disgrace on his office and his state." The *Houston Press* called Wallace "the principal menace to peace and order in Alabama." In Alabama, the *Anniston Star* accused Wallace of "reckless asininity."[31] But the unkindest cut of all, from Wallace's perspective, came from his sometime adviser and usual admirer Grover Hall in the *Montgomery Advertiser*:

> Wallace has dispatched state troopers to Mobile and
> Huntsville to usurp local power by force. . . . *The Advertiser*
> must sorrowfully conclude that, in this instance, its friend
> has gone wild. Alabama is not a banana republic. It is in no
> need of an adventurer to ride down upon local authority.[32]

Before dawn on Sunday, another bombing racked Dynamite Hill—this one at the home of the sixty-one-year-old black businessman A. G. Gaston. No one was injured, but Wallace's response was to go on statewide television that afternoon to reassert his determination to thwart public school desegregation. But he softened his tone slightly by saying, "We are going to resist . . . lawfully and legally, and we are going to have law and order." But no one, including Wallace, knew precisely what his next move would be. When he left the Birmingham television studio, he conferred at the Redmont Hotel with a quickly assembled panel of lawyers about the steps he might take. But the only hint of what action the governor might take was outlined by a panel member, the state Sen. James A. Simpson: "Let us go no further and no faster in the direction of error than we are forced to go by the overwhelming power of the federal government. As soon as the pressure is relaxed, let us recede as far and as rapidly as we can to a posture of common sense."

Local officials, like everyone else, remained in the dark. Authorities in all four beleaguered cities planned to open the schools on an integrated basis the next day, Monday. The Huntsville school superintendent said Wallace, in a telegram, had pledged not to interfere. The mayor of Mobile said his city's schools would open, but he admitted, "I don't know what to expect now. . . . The governor has not informed anyone of his plans, including those who must keep law and order." But Hall, in a Sunday editorial, predicted confidently that "a week of folly in Alabama is ended. Monday will see the state troopers again protecting motorists."[33]

Alas, Hall must have been talking to the wrong source at the capitol. As Monday's dawn was breaking in Birmingham, Wallace signed three executive orders permitting schools to reopen in Birmingham, Tuskegee, and Mobile—but directing troopers to bar entrance to the twenty black students assigned to attend previously all-white schools. (For unexplained reasons, he overlooked Huntsville; four schools were integrated peacefully there by four black children, who were unimpeded by state troopers. Years later, Wallace said he capitulated to the near unanimity of public opposition in Huntsville, a city with thousands of parents imported from many Northern and Western states to high-paying, high-tech federal jobs.)[34] Unlike Wallace's previous claims that violence over school integration was imminent, the new orders simply asserted, "forced and unwarranted integration of the public schools . . . will totally disrupt and effectively destroy the educational process and constitutes an abridgement of the civil rights of other children." The reasoning behind the executive orders was lifted from a decision handed down by a federal judge in Georgia—a decision subsequently reversed by the U.S. Court of Appeals for the Fifth Circuit.

Seemingly untroubled by adopting discredited legalisms, Wallace ordered Lingo to disperse his troopers at the schools scheduled for integration everywhere except Huntsville. At Murphy High School in Mobile, 175 troopers under Maj. Joe Smelley prevented two students—a seventeen-year-old boy and a sixteen-year-old girl—from entering. Within an hour, their lawyers obtained an order restraining Wallace from further intervention. In Birmingham, Lingo personally turned back the two black girls trying to enter West End High, and one of his captains denied entry to a third student. Lingo rushed to Graymont Elementary, where the two brothers had slipped in a side door the previous week before the schools were closed. This time, the boys arrived with their father, two lawyers, and Fred Shuttlesworth. As they approached the school entrance, Lingo held up his hands for them to halt. He handed one of the lawyers a copy of Wallace's order and said, "You will leave immediately." Ernest Jackson, one of the lawyers, told Lingo that a federal court had directed the admission of the students. "Do you have a copy of that order?" Lingo asked sternly. Jackson replied, "Would you obey that order if I had it?" "I will not," Lingo answered. In Tuskegee, the thirteen black students who arrived at the high school were turned away by another state patrol captain. But only 125 of the white students—fewer than 1 in 4 of those enrolled—turned up; before long, they would drop out, and Wallace would use them as a last-gasp ploy to weaken integration, if he could not stop it.[35]

On the heels of Wallace's defiant acts, Robert Kennedy requested Judge Johnson to issue a restraining order that would cover all of Alabama; Johnson responded within hours, and copies of his order were signed by the other four federal judges, whose authority spanned the entire state. The governor and his state troopers were enjoined from defying earlier federal court orders and from "harassing or punishing any students, teachers, or other authorized persons for having entered" the schools. Wallace was ordered to appear in court the following Monday. In Washington, President Kennedy said that federal action would be taken "only if Governor Wallace [compelled] it." He added, "So that [Wallace] may later charge federal interference, he is desperately anxious to have the federal government intervene in a situation in which we have no desire to intervene." That gave Wallace an idea: once the state patrol was prohibited from blocking black students' entrance to the schools, he called out the Alabama National Guard and directed it to replace the state troopers in anti-integration duty.

Once again playing hide-and-seek with federal marshals, Wallace refused to accept service of the court order when marshals appeared at the capitol on Monday night. "They hid in the bushes around the capitol," Wallace claimed, "and were going to confront me when I went out to get into my car and go home." So the governor remained holed up in his office and ordered a contingent of guardsmen to the capitol. When the soldiers arrived shortly after midnight, Wallace said, "They went around in the bushes, and, sticking their bayonets into the bushes, they flushed out about ten or fifteen U.S. marshals who were there to serve me. In one instance," Wallace chortled, "two or three of them were seen running down Capitol Hill." Wallace accepted service the following day, "but I was not going to accept service at ten o'clock at night," he said indignantly. By the time the guardsmen reached their positions on Tuesday, President Kennedy had federalized them. But instead of forcing another confrontation between federal troops and local parents and children, Kennedy ordered the troops to return immediately to their armories. Wallace, however, stuck to his script. After the additional twenty black students started attending the newly integrated schools, Wallace insisted again that he could not "fight bayonets with [his] bare hands," although not even soldiers, much less bayonets, were in evidence at any of the schools.[36]

Wallace would keep up his pesky hit-and-run tactics well into the following year. First, he moved for Johnson to recuse himself from hearing any more school segregation suits against the state on the grounds that Johnson harbored "personal bias and prejudice" against the governor because of Wallace's public attacks on him. Johnson was unpersuaded: "If statements made by a defendant against a judge could constitute a legal basis for asking a judge to disqualify himself, then any defendant could at his own will render [any] judge disqualified." In November 1963, Wallace tried to block the admission of a black man to graduate study at Auburn University on the grounds that the applicant had not graduated from an accredited college. Johnson saw through the Catch-22 facing the applicant: because the state failed to maintain any accredited black colleges, no graduate of a black college in Alabama could qualify for postgraduate education in the state.

Next, after all the white students had pulled out of Tuskegee High School, leaving only thirteen black students and thirteen black teachers, Wallace requested the state board of education (of which he was the president) to close Tuskegee High on grounds of insufficient finances and inefficiency. About a fourth of the whites had transferred to still-segregated high schools in the rural Macon County communities of Shorter and Notasulga; the remainder had switched to a hastily created private school—the state's first so-called "seg" academy—that was financed largely by state funds and to which most students were transported by state troopers. When the thirteen black students were assigned to other all-black schools in Macon County, Johnson stepped in and ordered that the black students be admitted to the Shorter and Notasulga high schools on the same basis as the whites had been. Wallace reacted by accusing Johnson of undergoing a "judicial tantrum" and called for his impeachment. Among other things, Johnson had directed Macon County school officials to provide transportation for the newly assigned black students, a move prompting Wallace to accuse the federal courts of "forced busing," a term he and others would use again and again in the years ahead, though no one else could manage to spit it out with quite the same venom.

Ultimately, thousands of whites throughout the state left the public schools for the segregated academies, but many eventually returned after the courts forbade further public assistance to private schools. Though Wallace was thoroughly thrashed by the courts, he still managed to score political points by revealing the "highpocrisy" of Judge and Mrs. Johnson: they were sending their son, Johnny (whom Wallace characterized as "a fine young man"), to a segregated private school that they had helped to establish. Wallace had a field day with Johnson—as he would with many national politicians and other federal judges in years to come—for sending his child to an expensive private school while "hard-working plain folks" were left to cope with the problems of court-ordered integration.[37] Wallace's own children attended public schools that, nominally at least, had been integrated.

But Wallace's tactics were greeted with far less than universal approval. The governor either dismissed Northern criticism or tried to fend it off with crude humor. When Harry Truman called Wallace "an ass," the governor told a reporter that "Truman's an authority on the subject; he sees an ass each morning when he shaves." And when his frequent adversary, Sen. Wayne Morse of Oregon, termed

Wallace "a punk," the governor replied, "I'd rather be a punk than a pink." When Wallace heard that a wire-service story reported him as saying, "I'd rather be a punk than a fink," he slapped his forehead and complained jokingly to his friend Dave Silverman, "There goes my Brooklyn Jewish vote."[38] But Wallace did not even try to deal with the more biting Southern critiques. Sam Ervin, leading the fight in the U.S. Senate against civil rights legislation, termed Wallace "the chief aider and abettor of those who would pass such bad legislation as this civil rights bill." And Grover Hall lamented sadly in the *Montgomery Advertiser,* "It is very hard, be certain, for *The Advertiser* to say it, but the fact is that Governor Wallace made a monkey of himself."[39]

■   ■   ■

All the talk, strategy, antics, and legal jousting through the summer and early fall had produced, mercifully, little more than delay, frustration, and minor skirmishes. But, given the unrelieved jab-jab-jab, punch-and-counterpunch battle that Wallace continued to wage in defiance of court-directed integration, pressure was bound to build; at last, the underlying tensions that Wallace had been fueling literally blew up in Birmingham on a cool, overcast Sunday morning, September 15, 1963, in the single most terrible incident of racial violence of the Southern civil rights movement. That day, four young black girls, dressed in their Sunday best, went to the Sixteenth Street Baptist Church to attend Bible classes and to participate in leading the eleven o'clock services to mark the church's Youth Day; thirty-eight minutes before the services were to begin, the children were blown apart by a powerful dynamite bomb.[40]

In minutes, the streets near the church filled with nearby residents, civil defense workers, policemen, and emergency medical teams. Looking for the missing children, authorities and volunteers dug with their hands and makeshift tools through piles of rocks, glass, and twisted metal. Then one of the rescue workers lifted a timber, exposing the bloodied corner of a white robe and a small hand. He shouted for help, and after others had joined him in frantically throwing off jagged slabs of concrete, they uncovered the four appallingly mangled bodies of Addie Mae Collins, Denise McNair, Carole Robertson, and Cynthia Wesley. As the bodies were removed and placed in ambulances, David Vann, an aide to Mayor Boutwell, was speeding to the scene; he screeched to a halt at a police barricade, jumped from his car, started toward the church, and then pulled up short. "There," Vann recalled later, "standing on the corner, was Robert Chambliss, looking down toward the Sixteenth Street Church, like a firebug watching his fire."[41]

Chambliss proudly bore the nickname "Dynamite Bob," given him by his Ku Klux Klan pals because he was involved with so many of the incidents that had given Birmingham the unenviable sobriquet of "Bombingham." Chambliss, a fifty-nine-year-old truck driver for an auto-parts company, was an organizer of a hate-filled, aggressively violent Klan clique that called itself the Cahaba River Group because its members met under a river bridge on the outskirts of Birmingham. Chambliss and an automobile mechanic named Troy Ingram built a bomb at Ingram's house. On the day before the deadly explosion at the church, Chambliss told his niece, Libby Cobbs, that "after Sunday morning" he would have "the goddam niggers in their place." And, he vowed, "they will beg us to let them segregate. Just wait and see." At nine o'clock on the fateful Sunday morning, a friend of Chambliss's wife, Tee, told a Jefferson County (Birmingham) Sheriff's Department detective named James Hancock that dynamite had been planted at a Birmingham church. Hancock, who played a key role in developing the information that ultimately put Chambliss behind bars, failed to act on the tip—some say because he lingered with the informant, likely engaging in a sexual encounter. (Hancock never denied the allegation but told questioners it was none of their "damn business" how he and the informant spent that Sunday morning.)[42] It was the first of several official blunders at the local, state, and federal levels that would delay justice for fourteen years—and, many believe, allow Chambliss's confederates to escape punishment altogether.

The next blunder was by Wallace, who "turned white with shock" when he heard the news and was eager—perhaps overly eager—to find the culprits.[43] A flustered Mayor Boutwell asked Wallace's help in quelling the disturbances and preventing further violence; the governor dispatched Lingo, along with three hundred state troopers, and placed five hundred National Guardsmen on alert.[44] He also offered a reward of five thousand dollars for information leading to the apprehension of the perpetrators. The reward was termed "blood money" by the president of the Americans for Democratic Action, John P. Roche. "Wallace," Roche said, "is as guilty as if he himself planted the bomb." Roy Wilkins of the NAACP maintained that Wallace's actions had "encouraged" the children's murder.[45] In Birmingham, many civic leaders were appalled by the bloody tragedy; Charles Morgan, Jr., a thirty-three-year-old lawyer, passionately told his peers at the Young Men's Business Club that all whites shared guilt. "Who threw the bomb?" he asked. "We all did it." Boutwell demurred, saying, "We are all victims."[46] Harsh criticism emanated from Washington. Sen. Jacob Javits of New York said that Wallace could not "escape some responsibility" for the killings. Sen. Thomas Kuchel of California argued that when elected officials "are bad leaders—when they flout the law—people are inclined to flout the law, too." Toughest of all was the suggestion by President Kennedy that Wallace contributed to the bombings: "It is regrettable that public disparagement of law and order has encouraged violence which has fallen on the innocent." The president's accusation was an only slightly gentler way of saying what Martin Luther King, Jr., told Wallace in an earlier telegram: "The blood of our little children is on your hands."[47]

For once, Wallace maintained a low profile rather than reflexively lash back at his critics. Expectedly, he felt wrongly accused. But he realized instinctively that anything he said in his own defense would appear disingenuous at best and heartless at worst. Instead, he made it clear to Lingo that he wanted action—and that he would like to beat the FBI to a solution. He told Lingo, "I cannot understand the feelings of anyone who would put a bomb under a church. At least, if justice prevails, it'll help to some degree."[48] The sentiments behind the state investigation were noble, but its execution was doomed by ineptitude and prejudice. Lingo started out convinced that Black Muslims were behind the bombing, and Wallace thought this was a reasonable idea. Fortunately, however, James Hancock, the detective who had been tipped about a bomb, ignored Lingo's theory and concentrated his efforts on the local Klan—particularly those members like Chambliss and Ingram who were reputed to have been responsible for past dynamiting incidents. With surreptitious help from Chambliss's wife, Hancock managed to install a listening device in Chambliss's kitchen. Some of the conversations, he said, "would curl your hair." Sample comments from the Chambliss kitchen included this from the Klan member Tommy Blanton: "I'll go to Fort McClellan and get a forty-five machine gun and step inside the door of the church and show you how to kill some niggers." And this from Chambliss: "We're going to have to kill a bunch of them sons of bitches before we bring them to their knees."

A state investigator, Ben Allen, also ignored his boss's hypothesis that the Black Muslims were behind the church bombing. Working separately, Hancock and Allen began pressuring some of the suspects—notably, Blanton and Ingram—and implied in time-honored investigative fashion that Blanton and Ingram were being blamed by their confederates, and the only hope for leniency was to cooperate. The investigators were convinced that these two suspects were about to break. Allen informed Lingo that Ingram had failed a lie-detector test and was close to a confession that would nail Chambliss and others. Lingo shocked Allen by saying he thought they had enough on which to base immediate arrests. When Hancock's superior, Sheriff Mel Bailey, heard that Lingo wanted to move, he called Lingo to protest; premature action, he warned, might destroy the case. Lingo ignored him and, two weeks after the bombing, ordered the arrest of Chambliss and two other Klansmen. Bill Jones summoned the press to announce that "state investigators expect to break the Birmingham church case within the next few hours." Off the record, Lingo and Jones reminded news reporters that the state had beaten the FBI to the punch. But after two solid days of questioning, Chambliss failed to crack; others in the case—notably, Ingram and Blanton—retained lawyers, who promptly told their clients to halt any further cooperation with local, state, or federal investigators. As a result, state authorities were forced to abandon their case; Chambliss and the two other Klansmen were charged with a misdemeanor—illegal possession of dynamite. To add to their humiliation, Lingo's investigators saw even that minor charge fall apart in court.[49]

If Wallace was abashed, he decided that he had held his peace long enough and that the best defense was a good offense. He revised slightly Lingo's preposterous notion that Black Muslims were responsible for the church tragedy by arguing that the state's failure in court may well have resulted from the Klansmen's innocence. While repeating his personal shock and dismay at the bombing, he argued that he was "not sure that this was the work of white persons. It could very easily have been done by communists or other Negroes who had a lot to gain by the ensuing publicity."[50] Wallace directed Lingo to step up the activities of the state patrol's unit to investigate "subversives" (formally known as the Investigative and Identification Division)—activities that included not only maintaining files on black leaders, Justice Department officials, and journalists and news organizations, but also attending, recording, and photographing dozens of meetings "suspected of teaching or advocating policies which were detrimental to the interests of the state of Alabama." The meetings in question almost always were interracial; state troopers even photographed every white person who attended the funeral of the four girls killed at the church.[51]

As unsavory as the activities of the Investigation and Identification Division may appear in retrospect, they were of a piece with the widespread national jitteriness about infiltration of Communists and subversives in the civil rights movement, an uneasiness encouraged by one of Wallace's icons, FBI Director J. Edgar Hoover. By the time of the church bombing in Birmingham, the FBI had staged nearly twenty known break-ins at the Atlanta offices of the Southern Christian Leadership Conference, during which files were examined and photographed and listening devices were planted. The bureau's paranoia was so great that Hoover, in the summer of 1961, ordered a full FBI investigation of King after reading in an agent's report that a Communist party official, Benjamin Davis, Jr., had donated blood when King had been seriously wounded in an attempt on his life in 1958.[52] Only weeks after Wallace had directed his spy organization to step up its activities, it would reward the governor with a major public relations coup.

■   ■   ■

A unit of Alabama's spy patrol was on hand when King arrived at the Birmingham airport on October 14, 1963, and maintained surveillance until 5:30 the next afternoon. At that time, according to the state patrol's official report, King "left Birmingham with four other colored males in a 1963 blue four-door Chevrolet Impala automobile en route to Selma," where he addressed a civil rights rally. The King watch was picked up in Selma by a state patrol unit there that, assisted by the sheriff, Jim Clark, stayed with King until he was chauffeured in the Chevy to Montgomery, where he boarded a plane for Atlanta. By the time King arrived home, Wallace's investigators already had determined that the Chevy in which King rode was a Hertz rental secured with a charge card issued to the civil rights division of the Justice Department. The next day, at Wallace's direction, state officials, condemning the use of taxpayer money to transport King, leaked the report to newspapers in Alabama—but withheld the crucial detail that they had examined the rental agreement and traced the charge card to the civil rights division. Justice Department spokesmen, unaware that Wallace's people possessed hard evidence, accepted the disavowals of their on-scene attorneys and subsequently denied the allegation as "either a gross mistake or a deliberate attempt to mislead the people."

Wallace then sprang the trap. He notified the U.S. attorney in Montgomery that he intended to order a state-level grand jury investigation to determine the facts because the Justice Department's denial had "impugned the honesty and integrity of state and county law officials in the performance of their official duties." When the U.S. attorney informed Washington of Wallace's intentions, Burke Marshall, the head of the Civil Rights Division, reopened his own inquiry. He then issued a statement backing away from the earlier denial, saying that it been based "on misinformation and, therefore, erroneous." He explained that the rented car was being used by a Justice Department attorney, Thelton Henderson, in connection with official business, but that on the night in question, Henderson had loaned the car to "a private citizen" who had driven King from Birmingham to Selma. Henderson himself had remained behind in Birmingham. "Nevertheless," Marshall's statement continued, "the use of the car for unofficial business was contrary to . . . regulations." More important, the statement continued, it was also contrary to Henderson's original story. Subsequently, however, Henderson, "came forward . . . and voluntarily gave a correct account of what occurred." Henderson submitted his resignation, which the department accepted.[53]

Just as when he had revealed that air force personnel had been taking part in civil rights demonstrations, Wallace vaulted upward in national popularity—not so much because of the consequence of his disclosures, but principally because he had caught the federal establishment unawares and guilty of misstatements. Wallace himself conceded that the incident was "rather insignificant," but he maintained that it "constituted a pattern" in Washington's antagonism to "state sovereignty." The reaction among many Americans was voiced by an Alabama editor: "If the Department of Justice—under present management—sometimes wonders why a lot of good Americans don't have much confidence in it, it should cease wondering."[54]

Wallace also helped himself rebound from criticism over the church bombing by aggressively spreading a positive message about his considerable accomplishments as governor in less than a year on the job:

- He had pushed through sizable raises in salaries for teachers—and the average pay of black teachers, due to their relatively longer tenure, was higher than that of whites.
- He had begun a major school construction program, including eight new junior colleges and trade schools for blacks.
- He had successfully sponsored a $100 million bond issue for roads and highways.
- He had attracted to Alabama a quarter of a billion dollars' worth of new industry that created twenty thousand new jobs, many of which were filled by blacks.[55]

Ironically, Wallace need not have risked blowing the case against Chambliss for want of besting the FBI; unknown to anyone outside the bureau, FBI Director Hoover did not want the agency to help break the case for fear of compromising an FBI informant within the Klan. The informant, Gary Thomas Rowe (see chapter 7), participated in several violent attacks on civil rights activists while in the pay of the FBI from 1960 to 1965, culminating in his complicity in the murder of Viola Gregg Liuzzo on the road between Selma and Montgomery in March 1965 (see chapter 12). Rowe was not charged in Liuzzo's killing; instead, he became the government's principal witness against the others involved. Therefore, when the FBI field office in Birmingham, two months after the Liuzzo killing, reported to Hoover that their investigation into the church bombing made it "apparent that the bombing was the handiwork" of Chambliss and several others, Hoover forbade the agents from furnishing their data to either state or federal prosecutors. In 1977, however, Chambliss finally was convicted—but because of renewed interest and efforts at the state level, not by the FBI; the investigation was resumed by Alabama's attorney general, Bill Baxley, who, with Wallace's support, directed the subsequent successful prosecution. But Baxley, who received minimal help from the FBI, was unable to gather enough evidence to bring anyone else to trial. As for Rowe, the FBI helped him start a new life with a new identity outside Alabama—even though he had twice failed lie-detector tests in which he denied participating in the church bombing, and had failed another lie-detector test where he denied firing the bullet that killed Liuzzo.[56]

■　■　■

Perhaps because the people of Birmingham, black and white, were stupefied by the enormity of the Sixteenth Street Baptist Church tragedy, the town quieted down. The funerals, presided over by King and Shuttlesworth, seemed to transmute rage into deep sadness and mourning. And the community's reaction to Wallace's speedy, if premature, apprehension of Chambliss and his alleged confederates, though ridiculed in the national press, was essentially positive. Wallace's swift response to the killings demonstrated to most citizens that he was eager to punish whoever was responsible.

Nonetheless, those who felt horror over the bombings branded Wallace as an agent of violence. Before he could seriously consider any kind of national political campaign, he had to ameliorate, if not eradicate, that image. The best way to do that, he believed, was to stand eyeball to eyeball with his toughest critics. He decided to embark on a national speaking tour and concentrate on appearances before those most likely to deride both him and his views—college communities. And he resolved to begin at the very fonts of intellectual liberalism where Wallace and everything he stood for were detested—the Ivy League.

With his surpassing self-confidence, Wallace believed he would acquit himself well before hostile audiences. For one thing, he sensed that most Northerners viewed the South in general (and him in particular) with disdain bordering on contempt, judging the South as a cesspool of poverty, ignorance, and hate. He reckoned that exceeding expectations so negative and deprecatory would require little more than speaking in complete sentences. And Wallace, in whose very core the South's system of segregation and devotion to white supremacy was deeply etched, felt certain that he could persuade Northern audiences to at least consider his points: that the South was far more hospitable to blacks than the North, that blacks preferred the real bars of segregation to the racial hypocrisy of the North, that racial harmony was evolving faster in the South than elsewhere, and that the true villain in the segregation drama was the federal establishment, whose intrusion was rushing integration too quickly, thereby fomenting racial hostility and slowing racial progress. He had, after all, done it before—as a peripatetic magazine salesman, a soldier, and a budding politician, he had convinced non-Southerners across broad chunks of America that white Southerners were decent, hard-working, smart folks who coexisted peaceably with, if separately from, blacks. And if Ivy League platforms seemed more imposing and inhospitable than the one-on-one campaigning, politi-

cal barnstorming, radio debates, and occasional congressional appearances that had theretofore marked his career, Wallace rightly
judged that he was now a far more consequential figure than he had
been earlier. Now, he was a governor, not merely a state legislator or a
small-town judge. And he was a governor who, by refusing to knuckle
under to the federal leviathan, and by transmuting the argument
against integration to one against national imposition on local custom, had fanned long-dormant sparks of individualism, chauvinism,
and racism in millions of Americans.

To many, he had become a powerful antidote to President
Kennedy—Tennyson's Mordred exposing the dark side of Camelot.
Grover Hall, in a letter to his fellow Alabamian Justice Hugo Black,
described Wallace as "an adventurer the same as Kennedy, the difference being they work different sides of the street." Hall wrote, "[Wal-
lace's] popularity with the masses is higher than ever and probably
will continue because he has the right enemies." Hall presciently
perceived Wallace's potential vote-getting strength in states like
Maryland, Ohio, and Indiana. He told Black that Wallace was "the
only visible, available protest symbol against the Kennedy civil rights
jihad."[57] Cognizant of Black's deep antipathy to Wallace, Hall tried
"to provide an insight to how an Alabamian might view him":

> Sometimes I think we might find an analogy in 1940 when
> London was under the terror of the blitz from night bombing.
> The antiaircraft guns in Hyde Park went off in systematic
> salvos. They did nothing but shower Londoners with falling
> shrapnel and didn't even annoy the German bombers. But the
> sound of the guns going off nevertheless made Londoners feel
> better.[58]

Wallace decided to open his foray behind enemy lines on November 4 at the citadel of American intellectualism, Harvard University. On his arrival in Boston the day before, however, it seemed like
anything but hostile territory. Aides to Endicott Peabody, the patrician governor of Massachusetts, greeted Wallace at the airport and
graciously welcomed him to the state. And a contingent of Boston
police officers, assigned to escort and guard Wallace during his visit,
were openly enthusiastic in support of their charge. "If the police
and the taxicab drivers were to choose the next president," the
Alabama reporter Bob Ingram wrote after the Northern trip, "it
might well be Wallace." In what would become a typical day for him
as he increased his national travels, Wallace conducted a general

news conference, participated in two half-hour radio and television interview programs, and dined with Alabama students at Harvard. He was joined in a televised news interview program by Gov. Phillip Hoff of Vermont, who advocated a national public accommodations law like the one in his state. Wallace interrupted to ask the percentage of blacks in Vermont. "Very small," Hoff conceded, and Wallace nodded vigorously to underline his point. Wallace thought so highly of his own performance that his staff obtained a filmed copy of the interview program and made it available to television stations in Alabama. After the show, station personnel continued to pepper Wallace with arguments against segregation. Wallace used his long-practiced tactic of throwing charges of racism back on the accuser. He asked how many black executives worked at the television station, and how many photographers, announcers, or salesmen? There were none. It turned out that even the janitor was white; there was not a single black employee. Wallace grinned, winked, and walked jauntily out the door.[59]

The next day, Wallace appeared on another half-hour radio news show, granted interviews to the *Harvard Crimson* and the campus radio station, and participated in a two-hour radio call-in show. The encounters strengthened Wallace's confidence. That night, undaunted by dozens of protesters who picketed outside the packed auditorium in which he would speak, he was ready.[60]

Wallace disarmed his audience early and often with gently captious comments about arch-rival Yale students who, a month earlier, had withdrawn their speaking invitation to Wallace at the request of the university's provost and soon-to-be-president, Kingman Brewster.[61] Some rebellious and enterprising Yalies arranged for a telephonic hookup between the Harvard theater where Wallace appeared and an off-campus hall in New Haven, Connecticut, that was crowded with interested Yale students. So when Wallace was introduced amid a chorus of loud hisses, he said, "Hello, there, Yale. I hope you're listening. Those hisses are for you, not me." The audience laughed and broke into applause. And they applauded again when Wallace chided Yale for refusing to allow him to appear not long after welcoming an American Communist party leader. "I suppose I'm more subversive than he is," Wallace said. "Of course, you Harvard boys and girls say that we live in a society that is supposed to be liberal where everybody can express his viewpoint. But at Yale, they mean that anybody can express his viewpoint—as long as they agree with it."[62]

Wallace then moved into his prepared speech, written largely by the Klansman Asa Carter (see chapter 8) under the firm direction of John Kohn. It described how the South was devastated in the Civil War, how it had endured "the unique distinction of being the only territory conquered by the armies of the United States" without having been "rehabilitated at the expense of the United States," as defeated foreign foes had been restored through the Marshall Plan and foreign aid. He was booed (as he would be at Dartmouth the next night) when he chanted racist dogma about how mulattos, having "inherited the mentality and personality of their white ancestor," were equipped to take college degrees and fill responsible jobs, but were "not representative in any true sense of their less capable African half brother." The latter, representing 40 percent of the South's population, Wallace described as "easy going, basically happy, unambitious, incapable of much learning." And, he contended, "the white man of the South, in addition to educating his own children, has attempted to educate [and] furnish public health services and civic protection" to blacks.[63]

But he quickly moved away from racist fulmination to the essence of his talk: an argument against a Supreme Court packed with unlawyerly hacks more interested in causes than in the law—men appointed by "tax, tax, spend, spend" politicians who kept their eyes glued to the growing impact of black voting blocs and the wishes of "the ultra-liberal controlled press" rather than to the U.S. Constitution. He attempted to show that the Warren Court's 1954 school desegregation decision (see chapter 5) had evolved from growing politicization of the Supreme Court, starting with FDR's appointment of Wallace's bête noire, Hugo Black. Here, he drew unplanned chuckles with an altogether improbable and metaphorically mixed formulation, obviously injected into the text by Kohn to impress the listeners with the governor's intellectualism:

> *Brown* did not, I assure you, as some seem to think, spring instantly into existence full grown and ready for action equipped with injunctive process, preferred appeal, set bayonets and all its accoutrements like Botticelli would have us believe Venus came to the shores of Greece full grown and full blown on the breath of Boreas.

But coming down from his flight of rhetorical fancy, Wallace gained the crowd's full attention when he cited an 1849 holding by the Supreme Judicial Court of Massachusetts that Boston had the authority to set up separate schools for blacks and whites—a Northern expression of the separate-but-equal doctrine nearly a half-century before it was nationally institutionalized in the Supreme Court's *Plessy v. Ferguson* ruling in 1896. During the question-and-answer period, Wallace received applause when he gave hecklers as good as he got; when a black man of uncertain connections declared that he was a candidate for president of the United States, Wallace evoked gales of laughter when he said, "Between you and me both, we might get rid of that crowd in Washington; we might even run on the same ticket."[64]

Those who counted said that Wallace was hissed six times and was applauded fifteen times. In the next three days, he spoke at Dartmouth College, Smith College, and Brown University, each time cutting back on his prepared remarks and increasing his participation in unrehearsed question-and-answer periods where his quips and off-the-cuff barbs at high-level officials proved popular and effective. He continued to leverage his appearances with radio, television, and newspaper interviews, even driving to New York after his speech in Northampton, Massachusetts, to do an ABC television interview at 1:00 A.M. Overall, he pronounced himself pleased—"much better than anyone, including myself, had expected," he said. "The North was getting a different, better opinion of Alabama." His complaints were with the press—"they misquote me and they say when I'm hissed but not when I'm applauded"—and with his own confessed ignorance of what made Northern college kids tick. Typical of his almost appealing naïveté was his comment at Dartmouth when the crowd of three thousand broke into laughter at what Wallace thought was a serious line—his assertion that scientific evidence proved that black children were damaged more by integration than by segregation. Wallace looked up with a quizzical smile and said, "I don't understand. You laugh when I don't think you will, and don't laugh when I think you will." The students laughed some more—but this time they applauded, too.[65]

Wallace boosters like Grover Hall were ecstatic. Hall wrote in the *Montgomery Advertiser* that the crowds in Massachusetts, New Hampshire, and Rhode Island who came to see Wallace were "composed of a superior element of America's young manhood" who were both "knowledgeable and probably adverse to the Wallace viewpoint." Nonetheless, Hall wrote:

Wallace disarmed them partially and wowed them entirely. . . .
Wallace seems now to have perfected a technique which his
friends believed he never would. And that is the deft, light
touch along with the tub-thumping. . . . If Wallace can disarm
and charm Harvard, how could he fail elsewhere? Wallace
plainly is a potent symbolism on the American scene. His
enemies, we predict, will make him yet more potent. . . .
Wallace is an uncommon man, made so by his spirit.[66]

And even allowing for a smidgen or two of hometown bias, the
Montgomery reporter Bob Ingram reflected a widely held view that
Wallace "hit a home run" in his Northern appearances. Writing of
the Harvard speech, Ingram said that Wallace "turned a hostile,
hissing audience of twelve hundred students into something closely
approximating a Wallace campaign rally. The ovation he received at
the conclusion rattled the rafters."[67]

■　■　■

Less than two weeks after Wallace triumphantly returned to Montgomery, President Kennedy was assassinated in Dallas. Wallace refused any further invitations until after the first of the year. He issued
a thoughtful, statesmanlike message:

We may disagree with people in public office because of
philosophy and attitudes, but this attack upon the chief
executive is an attack upon the American system, and I'm sure
that whoever did it had universal malice for all the people of
this country.[68]

Wallace paid his respects in Washington and attended the funeral services in the company of the world's mightiest people. The
one controversial incident was when Gov. Pat Brown of California,
with whom Wallace shared a car, told a reporter that Wallace had said
he really was against segregation but was forced to support it for
political reasons. Wallace denied he ever said such a thing. He maintains that he told Brown that segregation would have to end one day.
But the national scene had suddenly and violently changed for Wallace; he would not have the Kennedys to kick around as bogeymen as
the election year of 1964 dawned. Instead, a fellow Southerner now
ruled Washington and led the nation.[69]

Wallace thought long and hard about whether he would continue with his audacious plan to inject himself into the presidential campaign. At last, he told an aide that he would do it anyway. "It makes no difference who is the president," he said. "The issues are the same." On January 6, 1964, Wallace announced his support for independent electors in Alabama. He said he would decide later which Democratic primaries to enter. For the time being, he told his staff that he wanted to get back on the college circuit "and take advantage of all the news coverage" he could get. He called Jones and said simply, "You better get it set up."[70]

11

Shaking Their Eyeteeth

I*N JANUARY AND FEBRUARY OF 1964,* Wallace barnstormed the West and Midwest—and the more he traveled, the more he felt drawn by the magnetic pull of national notoriety. Hopping from one college campus to another, he honed both the style and message of what would evolve into his first presidential campaign.

In every locale, Wallace's point man, Bill Jones, arranged for a local news conference, a speech to at least one local civic group, and appearances on radio and television interview programs. Unlike the press-the-flesh, one-on-one approach to his Alabama campaigns, Wallace, on his national tours, eschewed plunging into crowds of shoppers, shaking hands of passersby on street corners, or mounting rousing rallies featuring tub-thumping oratory and country music. One reason was security; he was pursued by hecklers and pickets almost everywhere he traveled outside the South. Second, neither he nor his advisers knew how down-home campaign techniques would play in the North; such tactics might, they feared, reinforce the conviction (that Wallace believed was widely held north of the Mason-Dixon line) that Southern politicians, if not vicious bigots, were little more than worrisome bumpkins. But most of all, Wallace recognized that he could receive more exposure in more places in less time for less money by making one or two high-profile public speeches in each town to provide a news "peg," and then make as many appearances as possible on radio and television interview programs and call-in shows. It was a technique that Wallace would sharpen through four presidential campaigns and that national political candidates would come to emulate in the years ahead.[1]

As to his message, Wallace abandoned the academic, pedantic pretensions of his Ivy League discourses on the evolution of judicial activism in segregation. Audiences received those speeches tepidly at best and with downright boredom at worst. Also, taking his so-called historical approach required him to explain and defend the practice of segregation, inevitably leading to an exposition of discredited (and racist) anthropological views that mulattos were smarter, harder working, and more ambitious than full-blooded black people—and in the South, he contended, the latter far outnumbered their lighter-skinned brothers and sisters. While such declarations invariably evoked hisses from the crowds, Wallace found that he generated genuine audience enthusiasm with his extemporized assaults on growing federal intrusion into people's day-to-day lives. And he was aware that such attacks could be separated from the issue of race. So this time around, as he launched his swings through the West and Midwest, he decided to keep the message simple. Instead of wending along dusty paths of constitutional history, legalisms, and judicial theory, he drove straight toward a single target—a full-scale attack on the civil rights bill. And he would do it without denigrating blacks or even the goal of equal opportunity; he would attack the bill as a federal assault on individual rights, opening the door to the advance of communism in the United States.

■   ■   ■

In eight days in January and ten in February, Wallace raced through nine Western and Midwestern states and a Canadian province, playing everywhere to overflow crowds, which he found "courteous and friendly" for the most part, despite some boos and anti-Wallace pickets. He attacked the civil rights bill as "a federal power grab" over private property—a sure harbinger of socialism.[2] The only reason for the bill was to appease those who would "create national chaos." He continued, "We are witnessing the astounding spectacle . . . of high officials calling for the passage of a so-called civil rights bill for fear of threat of mob violence." Yet he and people like him who "believe in the rights of the individual states . . . who believe in fiscal responsibility . . . who object to [judicial] amendment of the Constitution . . . who object to socialist ideology" are, he said, "invariably . . . identified as the purveyors of hate."[3] The bill, he asserted, "is a prime example of what propaganda, misrepresentations, and misunderstandings can do to a governmental structure. Passage of this bill through a cloud of emotionalism will extend federal control over business, industry, and individuals."[4]

Wherever possible, he sought to demonstrate that racial problems in general and opposition to the civil rights bill in particular were not strictly Southern phenomena. In California, he reminded audiences that a local fair-housing bill had been defeated in Berkeley a year earlier. "People segregate themselves," he said. "The people in Berkeley talked like they wanted the bill—but when they voted, they voted just like the people in Alabama."[5] And he quoted a Los Angeles attorney, Lloyd Wright, a former president of the American Bar Association, as describing the civil rights bill as "ten percent civil rights and ninety percent extension of federal executive power."[6] In Colorado, Wallace described a "sleep-in" by black protesters at the offices of Gov. John Love as indicative of "the internal upheavals" that presaged Communist takeovers in other nations. When he was picketed and booed at the University of Denver, he told the students that Lincoln "would have been picketed for his views that Negroes shouldn't vote, serve on juries, or hold public office"—positions that Lincoln had enunciated in the fourth of his debates with Stephen Douglas in 1858 but with which he, George Wallace, disagreed. But he aligned himself with Lincoln's belief that blacks would gain full equality through time and education.[7] In Oregon, aware of a civic group's complaint that blacks faced discrimination in housing and employment in the city of Eugene, Wallace went straight to the point:

> The right to sell your property to anyone you want to will be taken away if the civil rights bill passes the Congress. The right to reject applicants for employment because of lack of qualifications is another right that will be taken away from store owners. . . . Politicians are misleading our [Southern] Negro citizens. They entice them with milk-and-honey talk into moving North into no jobs and poor housing. These politicians must share the blame for racial troubles in their areas.

The crowd of nine thousand at the University of Oregon field house grew so ardent that Wallace, carried away by the moment, shouted over them, "The Confederate flag will fly again!" They cheered wildly.[8]

At the University of Washington, Wallace repeated his contention: "When it gets down to the lick log, as we rednecks in Alabama say, the people of Washington will vote against something which affects them personally, just as we do in Alabama. And if the people of Washington want to remove racial and religious imbalance, as required by the pending civil rights bill, that's fine. But let the people of Washington and Seattle do it—not some socio-political theorist in Washington, D.C., four thousand miles away."[9]

At a Seattle news conference on January 14, Wallace said that when the Supreme Court handed down the *Brown* decision in 1954, "the ratio of black to white pupils in the Washington, D.C., schools was one in four. In 1963, it was nine in ten." He pressed on: "These same government officials who are trying to take over my school system have fled to Virginia or Maryland or put their children in private schools." Just before leaving the West to return to Alabama, Wallace said he might enter the 1964 Democratic primaries. "I know I can't win, but it will give me a chance to let the people know . . . the dangers they face from the encroachments of their own government."[10]

Less than a month later, he was off to the Midwest. While Western politicians had largely ignored Wallace, neither the people nor the press had.[11] But not so in the Midwest. Ohio's aging, acid-tongued Sen. Stephen Young excoriated Wallace—a "buffoon who has defied the courts of this nation, and who has abetted murder and violence in his state, and who has tarnished the image of our country throughout the world." Wallace sensed that this kind of attack signaled that he was gaining some strength in the Midwest; his subsequent travels in the region reinforced his belief.

In Cincinnati, on the day that Wallace was to speak, the Congress of Racial Equality coincidentally was leading a one-day boycott of the public schools. The unlikely confluence of events clearly heightened racial tension in the city—and the pickets outside the auditorium where Wallace was speaking did little to sweeten the temper of the audience. But they adored Wallace. He spoke for over an hour and was interrupted by applause forty-seven times. He denounced the civil rights bill as a ruse to destroy property rights: "The only place where there are no human rights is the place where there are no property rights." And he contended, "[Democratic government] now appears in the dress of a welfare state where government referees all rights and the individual is subject to the caprice and whim of an autocratic, all-powerful government structure." But then he started winging it, firing at whatever targets seemed to please the audience—namely, almost anything. They cheered when he said the racial disturbances in Birmingham had been Communist-inspired and warned that "the communists [would] take advantage of any unrest in America to foster their own goals."[12] They cheered when he complained that the federal government was ready to strike at Alabama, despite having "run off under a rock like a bunch of vampires" when Castro cut off the U.S. water supply at Guantanamo. They cheered when he said of Earl Warren, "You've got a chief justice of the Supreme Court who doesn't have the legal brains to try a chicken thief in my home county." And then he pointed his finger to where the pickets were parading outside, and he raised his voice:

> There are more good people like you in this country today than there are these little pinkos running around outside, but we must band together. When you and I start marching and demonstrating and carrying signs, we will close every highway in this country![13]

Leaping to their feet, hundreds in the audience shouted and pumped their arms in the air, then dozens started to the entrance as if to mix it up with the demonstrators and rip away their signs. Wallace was visibly shaken; he had never before moved a crowd so large to such a dangerous level of emotion. It would not be the last time that crowds would respond to a Wallace harangue with scarifying temper; though it filled him with an exciting rush of his own power, he also felt a flicker of fright. So he quickly acted, as he would in the future, to try to contain the crowd's excessive and alarming exuberance. He raised his arms and bellowed: "But wait! That's not the way you and I will fight. We will do it in the courts and in the field of public opinion, where more and more people are joining with us." The gathering cooled down, people returned to their seats, and Wallace picked up his themes, but with moderated rhetoric. Later, he admitted to his mixed feelings of elation and alarm at the incident. But the rousing response haunted him later when his staff reported they had neither the time nor the resources to collect, by the February 5 deadline, the requisite number of signatures to get his name on

Ohio's ballot for the Democratic presidential primary in June. He was convinced he would have carried the state.[14]

In Ohio, Wallace continued to attract excited crowds to his speeches, large turnouts to his news conferences, and more invitations for radio and television appearances than he could accept. At Ohio State University, where five thousand students had demonstrated the night before to protest the jailing of a coed for failure to pay a five-dollar jaywalking citation, Wallace captivated his audience as soon as he was introduced: "I wanted you to know," he began, "that I was a circuit judge—not a traffic judge." He enhanced his reputation for facing down his critics when he told a Sigma Delta Chi gathering, "The press doesn't occupy the place in American society it once did—and the reason is that many newspapers have failed to meet the demands of responsible reporting. People used to say they knew it was so because they read it in the newspaper, but you don't hear that said anymore." Wallace drew positive public response after he told a news conference that the federal government should concentrate less on integration and more on education. "They spend six million dollars to put one Negro in Ole Miss, and it could have been spent for training Negro children in Mississippi. But that kind of money goes to Rangoon or Ghana. If the schools are segregated, what difference does that make?" And when he was confronted with questions about the violence in Birmingham, he had ready answers: "In forty-five days of demonstrations in Birmingham, only sixty-nine people were hurt—and only twenty-two of those were Negroes. The others were policemen. More people were hurt last week in Cleveland in one day."[15] Then he added in grave imitation of his Northern critics, "I want you to know that the people of Alabama are very disturbed about the violence in Cleveland. I'm glad we don't have problems like you have here in the North." And when reporters pressed him on the unsolved bombings in Birmingham, Wallace continued scoring points with one-downsmanship: "Ohio has had more unsolved bombings than Alabama—over seventy in Youngstown alone." The Associated Press reported the next day that, in recent years, there actually had been eighty-two bombings in Youngstown (though not necessarily racially motivated), and all but one remained unsolved.[16]

Wallace flew to Chicago for an appearance on a popular television interview program hosted by Irv Kupcinet, a columnist for the *Chicago Sun-Times.* Wallace's growing stature was reflected by the other panelists whom Kupcinet had selected: Charles Percy, a business executive and candidate for the U.S. Senate; William Rusher, the publisher of the *National Review*, and John Kaplan, a professor of political science at Northwestern University. Rusher found himself frequently agreeing with Wallace about undue incursions by the federal government into areas best left to the private sector. Kaplan and Wallace argued over whether Alabama spent as much, on average, to educate blacks as whites. The answer was yes and no: the state spent less on black schools, but only because average daily attendance at black schools was lower. And Wallace succeeded in putting Percy on the defensive. "You know," Wallace said, "Martin Luther King said that Chicago was the most segregated city in the nation. Do you agree with that?" Percy answered indirectly by agreeing, "Hypocrisy didn't stop at the Mason-Dixon line; there is discrimination in the North." In other interviews before he left town, Wallace condemned violence in Chicago ("there's more violence in Chicago in one night than we have in Alabama in a year"); defended the integrity of Chicago's police (he said that reports of police brutality were "a Communist trick to try to undermine the police force"); and attacked the federal government for moving too quickly to end segregation (the problem, he said, would be resolved only by "common sense and massive education"). And before he left Chicago for speeches at the Universities of Minnesota and Wisconsin, Wallace reiterated his inclination to run in the Democratic presidential primaries. Demonstrating his political know-how by setting low expectations, he told reporters, "If I ran outside the South and got 10 percent, it would be a victory. It would shake their eyeteeth in Washington."[17]

It was in Wisconsin that Wallace's plans to jump into the presidential primaries began to jell. Wallace, understandably impressed by the abundance of favorable out-of-state mail that had poured into Montgomery since his school-house-door stand, conceded that he "fantasized that a Southerner could be elected president."[18] As early as the previous October, Grover Hall had seen the possibilities, especially in states like Wisconsin, Ohio, and Maryland.[19] But when he broached the idea to Wallace, the governor, though flattered, said, "It could be embarrassing to the state if I didn't get any votes at all."[20] But after his speech at the University of Wisconsin, where his adept handling of insistent interruptions by hecklers won him the sympathy, if not agreement, of most in the audience, several of his most ardent Wisconsin supporters buttonholed the governor and urged him to enter the state's April 7 primary. Wallace recalled one saying, "There are more people out there than you think who would vote for you and like what you stand for—and it would be a feather in your cap to make a good showing here in Wisconsin."[21] Among those most impressed by Wallace was a thirty-four-year-old Oshkosh home-maker named Dolores Herbstreith, who would single-handedly re-cruit the necessary number of delegates—sixty in all, representing each of the state's ten congressional districts, plus several chosen at large—by the March 6 deadline, a little over two weeks after the Wallace speech.

On the weekend after Wallace's speech, Herbstreith was at a party where one of her friends bemoaned the absence from the upcoming Wisconsin primary of a "true conservative"; the crossover race would be staged between two favorite sons—U.S. Rep. John Byrnes for the Republicans and Gov. John Reynolds, as a stand-in for President Johnson, for the Democrats. Herbstreith proposed that they invite Alabama's Wallace to Wisconsin. She thought so much of her own idea that the next day she decided to hire a housekeeper to take care of her three small children, and then started phoning and writing friends and acquaintances around the state to request their participation in and support of a possible Wallace candidacy. A few days later, on February 28, precisely one week before the filing deadline, Governor Reynolds, who had learned of her efforts, joked about it at a news conference. Asked what he thought of a possible Wallace run in the Wisconsin primary, Reynolds somewhat face-tiously directed all questions to Herbstreith.

The subsequent news report was the first that either Wallace or his inner circle had heard of Herbstreith or her endeavors. And it had an impact unintended by Reynolds: it generated dozens of serious phone calls to Herbstreith's home in Oshkosh—enough to complete the delegate slate. Immediately, she telephoned Montgomery with the news. Wallace's longtime friend Ralph Adams, now a member of the governor's cabinet, liked the idea, as did Bill Jones; the two of them, in fact, had been testing the idea among Wallace's intimates since returning from Wisconsin—and they knew that the prospect interested both Wallace and his informal adviser, Grover Hall. But now, Wallace had something more to grasp than mere straws in the wind: he had a tangible slate of delegates. He dispatched two friends from the legislature to meet with Herbstreith and confirm that both she and her delegate slate were legitimate. On March 4, they reported back that all was in order. On March 6, Wallace flew into Madison, where Herbstreith met him for the first time, and where the governor formally filed his primary candidacy. In his visit there just two weeks earlier, Governor Reynolds had graciously offered to accompany Wallace to the airport; Reynolds and Wallace had chatted cordially and warmly en route. At the time, neither knew that their relationship would turn decidedly sour—or that the Wisconsin governor's political future would be effectively ended in the bitter aftertaste of a vitriolic primary campaign against the man seated next to him.[22]

What Reynolds and most commentators would miss, however, was that the driving force behind Wallace's somewhat seat-of-the-pants entry into Wisconsin was not segregation but deeply held conservative convictions. Herbstreith was neither a racist nor a crazy, though Reynolds and newspapers made much of the fact that she was a native of Appleton, Sen. Joseph McCarthy's hometown, as if that were enough to suggest a conspiracy. Still, when Wallace opened his Wisconsin campaign in mid-March, he heaped lavish praise on the senator; he said that McCarthy's "warnings" about "the left-wing influence in the American government and all this 'mobocracy' around the world . . . [seemed] to be coming to pass in this country." But Herbstreith and her friends were less interested in race and the Communist menace than in sowing conservative seeds that began sprouting with Barry Goldwater later that year and flowered with Ronald Reagan in the 1980s. Her husband, Lloyd, was an advertising executive who was the chairman of a group that had tried vainly the year before to persuade the legislature to adopt a resolution calling for repeal of the federal income tax. And, as Herbstreith herself would explain her admiration for Wallace: "The appeal of Governor Wallace is not particularly his civil rights position. His appeal is as a conservative—and an articulate one. He upholds the Constitution, believes in states' rights, and limited federal government." She had never before been active in politics, but she recognized that Wallace was a harbinger of a potential conservative renaissance.[23]

Wallace's advance team, described by the Alabama writer Wayne Greenhaw as "a handful of country boys and a half-dozen tough-looking state troopers," opened the campaign with a total of eight hundred dollars. Later, when television stations demanded cash up front to purchase time for commercials, Seymore Trammel, who had ample personal financial resources, loaned the campaign twenty thousand dollars. Wallace justified using a state-owned plane for the bulk of his transportation by arguing that he was not only spreading Alabama's gospel throughout the North but also working to attract industry to his state. Other financial needs were covered—barely—

by small contributions from blue-collar workers (despite powerful opposition from AFL-CIO state and national officials), Wisconsin conservatives (still plentiful from the McCarthy days), and the large ethnic populations of Milwaukee.[24] The unsophisticated and inexperienced Wallace staff learned the exigencies of national campaigning as they went along. Scheduling tended to be helter-skelter, with Jones and Herbstreith trying, often vainly, to coordinate where and when Wallace would appear. Robert Kendall, an Alabama state senator who occasionally accompanied the Wallace entourage in Wisconsin, recalled that "Wallace would get into a car not having any idea where the hell he was going, except that it was someplace that Mrs. Herbstreith had scheduled."

Once, following a radio call-in show in Oshkosh that the governor felt had gone exceedingly well, a chipper Wallace decided—with startling consequences—to make an unscheduled stop at Oshkosh State College. As he walked about the campus, greeting students and faculty, word of his presence spread rapidly—and students were not pleased. By the time he climbed in his car to depart, a near-riotous mob had closed in on him. Students were shouting and brandishing hastily prepared anti-Wallace placards. Had the hurriedly summoned local police not restrained the students, Wallace might have been hurt. He would make no further unscheduled appearances. But the event gave Reynolds a false sense of security. And, underscoring his sense of Wallace's weakness and unpopularity, he looked at some early polls showing that Wallace would be lucky to receive twenty-five thousand votes. Feeling self-confident, Reynolds said that if Wallace got "a large number of votes in Wisconsin," that would "give heart to hate-mongers from coast to coast." Giving himself some room for error, he said that a hundred thousand votes for Wallace would be "dangerously high."[25]

Wisconsin's major institutions—government, religion, media, labor—were arrayed against Wallace, and their spokespeople were vociferous in their near-hysterical opposition. The state Democratic party chairman, J. Louis Hanson, said he did not recognize Wallace as a Democrat. "Given the election laws of Wisconsin," he said, "any kook—and I consider him a kook—can cause trouble. This man is being supported by extreme right-wing elements who are probably kookier than he is." Representative Byrnes, running unopposed as Wisconsin's favorite son to the Republican National Convention, wanted to discourage crossover votes in the state's open primary, so he urged Republicans to reject "hate and the hypocrisy," which he said Wallace represented, and he charged that Wallace was anything but "the true champion" of states' rights. Instead, asserted Byrnes, "[Wallace] poses a grave danger to those rights. . . . Governor Wallace and his wing of the Democratic Party have prostituted states' rights by using them to deny human freedom. We Republicans support states' rights as a means of preserving human freedom." The leaders of organized labor denounced Wallace in a battery of bulletins and press statements. John W. Schmitt, the state director of the Committee on Political Education, the AFL-CIO's political action arm, accused Wallace of coming to Wisconsin not as a political candidate, but as "an industrial pirate" who was seeking "to steal the jobs of [Wisconsin's] workers" and transport them to Alabama, where employees were underpaid and overworked. The state's AFL-CIO leadership branded Wallace as "a carpet-bagger, a bigot, a racist, and one of the strongest anti-labor spokesmen in America."

By far the most extensive vilification of Wallace, however, came from the leaders of all religious groups in the state. The *Catholic Herald Citizen*, the official newspaper of the Milwaukee archdiocese, told its quarter million readers, "Moral evil is invading Wisconsin; Governor Wallace of Alabama has come to our state . . . directed by an evil mind and motivated by an evil heart." A Lutheran minister in Milwaukee, Martin W. Bangert, warned, "[Wallace] has repeatedly and purposely spoken and acted contrary to everything about which God's word teaches and which we, as Christians, believe." Newspapers were almost uniformly opposed to Wallace's candidacy; typical of editorial opposition was a piece in the *Milwaukee Journal* claiming that Wallace had described various ethnic groups as "lesser breeds" than white Anglo-Saxons.[26]

Wallace allowed the widespread aspersions to bounce off as if he had the skin of an armadillo. This was a brilliant political ploy; it did not always win him friends, but it effectively turned away wrath. At a speech that opened his Wisconsin campaign in Appleton, he said, "I thought I would be ignored but, instead, I am getting more publicity than a man could buy." Then he smiled and added, "I guess you folks are sort of disappointed that I don't have horns after all you have read about me in the press." In response to attacks from organized labor, he produced a seventy-foot-long petition signed by Alabama union members. Following reports that he had maligned ethnic Americans, Wallace imported to Wisconsin a panoply of Alabamians of Polish, Russian, Greek, Jewish, Italian, and German origins.[27]

On the stump, he frequently encountered hostile audiences who booed, hissed, and waved placards with messages such as "Racist, Go Home" and "Wallace Doesn't Have Anything against Negroes—He Thinks Everybody Should Own One." Typically, Wallace would flick small salutes and maintain a broad smile while waiting for relative quiet. Then he would say, "I sense there is some disagreement between us." Invariably, the remark would generate laughter and applause. Then Wallace would add pleasantly, "But let us agree to disagree agreeably." Unfailingly, that did the trick.[28] Traveling the state over a three-week campaign, Wallace kept pecking away at the hobgoblins he maintained were threatening freedom—all of them emanating from the proposed civil rights act, which he insisted promoted federal usurpation of state and individual liberty:

> *On Communists:* It is an unvarnished fact of truth that the official Communist Party of the United States is an enthusiastic supporter of the civil rights bill.[29]

> *On states' rights:* We know . . . that the leaders of world communism intend to destroy our political system. We know that our [states' rights] system . . . is a frustrating roadblock to communism and its liberal forerunners. Hence, we have witnessed a venomous attack on all who believe in state sovereignty. We have witnessed a propaganda barrage of emotionalism that creates a climate of hysteria in promoting deliberate violations of those rights by judicial edict and physical force.[30]

> *On the Supreme Court:* The Supreme Court is an oligarchy. They legislate when they are supposed to adjudicate. Why can't you criticize a court? You can criticize governors—and they are just as sacred in the American system as judges.[31]

> *On government by fiat:* A Communist applauds government by executive or judicial edict [because] a president [or] a judiciary . . . may be deceived or brainwashed or corrupted. But . . . a Communist hates the Congress. . . . It is unwieldy. It is large. It has differing opinions, differing prejudices. It is rampant with debate and deliberation.[32]

When accused of opposing human rights by opposing the civil rights bill, he countered, "Property rights are human rights, too—and the civil rights bill threatens the destruction of property rights."

And then, at an Oshkosh meeting, he resorted to a favorite tactic of turning the tables on those critical of the South's racial tensions:

> Much of the hate and bitterness and ill-will in the country today is engendered by government hypocrites who preach one thing and practice another. In the South, we believe in segregation and say so. In other sections of the country, including Milwaukee, where integration is supposed to be in force, Negroes are demonstrating and threatening boycotts because they claim that segregation is still a way of life. I challenge you to visit Chicago, Baltimore, New York, and some of the other large Northern cities and then come to Alabama and see for yourself if there isn't more racial peace than in any city in the North.[33]

When challenged on the efficacy of segregated schools, Wallace would strike back with a non sequitur that nonetheless impressed many audiences: segregated schools, he pointed out, meant thousands of well-paying jobs for black schoolteachers; separate colleges for blacks and whites not only created opportunities for black academics, but for black college executives. "How many Negro college presidents do you have here?" he would ask derisively.[34] And when labor leaders claimed he was trying to hijack business from their state, he denied it; his goal was to encourage their industrial leaders to consider expanding into Alabama. Besides, he would add, the industry he lured to Alabama (its worth would total a half billion dollars by the end of 1964) had provided seventy-five thousand new jobs, more than a third of which had been filled by blacks.[35]

One antagonist in Oshkosh asked Wallace how he squared his antifederalism with his state's acceptance of an estimated $700 million in federal aid. "Well," he answered, "we paid about a billion dollars in income tax. It appears to me we've been short-changed." Then, unsure of his figures, he added, "There is no such thing as federal aid. Washington takes our money, pours most of it down various rat holes around the world, and sends back to the states the little that is left. All federal aid is taxpayers' money."[36]

The "rat holes" to which Wallace referred included "feeding and supporting half the Communist nations of the world" and "financing food for the Russians in order to ease their internal pressure"—programs that the United States might cut off or reduce while, in tandem with other industrialized nations, bringing "economic and political pressures to bear to negotiate freedom" for the Soviet-occupied nations of Eastern Europe. In the Western hemisphere, Wallace said the United States might offer military support to any Latin American government "to mop up the saboteurs, the fifth columnists, the rioters, and the Communist-trained street fighters."[37]

■   ■   ■

It cannot escape notice that Wallace's essential views—his virulent anticommunism, his dread of federal intrusion into private affairs, his belief that economic pressures could weaken the Soviet grip on its vassal states, and his willingness to support militarily the efforts of Latin American governments to suppress revolutions—all presaged official American policy, especially as embraced and practiced by President Reagan in the 1980s. And his pithy, if often simplistic, barbs aimed at the federal establishment were echoed for years to come by presidential candidates as dissimilar as Jimmy Carter, Ronald Reagan, and Ross Perot.

But Wallace carried some heavy personal baggage that would not burden his philosophical heirs—segregation and the ugliness that surrounded it. He had learned to avoid the issue of segregation whenever possible—but it was rarely possible. He tried, as he would all his life, to distinguish between being a racist (which he said he never was) and a segregationist (which he said he stopped being in the 1970s—and about which he said he had been wrong all along). "I am no racist," he told audiences. "I believe there is a God and He loves all men, and if I hate a creature that God made because of his color, that is evil. But I am a segregationist because I believe that segregation of the races is best for both peoples." Then Wallace would pause and, turning the question to his advantage, would add, "I am an Alabama segregationist, though—not a Wisconsin segregationist. If Wisconsin believes in integration, that is Wisconsin's business, not mine. That is why I'm here to tell you that Wisconsin has the right to choose the pattern it will follow in race relations. Alabama has the right to choose the path it will follow. And the central government in Washington has no right to tell either Alabama or Wisconsin what to do." (Here, there would usually be a mixed chorus of cheers and boos.) "So a vote for me in Wisconsin is not a vote for segregation. It is a vote for the right to run your schools, your business, your lives as you and you alone see fit." (Here, the cheers would almost always drown out the boos.)[38]

Wallace wanted to take his case directly to religious groups in Wisconsin, but nearly all of them turned him down. An exception was the Oshkosh Ministerial Association—clearly unfriendly to Wallace—and the confrontation produced an unexpected boon to the Alabamian. Several ministers, led by the association's president, a United Church of Christ pastor named Jack Lamar, peppered Wallace with harsh questions, including whether Wallace would object to his daughter marrying a black man. "I most certainly would," Wallace admitted. "I am against that." Lamar wanted to know why Wallace would object. Wallace said he did not think that "interracial marriages are good for either race." Lamar was not satisfied. "I think you are evading the issue," he insisted. Wallace became a bit riled. "I am against it," he barked. "That's not evading the question." Several ministers then started lecturing Wallace. One said that "the trouble in the South has caused all the trouble in the big cities. We didn't have any difficulty in Chicago until you had all that trouble in Arkansas, Alabama, and Mississippi." Wallace reminded him that a race riot in Detroit twenty years earlier had claimed thirty-four lives. "That occurred a long time before Little Rock and Birmingham," he said.

One minister, a Methodist named Ray Heilborn, surprised the group by supporting Wallace. "We're a bunch of Northerners whistling 'Dixie,' " he said. "We don't have any Negroes here at all and we are all scared to death that we might get some and not know what to do with them." That was more than most of Heilborn's colleagues could take. Several accused Wallace of ignoring the "basic human rights" of Alabama's Negroes. Wallace shot back, "You all might spend a little less time worrying about Negroes in Alabama and a little more worrying about the Indians in Wisconsin and the conditions they live in on the reservations." That last comment, when reported in several Wisconsin newspapers, electrified the state's population of twenty thousand Chippewas, Oneidas, and Winnebagos. Before the week was out, the consolidated tribes of Wisconsin presented Wallace with an elaborate American Indian headdress—and in the ensuing primary, Wallace received the bulk of votes cast by Indians; it was measurable in tiny Menominee County where all twenty-one of the votes cast by Indians went to Wallace.[39]

Wallace also planted seeds of doubt about the efficacy of the civil rights bill among many of his listeners by asking each audience for a show of hands on who had read the proposed law. As anticipated, very few had—so Wallace maintained they were not in a position to label his claims about the bill as false. Wallace would then proceed to excoriate the bill's provisions in apocalyptic terms, variously claiming that the bill virtually would eliminate state governments, that it would lead either to a police state or to massive illegality (as in Prohibition), that the government would assume power over all businesses and labor unions, and that it would give the federal government "power to investigate, to arrest, to charge and try a citizen without a jury of his peers." And, he asserted, "it will bring about the ultimate in tyranny. It will make government master and god over man."

After one such tirade before an unfriendly group at a Catholic school, a student said, "He's not as bad as I thought he was." A young priest said, "I am in sympathy with the objectives of the civil rights bill. But I haven't read it, and I must admit he raised some doubts in my mind." And when he told one audience that, under the bill, a person of Japanese extraction could demand a job at a nearby American Motors plant by claiming that not enough Japanese people were on the payroll, a man in the audience jumped up, identified himself as a member of Local 72 of the UAW, and asserted that Wallace had great support among his fellow workers who "don't like too much intervention by the federal government."[40]

■   ■   ■

Before the April 7 primary, Wallace tapped into two other areas of support—one accidentally and the other instinctively. After a news conference at a Kenosha hotel, as the entourage was leaving, two pickets swung their signs at Wallace. One missed entirely, but the second nicked the governor and banged against the head of one of his security officers. The attacker, a Kenosha architect, was arrested, but the charge against him of disorderly conduct was later dismissed. Both the assault and the failure to find guilt prompted widespread, sympathetic publicity in Wisconsin and in neighboring states. To be sure, Wallace did not tempt fate by seeking out hostile situations, but he learned to play to maximum advantage the belligerence that many crowds would display—particularly when heckling and interruptions would make them vulnerable to charges of throttling free speech.

Wallace's instinctive discovery was that ethnic groups were powerfully attracted to the message that the civil rights bill might adversely affect their jobs, their property values, the makeup of their neighborhoods, and children's school sites. Wallace was openly jittery about appearing at Serbian Memorial Hall in south Milwaukee as the campaign wound into its final week. Although he believed these people identified with his positions, he feared that he would look and sound too different to be entrusted with their votes. Then, as the evening opened with a Polish band playing the national anthem, followed by an off-key rendition of "Dixie," Wallace faced a new concern—a near explosion of racial tension in the hall. It began when two blacks in the audience failed to rise as the audience sang "The Star-Spangled Banner." The evening's host, Bronko Gruber, a hulking ex-marine and owner of a south Milwaukee tavern, ordered the two men to leave. Amid shouts and shoving, the two reluctantly complied. Then, as Gruber started to introduce Wallace, some other blacks shouted "police dogs" and other reminders of the violence in Birmingham. It was too much for the volatile Gruber, who shouted back, "Maybe we need some [police dogs] here," and then launched into an emotional verbal attack on blacks:

> Who was it that beat up an elderly white woman in my neighborhood a few weeks ago? They were three of your countrymen. Who is it that beats up newsboys, rapes our women, attacks old women? You know who it is. It's your colored brothers. How long can we tolerate this? Did I go to Guadalcanal and come back to something like this?

Wallace, standing in the wings, grew nearly frantic, certain the place would explode. He nudged two of his aides who knew Gruber and told them to go out there and calm him down. Then he signaled Bill Jones to tell the band to play. They struck up a reprise of "Dixie," drowning out Gruber as Wallace strode out to the podium. "My message is for all," he said soothingly, "and I want all of us to be in good humor tonight." He joked weakly that "Dixie" sounded "as good in Polish as . . . in English." Everyone laughed—even though no one had sung the lyrics in any language. Then he reminded them of his inaugural prayer in which he had asked God's blessing on all the people of his state, both black and white. When he sensed that the crowd's dangerous mood had eased, Wallace moved to his standard attack on the civil rights bill. His forty-minute speech was interrupted thirty times by applause, with the strongest ovations in response to his assertions that the bill would destroy job seniority, neighborhood school systems, and homeowners' rights to sell property to whomever they chose. He received a standing ovation when he closed by saying, "A vote for this little governor will let people in Washington know that we want them to leave our house, schools, jobs, businesses, and farms alone—and let us run them without any help from Washington." At the end, Wallace was mobbed by hundreds in the hall. They sought autographs, they made cash contributions, they wanted to touch him. Wallace felt their electricity—and, in Washington, President Johnson sensed it.

■   ■   ■

Until then, the president had remained above the fray, allowing Wisconsin's Governor Reynolds to carry the attack alone. But now he dispatched his postmaster general, John Gronouski, a Polish-American economist and academician who had been Wisconsin's tax commissioner, to do some quick fence-mending in the ethnic areas of the state.[41] Robert Kennedy, whose brother's Wisconsin primary victory four years earlier had helped propel him toward the Democratic presidential nomination, interceded also at the eleventh hour. He urged a "substantial victory" for Reynolds as a means of strengthening "the good fight for human dignity" on behalf of the civil rights bill. Johnson himself broke his silence with a wire, read at a testimonial dinner for Reynolds the weekend before the voting, calling the Wisconsin governor "a patriot and a leader in whom" everyone could "take pride." The powers that be were growing apprehensive. The state's director of elections predicted a turnout of more than a million voters—nearly as many as had turned out for the hotly contested 1960 primary between John Kennedy and Hubert Humphrey. Reynolds, who had raised his original estimate of Wallace votes from 50,000 to 100,000, started leaking numbers of 175,000 or even higher.[42]

In the end, Wallace struck a far heavier blow than even the most fearful among the Democratic professionals had anticipated. More than a million voters turned out, fulfilling the official prediction—and one in every four voted for George Wallace. Of the nearly 800,000 voting for either of the two Democrats in the open primary, 1 in 3 had voted for Wallace. Democratic politicians, in a word, were "stunned" by Wallace's showing. To be sure, many tried to suggest that there had been a heavy Republican crossover vote designed to embarrass the president and the Democratic governor. But Reynolds had given Wallace an outside chance to attract 10 percent of the vote; for whatever reasons—crossovers, veiled racism, repressed McCarthyism—Wallace received 25 percent of the total vote. And careful analysis demonstrated, as one report put it, "that nearly as many Republicans . . . jumped party lines to vote for Reynolds as for

Wallace"—voters who wanted to show their support for the civil rights bill that their man, Byrnes, had supported in the House of Representatives. Southerners, by and large, were "thrilled with [Wallace's] magnificent showing," as the new governor of Mississippi, Paul Johnson, put it. There were a few who tried to scotch over the results: Eugene Patterson, the editor of the *Atlanta Constitution*, maintained that "a food faddist could have entered the Wisconsin primary and picked up a good-sized vote if he had extolled the edibility of gourds." Atlanta's moderate mayor, Ivan Allen, dismissed Wallace's vote-getting ability in the North as having "no . . . basic significance." Those who did see significance tended to focus on the racial aspects of Wallace's appeal—a reaction against civil rights demonstrations, a manifestation of prejudice, or, as a black man, sipping a beer in a bar on Milwaukee's north side, said:

> Me, I'm glad he come up here and done what he did. He jerk the covers off these phonies up here. He say, "All right, boys, I'm for segregation today, tomorrow, and forever, and I know you cats are, too—but you too scared to admit it." So a quarter of a million of them admit it.

Almost none of the politicians or editorialists around the country saw anything beyond race in the Wallace vote—except Wallace himself, who exulted on election night, "We have won a victory and they know it. . . . The people of Wisconsin have done more to break the trend toward centralized government than they realize." To his eventual dismay, Reynolds did not see it that way. "All that Mr. Wallace has demonstrated," Reynolds said, "is what we've known all along. We have a lot of people who are prejudiced." The remark stung tens of thousands of Wisconsin Democrats who had supported Wallace in the presidential primary; in the fall, many of them organized a group that they named, with tongue in cheek, "Bigots against Reynolds."

In November, despite President Johnson's nearly two-to-one margin over Barry Goldwater in Wisconsin, Reynolds was defeated by his Republican challenger for governor. Wallace said that Johnson later told him jocularly, "You cost me a circuit judgeship." According to Wallace, Reynolds had asked for the post because he believed that his agreement to stand in for Johnson in the primary had irreparably damaged his chances for reelection. "I had hoped to give the judgeship to someone else," Wallace remembered Johnson saying.[43]

■   ■   ■

Even if few political leaders perceived the long-term significance of Wallace's showing in Wisconsin and his ability to stir nascent conservative instincts across the nation, politicians knew how to count votes—and "national leaders of the two political parties," as the news analyst Earl Mazo wrote, were "cautious and mostly apprehensive" about Wallace's future prospects in the North. They told Mazo they felt "the Indiana and Maryland primaries" that Wallace had entered would "clarify" whether the Alabama governor would "prove a formidable factor." To be sure, they were concerned about the immediate impact of Wallace's appeal to racist impulses, not about any growing conservative or antigovernment trends. And their interests were principally limited to short-term concerns—the effects that strong support for Wallace would have on the pending civil rights legislation in Congress and on the 1964 election. Still, they were onto something—something that Johnson's smashing victory over Goldwater would tend to obscure from moderate and liberal Democrats and Republicans for a number of years to come.[44]

Wallace's elation at his Wisconsin results was, if anything, surpassed by his Alabama constituents' exhilaration. At Montgomery's Dannelly Field, three thousand people greeted their governor's arrival from Wisconsin with "an outburst of fervor" in which they would "weep and shout and reach out [their] clutching hands to touch a conquering hero returning in triumph from the North." Many in the crowd had arrived in a three-hundred-car motorcade that had made the hundred-mile trip from Birmingham. Pumping his arm in the air as a victory sign, Wallace assured his supporters that his success would require both parties to "conservatize" their platform positions; he had demonstrated that there was widespread support in the North for containing federal power. Now, he told them, he was heading to Indiana, where he expected to strike another blow for individual liberty in the May 5 primary.[45] A week before the Wisconsin voting, Wallace's petitions to enter the Indiana primary were certified as acceptable by Indiana's Republican secretary of state. A few days earlier, the state's Democratic governor, Matthew Welsh, had tried vainly to have Wallace declared ineligible due to irregularities in his petitions, which, Welsh said, included among nearly six hundred signatures such questionable names as "Willie the Polack" and "Sam Sandwich." Wallace, whose associates believed they could round up the necessary five hundred Hoosier signatures in a couple of hours if they had to, found Welsh's tactics—and apparent discomfort—amusing; indeed, Wallace was "having the time of his life in Indiana." The Alabamian pointed out that Welsh previously had dismissed the Wallace candidacy with the japing remark, "Who's Wallace?" To which Wallace later replied, "He's not saying that now, is he?"[46]

Wallace believed that he might outperform his Wisconsin showing in Indiana because many Southerners, including numerous Alabamians, had migrated to Indiana in search of work after World War II. He viewed Hoosiers as "similar in thought and attitude" to Alabamians. An article in the *New York Times* by the journalist Claude Sitton buttressed Wallace's notion. Sitton wrote that Indiana was "the North's most Southern state" and thus would be "an admirable battleground for [Wallace's] purposes." A feature of Indiana was its "rustic rule and racial intolerance [that] approached equality . . . with some its neighbors to the South." Sitton described the historically strong support in the state for the Know-Nothings, the Ku Klux Klan, and "the far right wing [that] long ago moved into positions of power."[47]

Sitton's contention seemed validated when Wallace opened his Indiana campaign on April 15 with a news conference and speech to more than three hundred students at Butler University in Indianapolis. Reporters and photographers followed him in large numbers as he made the same case he had in Wisconsin—he was running to energize national opposition to federal encroachment on individual freedoms. It was just coincidental, he said, that the nation's central power was manifested by matters pertaining to race—school integration, the House-passed civil rights bill, and newly emerging efforts to alter traditional neighborhood school assignments to achieve greater racial balance in the public schools. At Butler, he was greeted by more than seventy student pickets; inside, a reporter from an Evansville, Indiana, newspaper said that "most of the student crowd . . . came to jeer the controversial Southerner." And jeer they did—especially when Wallace admitted ignorance on issues of foreign affairs (including his admission that he was not qualified to discuss Vietnam) and when he transformed questions about the economy into pat comments on how the civil rights bill would threaten union members' jobs. But slowly, Wallace's pungent, if glib, replies to questions designed to embarrass him won the crowd over. He was roundly applauded when, responding to a suggestion that his actions were damaging America's image among foreign countries, Wallace snapped, "It's about time we quit worrying about what they think of us and let them start worrying about what we think of them.

It's our money they are spending. We don't have to apologize for America. We have more civil rights per square inch here than they have in a square mile behind the Iron Curtain." When asked about the right of blacks to buy homes wherever they want, Wallace insisted that it was "a matter to be settled at the state level." "But six Negro families live in the same block as the executive mansion in Montgomery," he continued, "and they did not move out when I moved in—and I don't intend to move out until my term as governor is over." The students laughed appreciatively. But they saved their loudest applause for the governor's comment that he thought that fraternities and sororities should be free to admit or reject blacks as members. Later, the campus newspaper polled about 40 percent of the students who had heard Wallace; 56 percent said they would vote for Wallace, while the rest said they would vote for Governor Welsh.[48]

The inconsequential and meaningless poll nonetheless buoyed the Wallace staffers. A small team of neatly dressed aides set up headquarters in Indianapolis's aging Claypool Hotel and promptly began churning out and mailing campaign literature with benign slogans like, "A vote for me will be a vote to return the government to you—the people—where it rightfully belongs."[49] But if the Butler poll animated the Wallace team, it electrified Welsh—and he was determined to keep Wallace below the Wisconsin results.

Like Wisconsin's Governor Reynolds, Welsh began by sharply defining his opponent in harsh terms. At a Democratic meeting, Welsh declared that Wallace was trying to wreck the party and said, "[His campaign] smells sweet, but it has the taste of death." He then issued what *Time* described "as denunciatory a statement . . . as [had] been seen in U.S. politics in a long while":

> This [Wallace] is the man who tolerated the presence of billboards in his state before the assassination which demanded: "Kayo the Kennedys." This is the man whose beliefs were responsible for the deaths of innocent children in the bombing of a Sunday school class. This is the man who stood by while dogs were set upon human beings and fire hoses were turned on groups of peaceful demonstrators. . . . This is the man who is trying to destroy the political system of the United States as we know it and who seeks to discredit President Lyndon B. Johnson. This is the man who flies the Confederate flag over the statehouse in Alabama in place of the Stars and Stripes.[50]

It was tough stuff coming from anyone—but especially from the polished and ordinarily soft-spoken Welsh. But the jarringly vitriolic words—and there were more to come—were nothing compared to Welsh's political artifices designed to limit Wallace's vote. Unlike Wisconsin, Indiana was a highly politicized state, and its governor exercised real political power. State patronage employees—and there were thousands—were instructed to prevent appearances by or rallies for Wallace on state property, and they were directed to pressure individuals and organizations doing business with the state to refrain from lending any support to Wallace, including keeping any groups to which they belonged from sponsoring a Wallace speech. The state's AFL-CIO president, Dallas Sells, was a committed Democrat. While he knew there would be a widespread "silent vote" for Wallace from his members, he was nonetheless in a position to mobilize hundreds of men and women to pass out Welsh campaign literature and to ferry Welsh voters to the polls on the day of the May 5 primary. Finally, to discourage Republican crossovers into the Democratic primary, Welsh said any registered Republican requesting a Democratic ballot would be required to sign a pledge to vote for the Democratic party's nominees in the fall. In addition, the Democratic party's county chairmen in Indiana threatened to publish the names of anyone who crossed over—an embarrassment in a state where most people retained strong party affiliations. The Wallace people had not encountered a party juggernaut of that kind before. Early on, they jettisoned their initial plan to have Wallace stump Indiana much as he had Alabama. The best they could do was schedule the candidate for as many news conferences, call-in radio programs, and campus talks as possible; in addition, he managed appearances before a few extremely conservative organizations whose members were beyond Welsh's reach.[51]

But Wallace, who had learned in Wisconsin how to play the game of expectations, predicted, "I'll win this race in Indiana by getting any sizable vote at all." Ever-present "political observers" quoted in the newspapers were a little more specific: they told reporters that anything less than 100,000 votes for Wallace would be a "defeat"; he would need at least 150,000 votes to contend, as he had in Wisconsin, "We won without winning."[52]

Even deprived of what might have been his most effective campaign milieu, the big rally, Wallace adopted the attitude that his message would strike receptive chords in Indiana and that he would surpass expectations. His confidence was reflected in his relaxed response when his flight to Indiana on April 19 was forced to turn back due to rough weather. (Wallace's postwar anxiety about flying meant that flights in choppy weather made him doubly uncomfortable, as noted in chapter 3). As the pilot was turning toward Nashville to put in for the night, Wallace glanced out the window and correctly identified the city below as Bowling Green, Kentucky. Wallace insisted they land there instead of Nashville; Bowling Green had been one of the most successful stops on his itinerary when he was traveling the country selling magazine subscriptions. And before they took off for Indianapolis early Monday morning, Wallace took his aides on a tour of the town, pointing out some of his favorite haunts.

Wallace barely had touched down in Indiana a second time when Welsh was at him again, calling Alabama a "police state" where "scores of thousands of colored voters [were] denied their most precious right—the right to vote." Wallace handled allegations of that kind with benign equanimity, reacting as if Welsh, whom he described as "a fine man" for whom he had "the highest regard," simply misunderstood him and the South. He told students at Earlham College in Richmond, Indiana, that more blacks held professional jobs in Alabama than in their state. "The other day in Wisconsin," he said, "I saw a Negro Ph.D. sweeping the floor and I told him, 'You come on down to Alabama and you don't have to sweep floors. I'll see that you get a job in the school system.'" Defending segregation, Wallace said, "Take the beam from your own eye before you strike the mote from ours. If you want to talk about abolishing segregation in the schools, give us a good model and maybe we'll emulate you. When Chicago voted on whether to have integrated schools, they voted five-to-two against it. And Washington now has eighty-five percent Negroes in the schools. Is that what happens to integrated schools? Y'all talk a good game—but when it comes down to the fact, you don't do much." Maintaining that he was "religiously convicted [*sic*] that segregation is best for the welfare of both races," Wallace pressed his point: "You take Philadelphia. Anybody here from Philadelphia? You know, they can't even have night football games anymore because of the trouble between the races. And they have to play their games in the afternoon with no spectators. Now, who ever heard of such a thing, playing with no spectators. Anybody here from Philadelphia?" One boy raised his hand. "Well, it's true, isn't it?" Wallace asked. The youth nodded affirmatively.

"And that," Wallace said, aglow with triumph, "is the city of brotherly love."[53]

■ ■ ■

To be sure, Wallace had his rough moments, especially when confronted by issues of foreign policy. At Earlham, he was caught up short by a question about the Alliance for Progress. "You mean in South America?" he replied. "That's the one," the questioner smirked, and the audience burst into laughter. But Wallace kept his composure, joking self-deprecatingly that he recently learned that Vietnam was not in northern Alabama. And later, when he began an answer by saying, "The people of Alabama are intelligent, refined, and cultured people . . . ," the crowd cackled derisively. Wallace looked genuinely puzzled and hurt. But when he went on to complete the sentence, adding, ". . . just as the people of Indiana are intelligent and don't need somebody to tell them how to run their state," most of the students looked down at their hands as if somewhat ashamed of their arrogantly impolite outburst.[54]

In the ensuing two weeks, Wallace provoked a roller coaster of emotions: he was greeted with jeers and chants at Terre Haute, but with warm applause in Governor Welsh's hometown of Vincennes; he was booed and hooted at Indiana University, and alternately hissed and cheered at Notre Dame, where emotions ran high. Four hundred students, priests, and nuns picketed the packed field house in which Wallace spoke; the faculty issued a statement calling Wallace "the current lightweight champion of segregation, and America's number-one racist"; and catcalls interrupted him continually during his one-hour appearance. Midway through his speech, Wallace was forced to break off for ten minutes when 500 of the 5,000 people in the audience started shouting and pushing one another, some trying to drown him out and others insisting on freedom of speech; meanwhile, Wallace's antagonists sang the anthem of the civil rights movement, "We Shall Overcome." Through it all, Wallace retained his composure. During the stretches when singing and bellowing overwhelmed his attempt to speak, Wallace smiled, winked, snapped salutes, and signed autographs for dozens in the audience who either were admirers or were merely interested in a piece of history. When a large group, carrying and waving placards, started to march from the field house, Wallace cracked, "I accept the nomination." And when someone emitted a shrill yell from the rear of the hall, Wallace's schoolyard retort—"show that fellow where the little boys' room is"—was applauded.

Wallace's attacks on what he called "sweeping federal encroachment" and on nascent plans to bus schoolchildren to achieve racial balance were loudly cheered, as was his criticism of Northern hypocrisy: "What is termed a race riot in the South is called civil disobedience in New York or Chicago [and] in Washington . . . they are building a new bridge over the Potomac for all the white liberals fleeing to Virginia." When he departed, the automobile in which he was riding was banged and dented by protesters wielding their anti-Wallace signs.[55]

The next day, Wallace shared the spotlight with Roman Catholic Bishop Fulton J. Sheen in Washington, where both urged Congress to approve a constitutional amendment permitting school prayer. The widely published Associated Press photo in which Wallace and the nationally revered Sheen were smiling at each other provided Wallace with yet another symbol of respectability, and it—on the heels of the Notre Dame appearance—likely increased his strength in largely Catholic areas of Indiana and in his next primary target, Maryland. Wallace went out of his way to keep from embarrassing Sheen. "I wouldn't want to say the bishop agrees with me on all matters," Wallace told reporters. "I don't want to get the bishop in any trouble. In fact," he added, "I don't think he agrees with me on any matter but this one."

In his statement to the House Judiciary Committee, Wallace vigorously denounced the Supreme Court for its decision banning school prayer. "We are being manipulated by the courts in a gigantic socialist conspiracy," he said, contending that the Court had made a "hollow mockery" of the Bill of Rights in a decision "as sweeping and deadly as any ever issued by any dictatorial power." When he pointed out that the 1928 platform of the U.S. Communist party demanded the abolition of religious instruction in schools, he added "emphatically" that he was by no means suggesting that opponents of a school prayer amendment—who included the committee chairman, Rep. Emanuel Celler of New York—were themselves Communists. Wallace's language and demeanor were much more restrained during questioning. Asked who should designate prayers that students would recite, Wallace admitted that was a problem—but one he believed that could be resolved by "the common sense of local communities." He further stated, "Minority rights must be protected, but the majority have rights, too. No one should be compelled to pray. No one in school should try to convert anyone. But just to say, 'God bless us,' does not violate the Constitution."[56]

Back in Indiana, Welsh turned up the heat. The Democratic State Committee announced it would mount a $75,000 publicity blitz to defeat Wallace, whose own campaign planned to spend $50,000 to promote their man. Ted Kennedy traveled to Indianapolis for a news conference and a speech to three thousand adoring Democrats in which he said the nation was watching to see whether the state was "the home of extremism or the home of common sense." Indiana's two Democratic senators, Vance Hartke and Birch Bayh, wrote to thousands of constituents urging them to vote for Welsh as a stand-in for President Johnson and for the programs started by the martyred President Kennedy. Clergy of all faiths joined hands to oppose Wallace, and even some Republican leaders issued statements critical of the Alabama governor. Welsh even imported anti-Wallace speakers like Charles Morgan, the Birmingham lawyer who had blamed Wallace for the disorders in his hometown, and James McBride Dabbs of South Carolina who, as the president of the Southern Regional Council, could testify to the difficulties of registering blacks to vote in Alabama and the rest of the South. And with two weeks before the voting, President Johnson paid a personal visit to the state as part of what was billed as a "depressed areas" tour to Indiana, Kentucky, Pennsylvania, and West Virginia. As one journalist, Austin Wehrwein of the *New York Times*, put it sardonically, "The President's short visit was interpreted as a happy coincidence for the anti-Wallace campaign."[57]

But Wallace plowed ahead, sticking to the basic messages that he believed were winning him votes. In Richmond, Indiana, he called the civil rights bill a "back-door open-occupancy bill," contending that "a man who owns a home which is his castle ought to be able to sell it to people with blue hair and green eyes only. It's his house." He found a philosophical paradox in the bill's public accommodations section:

> They say [in the bill] you have a right to exclude anyone from your boarding house if it's five rooms or under—but if it's six or more rooms, it's unlawful. It's immoral to reject somebody or select your clientele with six or more rooms, but it's not immoral with five rooms or under. If it's a moral issue involved, it ought to be one room or all rooms.[58]

He invariably managed in every attack on the civil rights bill to rope in the Communist party and God. In Richmond he said:

> The bill has been endorsed and pushed by *The Communist Daily Worker* in every section of it and not a one of them believes man has a soul or has any afterlife and doesn't believe that man is made in the image of God. Every left-wing organization in America who doesn't believe in the existence of God is behind this bill.[59]

When he jumped on the courts, Wallace went beyond their rulings in civil rights cases. Throughout Indiana, he bemoaned the growing incidence of what he called "crime in the streets"—a term that Goldwater would pick up from Wallace a few months later during his presidential campaign, and a theme that would become Nixon's defining issue in 1968. Wallace put it thus in Terre Haute during the primary:

> Crime has risen in our country at an astronomical rate, and the court system now has ruled that you can hardly convict a criminal. If you are knocked in the head on a street in a city today, the man who knocked you in the head is out of jail before you get to the hospital. . . . And they can't tell me that we can't adopt a system in this country that will protect the individual liberties and freedoms of our people and, at the same time, incarcerate a man who is a self-confessed murderer.[60]

And whenever someone threw a curve at Wallace—most often, a question about foreign affairs—he managed to deflect it with candor and humor. In Bloomington, someone—obviously trying to demonstrate Wallace's limitations—asked for the governor's opinion on the ANZUS treaty (the mutual defense agreement among Australia, New Zealand, and the United States—hardly an issue of moment). Wallace remained unfazed. He admitted he was not familiar with the pact, adding: "I have no experience in this. But you all know what the country is like now. It got that way through experience. What we need in Washington now is a little inexperience."[61] One heard echoes of Wallace when, in a presidential debate during the 1992 campaign, Perot jerked a thumb at his two opponents and said, "They say I have no experience. Well, I don't have any experience running up a $4 trillion debt, that's for sure."

As the campaign drove toward the finish, Goldwater made it clear that he was keeping a close eye on Wallace and his popular appeal outside the South. Agreeing with Wallace, he told a news conference, "There is something to this term 'backlash.' . . . The people in the North and West, while they are eager for the Negro to have all his rights . . . don't want their [own] property rights tampered with. The people feel they should have the right to say who lives near them."

Like Wallace, Goldwater opposed the civil rights bill; he wanted issues like open housing, public accommodations, and fair employment dealt with at the state level. "I don't want to see a federal police state," he said, echoing a Wallace view. He anticipated that Wallace would do better in Indiana than the 25 percent he was widely expected to receive; Goldwater predicted that Wallace would receive 30 percent—which he did. Presciently, Goldwater added that Wallace would do even better in the May 19 Maryland primary. "There's a growing apprehension up there among Democrats that his vote is going to go very high."[62] On election eve, Welsh took a parting shot at Wallace by predicting that whatever votes he received would come from remnants of the Ku Klux Klan, friends of Southern White Citizens Councils, migrants to Indiana from the South, and right-wingers from the John Birch Society. Wallace, in typical fashion, snapped back, "I'm not like left-wingers. I believe in God."[63]

There was a second political contest on May 5 that demanded Wallace's attention—running his own slate of presidential electors against a slate of regular Democrats endorsed by Alabama's two U.S. Senators, Lister Hill and John Sparkman. Wallace flew back to Alabama and took to statewide television to plump for his slate. Wallace explained how the electoral system worked—that if the voters selected his slate and then backed it in the fall, their governor would control Alabama's ten electoral votes for president. He instructed the viewers to get pencil and paper, because voters could, if they wished, split their tickets, and Wallace wanted them to vote for each of the ten people pledged to him. He said that while someone was out of the room "fetching something to take down the information," he would review his strong showing in Wisconsin, discuss his accomplishments on behalf of "Alabama and the South," and point out how he would likely "win without winning" again in both Indiana and Maryland. When he assumed his audience was poised, pencils in hand, Wallace went through his list of electors, one by one, displaying their names on the screen and asking viewers to write down each name as he briefly described who each was.[64]

On May 5, Wallace celebrated two victories: he took 30 percent of the Democratic vote in Indiana and carried two counties in the state's industrialized and heavily unionized northwestern corner; and his slate carried in Alabama by an astounding five-to-one margin. Wallace's victory in Indiana's Lake and Porter counties, where he had not even made a personal appearance, covered the state's first congressional district and, under party rules, entitled him to three delegates to the Democratic National Convention. The state Democratic committee promptly changed the rules after the fact; delegates, they resolved, would be chosen at large rather than by congressional district. And in Alabama, where the Wallace slate of electors was expected to win, the political reporter Bob Ingram observed that "nobody—not even Wallace—anticipated such a sweep."

Despite efforts by leading Democrats to minimize Wallace's showing—President Johnson discounted the Wallace vote as "something less than an overwhelming endorsement"—most observers agreed that Indiana's governor did less well than hoped. And Southerners in Washington were delighted. The respected senator from Georgia, Richard Russell, said he was "utterly amazed at the strength (Wallace) has displayed." He and his colleagues believed that Wallace would run even better in Maryland against Sen. Daniel Brewster, who, as a stand-in for Johnson (who coincidentally planned a Maryland visit as part of his antipoverty tour), predicted that Wallace would be "overwhelmingly defeated."[65]

Wallace was tired and spent when he arrived in Maryland eleven days before the May 19 primary; partly for that reason and partly because of security problems—death threats against the governor were becoming almost routine—Wallace's staff planned what Bill Jones called "a campaign of illusion": ten speeches plus heavy advertising on radio, television, and in newspapers. And, because of his vote-getting successes, they had a political war chest of $100,000 to finance a media blitz.[66] A month earlier, however, Maryland's Democratic leaders had largely discounted Wallace's candidacy. The state's governor, J. Millard Tawes, had predicted that Wallace would not "get a vote of any significance" and would "be smothered." Tawes had stood aside for Brewster as a favorite son because a recent state income tax increase had sharply reduced the governor's popularity—and both organized labor and black groups, whose support would be essential, much preferred Brewster's strong civil rights record. But reports that Wallace might run unexpectedly well in Wisconsin, plus a large volume of constituent mail to Brewster opposing the civil rights bill, alarmed the party leadership in Maryland. As a result, Brewster canceled a planned nationwide speaking tour to support Democratic candidates elsewhere in the country. Instead, he launched a concerted drive to crush Wallace, mapping out an aggressive campaign schedule that included speaking appearances by a clutch of popular Democratic senators, including Ted Kennedy and Birch Bayh, plus Frank Church of Idaho, Daniel Inouye of Hawaii, and Abraham Ribicoff of Connecticut.[67] Brewster also added fire to his usually bland campaign style. In a speech to a Democratic group, he called Wallace "a professional liar, a bigot, and an aspiring dictator, and a certain enemy of the Constitution of the United States." And when the president visited Maryland on the eve of Wallace's arrival, he invoked Franklin D. Roosevelt, the American Revolution, and Maryland's tradition of respecting "the fundamental rights of man" for which he expected Marylanders to continue to fight.[68] Even Harry Truman got into the act. At a news conference in Washington, where he was honored by the Senate on his eightieth birthday, Truman was asked how he would handle Wallace. "I wouldn't handle him at all," Truman snapped, "because he will take care of himself. You don't have to handle a man who is always wrong."[69] Wallace's increasing notoriety even frightened the management of the Lord Baltimore Hotel, the site of Wallace's headquarters, into ejecting him and his staff. Their excuse was that Wallace had "made a farce" of a news conference at the hotel a week earlier; the room had been packed with Wallace partisans who booed reporters' questions and cheered Wallace's answers. Reporters complained and the hotel management feared negative publicity.[70] But when Wallace opened his campaign at Johns Hopkins University, he treated the incident lightly:

> Now, you know, they threw us out of the Lord Baltimore Hotel, and I want to tell you that that was their right. I don't feel offended at all. They said some of our people were getting kind of out of hand and making a fuss, and it was hurting business. So they asked us to leave, and we left. But under this [civil rights] bill, they couldn't do that. We could claim they were discriminating against us, and they couldn't act in the best interest of their own business without some federal bureaucrat in Washington telling them to go to jail.[71]

In his whirlwind Maryland campaign, Wallace adopted a tone described as "one of rustic reasonableness and injured piety."

He held forth on a range of topics.

On housing: "You may want to sell your house to someone with blue eyes and green teeth, and that's all right. I don't object. But you should not be forced to do it. A man's house is his castle."

On education: "Now, you may want to bus your children across to some other school just to meet the plans of some social engineer in Washington for racial balance in the classroom because they say that's good. I don't object to that if that is what you want to do. But you people here in Maryland ought to decide that for yourselves, not some bureaucrat sitting in Washington."

On unions: "Why, do you know that if this bill passes, union seniority won't mean a thing? If some social engineer in Washington decides your union doesn't have enough Chinese Baptists and Japanese Lutherans, they'll put them in there and put you out of work."

On small business: "Every businessman would have to keep records on the race, color, religion, and creed of his employees to prove that he is not discriminating. Because if he has one hundred employees and only two of them are Chinese Baptists, but there are 4 percent Chinese Baptists in the place where he lives, he is going to have to show some federal bureaucrat why he doesn't have four of them working for him—and then fire someone and hire them."[72]

The highlight of Wallace's campaign was a fiery speech on May 11 to nearly two thousand partisans in the racially troubled city of Cambridge on the Eastern Shore of the Chesapeake Bay. The six counties along Maryland's Eastern Shore were considered politically conservative, but none more than Dorchester, of which Cambridge was the seat; and Cambridge had been under modified martial law for nearly a year because of racial disturbances. The edict included a ban on demonstrations, yet a crowd of young blacks swarmed through town the night before Wallace's scheduled appearance, shouting anti-Wallace epithets and throwing bricks at houses and stores. The protesters were quieted by a black leader, Gloria Richardson, and contained by an augmented body of law enforcement authorities—in all, 400 National Guardsmen, 50 state patrolmen, and the local police force of 18—dispatched to Cambridge in anticipation of trouble surrounding Wallace's speech. No one was more worried than Wallace himself. Bill Jones, recalling Wallace's mien on the morning of the speech, said, "[He] was as tense as I have ever seen him." Wallace convened a staff meeting to discuss the possibility of calling off his planned appearances at a Veterans of Foreign Wars reception, to be followed by the big rally sponsored by the Dorchester Businessmen's and Citizens' Association, the group behind the earlier referendum to defeat a proposed public accommodations law for Cambridge. Wallace and some staff members were openly apprehensive about the effects of violence; there was not only the obvious danger to the governor, but also the potential political fallout, should Wallace be held accountable for whatever turmoil might ensue. But Jones argued strenuously in favor of Wallace keeping his commitment. The Eastern Shore, he said, would be a strong source of votes on May 19; he also maintained that if the threat of demonstrations forced Wallace to cancel the Cambridge speech, the governor's detractors might use the same technique to disrupt his entire speaking schedule in the limited campaign. Wallace checked news reports throughout the day; at three o'clock—the latest he could wait if he was to arrive on time for his VFW reception—he decided to go.[73]

The moment Wallace arrived for his speech, his mood improved. The audience was described by the *New York Times* reporter Ben A. Franklin as "wildly enthusiastic"; Wallace's fifty-minute speech was interrupted by cheers and applause thirty-five times. At the conclusion, he was mobbed by well-wishers. But after a few minutes, Wallace got word that black protesters were marching toward the hall; he was hustled into his car, which sped off toward Baltimore. Meanwhile, nearly five hundred blacks who had been meeting across town poured into the streets and started marching toward the Wallace rally. Led by Richardson and by eight priests from Catholic University in Washington, they marched to a National Guard barricade five blocks from where Wallace was concluding his speech. Troops donned their gas masks while their leader, Brig. Gen. George M. Gelston, urged the demonstrators to turn back. "The other meeting was a complete flop," he told them disingenuously. "Don't ruin your chances by going over there. It's not even half full." He conferred with Richardson, who succeeded in turning the crowd back to their meeting place. But many of that throng joined others, led by visiting officials of the Student Nonviolent Coordinating Committee (SNCC) on a second march toward the troops. This time, no one bothered to ask the protesters to turn back. Guardsmen, at the command of Col. Maurice Tawes, a cousin of Maryland's governor, started lobbing tear gas canisters and laying down a mist of tear gas from a converted flamethrower. Thirteen people were arrested and seven were slightly injured. Ironically, Wallace, the object of the demonstration, was long gone.

The next night, a two-month-old black child died in his house a hundred yards from the site where tear gas had been sprayed. His parents said the child had started choking when the scent of gas had entered the house—and at least one local black leader linked the death to Wallace. The governor, unnerved by the allegation, snapped at one of the staff, "I told you we shouldn't have gone to Cambridge"; in fact, he had never voiced opposition to the trip. But when an autopsy showed no signs of gas poisoning, but rather that the child had a congenital heart defect and a middle-ear infection, Wallace immediately perked up; he forgot his after-the-fact remonstrances and pronounced Cambridge a triumph.[74]

Indeed, it was all uphill after that, no matter what or who his opponents threw at him. He drew a crowd of nine thousand people on the campus of the University of Maryland, half of whom booed and half of whom cheered. Brewster, accompanied by Sen. William Proxmire of Wisconsin, had attracted just over three thousand at the university earlier in the day. Brewster renewed the charge that Wallace had portrayed Italians and Poles as "lesser breeds"—so Wallace went everywhere with his "ethnic row" or "U.N. squad" of Alabamians of Italian, Polish, Greek, and Jewish extraction. After Brewster claimed that Alabama's congressmen did not support Wallace, the governor trotted out eight of the nine members composing Alabama's delegation to the U.S. House of Representatives (Senators Hill and Sparkman were notably absent).[75]

As in Wisconsin and Indiana, Maryland's clergy—including the Roman Catholic archbishop of Baltimore and the Protestant Episcopal bishop of Maryland—openly supported Brewster. Organized labor conducted a massive campaign to portray Wallace as antilabor; those making personal visits to Maryland included the president of the United Steelworkers of America and the former president of the National Association of Letter Carriers. Milton Eisenhower, the president of Johns Hopkins and the brother of the popular former president, said he was "doing all" he could to defeat Wallace. Ted Kennedy and labor leaders accompanied Brewster into blue-collar, ethnic, and heavily unionized areas of Baltimore, where they invoked the name of John F. Kennedy and passed out free beer. Brewster's attacks on Wallace grew shriller as the primary approached; in one speech, he said Wallace was "against compassion and for cruelty, against honesty and for deception, against justice and for bigotry, against law and for anarchy, against order and for violence, against morality and for brutality, against enlightenment and for ignorance, against courage and for fear."[76]

Wallace's detractors spread word that he was backed by "professional haters," including the White Party of America, described by the American Nazi party leader, George Lincoln Rockwell, as "a bunch of disgruntled party members" who had "swiped [Wallace's] mailing list and defected." Gerald L. K. Smith, represented almost universally as an antiblack, anti-Semitic extremist, mailed out a letter urging his "friends in Maryland" to be "as loyal to Governor Wallace" as they had been in Wisconsin and Indiana. Newspapers quoted "authorities" saying that John Birch Society members were "operating under cover names" in support of Wallace. A bulletin of the National States' Rights party described Wallace as the "last chance for the white voter." Wallace blithely dismissed the notion that hate groups were supporting him. "I certainly don't approve of . . . anyone who would say anything that was mean and ugly," he replied to questions about this element of supporters. But, he added, "I cannot be responsible for everything that someone does who supports me." Despite the somewhat breathless tone of news stories alleging the presence of this element among Wallace's supporters, officials described as familiar with these groups said they were having little, if any, effect—principally because they were too extreme to attract a large following.[77]

In the final week before the balloting, Wallace's crowds consistently were in the thousands and Brewster's—even with big-name senators and labor leaders at his side—were in the hundreds. Wallace bought time for thirty half-hour television appearances across Maryland; Brewster, complaining of a shortage of funds, used TV sparingly and, when he did, relied on the thirty-second and one-minute spots then in vogue among politicians. Wallace was the first and, until the third-party candidacy of Perot in 1992, the only national candidate to rely on lengthy televised appearances to sell his issues and, more important, to sell himself. With his voice pleasantly modulated,

Wallace was an early master of the medium, the antithesis of the rabble-rouser many might have expected. In his half-hour Maryland campaign film—which was telecast daily for ten days from Washington, Baltimore, and Salisbury on the Eastern Shore—Wallace spoke about the inequities of the civil rights bill, repeating his familiar points about how it meant loss of privacy and property, how homeowners would no longer have the right to sell to whom they pleased, and so on. He said those in violation of the bill's provisions could be jailed summarily. Most of his claims were exaggerated, if not plain wrong; but he would read bits and pieces of the bill, lending credence to his assertions. As Attorney General Kennedy commented dryly, "If the civil rights bill was what Governor Wallace says it is, I'd be against it, too."[78] Later in his televised half hour, Wallace introduced his ethnic supporters, rolled out his seventy-foot-long petition containing the names of labor union supporters from Alabama, and assured viewers that he was not a racist. "Nazi Germany," he said, "is a good example of what happens when the states lost their power to the central government. If you folks give me a good vote on Tuesday, it will not be a vote against any segment of your population but against the people who are making all this noise about civil rights and don't care anything about anybody, black or white."[79]

Wallace felt the momentum and even dared—privately, of course—to think he might actually win. His confidence increased with every public appearance. On the Friday before Tuesday's vote, Wallace, interviewed on the NBC network's "Today" program by Neil Boggs in Washington and Hugh Downs in New York, was in top form. He took full advantage of an opening softball question by Boggs about why Wallace, despite being the object of condemnation by his opponents in all three primaries, had not returned the condemnation but, rather, had limited his criticism to the civil rights bill. "They try to obscure the issues," he said. "I'm not going to engage in personalities." He said he was in Maryland as a guest, that it would be "presumptuous" to criticize local officials, and that he wanted to stick to the issues. Even when asked to identify the "vociferous left-wing minority" he said was behind the civil rights bill, Wallace dodged and slid and described the group without naming a single name. Boggs pressed by asking if President Johnson and members of Congress who strongly backed the bill were part of the left-wing cabal Wallace spoke of. Wallace said he did "not mean, of course, to strike upon any member of Congress or the president or impugn their motives." Then he went on to quote from a speech in opposition to an earlier civil rights bill by then-Sen. Lyndon Johnson and added, "So I am taking his word for it. This bill is a bad bill." When challenged by Downs on the charge that the bill would limit those to whom homeowners could sell or rent, Wallace fell back on sources—including two former presidents of the American Bar Association—who maintained that the bill allowed for coverage of housing by executive order. "This bill is a tricky bill," Wallace said, "and it should be read very carefully, Mr. Downs, really."[80]

While Brewster ended his campaign Sunday night before a disappointingly small turnout of union workers, Wallace carried his drive for votes down to the wire in the Baltimore suburb of Glen Burnie at what a news correspondent described as "the most enthusiastic rally held for him in the Maryland campaign." (The next day, Wallace would carry Anne Arundel County, in which Glen Burnie is located, by a nearly two-to-one margin.)[81]

Like him or despise him, Wallace had indeed generated enthusiasm. Nearly half a million voters turned out, over 40 percent more than Maryland's previous record primary vote. Wallace received 43 percent of the vote—ten points more than Brewster privately had expected Wallace to receive. Every point over 33 percent, Brewster thought, would constitute a moral victory for the Alabamian. Brewster, a product of Maryland's wealthy hunt club society, conceded, "I made a definite mistake. I underestimated my opposition." And, one Maryland Democrat observed caustically of Brewster, "his supporters had overestimated him." Brewster had treated Wallace—not to mention the primary system—with haughty disdain, telling interviewer Robert MacNeil on "Today" two weeks before the election, "This little man has the temerity to challenge President Johnson. . . . He has no more chance of being nominated or elected than my six-year-old son." Then he sighed, "He makes life difficult for some of us these days, and he must be opposed." When Brewster and Wallace briefly crossed paths at a Baltimore television station two days before the vote, the gregarious Wallace strode across the room, stuck out his hand, and said, "Senator, I'm glad to see you again." Brewster eyed him coolly and replied, "I shake your hand out of respect for the system which allows you to be in the state, but I do not respect you or your principles." Wallace, obviously taken aback, just nodded, walked slowly back across the room, and sat down quietly.[82]

Wallace would have his revenge in the way he knew best—shaking some more eyeteeth. Although he did not realize the dream of actually winning the race, he carried 15 of the state's 23 counties.

For a time during the evening, it appeared that under Maryland's county unit rule, a sort of miniature electoral college, Wallace might carry the state's 48 convention votes. Under the county unit system, then being challenged in the courts, a candidate carrying a county was entitled to all that county's unit votes, a number equal to the county's allotted representatives in the state legislature. The county-by-county vote was decisive everywhere except in the state's most populous county of Baltimore. The results elsewhere gave Brewster 85 unit votes to Wallace's 79. Should Wallace win Baltimore, however, its 7 unit votes would give him a one-vote edge over the homeboy and entitle him to Maryland's entire delegate slate. Wallace was convinced the Democratic machine was stealing votes from him throughout the state, but if he could win Baltimore County, he could still claim victory, even if the unit vote system was later voided (which it was).

His big handicap was the huge black turnout in the city of Baltimore—twice as many as usual—and they voted forty-to-one for Brewster. But Wallace was winning 60 percent of the Catholic vote, which embraced most of the county's ethnic population, and he seemed to be getting most of the non-Catholic blue-collar vote as well.

At 10:30 P.M. Wallace could no longer contain his enthusiasm, and he claimed victory. A few minutes later, however, the vote tabulators announced there had been an earlier mistake; Brewster now was leading Wallace. Of the 95,000 votes cast in the county, Brewster was declared to be 324 ahead of Wallace.

In later campaigns, Wallace would tell rallies that when it looked as if he had carried Baltimore County and, under the old system, all the state's votes at the forthcoming convention, "they got on the television and asked for a recapitulation of the vote. Now, friends, I don't know what 'recapitulation' is, but I can tell you this: If anybody tells you they're going to 'recapitulate' on you, watch out, because they're fixing to do something to you."

Nonetheless, Wallace was elated, especially when analysts reported that he had won a bare majority of the white vote. In his exuberance, he made a rare mistake, saying within earshot of reporters, "If it hadn't been for the nigger bloc vote, we'd have won it all." He later claimed that he had said "nigra"—the purported "natural" Southern pronunciation of *Negro*. But the faux pas was lost in the postelection storm of analysis, recriminations, and estimates of the impact on the civil rights bill (which passed overwhelmingly in July after the Southern-led filibuster in the Senate finally was broken).[83]

Many liberals attributed Wallace's showing to what Senators Humphrey and Javits called his campaign of "distortion and misrepresentation." But Senator Ribicoff had a different view. "We should be candid with one another," he told his Senate colleagues. "Governor Wallace scored a big victory and we should not try to gloss it over. Governor Wallace has proved . . . that there are many Americans in the North as well as the South who do not believe in civil rights. The next twenty years," he warned, with Delphic insight, "will be years of strife and turmoil in the field of civil rights—and it will not be just in the South, but primarily in the North."

Ribicoff based his prediction on the movement from the South to the North of a million and a half blacks over the previous decade— a migration that he said would be accelerated by the displacement of another million Southern black tenant farmers by machines. When the civil rights bill became law, he said, "the problem of civil rights [would] be basically an urban, Northern problem." The solution, he said, would be education improvements and efforts to fight poverty and create jobs. Ribicoff sharply criticized Wallace because he sought "to divide rather than unite the nation" and appealed "to the basest instincts of the people." Nonetheless, he said he agreed with Wallace's contention that Northern liberals were hypocritical about civil rights. "In the cities of the North," Ribicoff said, "mass meetings are held concerning the problems of Mississippi and Alabama, and yet these very same people refuse to walk six blocks to straighten out their own problems."[84]

Wallace also was buoyed by thousands of write-in votes he received in states where he had not campaigned—including nearly four thousand in Illinois and an astounding twelve thousand in Pennsylvania.[85] He had sensed the potential for national influence more than a year earlier—two days before his inaugural, in fact, when some of the South's leading racist forces had gathered in Montgomery to organize a Southern free elector movement that would force the 1964 presidential election into the House of Representatives. A dozen men—including Wallace, Gov. Ross Barnett of Mississippi, Judge Leander Perez of Louisiana (see chapter 14), and the race-baiting publisher Roy V. Harris of Georgia—signed onto a plan in which slates of electors pledged to prosegregation favorite sons would be put forth in seven Deep South states with the intention of depriving the major-party nominees of a majority of electors. Wallace, of course, followed through; and in May 1964, Alabama named Democratic electors who, if they out-polled the Republicans in

November, would be controlled by Wallace. The Mississippi legislature enacted an independent elector law that would permit the inclusion of a state-controlled elector slate on the ballot. Later, after Wallace's powerful showings in the Northern primaries, Gov. Paul Johnson, who succeeded Barnett in Mississippi, agreed that a Wallace elector slate could appear in his state in addition to those of the regular Democratic and Republican parties; Louisiana's Gov. John McKeithen made a similar decision. Along with his staff, Wallace believed that he could meet requirements for November ballot positions in up to thirty-five states. He dispatched a team—Seymore Trammell, Cecil Jackson, Ed Ewing (Bill Jones's assistant), and John Pemberton (the clerk of the Alabama House)—to North Carolina with the task of obtaining in twelve days ten thousand signatures of registered voters to meet the state's ballot-position deadline. The rules for obtaining and certifying the signatures were stringent, and the four Wallace aides mapped out a carefully organized, centrally controlled plan that they could track for progress and check for accuracy. They brought in forty Alabamians and posted them in fourteen key cities throughout the state; these recruits, in turn, enlisted local Wallace supporters—men and women who had written favorable letters to Wallace in his year and a half as governor—as area captains to gather signatures. The Wallace forces included state employees such as top officials from the departments of labor, revenue, conservation, banking, insurance, and civil defense. In addition, there were many volunteers—among them, the mayor and the public safety director of Selma, lawyers, businessmen, a labor leader, and an architect—from all over Alabama. The secretary of North Carolina's board of elections flatly predicted that Wallace's name would not appear on the ballot. "There's not enough time for such a petition," he said. Wallace was on hand in Raleigh on the eve of the deadline; at a news conference, he triumphantly displayed twenty-six thousand certified signatures. In fact, his people had amassed three times that number, but there had been no need to go through the time-consuming process of having the additional signatures certified. As it turned out, Wallace would not exercise his right to a ballot position in North Carolina, but the operation proved to be a model that would serve Wallace well four years later.[86]

Through June and the first two weeks of July, Wallace kept himself in the public eye. He made page-one news at the National Governors' Conference when he discussed his presidential plans, and again when he launched his drive for a ballot position in North

Carolina and declared that when the civil rights bill became law, it would be up to the Justice Department, not him, to enforce it. He was invited to be the keynote speaker at the national convention of the U.S. Junior Chamber of Commerce, where he received an astounding five-minute standing ovation from all but a handful of the seventy-five hundred attendees. Though some Jaycee delegates from Connecticut and New York expressed "shock and disbelief" at the selection of Wallace as the keynoter, cheers interrupted the governor throughout his speech, in which he claimed that Washington had been taken over by "pure, brute, naked federal force" and that because of the Supreme Court, schoolchildren could not "even sing 'America' because it has the word 'God' in it."[87]

Another major public appearance, at a large Fourth of July rally at an abandoned stock car racetrack a few miles south of downtown Atlanta, nearly ended in disaster. The rally, billed as "American Patriots' Day," was clearly an observance for segregationists; ten thousand white people came to hear Wallace and Mississippi's Barnett, and to cheer the introductions of Calvin Craig, the head of Georgia's Ku Klux Klan, and an Atlanta restaurant owner named Lester Maddox.[88]

Barnett was first up, while Wallace waited his turn in a trailer behind the rostrum. As Barnett whipped up the crowd (he called President Johnson a "counterfeit confederate . . . who [might] someday resign from the white race"), three black men and a white girl, all SNCC members, started booing and hissing. Several people nearby shouted, "Kill 'em! Get 'em out of here!" Some jumped on the men and the woman and pummeled them. A few picked up metal chairs and crashed them on the heads of the black men. A Wallace aide on the stand raced to find the governor.

As the crowd rose with angry cries, Wallace hurried to the platform and urged the people to "settle down." At first, he was ignored, but as police rushed in and arrested four whites and dispatched the SNCC members to a hospital for treatment, he managed to quiet them. He went on to rouse the people with attacks on the pending civil rights law, on the Atlanta newspapers and its editorial voice of moderation, Ralph McGill, and even the National Press Club in Washington; after a speech to the press club a month earlier, its officers had withheld from Wallace its traditional certificate of merit: "They gave it to Khrushchev and Castro," Wallace spat, "but they kept it from me."[89] Wallace was on a roll. The president of Lions International, an Alabamian, invited Wallace to address the world assembly of ten thousand Lions Club members in Toronto in mid-July, which he did. During his visit, Wallace was picketed twice, was protected by the most elaborate security net in the memory of official Toronto, and was the impetus for a street-corner collection effort that netted five hundred dollars for Martin Luther King, Jr.'s Southern Christian Leadership Conference.[90]

■ ■ ■

By now, however, Wallace's presidential aspirations, if not his public relations successes, were winding down. Adding to the difficulties in obtaining a ballot position in a number of states was the increasing likelihood that the Republican party would nominate Goldwater for president—and Goldwater was popular among a number of Southern governors who earlier had pledged their support to a Wallace presidential bid. As the Republican National Convention opened in San Francisco, Goldwater told Southern delegates that Wallace was "a capable man . . . who had lots of wisdom" and that he hoped the governor would withdraw from the race. Nixon, who came to San Francisco as a Republican elder statesman whose active days as a candidate seemed over, took a different view of Wallace: he should remain in the race, Nixon said, because that would "leave the racist vote where it belongs—in that wing of the Democratic party."

With the nomination of Goldwater, however, Wallace realized that any further discussion was moot. His desire to stay in the race, in the words of his press secretary, "had gone out the door in San Francisco." He made a half-hearted effort to persuade Southern delegates to the Republican convention to weaken the civil rights plank in the platform, but nothing beyond that. He had a scheduled appearance July 19 on the CBS program "Face the Nation," and he decided to use it as the vehicle to withdraw.[91] Declaring that his "mission had been accomplished," Wallace opined, "I was the instrument through which . . . the high councils of both major political parties [were] conservatized." Goldwater, at least, was echoing a number of Wallace's views—a chilly attitude toward the civil rights bill (Goldwater voted against it), a concern about rising crime, and a disenchantment with the media.

On "Face the Nation," Wallace reinforced his own ideas. On crime he asserted, "You cannot even arrest a criminal in New York or any place else without the federal court system turning him loose on the public." And on the press he contended, "The American people are sick and tired of columnists and TV dudes who get on the national networks and, instead of reporting the news as it is and shame the devil, which is what they are supposed to do, try to slant and distort and malign and brainwash this country." After the program, the CBS reporter Dan Rather, one of the panelists, rushed up to Wallace and said earnestly, "Governor, if you ever have an instance where CBS has distorted news about you in any way, I want you to call me collect and let me know—and I will see that it is corrected." Wallace looked at him, grinned, and replied, "Dan, I can't do that; it would bankrupt CBS." Of course, Wallace's withdrawal would have little, if any, impact on the 1964 presidential election; Goldwater would carry only six states—five in the South (including Alabama) and his home state of Arizona (barely). But at the time, Wallace's action was seen as "a move of great political significance."[92]

For Wallace, it had been a brief but glorious run. Lyndon Johnson's overwhelming November victory obscured Wallace's messages of the spring: that there was important resistance by Northern voters to expanding federal powers; that large ethnic groups in and around big cities were aroused over what they viewed as blacks' encroachments on their jobs; and that many people in the suburbs were worried about federal intrusion in their businesses and schools.[93] For a few months, Wallace was courted by media throughout the country. He was even the subject of a *Playboy* interview—an interview in which he made one of his rare philosophical observations on the difference between the liberals he reviled and the conservatives he wanted to lead:

> Originally, a liberal was a believer in freedom. But the name has been taken over by those who believe in economic and social planning by the federal government to interfere in everybody's private business. The liberalism of today shows a loss of faith in the individual. Conservatives still believe in the individual, in private enterprise. Conservatives are not hostile to progress, however. Education, help for the aged and unfortunate, road building—that kind of aid to the people is a legitimate function of government. But just because I believe Alabama should do good things for her people, that the state should protect the people's welfare, does not mean I believe the government has the right to tell a businessman whom he can hire and whom he

cannot hire, a café or restaurant or motel owner whom he can serve and whom he cannot, a homeowner whom he must and must not sell his house to. A conservative tries to preserve freedom for business and labor.[94]

Inevitably, the election and the great events that were developing in America at home and abroad would relegate Wallace to the status of a fiery but short-lived meteor. When asked whether his campaign would soon be forgotten, Wallace replied, "That may be the case as far as I'm concerned. But the attitude of millions of people toward the trends in the country will not be forgotten."[95] He was right about the attitude of millions, but wrong about the durability of his own persona. In just a few months, his presence would thrust itself once more into the minds of Americans and onto their television screens—and he would wonder if a town named Selma might be his undoing in Alabama, and even more so across the nation.

12

Crossing the Bridge

THE DEFECTION BY MOST Southern governors to Goldwater's candidacy abruptly ended Wallace's somewhat chimerical presidential ambitions. Nonetheless, the Alabamian had firmly established his reputation as an exceptional campaigner—and, more important, as a politician sensitive to the concerns of white ethnic groups, blue-collar workers, and middle-class suburbanites.

Though Wallace's success in three primary campaigns clearly had demonstrated the ferment among large numbers of Democratic voters, the Republicans—not the Democrats—were the first outside the South to understand and exploit the rich political mother lode that Wallace had unearthed. In the general election campaign of 1964, Goldwater's antipathy to growing federal "intrusion" and his calls for "law and order" went largely unnoticed by Democrats who, in all likelihood, had grown politically complacent because of President Johnson's overwhelming popular and electoral victory.

Several Republicans who sought congressional seats in 1964 also took note of Wallace's unexpected Northern successes. In Texas, for example, U.S. Representative George Bush, seeking to unseat Sen. Ralph Yarborough, opposed the civil rights bill and explained, "I hate to see [the] Constitution trampled on in the process of trying to solve civil rights problems." He maintained, as had Wallace, that the bill would "make further inroads into the rights of individuals and

311

the states, and even provide for the ultimate destruction of our trial by jury system."[1] Indeed, Bush interpreted Wallace's strength in Northern primaries as a vindication of his own opposition to what he termed "unconstitutional" sections of the bill—requirements for fair employment practices and access to public accommodations. The Wallace vote, he said, "indicates to me that there must be a general concern from many responsible people over the civil rights bill all over the nation."[2]

Two years later, Ronald Reagan, running for the Republican nomination for governor of California, first struck the themes that would resound during the Reagan/Bush decade of the 1980s. In his 1966 campaign, Reagan, borrowing from Wallace, attacked crime in the streets, welfare, high taxes, swollen bureaucracy, government "planners," and the "spreading philosophy that the criminal must be protected from society and not the other way around."[3] Nixon's 1968 presidential campaign also centered on a law-and-order theme and, by 1972, the Nixon Southern strategy was in full flower. Not until Jimmy Carter won the presidency in 1976 with a campaign emphasizing that he was a Washington outsider who sought "a government as good as the people" did a Democrat embrace Wallace's appeal to what had become the swing vote in national elections—salaried people, most of them white, all of them self-described members of the "middle class," who felt pressure on their jobs, their security, and the quality of their lives because of a government they believed coddled the poor and winked at the excesses of the rich.

But it was the Republican Reagan who wholly subsumed the Wallace strategy—and Bush, his protégé, came close. Running for president in 1988, Bush condemned liberals and their Washington-centered, misguided "socialist" thinking learned from Harvard "elitists." Writing in *Newsweek*, the journalist Howard Fineman said that Bush sounded "suspiciously like" Wallace, and that "the key to [the 1988] election—and the rise of Republicans in modern presidential politics—[has been] the GOP's successful appeal to the kind of constituency George Wallace first laid claim to." George Bush of Greenwich Country Day School, Andover, and Yale's Skull and Bones Society seemed oblivious to the irony of his playing the "barefoot populist," as an observer termed it. But it worked for Bush, as it had for Nixon, Carter, and Reagan.[4] It would be 1992 before a Democrat running for president successfully shed the pejorative aspects of the "liberal" label and persuaded predominantly white, middle-class voters that he cared about their interests at least as much, if not more, than the interests of the super-rich, whom he said he would tax more fairly, or the superpoor, whom he said would no longer receive open-ended handouts. Bill Clinton effectively neutralized the GOP's claim to the Wallace constituency.

There was, however, an important difference between Wallace's anti-Washington stance and that of the Republicans who co-opted it. When Wallace said he opposed government intrusion, his antagonism was limited essentially to aggressive social policies—such as busing and federal requirements for minority access to public accommodations, housing, and employment—that had a distinctly, if not exclusively, racial connotation. The campaigns of Goldwater, Nixon, Reagan, and Bush also were hostile to social policies involving race. Beyond that, however, the Reagan and Bush administrations cannibalized the kind of programs with which Wallace was sympathetic, either as the Alabama governor or in national campaigns—aid to education, increases in the minimum wage and unemployment compensation, support for the elderly. And when it came to tax reductions, Wallace, in later years, was contemptuous of Reagan's so-called revolution. "He lowered taxes for the rich people," Wallace said in an interview, "and he raised them on the poor. That's wrong!"[5] And Wallace wanted government "off the backs" of "the little people—the restaurateur, the beautician, the truck driver, and the cab driver." He favored "reasonable" government regulation of big business—and the failure by Reagan and Bush to provide that regulation was, to Wallace, the direct cause of debacles like the costly collapse of numerous savings and loan institutions. "It happened on his watch," Wallace said of Reagan, "and he's got to take responsibility for it."[6]

Wallace possessed many of the traits of the classic populist: a belief that the well-to-do should pay their fair share of taxes, that the state had an interest in the reasonable regulation of big business, and what the scholar Robert McMath called "the simple idea that the producer deserves the fruits of his or her work."[7] Wallace also was the kind of magnetic campaigner who drew respect from, and was instructive to, professionals through the decades; James Carville, for one, who coordinated Bill Clinton's brilliant 1992 presidential campaign, considered Wallace "the best campaigner" of modern times. Wallace, as he said himself, "knew how to put the hay down where the goats can get at it."[8]

Wallace's growing celebrity, oddly, was helped by increasing racial violence in the nation, North and South, which seemed to underline his contention that education, not legislation, was the way to ease tension between blacks and whites. And he never missed an opportunity to point to Northern "hypocrites" who condemned segregation in the South but who supported suppression of black protests in their own cities and towns. More important, perhaps, was that the media spotlight was focused outside Alabama—at least, for a time. In 1964, for instance, resentment of police authority and discontent with poor housing conditions touched off outbreaks in New York City as well as in Rochester, New York; in the New Jersey cities of Jersey City, Elizabeth, and Paterson; in Philadelphia and Chester in Pennsylvania; and in several suburbs of Chicago. To Wallace's undisguised delight, civil rights groups issued charges of widespread police brutality in these Northern cities as the authorities there put down disorders, most of which conspicuously involved roving gangs of unemployed blacks. Martin Luther King, Jr.'s harsh criticism of the FBI's handling of civil rights complaints in the South provoked J. Edgar Hoover to brand King publicly as "the most notorious liar in the country." Wallace could not have hoped for a more important ally than Hoover in his efforts to persuade voters that King and much of the civil rights movement was of suspect loyalty.[9] And although the most chilling series of racial incidents in 1964 occurred in the South, they were not in Alabama—and, therefore, did not reflect on Wallace.

■   ■   ■

In the so-called Freedom Summer of 1964, during which hundreds of young volunteers flocked to Mississippi to encourage voter registration among blacks, the Ku Klux Klan and other white supremacists burned and bombed dozens of churches and homes of blacks, and beat, flogged, and even shot nearly one hundred people associated with voter registration drives. In mid-June, three of the volunteers—James Chaney, Andrew Goodman, and Michael Schwerner, all in their early twenties—disappeared near the town of Philadelphia, Mississippi, in Neshoba County. Sheriff Lawrence Rainey reported that the three had been stopped for speeding, had paid a fine, and had then departed in their late-model Ford station wagon. The next day, their burned-out vehicle was found fifteen miles northeast of Philadelphia. A huge FBI-led manhunt failed to locate the three; a widely held view among white Mississippians was that the young men were hiding out either in Communist Cuba or Democratic Chicago, seeking to embarrass the South and hasten additional civil rights legislation.[10] Even Gov. Paul Johnson seemed to support that implausible notion when, in late June, during a visit from Wallace, he deflected a reporter's question about the missing men with a weak and tasteless attempt at humor: "Governor Wallace and I are the only two people who know where they are, and we're not telling."[11]

But in August, acting on guidance from informers who had been paid nearly thirty thousand dollars by the FBI, authorities excavated the bodies from an earthen dam more than twenty miles in the opposite direction from where the car had been found. All three—one a black Mississippian (Chaney) and two white New Yorkers (Goodman and Schwerner)—had been shot to death. Six months later, based on their informants' leads, the FBI arrested Rainey, his chief deputy, and nineteen other local white men. Governor Johnson announced that the evidence was too flimsy for the state to prefer charges, but a federal grand jury indicted eighteen of the men, accusing them of violating the constitutional rights of the murdered civil rights workers. At the trial, it was determined that Klansmen had planned for days to kill Schwerner, one of the white New Yorkers, for having eaten and slept in the homes of blacks.

The deputy sheriff, Cecil Price, had arrested Schwerner and his two companions and, while holding them, had notified his Klan acquaintances. By the time the three had been released and had continued on their way, several carloads of Klansmen had been lying in wait. They had chased down the Ford, taken its occupants to a deserted dirt road, and brutally murdered them. Three years after their arrests, seven of the eighteen defendants, including Price, were convicted and sentenced to jail terms ranging from three to ten years, the maximum under then-existing law.[12] Sixteen years after the killings, many veterans of Freedom Summer were incensed when Ronald Reagan chose Philadelphia, Mississippi, of all places, as the unlikely site for a major speech early in his 1980 presidential campaign—not to recall the idealistic dedication to equality that had cost three young men their lives, but to declare his belief in states' rights and promise to "restore to states and local governments the powers that properly belong to them." William Raspberry of the *Washington Post* was among a number of commentators who suggested that the act implied sympathy with the murderers.[13] It is highly improbable that Reagan felt any such conscious or even unconscious commiseration for the killers; rather, he (or his handlers) felt impelled to follow the lead of successful presidential candidates Nixon and Carter (as *he* would be followed by Bush and Clinton) who had rushed in where Wallace had been first to tread.

■   ■   ■

But as 1965 dawned, much of the nation's attention turned to the central Alabama city of Selma, the seat of Dallas County—a city forty-nine miles due west of Montgomery that held important symbolic value for both whites and blacks. Selma, an important manufacturing center of powder, shot, and shell during the Civil War, had been sacked ruthlessly by Northern troops a hundred years earlier; the town had been burned, horses had been butchered, and a number of women had been attacked. Not surprisingly, Selma was the first Alabama city in which a White Citizens Council was formed shortly after the Supreme Court's 1954 school desegregation decision.[14] For blacks, Selma was, in the words of the civil rights leader Ralph Abernathy, an intellectual, cultural, and religious center.[15] More important to the civil rights movement, though, was that Selma was among the most rigidly exclusionary cities in Alabama and the South regarding black voter registration; while 67 percent of Selma's 14,000 prospective white voters were registered, barely over 2 percent of the 15,000 potential black voters—325 people—were registered. For two years, the Dallas County sheriff, Jim Clark—the man whose notorious posse had traveled the state to buttress local authorities in putting down black demonstrations in Birmingham and elsewhere (see chapter 8)—had effectively nullified, through intimidation and arrests, the voter registration efforts led by members of the Student Nonviolent Coordinating Committee (SNCC). SNCC workers, a number of whom were white, attracted little support from middle-class blacks, much less from the relatively moderate Selma mayor, Joe Smitherman. "Their dress," John Herbers of the *New York Times* wrote of the SNCC field-workers, "is usually rough and they make no attempt to emulate middle-class values."[16] Bill Jones was less delicate in his evaluation of SNCC members, terming them "beatniks [who] openly flaunted interracial couples before the unbelieving eyes of Alabamians. Their dress—the male variety's tight pants, Levis, jackets, boots, and beards; the female variety's form-revealing dress, wild, straight hair, unwashed look, small, white dungarees, and sloppy shoes—tended to inflame the Alabamian and to stiffen his resistance."[17]

The situation was ripe for Martin Luther King, Jr. On the evening of January 2, 1965, speaking to more than seven hundred people in Selma's Brown Chapel AME Church, King announced he would lead demonstrations—prohibited by a state judge's injunction—to dramatize white officials' refusal to register blacks as voters. The goal was to provoke mass arrests and, consequently, arouse national interest and concern. The first march on the courthouse on January 18 produced few fireworks. Clark's posse confronted the marchers and herded them into an adjacent alley, where they were told to wait until called in singly to register. After several hours of milling about, however, none in the group was summoned. So King resolved that the next day, no one would move. The crowd's intransigence inflamed Clark; he manhandled a woman at the head of the line when she refused his order. He then instructed his deputies to start arresting people, and nearly seventy-five people were hauled off to jail by the end of the day.

The resulting publicity caused Ralph Abernathy to exult that "the Selma campaign was at last on its way." He facetiously praised Clark with, "[He] did more for our organization this day than anyone else in the city of Selma." The next day, Clark's subordinates, with Alabama state troopers looking on, arrested another two hundred people who came to register. The marches, occasional beatings, and mass arrests continued into the next week when King and Abernathy made certain that, to maximize national interest, the two of them were among those arrested.[18] That prompted President Johnson to issue a strong public statement in support of the Selma protests, but he stopped short of saying he would propose voting rights legislation. And a few days later, when he met face-to-face with King, the president said he would send a voting rights bill to Congress "very soon."[19]

Actually, Johnson had no intention of sending such a bill to Congress until the following year. He thought that because of the contention over civil rights in 1964, everyone needed a breather— the people, to get used to the social changes wrought by the 1964 act; the Congress, to bind up the internecine wounds inflicted during debates; and the federal agencies, to familiarize themselves with their new duties and the administration of the new laws.[20] Events, however, would deny Johnson the luxury of delay. Not only did King strongly believe that voting rights reform was the only way to drive George Wallace from office, but, despite his natural inclination for moderation, he was feeling pressure from all sides to escalate the Selma struggle.[21] The courts were moving slowly. SNCC members were becoming jealous of King, and some were threatening to break off cooperation with King's Southern Christian Leadership Conference (SCLC). And much to the chagrin of King and his aides, Malcolm X came to town. Malcolm's black nationalism was repugnant to King's philosophy of racial integration and harmony. But King's aide, Andrew Young, allowed Malcolm to speak at Brown Chapel because "everyone has a right to be heard," and added, "The less about this, the better." Malcolm supported the Selma effort. "The black folks in this county . . . have an absolute right to use whatever means necessary to gain the vote. I don't believe in non-violence. The heroes of this country are not the ones who practice love for everybody. The white man should thank God for [King and his followers] because they are giving white people time to get things in shape. I don't think anyone expects sheep to go into the den of the wolf and love the wolf because the sheep would end up in the stomach of the wolf." After the speech, black leaders canceled a planned march of school-children, who they feared might have been moved to violence by Malcolm's words.[22]

But what ultimately persuaded King to propose a head-to-head confrontation with Wallace occurred in the town of Marion, thirty miles northwest of Selma. Early in February, black students cut school and, under the aegis of SNCC field-workers, tested public accommodations while nearly two hundred of their parents showed up at the Perry County courthouse to register to vote. Surprisingly, the students were served in a popular downtown café, and the adults were courteously greeted, seated, and registered. But when demonstrations continued the next day, the whites of Marion had run out of patience and goodwill; students were arrested at the café where they had been served the day before. And when they marched on the courthouse the following day, hundreds were arrested.[23] For two weeks, nightly meetings were conducted at black churches in Marion and Selma; after some meetings, blacks marched without incident.

Things seemed to look up for King when the courts at last directed county officials to register at least one hundred blacks a day. But during a march to take advantage of the court order, one of Clark's men punched and bloodied a King associate. From an angle, one photograph made it look as if Clark had struck the blow, though several black protesters who had been standing nearby said not. Clark denied it—but with racist bravado: "If I hit him, I don't know it. One of the first things I ever learned was not to hit a nigger with your fist because his head is too hard. Of course, the camera might make me out a liar. I think I have a broken finger."[24]

Through it all, Wallace had maintained silence, leaving it to Albert Lingo to act as his eyes and ears. After the punching incident in Selma, sympathetic blacks in Marion started marching nightly. Lingo and fifty troopers moved from Selma to Marion, and on the night of February 18, Clark, wearing sports clothes and carrying a nightstick, showed up in the neighboring county as well. "Don't you have enough trouble of your own in Selma?" someone asked. "Things got a little too quiet for me over in Selma tonight and it made me nervous," Clark replied.[25] At about nine-thirty, four hundred blacks concluded their rally and prayer meeting at Zion's Chapel Methodist Church and filed outside to stage a march on the Perry County jail to protest the earlier arrest of a civil rights worker. The local police chief, backed up by Lingo's troopers, stopped them and ordered them to disperse. When they did not, troopers waded in and started swinging their clubs. Many of the protesters rushed back into the church and were left alone by authorities. But about a hundred people who broke for a nearby funeral home and café were pursued by police. One of those who found temporary refuge in Mac's Café was Jimmie Lee Jackson, a twenty-six-year-old pulpwood cutter. Troopers rushed in, overturned tables, and started clubbing the huddled blacks, shouting for them to disperse and go home. One trooper struck Jackson's mother, Viola. When Jackson lunged at the trooper to defend his mother, the officer pulled his gun and fired. Jackson was hit in the stomach. Eight days later, he died of internal infections and other complications. In Washington, Nicholas Katzenbach, who had succeeded Robert Kennedy as the attorney general, started an investigation. In Montgomery, George Wallace announced his own investigation, saying he regretted the incident and promising "proper action."[26]

Shortly after Jackson was buried on March 3, King announced that the following Sunday, March 7, he would lead a march from Selma to Montgomery to take the issue of black voting rights in Alabama directly to Wallace. A telephone sweep by King's staff suggested that up to a thousand people would join the fifty-mile march.[27] Wallace was not amused. At a staff meeting, he and Lingo summarily dismissed a suggestion by Jones that the state allow the march to proceed. But Jones pressed his point, outlining a Byzantine scheme designed to win a propaganda war. He would leak to the press the false information that Lingo's troopers intended to prevent the march. Thus, Jones argued, the marchers would arrive at the starting point unprepared for a fifty-mile journey. And to make certain that King and his followers would, indeed, walk and not ride, Wallace would close Highway 80 to all vehicular traffic for "safety" purposes. The longer Wallace considered the argument, the better he liked it. By the time the meeting adjourned, Wallace told Jones to proceed with his leak.

But the next day—the Friday before the scheduled march—Wallace, clearly uncertain about what to do, asked advice from everyone who walked into his office. He then assembled his legislative leaders, most of whom liked Jones's plan. But one representative raised the specter of shootings of marchers or explosives planted along the march route—and that was enough for Wallace to change his mind. He summoned Lingo and some of his officers. He instructed Lingo to station his troopers on the eastern, or Montgomery, side of the Edmund Pettus Bridge, which was named for a home-grown Confederate general and U.S. senator and which spanned the Alabama River. They would halt the march at that point. If the demonstrators persisted, the troopers would raise their billy clubs in both hands and hold them defensively. If they were shoved, they were to fall back and reissue the order to disperse. If they were disobeyed again, they were authorized to use tear gas, but only enough to scatter the crowd. "Everyone in the governor's office," Jones said, "thoroughly understood the procedures to be used."

Saturday morning, Wallace called a news conference to say the proposed march would "not be tolerated." He said the march would interrupt Alabama's "orderly flow of traffic and commerce" and that there would be an "additional hazard placed upon highway travel"—concerns at odds with his later claim that the safety of the marchers was his primary reason for forestalling them. He also said he had instructed Lingo "to use whatever measures [were] necessary to prevent a march"—an overstatement he later said was designed to deter the marchers.[28] Wallace remained uneasy with his decision; he even telephoned the *Montgomery Advertiser* reporter Bob Ingram, seemingly to convince himself that he had made the correct decision. He told Ingram he "wouldn't let two hundred Boy Scouts march over the route—over hills and along swamps—much less blacks. [Wallace] said he didn't have enough men to try to arrest hundreds if they all went limp on the highway. He said he told the troopers to give the Negroes every opportunity to disperse peacefully" before using tear gas.[29]

Wallace summoned Lingo again on Saturday night; this time Lingo brought along Clark. "The meeting broke at midnight, twelve to fourteen hours before the events at the Selma bridge," Jones recalled. "And I know that Lingo and Jim Clark left the governor's office with instructions not to do anything more than to hold their nightsticks in front of them, and if the marchers pushed ahead, just to let them through. We thought the thing was in hand." Later, when a Montgomery television reporter phoned to ask the governor's reaction to the Selma clash, Jones was shocked. "Lingo violated the policy Wallace set down."[30] Actually, Wallace had asked Lingo to stay away from Selma altogether. "I ordered Lingo not to go to Selma," Wallace recalled, "because he had been taking pills for a bone marrow condition. I told Major [John] Cloud [a Lingo subordinate who would officially be in charge at the confrontation], 'Don't y'all let anything happen that will cause any sensationalism. If they want to march, go beside them and protect them.' But they told me there were reports of bunches of white people in trucks with rifles and they were afraid something would happen, so I asked them not to march."[31]

■   ■   ■

Black leaders never doubted there would be a brutish confrontation at the bridge. They believed that Wallace wanted to confine the protests to Selma, where any violence would be associated with Clark, and not him. They reasoned, therefore, that Wallace would turn Lingo loose to keep the marchers from leaving Selma. In addition, King had been receiving numerous death threats, so he decided to return to Atlanta rather than risk serious injury. Actually, King left on the Friday before the march, a day earlier than Wallace's announcement that Lingo had been instructed to use whatever means necessary to stop the march. But, in selective memory, King later said his aides, concerned for his safety, had urged him to leave after Wallace had implied that marchers would be met with force.[32] Publicly, King announced he was returning to Atlanta to keep church commitments and investigate "legal maneuvers to thwart Governor Wallace." Hearing that King was leaving town, Clark muttered, "I didn't think he'd have the guts to march."[33]

King's staff debated the wisdom of going ahead with the march on the grounds of safety and propriety. James Bevel, an aide easily identified by the embroidered skullcap he wore on his shaved head, argued that "it was time to go see the governor. We [had] already been to jail, tried to register, had done all these things. But Andrew Young tried to call it off and even told some reporters 'not to bother to come to Selma on Sunday because nothing is going to happen.' "[34] On leaving Selma on Friday, King had not decided whether to authorize the march. "You see what things look like Sunday," he told his principal march organizer, Hosea Williams, "then you let us know what you think."[35] But it appeared unlikely that either side— those wanting to march to dramatize their determination to get the vote, and those wanting to stop the march to demonstrate their commitment to continued segregation—could gracefully back down. A Birmingham reporter, Tom Lankford, later wrote: "It was like something rehearsed and predestined, the actors manipulated by unseen forces."[36]

■   ■   ■

By Sunday morning, marchers from Black Belt counties surrounding Selma had converged on the town, with their blankets and sleeping bags. In the driveway outside Brown Chapel, several vehicles were ready to accompany the march: a flatbed truck carrying four portable toilets, two fully equipped ambulances, and three hearses on loan from black funeral homes to serve as supply wagons. Four doctors and five nurses, sponsored by the New York–based Medical Committee for Human Rights, arrived at the church. Its leader, Dr. Alfred Moldovan, pale and precise, called a meeting of prospective marchers to discuss tear gas, which he described as "a panic gas." He explained: "It is not a dangerous gas, usually. It blinds temporarily, and it drives you into a panic. If tear gas hits you, go off to the side of the road and stand quietly. Don't panic. Discipline is the key to our success." Dr. Leon Redler, a red-bearded psychiatrist from New York's Metropolitan Hospital, showed the overflow crowd the distilled water with which he and others would wash out eyes stung by tear gas. A man accompanying the doctors, Frank Soracco, warned everyone "not to blow your cool." He continued, "Any means is justifiable to stop a howling, raging, unruly mob. The troopers want to turn us into just such a mob to justify severe action."[37] In Atlanta, just as Ralph Abernathy was about to step into the pulpit of West Hunter Baptist Church, he received a phone call from Hosea Williams in Selma. Williams claimed there were "thousands" of people "swarming all over the place" ready to march. He wanted Abernathy to secure King's authorization. Abernathy was skeptical; he thought of Williams as a man of "fiercely militant spirit" who craved "the challenge and glory" of the daring march. He phoned

King at Ebenezer Baptist Church, where the service had begun. But King had left word to be summoned from the pulpit, should Abernathy call. Both men discounted Williams's claim that "thousands" were ready to march to Montgomery. "But putting that aside," King said, "do you think we ought to let him go ahead?" Abernathy sighed and said, "If he wants to get his butt beaten, then let's let him do it, because if we don't, he'll blame us the rest of his life, saying he could have done this or that." After a long pause, King said, "Tell him he can go." Abernathy told Williams, "Hosea, go to it," and Williams cried out, "We're gone," and slammed down the phone.[38]

Williams rushed to join Bevel and Young to flip coins and determine who would share the march leadership with the SNCC chairman, twenty-five-year-old John Lewis. "I had heads," Williams said later, "and, bless your God, the others had tails." The marchers gathered on a playground in the George Washington Carver public housing project adjacent to Brown Chapel, organized into twenty-one groups of twenty-five people, each group with a marshal—546 people in all. Young called out for everyone to kneel for a brief prayer: "As we go through a wilderness of state troopers, go with us." Then the marchers, following Lewis and Williams, stepped off in groups in five (so as not to violate a local ordinance banning parades without a permit) at about 2:30 P.M. and headed for the bridge, where they planned to form a solid line, two abreast, and walk that day twelve of the fifty miles to Montgomery. Lewis wore a dark suit and striped tie under a raincoat and carried a khaki backpack containing a shirt, a change of underwear, a shaving kit, and a book called *American Political Traditions.* Williams wore jeans and a zip-up jacket, but did not carry anything; no need, he said later, because he knew that Lingo and Clark would not let them through. A quarter of a mile east of the bridge, 25 helmeted Alabama state troopers formed a line. Behind them were another 75 troopers and a posse of some 36 deputies, 15 of them mounted, all under Clark's command.[39] A hundred yards back, the ailing Lingo sat in a car after establishing with Clark that Major Cloud was in charge.[40] After eight weeks of demonstrations in and near Selma by those seeking the right to vote—eight weeks in which nearly thirty-five hundred people had been arrested and Jimmie Lee Jackson had been shot to death—the first full-blown confrontation between the forces of freedom and repression were about to collide.

The event was recalled and described vividly by a journalist who was present, William Cook of *Newsweek*:

A chilling southwest wind ripped through Selma, roiling the brown waters of the Alabama River under the arching Edmund Pettus Bridge on the eastern edge of town. The temperature, under a hazy sun, was barely forty-five degrees. . . . The Negroes walked slowly across on the left side of the gracefully arched bridge. All moving traffic had been stopped from both directions. A crowd of a hundred or more whites gathered to watch in front of the "Chick-N-Treat, Home of the Mickey Burger." More whites probably would have been on hand if Jim Clark hadn't been on the local radio station every half hour warning people to stay home. As we walked across with the Negroes, we stopped to chat briefly with a trooper. He asked me if I had a gas mask. When I replied negatively, he cracked, "You'll be hurtin' without one." The Negroes walked onto the grassy shoulder of the four-lane highway. . . . A bullhorn directed newsmen to assemble in front of Lehman Pontiac-Buick; "otherwise you will not be protected." [The] Dallas County possemen on horses patted their nervous mounts. The troopers started to put on their gas masks. The bullhorn blared again. The trooper in charge, academic-looking Major John Cloud, said: "This is Major Cloud. The march you propose is not conducive to public safety. If you continue, it will be detrimental to your safety. You are ordered to disperse. This march will disperse. You've got two minutes to turn around and go back to your church." Hosea Williams, standing about twenty-five yards away, asked politely, "May we have a word with the major?" "There is no word to be had." There was a brief pause. Then, less than a minute after the major had given the Negroes two minutes to disperse, he cried, "Troopers advance." The twenty-five troopers formed a flying wedge and started walking forward, picking up speed until, by the time they reached the head of the line, they were nearly running. They rammed into Williams and Lewis, pushing them backwards into the ones behind. The marchers were shoved along, like clothes on hangers pushed along a rod or, to pick another image, they were pushed backward and toppled like dominoes. The troopers rushed among the Negroes, flailing wildly with their clubs, knocking heads, as the crowd screamed. "God, we're being killed," someone shouted. "Please, no," another cried. Sheriff Clark's cavalry charged in, scattering more people. Then, the troopers moved in again and discharged tear gas. It billowed in a low, blue-gray cloud. Over the top of the cloud, billy clubs could be seen, thrashing like the rods in an infernal machine. . . . As the Negroes retreated, some up the bridge with the mounted possemen at their heels, they left a collection of debris like that seen on newsreels from Vietnam—shoes, sleeping bags, purses, hats [and] unconscious Negroes, others leaning against posts, rubbing limbs and heads. Mrs. Amelia Boynton [the woman whom Clark had manhandled at a demonstration in January] lay sprawled on the turf. . . . As someone tried to help the bulky woman, a trooper dropped a tear gas grenade by the fallen Mrs. Boynton. He then walked on, dropping smoking grenades by each fallen Negro. Through all this, the whites on the south side of the highway were cheering and clapping. . . . The initial encounter took just eighteen minutes. . . . "It was," said a veteran television cameraman who has covered Southern racial crises from the beginning, "the most brutal scene I've ever witnessed."[41]

In the lore of the civil rights movement, it came to be known as Bloody Sunday. Clark's posse chased the black marchers back to the public housing project and to Brown Chapel. Residents of the area then rained rocks and bottles on the riders, who retaliated by clubbing more blacks. Selma's commissioner of public safety, Wilson Baker, who supposedly had police jurisdiction in the city, while Sheriff Clark ruled Dallas County beyond the city limits, confronted Clark and argued that he and his police should assume control, now that order was restored. "I've already waited a month too damn long about moving in," Clark snarled. Baker, who enjoyed a reputation among black leaders and journalists as a racial moderate, nonetheless backed down and pulled his men out. The posse and some state troopers, armed with automatic carbines, pistols, clubs, shotguns, tear gas canisters, and grenade launchers, swarmed through the project and around the church. Some even rushed into private homes to flush people who they claimed had assaulted officers.

Meanwhile, the church parsonage was turned into a field hospital where the injured (fifty-five in all, seventeen of whom required hospitalization) were given first aid treatment before being shuttled to Good Samaritan Hospital, a Catholic institution open to blacks. Boynton, clubbed and gassed, was stretched out on the dining-room table; others sat on living-room chairs or were sprawled across the floors. Good Samaritan's emergency room was jammed with bleeding, gasping people. A nun circulated among them, taking their names, recording the nature of their injuries, issuing identification bracelets, and directing patients to available physicians or to the hospital dining room to wait their turn. Bleeding from a gash in his head, Lewis (who, it turned out, had suffered a fractured skull) insisted on addressing a crowd in Brown Chapel before going to the hospital. He called Wallace "a vicious and evil man . . . less than a man" and said, "He's responsible for all this." Then he turned on President Johnson: "I don't see how [he] can send troops to Vietnam; I don't see how he can send troops to the Congo; I don't see how he can send troops to Africa—and can't send troops to Selma, Alabama." Later, from his hospital bed, Lewis urged that the march be tried again.[42] It would be—this time in a swirl of national outrage, legal maneuvers, two more deaths, and a desperate political initiative by Wallace that, like so many of his encounters with Washington, would seem to have failed, but which he somehow transmuted into personal victory.

■   ■   ■

When he heard the reports from Selma, Wallace, as he remembered, was "very enraged"—especially because Lingo had ignored Wallace's order to stay away from Selma and "went anyhow," according to Wallace, who added, "and I think he may have been one of the ones that may have caused the trouble."[43] Though "furious at Lingo for the action of the state troopers," Wallace nonetheless thought it would damage police morale to dismiss him in the glare of national publicity and while condemnation was being heaped on both men. "Only the inexplicable loyalty which politicians have for their faithful," wrote Bob Ingram, "a loyalty which seems to extend beyond the point of reason, saved Lingo."[44] The governor continued to insist, "We saved their lives by stopping that march. There's a good possibility that death would have resulted to some of those people if we had not stopped them."[45] Despite his disclaimers that he had sought to avoid violence, most of the nation held Wallace responsible for the brutal attack. Some—including a militant black leader from Selma, J. L. Chestnut, Jr.—took him at his word. "He wanted to be president of the United States," Chestnut reasoned, "and he purposely gave vague instructions so he could capitalize on anything good and run from anything negative."[46] Ingram, in a friendlier voice, pointed out,

"Wallace is no fool. . . . [He] learned the hard way that both he and the state suffer anytime anyone is injured in a racial clash in Alabama. . . . Knowing this . . . Wallace is the last man [to] encourage . . . undue force."[47]

But to King and others, Wallace was an obvious and deserving target. The night of the Selma clash, King condemned the troopers, "under the sanction and authorization of Governor Wallace," for "degenerating to the lowest form of barbarity." King said that he and other leaders would ask the federal courts to restrain Wallace from impeding another "march of freedom" that he would lead two days hence, and he called "on religious leaders from all over the nation to join" the marchers.[48] The response was phenomenal. More than four hundred white ministers, priests, rabbis, and laypeople dropped whatever they were doing and streamed to Selma overnight; some were religious heavyweights like California's Episcopal Bishop James Pike, while others were unknown beyond their own orbits, like the Reverend James Reeb, who worked among the black residents in the Roxbury section of Boston. Protest parades seemed to spring up spontaneously everywhere—in Detroit, Chicago, Washington, Toronto, and Union, New Jersey. Lingo—chastened, but still making a public show of his authority—herded five hundred troopers into Selma, though he allowed Cloud to remain in titular command.[49]

■   ■   ■

Events surged ahead. On Monday morning, the day after the violence at Selma, lawyers representing King were in Judge Frank Johnson's court in Montgomery seeking to enjoin Wallace from interfering with a subsequent march; later, the Justice Department would file its own request for a sweeping court order to prohibit the state from meddling with peaceful demonstrations. To the surprise of both Wallace and King, Johnson ordered the plaintiffs not to march "until the matter [could] be judicially determined." He scheduled a hearing for Thursday. King later admitted to being "very upset" by the order. "I felt it was like condemning the robbed man for being robbed." He also faced two serious internal problems if he were to call off the march: he risked losing the support of the hundreds who had flocked to Selma in answer to his call, and he was certain to enhance the stature of the more militant leaders like Stokely Carmichael and Malcolm X who were critical of King's insistence on nonviolence.[50]

Meanwhile, Attorney General Katzenbach was having troubles of his own. Besides monitoring the events in Montgomery, he now faced another concern: should King try to march the next day as promised, the federal marshals would be required to force him to stand down. And, in an ironic turn of events not lost on Wallace, civil rights demonstrators who had been staging sit-ins at Katzenbach's office in the Justice Department were forcibly ejected by guards; to prevent further demonstrations, Katzenbach ordered the big metal doors at several of the building's entrances locked shut, with guards posted at the few open entrances to check the credentials of anyone seeking to enter.[51] Pickets also marched at the White House and demanded that President Johnson take immediate action to curb Wallace's intransigence; they were supported by many black leaders and white congressmen who called on the president to dispatch federal troops. During a White House tour, twelve protesters plopped down in a ground-floor corridor and refused to budge; on orders from the president, they were hauled off to jail—and Wallace chortled at what he called a double standard in which Southerners were condemned for breaking up demonstrations, but similar actions by the president and attorney general were overlooked. At the White House, with peace restored, the president told key staff members, "If I just send in federal troops with their big black boots and rifles, it'll look like Reconstruction all over again." Concerned about running for reelection in 1968, he said of sending in troops, "I'll lose every moderate—and not just in Alabama, but all over the South. . . . If it looks like the Civil War all over again, that'll force them right into the arms of extremists and make a martyr out of Wallace. . . . Now that Wallace, he's a lot more sophisticated than your average Southern politician, and it's his ox that's in the ditch. Let's see how he gets him out."[52] Wallace was trying his best to figure that out, keeping an almost round-the-clock vigil at the capitol so he could get reports on any further confrontations and decide how to handle them.[53]

With orders from the president to avert trouble at all costs, LeRoy Collins, the former governor of Florida and the head of the newly established federal Community Relations Service, was dispatched to Selma. On Tuesday morning, he shuttled back and forth between King and Lingo to work out a plan whereby King could march—sort of—without violating the court order or Wallace's prohibition against marches. While nearly all of the clergy who had journeyed to Selma wanted to violate Johnson's order against the march, Collins persuaded both sides to accept a compromise: King would march across the bridge to where blood had been spilled Sunday, be halted by the troopers, pray for a few minutes, and then return to Brown Chapel.[54] From Washington, Katzenbach instructed his marshal on the scene, Stanley Fountain, to stop the marchers at the foot of the bridge, read them the court order, and then back off; Katzenbach notified Johnson of his intent, explaining that the marchers would retreat after crossing the bridge.[55]

Fountain proceeded as instructed; after reading the court order, he said, "I am not going to interfere with the march. Let them go."[56] At the other end of the bridge, Cloud called a halt to the march and ordered the group to disperse. After repeating the order six times, Lingo took the bullhorn. "Stand where you are," he said. "This march will not continue." King then asked permission to pray, and Lingo nodded. For twenty minutes, hundreds of people knelt along the roadside as, first, Abernathy, and then several others intoned prayers on behalf of equality. When they were through, the troopers, on a signal from Lingo, moved to the sides of the highway, leaving the way open for King to proceed toward Montgomery in direct violation of the court order. King did not take the bait, and the throng of some fifteen hundred people followed him back to Brown Chapel. Most of the marchers clearly were disappointed. Some of the more militant could be heard accusing King of being an Uncle Tom. Still others mockingly sang the civil rights anthem, "Ain't Gonna Let Nobody Turn Me Around." James Forman of the Congress of Racial Equality called King's failure to reveal the compromise to the marchers "a classic example of trickery against the people."

King rushed from Selma to find solace in a few days of seclusion. But if he and the movement had been temporarily deflated, both would be tragically revivified that night when the bespectacled, bookish, thirty-eight-year-old James Reeb and two other white clergymen decided to dine in a dingy black-owned café near downtown Selma. When they emerged, a group of whites, shouting epithets, raced across the street from the whites-only Silver Moon Cafe and beat and clubbed the three ministers; Reeb's head was smashed with a three-foot club. Two nights later, he died in a Birmingham hospital.[57]

Reaction to the Reeb beating was as universal as the response to Bloody Sunday at the Edmund Pettus Bridge. In Montgomery, a thousand marchers blocked Dexter Avenue, the broad boulevard leading to the state capitol building, for nearly twelve hours. Wallace was besieged with wires and speeches on the floor of Congress holding him responsible for the murder.[58] On Thursday, the action moved back into Judge Johnson's federal courtroom. Lawyers for Clark were rebuffed when they petitioned Johnson to cite King for contempt of his order prohibiting marches. Little wonder. Having approved the compromise in advance, Johnson pressed King, who testified that he had known at the start he would turn around and not march to Montgomery. Johnson was to say later that King's march "was a symbolic sort of thing to save face for King." And when defense lawyers asked aggressive questions—as when John Kohn asked a black leader if he were being paid to "agitate"—Johnson reprimanded them for discourtesy. The hearing continued into the weekend, when Johnson clashed with Lingo, who testified he had authorized "necessary force" at the bridge because it was "futile" to make mass arrests. Lingo said that Wallace had instructed him to see that "no one would be hurt," but that he was "to restrain the marchers." "Regardless of what it meant to do it?" Johnson asked. "No," Lingo answered. "I did not mean to kill them but to use the least force possible to do it." The judge was unimpressed. "Regardless of what it is?" he asked. "Where were you going to stop?" Somewhat limply, Lingo said he had not wanted to use tear gas and that he was uncertain who, if anyone, had given the order to launch gas canisters. When the hearing ended, it seemed a sure bet that Johnson would rule for the plaintiffs. Yet the judge's wife and clerk would say later that Johnson "agonized" over the relative merits of, on the one hand, the state's obligation to maintain the safe and free flow of highway traffic and, on the other, the injustices done to blacks in pursuit of their constitutional right to vote. He would announce his decision the following Wednesday, March 17.[59]

Wallace was among those who were certain that Judge Johnson would allow the protestors to march from Selma. With Reeb's murder, demonstrators clogging Montgomery's streets, and a cascade of nationwide criticism coursing over him, Wallace decided he needed to move dramatically to regain the offensive. On Friday, March 12, he sent a long wire to President Johnson maintaining that street demonstrations "in defiance of lawful state and federal authority" were at issue, not voting rights, and that perhaps a solution could be worked out between him and the president at an early meeting. Johnson immediately agreed, and the meeting was set for noon the next day, Saturday, March 13.

The White House meeting turned out to be an extraordinary three-and-a-half-hour encounter. Precisely what happened throughout the session is hazy because aides for both men were in and out of the meeting, but none was present for all or even most of it. As might be expected, selection of the "winner" of the encounter depended on the speaker. Johnson's aides believed that the president simply overwhelmed Wallace, while Wallace's aides reported that the governor gave as good as he got.[60] In reality, both men came away with victories. The president used the meeting as a vehicle to dramatize the need for voting rights legislation; Wallace used it to demonstrate that he was a man of moderation seeking a peaceful resolution to the racial strife in his state and elsewhere. But there can be no doubt that Johnson held the upper hand with Wallace, as he did with almost everyone he encountered. For one thing, Wallace held an almost devout respect for the presidency; in the meeting, he apologized profusely for troubling Johnson and thanked him several times "for the opportunity to let" him come to the White House "and explain things to [Johnson] in person."[61] For another thing, Johnson's size and bulk made Wallace seem puny by comparison, especially when the president directed Wallace to a soft couch in which he sank to barely three feet from the floor while Johnson towered over the governor in a rocking chair that he pulled as close to Wallace as possible.[62] And Wallace admired Johnson, whom he described as "a big, strong, tall man ... very persuasive ... especially in a small crowd." And he would come to like Johnson, despite the president's public criticism of him, because of kindnesses to Lurleen as governor and during her illnesses (see chapter 13).[63]

Johnson sought to persuade Wallace that the civil rights demonstrations that both men disliked would end if Wallace would fully support black suffrage in Alabama. Wallace disagreed: "He [Johnson] was very concerned about the march and the need for the march. And, naturally, he was supporting universal suffrage and easier qualifications for electors and the civil rights proposals. And, of course, I was interested in maintaining law and order—and, of course, he was, too. But we were poles apart about our attitude toward those who marched. I felt that some of those who were involved in the march were not interested in solving the legitimate grievances, but interested in just creating chaos."[64]

Johnson's aide Richard Goodwin, Attorney General Nicholas Katzenbach, and Wallace press secretary Bill Jones were three who were present for part of the meeting. From what they, Wallace, and Johnson later recounted, here is a reconstruction of one of the more provocative exchanges in what Katzenbach described as "the most amazing conversation" he had ever witnessed.

JOHNSON: George, you see all those demonstrators there in front of the White House?

WALLACE: Yes, Mr. President, I saw them.

JOHNSON: Those goddam niggers have kept my daughters awake every night with their screaming and hollering night after night. Wouldn't it be just wonderful if we could put an end to all those demonstrations?

WALLACE: Oh, yes, Mr. President, that would be wonderful.

JOHNSON: Then why don't you let the niggers vote?

WALLACE: They can vote if they're registered.

JOHNSON: Well, then, George, why don't you just tell them county registrars to register those niggers?

WALLACE: I don't have that power, Mr. President. Under Alabama law, that belongs to the country registrars.

JOHNSON: George, don't you shit me. Who runs Alabama? Don't shit me about your persuasive powers. I had on the TV this morning and I saw you and you were talking and you was attacking me, George.

WALLACE: Not you, Mr. President. I was speaking against federal intervention.

JOHNSON: You was attacking me, George. And you know what? You were so damned persuasive that I almost changed my mind. George, you and I shouldn't be thinking about 1968. We should be thinking about 1988. We'll both be dead and gone then. What do you want left behind? You want a great, big marble monument that says, "George Wallace: He Built"? Or do you want a little piece of scrawny pine laying there that says, "George Wallace: He Hated"?[65]

With that, Johnson rose and strode toward the Rose Garden, where he had scheduled a news conference. He pulled Wallace along with him, stopping just before they went outside. "He wanted to discuss with me the things that we would say we talked about, because we did discuss many things in that conversation. . . . He wanted to talk about Vietnam, and he did. We talked about education. We talked about welfare. We talked about hospitals. We talked about medical care. . . . He said, 'I don't want them to think we spent three hours talking about niggers.' "[66]

At the ensuing news conference, Johnson courteously presented

Wallace to the White House press corps; in a brief statement, the governor said, "I hope we can come to a solution of our problems [and] a cessation of demonstrations." Johnson then stepped to the microphones and, to one observer, "never in his sixteen months in office was he more in command of the situation."[67] He said that he would send voting rights legislation to the Congress the following week, that he told Wallace he would "press with all the vigor at [his] command" to assure its passage, and that "the federal government would completely meet its responsibilities . . . in maintaining law and order . . . if state and local authorities [were] unable to function. He also warned Wallace "that the brutality in Selma . . . must not be repeated."[68] On the nationally televised program "Face the Nation" the next day, Wallace responded by continuing to assert that every eligible black person in Alabama could register, that state authorities reacted to extended demonstrations with greater tolerance than authorities in New York and Washington, D.C., and that incidents of brutality were few and far between, considering the extent and frequency of the protests.[69] President Johnson turned from the television set and muttered that Wallace was "a runty little bastard."[70] The next night, Johnson retained the high ground with a brilliant speech to a joint session of Congress—"Lyndon Johnson at his best: homely, compassionate, audacious, and noble."[71]

> At times history and fate meet at a single time in a single place to shape a turning point in man's unending search for freedom. So it was at Lexington and Concord. So it was at Appomatox. So it was last week in Selma, Alabama. There is no cause for pride in what happened in Selma. But there is cause for hope and for faith in our democracy in what is happening here tonight. . . . The cries of pain and the hymns and protest of oppressed people have summoned into convocation all the majesty of this great government. . . . Rarely in any time does an issue lay bare the secret heart of America itself . . . a challenge, not to our growth or abundance, our welfare or our security, but to the values and the purposes and the meaning of our nation. The issue of equal rights for American Negroes is such an issue. . . . The last time a president sent a civil rights bill to Congress . . . the heart of the voting provision had been eliminated. This time, on this issue, there must be no delay, no hesitation, and no compromise. . . . We cannot . . . refuse to protect the right of

every American to vote. . . . [Selma] is only part of a far larger
movement, one that reached North as well as South—the
effort of American Negroes to secure for themselves the full
blessing of American life. Their cause must be our cause, too.
It's not just Negroes, but it is all of us, who must overcome
the crippling legacy of bigotry and injustice. And we *shall*
overcome.[72]

The speech wrung cheers and tears from every civil rights advocate in America—from Representative Celler and Sen. Mike Mansfield, sitting in the House chamber, to Martin Luther King, Jr., watching on television in Montgomery.[73] Southerners were less than
elated. Louisiana's Sen. Alan Ellender slumped dejectedly in his seat
at the joint session, while Wallace's press secretary noted that, with
the speech, the president "took control of the civil rights movement
in the United States. He had now made the one hundred and eighty
degree turn from his Southern position as a Texas senator; he was the
nation's leading civil rights exponent."[74] Some black leaders, like
J. L. Chestnut, Jr., reached the same conclusion and "became uncomfortable." Chestnut said, "It suddenly dawned on me that King
was no longer the number-one civil rights leader in America; Lyndon
Johnson was. I was afraid we'd been outfoxed and were in danger of
being co-opted. Johnson [was] always advocating gradualism. . . . If
he . . . set our agenda, did this mean the end of the movement?"
Chestnut hoped for something soon that would allow blacks to steer
their own course and realize their own destiny.[75]

■ ■ ■

Another Johnson—Judge Frank Johnson—supplied that "something" on Wednesday, March 17. In a decision marked by the judicial
innovation that was to characterize his career on the bench, Johnson
ruled that although the planned march reached "to the outer limits
of what is constitutionally allowed," the "enormous" injustices visited on Alabama's black citizens by the state's officials "clearly exceeded" those constitutional limits. Johnson, in the words of his
biographer, decided "that the scope of a group's freedom to protest
its grievances depended on the virtue of its cause." Additionally, the
judge ordered Wallace to provide the marchers with adequate police
protection; if he and Alabama could not, he said, Wallace could
request federal assistance. The decision, Johnson's biographer wrote,

"far exceeded anything the [Supreme] Court had yet counte-
nanced."[76] As soon as the word spread, SNCC members in Montgomery organized a march; Assistant Attorney General John Doar
was on the scene and reported the events from a telephone booth to a
speaker phone in Katzenbach's office: "Now they are coming over
the hill. A few are carrying signs. The streets are filled with people."
But he told his relieved audience that despite what he called "lei-
surely" attacks on protesters, the police were maintaining order with
general restraint and that a repetition of the March 7 melee in Selma
did not appear to be developing. Katzenbach had been operating on
fewer than five hours of sleep a night for the previous week, and now
he wondered how Wallace would react. "Wallace may be a bastard,"
he said privately, "but he is not dumb." Katzenbach was sure that
Wallace would figure a way out—perhaps plead that Alabama could
not afford to protect the marchers and that the federal government
would be required to assume that burden. What worried him, he
confided to a reporter, was not that Wallace or Lingo would "unleash
the mercenaries or that organized bands [would] try to ambush the
marchers": "I fear most the sniper," he said.[77]

Wallace promptly announced he would address a joint session of
the legislature the following night and instructed his aides to arrange
for live television coverage. He denounced Johnson as "presiding
over a mock court [that] prostitutes our law in favor of mob rule." He
charged, "The call has gone out from the demonstration leaders for
every left-wing, pro-Communist, fellow traveler and Communist in
this country to be here." He even said darkly, "We have reliable
information that over two hundred nationally known entertainers
are coming into this state for this demonstration." Nonetheless,
Wallace said, "we will obey; we will do our duty. We will not abdicate
our responsibilities to provide protection as best we can. . . . Let's you
and I, the people of Alabama, see that this march is peaceful." But
he said that a survey he had ordered concluded that more than
six thousand people would be needed to adequately patrol the
marchers' route. So he asked President Johnson to provide "sufficient federal civil authorities . . . for the safety and welfare of the so-
called demonstrators." The president responded that the federal
government did not have civilian personnel in the numbers Wallace
said were required—but that the governor did have thousands of
National Guardsmen. Johnson said he would call them into service if
Wallace would not. Wallace responded with a resolution that the
legislature adopted making it plain, first, that Alabama could not

afford to activate the guard without "jeopardizing the essential functions of the state" and, second, that since the march was "sanctioned by a federal court . . . the financial resources of the federal government [needed to] be used to pay the cost of mobilizing the Alabama National Guard." The president complied, activating units of the guard, buttressed by regular army troops; he caustically noted that he was "surprised" Wallace had relinquished a state responsibility to the federal government.[78]

■   ■   ■

The march from Selma to Montgomery, largely symbolic once President Johnson had submitted his voting rights bill to Congress, stepped off at 10:00 A.M. on Sunday, March 21, with more than three thousand people from all over the nation; in the vanguard, in addition to King, Abernathy, and Lewis, were United Nations Undersecretary Ralph Bunche, nuns, students, clergymen, union members, and a man from Saginaw, Michigan, Jim Letherer, who completed the fifty-mile walk despite having only one leg. So many march participants had poured into Selma that many, unable to find hotel rooms, were put up in black churches.[79] "The impressive thing to me," Chestnut said, "was that no white person had decided there would be a march or where or how far it would go. Those were black decisions. . . . Blacks were in charge. . . . The march to Montgomery was the first enterprise I'd ever seen involving black and white people where the black people set the agenda and ran the show."[80]

And quite a show it was. The march director, Hosea Williams, organized teams to arrange for the complicated logistics to support thousands of people at the opening and closing of the march, and the three hundred that the court said was the maximum that could march on the two-lane stretches of highway. They rented four big tents and sent out committees to find sites on which the owners would allow the marchers to camp on the four nights they planned to be on the road. The women of black churches in Selma and Montgomery baked bread and cooked up fried chicken, fish, ham, collard and turnip greens, peas, sweet potatoes, macaroni-and-cheese casseroles, and pots of soup, much of it shipped to the marchers in shiny garbage pails that served as hot-food containers. They rounded up more than fifty support vehicles, including five latrine trucks, a six-hundred-gallon water truck, a mobile clinic, six ambulances, rubbish-pickup trucks, and cars driven by volunteers to ferry "excess" marchers (anyone beyond the three hundred permitted by the court order) from the line of march to either Selma or Montgomery. One of the volunteers was a thirty-nine-year-old housewife and college student from Detroit, Viola Gregg Liuzzo.[81]

The thousands of marchers—guarded by soldiers decked out in combat gear, while jeeps, lorries, and helicopters scoured the countryside along the line of march—completed a 7-mile leg in chilly weather on the first day. Thinned down to 300 people after that, the group traversed 16 miles in a punishing sun on the second day, 11 miles in a torrential downpour on the third, and 16 miles in balmy spring weather on the fourth day as they entered Montgomery, where they were joined by another 1,500 people as the highway widened.[82] Wednesday night, drenched by a sudden cloudburst, the throng camped out on the grounds of a Catholic church-hospital-school complex known as the City of St. Jude, where racial integration had been practiced (and overlooked) for years. But they were made inestimably more comfortable by a parade of entertainers (the very people Wallace had warned of) assembled by Harry Belafonte— talents like Mahalia Jackson, Tony Bennett, Billy Eckstein, Ella Fitzgerald, Pete Seeger, Nipsy Russell, Alan King, Ruby Dee, Joan Baez, and Sammy Davis, Jr., who called off a performance of his Broadway show *Golden Boy* to appear in Montgomery.[83]

The next day, on a muggy Thursday afternoon, a tidal wave of people, twenty-five thousand strong, rolled up Dexter Avenue to the capitol. They had wound through black residential sections of Montgomery to the downtown area, around the ornate fountain that anchored spacious Court Square and on up Dexter Avenue to the steps of the capitol. Wallace, who peered out a window of the office of Cecil Jackson, his executive secretary, had spent the week busily seeking ways to demean the marchers. He decreed that Thursday would be a holiday for all female employees because of the potential "danger." He toyed with (and then rejected) an idea that he close the capitol and replace the Alabama and Confederate flags with a black flag of mourning. Instead, he contented himself during the week with directing his legislative leaders to adopt a number of resolutions condemning the march in terms understandable to the governor's supporters: clergymen had no business participating in patently political demonstrations; "supposedly religious leaders from other parts of the United States" had been seen drinking liquor and heard using vulgar language; and there was evidence of fornication among the demonstrators and some "young women [would] return to their home states as unwed expectant mothers."[84] "All these segregationists can think of is fornication," John Lewis remarked. "That's why there are so many different shades of Negroes." It took nearly two hours for all the marchers to file up the avenue and gather en masse to hear King proclaim victory over the forces of oppression. Judge Johnson and John Doar watched the procession from the office of Judge Richard Rives of the U.S. Court of Appeals for the Fifth Circuit. Doar commented that it was "a beautiful sight." Watching the seemingly endless mass of people parading by the federal building, Rives turned to Johnson, smiled, and said, "This does indeed reach the outer perimeters of what is constitutionally allowed." Not everyone in the Johnson family or in white Montgomery was as riveted by the day's events as the judge; as the marchers converged on the capitol, Ruth Johnson and several friends played a round of golf at the Montgomery Country Club.[85]

Ralph Abernathy said, "It was a glorious homecoming for Martin and me"—back to the place where they had led the Montgomery bus boycott and the start of the movement just over nine years earlier. "I don't know what Governor Wallace and Sheriff Clark thought as they watched the spectacle of our celebration," Abernathy recalled, "but they should have recognized that their cause, whether states' rights or white supremacy, was doomed." King roused the multitude with some of the same thoughts in one of his classic speeches: "I stand before you this afternoon with the conviction that segregation is on its deathbed in Alabama—and the only thing uncertain about it is how costly the segregationists and Wallace will make the funeral." Then, to a steady and continually rising cheer that ended in an animal-like roar, King assured the masses that segregation's death would come soon:

> I know you are asking today, "How long will it take?" I come to say to you this afternoon: however difficult the moment, however frustrating the hour, it will not be long—because truth pressed to earth will rise again. How long? Not long—because no lie can live forever. How long? Not long—because you still reap what you sow. How long? Not long—because the arm of the moral universe is long but it bends toward justice. How long? Not long—because mine eyes have seen the glory of the coming of the Lord. . . . Our God is marching on.[86]

A delegation led by King supporter (and eventual successor) Joseph Lowery tried to deliver the petition for redress of grievances to Wallace, but they were denied permission to enter the capitol. By the time they persuaded the guards that it was a public building and that they were residents of Alabama and entitled to try to see their governor, Wallace already had departed; he would say later that he had no intention of dignifying a demonstration by meeting with some of its leaders.[87]

Depending on who was doing the talking, President Johnson and George Wallace both had won the day. The president's men had spread the word that Wallace had been trapped into asking for federal troops, thus sparing Johnson the political embarrassment of seeming to invade the South. Wallace's aides let it be known that the governor had sprung his own trap by maneuvering the president into sending troops to Alabama, thus forcing the federal government to bear the financial burden—and, should anything happen, the blame. "President Johnson got very upset with me," Wallace believed. "[Our] survey to determine what was needed for protection . . . showed it would take a lot more than we would be able to pay for—so many thousands of National Guard troops in addition to so many regular policemen, so many helicopters, so many portable toilets—and the state did not have the money to provide all of that. . . . And, of course, if something happened to anyone, and they had been hurt or shot, the law enforcement officials or soldiers were under the auspices of President Lyndon Johnson, and he would have to take the blame for any violence that took place in this march."[88]

■   ■   ■

But whoever set a trap for whom, everyone involved with the march— the president, the governor, the judge, the civil rights leaders, the soldiers, the police—was relieved that no one was hurt. Late that evening, the Justice Department's chief civil rights trouble-shooter, John Doar, was having his first meal of the day at the all-night Elite Café, when, at eleven-thirty, he was summoned to the phone. A few minutes later, he returned to the table and quietly informed his companions that it was the FBI telling him, "A Mrs. Liuzzo has been killed on the road back to Selma."[89] She was the eleventh person to die in Alabama in a racially connected incident since Wallace had taken office little over two years earlier.

Liuzzo was described in *Newsweek* as "a plumpish, perky blonde, belatedly a sophomore [in sociology] at Wayne State University [who] liked a cause. A mother of five, she had bolted to Selma with friends, departing in her blue 1963 Oldsmobile without even telling anyone good-bye; she had notified her husband by phone, spurning his entreaties not to go. "This is something I must do," she had told Anthony Liuzzo. In Selma, she had volunteered for the transportation committee, ferrying marchers back and forth to Selma and Montgomery. As the crowd had dispersed after King's speech in Montgomery, she had carried a carload of marchers back to Selma; on the return trip to pick up more people, she had been accompanied by Leroy Moton, a nineteen-year-old black civil rights worker from Selma. At eight o'clock, about a half hour out of Selma, they had been cruising along Highway 80, Moton fiddling with the radio dial and Liuzzo humming "We Shall Overcome." Just then, near the edge of Big Swamp in Lowndes County, about halfway to Montgomery, a red-and-white Impala had swept past and gunshots had rung out; at least six had torn into the Olds. Moton could not even remember having heard them; what he had seen though, was that Viola Liuzzo had slumped sideways, blood spurting from a head wound inflicted by a .38-caliber slug. The car had lurched to a halt against a wire fence beyond the shoulder. Moton had rushed down the dark highway, flailing his arms for help from passing cars; one had nearly run him down. He had returned to the car and assured himself that Liuzzo was dead, and then, emotionally spent, he had passed out for nearly half an hour.

After reviving, he had flagged down a pickup truck that had taken him back to Selma, where he had notified authorities. But he could identify neither the car nor the assailants. Nonetheless, shortly after noon the next day, President Johnson, flanked by Katzenbach and Hoover, went before television cameras to announce the arrest of four Klansmen from the Birmingham area; they were charged with an 1870 statute making it a federal crime to conspire to deprive persons of their civil rights. Speculation about how the authorities were able to strike so swiftly was laid to rest two weeks later when a federal grand jury indicted three of the four men; it was revealed that the fourth, thirty-one-year-old Gary Thomas Rowe, had been a paid FBI informant within the Klan for the previous five years (see chapters 7 and 10). Meanwhile, the three men were indicted by the state on murder charges. The first man to be tried, Collie Leroy Wilkins, twenty-one, was a hulking, pot-bellied auto mechanic who was accused of wielding the murder weapon. In the May trial, Wilkins was defended by a foul-mouthed Klan attorney, Matt Murphy, who was permitted by the judge to spew hatred through the court:

What kind of a man is this Gary Rowe? . . . What kind of a
man is this who took an oath and joined the United Klans of
America, took the oath [not to reveal Klan actions] with his
hand raised to his almighty God—and then sold out like
Judas Iscariot. . . . He sold his soul for a little gold. He's
worse than a white nigger. . . . I stand here as a white man
and I say we're never going to mongrelize the race with
nigger blood and the Martin Luther Kings, the white niggers,
the Jews, the Zionists who run that bunch of niggers. . . .
Niggers are against every law God ever wrote. . . . God
damned them and they went to Africa and the only thing
they ever built was grass huts.

The prosecution, in contrast, went straight to the only point.
"Forget the FBI," Joe Gantt, Alabama's assistant attorney general,
advised the jury. "Forget segregation, forget integration, forget
about white and black and Communists. . . . I'm talking about a
murder—a cold-blooded murder of a defenseless woman. She was
shot by a yellow-bellied coward."

Rowe, quietly and unblinkingly, told just how cowardly the act
had been. Early on the day of the killing, he had been invited to join
Wilkins and two others—Eugene Thomas, forty-three, and William
Orville Eaton, forty-one, both steelworkers—to drive from the Birmingham area to Montgomery to harass marchers by "head-
knocking." On the way back from Selma, they had been stopped on
Highway 80 for speeding, but had been let off with a warning. In
Selma, they had had some beers and had gone looking for more
marchers; once, they had started to "take two colored people," but
had been frightened off by an army truck. Then they had pulled up at
a stoplight and had spotted Liuzzo and Moton in their car. Rowe
continued with the bone-chilling tale:

Wilkins looked out the window and he said, "Looka there,
baby brother. I'll be damned. Looka there." Then Eaton said,
"I wonder where they're going?" Thomas said, "They're going
out to park someplace together." Thomas said, "Let's take
'em." As we were driving, Thomas reached into a
compartment by the front seat and got out a revolver.

They had chased the car onto the highway and almost overtook
it four times but had been forced back—once by a jeep with military
policemen, once when they had spotted a state-trooper stakeout for

speeders, a third time by a roadside crowd of potential witnesses, and finally by trucks in the oncoming lane. Rowe continued:

> I told Gene [Thomas] we'd better go back to Selma, we're wasting our time. Thomas said, "We're in the big time now. We're gonna take that car." Wilkins said, "You pull up alongside and we'll take it." I said to Wilkins, "How you going to stop them?" And Wilkins said, "Wait and see." Thomas passed his revolver back to Wilkins. We drew even to the car. And Wilkins said, "Give it the gas." Thomas moved the car up just a little bit. Wilkins rolled down the window. His arm went out the window—right out to the elbow length. There was a lady driving. She turned around and looked directly at us. Wilkins fired two shots. And Thomas yelled, "All right, men, shoot the hell out of 'em." Wilkins and Eaton emptied their guns. I made believe I was firing mine. We passed and the Olds seemed to be following. I said, "Good God, you missed. Wilkins slapped me on the knee and said, "I don't miss, baby brother. That bitch and bastard are both dead and in hell."

Liuzzo's car had then swerved off the road, and the Impala had sped back to Birmingham, where they had looked up a friend to establish an alibi. Rowe had slipped away to a pay phone to notify his FBI handlers, who had encouraged him earlier to go along on the ride. In the end, however, prosecutors managed to persuade only ten of the twelve Lowndes County jurors of Wilkins's guilt; the two who held out against conviction had been members of the White Citizens Council—and both said they had rejected Rowe's testimony because he had broken his sworn oath not to rat on Klan killers.[90] A second trial in October ended in outright acquittal for Wilkins. It was hardly surprising. Only a month earlier, a deputy sheriff who had gunned down "in self-defense" a white, unarmed civil rights worker and seminarian named Jonathan Daniels, had been acquitted in Lowndes County. Wilkins's jury this time included ten present or former members of the White Citizens Council, five of whom admitted they believed that blacks or whites who associated with blacks were inferior to the white race.[91]

It was in federal court in November that some sense of justice prevailed. For one thing, Judge Johnson allowed the government to exclude from the jury former White Citizens Council members; he similarly allowed the defense to strike NAACP members. Second, the defense was now represented by Arthur Hanes, the former mayor of

Birmingham; though a committed segregationist (he had tried to organize a "white march" to counter King's but had been dissuaded by Wallace), he was nowhere near the purveyor of unmitigated hate that Klansman Murphy had been. (Several months earlier, Murphy had been killed in an automobile accident, and Hanes succeeded him in the case.) Also, Judge Johnson almost certainly would not have allowed Murphy's kind of filth to be disgorged in his courtroom. Nonetheless, Hanes worked hard to win his clients' case by trying to impugn the character of the prosecution's principal witness, Rowe. As had Murphy, Hanes struck hard at the fact that Rowe had violated his Klan oath to "die rather than divulge" information about the organization's activities. In addition, however, Hanes forced Rowe to admit that he had not been supporting his five children from two marriages; that his pay as an informer ($22,000 in five years) was based on the extent of his activity on behalf of the FBI, implying that he might invent a story to get more money; and that he had partici-pated in the Mother's Day beatings of Freedom Riders in Bir-mingham in 1961.[92] But the government, represented by Doar and U.S. Attorney Ben Hardeman, an Alabamian, carefully recounted the facts and, as had state prosecutors, called on the jurors to put aside emotions and be "loyal to only one thing—[their] oath." Hardeman thundered, "Are we going to permit a star chamber court by persons . . . who are their investigators, their own witnesses, their own judges, their own jury, and, yes, their own executioner?" Judge Johnson, who had been incensed by the two state trials acquitting Wilkins, charged the jury for more than half an hour, lecturing its members that "the principles of justice and supremacy of the law [must] override any political or sociological causes or movements." But the jury, like the first Wilkins jury, announced after twenty-four hours of deliberation that it was hopelessly deadlocked. Johnson would hear none of it. "I think we're going to have to give the jury a little dynamite," he told his law clerk. The "dynamite" was the so-called Allan charge—a supplemental charge to a jury that, in 1896, the Supreme Court had upheld as constitutional. The charge came in a case where a judge had instructed a deadlocked jury that those members holding views contrary to the majority should treat the views of the others with proper regard and deference, asking themselves whether they might not reasonably doubt their own judgment. The judge told the jurors that there had been about fifty witnesses and as many exhibits, that the trial had been thorough and expensive, that they had not "com-menced to deliberate the case long enough to reach the conclusion" that they were "hopelessly deadlocked," and that there [was] no reason to suppose that the case [would] ever be submitted to twelve more intelligent, more impartial, or more competent people to decide it, or that more or clearer evidence [would] be produced on one side or the other." The judge's remonstrance produced results; four hours later, the jury returned with guilty verdicts. Johnson imposed the maximum ten-year sentence on each defendant and told the jurors, "All, right, gentlemen, if it is worth anything to you, in my opinion that was the only verdict that you could possibly reach in this case and still reach a fair and honest and just verdict."[95]

Johnson also blamed his old college friend for Liuzzo's murder—but culpability, in his view, extended far beyond Wallace. In later years, he told his biographer, Tinsley Yarbrough:

> I don't believe you would have any Wilkinses, Thomases, or Eatons if you didn't have leadership that gave them the idea that they could do what they did and do it with immunity. Oh, you'd have some isolated instances with fanatics, maniacs. . . . But these people were not maniacs. They were employed. . . . They had families. . . . I don't mean to blame it all on John Patterson or George Wallace. I blame a lot of it on the ministers [who] would condone putting . . . "goon squads" out in front of their churches to keep blacks from coming [and on] business leaders that refused to take a stand . . . when it was obvious to everyone that the laws of the land were being violated. . . . They refused to take a stand because they feared economic repercussions and they'd rather run the risk of some nondescript black organizing a black boycott than run the risk of being ostracized at the country club or losing some of their white clients. I use that word [clients] deliberately, because lawyers were just as bad in failing to take a positive stand on this as anyone else.[94]

Wallace, though genuinely shocked at and remorseful over the murder of Liuzzo (which he pronounced LOO-zee-o), remained combative as ever when he considered that Alabama was being singled out by politicians and in the media as a center of violence. The general opinion he faced was crystallized by Joseph Cumming, the native Georgian who was then *Newsweek*'s Atlanta bureau chief: "It really seems that Alabama, under Wallace—which means Al Lingo as public safety director—is really where the lurking, systematic apparatus for police brutality is most alive. . . . In Alabama, there is a sinister efficiency about the potential for police brutality."[95]

The day after Liuzzo's murder, Wallace, by prearrangement, appeared on NBC's "Today" show. He had intended to use the platform to contend that the Selma-to-Montgomery march in particular and civil rights marches in general were "communist-inspired and part of a plan to completely immobilize the nation" and were led by people who sought "redistribution of the nation's wealth through land reform and an attack on the established social and educational order throughout the nation, not just in the South." Clearly, Wallace was still mouthing phrases implanted by John Kohn; within the confines of segregation, his own educational and social policies in Alabama leaned heavily toward improving opportunities for the poor, including, of course, the large majority of the black population. But the "Today" program's interviewer, Richard Valeriani, quickly moved the conversation to the Liuzzo murder:

> WALLACE: Of course, I regret this murder. I would like to point out, though, that people are assaulted in every state in the union. It's still safer on Highway 80 than it is riding a subway in New York.
>
> VALERIANI: Do you think your own antagonistic statements about the march had invited or set the scene for violence?
>
> WALLACE: You can't blame any one individual about things that happen in Alabama any more than you can blame Governor (Nelson) Rockefeller about Malcolm X being slain in New York. And I regret this incident, but I can say with twenty-five thousand demonstrators in the streets and chanting and maligning and slandering and libeling the people of this state as they did for several hours on your network and the other networks, I think the people of our state were greatly restrained.[96]

Wallace issued a stronger statement later, calling the killing an "outrageous crime" and warning, "Such acts of cowardice will not be tolerated." At the Governor's Mansion that night, after the president had announced the arrests, Wallace told a reporter:

> I am as angry as I can be. I felt good last night when I went to bed. There had been no violence and the crowd had dispersed from the capitol area in an orderly manner. I thought it was all over. Then this thing happened—a tragic, tragic thing. One of

the main reasons I didn't allow this march at all was because of the possibility of something like this. The action of [those] fools, whoever killed her, certainly does not represent the people of Alabama. [The people] were represented by those who stayed away . . . as we had advised them to do. There had not been a single incident.[97]

■ ■ ■

Despite Wallace's public combative pose, privately he felt defeated or, at the least, helpless. He had lost his legal battle but, more important in his reckoning, he had lost the public relations battle. Lingo had seen to that at the Edmund Pettus Bridge in Selma on March 7. And whatever credibility he and the state may have regained from his highly publicized meeting with the president and the peaceable nature of the King march was destroyed the night of March 25 with Liuzzo's murder. So Wallace eagerly granted an audience to Joseph Lowery of the SCLC and a group of Alabama civil rights advocates; no Alabama governor—not even the racially moderate Jim Folsom—had ever before met with such a group. The delegation of sixteen men, all but one black, arrived at the capitol just five days after having been rebuffed by Wallace. Its members signed in as visitors and were escorted to the governor's office for a private meeting that lasted an hour and a half. Wallace greeted them and invited Lowery to read his petition. It was a lengthy appeal to Wallace for the right to vote, equal protection of the law, and an end to police brutality. Lowery, who had stood while reading the petition, resumed his seat as Wallace replied conversationally and fully, recounting his usual responses to civil rights criticism: he favored blacks voting if they met state-prescribed qualifications; the way to meet the qualifications was through education—and Wallace would take a back seat to no one in advancing education for both races in Alabama (his administration had increased average salaries for teachers, black and white, by 29 percent; a free textbook program would take effect in the fall; and the establishment of trade schools and junior colleges, which he had started as a legislator and was expanding as governor, included ten black institutions); education led to jobs—and at least a third of the seventy-five thousand new jobs he had created by luring industry to Alabama had gone to blacks; he had always directed law enforcement authorities to move with minimal force against demonstrators—and if they occasionally get out of hand, it is because they are human and must work long hours in stressful circumstances when there are demonstrations. Wallace made other assertions that were patently wrong but that he has always somehow managed to justify in his own mind: he had never made a speech that disparaged blacks; there had been no race riots in his administration—race riots being battles between whites and blacks, not police and blacks; he had wanted to prevent the march to Montgomery only to protect the marchers.[98] Throughout his career, Wallace always was able to rationalize the racist language of his 1963 inaugural as merely a prosegregation stance, police brutality as provocations by demonstrators, and the events at the Edmund Pettus Bridge as "just a shoving and pushing match—nobody got hurt, nobody went to the hospital." (In fact, seventeen had been hospitalized).[99]

But Wallace exuded an ingenuousness that imparted a sense of hope—so much so that, just as the group was leaving, King's aide James Bevel noticed a stack of photographs of the governor piled on a conference table. He asked if they were souvenirs for visitors. When Wallace said they were, Bevel took one and, quite to the surprise of everyone in the room, asked the governor to autograph it. Wallace delightedly complied, after which, the other fifteen civil rights delegates each claimed a Wallace portrait and autograph. At the end of the meeting, Wallace declined any comment beyond his aide's description of the session as "frank and friendly," but his mood was clearly upbeat. Lowery added only that he was "cordially and courteously received" and "given every opportunity" to be heard. "I hope," he said cautiously, "it will prove to be a fruitful conference."[100]

In many ways, it was. Wallace directed county registrars, who regularly met only two days a month, to open their doors for an additional ten days to register prospective voters. He also proclaimed his support for registration of "every eligible citizen." That summer, the voting rights bill became federal law and had an extraordinary effect throughout the South; twenty years later, the number of black voters in eleven Southern states had tripled to nearly 4.5 million, and hundreds of blacks had been elected to city, county, and state offices. Its immediate effect in Alabama was almost as dramatic. By the 1966 primaries in Alabama, the number of blacks on the state's voting rolls had doubled to nearly a quarter of a million. Four blacks were elected that year to local offices in two counties. In Selma, Jim Clark, seeking reelection as sheriff, was defeated by the relatively moderate Wilson Baker, who won an overwhelming majority of the black vote in Dallas

County (which had grown from barely over three hundred to more than ten thousand). In Birmingham, Albert Lingo, who had by then been dismissed by Wallace (in itself a positive sign), lost his race for sheriff. But his campaign had included an extraordinary appearance before a meet-the-candidates session organized by none other than the SCLC—and Lingo had even dropped a bill in the collection plate.

By the summer of 1968, nearly 60 percent of the adult black population of Alabama was registered to vote. Just as Wallace's schoolhouse-door stand had prodded President Kennedy to introduce the civil rights legislation enacted in 1964, Wallace's intransigence to the Selma-to-Montgomery march and the resulting melee at the Edmund Pettus Bridge had provoked President Johnson to send the voting rights bill to Congress in 1965. Years later, Rep. William Dickinson, who was a House freshman in 1965, encapsulated Wallace's influence on civil rights this way:

> George did more to bring about what he professed to oppose than any other three people I can name. Standing in the schoolhouse door—well, that gave him nationwide attention. But it sure did integrate our schools faster than any other state in the South. And this adamant, defiant attitude on the Selma march thing—whatever point they were trying to make, George just made it for 'em.[101]

But the point was made, and Wallace, who knew how to count as well as anyone, began crossing a bridge of his own—from being the nation's personification of segregation and racism to being named in a poll of Alabama blacks in 1986 the best governor in the state's history. It would be a slow crossing, to be sure; Wallace would continue to ply segregation for political gain in Alabama through 1970. But he would soon begin decelerating his strong anti-integration actions in the state, while broadening his efforts on the national stage to be seen as a man who opposed federal intrusion into everyday life, not a man who opposed blacks.

Indeed, after a twentieth-anniversary reenactment of the Selma-to-Montgomery march, Wallace welcomed its leaders, Coretta Scott King and Jesse Jackson, to his capitol office. Following a private hour-long meeting, the two symbols of civil rights had only praise for Wallace. Jackson said, "[Wallace] is a man whose attitude has changed, whose behavior has changed. I only wish that Ronald Reagan had the kind of sensitivity now being expressed by George Wallace."[102]

Through the spring of 1965, however, it appeared that George Wallace would soon be disappearing from the national consciousness. Given the worldwide opprobrium heaped on him and Alabama for the four racially motivated killings in the Selma area in just over a month; given the indelible images of troopers in helmets and jackboots, some on horseback, beating and gassing unarmed blacks; given the magnitude and utter triumph of King's march into Montgomery; and, just as important, given that he was approaching the final year in his term of office and could not by law be reelected— given these realities, it appeared that Wallace's meteor-bright candle would burn but briefly.

■ ■ ■

And it would seem that the final nails were driven into Wallace's political coffin on August 6, 1965, when President Johnson signed the Voting Rights Act in the room adjoining the Senate chamber where Abraham Lincoln had signed the Emancipation Proclamation 102 years earlier.[103] But only five days after the voting rights bill became law, a seemingly routine traffic arrest at the intersection of Avalon Boulevard and Imperial Highway in Los Angeles would spark fires that would reignite Wallace's rocket. A California highway patrolman stopped a twenty-one-year-old black man shortly after seven o'clock for reckless driving, a charge to which he would later plead guilty. But it was a hot night, and the residents of the predominantly black, densely populated area in which unemployment had reached a staggering 30 percent were easily agitated. Dozens of neighbors were attracted by the twirling red light of the police car; the young man's mother, who was among them, began to berate the policeman loudly. She jumped on his back as he pushed her son into the squad car; other police officers pried her loose—but then bystanders grew surly, complaining the police were too rough with a distraught mother. Backup police arrived, and as the traffic offender was carted off, they were forced to hold the crowd at bay with shotguns. As word spread (in greatly exaggerated form) that police were using force, more people spilled into the streets and began pelting the police with stones and bottles. By ten o'clock, the throng had turned into a mob that overturned cars, smashed shop windows, looted stores, and pounced on passing automobiles. Rioting and marauding continued until 3:00 A.M., when the rioters seemed to collapse en masse from exhaustion, and a semblance of peace returned to the neighborhood called Watts.

Sadly, the calm would last for barely more than fifteen hours. The next night, rioting started again—only this time, there was shooting and people were beaten. By the third day, 10,000 crazed bandits roamed a 150-block area, burning down buildings, attacking people in daylight, and sniping from rooftops at firefighters and police. The madness continued for six days and was quelled only after 14,000 National Guard troops and the entire Los Angeles police force had sealed off forty-six square miles of the city and had won a shoot-out with 36 gunmen at a Black Muslim mosque. When it was over, 34 people had been killed, 1,000 had been injured, and 4,000 had been arrested; the damage amounted to more than $40 million. In short order, serious racial disorders erupted in Chicago, San Diego, Hartford, and Springfield, Massachusetts, where a black official predicted presciently that "the civil rights struggle in the North [would] be longer, bloodier, and more bitter than in the South." Watts was the beginning of three summers of more than a hundred riots, nearly all in the North, that left 225 dead, 4,000 wounded, and $112 billion in property damage. President Johnson was numbed into disbelief. "How is it possible after all we've accomplished?" he asked. "How could it be? Is the world topsy-turvy?"[104]

Unfortunately, just as Wallace had been saying, Northern racial hostility was real and deep. As long as the civil rights movement had been focused on the South, as long as its leaders had been moderate and nonviolent, as long as the principal issues concerned had been voting, public accommodations, and de jure school segregation, a strong consensus among Americans of all races had held firm under President Johnson's leadership. But once the movement shifted to the North, once its leaders took on the "black power" demands of men like Stokely Carmichael and Floyd McKissick, and once the issues changed to housing, jobs, and de facto school segregation, the accord among whites and blacks started disintegrating.

Between 1964 and 1966, the percentage of Americans who thought that blacks were "trying to move too fast" soared from 34 percent to 85 percent—and 33 percent of the whites in the country felt less regard and respect for blacks. And when a Harvard professor named Daniel Patrick Moynihan issued an insightful report in November 1965 arguing that government should deal with blacks' problems that were the legacies of slavery—welfare dependency, a 25 percent rate of illegitimacy, a divorce rate 40 percent higher than that of whites—he was condemned as a "fascist" by black leaders and lauded by racists for "proving" the inferiority of blacks.[105]

The racial conflagrations, with the accompanying erosion of Northern white support for maintaining the pace of civil rights advancement, propelled Wallace from near-oblivion right back to center stage. With renewed confidence—and a rejuvenated belief that he could become a serious national force—Wallace decided to set the stage for an all-out third-party national presidential campaign in 1968. To do that, of course, he needed a platform; thus, it was necessary to retain his governorship. That meant running for reelection in 1966—and that meant changing the state constitution. If ever he had the power to do that, he had it now—or so he thought.

13

Lady in Waiting

"I *KNEW I HAD TO STAY IN OFFICE,"* George Wallace said simply, recalling his thoughts as his term was drawing to a close. "I wanted the continuity."[1] So in September 1965, Wallace called the legislature into special session with instructions to draw up a constitutional amendment to allow a sitting governor to run for a second consecutive term. The proposal would become effective if ratified by a popular majority of Alabama voters.[2] It was not a new idea; two years before, when Wallace's popularity had soared following his "stand" at the University of Alabama, he had proposed a similar constitutional amendment (see chapter 10). When he had run into a wall of opposition in the legislature, however, and a filibuster had threatened the rest of his legislative program, Wallace had quietly dropped the proposal—for the time.

But this was another time, if not another place. And this time, Wallace anticipated the opposition, much of which, he knew, would come from those legislators with gubernatorial ambitions of their own or who were lining up behind other prospective candidates. The early favorite for governor in the 1966 election was Ryan deGraffenried, the state senator who held relatively moderate views on race and who had been defeated by Wallace in 1962 (see chapter 7). The former governor John Patterson, despite the harsh racist record he had compiled in the four years prior to Wallace's election (he had not even permitted black high school bands to march in his inaugural parade), said he would run a "color-blind" administration if he were returned to office. Carl Elliott, who had lost his congressional seat in 1964, was considered perhaps the most moderate of all the gubernatorial aspirants. Also considering a run was the attorney general, Richmond Flowers, whose prosecutions of the killers of Viola Liuzzo and Jonathan Daniels, though unsuccessful, were gaining him support from the growing numbers of black voters as well as from white liberals like Virginia Durr (see chapter 6), who wrote her brother-in-law, Justice Hugo Black:

> Flowers certainly sounds fine. Everyone says he is a crook, but I feel that a little stealing is mild compared to the fact that law and order have broken down here to such a large extent. After I sat through Mrs. Liuzzo's trial, I realized that murder had become not only condoned but honored if it was against the "enemy"—and the "enemy" seems to be legion. Including us.[3]

Wallace also faced opposition from some erstwhile supporters, like state Sen. Vaughn Hill Robinson of Montgomery, whom Wallace had endorsed two years earlier in a thirty-second televised spot, despite a policy against individual endorsements. Robinson, facing a tight race, had prevailed on the governor to make an exception; yet, upon learning of Wallace's plan, Robinson had floridly denounced it: "Oh, what does this Caesar feed upon?" To that and similar criticisms, Wallace had replied in a statement: "To those so-called liberals who are voicing mock concern over what they call the growing power of tyranny and the washing tides of anarchy, I would suggest further that they are not concerned about me, but about the growing power of the people." Wallace had reason to make that charge. When one senator said he would support the succession amendment but only if it was to start with Wallace's successor, Wallace snapped, "What's the matter? You afraid to let the people vote on it?" And the senator replied, "Hell, frankly, yeah."[4]

■   ■   ■

But to most Alabamians, not to mention an increasingly broad spectrum of Americans in other states, North and South, Wallace had never been more popular—so he decided to take his case directly to the people. He planned a live, prime-time televised speech to the legislature to open the special session. In it he would glorify his 1964

Northern political excursions as having elevated Alabama and the entire South in the eyes of the rest of the country; if the people wanted him to continue his quest in their behalf, he must retain his governorship as a springboard to national importance. Speaking to a packed chamber, Wallace declared:

> I want to speak for you and champion what you would have me champion. I want to know that you are with me in our cause for the law and civilization. . . . If you send me again [to run nationally], I will go again. The liberals say George Wallace wants to be president. What's wrong with that? [And] if you feel a need for *me* in the job I try to do, then I want you to know I feel a need for *you.* . . . The issue is the right of the Alabama people to vote to amend or not to amend their own constitution. It is a precious right. I shall do all in my power to see to it that they do not lose that right. Let the people speak. I say, let the people speak![5]

The appropriate house and senate committees considered and approved the bill in less than a day; the full house membership passed it overwhelmingly, but fourteen senators immediately mounted a filibuster after their committee's decision. Wallace needed two-thirds, or 24, of the 35 senators to shut off debate, but only 18 were willing to go along. Wallace's prospects did not look good; even if the Wallace forces succeeded in a cloture motion, they would require 60 percent of the senate membership, or 21 votes, to pass a constitutional amendment. Wallace was thus 6 votes short of cloture—but, even then, 3 votes short of passage.

He knew only one way to fight back; a frontal assault. First, he tried to persuade the senators to change their rules by lowering the number of votes needed to stop a filibuster. When that failed, he turned to the Alabama Supreme Court, which summarily dismissed his somewhat ludicrous plea for the court to step in and rule filibusters unconstitutional. Then, using tried-and-true political ploys, he threatened to halt state-funded road projects in several of the filibuster participants' districts. One senator, Julian Lowe, said that Seymore Trammell had threatened the president of Southern Union College in Lowe's district with the loss of half a million dollars earmarked for the college unless Lowe joined Wallace's team. A house member, Ashley Camp, claimed he was told that unless he got behind the governor on the succession amendment, a school for the blind and deaf in his county might lose an appropriation. Wallace and Trammell denied having made any threats, and none—certainly, not against schools—was exercised in any event. But threats were made. "It was the way politics in Alabama worked in those days," Bill Jones recalled.

When bullyboy tactics failed, Wallace resorted to what he always did best—campaigning among the folks. He set out for every senatorial district represented by an opponent to the succession proposal; and everywhere he went, he was greeted by large, enthusiastic crowds—most of them showing up after only a day's or even a few hours' notice. In each district, he challenged the senator opposing him to debate the issue; some were foolish enough to try. In Limestone County, Wallace exhorted more than a thousand people to support him; when he was through and it was the senator's turn, the crowd simply disintegrated. In the blue-collar town of Roebuck, near Birmingham, the four thousand people surrounding the platform turned surly after Wallace's harangue; many charged the senator in opposition—and had Wallace not called them off, the legislator might have been seriously hurt.

But all Wallace's efforts were to no avail. The filibuster petered out nearly a month after the legislature had been convened, and on October 22, a vote was taken. The opposition fell into three groups: those who always fought Wallace on issues from race to road construction; those who had their own political agendas; and those who sincerely feared the accrual of power by a governor who could succeed himself. Together, they were too strong. Eighteen voted for the proposal, 14 opposed it, and 3 were no-shows. But the way Wallace counted, if you weren't with him, you were against him. He made it clear to all 17 members who had not voted for the succession amendment that he would do whatever it took to keep them from returning to public life. Ten did not even bother to run when their terms expired; 3 sought statewide offices and lost; the other 4 were defeated when they sought reelection. Wallace had his revenge—but his defeat left him, as Grover Hall observed, "crestfallen and melancholy." Wallace, Hall reflected, had "simply, as is the way of daring, resolute men . . . overreached himself." But if Wallace was down, he was not out. Immediately after being notified that the succession resolution had been voted down, Wallace rose from his desk; jabbed a cigar in his mouth; and, as he started out the door for an out-of-town engagement, turned to his staff and said simply, "My wife may run."[6]

■   ■   ■

The idea, as so many of Wallace's ideas, came on impulse—a whim he had neither discussed with aides nor even considered privately until the moment the thought left his brain and mouth simultaneously. Over the ensuing weeks, the staff put forward other possible surrogates who would act as de jure governor while Wallace actually pulled the strings. These included Wallace's handpicked speaker of the house, Albert Brewer, and the governor's brother Jack who had succeeded George on the circuit court bench in 1958. But none—not even brother Jack—could be counted on to be wholly manipulated. And only with Lurleen as governor could Wallace claim without contradiction to be not only the power *behind* the throne but also the cosovereign. And it was the kind of cheeky, audacious notion that Wallace loved best—the sort that a later generation might call "in-your-face" politics designed to thoroughly embarrass his antagonists. The more he thought about it, the more he liked it. A week after his legislative defeat, Lurleen shared the platform with George at a Huntsville appearance, and the crowd reacted jubilantly when she was introduced as "the next governor of Alabama." By mid-December, Wallace was issuing strong signals to out-of-state reporters that his wife would make the race.

The only problem, however, was Lurleen. She had grown accustomed to public life as Alabama's first lady, when she had played hostess for official dinners and receptions at the mansion and had supported various charitable benefits in the state. But she remained an essentially private person who was inestimably happiest fishing for bass or puttering around a vacation cabin humming Hank Williams tunes. Beyond ceremonial duties, however, Lurleen, in the words of her son, "felt very self-conscious because she had no college education. . . . She wanted to do it for Dad, but her life was her children and Dad. She was torn." But the largest impediment was her fragile health. When her daughter Lee had been born in 1961, the baby had been delivered by Caesarian section; during the operation, the doctors had discovered a small, abnormal mass attached to the uterine wall. Several pathologists had examined tissue samples but had not agreed over whether or not it was cancer. Wallace claimed that the doctors had said there was "no reason for her to take any kind of treatment" in any event, so she had not. In fact, no one had even told her there was a problem. But about a month after George first had raised with Lurleen the idea of her candidacy, her physicians had told her she had a pelvic tumor and needed a complete hysterectomy. Surgery was scheduled for the second week in January. According to

Lurleen's personal secretary, Catherine Steineker, the governor was ready to drop the whole matter. A few days before Lurleen's operation, Steineker recalled, Wallace told his wife, "Sugar, I have just decided that we're not going to run. We're going back to Clayton and you can fish all you want and we'll just get out of this thing." But Lurleen demurred. "Now, George," Steineker remembered her saying, "when you started all this mess, I was not very much in favor of it. But since that time, I have gotten real enthusiastic and I am going to run. And if you don't want to help me run, you can just sit down in that office of yours and I'll get out by myself." And just two days before the surgery, Lurleen told the reporter Bob Ingram that an operation was "imminent"—she did not say *how* imminent—but that it would not prevent her from running for governor if George wanted her to.[7]

The operation disclosed that Lurleen's tumor was, indeed, malignant—but the doctors assured her they had caught it in time. They "gave her a clean bill of health," Wallace insisted. "They said she was able to run for governor and that they had completely gotten rid of the cancer." Lurleen later told her biographer, Anita Hill of the *Birmingham News*, "[It was untrue that] George made me run. . . . He didn't force me into this." But a year later, weary from campaigning and feeling guilty over not seeing enough of her children, she confided to Wallace's aide Bill Jones that running for office was not high on her list of personal priorities. "Bill," she said quietly and directly, "I did it for George."[8] And her son was convinced that "had she known the tragedy that lay ahead, she would never have taken the remarkable step of running." More poignantly, George, Jr., recalled that toward the end of his father's term of office, Lurleen "wanted a place where *she* could truly feel at home—a house of her own, not a governor's mansion." She found a four-bedroom brick house on Farrar Street in Montgomery and kept her eye on it during the ensuing campaign, harboring a secret love for it—a desire to settle down to a nonpublic life sooner rather than later.[9]

But that was to be a dream delayed—though, of course, she had no way of knowing that it would be denied her altogether. Even as she was recuperating from surgery, her husband was surveying the field of potential opponents. Wallace had no doubt of his own political strength; and despite the unprecedented (and, among political professionals, unpopular) ploy of using his wife as a stand-in candidate, he believed that if he campaigned with his usual vigor, he could transfer much of his popularity to her. But he was not about to take anything for granted—and Ryan deGraffenried posed a legitimate threat. As 1966 opened, at least one potential challenger to de-Graffenried, Richmond Flowers, had decided to support him rather than oppose him. "I ran some polls," Flowers said, "and they showed him leading by a lot—in a position to win the election without a runoff." But the polls did not take into consideration Lurleen Wallace's candidacy. The political insiders simply refused to believe that George Wallace—no matter how angered over his legislative defeat, no matter how boundless his personal ambition—would go beyond reason to upset traditional practices of gubernatorial succession. DeGraffenried, like Wallace before him, had run a respectable, losing race for governor; four years later, he deserved the support of the establishment. Indeed, he already had built a strong coalition among editors, businessmen, educational leaders, and courthouse pols. However, he knew that Wallace still had the people.

In an attempt to shortcircuit Lurleen's candidacy and whatever popularity George could transfer to her, deGraffenried started campaigning early; he thought if he could build up enough public support before the month of February was out, George would have to back away from any idea he might harbor about having his wife run. DeGraffenried was flying around the state in a small, private plane from one speaking engagement to another. One evening in ridge-ribbed northern Alabama, the plane took off into gusty winds; the airport manager saw the craft hover over a mountainous area, corkscrew suddenly as if caught in a blast of spiraling air, and plunge toward the rocks below. DeGraffenried and the pilot were killed instantly. Much later, George conceded that deGraffenried had been the only candidate he thought might have a chance to derail Lurleen; when he died, the governor had no further hesitation. Once a respectable period had elapsed, Lurleen would announce her candidacy. On February 25, 1966, sixteen days after deGraffenried's death and just forty-five days after her own major surgery for pelvic cancer, Lurleen said she would run for governor and, if elected, would "let George do it."[10]

■ ■ ■

What followed was unquestionably one of the most unusual gubernatorial campaigns in American history. Only two women had been elected governors in U.S. history, both in 1924 and both more or less as surrogates. Nellie Ross of Wyoming had succeeded her husband in a special election after he had died in office; and Miriam Ferguson of Texas had been elected by pledging that her husband, a one-time governor who had been impeached and barred from running again for misappropriating funds, would really run things; the campaign slogan of the pair, who came to be known as Ma and Pa Ferguson, had been, amusingly, an early precursor of a commonly heard expression in the 1992 presidential race: "Two for the price of one."[11]

Wallace learned about the Fergusons shortly after Lurleen's announcement; his source, of all people, was the president of the United States during a White House briefing on Vietnam for the nation's governors. At a buffet luncheon, to Wallace's surprise, President Johnson beckoned Wallace to join him; "I wouldn't have been presumptuous enough," Wallace said later, "to have sat down without an invitation." Johnson told Wallace he had seen Lurleen's announcement on television and "had wanted to tell [Wallace] that he thought she handled herself so well." Then the president launched into the story of Ma and Pa Ferguson. It seems that despite the scandals leading to his impeachment in 1917, James E. Ferguson had possessed a strong streak of progressivism; in fact, in the 1924 race, he had promised that if his wife was elected, she would outlaw the Ku Klux Klan, a controversial position that nonetheless had tipped the scales in Miriam's favor by consolidating the votes of moderates and liberals. And when the legislation had been proposed and enacted the following year, its key supporter in the Texas House of Representatives had been none other than Sam Ealy Johnson, Jr., the president's father. Ever since, Lyndon Johnson had had a soft spot for the irrepressible Fergusons. James had been elected twice, impeached, then twice defeated (even though he probably should not have even been allowed on the ballot); after her 1924 election, Miriam had been defeated twice in the wake of her own administration's scandals, elected a second time in 1932, then defeated in a final run in 1940. James had died in 1944, but Miriam had reached the age of eighty-six before dying in 1961, just five years before Lurleen's candidacy. Then, Wallace remembered, Johnson regaled him with one of James's 1924 campaign speeches in which he had explained how the couple would operate if Miriam was elected: he would be her number-one assistant, he would say, but he would also "tote the wood and draw the water at the governor's mansion." Wallace knew a good line when he heard it—and he adapted it in every speech he would make over the next months:

How are we gonna operate? If she's elected, I'm gonna be her number-one assistant—and we're gonna go on doing things just like we've been doing them. But for the benefit of the *Life* magazine folks [or *Newsweek* or *Time* or whatever national publication was on hand that day], let's just say I'm gonna draw the water, tote in the wood, wind the clock, and put out the cat.[12]

With deGraffenried's death, candidates for governor seemed to sprout everywhere. John Patterson and Carl Elliott, already in the race, were joined by Richmond Flowers, state Sen. Bob Gilchrist (a leader against the succession amendment), the millionaire business-man Charles Woods, Jim Folsom (now just a melancholy shadow, rather than the hulking powerhouse he had once been), and three less well-known aspirants—nine men sharing the conviction that whomever else Alabama's electorate might prefer, the people were highly unlikely to choose a thirty-nine-year-old mother of four young children, a woman with little education and no political experience. Wallace instinctively knew better. "It was my time and her time," he said with piercing candor, "and nobody could have beat her. Nobody made any difference that year. All you had to do is go out and see the thousands of people who came to see her speech."[13]

And over the next two months, the Wallaces would put in twelve-hour days to see thousands who would gather at four to five full-dress campaign rallies every day, seven days a week, on behalf of Lurleen's candidacy. The campaign entourage sped over asphalt highways and wound through blacktop back roads—George and his aides in one car; Lurleen and a woman companion in another; five sound trucks transporting musicians, instruments, and sound equipment; two sta-tion wagons pulling trailers loaded with folding chairs, flags, and bunting; and a red truck hauling a portable speakers' platform. The stage would be set up near the courthouse or municipal building. The musicians, led sometimes by Sam Smith and other times by Hank Thompson, would appear first, twanging out popular country-and-western tunes that would help generate a crowd and then keep it happy until the principals would arrive. George and Lurleen, mean-while, would slip into the courthouse to greet local officeholders and functionaries, who would be waiting no matter what time of night or morning the Wallaces arrived. Then George and Lurleen would materialize in the midst of the crowd while Hank Thompson and the band would thrum two of Lurleen's favorites, "Slipping Around" and

"I'm So Lonesome I Could Cry." (George directed Thompson not to sing the lyrics to "Slipping Around," as they struck him as too suggestive for an Alabama rally.) Husband and wife would slowly wend their way toward the speakers' platform. Lurleen, with her light auburn hair softly sculpted around her pleasant, if unremarkable features, would be in a tailored skirt, turtleneck, and blazer. George, his face animated and eyes glowing as he pumped the crowd's out-stretched hands, would have his usual ill-fitting suit, shirt and tie, and slickly glossed pompadour. On signal, Thompson would play and sing a hymn, inviting the crowd to join in.

In the quiet that followed, he would introduce Lurleen amid whoops and applause as the band broke into "Dixie." She would read from a two-page typewritten script—a perfunctory statement express-ing "humility and gratitude" at the opportunity to allow her husband to indirectly continue to govern Alabama. She would always say "we" when expressing a position and would always ask the voters to elect a "Wallace administration." She would close by saying, "And now I give you my husband and your governor—the man who will be my number-one assistant in the next administration—George C. Wal-lace." George, still among the folks, would make his way to the platform amidst cheers and rebel yells that would get louder as he grasped Lurleen's hand and raised it aloft in the traditional political victory sign. She would then take a seat in a corner of the platform and more or less become invisible for the next forty-five minutes as George, abjuring notes or text, fired up his loyalists. He would usually begin by contemptuously poking fun at national publications op-posed to Lurleen's candidacy—but emphasizing that their very inter-est and frequent presence at Wallace rallies connoted Alabama's (and his) growing importance. "You know, the *Life* magazine come out against my wife. You know them, though. They think you're degenerates. . . . And the *Saturday Evening Post* [is] with us here today. They take a lot of pictures, then they pick out the worst one and put it in there. . . . The *Wall Street Journal* made fun of my wife on the front page because she used to be a dime-store clerk and her daddy was a shipyard worker." Then he would pull it together: "The liberals and beatniks and socialists have gotten together and said, 'We're not gonna have any more of Wallace,' and that's why the national press is here—to see if you are going to repudiate what we have done. I'm not fighting the federal government. I'm fighting this outlaw, beatnik crowd in Washington that has just about destroyed the federal government—and I'm trying to save it."[14]

As the campaign wore on, Lurleen's presentations grew more relaxed and conversational, but George remained the main attraction. What criticism there was of her tended to focus on her gender rather than her lack of experience—and certainly not on her character. Rep. Edith Green of Oregon feared that Lurleen's evident role as her husband's pawn might set back the movement toward women's equality. George, in speeches, would snarl, "[My opponents] say they don't want no skirt for governor of Alabama; that's right—no skirt. Well, I want you to know I resent that slur on the women of this state." Even an enlightened publication like the *New York Times Magazine* let pass an article that asked, in apparent seriousness, "[If Lurleen is elected], who will actually sit in the governor's chair and attend the governor's conferences? Will she be called 'Governess'? Or perhaps 'Gubernatrix'? Who will address the legislature? Will this mother of four sign the paper which can end or save the life of a young man condemned to the electric chair?"[15] Serious criticism—to the extent that there was any—was reserved for the governor. Flowers, openly courting the black vote, continued his four-year-long condemnation of Wallace's intransigent defiance of integration laws; he even struck out at Wallace's insistence that only the Alabama and Confederate flags fly atop the state capitol while the American flag be displayed on a pole to the side of the building. "This is no act of reason," Flowers said. "This is a gesture of defiance that must be put behind us. I intend that such gestures become a part of our past." Bob Gilchrist tried to drive home the reality that Wallace's intractability in racial matters had, in fact, sped integration. "No two men in America," Gilchrist would thunder, "have done more for one another, need one another more, than George Wallace and Martin Luther King."[16] It was a shrewd insight on how each man, and the movement represented by each, had profited by painting the other as the incarnation of all that was wrong in America. But Gilchrist's observation, however true, carried little weight with Wallace supporters because, even as states' rights and segregation were being rolled back in Alabama at least as quickly as the rest of the South, Wallace gave Alabamians a sense of being unfairly overrun—a sense that they, in fact, held the moral high ground.

In any event, George generally ignored the criticism. Throughout the campaign, he studiously avoided using the word *segregation*, and both he and Lurleen carefully and correctly pronounced the word *Negro*. Instead, George talked about the erosion of local control of schools and of state and local government because of the ever-increasing power of the federal government. And he let his actions speak louder than his words on the stump. When Alabama's public mental hospitals integrated their facilities voluntarily, Wallace rescinded the action as soon as he learned of it. He mobilized resistance to federal school integration guidelines and directed any public schools that had integrated their faculties without a court order to reverse their actions. Over the unexpected objection of the Alabama Education Association, Wallace pushed through the legislature a bill allocating state funds to replace whatever amount public schools might lose in federal aid if they refused to adopt and implement integration guidelines—a potential $38 million a year (although the real figure would be much less because only 20 percent of the state's school districts had failed to adopt integration programs, however modest). "Uppermost in our minds," Wallace intoned, "is the welfare and safety of the school children of this state." Even Gilchrist had to fall in line. "Liberty never came cheap," Gilchrist said. "We may lose some money, but it is not going to be forever. Let us not surrender constitutional rights without a fight."

Sooner or later, Wallace knew, Frank Johnson and the federal courts would step in and place the entire state under a court order; but, as always with Wallace, what mattered most was putting up what he perceived to be the good fight. In fact, in the midst of this latest school integration brouhaha, George Wallace, Jr., then fourteen, entered newly integrated Bellingrath Junior High School in Montgomery, enrolling on the same day as sixteen black students. "It just so happens," Wallace blithely explained, "that many working people can't afford private schools. My son has to bear the burden of school desegregation along with the rest of the people." Then he pointed out that Johnson's son attended an all-white private school. He quickly added, "I'm not reflecting on the son at all; he's a fine young man. But I'm just talking about his daddy."[17]

Most important, George kept reminding voters that support of Lurleen meant support for him on the national stage. And in nearly every speech, he emphasized the overriding importance of supporting him as he sallied forth to slay the dragons of federalism and immorality that were infecting the country:

> And we've always said that we wanted to be able to let people
> in other parts of the country know what we stood for. We are
> not against any of our people. But we want someday to see
> local government returned—and you never gonna get it

returned . . . unless we carry on this matter throughout the nation and other parts of the country.

Then he would launch into a diatribe against opponents to the Vietnam War, reserving special venom for college students who he said were trying to organize a Freedom Brigade to go to Vietnam to fight against the Americans:

> We still defend our nation's servicemen in Vietnam, and I'm proud to say that the college students in our state have no organization to raise money and blood and clothes for the enemies of our country. . . . Sometimes I wish they'd organize that brigade and get all the dirty beatniks that march in these [antiwar] shindigs and get 'em over there and let 'em do a little fightin' and get rid of 'em.

Finally, he would wind up by making certain that people understood what the election was really all about—the unending fight to bring Alabama's truth and the respectability of its people to the entire nation:

> These big newspapers say you got to change your image. We don't got to change any such thing. We got just as good people right here in Alabama as any place else. Why should we change our image to suit some communist Hottentot ten thousand miles from here? . . . We can win someday 'cause we're not alone. You know that; the Lou Harris poll tells you that. . . . We've got support in California and Wisconsin and Maryland and all over this country. . . . I spoke at the long-haired college of Harvard. . . . I made the best speech they ever heard up at Harvard and, you know, the next day hundreds of 'em got their hair cut. . . . If you want us to continue, we'll continue . . . and if you elect my wife the governor of the state, we will continue to be able to stand up in places all over our country and say this: "I come from a state whose people are just as refined and cultured and intelligent and righteous as the people in any state of this union and don't you forget it." . . . An Alabamian would make as good a president as somebody from New York and maybe a darn sight better than somebody from Texas.[18]

■   ■   ■

The Wallaces pose in the back-yard of the governor's mansion in 1965 with two of their children, Peggy Sue, fourteen, and Lee, four.

George, Jr., ten, steadied by his father's hand, stumped for Wallace in 1962 as he had four years earlier. "With God's help," he would say, "my daddy will make you a good governor."

A huge throng welcomed Wallace to Newark during the 1968 presidential campaign. Scorned by a writer as a "cultural Moon Mullins," Wallace retorted, "The Moon Mullins vote is in the majority."

Wallace backers in Kansas City in 1968 typified the backbone of his support— blue-collar and middle-class whites. Wallace's articulation of the "little man's" concerns earned him the sobriquet of "the Cicero of the cab driver."

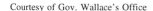

Wallace rally crowds, as this one in Kalamazoo, often included antagonists and hecklers, whom Wallace used to advantage. "These are the so-called free-speech people," he would sneer when protesters booed and shouted epithets.

Courtesy of Gov. Wallace's Office

In a meeting during the Selma crisis in 1965, President Johnson suggested that if Wallace backed away from segregation, he would be remembered by "a great, big marble monument that says, 'George Wallace: He Built.' "

Wallace's denunciation of increasing crime, civil disorder, and growing federalism gained wide popularity, but his ultimate campaign weapon was the electricity he generated working the crowds.

AP/Wide World Photos

In 1970, Wallace reverted to racism in recapturing the governorship from Albert Brewer, who succeeded to the office on Lurleen's death in 1968.

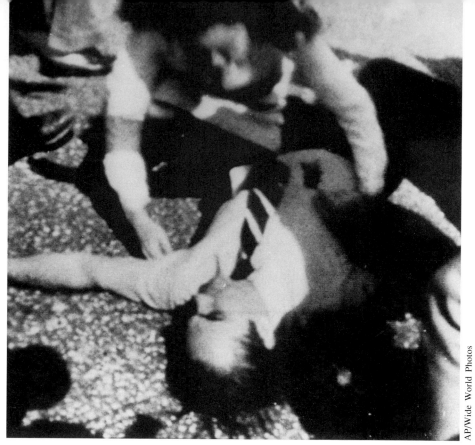

Cornelia Wallace crouches over her husband, who had been shot during a 1972 rally in a Laurel, Maryland, shopping center. The assassination attempt crippled Wallace for life and effectively ended his national aspirations.

Maryland police subdue Arthur Bremer (center), who had just pumped five bullets into Wallace. Subsequently convicted and sentenced to sixty-three years in prison, Bremer had stalked President Nixon before targeting Wallace.

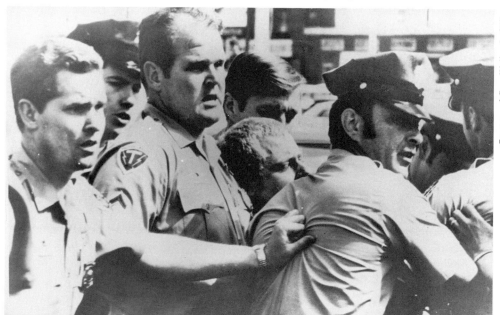

At the 1972 Democratic National Convention, Wallace warned the party to adopt his positions on crime and middle-class tax relief or face years out of power.

Nixon confers with the wheelchair-bound Wallace during a 1973 trip to Alabama, ostensibly to visit federal installations. In reality, Nixon was eager to build his Southern strategy by appearing with Wallace.

A decade after trying to bar blacks from entering the University of Alabama, a "new" Wallace crowned its first black homecoming queen.

On his last day as governor in January, 1987, Wallace gazed at a bust of Lurleen in the capitol rotunda. In the previous quarter century, he controlled the Alabama governorship for all but two years and had run for president four times.

The Reverend Jesse Jackson (seated, center) was among a number of black leaders heartened by Wallace's public renunciation of his segregationist past and subsequent efforts to expand opportunities for Alabama's black citizens.

When primary day arrived on May 3, George was certain that Lurleen was in the lead—but neither he nor any pundit in politics or the press had any notion of just how far in the lead she really was. Under Alabama law, if no candidate received a majority of the vote, the two top vote getters would face off in a second primary. That was the historical rule, rather than the exception, in the state's gubernatorial elections. In 1958, John Patterson had defeated Wallace in a second primary. Four years later, Wallace had won in a second primary. But this time, there would be no second primary. Nearly 900,000 people cast their ballots, an Alabama record. The total included 180,000 blacks, more than 75 percent of all the blacks registered (and about 65,000 more than had been registered less than a year earlier when the Voting Rights Act had become law). But, beyond even George's most optimistic projections, it was, indeed, Lurleen's time and Lurleen's day. In the field of ten candidates, Lurleen received an astounding 54 percent of the vote. Her total of 481,000 votes was nearly triple that of her nearest contender, Flowers. But Lurleen's support was not universal; Flowers actually ran ahead of Lurleen in the band of central Alabama counties called the Black Belt (for its rich soil), where black voting was heaviest, and finished with less than a majority in the ten major urban areas of the state. But in the small towns of Alabama, where the black population was about 15 percent to 20 percent, Lurleen won by drawing nearly 70 percent of the vote. And she simply could not have run that powerfully without an attraction that went beyond her husband's popularity.

Even though she had pointedly taken a back seat to her husband during the campaign, she drew whoops and hollers and hugs on her own; she clearly projected a warmth and honesty and down-to-earth character that appealed to many and, just as important, deflected any thought that she might be an embarrassment if actually representing the state to the nation. The governor's brother Gerald said, "In the beginning of the campaign, people were voting for George. But as the campaign progressed and more people saw Lurleen, they were voting for her." And Catherine Steineker added that "there were people who couldn't stand George C., but they all loved Lurleen." It remained difficult for many commentators to believe that this quiet, unassuming homemaker and mother would *really* be elected. A typical observation (this one made in *Newsweek*) was that in the face of Lurleen's primary landslide, her Republican opponent in November's general election, Rep. James Martin "sank overnight from favorite to an even-money choice at best." Alabama had voted strongly for Goldwater in 1964 and had elected Republicans to four of its eight House seats, but with nearly as great a voter turnout in November as in May, Lurleen raked in the chips from anyone foolish enough to have taken that even-money bet on continued GOP bullishness. She won 63 percent of the vote (including, this time, a majority of the black vote—an anomaly that Wallace would cite years later as "evidence" that, despite his support of segregation, he was no racist—that, had he been, blacks never would have supported his wife and, in later years, him).[19]

George Wallace wasted no time in flexing his bulging political muscles. Less than a week after his wife's overwhelming primary victory, he summoned Alabama's entire congressional delegation— including Senators Sparkman and Hill and Rep. Martin—to Montgomery to discuss resistance to the new federal guidelines on school desegregation. At first, the congressmen balked; they wired Wallace, saying, "It is our considered and unanimous opinion that the best results can be had by a joint meeting in Washington with the United States commissioner of education." By return telegram, Wallace informed them he had no intention of going to Washington. End of conversation. Four days after the initial call for the meeting, all ten members of Alabama's congressional delegation, none foolhardy enough to risk offending Wallace's unquestioned political power, were in his Montgomery office. At the end of the meeting, all ten stood docilely by as Wallace read a joint statement that described the federal guidelines as "illegal" and "totalitarian" and that pledged to mobilize opposition to their effectuation.[20] At his apocalyptic extreme, Wallace called the guidelines "a blueprint devised by socialists which has as its objectives the capture and regimentation of our children and the destruction of our public education system."[21]

Throughout the South, politicians flocked to bask in Wallace's glow. In an October trip by Wallace to Mississippi, even the venerable Sen. James Eastland, challenged by a Goldwater Republican who claimed incredibly that Eastland was relatively "moderate," rushed "as fast as dignity would permit when [Wallace's] Aero Commander rolled up" to the airport gate. Wallace had come to the Mississippi–Alabama Fairgrounds near Meridian to boost Eastland's candidacy for a fifth term—and, not incidentally, to parade himself as a national candidate. It was there that Wallace coined one of his most effective pejorative descriptions of the major political parties:

You can put LBJ in the sack. You can put HHH in the sack. And you can put Robert "Blood-for-the-Vietcong" Kennedy in the sack. You can put Earl Warren in the sack; Warren doesn't have enough legal brains in his whole head to try a chicken thief in my home county. You can put wild Bill Scranton and the left-wing Governor Romney and Nelson Rockefeller, that socialist governor, in the sack. Put 'em all in the same sack, shake 'em up. I don't care which one comes out, you stick him back in—because there isn't a dime's worth of difference in them.[22]

Wallace reserved special invective for Richard Nixon because Nixon, as Wallace saw it, had insulted Lurleen and the entire state of Alabama by sneering that Alabamians had nominated "a dime-store girl for governor." Wallace thought it was a damned sight better to vote for a dime-store girl than for Nixon, a man Wallace portrayed as "the general at Little Rock when they put the bayonets in the backs of Southerners and set the precedent for the Kennedys at Oxford." (Nearly a decade had passed since the Little Rock crisis, throughout which Nixon, who had not even held public office for six years, had remained virtually invisible; but Wallace knew that it was quite enough simply to remind ever-sensitive Southern audiences that Nixon had been vice-president at the time.) No one on the national scene—except perhaps Senator Russell of Georgia—was good enough or conservative enough for Wallace. Goldwater "ought to stay in Arizona and help all those Indians out there get their civil rights." Reagan "used to be a liberal. Now he's a conservative and he might change back again." Wallace had no "burning ambition" to be president, but if neither party offered "a clear choice" who would support "restoration of local government," then Wallace vowed to "be in that race."[23]

Even after Lurleen's overwhelming victories in the primary and general elections, George remained the focus of press attention. At her victory news conference in November, national media representatives took note that she was clad in a knit, off-white suit and that she briefly thanked the voters. The rest of the coverage was devoted to George and his presidential aspirations.[24] And he played his part to the very end of his legal term. Again using his favorite forum, a joint session of the state legislature, Governor Wallace issued a report on his four years in office. The first half of the speech was devoted to his administration's considerable achievements, which included:

- Doubling public education appropriations, which included providing free textbooks to all students in grades one through twelve and increasing teachers' salaries by more than 40 percent.
- Opening 14 junior colleges and technical schools and adding 15 new trade schools to the 5 that State Representative Wallace had been instrumental in establishing nearly two decades earlier.
- Expanding the University of Alabama Medical Center and establishing the University of South Alabama at Mobile—the state's first new university in nearly a century.
- Luring to Alabama nearly $2 billion in capital investment in new and expanded industry, resulting in a hundred thousand new jobs and helping to make Alabama second in the nation in the rate of increase of per capita income.
- Implementing the state's largest-ever highway construction and maintenance program.
- Launching statewide programs to benefit the mentally retarded and arrest water pollution; increasing support for the state's mental institutions and prison system (soon to become objects of controversy); and increasing medical benefits to the aged and indigent.
- Instituting rigid ethical standards in competitive bidding for state projects while abolishing the "whisky agent" system, through which previous governors had enriched their cronies by requiring payoffs from liquor companies for shelf space in state-controlled liquor stores.

In addition, Wallace offered a number of "recommendations" for the new administration, which everyone understood to be Lurleen's proposed legislative program: requiring banks to pay interest on state deposits; expanding competitive bid laws to cover all state agencies and local government contracts involving state aid; significantly extending the state's highway construction program by issuing bonds; improving state parks; and strengthening all levels of education and aid to the aged, the infirm, and the mentally ill.[25]

To a large extent, Wallace's achievements as governor were ignored or cheapened by critics. His opponents were unable psychologically to attribute leadership and progress in education, health, the economy, and the environment—advances they ordinarily would have applauded—to a man whose racial politics they found so despicable. So the tendency among opinion molders in politics and the media was to belittle Alabama's (and Wallace's) attainments through the very unliberal practice of blaming the victim—condemning Alabama for the entrenched poverty to which it and other endemically poor states had been sentenced by nature and by changing economic dynamics.

To be sure, it was Wallace's own nature and ambition to make himself a target. He would delight in waving the red flag and provoking the bull to charge. And in the second half of his end-of-term "report" to the legislature, he made certain he would arouse angry snorts from all those he sought to inflame, because he firmly believed that his adversaries were increasingly irritating large and growing segments of the American people. Wallace took shots at his usual bêtes noires:

> The people of this country are simply fed up with the antics of strutting bureaucrats lording it over them—telling them when to go to bed at night and when to get up in the morning. They are fed up with bureaucrats telling them that they haven't got sense enough to run their own schools and hospitals and local governments. They are disgusted by the spectacle of federal officials running around the country urging people to "peacefully" take to the streets [encouraging] assault with guns, rocks, and Molotov cocktails upon policemen, firemen, and others trying to protect life and property in their communities. . . . They are beginning to sense that the underlying source of these complaints is an incompetent, unrestrained federal judiciary. . . . [Judges] believe that God is dead. . . . [And] what can members of our armed forces think when they see freedom of speech distorted into license to conduct pep rallies to encourage other youth to burn draft cards? . . . Laws of Congress are now amended, supplemented, or repealed at will by mimeographed regulations and guidelines—by oral directives and penciled memorandums issued by faceless petty executives of a department of federal government.[26]

Time and again, Wallace addressed his remarks to "the people of this country," or to "all sections of the nation," or to "the people of the United States," or to "American citizens." He never mentioned segregation by name and only alluded to it twice—when disparaging bureaucrats for trying to run local schools. It was a measure not only of the changing electoral landscape in the South but of the broadened constituency Wallace was aiming to build. Wallace perceived that more and more Americans were coming to his view that government interference in their lives, especially from the federal bureaucracy, was moving well beyond matters involving de jure segregation. Not only had the Supreme Court outlawed school segregation, but it had issued a series of landmark decisions protecting the rights of Communists and criminals, while prohibiting school prayer and dictating how the states must apportion their legislatures.[27]

■   ■   ■

After Lurleen's inauguration, she moved into the governor's office suite (number 100), while George moved in across the hall (number 101) but retained a key to the private entrance to Lurleen's office. Lurleen kept George's cabinet intact except for the press secretary, Bill Jones, who left the executive offices to open Wallace's presidential campaign headquarters a couple of blocks away on Hall Street.[28] In all important aspects, the government of Alabama remained firmly in George's hands, but Lurleen, by all accounts, including Wallace's, "had ideas of her own." She even asserted herself early, if playfully. As she and George left the mansion on her first morning as governor, George climbed into his usual place in the limousine—the right, rear seat. Lurleen, outside the car door, leaned over and said, "Move over, George. I'm the governor now; I ride on the right side and you ride on the left." The state troopers assigned to Governors George and Lurleen, as they came to be called, cackled appreciatively as George slid over. Not long after, when George let himself into Lurleen's office, he came upon Lurleen meeting with about fifty people. "What can I do for you, George?" she asked with a small smile. "Oh, I just came by, honey," he said. "We're busy now," Lurleen replied with mock severity, "but I'll be glad to see you later." Wallace raised his eyebrows, shrugged, smiled, and backed out as the room erupted with laughter.[29] As expected, Wallace guided key issues in the state such as highway construction and education development, while the cabinet ran day-to-day operations. While Governor Lurleen saw primarily to ceremonial duties—signing proclamations, welcoming visitors, swearing in public officials—Governor George arm wrestled with the legislature. In one instance, George worked out a compromise when a $160 million bond issue for highway construction was being held hostage in the legislature because Lurleen was reluctant to sign a legislative pay-raise bill. George explained privately to house and senate leaders that Lurleen could not sign the bill because of her campaign pledge to run a frugal administration. But, he said, a deal could be cut. Lurleen would veto the bill but would instruct her floor leaders not to raise a fuss, should anyone try to override the veto. The agreement was made: Lurleen vetoed the pay raise, the legislators overrode it, and then they passed her highway construction bond issue. Although George thought it would stretch propriety for him to conduct news conferences (which Lurleen avoided assiduously), hardly a day passed that he did not join Alabama reporters at lunch in the capitol basement's restaurant for state employees. Over fifty-five-cent specials of fried steak, boiled okra, corn bread, and iced tea, Wallace made known current state policy.[30]

Still, Lurleen, as governor, played a more substantial role than perhaps even she had expected, though in limited areas. Public recreation and mental health were the two issues that she decided to concentrate on in the 1967 session of the state legislature. After her nomination for governor in the spring of 1966, Lurleen had accompanied George to the Southern Governors' Conference at a public resort in Kentucky. During a steamboat ride with other Southern governors and their wives, Lurleen had been struck with the thought that Alabamians ought to have similar parks of their own—places to fish, hike, dine, spend the night, and perhaps have access to other recreation. "Well," George had told her, "you're going to be the governor." Once in office, she pursued the idea vigorously by authorizing a study of the kind of public parks Alabama might establish, their number, and their location. The legislature appropriated $43 million to dot the state with public parks over the next four years; when George returned to power in 1971, he added $16 million more to complete the project—and had one of the parks named for Lurleen. She launched a crusade to improve conditions for the mentally ill and persuaded the legislature to float a $15 million bond issue and enact a two-cent-a-pack cigarette tax, earmarking all the funds for building and improving facilities for mental patients. "I always felt," George Wallace, Jr., said, "that Mother was able to speak with a moral force on these issues that a man mightn't have been able to."[31] George himself would come to agree with that judgment when his own, later efforts to increase funding for mental health would be turned away. Regarding mental health, George complained, "When Lurleen was for something, every single legislator said, 'Yes, ma'am.'

When I go and ask them for something, sometimes they say, 'Uhh.' Lurleen had a woman's touch."[32] In 1967, a Gallup poll listed Lurleen as the sixth most admired woman in the country.

The Wallaces' efforts to improve mental health facilities and treatment in Alabama, and the condescending reaction to those efforts by Wallace's enemies, provide a representative illustration of how even the smallest acknowledgement of George Wallace's accomplishments would choke in his critics' throats. In the 1970s, Judge Johnson issued a series of orders requiring expensive improvements in the state's mental institutions, based on his finding that patients had a constitutional right to adequate treatment. A civil liberties lawyer prominent in the litigation on behalf of mental patients, George Dean, scoffed at Lurleen's advances in mental health. Referring to her tours of mental facilities, one of which had brought tears to her eyes, Dean sneered, "Shortest sentence in the Wallace Bible: 'Lurleen wept.' " And when George tried to divert $24 million in surpluses from the teacher retirement fund to benefit mental institutions (but was turned back by the legislature), Dean dismissed the attempt by pointing out that the state spent more than that on "unnecessary or non-essential" functions such as livestock shows, beauty pageants, athletic events, and Confederate memorials. In a filing in Johnson's court, Dean wrote that the state's mental patients "feel that they may have been better provided for if they were athletic and photogenic cows of Confederate ancestry." Said Dean: "George Wallace is just a bad little evil man. He's just a simple demagogue in the classic Greek definition. Absolutely nothing but whatever madness the crowd wants to hear at the time, George Wallace feeds to them. That's all he is. He has no philosophy. . . . If we had not the word 'demagogue,' we would have had to invent one for George." Yet Dean and those who shared his attitude toward Wallace seemed blind to unethical acts of people, such as Frank Johnson, whose views coincided with their own. Dean once revealed that Johnson had taken judicial reprisals against him until he dropped a case to expose usury by the judge's brother. After settling the case quietly and returning to the judge's good graces, Dean passed off the incident as evidence of Johnson's deep feelings for his family. Dean also knew that Johnson had played a pivotal role in having a woman wrongfully committed to a state mental institution because the judge had disapproved of the woman's relationship with his emotionally disturbed son, Johnny. The judge had sent lawyers to threaten her with commitment if she did not leave his son alone—and she had, indeed, been committed subsequently by her family. From the hospital, the woman had succeeded in reaching Dean, who had secured her release. Dean's assessment of Johnson's behavior again lacked the righteous passion that he could work up for Wallace: "If I had been Johnny's daddy," he said, "I'd have been upset about it. . . . But the woman didn't belong . . . in prison or in the hospital, so I got her out."[33]

Had the George Deans of the world the smallest inkling that George Wallace might have influenced a criminal case against his own brother, or might have caused the commitment to an asylum of someone he considered a threat to his family, headlines would have rightly screamed of the man's perfidy. There was more than hypocrisy at work here. There was a moral and ethical void—the same kind in which Virginia Durr could excuse Richmond Flowers of taking graft because, compared to Wallace, he seemed to her the lesser of two evils. It was simpler to avoid the complexities and inconsistencies of democracy and, instead, to categorize people as good guys and bad guys, white hats and black hats, divinities and demons. And subconsciously, it surely added a sense of moral superiority to those who could point to others as representing evil; in a black-and-white world, that automatically made the moralizers symbols of goodness.

■   ■   ■

The critics had a harder time finding evil in Lurleen, so they snickered—meanly, if with cause—at her lack of experience and education. But at the outset of her term, Lurleen's betterment of the lot of Alabama's mentally ill was cheered by progressives everywhere; only later, when her efforts seemed little more than a brave but ineffectual solution to a monumental problem did Wallace critics (with Lurleen gone from the scene) feel it necessary to dismiss her altogether—and unfairly so. But if her gender and obvious gentleness afforded her a brief honeymoon, her early popularity was challenged by the baggage of school segregation, a burden she inherited from her husband but carried uncomplainingly. On March 22, a special three-judge federal panel, in an opinion written by Johnson, imposed a statewide desegregation order similar to one he had issued three years earlier. George had sidestepped the 1964 order by providing private school tuition grants to parents who believed that public school attendance might impair their children's "physical and emotional health." The new order imposed strict directions for integrating the public schools, invalidated the private school tuition plan, and warned that if another private school scam were adopted, the court might well require *their* desegregation, too. A week after the initial decree was handed down, Lurleen went before her first joint legislative meeting to give Alabama's answer.[34]

The governor's number-one adviser was in full charge of the proceedings. In the days between Judge Johnson's decree and Lurleen's public reply, George conducted a series of meetings at the capitol with school superintendents, school board members, the heads of state colleges, and state school officials to elicit their support of whatever decision Lurleen would announce on the evening of March 30. When some of the school leaders balked at handing George an open-ended endorsement of they-knew-not-what position, he bristled and assured them that it would be a position in the state's best interest. In the end, they all fell in line; they all knew that George Wallace's view was preordained. "He feels impelled to do something," said Austin Meadows, Alabama's former state school superintendent. "The folks elected him to do something." In fact, they had elected *Mrs.* Wallace, but that, as everyone knew, was a mere technicality. She had stayed home at the mansion that day so she could be well rested when she delivered her speech that evening; the speech would be carried over the state on seventy radio and television stations.

A little past four o'clock, George and his aides completed their finishing touches on the document; one assistant scuttled out a side door of the capitol to rush a copy to Lurleen for her perusal and rehearsal. At four-thirty, George invited some news reporters into Lurleen's office. One of them, Gerald Lubenow of *Newsweek,* remembered the encounter this way:

> Ensconced behind his wife's desk, Wallace was sipping a Coke, flipping cigar ashes in the general direction of the waste basket, and absently ruffling through the speech that his wife would deliver three hours later. He was buoyant, like a man breathing easily in the eye of a hurricane—which he had invoked. Progress for Wallace comes about only in a series of violent clashes, hot glandular action and reaction—and now the battle was joined. Around him the fond old familiar alarums and gallumphing were sounding, and he was conspicuously of the moment. Alternately, he compulsively plunged about the paneled office and then plopped in a chair at his wife's littered desk, all the while gustily flailing away at

his most cherished dragon, the federal courts. . . . Flourishing his cigar, Wallace quipped, "Six other states are in the same spot we're in, so some of the legislators have asked me to be president of the Confederacy—but, of course, I don't know that I want it. But you just stick around; we may secede."[35]

George may have been joking, but Lurleen's speech was as tough in its language as anything George had delivered from his own lips. As he watched the proceedings on television in his own capitol office, Lurleen, looking like a college glee club member in a blue skirt and her trademark blazer (this one blue with white stripes) made ready to enter the Alabama House chamber. She scowled fleetingly (and a number of legislators guffawed) as Lt. Gov. Albert Brewer mistakenly announced her as "George" Wallace before quickly correcting himself. The laughs turned to cheers as she approached the lectern, and one ecstatic lawmaker bawled loudly, "It's gonna be 'hallelujah time' here in a bit." In her half-hour speech, Lurleen, appearing solemn and speaking with assurance in her well-modulated drawl, was interrupted twenty times by wild cheering, lusty applause, and a generous smattering of rebel yells.[36] The words, if not the manner, bore the clear imprint of George Wallace:

> I want the people of Alabama to know, the people of this country to know, and the people who would attack our children and our institutions to know that Alabama and its elected officials dare defend our rights. . . . This order [directing statewide school integration] takes over every single aspect of the operation of every school system within the state of Alabama. It destroys the authority of the local school boards, the state board of education, the superintendent of education, and the governor. It reduces the constitutionally elected officials of your state to mere agents of the district court who must execute the commands of three judges who would determine all matters of educational policy. . . . It requires in every area of Alabama transferring of students back and forth to achieve so-called balance . . . [and] the closing of every Negro college, junior college, and trade school, and every all-Negro elementary and secondary school in the state. . . . This order forces white children to go to all-Negro schools and Negro students to go to predominantly white schools. . . . The only way we can force children to attend . . . is to put their parents in jail. We in Alabama will not put parents in jail. And

we cannot and will not deprive our Negro children and college
students of an education by closing all Negro schools. . . . If
they are closed, the federal courts will have to close them.[37]

That line, reporter Lubenow observed, "lifted the capitol dome at
least two inches."

The speech's end-of-the-world vision was highly questionable;
the order had not, of course, directed the closing of all black schools
and colleges. It had included detailed standards to which each local
desegregation plan must conform and, for the first time, had denounced "freedom of choice"—the basis of nearly all previous
school desegregation plans in Alabama—as "a fantasy;" nearly all
white students chose white schools, and nearly all blacks who braved
community pressure and chose white schools were told that the white
schools were overcrowded. Just enough blacks were admitted to white
schools to allow the school systems to claim they had begun a plan of
integration. So Johnson had written that "the measure of a freedom-
of-choice plan—or, for that matter, any school plan designed to
eliminate discrimination based on race—is whether it is effective."
Lurleen (or, more likely, George) carried the dictum to its ridiculous
extreme by suggesting that the only "effective" integration plan
would require closing black schools and mixing the students in the
white schools. The irony that seemed to escape the Wallaces' notice
was their indirect admission that black schools must, in fact, be
inferior to white schools. The numbers bore that out. The per pupil
property valuation of white school facilities in 1967 was about six
hundred dollars, twice the per pupil valuation of black schools;
nearly all white high schools were accredited, while one in four black
high schools remained unaccredited.[38]

Still, Lurleen's fiery words—odd though they seemed, coming
in honeyed accents from the demure, preppy governor—succeeded
in reaching their intended audiences: the majority of white Alabamians and the growing legions across the country who were starting
to feel steamrollered by "big government." Had the bombast come
instead from her husband, with his patented combativeness and surly
sarcasm, it could not have elicited louder or more enthusiastic responses. Lurleen's administration appealed the court order, but in
April the judicial panel refused to delay enforcement of its order. The
only semblance of victory in the courts for Lurleen was when the
three judges—Johnson, Hobart Grooms, and Richard Rives—
forbade federal authorities' withholding of funds from those school

districts that made a good-faith effort to comply with court-ordered integration; Washington had wanted to cut off school aid across the board, until the entire state had acquiesced.

The minor victory turned sour only ten days later when a bomb shattered several windows in the Montgomery home of Judge Johnson's widowed mother. Though she was uninjured, the incident aroused the anger of Alabama's media and bar. The *Birmingham Post-Herald* went so far as to condemn "verbal assaults on the courts and undocumented charges of lying against federal judges" as "un-American. We wish they were un-Alabamian." Ray Jenkins in the *Alabama Journal* suggested that guilt for planting the dynamite went beyond the individual culprit (who never was found): "Every society, of course, has its deranged element capable of criminal violence. But the test is whether the whole community will endorse the act by allowing the criminal to go free. When we do this, we allow madmen to speak for all of us."[39]

To her credit, Lurleen did not wait for the public outcry before responding forcefully to the violence. She offered a reward of $5,400 for information leading to the culprit's apprehension, saying it was "difficult to find words to express [her] abhorrence and scorn" for the "cowardly" act, adding, "This is not the American way or the Alabama way to protest [court] decisions."[40]

All of the Wallace scheming was an empty charade, of course; there was no way to stop integration. But most of the other Southern governors had found that, by giving lip service to integration, they effectively delayed its implementation. Too, both Washington and the federal judiciary were quite content to avoid head-on confrontations, and happily allowed governors who were viewed as progressive or realistic—and who did not make verbal waves—to integrate at a snail's pace. The squeaky wheel, George Wallace, got the federal grease—greased skids to desegregated schools through court orders and threats of drying up federal largess. But Wallace believed that slowing the inevitable was less important than giving voice to the fears and frustrations of those in the state who could not afford a way out of integration. He maintained that the rich and middle class could send their children to private schools, including the segregated "Christian academies" that sprang up over the state. But poor white people, Wallace argued, had to accept integration. Wallace believed he could ease their inescapable future by letting them see that he understood their plight.[41] What he understood was that the system of segregation made these people—despite their often squalid, nearly hopeless lives—automatically superior to about half the other people who lived in town—namely, the black half, even if some of those folks were doctors or lawyers or teachers or preachers. Wallace believed that his clamoring on poor whites' behalf, however counterfeit, provided an outlet—a nonviolent, if not wholly pacific outlet—for their smoldering rage. To be sure, it also provided *him* with a devoted following that stretched well beyond Alabama's white poor; those who could afford to buy their way out of integration also appreciated Wallace's taunting of Goliath.

■   ■   ■

But George already had turned his eyes to the national scene (see chapter 14). After Lurleen's rousing (and meaningless) speech of defiance, George's attention span, where state matters were concerned, grew shorter and shorter—to the point that Lurleen actually was making a number of decisions on her own. For example, she refused to support the trucking lobby on a bill favored by her husband to allow tractor-trailers to hook up so-called piggyback trailers. The piggybacks would double the hauling capacity of each truck, thereby doubling productivity. But critics contended that the long and unwieldy trucks would increase ordinary motorists' driving hazards and would likely escalate wear and tear (and, therefore, maintenance expenses) on the state's roads and highways. Wallace would come home to the mansion at night and ask Lurleen, "Honey, you haven't changed your mind on that trailer bill, have you?" She had not. "If they would just have them on the interstates," she said, "it would be fine." But, of course, the trucks would traverse smaller roads and city streets to reach and leave the interstates, so she continued her opposition.[42]

The inherent complications of the mom-and-pop gubernatorial operation was not lost on those closest to Governors George and Lurleen. In a letter to a Montgomery organization that had invited George to speak, Bill Jones apologized for his delay in responding:

> But I believe you can understand that we have quite a
> transition problem in moving our headquarters from the state
> capitol into another building. Although Governor [George]
> Wallace still carries on the functions of the governorship of
> the state, he actually is no longer governor—and this has
> given us some problems that are right difficult to handle.[43]

As early as March 1967, Wallace and his key campaign aides started traveling to build an organization for the 1968 presidential campaign, thus assuring Lurleen—like it or not—of a larger role at home. The principal objective was to attract leadership groups across the country that would spearhead efforts to put Wallace's name on all fifty state ballots. And Wallace attracted an odd lot. In Cleveland, Ohio, his early point man was Robert Annable, a Klan-connected book dealer who peddled Klan publications such as *The Fiery Cross* and bumper stickers urging membership in the North American Alliance of White People. But in Columbus, Ohio, Wallace's volunteer leader was Bobby Stevens (who, as an undercover operative for the Columbus Police Department, penetrated the Ohio Klan and testified in February 1966, on its activities—including those of Robert Annable—to the House Un-American Activities Committee). Another early supporter in Ohio was a former Hungarian freedom fighter and chemist, Louis Molnar. In Hawaii, a salesman who had graduated from Southern Methodist University, James Dennis, volunteered for the Wallace effort because he believed the Alabamian was the best hope for "throwing the bureaucrats' briefcases into the Potomac." In Reno, twenty-six-year-old Daniel Hansen—a Mormon, a Bircher, and a graduate in political science from the University of Nevada—was the state vice-chairman of Wallace for President. He explained his support: "The country is moving toward anarchy at home and appeasement abroad. George Wallace is for winning the Vietnam War; for local government and states' rights; against graft, corruption, and lying in government; against high taxes, socialist programs and a Supreme Court that's soft on crime and communism." In Omaha, Wesley Trollope, age forty, thought Wallace could do something to control lawlessness. A farm manager, Trollope thought Wallace was the only candidate not controlled by the "Eastern establishment." Small businessman Christian Glanz in Kentucky saw Wallace as the only candidate who represented "the desires of the little man, the working man." Wallace, he said, would challenge "those people sitting in their mansions who [were] willing to pacify belligerent groups with aid and civil rights laws." And in the state of Washington, Haskell Davis, a sixty-four-year-old real estate salesman, thought the country was "in a very bad way" because of those who were "circumventing the Constitution." And, without apology, he added, "I am a racist. I don't even believe in Irish marrying Germans." Before long, grassroots organizations for Wallace were springing up widely, but not everywhere. In Great Falls, Montana,

Wallace's aide Tom Turnipseed advertised a meeting to organize a Wallace for President group. No one showed up, and Turnipseed left the state.[44]

But Wallace drummed up business the old-fashioned way—he went after it personally. He filled Syracuse University's Manley Field House beyond its 4,500-seat capacity while thousands more milled outside but were denied entrance by the fire marshal. Characterized by a reporter as taking "a moderate stand on racial issues," Wallace drew jeers and boos, but also applause. The loudest and most sustained ovation came when he suggested, "Anyone who offers aid to the Vietcong is guilty of treason." He backed away from his "segregation forever" pledge, maintaining that it was meant only for Alabamians—and that his state's schools were "no longer segregated, anyway."[45] The next night, Wallace attracted a record turnout of more than nine hundred important business and professional men to Pittsburgh's Penn-Sheraton Hotel for the prestigious Amen Corner dinner. He amused them by saying it felt unusual "to speak to an orderly crowd" and that Lurleen had appointed him, as Lyndon Johnson had appointed his spouse, to head the highway beautification program. His attacks on institutions—big government, the national press, an unrestrained federal judiciary, and universities where professors advocated aid to Hanoi—elicited a warm, if not overly enthusiastic, response.[46]

■　■　■

Back in Montgomery, Lurleen fell into a comfortable routine in which her husband's team of experienced aides handled day-to-day operations while she spent much of her time in personal appearances, plumping for public support of her mental health and state parks initiatives. In May, however, Lurleen was thrown into an unexpected tizzy by an invitation to the White House for another of President Johnson's Vietnam briefings for the nation's governors. It was not what official Washington refers to as "a spouse event"—that is, neither the states' first ladies nor Alabama's first gentleman was invited to accompany the governors to the briefing, but would join them at an evening state dinner. The morning of the briefing, Lurleen momentarily considered making her excuses. "She naturally was a little nervous about being the only woman present," Wallace recalled, "and I reckon most governors are nervous anyway the first time they go to a conference with the president because of the position he occupies." Wallace tried to calm her. "I told her, 'You know most of the governors. You've been with them, you've been with their wives.' " Wallace speculated that Johnson would be "especially solicitous and kind" to Lurleen. "You just don't have a thing to worry about," he assured her. "You're going to enjoy it, and you're going to be glad you're here." Wallace had judged Johnson correctly. Lurleen was seated in the front row, and Johnson, she said later, "paid attention to me and even called my name." Later, when they posed in the Rose Garden for group photos, Johnson saw to it that Lurleen stood next to him. When the group headed in for lunch, Johnson excused himself from the other governors, took Lurleen aside, and asked, "Lurleen, do you want to go to the little girls' room?" Lurleen said she did, and the president took her to the elevator and accompanied her to the family quarters, where he directed her to Lady Bird's private bathroom. He waited for her and escorted her back downstairs to the luncheon. At the dinner that night, Johnson (who fully expected at that time to seek reelection in 1968) joked that he "had learned something from the Wallaces" and that "maybe Lady Bird would run in '72" when he would be barred from seeking another term.[47]

■　　■　　■

With Lurleen running the state and George running for president, the Wallace children found themselves under what George, Jr., called "doubly rough" pressure. Daughter Peggy Sue recalled, "We used to have to make a mental list of what we wanted to ask her when she was home because she was gone so much. And living in the public eye is just a real difficult thing to do, as far as the personal family life goes. . . . The older you get, the more you realize that it's not going to change, no matter how bad you want to have three meals together . . . [or] worship on Sunday together. It just can't be. . . . You really can't make up for the frequent separations." It's likely that the strains his parents imposed on his childhood left George, Jr., with lasting scars. By 1993, he had been married and divorced three times. Two of his marriages lasted less than a year; and one, in which his wife bore him two sons, ended after two years. His third wife, Angela Shoemaker, whom he divorced in May 1991 after eleven months of wedlock, said that George, Jr., was given to frightening fits of anger in which "one minute he'd be sweet and loving and the next he'd be furious, in a rage, screaming at me, calling me a whore and saying he hated me."[48]

In the summer of 1967, Lurleen knew that cancer had returned. She told her secretary, "This cancer is back. I won't live." Catherine Steineker tried to persuade her that it was just nerves from all her public appearances. In July, her doctors found another abdominal growth and sent her to Houston's M. D. Anderson Hospital for removal of that lemon-sized malignant tumor and another malignancy in her colon. George took an apartment in Houston and arranged his campaign travels so that he could return there at least two days a week while Lurleen was hospitalized during much of the summer (see chapter 14). She returned to Montgomery and was well enough to go to her office for a few weeks. But in September, she started to weaken again. George, Jr., recalled that "she would come in from a function, and smile and walk in the back door and literally collapse at the back steps, and we'd have to carry her up the stairs." George said, "She was suffering so badly one night, I had to call the ambulance to take her to the hospital." She returned to Houston on September 10 for cobalt treatments, remaining there until November 1. By now, George was spending most of his time in California, trying to get on that state's ballot, but he would return to Houston as often as he could. Lurleen roused herself between treatments to accompany George to Dallas and Fort Worth for ceremonies to open his campaign offices. And despite feeling weak and nauseated from the cobalt, she traveled to California for appearances and brief speeches at several rallies. She returned home for Christmas and insisted on joining a team of volunteers in wrapping hundreds of gifts for children's homes in Alabama; she even personally delivered many of the gifts to several homes. But on January 3, 1968, another pelvic tumor was discovered; it was treated with betatron radiation in Houston. A week later, she appeared at the opening of the Houston headquarters of her husband's presidential campaign. In February 1968, constant pain necessitated prescribed doses of morphine. She decided to return to Montgomery, where, on February 22, she was rushed to St. Margaret's Hospital; surgeons there removed an intestinal obstruction. She would stay in the hospital for two months as her condition deteriorated.[49]

Lurleen had a hospital suite with a sitting room, and an adjoining room was provided for George so that he could spend the night whenever he wished. For a time, George ran the state from the governor's office, but Lurleen would phone and ask him to come and spend the day and night with her. So the hospital set up an office across the hall from Lurleen's room where George could prepare papers for her signature. One day, George walked into her room and was jolted to see an intravenous needle inserted into her neck; the veins in her arms could no longer accommodate the needles. Involuntarily, George started to cry. "Ah, don't cry, George," Lurleen said. "This is nothing. They do this with a lot of people. Honey, don't get upset." But he was—and he became more despondent when one of the doctors told him that Lurleen would not make it. He told them he had read that the Japanese had made a breakthrough in cancer research; he offered to charter a jet to fly the doctors to Tokyo to see if they had found a medication that would help Lurleen. The doctors persuaded him that he was grasping at straws.[50]

On April 13, Lurleen pressed the doctors to let her return home in time for her daughter Lee's seventh birthday. A hospital bed and medical equipment were moved into the mansion, and nurses attended Lurleen around the clock. Her close friend, Mary Jo Ventress, moved into the mansion so she could be with Lurleen almost constantly. Little Lee would sit in her mother's room to watch television. George, Jr., now sixteen, would visit his mother early in the morning before going off to school. Peggy Sue, an eighteen-year-old high school senior, would visit after class; mother and daughter made plans for Peggy's graduation and senior prom that fall, events that Lurleen was more and more convinced she would not live to see. She began to talk more and more of death. She recalled a movie in which a dying man told his family they would all meet in heaven. "Honey," George said, "you are not going to go to heaven now, because you're going to get well." Wallace later recalled, "She did not believe it was true; then, on the other hand, she wanted to believe it. We both did. It's the way nature takes—realizing you're dying but still not accepting it." Soon, she could not eat; she shriveled to sixty-eight pounds. One morning, George, Jr., snapped at his mother when she did not touch her breakfast. "Mother, just eat it," he exclaimed. "Just make yourself eat it." She looked up and, in a pitifully weak voice, replied, "Son, I would if I could." On May 1, another abscess formed. George wanted the doctors to operate; maybe, he said, it would "prolong her life a day or two or three or four, and maybe something would come out in the papers that would show they had something to cure cancer." The doctors explained gently that surgery would simply lengthen her suffering. One said, "It would be unfair for us to do this when we know it would do no good. You know yourself just from looking at her that she is dying; she'll die in the next few days."[51]

On Monday morning, May 6, Lurleen pleaded with George to

spend the day with her. "I feel like something's going to happen to me," she said. "Please stay with me." Her pain worsened through the day, and the doctors told George that death was not far off. By nightfall, the entire family had gathered at the mansion. About ten-thirty, Lurleen fell into a coma. George took her hand and quietly talked to her, naming the children who were there with her, telling her that when she got well, they would all go to the lake together and fish. "Darling," he said, "squeeze my hand if you can hear me." And there was a slight squeeze. Over the next two hours, as George talked to Lurleen, he would occasionally squeeze her hand, and he would feel a slight pressure in return. By midnight, Wallace remembered, "her little hand began to loosen. There was no squeeze from it at all. And then, she began to take long breaths—and it seemed like minutes before she would take another one. She did that twenty or twenty-five times, with the breaths getting farther apart, until the last one—and there were no more." He looked up at the attending physician, Hamilton Hutchinson. "Is she gone?" he asked. The doctor put his stethoscope to Lurleen's chest, then checked her pulse. He nodded. Everyone filed silently into the hallway and comforted one another. Then George went back in alone to await the funeral home attendants. He sat on the side of Lurleen's bed and talked to her. "Honey, you've been a great wife; you've been a good governor; you've been the greatest mother of anyone. Oh, how much we love you." He ran his fingers through her hair, kissed her lightly on the forehead, took her hand, and said, "Good-bye, sweetheart."52

■　■　■

Through the weekend, Lurleen lay in state in the capitol rotunda; only Jefferson Davis, his body en route to its final resting place in Richmond, had been so honored before. Thirty thousand people wound past the open casket to pay their last respects. (Lurleen, aware of the extent to which she had withered, had left instructions for her casket to remain sealed; the funeral home had restored her looks so effectively, however, that Wallace decided to countermand her wishes and allow mourners to view her.) Through her minister, Lurleen had requested that Elizabeth Barrett Browning's sonnet beginning "How do I love thee?" (sonnet 43, *Sonnets from the Portuguese*) be read at her funeral and that selections from Handel's *Water Music* be played;

unfamiliar with the Handel piece, a military band assigned to the funeral practiced through the night to learn it in time for the service. Senators, congressmen, and governors were there by the dozens, and President Johnson sent Price Daniel, a former governor of Texas, to represent him. So many people across the country had sent floral remembrances that back orders enabled the cemetery to keep fresh flowers on her grave for a year and a half.[53]

George was forlorn. He openly wept in his daughter's arms. He played records of Lurleen's favorite tunes over and over. Albert Brewer was sworn in as governor, but he gave the Wallaces a few days to move out of the mansion they had occupied for the previous five and a half years. Fortunately, they had a place to go to. Before her inauguration, Lurleen had persuaded George to buy the house on Farrar Street; George had indulged her, despite his belief that they would be living in the mansion for another eight years. Quietly, out of the public view, Lurleen had used the house as her touchstone, a way to bridge the trappings of politics that had defined and confined her, to reach what to her was genuine but always just beyond her grasp— the life of a wife and mother. Her son was glad in many ways that Lurleen had endured the pressures and physical challenges of the governorship. "She grew as a person. Had she not done it, she might never have realized that she had all this ability and talent." And there was no doubt that her brief administration was widely admired. Jackson Stell, the curator of the Lurleen B. Wallace Museum in Montgomery, said, "Unfortunately, people will generally think of her only as someone who stood in for her husband. But the programs she began in mental health, youth services, and state parks have been a great help to the state of Alabama. No one was ashamed of Lurleen Wallace as governor." But George, Jr., knew as well as anyone that Lurleen's heart was more often closer to the brick house on Farrar Street than to the mansion on Perry Street:

> Dad didn't see why they needed a house right then, since they'd be living in the mansion for some time. But he bought it to please her. And while Mother was governor, she loved to spend time furnishing the house on Farrar against the day when she and Dad could move in. She never did get to live in the house. But the week before she died, she visited it one last time to admire some new living room and dining room furniture she'd asked Dad to buy for it. It seemed to be her

one hopeful link to a normal life as a housewife in a future she would never see.[54]

Wallace suspended all activities and went into virtual seclusion for a month. His daughter recalled that he lay about, depressed, playing no role in day-to-day family life. But, as Peggy Sue noted, "I think his politics probably was the best cure for that. It got him back in the swing of things."[55]

In June, Wallace returned to the campaign trail—and to a crucial role in what must rank among the most turbulent political years in American history.

14

Waking a Sleeping Giant

GEORGE WALLACE HAD SAID REPEATEDLY during Lurleen Wallace's 1966 campaign for governor that her election would provide the platform he needed to keep "the views of Alabamians" before the entire nation. Everyone knew that meant he would run for president again in 1968—only this time, he would be in for the long run, extending his flaming, furious sprint of 1964 to a steady yet powerful cross-country lope. There was a sleeping giant out there and—for good or ill—he meant to wake it.

But how to make the race? As a Democrat entered in key primaries, in hopes of gaining leverage (if not the nomination) to change the direction of the party? Or as a third-party candidate thumbing his nose at "national" Democrats and Republicans and perhaps depriving either party's nominee of an electoral majority?

Wallace's top staff members—Seymore Trammell, Cecil Jackson, Earl Morgan, and Bill Jones—insisted that the requirements of a national campaign demanded that Wallace make an immediate decision. They braced him the day after Lurleen's inauguration in his new office across from Governor Lurleen's and said they would not leave until George told them how he planned to run.

The aides all argued for a third party. It was possible, they reasoned, to embarrass President Johnson by defeating him in one or more primaries. But the president controlled the party machinery, and it was foolhardy to think they or anyone else could deprive him of the nomination. Johnson might throw Wallace a bone or two in the party platform to muzzle him during the general election campaign, but it would be small compensation for the time and expense devoted to running in a dozen or so primaries.

Besides, they believed that much of Wallace's support would likely come from Republicans disgruntled with their party's drift to the left following Goldwater's massive defeat in 1964. Although some would be allowed to cross over and participate in a few Democratic primaries, many more would be lost to Wallace. And as a third-party nominee, they reasoned, Wallace would be wholly free to condemn the policies of both his Democratic and Republican opponents. Further, as an independent, he would remain in the spotlight for the duration of the campaign—all the way to election day in November 1968. The downside, of course, was that his campaign might lose steam, that the opprobrium heaped on him from all sides might diminish his appeal, that a poor showing in November would make him a laughingstock and might effectively end his political career in Alabama as well as in the nation.

But the staffers wanted—needed—a prompt decision on whether Wallace was willing to take the risk. If Wallace were to run as an independent, they would have to act immediately to succeed in the arduous—perhaps impossible—task of placing his name on enough state ballots to make a difference in the election. If Wallace would give them the go-ahead that day, the staffers said they were confident they could qualify him in thirty states, and perhaps in two or three more. The goal, of course, would be to attain ballot position in all fifty states, but that objective might be beyond reach.

The decision, they emphasized, would be irreversible; it was important that Wallace, given his propensity for changing his mind, understand that once people started committing their time and money to put him on state ballots, it would be political suicide to abandon them. Wallace asked a few questions and then made his decision; he would travel the third-party route in 1968.[1]

Within a week, Jones opened a campaign office a few blocks from the capitol. The task of getting Wallace on all the state ballots would be formidable, as anticipated. Rules, deadlines, and the number of required signatures differed from state to state, the latter ranging from just 300 in North Dakota and Colorado to 433,000 in Ohio.

Although California required only 66,000 signatures, it would be the most challenging. It had the earliest deadline of any state—midnight, December 31, 1967. Each of the signatories was required also to register as a member of Wallace's new party. Obviously, that would discourage many people from signing up and probably would confuse others. Trammell agreed with Jones that if the Wallace forces could succeed in California, the achievement would inject an enormous emotional lift into the campaign just when it was likely to need one—at the dawn of the election year.[2]

Jones started the long, laborious mission of developing Wallace organizations in California and elsewhere by using the meticulously kept records of the million-plus supporters around the country who had written or contributed to Wallace over the years. State-by-state lists were compiled and distributed among Alabamians who had signed on as campaign volunteers—lawyers, legislators, and students, for the most part—and about a dozen people on the state payroll but detailed to the campaign. The Alabamians wrote, telephoned, and sometimes personally visited key Wallace supporters around the country and enlisted them as local coordinators. These people were asked to start a chain of support, enrolling friends who would draft their friends, and so on. Along the way, each was requested to sign petitions and contribute anything he or she could afford. Whenever necessary—usually, if factional disputes or special difficulties in obtaining ballot position arose—Jones or Trammell would travel to a state personally.[3]

■ ■ ■

Wallace launched his campaign, more or less officially, with an April 23, 1967, appearance on "Meet the Press." Wallace said, "There is more chance that I will run than I will not run"—about as close to a formal announcement as any politician makes more than a year and a half before an election. He insisted he was not a racist, that he did not dislike any person because of color, that he did "not recommend segregation in any phase of our society in any state in this union" but rather "that the states . . . continue to determine the policies of their domestic institutions themselves, and that the bureaucrats and the theoreticians in Washington let people in Ohio and New York and California decide themselves . . . what type of school system they are going to have." He rejected the notion of a "white backlash" in the country. "There's not any backlash among the mass of American people against anybody because of color," he insisted. Rather, he said, "there's a backlash against big government in this country." He elaborated:

> This is a movement of the people, and it doesn't make any difference whether top, leading politicians endorse this movement or not. And I think that if the politicians get in the way . . . a lot of them are going to get run over by this average man in the street—this man in the textile mill, this man in the steel mill, this barber, the beautician, the policeman on the beat . . . the little businessman. . . . They are the ones. . . . Those are the mass of people that are going to support a change on the domestic scene in this country.[4]

The impact of Wallace's words was stunning. Throughout the country, thousands were mobilized. They wrote letters, sent cash or checks ranging from a dollar to a hundred dollars, and volunteered to help put him on their respective ballots. Some did not wait for direction from Montgomery but on their own started circulating petitions in Wallace's behalf. Wallace's influence on TV viewers was exemplified in Pinole, California, a working-class community twenty miles northeast of San Francisco, where Mary Marshall, a homemaker in her mid-forties, watched "Meet the Press" in the living room of her small, single-level, pink stucco house. "I was so inspired by him," she said, "I got up and wrote him a letter and drove down and mailed it that same day. I told him that I felt there were certain times in history for certain men. 'This is the time and you are the man to lead us.' " Mary and her husband, Carl, a worker in an oil-company refinery, were concerned, as they put it, about law and order, welfare cheats, Communists, hippies, and the decline of public education and public morality. Before long, Wallace supporters in California invited the Marshalls to meetings and appointed them deputy registrars; by the deadline at the end of the year, they had registered six hundred people for Wallace's third party. They worked all Christmas afternoon getting signatures; they worked until eleven at night on New Year's Eve. "One night about a quarter to one," Mary Marshall recalled, "the phone rang. A man wanted to register. So we got up and dressed and got out our books and went and registered him." Well over half the people the Marshalls registered had been working-class Democrats like themselves—a clear portent of elections to come.[5]

Lurleen had explained George's popularity simply: "He speaks out for the people. He says what they think. When he's on 'Meet the

Press' they can listen to him and think, 'That's what I would say if I were up there.' " Grover Hall, who had moved on from Montgomery to edit the *Richmond News-Leader,* saw the same phenomenon from Wallace's perspective: "He can read your insides quicker than any man I ever saw."[6]

Wallace continued to stir the pot of speculation by welcoming national publications to Montgomery for in-depth profiles. He gave reporters full access to his activities: he allowed them to sit in on all his meetings, follow him around, eat with him,[7] and interview any of his aides and family members. All found him an irrepressible bundle of energy. Tom Wicker of the *New York Times* said Wallace would fidget whenever he was seated, would regularly dash from behind his desk to greet nearly any visitor to the capitol, and would compulsively telephone aides and supporters, seemingly for no reason except to hear a friendly voice.[8] The syndicated columnist Jack Kilpatrick said, "[Wallace] can strut sitting down. . . . He is full of a nervous stage business: standing up, sitting down, the horn-rimmed glasses on, the glasses off, lighting his cigar, licking his cigar, spitting in the waste-basket. There is never a moment of stillness. . . . I have met some mighty talkers. But George Wallace is the greatest nonstop talker of them all." Traveling, dining, and chatting with Wallace during one concentrated period, he said, "was like spending seventeen hours in the middle of a juke box."[9]

Wallace was ebullient in the last week of April when, in the company of a dozen reporters from national publications, he made his first campaign foray—a Northern expedition that Wallace eagerly anticipated despite his expectation that it would be "a hostile trip," especially during campus visits. "There'll be pickets and heckling," he predicted. "We never do well on college campuses. The professors always oppose us. You can tell the number of people against us by counting the bicycles."[10] Wallace, in fact, did very well on college campuses—and usually when picketing and heckling reached their zenith.

The trip began at Syracuse University, where, at an airport news conference, he was asked his reaction to being described by a national columnist as "a cultural Moon Mullins [who] cares nothing for sports, books, the dance, the drama."[11] Wallace smiled. "Moon Mullins is pretty widely read across the country," he said. "I don't know how much culture Moon Mullins has, but the Moon Mullins vote is in the majority—so I'll stick with the Moon Mullins folks." When he appeared before forty-five hundred people in the university's dirt-floored, domed, circular field house, he forecast accurately, "There's gonna be a hot time in the old town tonight." A hundred blacks, some of whom masqueraded as Klansmen, walked out chanting, "Black power!" as the audience cheered. His remarks were frequently drowned out by catcalls and boos. Some two hundred students in the aisles and along the walls sang and shouted slogans of the civil rights movement. One student, standing just below the platform, shouted repeatedly, "Get your ass back down South, you son of a bitch." The intensity of the heckling derailed Wallace's train of thought several times, but he managed to squeeze in—to loud ovations—his denunciations of big government, lawlessness, open housing, and those "guilty of treason" for raising money and donating blood for the Vietcong. The television journalist Nelson Benton observed that "the only difference between this and a bullfight is that the bull lived." But later, when a group of Syracuse students came to Wallace's motel to apologize for the misbehavior of their peers, Wallace brushed it aside and insisted, "We did a lot better than you thought we'd do, didn't we?"[12]

He received a much friendlier reception at Rose Polytechnic Institute in Terre Haute, Indiana; and in Pittsburgh, he scored well with 1,300 business, civic, and professional leaders at a formal dinner.[13] He was picking up steam with every appearance and with every heckler. Gallup had him at 13 percent even before his Northern trip. The poll showed that without Wallace in the race, Gov. George Romney of Michigan would defeat President Johnson (52 percent to 43 percent), but with Wallace in the race and drawing 13 percent, the president emerged the winner (43 percent to 35 percent). Richard Nixon tied Johnson in a two-way race but, with Wallace in the mix, lost to him by ten percentage points.[14]

Immediately, Wallace's rivals started to react. Romney, in his first Southern appearance, thought a third-party effort would be "tragic" in its effect on the traditional two-party system. And Johnson started devising his own Southern strategy, in which he sought to obtain the loyalty—or, at least, the neutrality—of Southern Democratic governors. His initial gesture in that direction was dispatching his vice-president, Hubert Humphrey, to Georgia, where the long-time civil rights champion compromised his stature by posing arm-in-arm with Gov. Lester Maddox, the one-time restaurateur who had risen to political prominence by vowing to shoot or beat any black people who tried to eat at his Pickrick Restaurant; Humphrey described Maddox as "a good Democrat" for whom there was "lots of room" in the party.[15]

Throughout the spring and summer of 1967, Wallace ferried back and forth between Alabama and speaking engagements likely to attract national coverage. He also made himself available to journalists for national media. The eminent correspondent Stewart Alsop wrote a Wallace piece for the *Saturday Evening Post*; the columnists Rowland Evans and Robert Novak prepared a major piece for *Look*; interviewers from network and out-of-state TV stations came and went regularly; more than a thousand speaking invitations from universities, clubs, and political organizations were awaiting responses.[16]

The notice given Wallace's sporadic journeys outside the South was enhanced by his shrewd selection of key audiences. These included an American Legion post in Wisconsin, a harvest festival in Ohio, a "bosses' night" banquet in Florida, a "parents' day" gathering in Indiana, a Kiwanis Club youth rally in New Hampshire—real Americana. Every chance, he would conduct a rally, speak at a university, address a press organization, and drum up interviews. But the center of his trips would always be the "folks."[17] And every time a college crowd got out of hand, it would redound to Wallace's benefit. At Dartmouth in May 1967, after being drowned out by a particularly raucous and unruly student audience of fifteen hundred, a mob bent on violence menaced him as he was leaving the auditorium. Some five hundred students pinned him in his car, then started rocking the car and banging on the doors and hood. A phalanx of policemen managed to extricate Wallace and tried, unsuccessfully, to spirit him, unnoticed, to another car. He managed to get inside, but the students quickly swarmed over it and started whacking and shaking it, as they had the other one. This time, the police mixed it up with the kids, and during the melee, Wallace's driver managed to pull away. The dean, Thaddeus Seymour, wired his apologies to Wallace, saying that "there [could] be no justification of the abusive behavior" displayed by the undergraduates. In the campus daily, the dean also lamented, "We gave away quite a bit of Dartmouth College last night." But he astutely judged that the riot added perhaps 100,000 votes to Wallace's candidacy.[18]

■   ■   ■

Wallace was on his way. In June 1967, with the national political conventions still a year away, 72 percent of the American people could correctly identify Wallace; by contrast, only six months before the 1964 Republican National Convention had chosen Goldwater as its nominee for president, just 61 percent of Americans could identify Goldwater. To be sure, 58 percent of the people judged Wallace to be antiblack, narrow-minded, arrogant, and even stupid. But 24 percent lauded his sincerity, directness, independence, and courage.[19]

Wallace's rapid rise was making many lawmakers jittery. Several congressmen, including Representatives Charles Goodell, a New York Republican, and Morris Udall, a Democrat from Arizona, proposed constitutional amendments to replace the electoral college with direct, popular election of the president and vice-president.[20] The wily Senate Republican leader, Everett Dirksen of Illinois, abandoned his long-standing support of the electoral college in favor of direct presidential elections when the polls suggested that, under the existing system, Wallace's third-party candidacy might keep a Republican from unseating President Johnson.[21] Johnson himself got into the act by proposing federal financing of presidential campaigns, but the candidates of minor parties could be reimbursed for expenses only *after* the election—and then only if they compiled more than 5 percent of the popular vote. (In 1948, Strom Thurmond's Dixiecrats had gathered thirty-nine electoral votes, but only 2.5 percent of the popular vote.)[22] In proposing his financing scheme, Johnson was dropping the second shoe of his so-called Southern strategy. To carry at least some Southern states, he wanted Wallace to split the Republican vote in the South; but to prevent Wallace from becoming strong enough to sweep the South and deprive the Democrats of potentially crucial electoral votes, Johnson sought to starve Wallace of funds. It may have been a good idea, but it did not work.

Seymore Trammell had devised a time-payment pledge plan; by the end of 1967, more than twenty thousand supporters had signed up to make contributions, for which they were billed monthly. Those who could not afford to contribute money enlisted in Wallace's fundraising army. Some would pledge ten hours a week, with a goal of collecting $100 each week. Others opted to set a target of persuading at least eighty-five families to give ten dollars each. Everywhere Wallace traveled, fund-raising dinners were de rigueur; $25 a plate was the usual rate, though sometimes the tariff was $100 or more. And at rallies, "Wallace Girls," bedecked in boaters and bright sashes, invaded the aisles carrying yellow plastic buckets while speakers implored the faithful to fill them with dollar bills or even fives and tens. Additionally, bumper stickers, campaign buttons, banners, photos, and other paraphernalia were sold at Wallace rallies, rather than following the tradition of giving them away.[23] In later years, the major parties would borrow a number of Wallace's fund-raising techniques.

It would be a quarter of a century before other presidential candidates would fully embrace Wallace's campaign practices of participating in local television talk shows (then called "informal chatter" programs), speaking to local business and professional groups (thus increasing his local-area coverage while other candidates played to the networks and national publications), granting on-air interviews to local radio disc jockeys, and appearing on radio call-in segments (called "dial-a-question" programs in their early manifestations). In Oklahoma City, Wallace was a guest on a local country music TV show. He greeted and lauded the band and, to the delight of the studio audience of a hundred (not to mention the thousands watching on television), proclaimed, "People that listen to the kind of music you are playing tonight are the people that are going to save this country." In St. Louis, the host of a radio call-in show said that during Wallace's forty-five-minute segment on the program, a record two-thousand-plus callers had tried to get through—and they were overwhelmingly favorable to Wallace. "Those kinds of shows," Wallace said, "reach the man in the street—your steel workers, your oil workers, building trades workers, beauticians, little businessmen, and farmers, and your policemen and firemen. Those are my kind of people." It was not empty rhetoric. In Bethany, Oklahoma, Wallace popped into a beauty shop and engaged both the proprietors and their customers, most of whom beamed from under dryers while their hair was rolled tightly in curlers. Then he stopped to chat with the policemen who were escorting him around town. "You know," he told them, "there's nothing wrong with this country that we couldn't cure by turning it over to the police for a couple of years. You fellows would straighten it out." In San Francisco, Wallace refused to cross a picket line to make a television appearance. Wallace's "identification with the 'common man' [is] so complete," the reporter James Dickenson observed, "that it often seems that he believes that he embodies the very will and being of the common man. George Wallace is the Cicero of the cab driver." It was the average cab driver, Wallace maintained, who could cut through "pseudo-intellectual" ideas. "They come into fierce contact with life," he told a California audience. "They knew Castro was a communist long before *The New York Times*.

They knew it by looking at him and listening to him. You know what *The New York Times* called Castro? They called him the Robin Hood of the Caribbean."[24] Many of those who knew Wallace believed some mystical quality enabled him to know an audience's deepest concerns. "He has a special knack of adjusting to the feel of a crowd as he is speaking," one said. "He modifies his speeches according to the reaction he senses." And a legislative colleague, Pete Mathews, marveled, "George is able to convince people that they believe what he believes."[25]

By the summer of 1967, the national media had elevated Wallace to legitimacy; when most publications reviewed positions on key issues of the people considered potential contenders against President Johnson, Wallace invariably was included. Describing Vietnam as "the big issue" facing presidential hopefuls, *Newsweek* sought the views of the seven men it considered likely candidates. The list comprised one Democrat (presciently, Bobby Kennedy), five Republicans (Governors Reagan, Romney, and Rockefeller; Sen. Charles Percy of Illinois; and Richard Nixon), and Wallace. Kennedy and Rockefeller declined to participate. Romney, Percy, and Nixon all straddled the question by opposing unilateral withdrawal on one hand and massive military escalation on the other; ironically, Nixon warned, "If we continue President Johnson's policies, we are confronted with a war that could last five years." Reagan's and Wallace's expressed convictions were similar—and considerably tougher than those of the presumed mainline candidates. Reagan said, "The way to win a war is to win it . . . as swiftly as possible; attrition over the long period of time will cost more in lives than a sudden strike for victory." Wallace insisted that the government "show the enemy [U.S.] resolve" to earn "the respect of friend and foe alike. Strength, respect, and power are deterrents to war." Interestingly, however, Wallace was somewhat more muted than Reagan when it came to the possible use of nuclear power. Wallace said that, as president, "I will not rattle rockets and sabers." But Reagan, while saying that no one "would cheerfully want to use atomic weapons," added, "The last person in the world that should know we wouldn't use them is the enemy. He should go to bed every night being afraid that we might."[26] A comparable position on the use of nuclear weapons enunciated a year later by Wallace's running mate Curtis LeMay would nonetheless be attacked in the media as irresponsible and would cost Wallace some votes (as discussed later in this chapter).

In the fall, Wallace faced a dual crisis—his wife's failing health and the growing difficulty in qualifying for the California ballot. In late October, Bill Jones learned that the firm he had retained to collect the needed 66,000 signatures and registrations had obtained fewer than 2,000. "We had to start the campaign practically from scratch," Jones said. "We had two months. We needed offices, TV spots, logistics for the governor to tour the state, times and places for rallies, advance work." He called Trammell and told him the situation was desperate. Without hesitation, Trammell authorized Jones to spend a million dollars. A few minutes later, Jones phoned again "to make sure Trammell knew what had to be done." Jones recalled saying, "Trammell, dammit, listen to me. I'm telling you it's going to take a million dollars to do this." And Trammell said, 'Well, goddammit, you ain't listening to me. Get going.' Within a day, he signed the notes personally with the Central Bank of Birmingham to get the money. . . . Then [Jones and Trammell] told the governor he'd have to spend a solid thirty days out here in December.' "27

California was not Wallace's only problem; Ohio's draconian third-party regulations required gathering more than 400,000 signatures in a ten-week period that would end early in 1968. Accordingly, Wallace opened an eight-day blitz in Ohio in November 1967, before starting a twenty-one day, fifty-city, eighty-speech barnstorming tour throughout California, where he had just until the end of the year to qualify. In Ohio, Wallace's supporters somehow surpassed the required number of signatures, perhaps by as many as 100,000. But Ohio's secretary of state, Ted Brown, declared that the petitions were null and void on the grounds that they had been filed after the deadline. An appeal to a three-judge federal court merely reinforced Wallace's mistrust of the federal judiciary; the court refused to order Wallace's name placed on the Ohio ballot because, the judges ruled, Wallace's American Independent party was a "fictional party." A real party, the court declared, developed from the bottom up in search of a leader; the Wallace party, by contrast, appeared to have been organized from the top down.28 The Wallace forces then did the unthinkable—they appealed to the U.S. Supreme Court. With only a month to go before election day in 1968, the high court ordered Ohio to place Wallace's name on the ballot, giving the state's eighty-eight counties barely enough time to receive more than six million corrected ballots from the printer.29

But it was Wallace's challenge in California to which both the nation and the Wallace campaign were riveted. California's ballot-qualifying deadline came earlier than Ohio's; the hurdle of getting people to complete a two-page, legal-sized form to register as members of Wallace's American Independent party seemed insuperable; and California's size and political importance drew media representatives like a magnet.[30] For the month of December, wrote the *Wall Street Journal*'s Neil Maxwell, "the capital of Alabama is not Los Angeles, but it might as well be." During much of the month, Los Angeles became headquarters for Governors George and Lurleen (when she was well enough to leave the hospital in Texas), her executive secretary, her press secretary, the director of the Alabama labor department, the state banking director, executives from the state's banking and insurance departments, the deputy prison commissioner, the clerk and assistant clerk of the state's house of representatives, a steady stream of state legislators, and a dozen state troopers. Other state officials worked full-time in campaign headquarters in Montgomery. Trammell, who remained the state finance director under Lurleen, had not seen his capitol office since mid-October. Other officials, such as Stan Sikes, a legislative recording secretary, conceded they were "moonlighting" at their state jobs while putting in most of their working hours at Wallace campaign headquarters.[31]

Wallace's justification for appropriating a sizable chunk of the state's payroll (estimated to total nearly $200,000, excluding the salaries of the state troopers who acted as bodyguards) was a transparent concoction. The troopers were responsible for protecting members of the governor's family, he explained, and he certainly qualified as a family member. As for the other employees in California, he said, they simply were on hand to support Lurleen, who had been making a number of visits to the state. And the state employees working in the Wallace for President headquarters in Montgomery? Well, state government can be carried on anywhere, not just in the capitol. Predictably, the national media—and even most of Alabama's press—were outraged. Even a friendly editor in Montgomery complained—but with a smile:

> Aw, come on, California, let our people go. . . . You've got all
> the politicians you can ever use. Yet you are tying up the
> political leadership of Alabama, holding our legal governor,
> our *de facto* governor, our *ex post facto* governor, and heaven
> only knows how many aides, flunkies, and sycophants. . . . Step
> forward [and sign Wallace's petitions] before Alabama
> collapses through chronic absenteeism.[32]

But Wallace needed all the help he could get to qualify for the California ballot. Re-registration, as Tom Wicker pointed out, was "a task infinitely more difficult than merely getting people to sign petitions."

Wallace extended his California drive from thirty days to six weeks—and he far exceeded his planned eighty speeches. Just before Christmas, he gave his hundredth speech to a white, elderly crowd of about eighty people in a Los Angeles suburb. As always, he flayed "pseudo-intellectuals" and growing lawlessness. He condemned college professors for "drawing down thirty or forty thousand of [the voters'] hard-earned tax dollars" to stir up opposition to American soldiers fighting in Vietnam. He contended, "You can't even walk in the shadow of the White House in Washington, D.C., unless you got two police dogs with you." But he said that "pseudo-intellectuals" would absolve a criminal because "his daddy didn't carry him to see the Los Angeles Rams play when he was a little boy—and [so] he's all messed up." And he warned that protesters or "hippies" who dared lie down to block his car would learn it would be the "last car they ever blocked." The crowds—large and small—ate it up. But signing up converts remained difficult. A Birmingham steelworker who had volunteered for the effort said, "[People] give you all sorts of reasons for refusing, but the main one is they're afraid that if they register, they'll go on jury duty."[33]

At Christmas, California officials had certified that Wallace's American Independent party had acquired less than 42,000 adherents; they had just a week to get 24,000 more. The frantic final week started producing a torrent of signatures. But the stepped-up activity and aggressiveness of an army of new registrars, many of whom poured into neighborhoods and knocked on doors, stood on street corners, and invaded shopping centers, generated an upsurge in opposition and hecklers. At one rally, three youths stuffed eggs into their jackets with the apparent intention of throwing them at Wallace. But a couple of Wallace's guards had noticed. When the boys moved into range, the guards stepped up and, on the pretext of conducting a search, slapped their hands over the boys' pockets, splattering the eggs over the would-be offenders.[34]

By the deadline, California authorities announced that the Wallace forces had surpassed the target of 66,000 signatures by at least 10,000; in fact, the final tally would show that more than 100,000 Californians had switched party affiliations to sign up as followers of the American Independent party—and, to the surprise of many observers, nearly 65 percent of them had been Democrats. By any reckoning, it was an extraordinary achievement—a "nearly impossible feat," one political scientist exclaimed. Wallace was so elated that he threw traditional political caution to the winds and predicted flatly that he would be on the ballot in all fifty states.[35]

The accomplishment also started making believers of a number of people who earlier had shrugged Wallace off. "George Wallace is a serious political candidate," said James Farmer, the immediate past director of the Congress of Racial Equality. He added, "[Wallace is] an articulate, intelligent man who has a message to sell and is selling it very effectively."[36] Wallace reached a new, estimable plateau among members of the Eastern establishment when the *New York Times* columnist Russell Baker made him the subject of a satirical piece describing how Wallace might have retold Mother Goose stories:

> I want to tell you good folks about a little girl named Mary [whose] lamb followed the little girl to school and do you know what those pseudo-intellectuals at the schoolhouse said? They said, "You can't have no lamb following you to school because it's against the rules." . . . You take a blackjack to school . . . and all they say is, "Oh, that poor fellow with the blackjack! We got to do something for him! His daddy wouldn't give him a Cadillac when he was a little boy and now he's all messed up."[37]

Florida's Gov. Claude Kirk, hoping to weaken Wallace in the South, unconvincingly portrayed him not as a redneck racist of the right, but as "a flaming liberal when it comes to spending."[38]

On February 8, at a news conference crammed with seventy-five reporters and television cameras at Washington's Sheraton Park Hotel, Wallace formally announced his independent candidacy for president. It was, one reporter commented, "the anticlimactic fulfillment of a long-standing threat. . . . With little pomp and less drama, [it was] the most significant political development to date of [that] election year."[39] Wallace used his surroundings to renew his condemnation of federal officials as representatives, to most Americans, of bureaucracy and crime. He said he would gather "all [the] briefcase-toting bureaucrats in the Department of Health, Education, and Welfare . . . and throw their briefcases in the Potomac River." And he said he would make it possible to walk Washington,

D.C.'s streets safely, even if he "had to keep thirty thousand troops standing on the streets two feet apart and with two-foot-long bayonets." (Twenty-five years later, Mayor Sharon Pratt Kelly of Washington, D.C., asked President Clinton to activate the National Guard to help fight crime in the nation's capital.) Urban rioting and open support for America's Vietnamese enemies, he said, were led by "activists, anarchists, revolutionaries, and communists" whom he would put behind bars.[40] But when he said that Americans were "hungry for a change" and "concerned and disgusted" with national trends, he was putting his finger on the anger rising in the land.[41] The "long, hot summer" of 1967 that had ravaged Newark, Detroit, and many other cities truly had frightened millions of Americans, black and white alike; and the national caldron—already bubbling because of rioting, growing crime, and the war—was about to boil over.

Politicians, the press, and professors were increasingly uneasy about Wallace. Sen. Percy found support for Wallace "surprisingly stronger than [he] thought it was" and feared the election might be decided in the House of Representatives because no candidate would win a majority in the electoral college. Sen. Thomas Kuchel of California said electing the president in the House "could be as bad for our country as a dictatorship."[42] Wallace claimed that the decision would never reach the House; he would direct his electors to vote for the major-party candidate who allowed Wallace a say in selecting the Cabinet and future Supreme Court nominees.[43] Rep. Jonathan Bingham of New York proposed a constitutional amendment for a runoff election between the two candidates who received the most electoral votes, should no one receive a majority.[44] A political science professor, fearing that Wallace's candidacy put the U.S. "democracy in serious danger," suggested that President Johnson and Governor Rockefeller form a coalition ticket, announcing in advance their intention of appointing prominent Democrats and Republicans to the cabinet.[45] And on the eve of Wallace's planned three-day drive to acquire the more than ten thousand signatures he needed to put him on Pennsylvania's ballot, one of that state's senators, Hugh Scott, asserted, "[Wallace would be] dangerous to both parties. George Wallace is a menace to everybody. He's a menace to himself; he's a menace to Alabama; he's a menace to the United States; and he's a menace to the Democratic and Republican parties. I think if he bit himself, he'd die of blood poisoning."[46] The next day, in Pittsburgh, Wallace introduced reporters to his four bodyguards by saying, "I have them here to keep me from biting myself."[47]

Meanwhile, Wallace made prompt moves in California, South Carolina, and elsewhere to scotch local supporters' efforts to run their own candidates for statewide, congressional, or local offices; Wallace feared that local aspirants for office, as one observer put it, "might turn out to be embarrassing extremists."[48] Clearly, Wallace was feeling growing national strength and was trying mightily to temper his harsh image.

■   ■   ■

The turbulence that Americans were feeling and fearing was further reflected by the entrance into the presidential sweepstakes of the strongly antiwar Sen. Eugene McCarthy. Two weeks before the May 12 presidential primary in New Hampshire, a *Time* magazine poll gave Senator McCarthy just 11 percent of the vote. But pollsters reported widespread anxiety among voters in that state—concern over the war, the economy, and the general sense of too much disruption in the country. McCarthy himself began to think he had "a chance . . . when [he] realized that you could go into any bar in the country and insult Lyndon Johnson and nobody would punch you in the nose."[49]

In New Hampshire, at least, people were decidedly anti-Johnson rather than pro anyone in particular. Sensing that mood, Johnson, who had not bothered to have his name placed on the ballot, directed his political operatives to mount an intensive write-in campaign among loyal Democrats and those who could be persuaded that a vote against Johnson amounted to a vote for McCarthy "peaceniks," on one hand, or Wallace "racists," on the other.[50]

Another major blow to Johnson's popularity was the issuance of the fifteen-hundred-page report of the National Advisory Commission on Civil Disorders—the Kerner Commission—just a week before the primary. The report made the now-famous assertion, "Our nation is moving toward two societies, one black, one white—separate and unequal." It also maintained that institutionalized racism—barring of blacks from decent employment, education, and housing—had triggered the riots of the previous summer. The report proposed a huge federally financed program of jobs creation, on-the-job training, open housing, construction of low-income housing, and, of course, elimination of de facto school segregation.[51]

The response from Southerners like Rep. F. Edward Hebert of Louisiana, who termed the report "propaganda *ad nauseum*," was predictable. The response from Richard Nixon, who was seeking New Hampshire's Republican votes in the primary, was, perhaps, more surprising. In what was to be a major turning point in Nixon's 1968 presidential campaign, the former vice-president used the Kerner Commission report as a springboard for embracing as his own the pith of George Wallace's powerful appeal—the denunciation of a myopic big government that saw "crime in the streets" and other societal ills as something for which the victims were responsible. In a March 6 radio interview in Keene, New Hampshire, Nixon said, "[The report], in effect, blames everybody for the riots except the perpetrators of the riots." And the next night, in a nationwide radio address, Nixon went much further—further, it might be argued, than Wallace had. Regarding domestic violence, he said, the government should meet "force with force, if necessary," and provide "retaliation against the perpetrators and planners of violence." As the campaign wore on, Nixon espoused more and more of Wallace's core campaign; in addition to the Wallace positions on crime, Nixon spoke out against school busing, federal enforcement of school desegregation, antiwar activists, and the federal judiciary. Where Wallace had opposed school busing by contending it would ruin neighborhood schools and heap physical stress on small children, Nixon aimed his argument squarely at those who feared that the education of white children would be impaired if they attended classes with blacks.

In September in Anaheim, California (not in Wallace's de jure segregated Deep South), Nixon said, "I do not believe that education is served by taking children who are two or three grades behind and busing them across to another district." The same month in a television interview beamed throughout North Carolina and South Carolina, Nixon attacked the federal government's attempt to enforce integration. He maintained, "When you go beyond [the 1954 Supreme Court decision banning school segregation] and say that it is the responsibility of the federal government and the federal courts to, in effect, act as local school districts in determining how we carry that out, and then use the power of the federal treasury to withhold funds or give funds in order to carry it out, then I think we are going too far." In October, Nixon's vice-presidential running mate, Gov. Spiro Agnew of Maryland, said on "Face the Nation" that demonstrators—including those who had participated in the Montgomery bus boycott some thirteen years earlier—"should not be tolerated" because "they let individuals decide which laws to obey or break." And in November, Nixon accused Democrats of "giving aid and comfort to those who [were] tearing down respect for law by burning their draft cards." In the same speech, he pledged to appoint "strict constructionists" to the federal bench "who saw their duty as interpreting the law and not making law . . . not superlegislators with a free hand to impose their social and political viewpoints upon the American people."[52]

When the polls closed in New Hampshire, McCarthy's showing of 42 percent astounded the pundits, nearly all of whom hailed McCarthy's "victory" as an indication of the public's reversal on the Vietnam War issue. That perception, pounded into the American consciousness by an unremitting media exegesis on the primary, changed the course of history: it provided the impetus for Robert Kennedy to enter the presidential race; it likely hastened Johnson's decision to launch a peace offensive in Vietnam without waiting for an initial overture from Hanoi that, in the opinion of Henry Kissinger, for one, might have facilitated a compromise and a quicker end to the war; it persuaded opinion molders like the journalist Harry Reasoner that the New Hampshire results signaled "the final realization that basic Middle America did not believe in that war anymore." The truth—at least as far as New Hampshire was concerned—was far different from the perception. To begin with, McCarthy's 42 percent represented less than twenty-three thousand voters—not exactly a major chunk of Americana. Second, Johnson, as a write-in candidate, outran McCarthy by six and a half percentage points, or thirty-five hundred votes. Third, three out of five people who voted for McCarthy said they believed that Johnson should exercise *more* force in Vietnam, not less. And finally, a plurality of those voting for McCarthy in New Hampshire in March ended up voting for Wallace in November.[53]

The spring and summer of 1968 became a blur of shock and tragedy for the nation and for Wallace. The initial jolt was President Johnson's announcement on March 31 that he would "neither seek nor accept" renomination, throwing the Democratic race wide open. Four days later, Martin Luther King, Jr., was assassinated, touching off dozens of urban riots. Barely a month after that, on May 7, Lurleen Wallace died; and beyond Wallace's personal loss were the prospective corollary losses to his campaign precipitated by Lurleen's death. The first was whether Lurleen's successor, Lt. Gov. Albert Brewer, would allow dozens of state-employed "volunteers" to continue working for the presidential candidate (he did—until about a month before the election). The second was whether the counsel of the Wallaces' minister—namely, that propriety required Wallace to stay off the campaign trail for thirty days after the funeral—would cripple the third party's finances (it did not, despite Wallace's absence from about twenty rallies.) Then, just as Wallace was emerging from what he termed his period of self-imposed "seclusion," Robert Kennedy was murdered. Ahead lay the tumultuous Democratic National Convention in Chicago. But through it all, Wallace sensed correctly that the national churning was strengthening his hand.[54]

Each time a Wallace rally was accompanied by some disorderly protest—which occurred more often than not—the Alabamian gained new sympathizers. In Omaha, about a hundred hecklers threw placards, chunks of wood, and coins in the direction of Wallace, who cried out, "These are the free speech people." Then police waded in, triggering what one observer called a "wild, bloody, and sometimes brutal clash." Wallace was whisked from the auditorium, but a night of rioting swept Omaha. In a typical reaction, Eva Chess, a seventy-year-old widow who witnessed the disruption, declared her support for Wallace because she said that the major-party candidates were "too permissive" toward criminals and needed "a little push to make them realize that people [were] tired of crime in the streets."[55]

At a Minneapolis rally, demonstrators grabbed a stack of signed petitions from a desk and ripped them to shreds. In the ensuing struggle, an Alabama state trooper was thrown to the floor; he pulled his gun and cracked it over the head of a demonstrator, knocking him unconscious. The fracas was quelled without further injury. The next day, the airwaves and newspapers were filled with apologies to Wallace and admonitions against violence-prone hecklers.

Turmoil in the nation also made Wallace's candidacy more attractive to the members of groups and organizations whose very lives depended on orderliness, such as the police and the military. The Fraternal Order of Police invited Wallace to keynote their national convention; when he spoke, Wallace for President banners were unfurled throughout the hall. Wallace had the crowd on its feet almost continuously, telling the delegates that if the police "were allowed to carry out the law and were backed up by the judges and the courts [they would] cut out [the] tremendous increase in crime on the streets." He predicted darkly (and presciently), "[In future years] a woman driving a car when she comes to a traffic light, and a car comes up beside her with several men in it, she'll have to lock her doors and be skittish and worry about what they might do. It's just a terrible situation we've got in this supposed civilized nation. People cannot walk the streets at night without fear of bodily harm."

The major veterans' organizations—the American Legion, the Veterans of Foreign Wars, and the Disabled American Veterans— enthusiastically received Wallace (a member of all three). Besides issuing the sure applause lines about traitorous college professors and draft-card burners, Wallace insisted that the federal government was obligated to increase programs for veterans—including those then fighting in Vietnam—and provide nursing homes when they grew old. "It's going to be a strain on the budget," he said, "but we should look after those who saved our country from being destroyed."

A sense that America was losing its bearings led Ezra Taft Benson, a Mormon leader and Eisenhower cabinet member, to endorse Wallace personally and sponsor his appearance before a standing-room-only crowd of more than fourteen thousand at the Mormon Tabernacle.

Among the ethnic groups that were drawn to Wallace for a variety of reasons, one in particular seemed to view him with special affection—American Indians. As noted in chapter 11, the attraction had begun in Wisconsin in the 1964 primaries when Wallace had chided liberals for weeping over Southern blacks while ignoring the plight of the Indians in their own state. In 1968, several tribal chiefs and their wives sat on stage with Wallace at the riotous Omaha rally; one of the chiefs, a large, athletic man, waded into the crowd on Wallace's behalf and, the candidate recalled, "floored every [heckler] that came by with his fist."[56]

Wallace faced real problems, though, while he observed a formal period of mourning throughout May. The nature of the publicity surrounding his wife's death—nearly all of it focused on the impact it would have on the presidential campaign—called into question Wallace's sensitivity. Even when a news story alluded to Wallace's sorrow, the tone was of genuine surprise, as in this commentary by Ben A. Franklin of the *New York Times*:

Last week, the human Wallace emerged—briefly. Close observers of the Wallace cult in Alabama discerned grief in the former governor's face and manner as he attended to the state funeral and family arrangements following the difficult and lingering death of his wife, Lurleen, at the age of forty-one. It

was a natural and affecting—but nonetheless novel—
revelation.⁵⁷

The media greeted Albert Brewer with faint praise—colorless,
but at least someone who would give Alabama and the nation some
respite from Wallace—"the vivid, tough, cigar-chewing, constantly
calculating, segregationist, and demagogical politician."⁵⁸ Brewer,
reporters wrote, was "far less inclined than Mr. Wallace to pick
fruitless feuds with the federal government to enhance his image of a
cocky, bantam rooster fighter held dear by the voters at home."⁵⁹

In addition to Lurleen's death, Wallace was distracted by
charges that his top campaign adviser, Seymore Trammell, had been
forcing asphalt companies to pay "commissions" and make political
contributions in return for state highway contracts. A few days before
Wallace returned to the campaign trail, a federal civil suit brought by
some companies was settled out of court, on undisclosed terms; but
Judge Frank Johnson required Trammell to pay the court costs.⁶⁰ It
was the first intimation (but not the last) that Trammell, so valuable
to Wallace in raising money, might be in business for himself.

Of more immediate concern to Wallace's ultimate vote-getting
ability was the increasing number of major-party politicians who were
beginning to steal his thunder. During Wallace's mourning period
in May, for example, Governor Reagan of California toured the
hustings—and, but for the accent and polished, scripted delivery, he
might well have been mouthing Wallace's lines. In New Orleans
on May 19, Reagan called campus dissidents "rabble rousers and
hate-mongers, members of the New Left who are really unwashed
members of the old right practicing storm trooper tactics." Their
demonstrations, he said, "have nothing to do with civil rights or
equal treatment; they know it and we know it." He also condemned
college administrators for having "abdicated their authority" by refusing to act against students who participated in disturbances. In
Washington, D.C., the next day, Reagan described a demonstration
by poor people in the nation's capital—the Poor People's Campaign—as a "fraud on the poor" because it engendered false hopes.
Winging to Florida, Reagan evoked the images of riots in Newark and
Detroit, tied them to what he described as failed federal policies, and
asserted that the duty of government was "to protect society from
lawbreakers instead of the other way around."⁶¹

■   ■   ■

Wallace emerged from seclusion on June 11 for a rally in Memphis. If gaining ballot position in California had demonstrated the Wallace campaign's viability, then the Memphis rally displayed its authenticity. After California, the Wallace campaign was a million dollars in debt—the amount that Trammell had borrowed personally to finance the massive California petition drive. The publicity generated by Wallace's unlikely success in California triggered an outpouring of contributions that kept the campaign in the black for the duration. The Memphis rally, on the other hand, went relatively unnoticed by the media—but not by Wallace campaign directors. It was the start of an eight-state, eleven-day campaign swing through Dixie in which the opener at Memphis was downplayed by the staff to dampen media expectations. It was suggested, not unreasonably, that Wallace would need a few days back on the campaign trail—and the publicity accompanying his return—to rekindle the sort of widespread enthusiasm he had generated before Lurleen's death. Wallace, knowing that a month out of the headlines was an eternity in a political campaign, was apprehensive about the crowds he could draw in Memphis. Bill Jones recalled:

> It was the first rally after Lurleen's death, and I had set up a $100-a-plate luncheon, a $25-a-plate dinner, and rented a hall that seated thirteen thousand. The governor almost beat me out of Montgomery when he found out I'd rented that hall. He swore we couldn't get thirteen thousand in Memphis. I told him we've either got to go all the way or get out. When we got to Memphis, we had a full house for the dinner. And when we got to the rally, people were hanging off the rafters. . . . We set out to raise $50,000. We raised over $100,000. . . . That's when I knew we were on our way.[62]

"The remarkable thing," the *Newsweek* correspondent Joseph Cumming noted as he followed Wallace's campaign swing, "is that Wallace has scarcely added to or changed his spiel since the time before all recent events"—King's assassination, Johnson's withdrawal, Lurleen's death, and Robert Kennedy's murder. In Chattanooga, where Wallace drew six thousand people to his rally, Cumming observed, "He still talks about the two parties as tweedledum and tweedledee, raises hell with the Supreme Court and pseudo-intellectuals (and professors) with pointed heads who can't even park their bicycles straight. . . . Breakdown of law and order is still the fault of the country's permissive liberals who say, 'We've got to remove the *causes*'—(heavy sarcasm)—'Well, there is no cause ever for anyone burning down and looting an American city . . .' While Wallace was saying the same old things, the same old things apparently were on people's minds because he got the same old snap-clapping response."[63]

Wallace's campaign style had not changed either. Wallace would arrive in town at ten in the morning and conduct an airport press conference that would get him on the front page on the late editions of the afternoon newspapers. He would go directly to his hotel for a private lunch with "big" contributors whose identities were kept carefully shielded from the press. Wallace aides allowed the reporters to think that the average attendee gave a thousand dollars; more often than not, however, it was a hundred. And the fifteen to twenty who broke bread with Wallace often included, as one observer described it, "Jewish merchants, John Birch doctors, and wealthy right-wingers."[64] Rumors of a Mister Moneybags persisted throughout the campaign and, indeed, throughout the next four years. One important supporter was Leander Perez, a long-time political power in Louisiana whose unremitting racism resulted in his excommunication from the Roman Catholic church. Wallace said that Perez raised "quite a bit of money" for his presidential race. And he had a few Hollywood performers, including Chill Wills and Walter Brennan, in his camp, but there is no indication they offered much financial assistance.[65]

The person most often mentioned as the shadowy source of big money was the Texas oil tycoon H. L. Hunt. But no major contributions from Hunt ever were reported, and it is unlikely that Wallace would have risked breaking the law—especially as his campaigns drew sufficient funds from legitimate contributions and, in fact, showed surpluses. The historian Dan Carter wrote that Trammell, in a 1990 interview, claimed that in 1968, Hunt had handed him "a suitcase filled with three thousand $100 bills," but there is no evidence to back up Trammell's assertion. No one else connected with the campaign—neither Wallace, Jones, Joe Azbell, Charles Snider, nor anyone else—has lent the story any credence. And though H. L. Hunt's son, Bunker, contributed heavily to Wallace's gubernatorial campaign two years later, Snider, then in charge, said he received nothing then or later from the elder Hunt. Besides, Trammell, who first made the allegation more than twenty years after the event—may have been seeking a measure of revenge against Wallace for his refusal to support Trammell in fighting kickback charges (see chapter 15). Carter himself concluded that, whatever the truth of Trammell's assertion, "the real source of [Wallace's] campaign kitty was the hundreds of thousands of low- and middle-income Americans who mailed ten- and twenty-dollar contributions." Carter said the Wallace campaign modeled its direct-mail fund-raising efforts on one of the first successful radio and television evangelists in the country, Billy James Hargis.

More money poured in from Wallace's $25-a-plate dinners— $10,000 in Chattanooga, $12,500 in Atlanta, $15,000 in Jacksonville—and from his rallies at which campaign materials would be hawked throughout the evening (Wallace neckties, tie clasps, bumper stickers, lapel pins, souvenir coins with a likeness of the candidate, record albums with speech excerpts from Governors George and Lurleen) and where pretty Wallace girls would pass plastic money buckets up and down the crowded aisles.

"There is an old-fashioned quality about Wallace's campaign," Cumming observed. "The heat, the rebel yells, the flags waving, and little children dressed up [wearing] signs and looking dumbfounded. It is, in other words, a museum piece—except, before it gets roped off with red velvet festoons, it is going to scare the hell out of America's political establishment." He continued:

> It is easy to discount the crowds that follow Wallace—
> psychologically threadbare people whose anxiety with change
> draws them to Wallace; or sly old politicians who lost out
> somewhere back there and enjoy the smell of action and long
> hope of power again. But everyone senses the unease in
> America . . . and Wallace's "movement" speaks to that
> unease. . . . Just counting freckle-bellies and sapping-paws, like
> he says, "there're more of us than there are of them."[66]

A lot more than the "freckle-bellies" intended to vote for Wallace. Just before the major-party national political conventions, the pollster Louis Harris projected that, if the election were held then, Wallace would receive ten million votes, 53 percent of which came from Democrats, and 29 percent from Republicans; 59 percent of the Wallace supporters were high school graduates, and 18 percent were college graduates; more than 60 percent lived in cities, suburbs, and towns; and 75 percent of the respondents, rather than believing Wallace merely reflected any popular passing fancy, agreed instead that he had "the courage to say what he really" thought.[67]

Wallace's growing strength made him the top attraction at the

1968 Southern Governors' Conference in Charleston, South Carolina—even though he was neither a governor nor any longer the spouse of a governor. Wallace had arranged a rally in Charleston to coincide with the conference, and he impressed his one-time colleagues by packing the county hall with forty-five hundred shrieking supporters. Wallace's news conference attracted a hundred reporters as well as three of the seventeen governors attending the conference—Alabama's Brewer, Georgia's Maddox, and Mississippi's John Bell Williams. Nearly all the other governors passed up the news conference but made clear to reporters that they considered Wallace a personal friend. The only openly anti-Wallace notes were sounded by Governors Winthrop Rockefeller of Arkansas and Spiro Agnew of Maryland. Rockefeller called the Alabamian a "demagogue"; Wallace, asked to comment, said, "I know and he knows anybody in political life gets called a lot of names. I guess Governor Rockefeller has been called a few things. The Rockefellers are rich folks, and we in Alabama helped make him that way. We bought a lot of his kerosene when I was a boy in Alabama."[68] Agnew, polishing his image as a moderate Republican who might be tapped as a vice-presidential nominee, expressed "confidence in the good sense of the American people," saying, "I know they will not support a man like that." Carl Sanders, Georgia's former governor who dropped by the conference, was not so sure. He said, "[Wallace] is getting a free ride. No one here is taking issue at anything he says. He is gaining momentum every day and he is taking all the steam out of the Democratic Party in the South. If we continue to [stay silent], I don't see how anyone can cry on election day." Wallace saw no valid reason to disagree with him, saying, "I'm more attuned to the people. I know a lot more about what and how they're thinking than anybody else who wants to be president. I know they're tired of what has been going on."[69]

■   ■   ■

Mainline political organizations in the North continued to try to block Wallace's access to the ballot. In Massachusetts, Wallace needed more than 60,000 signatures to qualify. But a cabal of state and local officials threw out from 40 percent to 70 percent of the signatories on technicalities—omission of a middle initial, a seeming spelling disparity, or the slightest variation in handwriting—or because the signers were not registered as independents. But the Wallace people waged a successful publicity campaign pointing out that the Massachusetts law did not require re-registration.[70] In the end, state officials backed off and placed Wallace on the ballot. In Texas, Wallace needed only 14,000 signatures, but the law required that anyone signing up must forego voting in the Republican or Democratic primaries; he received 98,000. And in Georgia, where Wallace needed 84,000 petitioners—more than 7 percent of the vote in the 1964 presidential election—he obtained 180,000.[71] Respected Washington insiders like Robert Spivack started taking Wallace seriously; he predicted (generously, he thought) that Wallace would make the ballot in thirty states. Even so, he said that Wallace's strength outside the South was growing—and that the growth was not due to racial animosity:

> In large Northern industrial centers, his strength is among trade unionists and other lower middle-class workers who have been hard-core Democrats backing liberal social legislation almost all their lives. Now they feel so threatened by the breakdown of "law and order," or what he insists is "softness" in coping with disorders, that they are ready to vote against their own economic self-interests for a Wallace, or preferably a Ronald Reagan, or, less enthusiastically, for Richard Nixon.[72]

Spivack observed that Wallace was gaining respectability but pointed out that it was still not "fashionable" for long-time blue-collar Democrats to admit openly a preference for Wallace. And he shrewdly suggested that by election day, many of those leaning toward Wallace might well end up backing Nixon, as distasteful to them as that may have seemed.[73]

Labor leaders shared Spivack's view. They feared that rank-and-file union members were deserting Hubert Humphrey, who had recently been nominated for president at the tumultuous Democratic National Convention in Chicago, and flocking to Wallace. Polls of United Auto Workers locals in New Jersey and Illinois gave Wallace 80 percent of the total in one, and 90 percent in the other. Textile Workers Union members in the Carolinas and New England flocked to Wallace rallies, and many steelworkers in Gary and Pittsburgh were signing up as Wallace volunteers. The reasons, though racially related, were at bottom economic. The general complaint among white unionists was that management, to comply with federal regulations regarding government contracts, was hiring many unqualified blacks and training some for jobs that would advance them over more experienced workers. One spokesman for the United Steelworkers said he strongly supported job opportunities for blacks, but he added, "It's got to be *true* equality. Our guys have their rights, too. They've earned them." Just as important as traditional labor issues, however, was concern among working families with the growing incidence of crime and turmoil created by civil rights and antiwar protests. "The problem in the streets is more important" than labor issues, a unionist said in an interview. "Wallace seems to be the man who can straighten the country out."[74]

■ ■ ■

There was no way, however, that Wallace could shed his segregationist past. Jules Witcover, writing in the *Progressive*, spoke for most other national media representatives when he said, "[Wallace's] potential for creating mischief and for fanning passions in both North and South rests not only on the state of racial unrest in the big Northern cities and the country at large. It is bolstered by this clever and cocky little man's considerable talent for wrapping racism in rationalizations that permit many voters to go along without much nagging from their consciences. . . . He never mentions racism and, increasingly, he has put his candidly segregationist views on the back burner. Defending 'property rights' is just as effective and the message just as clear."[75] It would become an article of faith among national journalists, Northern Democrats, and liberal Republicans that anyone criticizing growing federal involvement in housing and business, ballooning welfare costs, or increasing crime rates was, by definition, a closet racist.

As Wallace continued to climb in the polls—9 percent in April, 14 percent in May and June, 16 percent in July—journalists started considering that white people supported him for reasons beyond racism, although overlooking the reality that problems of crime and taxes affected citizens of all races. "Rather surprisingly," Susanna McBee wrote in *Life*, "Wallace raids into the alien North have found a welcome among many people of substantial place and means." She continued:

> But his primary pitch seems targeted dead center on middle-class and on lower-middle-class whites. Here lie resentments about high taxes, inflation, and crime, along with the sullenness of people who feel that they are left out in the cold while the country's leadership pampers the undeserving

shiftless. Both North and South, Wallace appears to be
tapping a powerful underground stream of frustration and
discontent.[76]

Without question, Wallace's tough talk endeared him to those
people both outraged and frightened by street crime and riots. When
hecklers, often blacks, tried drowning him out at rallies, as they did in
a suburb of Providence, Rhode Island, he would snarl at the clique
and then shout, "These are the folks that people like us are sick and
tired of. You've been getting a good lesson in what we've been talking
about. They talk about free speech but won't allow it to others." He
told reporters he would stop urban riots by shooting looters and
arsonists on the spot. Wallace's law-and-order rhetoric inevitably attracted right-wing militants (who were dropped from official campaign positions when they expressed their views publicly). But it also
spurred both Nixon and Humphrey to parrot much of Wallace's
language. "There are three men running for sheriff of the United
States," a one-time McCarthy supporter said in September, "and no
one running for president." As the election loomed closer, however,
Nixon decided to make the law-and-order theme central to his campaign in an overt quest to appropriate the issue from Wallace; he
would succeed, he thought, because voters would soon realize that
Wallace could not be elected and would switch to Nixon as the
electable law-and-order candidate.[77]

Ultimately, both Nixon's calculated appeal for the law-and-order
vote and Humphrey's late emotional crusade for the return of traditional Democrats would cut sharply into Wallace's support. But moving into mid-September, Wallace was still gaining in the polls—and
without benefit of a strong campaign organization or traditional
media blitzes. In Michigan, the journalist Jon Lowell marveled, "Despite an almost invisible Wallace campaign, at least in the populous
urban areas, Wallace's strength has doubled—from eight percent of
the vote just preceding the GOP national convention to sixteen
percent in a poll completed prior to the events [at the Democratic
National Convention] in Chicago." Wallace's big Michigan upsurge
came after the publicity attending his speech at the national convention of the Veterans of Foreign Wars and his subsequent appearances
on a number of local radio and television interview and call-in programs. (In the end, Wallace fell to 10 percent of Michigan's vote, and
it appeared that the bulk of the defectors provided Humphrey with
the winning edge in that state.) In Illinois, the reporter Don Holt

concluded, "The Wallace campaign in Illinois is like the air. You can't see it, but it is all around you. There is no visible campaign structure—no headquarters, no billboards, no media advertising (except for a one-time, thirty-minute television special appealing for funds). But he will be on the ballot in Illinois and the best estimates are that he will get sixteen percent or better of the Illinois vote." (Wallace fell to 8 percent by election day, but he retained enough usually Democratic votes to deny the state to Humphrey, who lost by three percentage points.) The old-line segregationist and political dabbler Roy V. Harris, Wallace's campaign director in Georgia, explained bluntly, "We haven't got much organization; we don't need it."[78]

The journalist Marshall Frady, who had spent nine months in Montgomery and "countless hours" with Wallace in preparation for a book on the Alabamian, believed that Wallace had instinctively discovered "a new politics of his own—at once absurdly simple and ingenious: he [was], in his own way, dealing in 'people politics,' that general phenomenon of our time."[79]

> Power to him does not lie in the traditional equations of press and business and political establishment support. He operates outside the conventional political wisdom, has bypassed the classic brokers of political power [and] could even be called a revolutionary. If the cliché were ever true of a significant political figure in this country, he has nobody but the people—and just how many of his people there are in this nation is, aside from the dishevelment he may cause the normal presidential election process, the most unsettling specter raised by his candidacy.

Except for his overheated vision that Wallace might usher in a fascist era in America, Frady came closest among the journalists of that time to understanding the secret of Wallace's success:

> It's doubtful any other recent national figure—I mean this—has operated with the uncanny and total and undistracted instincts for the primitive dynamics of the American democratic system as [Wallace] has. That's why he is—almost innocently and accidentally—the absolute product of the democratic system. But then, the ultimate democratic politician is probably the demagogue anyway. But, as I said, his formula is almost childishly naive: power lies with the folks and

nothing else. . . . The thought of George actually occupying the White House is still like an Ionescan nightmare. But one of his fundamental strengths throughout his national adventuring [is] that he has been consistently underestimated. He has just been too baroque for most of the conventional custodians of reality—the pundits, etcetera—to accept, which may come to testify to a profound chasm that has existed all along between what most of us thought this nation was and wanted, and what it actually is and wants.[80]

■   ■   ■

In early September, Wallace's American Independent party still had no platform, though Wallace promised it would develop one soon. So the *Miami News* offered one in a cartoon showing Wallace as a barefoot country boy reading a scroll labeled "Wallace Platform":

- 1. Run over hippies with yore car.
- 2. Win war—somehow.
- 3. Throw bureaucrats' briefcases in Potomac.
- 4. Run over Yippies with yore car.
- 5. Throw bureaucrats in Potomac.
- 6. Wave yore flag.
- 7. Put crooks in jail.
- 8. Put Supreme Court in jail.
- 9. Put pink press in jail.
- 10. Get law and order.
- 11. Get a dime's worth of difference.

But Wallace was no joke, and many of his critics were beginning to exhibit primal fear of his potential power and the national disaster they believed it portended. Charles Morgan, a one-time Birmingham lawyer who had become an executive of the American Civil Liberties Union, said ominously, "He is the anti-Christ." The journalist Robert Sherrill, who earlier had tried unsuccessfully to damage Wallace by reporting about his cronyism and alleged Klan connections, now pleaded for Wallace's opponents to somehow "crush him as Orval Faubus was crushed at Little Rock, [so] his career [would] never again seriously seep past the boundaries of Alabama."[81] The Wallace movement prompted the militant black leader Stokely Carmichael to predict, "[Whites] are getting ready to commit genocide against us"; and even the black intellectual and author James Baldwin wrote,

"White America appears to be seriously considering the possibility of mass extermination."[82] But Wallace's opponents were so preoccupied with his racist origins that they tended to ignore the deeper, stronger bonds he was forming with the electorate. *Newsweek*'s Joseph Cumming, a Southerner himself, offered this penetrating analysis of how Wallace was exploiting a torrent of liberal proposals flowing from Congress and a proliferation of Cassandra-like academic reports on national problems:

> No one seemed to notice the mystical communion Wallace was developing with thousands, then millions, of quietly panicked Americans. The left wing was where all the action was taking place with its new doctrines of "participatory democracy." But that very ideal was being threaded together by Wallace and used to give a form of protest to citizens impatient with the intellectualization of problems, of commissions and their grave improbable findings, of a sociological jargon too "new fashioned" to grasp.[83]

Wallace's support seemed to turn up in unlikely places. When the candidate walked into the decorous Fleur de Lis restaurant in Miami's Fontainebleu Hotel, the diners (many of whom were vacationing New Yorkers) spontaneously burst into applause. And after Senator McCarthy dropped out of the presidential race, a number of his "Clean for Gene" backers on college campuses switched, amazingly, to Wallace and handed out literature on his behalf door-to-door and in shopping centers. One of the new Wallace volunteers, an Illinois college student, explained that he had been disillusioned and embittered after the Democratic National Convention; he wasn't so much pro-Wallace as antiestablishment.[84] The most bizarre group of Wallace supporters turned up in Albany, New York—Hippies for Wallace, some fifty long-haired, sandal-clad young people carrying signs reading "Wallace Is a Good Trip" and "Freak Out with George." A reporter thought it was a put-on until one of the group told him, "Wallace is straight, man. He tells it like it is. We need law and order. It's tough enough walking on the streets when you look like I do." When hecklers nearby started shouting, "*Sieg heil,*" the self-styled hippie called out, "Like, shut up, man, you're ruining my thing."[85]

Wallace attracted some support he would rather have done without. At one of his twenty-five-dollar-a-plate dinners in the town of Eutaw, Alabama, the Ku Klux Klan imperial wizard, Robert Shelton, was among the paying guests. When an ABC cameraman filmed Shelton being greeted by Wallace, a Wallace bodyguard confiscated the film. But Wallace wired his apologies to ABC for the incident and assured its news executives that he welcomed the network's coverage of the campaign.[86] And during a campaign swing through Indiana in August, Dick Smith, one of Wallace's chief fund-raisers, was persuaded by a shapely, fortyish model named Ja-Neen Welch that she was the original Miss Dodge Rebellion (of a recent and successful series of television commercials) and that she would add some glamour to the Wallace rallies. Dressed in skin-tight cowgirl outfits of gold lamé, she would rush to a microphone and, after Smith had implored the faithful to fill up the plastic money buckets, coo suggestively, "The Wallace rebellion wants you!" Smith started souring on Welch within a month when he was told by reporters that the Dodge public relations office had never heard of her; apparently, Welch had made some commercials for local Dodge dealers in which she impersonated the model in the network ads. And, in Alabama, after Welch posed with a congressional candidate who was seeking to identify himself with Wallace, Smith instructed her to dissociate herself from the campaign. Wallace at first had thought that having the Dodge Rebellion girl in his entourage was a coup (even though, after meeting her up close, he allowed to a security guard, "I reckon television makes you look younger than you really are," to which the guard replied, without gallantry, "She must have been Miss Dodge Rebellion of 1928"). But Welch persisted. She followed the campaign to Florida, was seen shepherding Wallace's seven-year-old daughter Lee around an Orlando hotel, and finally called a news conference to announce her impending marriage to the former governor. Fortunately for Wallace, no one in the press corps took her seriously; Wallace instructed his staff and Secret Service agents to keep her far away from him, and Welch, seemingly satisfied with her fifteen minutes of fame, finally gave up.[87]

■ ■ ■

The campaign itself started taking on a sleeker, sharper look. In addition to guitar pickers and country singers, the twelve-piece brass band from Alabama's Troy State College joined the candidate in campaign rallies around the country.[88] Lissome, long-tressed Alabama coeds traveled from rally to rally to help plump for contributions, while a rotating company of 125 more college students from Alabama, Georgia, Florida, and Louisiana volunteered to help with advance preparations for upcoming Wallace campaign stops. A rickety prop-driven DC-6 was traded for an only slightly better DC-7, but later for two Lockheed Electra prop-jets. Wallace crowds, according to one reporter, were "improving in class as well as size," encompassing stylishly dressed men and women—doctors, lawyers, engineers, insurance underwriters, and realtors—as well as those in overalls and cotton dresses from the mills and the farms, the ones Wallace described as the "peapickers, peckerwoods, crackers, and rednecks" who composed the foundation of his support. Even the press badges, on which names had been scrawled by hand, were replaced by arty printed versions.[89]

The new badges were small comfort to reporters used to the nurturing care and feeding they enjoyed when traveling with the major-party candidates. Wallace's campaign plane carried no alcoholic beverages and only snack food: liquid refreshments were confined to Cokes, orange juice, and milk (no hot coffee); snacks were limited to cookies, Tom's Peanuts, Cracker Jacks, and candy bars. Because no schedules were issued to the press, reporters relied on word of mouth to find out when the plane would depart for the next stop—and often received different information from different aides. As a result, reporters were left behind occasionally; twice in one week in late September, the Wallace plane took off without the correspondent from *Time* magazine. Once on the ground, reporters frequently found that the bus to transport them from the airport had left prematurely or failed to show up at their hotel to take them to the evening's rally. Wallace apologized profusely; he responded to press complaints by assigning a Secret Service agent to shepherd the reporters on and off the press plane and to and from campaign sites. Still, when arriving at an airport, Wallace would risk missing media deadlines by rushing past waiting reporters to greet cheering, sign-waving supporters behind security barricades; his airport news conferences would begin only after he had touched every extended hand in the crowd.[90] Most other candidates planned their campaigns around news deadlines so they could "go from one media center to another . . . to be seen shaking hands" with or visiting prospective voters, as Jimmy Carter observed years later, making the point that it is less important for a politician to see the people than it is to be *seen* seeing the people.[91]

Nonetheless, an atmosphere of grudging respect developed between Wallace and the entourage of reporters following his campaign. When he chided the press during campaign speeches, he would pause, gesture to the press table below the podium, and add, "Course, now, I don't mean to include these fellas who been traveling with me. They're all good fellas." And when the reporters jokingly demanded whisky on the press plane, Wallace replied, "I can't handle you fellas sober. I don't know what I'd do if you were all drunk." (Actually, national reporters with generous expense accounts carried their own bottles aboard and shared the liquor with their less-well-heeled colleagues.) But Wallace worked hard to win the reporters' friendship. Aboard the press plane, a reporter need only plop down next to the candidate to ask a question or two; the other candidates were usually unapproachable without prior permission from a key staff member. On the road, Wallace would usually rest between appearances; but if he was not asleep, he would make himself available in his hotel room to any journalists who had asked to see him. As one reporter put it, "The best source is Wallace himself."[92]

But if those following the campaign began to see a gentler, kinder Wallace, nothing had changed in his aggressive attacks on the federal establishment or in his capacity to galvanize his supporters with rousing, confrontational oratory, as in this mid-September speech at a rally in Cape Girardeau, Missouri:

> When [politicians] succumb to anarchists in the street, then
> they haven't got what it takes to lead us out of the morass. . . .
> We're going to take some of these students by the hair of the
> head and see if we can't stick 'em under a good federal
> jail. . . . I'm sick and tired of some professors and some
> preachers and some judges and some newspaper editors
> having more to say about my everyday life . . . than I have to
> say it about it myself. I am going to give the moral support of
> the presidency to the police and firemen in your city and
> through your state. Let me tell you something: if it wasn't for
> the police and firemen in your city, you wouldn't be able to
> even ride down your streets, much less walk down them. . . .
> I'm going to take every communist out of every defense plant
> in . . . every state in the union. Let me tell you something else:
> when I become your president, I'm going to ask my attorney
> general to seek an indictment against any college professor

who calls for a communist victory [in Vietnam]. . . . That's not dissent. That's not free speech. That's treason.[93]

"The ensuing tumult," reporter Jim Hampton of the *National Observer* said following a Wallace speech in Dallas, "is louder than Richard Nixon or Hubert Humphrey will ever hear."[94] Wallace's rallies rarely drew crowds of fewer than 4,000 people; sometimes he drew throngs at outdoor rallies: 13,000 at Burnett Park in Fort Worth and 20,000 at the Boston Common.[95]

■   ■   ■

Wallace continued to oppose civil rights, voting rights, and open housing laws, but he insisted that his objections represented aversion to federal control, not hostility toward blacks. He said he favored civil rights as defined in the Constitution—freedom of speech, press, religion, and assembly, and the right to a jury trial. He opposed the government "in the name of civil rights trying to control the property rights of people [and] the seniority list of labor unions [or] telling [restaurateurs] who they must serve." Personally, he said, he would not object to any hotel or restaurant serving blacks. He thought the Voting Rights Act was "tragic" because it meant that illiterates could vote in five Southern states—"but," he said, "if the same illiterate moves to the state of New York, he cannot vote, and that is unfair." Wallace promised to repeal the recently passed fair housing law because he said it put "people in jail" unless they sold or leased their "property to someone that a bureaucrat or a judge thought [they] ought to sell or lease it to." He said he would not advocate school segregation but, if elected, would say to the states, "You run your schools yourselves." But he strongly condemned busing to achieve racial balances in schools. In almost every speech, he would say, "If you people want to take your children and send them all the way to Montreal, Canada, to go to school, it's all right by me. . . . [But] when I am president, not one dime of federal money will be spent for busing one single student."[96]

Wallace's insistence that race had nothing to do with his positions was, of course, a sham. No one knew better than he that without federal intervention, blacks in the South would not be permitted access to public accommodations, could never hope to buy a home or rent an apartment in areas reserved for whites, would rarely be considered for job promotions over whites, would be discouraged from registering to vote, and would be effectively barred from attending the better public schools, nearly all of which were white. (And, of course, court-ordered busing for racial balance was financed locally, not federally.) Once during the campaign, he allowed his mask to slip. On September 20, returning to Montgomery from a campaign rally in Orlando, Florida, he told reporters that if he lost the election, people might "physically take over the schools through the police power" of localities. Referring to the Orlando rally, he asked rhetorically, "Did you see those women in there? They were hysterical about their children. Folks are mad about law and order and about schools. . . . Race mixing doesn't work. Show me a place where it's worked." Later, he insisted that he meant there would be a political takeover without violence—that people would "rise up at the ballot box."[97]

But what Wallace also understood, and what few others in politics or the press seemed to, was that antipathy to blacks was not central to Wallace's growing popular appeal. Widespread fear and a sense of dislocation were propelling more and more people to find someone in politics who seemed to understand them. People feared so-called hippie demonstrators every bit as much as civil rights demonstrators, if not more. They feared what seemed to be growing lawlessness, not just among the poor and disfranchised but among the privileged and well-to-do. The assassinations of King and the Kennedys made people feel vulnerable and exposed, fearful that all sense of order in their nation was coming apart. Urban riots and open sexuality on campuses shocked them. Vocal opponents to the Vietnam War were staging marches and protests that seemed to millions of others—many of whom shared their doubts about the war—to border on cowardice and treason; the fact that some of the more extreme protesters at the Democratic National Convention and at the Pentagon screamed obscenities at authorities and urinated and defecated in public only exacerbated their revulsion.

By the final weeks of the campaign, Wallace obviously had drawn his opponents to his own turf. In the words of one national correspondent, Wallace had "made law and order the controlling issue"— one that Nixon latched onto with gusto by making it the centerpiece of his national television commercial blitz. Nixon went further into Wallace territory by promising he would not withhold federal funds from segregated schools. And Humphrey, even after renouncing his president's Vietnam policies, condemned "anarchists" for domestic disruptions.[98]

Had the election been held in the first week of October, Wallace would have collected more than 15,300,000 votes and, according to a *New York Times* survey published on October 6, seemed destined to win twice as many electoral votes as Humphrey.[99] If he kept climbing in the final month of the campaign as he had in the late summer and fall, it appeared that he might well realize his goal of denying the major-party nominees a clear electoral victory.

Reporters and pollsters also found that people outside the South who earlier had been reluctant to express their pro-Wallace views publicly were beginning to speak out forcefully and unashamedly for their man. In the tobacco-belt counties in eastern North Carolina that traditionally had voted Democratic in numbers greater than Mayor Daley's Chicago, three of every four Democrats interviewed by the perceptive political observer Samuel Lubell announced they would vote for Wallace with comments like, "Wallace is the man to straighten this country out," and "he's the only one who is really for law and order."[100] In Milwaukee, several one-time McCarthy supporters had switched to Wallace—and many of them, unlike a number of college students who had made a similar leap earlier in the campaign, not entirely as a protest. "I know it's a drastic switch," Wally Porterfield, Jr., one ex-McCarthy supporter, explained, "but there are no leaders in the major parties." Another said that McCarthy "was a very honest fellow, just like Wallace." And a third, Paul Herman, added, "The major-party candidates all owe something to someone; they're afraid to step on any toes. Wallace is the only one for the people. When he speaks at a rally, you feel so close to him."[101] And in the heart of New York City, Wallace filled Madison Square Garden to the rafters with twenty-five thousand people dancing in the aisles, climbing over chairs and one another in their eagerness to toss ten-dollar bills into the collection buckets (in addition to the fifteen dollars each had paid for admission), and responding again and again with full-throated roars to Wallace's by-now patented assaults on the federal establishment. It was the high point of the long and arduous campaign. A veteran police official called it "the greatest crowd response [he'd] seen in the Garden since Franklin Delano Roosevelt" in 1936.[102] And when a Gallup poll of America's most admired men was published, Wallace placed seventh—just below Pope Paul VI and just ahead of Richard Nixon. Hubert Humphrey did not make the list.[103]

■   ■   ■

But then, perhaps inevitably, Wallace's support began to erode. A relatively small but perceptible drop was attributable to his selection of a running mate, a decision he put off as long as possible. For most of the campaign, an old friend and a former governor of Georgia, Marvin Griffin, allowed his name to be used in states where Wallace needed a vice-presidential nominee to qualify for a position on the ballot. But Griffin had no desire to be anything more than a stand-in, did more fishing than campaigning, and went for weeks at a time without even speaking to Wallace.[104] When Wallace learned that A. B. "Happy" Chandler, a former Kentucky governor, U.S. senator, and commissioner of major league baseball, would be willing to run as his vice-president, the Alabamian promptly invited him onto the ticket and aides leaked Chandler's name. Overall, the response was positive. But, according to Wallace, four state delegations of electors, including those from Kentucky, threatened to resign if Chandler remained on the ticket—and the threat demonstrated that many Wallace supporters were, indeed, fierce racists. Reportedly these electors objected to Chandler's passivity regarding two major integration developments: as baseball commissioner in 1947, he had not objected when the Brooklyn Dodgers had brought the first black player, Jackie Robinson, into major league baseball; and as governor in 1956, he had not tried to block the integration of Kentucky's public schools. The deadlines had passed for the selection of new electors, so the choices were to run in 46 states with Chandler or in 50 states with someone else. Wallace's decision showed he was dedicated less to moderating his racist image than to underlining his personal political strength.

He dumped Chandler, and he shrank from confronting him even by telephone. Instead, he dispatched three aides to Chandler's home in Versailles, Kentucky, to break the news. Afraid to generate publicity that would add to Wallace's racial patina, they blurred the reasons for pulling the rug from under the Kentuckian, leaving the impression that some well-heeled Southwestern oil interests had threatened to withdraw their support from Wallace with Chandler on the ticket. Chandler, an old pro, took the disappointing news in stride—but thought Wallace had made a mistake; in fact, Chandler believed that his record as a moderate on integration would stand Wallace in good stead as "a counterbalance" to Wallace's own harsh positions on race. And on just about every other issue, the two men were in sync—law and order, greater fiscal responsibility, less federalism, and a "win-or-get-out" Vietnam policy. In later years, Wallace defended his judgment that the symbolic importance of running in all fifty states had outweighed his commitment to Chandler. "But to come off of him without talking to him myself," he recalled with shame, "was something I will always regret. . . . I did not write him or see him," he added, his voice trailing off.[105]

It took nearly a month to repair the damage of the Chandler affair. On October 3, Wallace announced that Curtis LeMay, a former air force chief of staff would be his running mate (see chapter 3). Prior to a nationally televised news conference, Wallace, who had repeatedly told interviewers that he would not use nuclear weapons in Vietnam, anticipated that the media would press LeMay on that question. There were obvious reasons for his concern. LeMay had long been a superhawk on the U.S. role in Vietnam. In early 1964, he urged President Johnson to initiate bombing raids on North Vietnam in language the president could understand and identify with: "We are swatting flies," LeMay said, "when we should be going after the manure pile." And in a 1965 book, *Mission with LeMay*, the general had said he would end the war by telling the North Vietnamese "to draw in their horns and stop their aggression" or the United States would "bomb them back into the Stone Ages."[106] Wallace tried to prepare LeMay for what he was certain would be the principal thrust of the reporters' questions:

> General, you are used to giving orders and they would always be obeyed. But in this case, we are out here among a bunch of hungry media wolves and they want to trap you into saying you would drop nuclear bombs. One of them is going to ask you a question like this: "If the . . . United States is in danger of being obliterated from the face of the earth, would you drop nuclear bombs?" Of course, any man . . . would say, "Yes, I would drop a bomb to save our country from being annihilated." I would certainly drop a bomb. But you don't give that answer. The answer you give is this: "Listen, my friend, you are asking a purely hypothetical question . . . that would never have to be decided because we are going to be so strong under President Wallace that . . . no nuclear bomb will ever have to be dropped in our administration."[107]

LeMay tried to adhere to Wallace's cautionary advice, but he was no match for the press corps. He said, "[We] would use anything that we could dream up, including nuclear weapons, if it was necessary [but] I don't think it's necessary in this case or this war." Wallace stepped in and tried to explain what LeMay meant: "If the security of the country depended on the use of any weapon in the future, he would use it [but] we can win and defend in Vietnam without the use of nuclear weapons." LeMay tried to reinforce Wallace's comments but only got himself in deeper. He kept repeating that he did not think nuclear weapons were needed in Vietnam, but he also insisted on qualifying his statement by saying, "I would use any weapon . . . in the arsenal that is necessary. . . . I am certainly not going to . . . tell our enemies that I advocate that under all circumstances I'm not going to use nuclear weapons." The damage was done. Despite Wallace's repeated disclaimers—he said he would pull out of Vietnam before he would use nuclear weapons—Nixon, Humphrey, and dozens of editorialists and commentators painted the Wallace-LeMay ticket as reckless and dangerous.[108] For the next three days, the drumbeat of press criticism continued as LeMay joined Wallace in campaign appearances in the industrial Northeast, although the two did not travel together. LeMay would not fly on an Electra, so the campaign's transportation coordinator, Charles Snider, acquired a Boeing 727 jet for the general's exclusive use; "it cost more for a day than both Electras for a week," Snider recalled, "but it kept him quiet." When he told Wallace what they were spending for LeMay's 727, the governor shook his head and sighed, "Goddam, he's either spending all our money or dropping atomic bombs."[109] Then Wallace hit on a way to employ LeMay and simultaneously take him off the front pages; he sent him to Vietnam on "a fact-finding mission." (A member of Wallace's press entourage quipped, "I understand LeMay will be flying over and sailing back—on a slow boat.")[110]

Whatever loss in support Wallace's running-mate gaffes may have generated, they were nothing compared to the slippage caused by Nixon's and Humphrey's efforts to persuade the electorate that a vote for Wallace was a wasted vote. In a Gallup poll conducted in the week ending October 12, Nixon led Humphrey by 43 percent to 31 percent, and Wallace had slipped slightly to 20 percent of the vote.[111] Just a week later, Humphrey moved from twelve to eight points behind, but Wallace's support dropped precipitously to 15 percent. By election eve, Lou Harris showed Nixon and Humphrey only three points apart—a statistical standoff—but Wallace's support showed "real signs of slippage, most sharply among Northern union members."[112]

Additionally, strategic differences between Wallace and Trammell were pivotal to the candidate's chances of turning the tide.

Trammell wanted to pour every dollar available into television time and newspaper space during the closing days of the campaign—a million-dollar media blitz concentrated in states where Wallace was running close enough to Nixon to have a chance to win (Arkansas, Florida, the Carolinas, and Tennessee). He argued that with Humphrey closing fast on Nixon in the North, Wallace victories in a few Southern states besides the four he was certain to win (Alabama, Georgia, Louisiana, and Mississippi) might keep anyone from an electoral majority. But Jack Wallace and Ralph Adams contended that Nixon's electoral-vote lead in the polls was insurmountable, and that the GOP's likely expenditures in those same states for the same reasons would cancel out Wallace's efforts. But they won over Wallace by suggesting that the million dollars Trammell would lavish on advertising could be squirreled away instead to provide Wallace future options: a run for governor in 1970, seeking John Sparkman's seat in the Senate in 1972, or preparations for another national campaign.[113] Wallace went along with his brother and old friend. He reasoned that he had gotten as far as he had in 1968 with minimal advertising anyway and saw no reason to change; besides, though he had assured Albert Brewer that he had no intention of opposing him for governor two years hence, he was starting to reassess that commitment.[114] Jack Wallace and Adams took over the campaign's finances in the closing weeks. In the end, the campaign raised close to $10 million and spent just under $8 million; whatever happened on election day, November 5, Wallace could contemplate his future political options with a war chest of nearly $2 million.[115]

But though Wallace imposed spending limits on advertising, he tried to make up for that by stepping up his whirlwind personal campaigning. Everywhere he went, he drew huge crowds: 2,000 in Wichita Falls, Texas; 3,000 in Providence and in Cape Girardeau, Missouri; 4,000 in Dallas; 5,000 in Milwaukee and in Canton, Ohio; 5,000 in Kalamazoo and Lansing, Michigan; 6,000 in Daytona Beach and in Indianapolis; 7,000 in Tulsa, in Toledo, and in Cicero, Illinois; 8,000 in Buffalo, in Tallahassee, and in Grand Rapids, Michigan; 9,000 in Lexington, Kentucky; 10,000 in Pittsburgh and in Orlando; 11,000 in Flint, Michigan; 13,000 in Forth Worth; 15,000 (at ten dollars a head) in Montgomery; 20,000 in Boston; and 50,000 in a nine-block noontime motorcade in Chicago.[116] He was now speaking four times a day—at ten, noon, two, and four—before appearing at his twenty-five-dollar-a-plate dinners and his climactic evening rallies. He would return to his hotel at midnight with that

peculiar mixture of exhaustion and exhilaration common to politicians and performers after successful appearances. He would take a
quick shower, pull on his pajamas, and prop himself up in bed while
one of his cronies—Ralph Adams, Glen Curlie, Oscar Harper, and
Dave Silverman were among the small coterie in Wallace's inner
circle who took turns traveling with him—would sit in the room and
gab until two or three in the morning until Wallace finally nodded
off.[117]

■   ■   ■

On election day, November 5, Wallace's support had eroded to just
over 13.5 percent of the popular vote. He carried five states, winning
Arkansas along with his Deep South bastion of Alabama, Georgia,
Louisiana, and Mississippi; they were worth forty-six electoral votes.
He ran second in the Carolinas and Tennessee and, despite receiving
31 percent of the vote, third in Florida. Humphrey's surge had
carried him to within seven-tenths of a percentage point of Nixon,
but Nixon's 301 electoral votes were 31 more than needed for victory.
Wallace believed that he had deprived Humphrey of the victory, and
he was not alone in that belief. A number of analysts thought, as one
put it as recently as 1992, that Wallace "ensured the defeat of Democrat Hubert Humphrey and gave the election to Republican Richard
Nixon."[118] The view is based on exit polls suggesting that had Wallace not been in the race, enough of his supporters in Ohio, Illinois,
New Jersey, Missouri, Wisconsin, and Kentucky would have switched
to Humphrey to provide Democratic victories in those states. Even if
all the Wallace states had supported Nixon, Humphrey still would
have held a margin of victory. The flaw in the theory is that it seems
likely that, but for Wallace, Texas would have opted for Nixon rather
than Humphrey—and that switch would have given Nixon the election despite the loss of the other states.

The national press seemed eager to write Wallace off. Inside
Wallace's Montgomery headquarters, wrote one journalist, "there is
the emptiness of defeat."[119] Another described Wallace "in his windowless office" trying "wearily . . . amid the debris of defeat to determine just how badly he . . . had been hurt. The answer, in terms of
national stature and the foreseeable future, seemed to be fatally."[120]
He said he had no intention of running for governor, but he would
not rule out another try for the presidency—leaving open the possibility that he might even run as a Democrat.[121] But in fact, Wallace

was already aiming for the governorship; he simply did not want to alert Brewer too early. Financially, with his huge campaign surplus, he could afford to bide his time. He asked his long-time aide Taylor Hardin to act as the executive director of a continuing organization called "The Wallace Campaign"—an enigmatic title that would suggest action without indicating what Wallace was campaigning for. The newspaperman Joe Azbell agreed to lend his prolific writing talents part-time to the group, and Charles Snider, the thirty-eight-year-old Montgomery businessman who had coordinated transportation and travel in the 1968 campaign, stayed on full-time to coordinate the Wallace Campaign's day-to-day activities. Snider sold his construction business, established Wallace Campaign headquarters in a new two-story building on the south side of Montgomery, hired two clerks and a secretary, enlisted a few volunteers, and went to work consolidating and updating mailing lists of the people who had contributed to Wallace during the campaign.

Within a few months, there were twenty-two full-time staffers—more than were employed by the Democratic National Committee in Washington—assisting Snider, sorting and answering mail, receiving visitors, and responding to telephone requests for information. Azbell started grinding out a monthly newsletter that carried a page-long message from Wallace and articles about national problems ranging from campus unrest to the Vietnam War to high taxes. The first issue of the newsletter, in which Wallace vowed to continue his crusade, was sent to a million people on Snider's growing mailing list; the recipients were invited to subscribe for twelve dollars a year. Before long, there were forty thousand subscribers; the number would reach a quarter of a million during the 1972 presidential primaries. For his part, Wallace gave a speech or two a month before professional or civic groups around the country, and the accompanying publicity helped to keep his name before the voters. But he spent most of his time roaming Alabama, calling on old political allies, or holding court at his new Montgomery offices for the streams of politicians and well-wishers who dropped by.[122] He took special pleasure in telling callers that two of his most prized accomplishments of the 1968 race were winning a plurality of the absentee ballots cast by American soldiers in Vietnam, and carrying Alabama's Jefferson County, which encompasses Birmingham, for the first time.[123]

While much of the media were eager to bury Wallace, others knew he would be back. As noted in chapter 15, Nixon spared no expense in trying to block Wallace's national comeback in 1972 by financing Wallace's state-level opponent in 1970. And one of the most incisive political analysts of the day, the one-time Census Bureau chief Richard Scammon, perceived that Wallace's message was too effective not to be reprised. He said that Wallace had struck a deep chord in Americans with his broad condemnation of central government and bureaucracy, and with his defense of hard work and free enterprise, which were supposedly being undermined by his ever-present gallery of villains—"Communists, anarchists, beatniks, and hippies." But, Scammon wrote, "most of all there is the appeal for law and order, the demand for a return to domestic tranquility."

Predicting that the Wallace "phenomenon" would be seen again in 1972, Scammon said, "Wallace is a campaigner, and a good one. He is a politician, and a first-rate one. Above all else, he is an authentic spokesman for millions of Americans."[124]

Wallace enthusiastically agreed with Scammon's conclusions, with a single exception: he did not think there was anything phenomenal about his political strength. "A phenomenon is something you can't explain," he told me ten months after the election. "I can explain it."

> When the government tries to force masses of people against their will to conform to certain guidelines involving their children, their taxes, their labor unions, their property, it would have been a phenomenon if they had not given vent to their antagonism and anger at this drive to try to make everyone conform to what the pseudo-intellectual thought the average citizen should conform to. . . . My vote was only the tip of an iceberg. . . . Now there are others I'm responsible for— [Sam] Yorty, [Charles] Stenvig, [Ed] Koch. They were making Alabama speeches with a Los Angeles, Minneapolis, and New York accent. The only thing they omitted was the drawl.

He said that many members of Congress were starting to sound more like him as well—people like Edith Green of Oregon, Roman Pucinski of Illinois, and Wayne Hays of Ohio, indicating that the Wallace message went beyond racism. Racism had increased in America, he maintained, but not because of him; it was exacerbated by big government. He formulated a theorem of sorts: "Racism has grown in proportion to the rapidity of the coercion exerted by the government through the influence of the liberals to make the masses do that which they didn't want to do." He conceded that government pressure had "brought about some things [for blacks] that wouldn't have come about" and said rhetorically, "but when you lose peace and tranquility, and ill will exists among the races as a result of some so-called improvements, then, really, have you had improvements?" He then insisted that race was not the problem in America, merely a symptom of general frustration over the Vietnam War, school busing, increasing crime, higher taxes, and overall resentment of an intrusive government.[125]

■   ■   ■

The remedy, Wallace said immodestly, was him. "People all over this country want to keep the movement alive. If I've got to run for governor to do that, I will. If I've got to run for president again, I will."[126]

The cat was out of the bag. Despite his earlier insistence to the contrary, Wallace would run for governor and use the job as a springboard to another national campaign. To justify breaking his promise to Brewer, Wallace asserted improbably that had Brewer campaigned for him in Brewer's native Tennessee he might have carried the state. Never mind that Brewer had been a stand-in for Wallace at numerous twenty-five-dollar-a-plate dinners; he only did that, Wallace declared, to "ingratiate himself" with Wallace's supporters.[127]

Explanations, however empty, out of the way, Wallace set about to reclaim the governor's chair that, but for his wife's death, still would have been occupied by a Wallace. He thought it would be easy. It would be anything but. Ironically, though he had detected widespread unhappiness across America with the politicians in Washington, he was unaware of forces gathering against him right under his nose in Alabama.

15

Triumph and Tragedy

$\mathbf{A}$*LMOST FROM THE DAY AFTER* the 1968 election, George Wallace knew that his continued national stature depended on a successful run for governor in 1970. Without the governorship, he would have no launching pad for another presidential campaign in 1972. But should he lose the race in his own state, his national political career would be over. His thirst for the national spotlight overwhelmed any risk, however, so George set his sights on taking back his and Lurleen's job from the lusterless, mediocre incumbent, Albert Brewer. Despite Wallace's persistent disclaimers of interest in challenging his one-time acolyte, Brewer was virtually the only Alabama politician who was, like the cuckolded husband in one of Boccaccio's tales, gullible enough to believe him.[1]

The veteran Alabama political reporter Bob Ingram, who had become Brewer's finance director, remembered Wallace telling Brewer, "The only Wallace candidate who will be running for governor in 1970 will be you." But Wallace provided visitors to his perpetual campaign headquarters with varying reasons why he might change his mind; if one reason did not seem credible to the listener, he would come up with another. The selection included: Brewer's failure to campaign in Tennessee for the Wallace-LeMay ticket (as if that alone would have made up Wallace's thirty-five-thousand-vote deficit there); Brewer's failure to take a hard enough line against federal imposition of integration (as though Wallace was not trying to soften his own segregationist stance); Brewer's hiring of several supposed "enemies" of Wallace (although Wallace would not name any); Brewer's supposed spending of "big money" to promote his candidacy for reelection (as if that were somehow dirty pool in Alabama politics).[2] Wallace offered one justification for breaking his word to Brewer that, because it involved a candid admission of impropriety, at least had the distinction of sounding plausible: supposedly, Brewer had refused Wallace's request to use the perquisites of the governor's office for his upcoming presidential campaign. Wallace said that he had confronted Brewer early in 1970 and had told him, "When you get in line with [my opponents] and don't let me use the office of governor [to] help me as a jump-off [point] for running in primaries, well . . . I told you I wouldn't run for governor under certain circumstances; those circumstances don't exist anymore."[3] But if such actions had meant not having to face Wallace in an election, Brewer would have willingly opened the state treasury to the 1972 Wallace presidential campaign, just as he had continued Lurleen's practice of furnishing state-paid personnel to Wallace's 1968 campaign.

Besides, Wallace and Brewer could not have clashed in early 1970 over what support he could expect during the primaries; Wallace did not decide until sometime in 1971 that he would, indeed, compete in the Democratic presidential primaries.[4]

■   ■   ■

Though the obvious first order of business was to campaign for governor, Wallace never took his eyes off the big prize. Taylor Hardin oversaw campaign office functions (including finances after Jack Wallace and Ralph Adams returned to their regular jobs) and meaningfully changed Wallace's headquarters address in Montgomery from P.O. Box 1968 to P.O. Box 1972. Charles Snider, who was given the title of campaign chairman, was refining his million-name mailing list, categorizing supporters by zip code, sex, age, occupation, and principal issue concerns. Joe Azbell produced the Wallace newsletter and started laying plans for additional communiques aimed at diverse groups that could be isolated by Snider's increasingly sophisticated mailing lists. And a young South Carolina lawyer named Tom Turnipseed, who worked as a state organizer for Wallace's ballot-position drive in 1967 and 1968, was added as the campaign director;

Turnipseed was to start traveling the country to revivify Wallace's state organizations.[5]

By any measure, Wallace's most spectacular self-propelled thrust back toward the national spotlight came with his visit to Vietnam in mid-November of 1969. To Paul Brinkley-Rogers, *Newsweek*'s correspondent in Saigon, watching "George Wallace pumping hands, George Wallace hugging babies, George Wallace beaming in his battle fatigues, George Wallace on the war's front line . . . [made it seem] for one hallucinatory moment [as if] the presidential elections of 1972 were only moments away." But journalists missed most of Wallace's six-day visit to Vietnam because, the journalists were convinced, the White House had ordered government officials to minimize publicity. To this end, such officials refused to divulge Wallace's itinerary or whereabouts and failed to provide transportation for the press, as was customary during foreign visits by dignitaries. But what little the print reporters and television cameras were able to record redounded to Wallace's benefit. When he stepped off his chartered jet in Saigon, Brinkley-Rogers recalled, a Green Beret near the apron shouted, "Alabama!" Wallace, en route to a news conference in the VIP lounge, "turned in his tracks and lunged toward the soldier; he gripped him by the hand and embraced him. Wallace wanted to get close to the troops and, when he saw them, he closed in on them—black and white—with a flurry of salutes, handshakes, hugs, and 'Hi, y'all! You're doing a fine job, y'hear? Hope to see you back home real soon.' "

The soldiers—black and white—succumbed to Wallace's gregariousness and enthusiastic support. And from the little observed by journalists, so did every stratum of the Vietnamese people, from high-level officials to rank-and-file soldiers to civilians to young refugee children, a gaggle of whom swarmed over him with hugs and kisses. Wallace did not even allow a soaking rain to prevent him from walking through a housing project to shake hands and wave to its Vietnamese residents, who enthusiastically waved back from the shelter of porches.

The U.S. embassy's attempts to prevent the press from recording the widespread zeal for Wallace was sometimes ham-handed. The embassy's protocol officer told reporters to be in front of Wallace's hotel at nine o'clock if they wished to accompany him on a day-long trip to see Vietnamese army units and their American advisers in the field. A large group of journalists showed up—only to be told that Wallace had been whisked away to an "unscheduled" breakfast with

Gen. Creighton Abrams, Gen. William Westmoreland's successor as the U.S. military commander in Vietnam, and had left on his tour immediately thereafter.[6] As a liaison officer confided to Brinkley-Rogers, "I advised the embassy that many members of the press wished to cover the Wallace visit, but I was told, 'We have been ordered by the highest circles imaginable not to get involved in the Wallace trip.' "[7]

Wallace took it all stoically, telling reporters in Saigon to "draw [their] own conclusions" as to whether the White House had tried to limit press coverage of his excursion. Despite any disappointment he may have felt, Wallace remained exuberant when encountering GIs and Vietnamese. Besides, he was amassing much-needed credibility for any future pronouncements on the war; additionally, his subsequent side trips, where he met with officials in Taiwan, Hong Kong, Singapore, Malaysia, Thailand, Cambodia, Laos, and South Korea, increased his standing as a spokesman in foreign affairs.[8] And what he lost in day-to-day coverage abroad he regained in interviews and television appearances on his return, including yet another guest spot on "Meet the Press," where he asserted that the war was "winnable" and said, "The enemy must be defeated . . . before [U.S.] combat forces can be withdrawn." He called for bombing Cambodia where forty thousand North Vietnamese regulars were in staging areas; neither Wallace nor the American public realized that Cambodian "sanctuaries" had been under massive attack by American bombers for more than eight months and would continue to be targets for another six months. (A revelatory *New York Times* article on the Cambodia bombing had appeared the previous May but had been generally ignored by politicians, the rest of the press, and the people.)[9] Later, Wallace would embrace a "win-or-get-out" policy, saying that if he were president, he would allow the military ninety days to win the war (using only conventional weapons) or withdraw from Vietnam.[10]

■   ■   ■

In February 1970, Wallace announced that he intended to run for governor—not because he found fault with Brewer but because a Wallace candidacy would "be a thorn in the side" of President Nixon. "I'd be derelict in my duty in *not* running for governor," Wallace said with more than a whiff of hubris, "knowing that my election would bring back . . . control of public school systems to the state. . . . My election will tell Nixon, 'You can either put up or shut up.' Nixon's worried about the future, and there won't be any future for him unless he gives us our schools back."[11]

Aware that he was opposed by liberals, blacks, regular Democrats, and even Republicans (led by Nixon's postmaster general, the Alabama businessman Winton Blount), Wallace clowned during his formal announcement by pretending to peer under an imaginary bedsheet to identify his political enemies: "There's the Humphrey-Muskie Democrats; and there's some militants; and look-a-there— there's a cabinet officer; and over yonder in the corner are some big-city newspapers . . . ."[12]

But the old magic did not seem to be working—at least, not at first. Long-time Wallace supporters were telling visiting journalists that they might defect. "People's wore out," an elderly sign painter told the reporter William Greider. "They've heard it all before. The idea that he's going to fix the schools. Everybody knows he ain't gonna do that."

And Ralph Sears, the publisher of a weekly newspaper in Shelby County, a solid Wallace area, explained, "Brewer is cooperative [with federal officials] where Wallace is strictly belligerent. I think the people have had enough fighting. They want to settle down to peace and prosperity."[13] But Wallace had Nixon pegged correctly; a successful comeback by Wallace would, in fact, trigger a Southern strategy and a broad Republican withdrawal from aggressive civil rights policies for the next quarter century.

Nonetheless, to his surprise and chagrin, Wallace found himself playing catch-up politics. Polls in mid-March showed Wallace trailing Brewer by a wide margin. The forty-one-year-old governor, nearly ten years Wallace's junior, was scoring points by pledging to be Alabama's "full-time governor," something for which Wallace clearly had little inclination. At rallies, at which he invariably was well received, Brewer spoke of local bread-and-butter issues, such as a new highway interchange for Birmingham's airport, a new park for Jefferson County, and a new state car-pool system that already was effecting savings. Then Brewer would launch into his softly modulated, coded critique of Wallace, as in his comments at one small, blue-collar town south of Birmingham:

> You know, folks, you don't hear much about law and order in Alabama these days because we've got law and order. I'm telling you we can't grow and prosper and get new industry

and educate our children as long as there's an atmosphere of
strife and turmoil and confusion. . . . I promise as your
governor I won't do anything to embarrass you or make you
ashamed you voted for Albert Brewer.[14]

Brewer flooded the state with TV commercials, print ads, billboards, bumper stickers, and formal get-out-the-vote efforts. He
seemed to have no money problems; reporters at the time assumed
that big out-of-state contributions were coming from organized labor
and Republican fat cats acting at Winton Blount's behest to help
Nixon indirectly by defeating Wallace.[15]

In fact, Nixon had a direct hand in trying to beat Wallace, as
the nation would learn three years later. In testimony before the
Senate Watergate Committee on July 17, 1973, Herbert Kalmbach,
Nixon's personal attorney, disclosed that, on instructions from
White House Chief of Staff H. R. Haldeman, he had made secret
payments totaling $400,000 to the Brewer campaign. Kalmbach
testified that he had stashed hundreds of thousands of dollars left
over from Nixon's 1968 campaign in safe-deposit boxes across the
country. Prior to Alabama's May 5, 1970, gubernatorial primary,
Kalmbach, who lived in Orange County, California, flew to New York
and got $100,000 in cash from a safe-deposit box at the Chase
Manhattan Bank in midtown Manhattan. He then took the bundle
in an attaché case to the lobby of the tony Sherry Netherlands Hotel
to await a person whom he said he had never seen before. That
person—who turned out to be Bob Ingram—simply walked up to
Kalmbach "and identified himself as being from some place." But
Kalmbach testified, "I don't recall where it was . . . I think I was in a
particular colored suit . . . I was advised at a later date that I had
given the funds to the right person."

The cavalier attitude toward such large sums astonished the
senators—but Kalmbach then amazed them even more. He said
that he later withdrew an additional $200,000, but, unable to make
the delivery personally, he gave the cash to his brother-in-law
and told him to give it to yet another stranger who would approach
him in the Sherry Netherlands lobby. Kalmbach made a final
$100,000 cash delivery to a Brewer representative whom he did not
know—this time in the lobby of the Bank of California in Los
Angeles.[16]

■   ■   ■

For his part, Wallace relied on his tried-and-true, old-style, hand-pumping, stump tours with country musicians warming up the crowds from flatbed trucks. "Over a period of time," Charles Snider said, "we hired Nashville, Tennessee."

Wallace crisscrossed the state with four-a-day rallies in the so-called branch-head towns like Florala, Andalusia, Enterprise, New Hope, and Albertville (where he drew 2,000 of the 12,000 townspeople) and occasional large gatherings in the major cities (he attracted 11,000 to his kickoff rally in Mobile). The Wallace message had not changed much, either. At Albertville he said:

> They call us a redneck state. I told them, if you mean by a "redneck" people who go out and do an honest day's work in the sun, why, we've got lots of them. . . . It's the Birmingham newspaper editors who worry about Alabama's image while they sit out at the country club and drink tea with their little fingers stuck up in the air. I think Alabama's image is just fine the way it is. [But] if I'm not elected governor, this administration in Washington is going to go so far to the left they'll be out of sight. But if you make me governor, we can keep the pressure up, the foot in the back of the president and Congress. We are the balance of power.[17]

And in response to Brewer's pledge to be "a full-time governor," Wallace promised he would work "double-time" for Alabama.

Except for allusions to the growing number of registered blacks as the bloc vote that would likely support Brewer overwhelmingly, Wallace steered clear of obvious appeals to segregationists. He did not think it was necessary; with mounting racial discord in the country—growing militance epitomized by the Black Panthers, shoot-outs between blacks and big-city police, disgruntled black college students taking over campus buildings (a group armed with rifles emerged from one building at Cornell)—he felt as if headline writers were doing his talking for him. Instead, Wallace relied on his stock populist promises to squeeze more money out of the utilities, increase old-age and unemployment compensation, and remove the sales tax from drugs and food. Given the size and enthusiasm of his crowds, Wallace felt that he was cutting into Brewer's early lead.[18]

But Wallace, who had not employed a pollster, was flying by the seat of his pants. Brewer, on the other hand, had engaged Oliver Quayle, one of the nation's best-known pollsters. And Quayle knew that Brewer had a decent chance to achieve what would have been considered impossible just two years earlier—beating George Wallace without a runoff. But he also knew there were two major obstacles to Brewer's chances of pulling it off. The first was Charles Woods, a forty-eight-year-old businessman from Dothan, Alabama, who had grown up in an orphanage but had made millions building houses and investing in television and radio stations. As a bomber pilot in World War II, Woods had been hideously disfigured when his plane had crashed and exploded. After Woods had spent five years in military hospitals and undergone sixty operations, his face remained a mask of scars and skin grafts; his hands were square slabs with stubs where his burned-off fingers used to be. As one of Lurleen Wallace's numerous opponents in 1966, he had applied his considerable resources to tell his story on television—that of a man who had overcome poverty, pain, and disfigurement to achieve financial success. Some were repelled by the sight of Woods; others were fascinated. But nearly everyone admired his courage and grit, as well as what was seen as the inner strength to appear in public without apology or embarrassment. And his ideas, every bit as populist oriented as Wallace's (in 1966 he had advocated, among other things, shifting the tax burden onto "big business and big landowners," passing a strong antipollution law, and ending controlled milk prices), seemed especially credible because they came from an "antipolitician" millionaire businessman. He had run fifth in the crowded pack against Lurleen. But in 1970, repeating his media blitz, he picked up higher-than-expected support from people who could not decide between Brewer and Wallace.[19]

The second obstacle facing Brewer also redounded to Woods's benefit—namely, a dispute among the state's black leaders about their election strategy. By 1970, there were nearly 300,000 registered black voters in Alabama, about 20 percent of the total electorate, and the politically active among them were split into two major groups. The larger and more moderate group was the Alabama Democratic Conference, headed by Joe Reed, the assistant director of the Alabama Education Association. Reed was instrumental in raising union money for Brewer and organizing election-day voter transportation on Brewer's behalf, although leaks to the press of Reed's activities may have hurt Brewer among some white voters. The second, more militant black political group was the National Democratic Party of Alabama (NDPA), controlled by John Cashin, a Huntsville dentist. Cashin, who claimed an NDPA membership of eighty thousand, urged his followers to sit out the election or to vote for one of the also-rans like Woods. Borrowing a page from Wallace's 1968 strategy book, Cashin reasoned that if neither Wallace nor Brewer won a first-primary majority, they would be forced to deal with Cashin to deliver a second-primary margin of victory. Said Cashin with ill-concealed mockery: "I'll deal with Wallace or Brewer. There's not a dime's worth of difference between the two of them."[20]

■   ■   ■

As May 5 dawned, the Wallace camp predicted its man would fall short of a first-primary clear majority but would lead the pack by 50,000 votes. By day's end, the overconfident Wallace was plainly shocked: there was no 50,000-vote lead; there was no lead at all. Wallace finished 7,000 votes behind Brewer, who drew 421,000 votes. Woods attracted a wholly unexpected 148,000 votes, and that proved to be the crucial difference that kept Brewer from capturing the governorship in the first primary. An April poll revealed that Brewer was the second choice of 90 percent of the people who planned to vote for Woods. Had just 75 percent of the Woods vote gone to Brewer, there would have been no need for a runoff. In the second primary, Brewer expected to win the big chunk of white voters who had supported Woods; he also could reasonably depend on the vast majority of Cashin-influenced voters, though he could not risk offending whites by openly seeking Cashin's support. As for Wallace, the course was clear. "There weren't any meetings," Tom Turnipseed said, "no brainstorming. We all knew what the governor [Wallace] had to do: promise them the moon and holler 'nigger.' "[21]

Wallace proceeded to do just that—and more; the next thirty days degenerated into the dirtiest campaign in Alabama history. Where he had decried Brewer's "bloc vote" in the first primary, he added a clarifying word in his post–May 5 speeches to make certain that no one missed the message: now he disparaged Brewer's "black bloc vote." His campaign staff quickly organized a registration campaign among less affluent whites who had failed to enroll for the first primary, warning them that a Brewer victory would signal black-dominated politics in Alabama for fifty years.

At the Montgomery County courthouse, one young white woman waited in line with her two small children from noon until four o'clock so she could be eligible to vote for Wallace. In Etowah County, where Wallace had run third, a union member on strike at the Goodyear plant registered for the first time, explaining that "only niggers" had voted in the first primary. A stream of hate literature and race-oriented ads began spewing from Wallace supporters; if, as Wallace maintained, he had not authorized it, he did not do anything to stop it, either. In Anniston, a radio commercial reminded listeners that some black leaders had demanded integration of the Alabama Highway Patrol. "Suppose," the announcer intoned, "your wife is driving home at eleven o'clock at night. She is stopped by a highway patrolman. He turns out to be black. Think about it. Elect George C. Wallace."

A Wallace ad that ran in several newspapers pictured a four-year-old golden-haired white girl sitting on a beach surrounded by seven grinning young black boys. The caption read, "This Could Be Alabama Four Years From Now. Do You Want It?" Even Wallace, usually assiduous in avoiding epithets in public when referring to blacks, let slip while talking to workers at a plant gate in northern Alabama. Apparently forgetting that he had been fitted with a wireless microphone by an ABC-TV film crew, Wallace was overheard saying, "Of course, 300,000 nigger votes is mighty hard to overcome."

And there were anti-Brewer dirty tricks as well. An unsigned circular accused Brewer of being a homosexual; Wallace himself frequently referred to Brewer as a "sissy-britches." The same sheet asserted that Mrs. Brewer was an alcoholic and that her two daughters had been carrying on sexual affairs with black men. The hastily organized Women for Wallace, whose principal task was to telephone thousands of prospective Wallace voters in a get-out-the-vote campaign, engineered a scam on the side to embarrass Mrs. Brewer. Some of the Wallace women telephoned nursing homes around the state and, pretending to be Brewer staffers, announced that Mrs. Brewer would be dropping by the home the following day. "You know how it is at a place like this," a Birmingham nursing home director said. "The women got all gussied up and we even planned to sing, 'For She's a Jolly Good Fellow.' They were all so excited. Then Mrs. Brewer never showed up." Eventually, Mrs. Brewer issued a form letter to all the nursing homes in the state explaining that the "appointments" made in her behalf had been cruel frauds.[22] Wallace even openly appealed for Klan votes; thousands of copies of an official Wallace brochure was made available to the state's Klan organization, inserted in the organization's monthly magazine, and mailed to its membership.[23]

Brewer, to be sure, was not exactly playing according to Hoyle, either. In addition to large, secret cash infusions into his campaign from what came to be known as Nixon's Watergate slush fund, Brewer tried to pin down and publicize rumors that Gerald Wallace had grown rich by peddling his influence during the administrations of his brother and sister-in-law. One bizarre attempt to disparage Gerald was when Brewer directed his press secretary to photograph Gerald's supposedly opulent farm from a state-owned helicopter; the helicopter malfunctioned, however, and crash-landed near one of Gerald's fields. The press secretary and the pilot were unharmed, and neighbors observed them racing across the field in a vain attempt to get away unobserved.[24]

Another attack on Wallace bore the sinister stamp of a White House abuse of power. Eager to remove Wallace as a potential threat to Nixon's reelection in 1972, Haldeman, shortly after Wallace announced his intention to run for governor, directed the Justice Department to set up a special unit, on the pretext of investigating public corruption. In reality, it was created to investigate Wallace, his wife, their staff members, their contributors, and—most particularly—Gerald Wallace.[25] The unit was headed by William Sessions, a Texas lawyer who had joined the Nixon Justice Department as the chief of the government operations section of the criminal division and later became FBI director.[26] In addition to overseeing the attorneys assigned to his section, Sessions coordinated the investigative efforts of more than a dozen Internal Revenue Service agents and a team of lawyers in the U.S. attorney's office in Montgomery. While Sessions was launching his probe, Clark Mollenhoff, an obstreperous investigative reporter–turned–White House assistant, was prowling through tax returns at Nixon's behest for dirt on Democratic officeholders—and the Wallaces, including Gerald, were high on his list.[27]

Without question, Gerald Wallace was an irresistible target for anyone trying to uncover governmental turpitude. Hard-drinking and indiscreetly talkative, Gerald, though never a state employee, frequently bragged to anyone within earshot—even while tippling with reporters—about his clout with state government. And Gerald was anything but bashful about selling his presumed access; soon after George's election in 1962, Gerald had bought a 25 percent interest in an asphalt company that procured $3 million in state contracts in the five and a half years that George and Lurleen held office. But despite allegations to the contrary, no improprieties concerning the asphalt company ever were established; indeed, over the years, Gerald appears to have accumulated most of his money more on the perception of his leverage with George than on its reality.[28]

Nonetheless, the White House believed that Gerald might well be George's Achilles' heel, and Mollenhoff sought regular updates on the status of the investigation into Gerald's taxes. On April 2, a month before the Alabama primary, IRS Commissioner Randolph Thrower sent Mollenhoff a brief memo on the Wallace inquiry. Mollenhoff sent a copy to Haldeman, and on April 13, portions of the memo appeared in the syndicated column of the muckraking journalist Jack Anderson. Anderson wrote, "Confidential field reports made available to this column quote Alabama informants as saying that Gerald Wallace has boasted of receiving four hundred thousand dollars in commissions on state liquor sales."[29] Perhaps because the leak had White House fingerprints all over it, or because the unnamed "Alabama informants" were assumed to be Wallace's political enemies, or because most Alabamians recognized that an alleged boast is a long way from proof, the episode failed to generate significant anti-Wallace feeling in Alabama's electorate.

As with other charges against Gerald to that point, this one also came to naught. Ira DeMent, who had been the U.S. attorney in Montgomery during the Justice Department–IRS investigation of the Wallaces, said, "I'll say this for Gerald. He damn well paid federal income taxes on every dime he received."[30] (That was then. Nearly twenty years later, Gerald's lifelong propensity for skirting the edges of ethicality and legality would catch up with him; in 1990, he would be fined heavily for failing to report and pay taxes on income of $165,000 in 1984 and 1985. George had been the governor then, but the money had not come from any work related to state government.) But in the federal investigation that started in March 1970 and continued for more than a year, Gerald had dodged the bullet.[31]

The federal investigation was suspended in May 1971, without any action being taken.[32] But it was resumed in September and continued for another year when, despite having cast a wide net, the investigators ended up by hooking only one fish—Wallace's one-time finance director, Seymore Trammell, already too far removed from Wallace to cause any damage.[33] Trammell was convicted of failing to pay $5,000 in federal taxes on a $22,000 home swimming pool, which had been a gift from a grateful recipient of state contracts during Lurleen's administration. George refused to appear as a character witness at the trial of his old Barbour County friend and close adviser;

years later, he snarlingly dismissed Trammell as nothing more than "a common thief."[34]

To George, the investigation of Trammell and his brother was a matter of concern. George had suspected for some time that Trammell might be involved in payoffs from state contractors, but he feared that Gerald might have dirtied his hands as well. Gerald regularly assured him he was clean, and when George asked DeMent what, if anything, the investigation had turned up on anyone in the family, DeMent answered, "Not a damn thing."[35] Beyond that, the inquiry proved to be little more than a major annoyance.

"They had fourteen Internal Revenue men looking into my records, and they spent a million dollars trying to find something," Wallace said, with obvious disdain, some two years after the 1970 primaries. "If there'd-a been anything wrong, you'd-a known it by now." Wallace had precious little income to declare. He and Lurleen had lived on their salaries; after her death in 1968, he had made himself the editor of the Azbell-produced newsletter *The Wallace Stand* and had received $14,000 for that. In 1969, he had taken another $14,000 for the newsletter editorship and had earned an additional $11,000 from speeches and from his contributions to a book about Lurleen. His 1970 income also totaled around $25,000, though he managed to defray most of his expenses—quite legitimately, as it turned out—by charging them to the campaign. "It really drove our family nuts, being investigated during the campaign for governor," he complained. "They even asked me to cut some speaking dates so I could meet with them. I told them they better get a court order for me to do that, because I was running for governor and had a schedule to keep." He said he accused the IRS and Justice Department inquisitors of participating "in a purely political venture." "I wasn't going to do anything about it," he explained, "but as long as they were being so shit-assey, I filed a new return claiming myself as the surviving spouse after my wife died, 'cause my lawyer said Lurleen was the family breadwinner at the time of her death." Then he paused triumphantly. "It ended up with *them* having to give *me* an $800 refund."[36]

■   ■   ■

In the closing three weeks of the campaign, Brewer, thinking himself safely ahead, turned his campaign down a notch. He planned only a half dozen rallies instead of the three or four per week that he had conducted previously, and at the rallies he dropped his hillbilly band as undignified overkill. He concentrated on slick TV and newspaper ads and quiet handshaking tours. Neither he nor his staff was concerned about dropping off the front pages; every major daily in the state supported him and shamelessly skewed its coverage to emphasize Brewer's virtues and Wallace's vices.

In addition to black voters, most of whom lived in Alabama's southern Black Belt region, Brewer's first-primary strength had derived from populous northern Alabama—Birmingham, Anniston, Gadsden, Huntsville, and his hometown of Decatur, where he held his last rally of the campaign.[37] He emphasized the low-key, dignified approach of his campaign, which, by extension, indicated how he would comport himself as governor, compared to his opponent:

> This gutter-type politics is a campaign of desperation, an
> attempt to scare you. Don't let them put hate in your hearts. I
> said when we began that I would conduct a clean, honest,
> forthright campaign that would befit the office of governor.
> But the opposition became desperate, frantic, and they went
> wild. This turned out to be the dirtiest campaign in history.[38]

It was. But Snider, Wallace's campaign chairman, conceded, "That was the only way we could win it." And Wallace pursued his come-from-behind victory at the only speed in his repertoire—flat out. He maintained his rally-a-night schedule across the state; authorized spending up to $7,500 a night to attract star country performers like Roy Clark, Billy Grammer, and Marty Robbins; increased advertising; approved diverting precious resources to organize a statewide get-out-the-vote campaign; and turned a blind eye to the scurrilous, often-racist, anti-Brewer literature disseminated in his name with increasing frequency.[39]

For the final week's push, Wallace scrapped his original schedule, which, in keeping with conventional political wisdom, called for him to tour his areas of strength in the southern part of the state. Instead, he made an unusual move that turned out to be critical to the election's outcome; he decided to spend the closing days in northern Alabama, where he had run poorest on May 5—in some counties, even behind Woods. He reasoned that there was nothing left to do in southern Alabama; more blacks than usual likely would turn out to vote for Brewer, but Wallace was sure his own tactics would attract sufficient white votes to offset them.

Wallace crisscrossed the area, maintaining his clip of four-a-day outdoor minirallies at which he spoke from the back of a flatbed truck, and he starred at major rallies in the region's population centers like Birmingham and Huntsville. Wallace brazenly scheduled his final Monday night rally in Gadsden, the seat of Etowah County, where he had run third, behind Brewer and Woods. Twelve hundred stomping, cheering partisans filled Convention Hall in the industrial town that perched on a bend of the Coosa River in the northeastern quadrant of the state. Country singers warmed up the crowd— women and children, most of them wearing their churchgoing best, and men whose attire ranged from well-tailored suits or sport outfits to plaid shirts and hiked-up overalls. Some were puffing cigarettes, and picking their teeth with paper matches; others, with kids perched on their shoulders, behaved with Sunday School restraint. But when Wallace entered to the strains of "Dixie," the crowd was as one—on its feet, whooping and cheering, fists pumping in the air, sometimes close to hysteria as when one man in his forties, his head lolling in Holy Roller ecstasy, shrieked, "God, let him win!"[40]

Wallace gave them their money's worth with a classic Wallace stemwinder—a pastiche of promises and attacks. First, he reminded his audience that his election would have national consequences:

> These last few days, all the networks have been here—Roger Mudd and Bill Lawrence and all those fellers. And I rode down here with some newsmen from Chicago. And we've even had French and British newsmen here. They know this election is important, and so do all of you. . . . There's been a lot of talk about smears in this campaign. Well, I've been smeared from heck to breakfast, from Concord, New Hampshire, to San Diego. I don't *cry* about it. If you can't stand hot grease, get out of the kitchen. I'll take it from the *New York Times* and the *Newsweek* which writes when I eat, I make a sucking sound with my teeth. They've called me racist, bigot, the American Hitler. But I took all that, because someone's got to speak for you. I've been on national TV—"Meet the Press," "Face the Press," something like that, with supposedly the smartest newsmen in the country. I don't want to sound immodest, but when I got through with them, they didn't know if they were upside down or out. . . . We stirred something up in this country. If I'm elected, Nixon will turn in our direction. The people of Alabama are being paid more attention to than any other state.

They quieted down the school business 'cause I'm running for governor. If I'm defeated, you watch out. They gonna run the public schools. . . . The federal government has taken control of restaurants and stores; they took control of your unions, and then they controlled your homes. Now they want to control your schools—all to please a group of people who voted in a bloc.[41]

Wallace was not engaging in mere self-puffery by underlining his national stature; State Democratic Chairman and Wallace foe Robert Vance was among those who believed that national press attention to the campaign brought hordes of additional Wallace voters, energized by chauvinism, to the polls.[42] And Nixon had indeed ducked for cover on segregation, implementing his "Southern strategy" in reaction to Wallace's prospective candidacy for president. Nixon fired his education commissioner for publicly urging the administration to speed up school integration. The president eschewed sending "vigilante squads" to the South to enforce court rulings. Instead, he announced he would rely on local Southern school officials to comply with court orders. He said he would not compel communities to compensate for established residential patterns by integrating schools through busing. Worst of all, the Justice Department filed a brief in a Mississippi case supporting the contention that segregated private schools should keep their tax-exempt status.[43]

The department's position encouraged the rapid formation of so-called seg academies throughout the South. Numerous white parents pulled their kids out of public schools, pooled their resources to buy a few books and hire administrators, set up shop in congenial churches, and usually filled teaching positions themselves. Few came close to meeting state education standards, but sympathetic state governments accredited all but the most egregiously unqualified of the academies. And, though the courts regularly turned back Southern legislatures' efforts to provide direct support to private schools, tax deductions for tuition, supplies, and contributions to the schools by benefactors provided considerable indirect support. And audacious politicians like Wallace found ways to encourage personal contributions to the private schools. "Hell, I raised about a half million dollars for the private schools in Alabama," he once crowed. "Some fella would want to sell some insurance to the state or do some legal business. I'd suggest he make a nice contribution to the private schools." Asked if such actions might not constitute illegal shake-downs, he replied, "Shee-it, that wasn't no shakedown. I mean, it wasn't going in *here*, in *my* pocket. It was going to the children."[44]

After establishing the national implications of the election, Wal-lace next turned to the issue of race:

> I have never injected race in this campaign. A bloc vote joined with the moneyed interests, the national Republicans, and the Humphreyites to support my opponent. I ask this: What will you promise for 250,000 [black] votes? In places like Cleveland, Ohio, this one group controls every political decision. If this black, bloc vote determines who will be governor of Alabama this year, they'll determine every governor of Alabama for the next fifty years. We don't want any one group to control government because that's bad government. Don't let this happen. Because, then, who will stand up for you? They want your voice stilled and silent. You've got to say "no" to busing your little children and closing your neighborhood schools.[45]

With breathtaking gall Wallace exhibited his uncanny ability to inject racism in the campaign by denying it. And the demagogue shone through in his mastery of fallacious reasoning: Brewer's election would mean, ipso facto, that blacks now controlled Alabama's politi-cal process and would continue to do so for half a century; it was bad government to allow any one group (except, of course, segregation-ists) to control state politics—at least, not if the "one group" caused Wallace's defeat and deprived white people of their self-proclaimed champion. If that happened, busing would increase and neighbor-hood schools would disappear.

So, Wallace asserted, only his election would prevent federal power from overrunning Alabama in a sort of second Reconstruc-tion. But, of course, Wallace would do much more than defend Alabama from Washington-inspired incursions. He would continue and enlarge the sort of popular programs that his and his wife's administrations had promulgated in the past:

> When I was governor, teachers got a 42 percent raise and your children got free textbooks. . . . Now we're gonna provide higher education for the average working man. In my administration, we raised old-age pensions and we started Medicaid in Alabama and unemployment compensation was

raised. . . . Now we're gonna raise old-age pensions again,
take the tax off of drugs, provide a sixty-dollar minimum
weekly unemployment compensation where you'll start to
draw in the first week you're out of work and not have to
wait till the third week. We're gonna investigate the high cost
of liability insurance on automobiles. We're gonna take the 4
percent utilities tax off of your bills and put it on the
utilities themselves and make them lower their rates. We're
gonna get a strong pollution bill. All these big industries
have been killing fish up and down the river and polluted
the air. They've got the money to do it and they ought to go
ahead and do it.[46]

Wallace conveniently failed to mention that many of his programs relied to a large extent on federal largess (to which, in any
event, he claimed the state was entitled because of its contributions in
federal taxes); or that he had been the first to advocate concessions
to attract industry to the state; or that he knew that many of his other
pledges would fail, as they had in the past, due to lack of sufficient
state funds, legislative recalcitrance, or both. As if anticipating such
objections, he moved to his finale, his coup de grace, by pointing to
the real villains—those with enough money, privilege, and power to
block his populist programs:

Alabama has never had a governor to attack the special
interest groups. Management gets too much of the profits, not
the working man. The workers pay through the nose—but the
Rockefeller Foundation and the Ford Foundation and the
Mellons and the Carnegies get the laws passed they want so
they don't pay taxes. We're gonna take taxes off food and put
it on somebody's got the money to pay it. Mountain Brook
[the posh town near Birmingham] voted twelve to one against
Wallace. They're saying, "Be quiet, you rednecks. Don't
complain about busing your children fifteen miles to some
school. Don't complain about high utility rates." Why should
they complain? They've got the money to buy their way out of
anything. . . . There's people who can't stand me and there's
people for me 100 percent. But there's no middle ground on
George Wallace.[47]

Wallace's denunciation of the rich and powerful never failed to
pull an audience into a sense of oneness, a feeling of "us against

them," and a belief that Wallace was the best man to protect them from Alabama's mighty and to protect Alabama from Washington's leviathans. And Mountain Brook was the perfect target. The town ran its own private school system and accepted no state or federal money; no black students attended any Mountain Brook school.[48]

It was a masterful performance that crowned a week of exceptionally successful appeals reaching beyond the Wallace faithful to those who previously had voted for one of his opponents or had not voted at all in the first primary. He knew he needed to be at his best. Arrayed against him were the Republicans, "loyalist" Democrats, Brewer's precinct-level organization, the young (overwhelmingly against Wallace in the polls), the "establishment" (comprising leading newspapers, banks, and utilities), the "new respectables" (those thirsting to shed the redneck image Wallace conveyed), the blacks, and, of course, Brewer himself, with his modestly successful record and promise of tranquility. But even before the first primary, the singularly perceptive journalist Stewart Alsop understood Wallace's almost mystical hold on Alabamians. After observing a Wallace rally in rural Alabama, Alsop noted that, as expected, Wallace won points when he hung the black vote, like an albatross, around Brewer's neck. Then Alsop noted:

> But more effective still is George Wallace's quite genuine star quality as a campaigner. . . . You could feel the electric current generated by a great demagogue pass through the crowd as Wallace denounced the banks and utilities, and the rich on Wall Street who don't pay their taxes. . . . He is also a populist, an anti-establishmentarian—and his attacks on the big newspapers, the banks, and the utilities account for that electric current in his shirt-sleeved crowds at least as much as the race issue. His opposition has never been more formidable. But little George Wallace, all the same, may get his chance to 'keep my foot in Mr. Nixon's back' so that Mr. Nixon will 'keep his promise to give your schools and your children back to you.'[49]

On election day, Wallace was tired but in good spirits. He drove to Barbour County to vote, and while lunching with two reporters in Clayton, he paraphrased Richard Nixon: "If I lose, I'm gonna say in my concession statement, 'Well, I won't have all you newsmen to kick around anymore.' " That evening, he returned to his Farrar Street home to watch the returns on a color television set in his pine-paneled family room. The only guests, other than family, were five reporters: Jules Loh of the Associated Press, Don Farmer of ABC, Jim Wooten of the *New York Times*, Phil Garner of the *Atlanta Journal,* and me, representing *Newsweek*. Wallace pointed out the bathroom to everyone, then offered Cokes all around. Wooten complained jokingly, "Governor, if we're gonna keep coming 'round, we've got to make some new drinking arrangements." When Wallace repeated his usual line about the need to keep reporters sober, I responded, "Governor, we've not done too well by you sober; why don't you try us drunk?" Wallace smiled and said quietly and incisively, "Y'all have done all right by me."

He betrayed no signs of nervousness as the returns started coming in. Well-wishers phoned steadily. "You just keep plugging, hear?" he would say. Or, "Tell everybody hello up there, hear?" With 29 percent of the vote in, Wallace led by 17,000. "Not enough," he muttered. "Just not enough to get over that Jefferson County vote." But by eight-thirty, with some votes in from Jefferson County, Wallace's lead swelled to 55,000, and he was growing visibly excited. "Fifty-five thousand would be pretty much to overcome, don't you boys think?" he asked the reporters over and over. The journalists agreed and headed for the Governor's House Motel to await Wallace's formal victory statement. As he chatted with me at the door of his home, Wallace admitted, "Well, I suppose there was some of what you could call a backlash vote . . . [but] racism and a white backlash against bloc voting are two entirely different matters." He said he now was in a position to insist that Nixon keep his "commitments" to permit freedom of choice for all students and to prohibit busing. The final vote, in Alabama's greatest turnout for a governor's race, was 560,000 to 526,000.[50]

In the campaign's closing days, Wallace had trusted his political instincts, which did not fail him. Ten counties carried by Brewer in the first primary had switched to Wallace in the runoff, and seven of those were in northern Alabama. They included Etowah—one of only seven Alabama counties with a population of more than a hundred thousand—where Wallace earlier had placed third. Wallace had picked up votes on Brewer everywhere except in Jefferson and Montgomery counties and in black-majority counties where black voters had stayed home in the first primary.[51]

About half past midnight, a bitter Albert Brewer went before the cameras to concede defeat. He said he knew from the start that if race became the chief issue in the campaign, he "couldn't win." He continued: "It was the issue—and I'm glad we didn't run that kind of campaign. I'd rather not win than do it with the race issue. . . . This has been the dirtiest campaign I've ever observed in Alabama. . . . To those who had to stoop to these kind of tactics to try to advance the cause of their candidate, I'll ask: 'Was it worth it?' " ("Hell, yes!" shouted a Wallace supporter watching TV from a bar stool at the Governor's House Motel.) "All of us have tried to give Alabama something better. We didn't get lower in the gutter and we didn't depend on hate."[52] The words were noble, but the tone was churlish, and Brewer never was able to shake either his resentment toward Wallace or his reputation as a sore loser who refused to rejoin the team, as Wallace had after his loss to John Patterson (see chapter 6). Brewer attempted a comeback in a run for governor in 1978 and was considered the favorite until one of the candidates, State Attorney General Bill Baxley, repeatedly excoriated him for accepting Nixon slush-fund handouts, which by then had been revealed publicly through Senate Watergate Committee hearings. Brewer finished third behind Baxley and the winner, an Opelika businessman named Fob James. After that, Brewer, even more embittered, dropped out of the public eye for good, confining himself to the practice of law in his hometown of Decatur.[53]

■　　■　　■

Wallace was about to return to the power in which he had luxuriated. And, because of a constitutional change under Brewer that Wallace had been unable to engineer four years earlier, he could try to succeed himself in 1974 fairly and squarely—no surrogates need apply. But Wallace already had cast his eye beyond Montgomery. He shut down his state campaign organization, housed in a one-time Elks lodge, and donated the building for use as a seg academy. Turnipseed, Snider, and Azbell turned their attention from state politics to the national Wallace campaign, and first on their agenda, ironically, was concocting ways in which Wallace might shed (or at least diminish) his racist image.[54] But even Nixon's Southern strategist, the political theorist Kevin Phillips, believed that the Wallace threat was fading. "Wallace," Phillips said, "has become too gross for the Southern middle class. Where before he was a conservative regional candidate, he had to get down to his cracker base to win in his home state."[55] The journalist R. W. Apple echoed the belief that Wallace's retreat from having "tried very hard in 1968 to rid himself of the racist label . . . [might] not stand him in good stead [in 1972] outside the Black Belt."[56] So Wallace's brain trust urgently drew up a list of suggestions on how their boss might move back toward racial respectability outside the South as well as among the growing number of white Southerners who preferred accommodation with blacks to continued acrimony and disruption. Their ideas included dropping hard-and-fast defense of school segregation in favor of freedom of choice—an option likely to result in widespread, though token, integration; emphasizing that opposition to busing was based on safety and neighborhood integrity rather than race; keeping racial themes out of the inaugural; twisting arms to get blacks to participate in inauguration activities; or appointing blacks to minor state offices.[57] Wallace thought they were all good ideas, but he dawdled in making decisions; he frankly admitted that he was distracted by a major development in his personal life, namely, his relationship with Cornelia Ellis Snively.[58]

Cornelia, the lissome, stunning, then thirty-year-old niece of Jim Folsom, had met George at a campaign rally in May 1970, only four months after her divorce from a Florida business executive. George had been captivated immediately by her sensual good looks, her youth (she was twenty years his junior), her obvious interest in him, and her ready laugh and unreserved expansiveness. At that rally he had been charmed by her story of how they had met once before: "We hugged," she had said—and, as Wallace had lifted his eyebrows in puzzlement, she had added suggestively, "and I was in my nightgown." She had laughed at Wallace's wide-eyed, slack-jawed reaction and had quickly explained that she had been only seven and Wallace had been a recently elected state representative of twenty-seven; it was 1947, shortly after the widowed Jim Folsom had been elected governor and had installed his sister, Ruby Folsom Ellis, also widowed, as the official hostess at the Governor's Mansion. At a party for the legislators and their wives, Ruby's daughter, Cornelia, had dressed for bed and then peered at the arriving guests through the balustrade at the top of the mansion's ornate central staircase. One of the legislator's wives—petite, pretty, and not yet out of her teens— had spotted the girl, cooed maternally, and, dragging her husband

along, climbed the stairway. She had introduced herself as Lurleen
Wallace, embraced the girl, directed George to do the same, and
then had cautioned Cornelia not to stay up too late.[59]

Cornelia had grown into a woman different from Lurleen in
every observable respect, and it aroused George's interest and ardor.
Where Lurleen was diminutive, trim, fair, quiet, demure, and wholly
committed to her family, Cornelia was tall, lithe, raven-haired, viva-
cious, gregarious, and personally and politically ambitious.[60] Cornelia, too, was attracted by the contrasts she saw between George and
her first husband, John Snively III, the heir to one of Florida's largest
citrus operations, who loved horses, water sports, and his privacy.
George on the other hand, had always scrambled for income, had
liked physical sports such as football and boxing, and had come alive
in crowds and in the spotlight's glare. But the mutual attraction
between George and Cornelia was practical as well. Cornelia, George
observed frankly, "made a good public appearance"—someone who
would be an asset on the national scene.[61] For her part, Cornelia
craved a new adventure, financial security (John Snively was supporting their two young sons, but not Cornelia), and, most of all, a public
stage for herself.[62]

■　　■　　■

From her youngest days, Cornelia's life had resembled a pinball:
rebounding from one lighted bumper to another, landing occasionally in a pocket, only to be ejected; receiving a helpful flip
upward now and again; but, even as the score was ringing higher,
rolling slowly, inexorably, toward the bottom of the game board and
the exit slot. After her father's early death from cancer, she became
the object of her mother's single-minded devotion. Cornelia, more
than her brother, Charles, was always at Ruby's side, "growing up in
politics," as she said. She accompanied her mother to nearly every
activity that revolved around her Uncle Jim's burgeoning political
career—sitting in on smoke-filled strategy sessions, handing out leaflets on street corners, passing the money buckets at campaign rallies.
And when Jim was elected governor, Ruby and Cornelia moved into
the mansion and found themselves living in the midst of an almost
never-ending rush of visitors, conferences, dinners, and balls. Ruby
encountered the rich and the famous: she sipped Jack Daniels with
Tallulah Bankhead, another Alabamian; met Queen Juliana, of the

Netherlands; had tea, by invitation, with Eleanor Roosevelt; and laughed with Bess Truman.

Ruby lived at a continual high, both literally and figuratively: flamboyant, unreserved, and loud—but funny, warm, and generous. She loved parties, bragging that she "could dance everyone clear off the dance floor." She surprised new acquaintances—shocking some, delighting others—by yanking them to her expansive bosom in a friendly bear hug. An alcoholic who sought treatment but backslid often, Ruby explained that she and her brother "had a hollow leg." "When I die," she said, "instead of a lily in my hand, give me some branch water and Jack Daniels—and they'll all know I died happy." She also entertained a steady stream of boyfriends, one of whom became her second husband. When he, too, died of cancer, Ruby resumed her search for a new mate. She talked so often, openly, and suggestively about her quest for male companionship that Cornelia, then dating Wallace, tried to stifle her. "Next thing you know, Mama," she scolded, "people will think you'll want to take George away from me." Ruby, who stood almost five-eleven in her bare feet, snorted, "Hell, honey, no way would I want George. Why, he don't stand but titty-high."[63]

Cornelia was her mother's daughter—gregarious, accessible, sassy, and salty. At eighteen, with a crush on Wallace, she wrote a jingle to the tune of "Sugartime" for his 1958 campaign; the staff rejected it as too racy: "Wallace in the mornin', Wallace in the evenin', Wallace at supper time . . . " Years later, appearing as Alabama's first lady on Dick Cavett's TV talk show, she said, with a broad wink, that given her proclivity for driving fast, "George is going to have to put a governor on me." And when Wallace was distracted by a buzzing fly during an interview at the Governor's Mansion, Cornelia remarked twittingly, "Don't worry with it, George. It shouldn't bother you. It ought to remind you of home in Barbour County."[64]

If Cornelia inherited her mother's tongue, she also came into Ruby's love of lights and glitter and the desire to pursue them. Ruby had filled Cornelia's head with notions of becoming a movie star or a great singer. As a teenager, Cornelia was a majorette and cheerleader in high school, played the organ in church, and took lessons in dance, piano, guitar, voice, and equitation. She lived in New York a year and studied with a voice coach named Carlo Menotti (not the composer and conductor Gian Carlo Menotti). She toured Australia with a country music group featuring Roy Acuff. She tried composing and recording her own songs, but with no success. She became an accomplished water skier at a summer camp and then won a place on the water ski performance team at Cypress Gardens in Florida. A regular presence at Cypress Gardens was young John Snively, whose father had helped to bankroll its establishment in 1936 as Florida's first tourist attraction; there, he met Cornelia and courted her. By summer's end, they were married. Cornelia, at twenty, became a young society matron. She gave up work, stayed at home, occasionally showed horses, joined the garden club, and bore two sons.

Inevitably, Cornelia grew restless with her secure, quiet, dull existence. A divorce followed, and, at age thirty, Cornelia returned with her sons to Montgomery and moved into Ruby's house. Because Ruby had her hands full nursing her dying second husband, Cornelia found herself on her own, with no one to care for her or support her, for the first time in her life. She did not much care for that reality. "It was the hardest time in my life," she whined in 1971, before, sadly, experiencing *really* hard times some years later. "I was stranded with the children. I car-pooled them, but the maid left at three and I was really tied down—more than any time in my life. I was right stranded."[65]

But then came George. They dated sporadically until after the victorious June primary, and then they were virtually inseparable, though discreet. By the end of June they were traveling together outside the state, occasionally accepting the hospitality of wealthy friends at their secluded estates. By the end of July the two were such an item among Cornelia's friends that they spoke to her of George as "your governor." Several were bold enough to ask Cornelia to put in a good word with George concerning jobs they were after or programs they were supporting. By August she was coyly asking friends their advice on the match; one urged her to "go ahead and get married as soon as possible to stop speculation."[66]

They decided to wait until after the November election, then a formality in Alabama, to announce their plans. The couple believed a pre-election announcement would provoke greater media attention and personal intrusions. Also, they wanted to give their respective children a chance to get to know one another and get used to the idea. On Christmas, Wallace announced the impending marriage; other than saying it would be in January, he kept secret the details of where or when. Only family members attended the January 4 wedding; 30 other people managed to learn of the plans—and waited outside the church in a misting rain during the ten-minute ceremony.

They rushed to congratulate the two when they emerged from the Trinity Presbyterian Church (the same church at which Cornelia and John Snively had been married).[67]

■   ■   ■

Wallace had been seen publicly only infrequently between June and January, and the change in him was perceptible, in both style and substance. Cornelia's influence was obvious in his appearance. His sideburns were longer; his tacky, rumpled suits had given way to Edwardian cuts with bright, color-coordinated shirts and wide ties; and, at the risk of others calling *him* sissy britches, hair spray had replaced the gobs of brilliantine with which he had slicked down his black, dandruffed hair. More important, from the day of his inauguration two weeks after his marriage, Wallace demonstrated his awareness of a crucial sea change in the South's demographics—the increasing importance of the black vote that had come so close to beating him in the recent election.

Wallace's inaugural address did not contain the word *segregation* or any reasonable facsimile; instead, Wallace said that government must be "for the weak, the poor, and the humble as well as the powerful." He even added, "Alabama belongs to us all—black and white, young and old, rich and poor alike." Blacks marched in the inaugural parade for the first time. And if anyone missed the message, Wallace summoned reporters and photographers to his office a few weeks later to record him conferring on Norman Lumpkin, a Montgomery television reporter, the title of honorary lieutenant colonel of the state militia. Lumpkin was black.[68]

■   ■   ■

Wallace's conscious devaluation of the segregation issue was designed, first, to enhance his national acceptance and, second, to send out signals that, sooner rather than later, he would want a rapprochement with those who controlled the black votes in Alabama. But moving away from the politics of race had its price. Shortly after the inaugural, a group of whites demonstrated near the capitol; they carried a Confederate flag and complained they had been sold out by Wallace on segregation.[69] Of greater concern than the loss of pockets of his traditional constituency was whether his strong grip on the legislature would weaken once he dropped his longtime pledge to fight integration with all his power. In the past, when Wallace had needed votes for controversial programs such as funding improvements for prisons or mental institutions, he had threatened to oppose the reelection of legislators who failed to support him. His leverage had been his almost mystical hold on voters emanating from his dramatic and highly publicized stands for segregation. But with Wallace's retreat, legislators knew instinctively that he could no longer generate the same level of influence. When the legislature convened, filled with Brewer supporters still bitter over Wallace's no-holds-barred campaign tactics, Wallace found his pet proposals—abolishing garnishments, outlawing finance companies from charging interest on interest, prohibiting merchants from seizing property for missed payments but still requiring full payment of contracts—going absolutely nowhere. Most troubling, the legislature refused to approve Wallace's state budget.[70]

Uncharacteristically, Wallace was not meeting the crisis by working all day and, if needed, all night, scratching backs, twisting arms, arguing, cajoling, calling in IOUs, or doing whatever it took to press his case. In addition to spending more time at home with Cornelia and the family than he had ever spent with Lurleen, his attention was divided between the legislature and his nascent national campaign—and he was succeeding at neither. Not only was the legislature balking at the Wallace agenda, but there was dissension among leaders of the Wallace Campaign as well.

There was contention over money matters, as there had been in 1968. The old guard—men like Ralph Adams and Jack Wallace—argued, as ever, for frugality, while the newer, younger professionals—principally Tom Turnipseed and Charles Snider—urged more open-handedness, especially in wooing the media and in modernizing the campaign's transportation, fund-raising techniques, and advertising operations. But there was a more fundamental dispute that went to the heart of the campaign's underlying philosophy: Was Wallace principally a politician seeking national office, or was he the leader of a sociopolitical "movement" to establish a third party based on antifederalism?[71]

Turnipseed embraced with an almost religious fervor the notion of a Wallace-led political movement. In a December 1969 memorandum to Wallace, he wrote, "We must continue and strengthen our nationwide political movement which is the ultimate hope for relief from the federal takeover. . . . The same solution is also the last, best hope for righting all the other wrongs brought upon us by the federal government [and] George Wallace is the man who will lead the people in the movement."[72]

Wallace was uncomfortable with purple descriptions of his presidential quest as a "movement" or "crusade" or "cause." As a rule, he found that his more emotional followers often made outstanding gofers willing to work day and night stuffing envelopes or running errands, but they made lousy political strategists or advisers.[73] Turnipseed, however, was an exception to the rule. He was, indeed, a true believer who worshiped both the Southern myth (he named his first son Jefferson Davis Turnipseed) and George Wallace, whom he saw as its prophet. Nonetheless, he never allowed his passion to blur his keen-eyed political vision. He was a cool-headed, brilliant tactician who laid out Wallace's winning approach to the 1970 campaign.[74] In his ten-page memorandum of December 1969, Turnipseed cautioned against holding out "false hope" for continued school segregation, advocated pressing instead for freedom of choice, and proposed holding up as the real devil-in-disguise not integration per se but busing. After all, Turnipseed noted, just a few months before, the New York State legislature had prohibited busing schoolchildren against their parents' wishes. Turnipseed's most important contribution to the Wallace victory was the insight that Wallace's greatest strength in Alabama was not his considerable record as governor but his national stature. As Turnipseed saw it, Brewer's charge that Wallace would use the office of governor as a stepping stone to national power played right into the Wallace camp's hands:

> The so-called national issues—school integration, local control of local domestic institutions, taxes, inflation, law and order, and Vietnam—are the most important issues to the average Alabamian. Wallace's strength in Alabama is built almost totally on his ability to stand up for the people of Alabama against the wrongs perpetuated [sic] against them in these vital areas by the federal government.[75]

Turnipseed, looking toward a third-party race, assigned Charlie Snider the task of determining the requirements to put Wallace on all fifty ballots in 1972. Snider determined that, overall, the job would be far easier than it had been in 1968; in most states, Wallace's 1968 showing had been sufficient to place his party on the 1972 ballot. The only essential was to keep an acceptable party structure alive both nationally and in each state. Toward that end, Turnipseed, with Wallace's blessing, started traveling the nation to reconstitute the

American Independent Party. Despite contrary opinion among several of his key advisers, Wallace leaned heavily toward Turnipseed's viewpoint; the young man had been dead-on in his guidance for the gubernatorial run, and there was no reason to doubt him now. But Turnipseed's newly acquired rank—he was incontestably in charge of the campaign—may have proved too heady for someone so callow. Wallace received reports that Turnipseed, in his travels, had been dispensing money with abandon, staying in the best hotels, hosting dinner parties nearly every night, and acquiring a reputation as a playboy. Over the weeks, Wallace grew increasingly apprehensive, but his respect for Turnipseed's perspicacity stayed his hand. But the last straw came with a party Turnipseed threw in Florida for hundreds of reporters and supporters. Turnipseed was reported to have gotten "pretty well looped," according to Snider, "and was handing out fifths to the reporters"—bottles for which the hotel was charging fifty dollars each. The tab ran into the thousands. "Tom was called back," Snider said. "Troopers carried him to the governor. Tom didn't want to go; he was looped again." Wallace asked for an explanation. Turnipseed, Snider said, "told the governor to go to hell." Not long after, Tom and his young family were heading back to South Carolina. Wallace turned to Snider, making him acting campaign director. Snider pored through the books and found the campaign deeply in debt. When he went over the situation with Wallace, the governor asked Snider to officially take over the 1972 campaign.[76]

■   ■   ■

Snider agreed to take the job, but he laid down two conditions. First, he did not want to handle the money. He said he would participate in fund-raising activities, but he did not want to sign checks or be involved in any activity that could suggest impropriety on his part. Wallace agreed; he said he would bring his brother-in-law, the businessman Alton Dauphin, into the campaign to handle finances. The second condition was that Wallace run on a major ticket rather than as an independent. Snider said that he "would not be part of another third-party effort." "It didn't have a chance in hell," he contended, "and why get out and beat your brains out and run up and down the country, take the chance of going down in an aircraft? We didn't have a chance. He said he'd think about it, and finally he decided he'd run in the Democratic primaries."[77]

Because the federal investigation of Gerald Wallace was suspended in May 1971, and because George subsequently ran as a Democrat in 1972, there has been speculation for years that Wallace must have cut a quid pro quo deal with President Nixon—that if the federal government quit hounding Gerald, George would add to the Democrats' troubles by running in their primaries and then forgo running as a third-party spoiler. The fact that George's decision to run in the primaries came a month before the investigation was suspended might deepen those suspicions. With millions of Nixon administration documents unavailable to scholars or the public in the mid-1990s, and given the Nixon White House's established record for duplicity and criminality, it is no wonder that uncertainty about a Nixon-Wallace deal refused to go away.

But the available evidence suggests strongly that there was no deal. All the principals who might have been involved in such a pact deny there was one. The fact that Snider had insisted that Wallace run in the primaries as a condition for agreeing to direct the campaign further suggests the absence of a deal. William Sessions, in an interview shortly after his dismissal as the FBI director, conceded that, regarding the Wallace investigation, "there has been speculation for years of some heavy hand saying, 'Stop! Do not go any further.' " But Sessions, who ran the investigation with special attention to Gerald Wallace, said emphatically, "I never knew of any such direction [to stop], I never heard of any, I never suspicioned [sic] any." In all of his investigations of corrupt practices, he said, "I was so convinced we were absolutely correct, that if there were no adoption of my recommendation [to prosecute or not], I would have gone back to Texas." He recommended dropping the Gerald Wallace investigation; he later resurrected an investigation against one-time Wallace aide Seymore Trammell, who subsequently was convicted and imprisoned.[78] Two of the top investigators on the case, Ira DeMent and D. Broward Segrest, emphatically maintained that nothing ever was found on Gerald—at least, nothing that would have justified prosecution. Also, George Wallace never completely abandoned the possibility (or threat) that he might run as an independent in the fall, should the Democrats dismiss out of hand his key proposals for the party platform.

If Wallace had known all along that he would sit out the general election, it seems logical that he would have been preparing reporters for the inevitable by telling them that, for whatever reasons, he had ruled out a third-party run. But as late as December 1971,

Wallace told me, for one, that his plan was to make a major splash during the Democratic primaries by demonstrating wide support for his views—and then likely move into a third-party mode; he could afford to bide his time, he said, because his 1968 showing would have allowed him to qualify easily or automatically in nearly every state.[79] Lastly, when the remnants of the American Independent Party convened late in the summer of 1972 and called on Wallace to head its ticket, even from a wheelchair (see later in this chapter), Nixon dispatched Secretary of the Treasury John Connally to Birmingham, where Wallace then was hospitalized, to dissuade him from accepting. "I had a lot of pain and was about to die. They [the Nixon administration] didn't have to offer me nothing not to run for president. . . . I was thinking about getting well."[80] Had an earlier deal been struck, Connally's late-summer plea would not have been necessary—and by that time, with the investigation into the Wallace administration long since concluded, there was not much that Wallace could have been offered to stay out of the race.

■   ■   ■

Because Wallace had resolved to run in the primaries, Snider and his team—there were now six campaign workers on board full-time— were obliged to proceed with alacrity. Their ultimate target, election day in November 1972, had been moved up eight months to March, when Wallace would compete in his first primary in Florida. And it was now necessary to jump-start all the vital support tasks of the campaign as well—finance, organization, publicity, and, of course, the candidate's travel and speaking schedule.

But first and foremost, the campaign needed money. In the past, the most successful fund-raising technique by Wallace had been through direct mail; Snider had been updating the mailing list, but his new responsibilities had prevented him from completing the job and putting it into action. Besides, it took a lot of up-front capital— money that now had been drained from the campaign—to finance the initial mailings seeking contributions. And, Snider asked himself, where would he get the staff to handle millions of pieces of mail? He turned for advice to a strange bedfellow, a dedicated progressive in racial and political matters, Morris Dees. Dees had made millions in the direct-mail business and now was using his fortune to promote liberal causes, including integration. But he was an old acquaintance, and Dees, who would successfully raise money through the mails in 1972 for George McGovern, was imbued with the Southern convention of dealing honorably even with those friends whose views were diametrically opposed to one's own; after all, one did not attack an unarmed man—and Dees did not turn Snider away without offering him a weapon. To be sure, Dees refused to get involved personally with Wallace's campaign. But he directed Snider to a rising star in the direct-mail business who he thought might prove to be a kindred spirit—an intensely devoted conservative named Richard Viguerie.[81]

Viguerie had started making a name for himself in conservative Republican circles by raising funds in 1970 for a U.S. Senate race in Florida by G. Harrold Carswell, a rejected Nixon nominee for the U.S. Supreme Court. Viguerie's breakthrough, however, would come with Wallace. Visited in his offices outside Washington, D.C., by Snider and Azbell, Viguerie agreed to put up the front money for packaging, mailing, and postage. But Snider insisted on some tough provisions. All the contributions would be remitted directly to Montgomery; the campaign would do all the accounting, thus requiring Viguerie's trust. In addition, the campaign would have to retain all of the initial contributions to pay off accumulated debts and initiate essential campaign activities. Third, Snider declined to pay Viguerie on a percentage basis, but rather would compensate him a dime per package, plus postage. In return, Azbell would be available to Viguerie to write the contents of each appeal, and—perhaps most important to Viguerie's future fortune—Snider gave Viguerie the Wallace mailing list of, by then, nearly three million supporters; Viguerie would update, purge, categorize, and computerize the list, which he could use after the election at his discretion in his other fund-raising activities. Viguerie started sending out appeals in June, reaching the entire list every sixty days; to save overhead costs, he would continually cull noncontributors from the list. By Christmas, he was focusing on a million people whom he judged to be the most responsive; the December appeal to that group grossed $800,000. Viguerie invested nearly $500,000 of his own money before he recovered his first dime from the Wallace campaign. By the time Wallace was effectively out of the presidential race a year later, Viguerie had raised more than $4 million, the most effective fund-raising operation among Democrats to that point in the campaign. (Dees was running a close second.) About $2 million was retained by Wallace, $1 million went for expenses, and the other $1 million to Viguerie. (Wallace's net of about 50 percent of the proceeds was high for Viguerie's clients, who, for the most part, netted only about 25 percent.)[82]

The Wallace newsletter evolved into a slick-paper, four-color publication; at twelve dollars a year per paying subscriber, *The Wallace Stand* grossed about $2 million a year. Much of the income was used to underwrite a slew of other publications that gushed from the typewriter of the prolific Azbell: *Labor Action,* directed to trade unionists; *Impact '72,* for voters under twenty-five; *Women for Wallace,* extolling the importance of women rather than focusing on specific issues; *Wallace Hoy,* for Spanish-speaking voters; and *The Wallace Digest,* which collected the sayings of Chairman George every month or so. Azbell also produced special tabloids for seniors and various ethnic groups. In addition, Azbell churned out three books with an initial press run of a hundred thousand copies each: *Journey with Courage,* a compendium of Wallace quotes over the previous decade; *A Time for Courage* (obviously a favorite Azbell word), an assemblage of Wallace's views on current issues; and *Wallace: A Man for America,* the authorized biography for the 1972 campaign.[83]

Over the course of 1971, Wallace headquarters mailed out a million questionnaires to determine voters' gripes, gauge their greatest concerns, and get their suggestions for a Wallace running mate, should he run as an independent (Lester Maddox, the race-baiting former governor of Georgia, finished first, and Paul Harvey, the conservative radio commentator, was a close second).[84] Wallace rallies and dinners were additional sources of income, as was the sale of campaign paraphernalia such as Wallace watches, tie pins, cuff links, and bumper stickers. The campaign bought an old C-46 and hired off-duty or vacationing Delta Airlines pilots to shuttle people and supplies around the country.[85] But the campaign managed to stay in the black. "You know why?" Snider asked rhetorically. "Because no one will extend us credit—the phone company, hotels, motels, the airlines, Avis, Hertz—no one. We've *had* to stay current."[86] Other candidates enjoyed the luxury of credit—and, often, the profligacy of write-offs. At the end of 1969, airlines wrote off Democratic National Committee debts of more than $200,000. At the same time, the Republican National Committee had unpaid airline bills of more than $100,000. Nixon's airline debts were $69,000; Humphrey's, $138,000; and Robert Kennedy's, $415,000.[87] The noise that Wallace, among others, made about these hidden campaign contributions by airlines, the phone company, Western Union, and other travel and communications enterprises led to a change in the law to forbid corporate write-offs of unpaid campaign bills.

■   ■   ■

Before long Wallace began acquiring the trappings of political respectability. Hubert Humphrey, back in the U.S. Senate and the chairman of an agriculture subcommittee, called on Wallace in Montgomery to discuss a rural development bill.[88] President Nixon flew to Alabama, ostensibly for the dedication of the Tennessee-Tombigbee Waterway to open up an extensive river-transport system among five states and the Gulf of Mexico. "But it is safe to assume," *Newsweek* opined, "that the president's main motive was the opportunity to show his face and muster his forces in the midst of George Wallace country." Wallace greeted the president on his arrival near Mobile, and the two swapped cheerful badinage during the dedication ceremony. At a later meeting in Birmingham with editors and publishers from a dozen Southern states, Nixon did his Wallace imitation: "I have nothing but utter contempt for the double, hypocritical standard of Northerners who look at the South and point the finger and say, 'Why don't those Southerners do something about their race problem?' " He maintained that the South had made important strides toward school integration in the previous three years, while the North had made no progress in combating de facto segregation.[89]

National antipathy to busing proliferated after the Supreme Court ruled in April 1971 that it was constitutional to transport children out of their neighborhoods for the purpose of dismantling a racially dual school system. Nixon damned the decision with faint praise, saying that he supported it but that busing for integration was not "in the interest of better education." When, in August, the president disavowed a busing plan painstakingly worked out between his own government and Austin, Texas, school officials, Wallace pounced.[90] With a look of devilish merriment, Wallace announced he was going to help implement Nixon's latest antibusing pronouncement. He reassigned a Birmingham girl to a school closer to her home than the one she had attended eighteen miles from her home. He invoked the "police power" of the state to order a school system to reopen a black school closed by federal court order; later he directed two other school systems to ignore federal court orders. In the end, school officials obeyed the courts, but Wallace's showboating not only caught the nation's attention but drew widespread approbation. The beleaguered Austin school superintendent said Wallace had demonstrated that Nixon had spoken "with a forked tongue." An official with the Department of Health, Education, and Welfare grumbled, "This is one time I don't blame Wallace one damn bit." Jody Powell, then the press secretary to Governor Jimmy Carter, conceded, "If the militant approach works rather than the traditional methods, then we'll be faced with taking similar steps." ("Traditional methods" meant going along with court orders—very slowly.)[91]

"Who ever heard of a good old boy from Barbour County, Alabama, having the impact I've had?" Wallace asked a reporter. "All I'm trying to do is help the president and the attorney general . . . to do what they say they all want to do—and that's stop busing. That's all I'm trying to do—just make these judges stop toting our kids all over creation." Then, with what a reporter described as "a quick wink and a sly smile," Wallace asked, "How am I doing?" The consensus among reporters, politicians, and government officials who were watching Wallace's early campaigning was that he was succeeding.[92]

And, when Wallace was asked on NBC's "Meet the Press" whether he was defying the Supreme Court by trying to spike its busing orders, Wallace replied with uncharacteristic conciliation: "I am not defying. In fact, I don't believe anyone should defy a court order or should defy any law. We must obey the law whether we like it or not."[93] One wonders how the course of American history might have been altered had Wallace struck that same tone in 1963. But if Wallace was moving to the mainstream by endorsing obedience to court orders, he believed he was also on the cusp of public opinion when it came to busing—and, court orders or no, he was not about to let the issue slip away. If he opposed the courts on busing, he did so, he insisted, only within "common law" requirements for a governor to protect the health and safety of a state's citizens. He seized on the chief justice's language in a busing order that suggested one could validly object to busing where excessive distances might impinge on a child's health or education.[94] "This issue is not an issue of black and white," Wallace maintained. "It's not race at all. It's a matter of equity and health and safety." In a speech to the Alabama legislature, his favorite forum, he read from a dozen letters in which black and white parents and students complained about busing—a black mother in Birmingham who could not afford the twelve dollars a week in bus fares for her children; a white couple in Tuscaloosa whose son and daughter were legally adopted by grandparents to avoid busing; a boy who bought a forty-dollar class ring and then was transferred to another high school.[95]

Wallace's busing stand was also securing him grudging support from many Alabama legislators who earlier had successfully blocked his program by adjourning the 1971 session without approving a budget. Wallace felt strong enough to move boldly when he lacked money to meet the state's October payroll. He patched together a deal with the state's three largest banks: the banks would issue a loan to each state employee in the amount of his or her salary; the state would repay the loans—without interest—as soon as the legislature enacted a budget. In return, Wallace signed into law a bill containing his proposals to outlawing loan-sharking practices, plus a provision the banks wanted—increasing the limit on consumer interest rates. Wallace called a special session, daring the legislature to continue to oppose him. It backed down and enacted a record billion-dollar budget. "What the man has done," complained John Ripp, a consumer advocate opposed to the interest-rate increase, "is to thwart the legislative branch of government. It would be like Chase Manhattan giving Nixon money for programs the Congress had refused to finance."[96] (Ripp was onto something: other than its being public, Wallace's ploy was little different from Ronald Reagan's secret deals with oil-rich sheiks to finance the Nicaraguan contras after Congress had cut off funds for the rebels.)

■   ■   ■

By the end of October, Wallace decided (but did not announce) that he would enter the Florida Democratic primary, and a little-noted statewide referendum there in the first week of November convinced him that he could win it. Floridians overwhelmingly approved a 5 percent corporate income tax, the first in the state's history, despite organized and bitter opposition from big business. Wallace believed the vote in Florida signaled a likely positive response there to his own populist stances; he believed, too, that by adding to his hard-core following those voters who might be attracted to his populism could well lead to his first-place finish in the fractionalized Democratic field expected to participate in the March 14 primary.[97]

Another encouraging sign was that Wallace's "appreciation" dinners were big draws. In Los Angeles, fourteen hundred paying guests included the consul general of Taiwan, the comedian Pat Buttram, the actor Chill Wills, and the TV actor George Lindsey.

Wallace's New York dinner attracted twelve hundred (at fifty dollars a head, twice the tariff of the Los Angeles dinner); among the diners were several building-trades union officials, delegations of Chinese and Czechoslovak ethnic groups, and vice-presidents of two major banks.[98]

For his late-November Houston dinner, the campaign sold twenty-six hundred tickets; attendees included the local police chief, Herman Short; the football star Dickie Moegle; and the president of the longshoreman's local. As Wallace boarded his chartered jet for the flight to Montgomery, he chortled over a banner rigged by the maintenance crew: "George Wallace All the Way.   Give Them Hell, George." As he settled into his window seat, he turned to a reporter and said, "Man, these are straws in the wind, straws in the wind."

Wallace was so ebullient that, during the flight, he agreed to "play president" and provide a public preview of what a Wallace cabinet might look like. Wallace's only caveat was that in any subsequent article, it be made clear that Wallace, who had not given the matter deep thought, was simply mentioning names to personify his views of various issues. He well understood that he was a political leper even to those like Nixon, Spiro Agnew, and Washington State's Senator Henry "Scoop" Jackson who were echoing many of his views, and he wished neither to stigmatize nor embarrass anyone. "I don't want to get none of these fellas into trouble, now," he said. "You know, they might all have to come out with statements that they wouldn't serve with me. So you make it clear now that these are just the kind of people I admire." Then he added, a bit plaintively, "You know, they might not like me or vote for me." His selections included:

> *Secretary of Defense*: Congressman F. Edward Hebert of
> Louisiana, the chairman of the House Armed Services
> Committee. Wallace explained, "I want a man who believes in
> superiority in our offensive and defensive capability—not like
> these liberals who are trying to unilaterally disarm this
> country. The best way to stop World War III is to talk from a
> position of strength with the Russians and the Chinese."

> *Secretary of Health, Education, and Welfare*: Max Rafferty, the one-
> time controversial California superintendent of education
> whom Wallace had imported to Troy State College (in Troy,
> Alabama) as the dean. "He's a fundamentalist on education.

He believes in the three Rs and the basics—not this permissiveness stuff that turns these kids into radicals."

Secretary of the Treasury: Congressman Wilbur Mills of Arkansas, the chairman of the House Ways and Means Committee, or the economist Milton Friedman. "I would want somebody who was ignorant, like I am—I mean, who doesn't understand how you can run up a hundred-billion-dollar deficit and yet everybody in the country's gonna get rich. See, we don't understand that in Alabama. And I'd want somebody who would tax these super-rich foundations and church-owned commercial property because the people have had it up to here with taxes."

Attorney General: Former U.S. Supreme Court Justice Charles Whittaker or Senator John Stennis of Mississippi. "I'd want the attorney general to be strong for local law enforcement. We don't want any national police force. And, except for national security, where you'd make a sworn statement to a judge that that's what it's for, I don't like this wiretapping."

For secretary of state, Wallace liked William James Porter, a career diplomat who, for the previous four months, had been the chief negotiator at the Paris peace talks to end the Vietnam War. Porter had been the ambassador to Korea when he and Wallace had met during the governor's Southeast Asia tour in 1969. At that time, Wallace asserted, Porter had told him he had recommended to Nixon that U.S. bombers destroy North Vietnam's system of dikes controlling the flow of water to rice paddies. "They couldn't have kept on fighting without that rice crop," Wallace contended. "They say it would have drowned thousands of people and that it would be cruel. But I don't think that's cruel, do you? When you're fighting a war?"

Herman Talmadge, the Georgia senator and Agriculture Committee chairman, would champion a higher parity level for farmers as the agriculture secretary; Wallace's interior secretary (for which he did not suggest a name) would have to recognize both the country's energy requirements and the "gigantic" size of the pollution problem; his labor secretary would be the AFL-CIO's George Meany or the UAW's Leonard Woodcock ("but they'd have to be objective and willing to say when there have been excesses on the part of labor as well as on the part of industry"); and Nixon Supreme Court selections Lewis Powell and William Rehnquist represented the type of people Wallace would choose for the Court.[99]

Wallace's hypothetical choices prompted the *Washington Post* to comment: "It was . . . the business-as-usualness of it all that struck us as interesting about Governor Wallace's list. . . . *Plus ca change*, as they say in pointy-headed circles, which, roughly translated, means: 'There's not a dime's worth of difference.' "[100] But there *was* a difference—a crucial difference—with Wallace. He may not have governed much differently from his competitors for the Oval Office, but he certainly *talked* differently. And it was meaningful to millions of people to hear someone of importance articulate their hopes and frustrations. Like Starbuck in *The Rainmaker* or Professor Henry Hill in *The Music Man*, he was selling the people a dream. But instead of a dream of rain in a parched piece of the Southwest, or of a sparkling school band in River City, Wallace offered a vision of bringing to heel the mighty who controlled the nation's wealth and the government and who preyed on the hardworking "little people" by keeping them underpaid, overtaxed, and harried by interference in their day-to-day lives. Yes, Wallace warned, there *was* trouble in River City—and that starts with *T* and it rhymes with *P* and that stands for *Politician*. And like the denizens of River City, the millions who flocked to Wallace derived almost as much satisfaction from hearing him validate their dream as they might have from seeing him realize it.

"People can let off steam with me," he said in a 1971 interview. "They get mad—like this New York cab driver who says to me, 'These niggers been robbing me blind, and I'm gonna vote for you.' Well, he goes in that booth and—*yennnhhh!*—he yanks that lever and he gets to feeling better. That's better than if he went out and got himself all frustrated or got in a fight or hit somebody over the head."[101]

■   ■   ■

On January 5, 1972, a week before he formally entered the Florida Democratic primary, Wallace said, "I have no illusions about the ultimate outcome. But we gonna shake up the Democratic party. We gonna shake it to its eye-teeth." He would be one of eleven candidates seeking Florida's delegates, and a Wallace poll conducted fully two and a half months before the March 14 vote showed him getting 45 percent of the vote and carrying sixty-five of the state's sixty-seven counties. No one believed it, not even Wallace. He spent fifty-two of the next seventy-five days in Florida, conducted a hundred rallies in as many cities and towns, and spent a quarter of a million dollars.

Wallace doggedly pursued the style and olio of issues that had been working for him for more than a decade. He concentrated on the big rally, as opposed to the dozens of smaller meetings and hand-shaking tours favored by the other candidates. But none of the other candidates could risk staging a rally for fear of not drawing a crowd. Wallace packed them in—6,000 in Jacksonville, 3,500 in the Miami Beach Auditorium on a rainy night; 5,000 who waited two hours in ninety-degree heat at a Lake City park—a crowd that represented nearly a third of the city's population. His country musicians would entertain until George Mangum, a thirty-eight-year-old, beefy, white-maned Baptist preacher from Alabama would take the podium to whip up enthusiasm and plead for contributions. Mangum had been a Wallace campaign fixture since Lurleen's run for governor in 1966, and his pitch, like this one to 2,000 adherents in Bradenton, was down-home sermonizing: "If you believe-ah in what George Wallace is trying to do; if you believe-ah in this moment; if you believe-ah he should continue doing what he's doing—then we need your money."[102]

When Wallace would walk on stage, the crowds would go wild; he enjoyed the same sort of passionate public response that no political candidate, save John F. and Robert Kennedy, had provoked over the previous dozen years. Those screaming and yelling admirers were hardly confined to the rednecks or hardhats, though both groups generally predominated at his rallies. But there were identifiable knots of young people, some sporting full beards (at the time, a badge of youthful assertiveness, if not dissent) and some ecstatic teenyboppers; elderly people; disabled veterans in wheelchairs; union members; and white-collar workers. His appeal was to that broad band of the electorate that hungered for recognition—and Wallace provided it, praising their intelligence, foresight, intuition, traditional ethical and moral values, compassion, and willingness to work hard for what they got.[103] He told the Bradenton crowd:

> We're here tonight because the average citizen in this country—the man who pays his taxes and works for a living and holds this country together—the average citizen is fed up with much of this liberalism and this kowtowing to the exotic few. The big-time news media is here, too, and they're not here because of me but because of you. The other day on NBC, Mr. [David] Brinkley said that Governor Wallace

represents the average citizen of this country more than any other candidate. Sometimes these big-time newsmen, they ask me: "Haven't you changed?" Well, I haven't changed and you haven't changed. What's changed is they didn't listen to us in the past—but they have to listen now.[104]

At the Martin County Fair in Stuart, Florida, he told fifteen hundred cheering adherents:

When the theoreticians and bureaucrats in Washington said we ought to keep giving away our money because we'd get rich, you people—the average citizen, the little businessman—said, "No, we'd go broke that way." Well, you were right and they were wrong. . . . When the *New York Times* said old Castro was the Robin Hood of the Caribbean, they were wrong—and the average Alabamian or Floridian or American could just look at old Castro and tell by intuition he was a Communist."[105]

Privately, Wallace remained nearly as intense as he was on the platform. Politics was all there was for him. He had no hobbies, and he read little beyond history (especially about the Civil War) and press clippings or articles about himself. (On his occasional forays into fiction, he would tend toward the classics, such as Tolstoy's *Anna Karenina*, which he pronounced "Anna Ka-REE-na." "Why do you suppose," he said once, "that she threw herself under that train? You'd think she could have worked something out.")[106] And he rarely saw his family, even Cornelia, except on the stump. As Eleanor Clift of *Newsweek* observed, George often seemed oblivious to Cornelia—or, when he noticed her, downright rude. Before she was about to meet a group, he admonished, "Get the hair out of your eyes." While Cornelia was talking to Clift as the campaign plane was taking off, George said gruffly, "Hush! I don't want to have a wreck because you're running your mouth." But he was often solicitous, referring to Cornelia as "doll" and his "striking black-headed girl." He talked often of how happy he was, but he rarely showed any affection in public, would often summon Cornelia by barking her name, and would sometimes even neglect to introduce her to people. "He can't pull me around like a doll," she once snapped angrily. But, as time would tell, she was to stand by her man for several years in trying circumstances.[107]

Privately, he also excoriated his opponents. While downing breakfast at NBC's Washington studio after a "Today" show interview, he jabbed his finger at the Formica tabletop and said, "Teddy Kennedy doesn't have any more feeling for people than this table. Hell, he goes to Switzerland to ski for five days, probably spent fifty thousand dollars. Why don't he give that to the poor if he's so interested in them?" Later, when Muskie was mentioned, he said, "You know what they saying about Muskie? If you don't vote for him, he'll cry," a reference to Muskie's choked-up response in New Hampshire to allegations that his wife was an alcoholic. Then he added, "No, he's a high-type individual. . . . They all high-type individuals. They ain't worth a damn politically. Now, I say that in all good humor, but they never say nothing nice about me."[108]

In Florida (and, later, in Michigan and a few other states) school busing was the key issue. At Vero Beach, Wallace said:

> Now, on this busing. I said many years ago, if we don't stop the federal takeover of the schools, there'd be chaos. Well, what've we got? Chaos. This thing they've come up with of busing little children to schools is the most asinine, atrocious, callous thing I've ever heard of in the whole history of the United States. Why when President Nixon was in China, so I hear, he and Mao Tse-tung spent half their time talking about busing. And I hear Mao Tse-tung told him, "Well, over here in China, if we take a notion to bus 'em, we bus 'em, whether they like it or not." Well, Mr. Nixon could have told him that we about to do the same thing over here.[109]

Being against busing, he insisted, was not being for segregation or against blacks. He was fond of telling the story of when an NBC crew headed by the correspondent Sander Vanocur was doing a story on Wallace's hometown of Clio:

> We drove by Willy Wilburn's. That's a black nightspot in Barbour County. And I said, "Let's pull up here." And some of them New York boys, they didn't want to stop because there's three or four young blacks, tough-looking with mustaches, standing outside. But I walk up and they smile and they shake my hand, and then Willy comes running out and hugs my neck and says, "Governor, I thought you never coming back after they sent you up yonder," and he turns and hollers, "Louise, come see Governor Wallace"—Louise, that's his wife. Shoot, them New York boys like to died. I said, "Now, when I'm in New York, you gonna take me to see some of your black

nightspots?" And they said, "No, sir. We're liable to get killed."[110]

In states like Wisconsin, where busing was not a serious factor, and even in Florida, Wallace emphasized another part of his litany— tax reform, an issue he insisted was more important to him than busing. Here's how he put it at a Tallahassee rally:

> We're sick and tired of the average citizen being taxed to death while these multibillionaires like the Rockefellers and the Fords and the Mellons and Carnegies go without paying taxes. They got billions of dollars in tax-shelter foundations and they don't pay as much tax as you do on a percentage basis. And the church commercial property—the churches own businesses, shopping centers, hotels, skyscrapers, all competing with private enterprise. A fair tax on this two hundred billion dollars in untaxed wealth would bring in twelve billion dollars to the treasury. We've got to close up these loopholes on those who've escaped paying their fair share so we can lower taxes for the average citizen— the little businessman, the farmer, the elderly, the middle class.[111]

He remained tough as ever on law and order, praising the police and condemning the courts: "These federal judges don't get elected," he said at Leesburg, Florida, "they're not responsible to the people, and they've got more power than all your elected representatives put together. And if one was sitting next to you, you wouldn't recognize him. We ought to send a message to Washington that we want Supreme Court judges reaffirmed by the Senate every six years. And we want these district court judges elected by the people." And welfare remained a bloated target, as he said in Orlando: "Up in New York City, they got 1,270,000 people on welfare. But they say you can't ask him whether he works or how much money he makes or you might hurt his dignity." And, of course, as he mentioned in Lake City, "The average citizen is fed up with this foreign aid . . . to countries from Afghanistan to Zanzibar."[112]

■   ■   ■

Wallace's messages brought his supporters up out of their chairs, but the fundamental message—the one that precipitated guttural roars as if from the throng's buried soul—was Wallace's passionate apotheosis of the frustrated, overlooked middle class:

> This is a people's awakening. Those pluperfect hypocrites in Washington don't know what's coming over you. Well, if they'd gone out and asked a taxi driver, a little businessman, or a beautician or a barber or a farmer, they'd have found out. But no, they don't ask those folks when they make their decisions. They ask some pointy-headed pseudo-intellectual who can't even park his bicycle straight when he gets to the campus, that's who they ask. But they're not ignoring you now. You're tops. You're the people.[113]

Some called it demagogy: "Flattery pure and simple forms a major part of Wallace's magic with crowds, as does the crudely simplistic fashion in which he evokes the public's gripes," said *Newsweek*.[114] That in itself seemed a crude assessment; after all, what politician does not flatter his or her adherents? And one person's crude simplism might be another's raw honesty. During the Florida campaign, Humphrey admitted to changing his positions on busing and tax reform to get closer to Wallace's views, although that did him little good.[115]

Wallace took 42 percent of the vote (more than half a million votes) and carried every county in the state, including urbanized Dade County (Miami), suburban Broward County (Fort Lauderdale), and posh Palm Beach County, plus the rural counties.[116] His nearest competitor, Sen. Hubert Humphrey (Minnesota) received 18 percent; Sen. Henry "Scoop" Jackson (Washington) took 13 percent. Sen. Edmund Muskie (Maine), already weakened in New Hampshire (where he had won, but where the media had portrayed Sen. George McGovern's better-than-expected second-place showing as the "real" victory) received only 9 percent, and his bile-filled denunciation of the results essentially eliminated him from the race in which he had once been considered the front-runner. "This shows," Muskie said of the Florida results, "that some of the worst instincts of which human beings are capable are all too prevalent in our elections. George Wallace is a threat to human decency."[117] Other candidates, however, either held their tongues or openly identified with Wallace's views.

In a postprimary interview on the "CBS Morning News," not only did Humphrey refuse to reject Wallace as a prospective running mate, but he made comments on busing that might have been scripted by the Alabama governor: "People don't want their children to be bused hither and yon," Humphrey said, "from a good school to a bad school, from a good neighborhood to a neighborhood filled with crime."[118] Two days after the election, the president of the United States declared on national television that people do "not want their children bused across the city to an inferior school just to meet some social planner's concept of what is considered to be the correct racial balance."[119] Most important to Wallace's stature was Nixon's strongly worded denunciation of those who associated anti-busing views with racism. After Nixon's statement, it required extraordinary mental gymnastics to maintain that Wallace's condemnation of busing encompassed coded racism, but Humphrey's and Nixon's did not.[120]

■ ■ ■

Other critics rejected the conventional description of Wallace as a populist. "Wallace's spiel . . . is populist," Frank Trippett wrote in *Life*, "only in its lurid sheen. Its body lacks the detailed critique of the system's inequities that was the hallmark of the authentic populist movement. It is utterly without a populist prescription of specific remedies."[121] Granting the frequent misapplication of the term *populist* to any politician who appeals to popular whim, such wholesale censure of Wallace's populism clearly was a response more to Wallace's racist past than to an examination of his political present. Wallace, like the original populists of the 1890s, distrusted banks and the rich while advocating tax reforms that would favor farmers and working people. And his proposals were as specific—often more so—than those of his opponents. His suggestion to tax foundations and church-owned property went far beyond anything offered by any other candidate. His advocacy of public school choice, dismissed by his opponents as a dodge to avoid integration, was twenty years ahead of its time as a mainstream proposition. One need not agree with school choice, whatever Wallace's motive for supporting it, to understand that its application is theoretically egalitarian and democratic—and fully populist. And it is difficult to think that the hardworking, somewhat nativist early populists, had they lived in a later time, would have objected to Wallace's insistence that able-bodied welfare recipients go to work, or that nations denouncing the U.S. in world councils be stripped of U.S. foreign aid.

Postelection polls in Florida demonstrated that the people

viewed Wallace as a populist rather than an extremist, and he carried his new respectability with him to Wisconsin.[122] The day after the Florida primary, Wallace told his staff he ought to test his strength in the North by entering the Wisconsin primary. When his polls came back, showing him receiving 8 percent of the vote (about the same he had received in the 1968 general election), he almost regretted his decision. He agreed to appear at four rallies and put up a token campaign. He returned to Alabama for more than a week and did not enter Wisconsin until March 23, leaving him only eight days to campaign before the April 4 primary (Wallace did not conduct Sunday rallies). But when his first rally in Milwaukee drew a standing-room-only crowd, Wallace told Charles Snider, "See if we can't get into some more cities." In the end, he staged eleven rallies and submitted to as many TV interviews as possible—and he ended up with 22 percent of the vote. That put him in second place, eight points behind McGovern and a nudge ahead of Humphrey. Wallace had shown quick adaptability, shifting from the Floridians' key concern over busing to the Wisconsinites' primary worry about high state and local taxes. He reminded the voters how his strong Florida showing had sent a message to Nixon, who had swiftly jumped off the school bus. A good vote in Wisconsin, he pledged, would bring "a move for meaningful tax relief" even before the general election in November.[123]

The other candidates followed suit—wisely, as it turned out. A postelection survey found that economic issues accounted for the one-two finish of McGovern and Wallace; in fact, a large number of Wallace voters reported that McGovern was their second choice.[124] But the Wisconsin results also revealed Wallace's essential weakness—unfamiliarity with the delegate-selection process developed by party pros after the 1968 election. Because Wallace had swept Florida and all its counties, hardly anyone raised an eyebrow over Humphrey having been awarded 6 of the state's 81 delegates. But the Wallace people were virtually unaware that the rules there, as in a number of other primary states, awarded delegates to candidates carrying pluralities in congressional districts, not by apportioning delegates on the basis of the popular vote. So in Wisconsin, Wallace's 22 percent of the popular vote did not translate into a single delegate. Third-place Humphrey, however, received 13 delegates, while McGovern's 30 percent translated into 54 delegates. In Pennsylvania, Wallace conducted only one rally; he came in second with 21 percent, a result he termed, with some justification, "the most phenomenal victory of [his] entire career." But he received no delegates. McGovern, who finished just a few votes behind Wallace, nonetheless received 37 delegates; Muskie, in fourth place, acquired 29 delegates; the winner, Humphrey, who won 35 percent of the popular vote, obtained 57 delegates. Indiana was much the same. Humphrey won with 47 percent of the vote, with Wallace a strong second at 41 percent. But Humphrey took 54 delegates and Wallace only 21. "We didn't know the rules the way the McGovern [and Humphrey] people did," Snider admitted belatedly.[125]

■   ■   ■

Wallace won big in Tennessee and North Carolina (though a number of delegates threatened to ignore the requirement to vote for Wallace). He took a plurality of Texas delegates elected in convention; in Houston on the night of the Indiana primary, he was accorded a frantic, heated two-minute ovation when he announced he was running a close second in the Hoosier state. And, despite a strong effort by his opponents to embarrass him in the Alabama primary (criticizing his long absences and renewing allegations of corruption in his administration), Wallace won overwhelmingly and received 37 delegates.[126]

With his polls showing that he would do well in Michigan and Maryland (which would be his last two major primaries; his people had failed to qualify him for the Ohio and California contests), he felt confident that, despite the campaign's failure to focus on delegates rather than on popular votes, he would enter the Miami convention with 300 to 400 delegates—perhaps enough to block a first- or second-ballot nomination of his remaining chief rivals, McGovern and Humphrey. Then, he felt, he would have a chance to broker the convention or—it was not beyond possibility, he thought—even get the nomination himself.[127] At the least, he believed, he could force the Democratic party to move to the right.[128]

And he was not alone in believing that "right" clearly was the direction in which the party had to move if it wanted to win. The demographers Richard M. Scammon and Ben J. Wattenberg, in a remarkable 1971 analysis of the American electorate called *The Real Majority*, doubtless had Wallace in mind when they offered this prescription for a Democratic victory in 1972:

Do *not* say, "Well, I don't agree with the Students for a

Democratic Society when they invade a college president's office, but I can understand their deep sense of frustration."

Do say, "When students break laws they will be treated as lawbreakers."

Do *not* say, "Crime is a complicated sociological phenomenon and we'll never be able to solve the problem until we get at the root causes of poverty and racism."

Do say, "I am going to make our neighborhoods safe again for decent citizens of every color."[129]

Wallace (and the occasional political scientist like Scammon, Wattenberg, or Kevin Phillips) warned that unless Democrats reversed their leftward trend, they could forget about winning the White House. As Wallace prepared to close out his Maryland campaign the day before the May 16 primary, he believed that, at the Miami convention, he would persuade the party that he was correct.

■　　■　　■

On Monday morning, May 15, Wallace awoke in the ornate bedroom of Alabama's Governor's Mansion at seven-thirty, donned his scarlet bathrobe with black satin lapels, shuffled downstairs, and announced he was ready to eat. He was already reading the Montgomery and Birmingham newspapers when Cornelia joined him for breakfast. Wallace asked for toast rather than his usual biscuits because he thought he was putting on weight. Afterward, he dressed quickly, checking with his wife to see if his tie matched his suit and blue shirt. By 9:00 A.M. they left the mansion for the flight to Maryland and his final rallies of the primary campaign.[130]

Wallace had been voicing some unease over the growing intensity of demonstrations at his recent rallies. While campaigning in Michigan early in May, he had told Michael F. Wendland of the *Detroit News* that he was not especially concerned about hecklers from college campuses. "Hell," he said, "I don't mind the kids. They're just young and full of spit and vinegar. They ain't the ones I fear. The ones that scare me are the ones you don't notice. . . . I can just see a little guy out there that nobody's paying attention to. He reaches into his pocket and out comes the little gun, like that Sirhan guy that got Kennedy."[131]

His Maryland campaign had intensified his worry. "Somebody's going to get killed before this primary is over," he had said, as quoted in *Time*. In the first week of May, two hundred blacks in Hagerstown, Maryland, shouting slogans and obscenities, had forced Wallace to cut short his speech; on May 11 in Frederick, Maryland, he had been hit in the shoulder by a rock thrown by a demonstrator. Later the same day, University of Maryland students had thrown Popsicles at him. On May 15, his first rally was at a park in Wheaton, a sprawling suburban community in Maryland's affluent Montgomery County, outside Washington, D.C. He faced a boisterous, restless crowd of three thousand; the hecklers among them shouted "remember Selma" and "Hitler for vice-president." Halfway through his speech, a barrage of coins, rocks, oranges, and tomatoes flew toward Wallace's eight-hundred-pound, bullet-proof lectern that the campaign transported from rally to rally. Security guards deflected most of the missiles with table-sized metal shields they had begun carrying in Maryland a few weeks earlier. Meanwhile, Wallace deflected most of the taunts. To the cries of "bullshit, bullshit," he commented that he expected a broader vocabulary from college students. To one (fortuitously) errant tomato thrower he suggested that the Baltimore Orioles might want to sign him to pitch for the opposition.[132]

Standing close to the stage was Arthur Bremer, a well-groomed, clean-shaven, twenty-one-year-old man wearing a Wallace button on his jacket lapel. He applauded Wallace loudly and often and asked a Secret Service agent if he could induce the governor to come down and shake hands. A television newsman, Fred Farrar, saw Bremer standing there and thought to himself, "This guy is weird. That smirk of his was almost spine-tingling." He instructed his cameraman to get Bremer on film. But the governor, after curtailing his speech by about fifteen minutes, was hustled directly to his car; his security people prevailed on him to forgo working the crowd because of the hecklers' number and temper.[133]

The Wallace caravan sped to the town of Laurel in adjacent Prince Georges County and, before heading to the Laurel Shopping Center, stopped at a Howard Johnson restaurant for a lunch break. The unpleasantness in Wheaton had not dulled Wallace's appetite; his bill of fare included a hamburger steak doused in ketchup, mashed potatoes, boiled carrots, apple pie, milk, and iced tea. While Wallace was eating heartily, Bremer drove his dusty blue coupe, an American Motors Rebel, to the Laurel Shopping Center and found a place close to the stage, just as he had in Wheaton. It was about three o'clock when the Wallace entourage set out from the restaurant for the shopping center. In the car, Wallace started coughing, and a concerned Cornelia asked an aide to get a jar of honey so the governor could soothe his throat. But by the time he brought the jar and Cornelia had poured some into a cup, Wallace had taken the stage.[134]

His voice cracked occasionally, and he repeatedly referred to the people of "Princess George County," instead of Prince Georges County, eliciting guffaws from collegians in the crowd. But when he finished his fifty-minute discourse on the evils of big government, the federal courts, the national media, social planners, bureaucrats, and pseudo-intellectual college professors, he drew thunderous applause.[135] He descended from the stage, signed some autographs, and turned toward the blue station wagon that had carried him and Cornelia to the rally. But many in the crowd implored him to approach the rope barrier so they could shake his hand. Wallace, never needing much encouragement to plunge into a crowd, handed his suit coat to an aide and moved to the folks. He grabbed the hand of Clyde Merryman, a horse exerciser at Pimlico, and that of Clyde's mother, Maryellen Snodgrass, and greeted Ross and Mabel Spiegel. At that point, Bremer pushed between the Spiegels and started firing a .38-caliber revolver. He emptied all five shots into Wallace before Merryman and Spiegel wrestled him to the ground and started beating and kicking him. Wallace fell on his back, with his arms flung out to either side. Cornelia rushed to him, stooped down, and pressed against him, soaking up some blood on her yellow suit jacket. Two doctors in the crowd reached Wallace and lifted Cornelia from her husband; he was having trouble breathing, and the doctors urged that the agents not even wait for an ambulance but take Wallace to a nearby hospital in the station wagon.

Prince Georges County policemen had grabbed Bremer from the mob and stuffed him, bruised and bleeding, into the back of a squad car. At the podium, George Mangum exhorted the crowd to back away from Wallace and give him room to breathe. Fights broke out between Wallace supporters and hecklers. Some people screamed and others wept. Amid the mayhem, it was only belatedly that someone noticed three others down: Secret Service Agent Nicholas Zarvos, with a throat wound; Dora Thompson, a local Wallace volunteer, with a bullet in her right leg; and Alabama State Trooper E. C. Dothard, with a slight stomach wound. All three were hit by bullets that had also struck Wallace.[136]

An ambulance arrived moments after Wallace had been placed

in the back of the station wagon. A volunteer rescue squad worker had been applying oxygen to the governor until he and Dothard were transferred to the ambulance and placed side by side for the fifteen-mile trip to Holy Cross Hospital in Silver Spring; a Secret Service staff car carried Zarvos and Thompson to Leland Hospital, closer than Holy Cross, but not as well equipped to deal with the severe wounds Wallace had suffered. Cornelia climbed in the ambulance's back seat, from which she leaned over and stroked her husband's head. Three Secret Service agents and a Wallace aide hopped aboard; two medical technicians applied oxygen to Wallace and intravenous medications to both wounded men. As the ambulance raced to Holy Cross, Cornelia alternated between periods of composure and grief. Dothard repeated over and over, "Take care of the governor, take care of the governor." Wallace seemed bewildered but did not lose consciousness. He pushed the oxygen mask away several times, and asked, "Am I shot?" "I'm in pain," he uttered twice. Then, presumably anticipating uncomfortable surgery, he said, "Make sure they knock me out."[137]

At the hospital, a team of surgeons started working on Wallace shortly after five o'clock. More than five hours later, he was wheeled out of surgery into the recovery room. He had been struck twice in the right arm and once in the left shoulder blade. One bullet had crashed into his abdomen, perforating the stomach and large intestine; enough of Wallace's undigested lunch had splattered into his body cavities to cause several serious infections. But the real problem was that a fifth slug had penetrated the spinal canal and had severed a bundle of nerves carrying impulses from the lower body to the brain. Wallace would never walk again. He would never have control over his bladder or bowel functions.[138] He would no longer be sexually active. And what would prove to be most psychologically debilitating of all, he would never have another day without grinding, insistent pain—pain that neither drugs nor acupuncture nor sophisticated neurological surgery would eradicate.[139]

Cornelia met the press that night to say that George was in "very good" condition. She said he had suffered an abdominal wound, but she neglected to mention his paralysis.[140] But apparently she knew, because when Snider arrived at the hospital after flying up from Montgomery, Cornelia greeted him by saying, "Well, Charlie, it looks like we've got another FDR candidate on our hands."[141] The next day, Wallace's chief physician, Joseph Schanno, asked about Wallace's future viability in politics, made the same comparison between

Wallace and FDR.[142] A couple of days earlier, anyone making such a linkage would have been fitted for a straitjacket.

■ ■ ■

Had the calamity of May 15 not intervened, rendering Wallace physically unable to continue his fiery campaign (the success of which relied almost exclusively on Wallace's physicality), he may well have succeeded. But the power of ideas alone, divorced from a convincing sachem crusading for them, has rarely been enough in American politics to forge a wide and stable constituency.

Still, the bullets that had ripped into Wallace had a politically cleansing effect. In the ensuing weeks, he was visited in the hospital by a parade of notables—including Nixon, Humphrey, McGovern, several of the Kennedys (Ted, Joan, and Ethel), Democratic Party Chairman Lawrence O'Brien, and a host of governors, many of whom would not have touched a healthy Wallace with a ten-foot pole. Not only had he joined a frighteningly expanding list of political martyrs, but the Democrats now thirsted for his followers. Jimmy Carter, who had been trying to walk the line between Wallace and an image of moderation, said, "[The Wallace voters are] now somewhat detachable from Wallace himself, and they must be kept in the Democratic Party."[143] Carter would attract most of them four years later because he was a Southerner and because, like Wallace, he ran as an outsider who denounced the Washington establishment and its entrenched bureaucracy. But Ronald Reagan would snatch the Wallace adherents for the GOP in 1980. By then, the Wallace issues had become part and parcel of mainline Republican politics, and it would not be until 1992 that the Democrats finally caught on.

But Wallace was finished as a personal force. His assailant turned out to be an emotionally stunted, impenetrably twisted man who had set out to kill President Nixon but, when he could not catch up to him, considered shooting McGovern, and finally switched his target to Wallace. "I have to kill somebody," he confided to his diary. "I am one sick assassin." An hour after the shooting, Secret Service agents, without a search warrant, entered Bremer's cluttered Milwaukee apartment and found Wallace campaign buttons, Black Panther literature, an old high school theme in which Bremer fantasized that his father had married Donna Reed, and a scribbled note about masturbation; incredibly, no one objected when several reporters entered the apartment and, in some cases, made off with some of

Bremer's possessions. The Prince Georges County police officers who searched Bremer's car parked at the shopping center found, among other things, two books about the assassination of Robert Kennedy.[144]

Within two minutes of the shooting, the presidential aide H. R. Haldeman had been notified and had relayed the information to Nixon. About the same time, Assistant FBI Director W. Mark Felt called another of Nixon's aides, Charles Colson, to inform him that his boss, Acting Attorney General Richard Kleindienst, had instructed the FBI to establish its jurisdiction by moving agents to every investigative locale, including Bremer's apartment. Felt told Colson that his agents would not enter the apartment until they obtained a search warrant. Colson rushed to the president's office, and the two men quickly hatched a bizarre plot that far surpassed in its base criminality anything of which Nixon subsequently was accused in the Watergate-inspired articles of impeachment: Colson operative E. Howard Hunt, a retired CIA agent, would break into Bremer's apartment and plant pro-McGovern literature there. Authorities and the media would be convinced that the attempted assassination was rooted in left-wing Democratic politics. Colson prepared the ground by phoning Felt to pass along "rumors" that he and Nixon supposedly had heard that Bremer "had ties with [Ted] Kennedy or McGovern political operatives [and] that obviously there could be a conspiracy." Within an hour, Hunt's bags were packed, and he had made a plane reservation. But the FBI had moved too quickly; before Hunt departed, agents had obtained their warrant and had sealed off Bremer's apartment. Nixon upbraided Colson for not having slowed down the FBI; he later complained that the agency's sudden competence had resulted in a lost opportunity to damage his likely opponent in the fall.[145] (Disclosure of the incident by the journalist Seymour Hersh in December 1992 prompted Wallace's son to request a federal investigation into the possibility of a Watergate-related conspiracy to shoot his father.[146] Nixon reportedly was worried that a member of his reelection campaign might have been involved. Two years later, as the net of impeachment was enmeshing Nixon, Vice-President Gerald Ford, presumably anticipating having to deal as president with a deposed Nixon, asked Nixon's lawyer, James St. Clair, if the White House had been involved with Wallace's shooting. " 'Is there anything to it?' " St. Clair quoted Ford. " 'Is there a problem? Was the White House behind the Wallace shooting?' I said no."[147] The thousands of pages of FBI investigative documents on the shooting, obtained under the Freedom of Information Act, have revealed no credible evidence that Bremer even knew, much less acted with, anyone connected with the White House or Nixon's reelection campaign committee—or with anyone else, for that matter.[148]

■   ■   ■

Bremer was sentenced to sixty-three years in jail; Wallace got life, imprisoned in his own body.[149] But the day after the shooting, Wallace's already impressive campaign was crowned with an exceptional double victory. In Maryland, Wallace took 39 percent of the vote to Humphrey's 27 percent; McGovern was third with 22 percent. In Michigan, Wallace attracted 51 percent of the total vote. McGovern finished second with 27 percent, and Humphrey drew a disappointing 16 percent, boding ill for the all-important, winner-take-all California contest three weeks away.

School busing was a big issue in Michigan, and two-thirds of the voters in both states named crime and violence as a primary concern. Exit polls demonstrated further that few voters switched to Wallace in sympathy over the shooting. A *Time* correspondent in Michigan, Gregory Wierzynski, said that interviews with Wallace voters suggested that they viewed him as "something much bigger than [a] regional candidate.... People expressed genuine admiration, almost reverence, for Wallace."[150] By day's end, Wallace, of all the Democratic candidates, was by far the popular choice among the voters. Overall, he had amassed more than 3,300,000 votes—700,000 more than Humphrey and over a million more than McGovern.[151]

In the six remaining primaries, Wallace, represented inadequately on the stump by Alabama state legislators and staff members (Cornelia, who might have been more effective, refused to leave her husband's side) accumulated 54 more delegates and an additional 400,000 votes, including 216,000 write-in votes in California, which placed him third. McGovern won there with 44 percent to Humphrey's 39 percent. But under the rules, McGovern was awarded all 271 California delegates.[152] That left McGovern a bare 50 votes short of achieving 1,509 delegate votes—the absolute majority needed for the nomination.[153]

McGovern's opponents coalesced into a loose federation to try to stop his nomination. They won an initial victory at the credentials committee on June 29; the committee voted seventy-two to sixty-six that, in keeping with the party's efforts at fairer, more democratic representation at the convention, the California delegates should be allocated proportionately to the popular vote.[154] In effect, the ruling deprived McGovern of 151 votes and left him more than 200 votes short of the number needed for nomination. It also meant that Humphrey and Wallace now owned a combined vote of just under 900—400 behind McGovern but certainly within striking distance.[155] Humphrey began thinking about an unlikely coalition to stop McGovern and to give the Minnesotan a second chance against Nixon.

Actually, Humphrey had started putting out feelers for Wallace's support a few days before the fateful shooting. An overture had been made two weeks after Wallace's astonishing second-place finish to Humphrey in the April 25 Pennsylvania primary, and when polls had shown Wallace leading in the forthcoming contests in Maryland and Michigan. A Southern supporter of Humphrey, the insurance company executive John Amos of Columbus, Georgia, had arranged a meeting with a longtime Alabama politician and Wallace friend, Jimmy Faulkner. According to Faulkner, Amos had said he was representing Humphrey, who wanted "to open a line of communication" for Wallace's support; in return, Humphrey was "willing to consider such things as letting Wallace suggest the vice president . . . or help nominate cabinet members." Faulkner had replied that the only way to assure Wallace's support was to make him part of the ticket. Amos had answered that he was not authorized to go beyond what he had said, and he had asked that Faulkner carry the message to Wallace, who was then campaigning in the Midwest. After spending a day in Montgomery, Wallace would go to Maryland and remain through Tuesday's results. Faulkner had made an appointment to brief Wallace for the following Friday, May 19.[156]

On Monday, May 15, Wallace was gunned down; on Tuesday he won Maryland by a wide margin and Michigan overwhelmingly. On Wednesday, Amos telephoned Faulkner and, as Faulkner recalled, "said Humphrey had called him and they were willing to take George Wallace on the ticket on crutches, in a wheelchair, or any way." He asked Faulkner to pass the message on to Wallace as quickly as possible. Faulkner was able to see Wallace on May 25. When he told him of Humphrey's offer, Wallace was delighted. He asked Faulkner to serve as his liaison to Humphrey at the convention.[157]

■   ■   ■

By the time the convention opened in July, Wallace had been transferred from Holy Cross Hospital to a Birmingham hospital. Nixon, in
yet another manifestation of how the shooting had raised Wallace's
stature, sent a Navy DC-9 hospital plane to transport Wallace to the
Democratic National Convention. The governor was in some pain
and it increased during the week; his doctors would discover in a few
days that he had developed severe peritonitis; Snider said later, "It
almost killed him; he never should have come." But Wallace was
determined to accept Larry O'Brien's invitation to address the convention, a first for a presidential candidate.[158]

Meanwhile, Snider worked with top campaign aides to other
presidential candidates in an attempt to block McGovern's nomination. Humphrey's and Scoop Jackson's people worked in lockstep
with Snider; Muskie, on the other hand, could not decide whether or
not to encourage his 208 delegates to join the effort—and his hesitation would work to McGovern's favor.[159] The key to the cabal was
California. The convention would vote Monday night, July 10, on
whether to accept the credentials committee's decision to apportion
California's delegation according to the popular vote. Upholding the
committee's ruling would give Humphrey a fighting chance at the
nomination; overturning it would virtually assure McGovern's nomination. On Sunday, O'Brien made it easier for McGovern's forces to
negate the committee's determination. He decided that the 151
delegates in dispute—those taken from McGovern and awarded to
Humphrey, Wallace, and others on the basis of the proportional
distribution of delegates—would not be permitted to vote on the
California question. Conversely, the 120 pro-McGovern delegates in
California would be allowed to vote. In addition, a simple majority of
those voting, rather than an absolute majority of delegates, would be
sufficient to upset the credentials committee's recommendation.
O'Brien's action lowered the bar for McGovern by some 200 votes: he
would have his 120 votes from California, and he would need 76 fewer
votes to obtain his majority.[160]

Snider and his allies tried to fight O'Brien. They secured a
meeting with the party chairman the night before the vote. The
credentials committee's ruling, Snider argued, was based on the
party's reform rules of fair apportionment—rules that should have
taken precedence over the prior decision of the California Democratic party to conduct a winner-take-all primary. O'Brien curtly told
Snider, "You are playing in the major leagues; you can't change the
rules of the game after it starts." Snider rejoined, "Yes, sir—but this

is the first ball game we've been in where the umpire gets up to bat."
O'Brien snorted, said he would consider their views, and left.[161]

At almost the moment Snider was being rejected by O'Brien,
Faulkner was being received warmly by Senator Humphrey. He remembered Humphrey saying that he and Wallace "would make a
winning team." Humphrey said, "Wallace would be good for me and
I think I would be good for him." Humphrey said he would "finalize
the arrangements" after consulting three people whom he did not
identify. He added, however, that should the convention vote the next
night to give McGovern all 271 California delegates, the idea of a
Humphrey-Wallace ticket would, of course, be moot.[162]

Even with O'Brien stacking the deck for McGovern, nearly all
those participating in the convention expected the California vote to
be close. Those who knew better were McGovern's political operatives, headed by Gary Hart and Frank Mankiewicz. They had been
quietly and persistently making inroads among delegates supporting
other candidates but willing to lend support on the California vote.
McGovern operatives made face-to-face calls on delegates in their
beach-front hotels; party regulars, now lined up with McGovern, won
over delegates by inviting them into the inner sanctum—O'Brien's
posh convention headquarters suite—for cocktails and personal introductions to the party's leading lights. Their biggest cache of votes
came from Muskie delegates who, absent Muskie's guidance, agreed
to help McGovern on the California vote. By the time the wavering
Muskie, feeling himself ill treated by the McGovern forces, announced that he would support upholding the credentials committee's decision, it was too late; most of his delegates had pledged to
back McGovern on the issue. One of Humphrey's floor leaders later
said bitterly that McGovern would probably appoint Muskie to be
ambassador to Elsinore.[163]

In the end, the McGovernites rolled up 1,618 votes to overrule
the credentials committee—185 more than the required majority,
and 109 more than an absolute majority. But he would have lost had it
not been for O'Brien's manipulation of the voting rules. Had the 120
Californians for McGovern been barred from voting, as had the 151
backing other delegates, McGovern would have received 1,498
votes—65 votes more than a majority of those eligible to vote, but 11
votes short of the absolute majority of 1,509. Without O'Brien's
parliamentary sleight of hand, McGovern would have lost the California vote and Humphrey might well have been the party's nominee.[164]
The next morning, Humphrey telephoned Wallace to tell him he was

withdrawing and would not have his name placed in nomination. Wallace said, "I'm sorry, Hubert, because I think we would have made a good team."[165]

Had Humphrey secured the nomination, would he have actually gone ahead with his plan to put Wallace on the ticket? None of the several former Humphrey aides I interviewed thought so; indeed, none believed that Humphrey had, in so many words, offered the second spot on the ticket to Wallace. Humphrey's longtime press secretary, Norman Sherman, thought Wallace's claim was "nonsense." Sherman said he personally abhorred John Amos, now deceased, but he conceded, "For some reason, Hubert liked him. . . . I'm sure [Amos] went away from Hubert thinking he had a mission to work out an alliance with Wallace. Hubert probably said something like, 'It sounds like a good idea, John,' and then forgot about it."[166] But Sherman and other former Humphrey aides to whom I spoke agreed that Humphrey had shown himself quite capable of Machiavellian politics, as when he had toadied to Gov. Lester Maddox of Georgia for his support in 1968, or when he had run radio commercials in the 1972 Florida primary excoriating "welfare loafers."

And more than a dozen Democratic governors, several of whom (including Jimmy Carter) thought that a Humphrey-Wallace ticket would have carried the South, went so far as to raise the possibility of a McGovern-Wallace ticket. Carter, South Carolina's John West, and Minnesota's Wendell Anderson were among those who called on Wallace after the California vote. It was an unofficial delegation to see if Wallace would consider running with McGovern; if so, they would sound out McGovern on the idea. Wallace was not interested, and the matter died.[167]

■   ■   ■

On the night of Tuesday, July 11, George Wallace reached the pinnacle of his political career. Two Secret Service agents and an Alabama state trooper lifted the governor in his gleaming, chrome wheelchair to the convention platform. Most delegates stood and applauded. Many, however, remained seated and silent. For the next nine minutes, despite fierce pain, he spoke in a strong voice, summarizing his views on how to make the Democratic party "become what it used to be—the party of the average working man."[168] His speech concentrated on the Wallace planks advocating tax reform and tax relief for the middle class (to be financed, in part, by taxing foundations and

church-owned property), prohibition of busing for school integration, restoration of school prayer by constitutional amendment, a
firm stance on law-and-order, support for a strong military, and linkage of U.S. withdrawal from Vietnam with the return of all American
POWs. The Wallace positions prompted Kevin Phillips to describe
Wallace, some years later, as "the first national tax-revolt leader [and]
the man also in the vanguard of so many other populist causes."[169]

All the minority platform proposals were overwhelmingly defeated by thundering choruses of nays. The McGovernites, in their
summary disavowal of the concerns eating at millions of voters, had
inadvertently solidified the conservative presidential majority established in 1968 when Nixon and Wallace together won 57 percent of
the vote. Nixon—and every successful presidential candidate
since—found the winning formula by appealing to the growing mass
of voters who may have supported the abstract principle of racial
equality but who, in the words of the journalist Thomas Edsall,
rejected what they saw as a government-imposed "liberal, authori-
tarian, statist agenda ... directed by the courts and the federal
regulatory bureaucracy."[170]

■   ■   ■

Wallace was nominated for president on July 12 and received nearly
four hundred first-ballot votes. (He would have accumulated more
than four hundred had Jimmy Carter not reneged on an earlier
bargain—that if Wallace stayed out of the Georgia primary, Carter
would deliver Georgia to him at the convention, provided Wallace
had amassed three hundred delegates or more. Carter, who already
was hatching his own national plans, established his moderation by
distancing himself from Wallace; Carter was among those nominating Scoop Jackson.) The day after making his speech, Wallace was
rushed back to Birmingham for emergency operations to clean out
his internal infections. As he slowly recovered in Alabama, national
politics went on without him for the first time in a decade. He refused
to endorse McGovern, not that it would have made much difference.
McGovern later blamed his crushing defeat partly on the growth of
Wallaceism in America. He was right, of course—but few Democrats
grasped that Wallaceism no longer meant racism. As a result, they
moved farther and farther away from the party's traditional constitu-
encies, which, by default, reached out to the Republicans; the GOP
grabbed Wallaceism and ran with it.

One Democrat who understood the message was Jimmy Carter. After Wallace's speech to the convention, Carter said that a Democrat who "campaigned hard . . . and managed to avoid alienating the Wallace constituency could win." Four years later, Carter would do just that. But then Ronald Reagan out-Wallaced Carter and, later, Walter Mondale; George Bush followed suit against Michael Dukakis. In 1992, Bill Clinton ran as a "new kind of Democrat" and won on the promise of caring for the middle class with jobs, training, health care, and tax relief while reducing wasteful government spending and reforming welfare.

From 1968 to 1992 no person was elected president without clearly embracing and articulating (though not necessarily implementing) the Wallace issues. George Wallace understood the real America of his time. It is impossible to know, had he not been shot at the peak of his political power, whether he could have been nominated or elected president. My own belief is that he could not—that most voters were eager to use him as a vehicle for their messages but would have drawn away from putting into the Oval Office someone so closely identified with one of the meanest chapters in American history. But the truth is that he did realize his dream of brokering national elections—indirectly, perhaps, but no less effectively than he originally hoped. George Wallace's wish to be "rehabilitated" by history may or may not be realized—but history already has substantiated his idea of America.

Epilogue

The Last Political Mountain

GEORGE WALLACE WAS BY NO MEANS THROUGH—
neither as a politician nor as a man—after the 1972 Democratic
National Convention. Over the next fifteen years, he was elected
governor of Alabama twice more, the second time with extensive
black support, and his administrations compiled a more than credita-
ble record in race relations, education, and industrial development.
In 1976, he mounted his best-financed, best-organized presidential
campaign—but, by then, with the absorption of his issues by every
leading candidate and his confinement to a wheelchair, he did not
have a chance. His marriage to Cornelia collapsed amid scandal in
1978; three years later, he married Lisa Taylor, thirty years his junior,
but they split in 1987, shortly after he left politics for good.

In those fifteen years and beyond, he became something of a
national political icon, a man to whom it was obligatory for candidates of both parties, from Ted Kennedy to Nelson Rockefeller to
Jesse Jackson, to pay homage en route to their quests for Southern
votes. But Wallace would never again be a personal force in national
politics.

■ ■ ■

In the months following the shooting, Wallace spent 140 days in
hospitals and underwent a dozen operations. It was a full year after

the assassination attempt before he started functioning again as a leader. He decided to seek reelection in 1974, since the Alabama constitution by then allowed incumbent governors to succeed themselves. After that, as a now-legitimized and important figure in the Democratic party, he thought that he might well run for president again in 1976. But first, he needed to raise money to wipe out the quarter-million-dollar debt that had piled up since the shooting and to start building a war chest for the future. Over the next two years, under the guidance of Richard Viguerie (see chapter 15), Wallace's coffers swelled by $4 million; by July 1975, he was grossing more than $300,000 a month in contributions.[1]

Wallace's first broad objective was to attract Alabama's black voters. Blacks now constituted more than a quarter of the state's electorate, and Wallace wanted to eradicate his racist reputation once and for all. When University of Alabama students, a decade after Wallace's "stand" in the university's door, elected a black coed as homecoming queen, Wallace traveled to Tuscaloosa to crown her. He started appointing blacks regularly to state positions and speaking to a number of black groups—one of which, a conference of Southern black mayors, gave him a standing ovation. When he announced he was seeking reelection, Wallace won endorsements from a number of black public officials, a couple of black voter groups, and an important black community newspaper, the *Birmingham Times*. In repayment, Wallace later named black men and women to key jobs, including his personal staff. In Mississippi, Charles Evers said that he could support the "changed" Wallace for vice-president in 1976. In the Alabama gubernatorial primary, Wallace received more than a half million votes—64 percent of the total cast. Though the outcome had never been in doubt, the fact that Wallace had received about 25 percent of the black vote, not to mention a number of key endorsements from blacks, would prove to be of critical importance to him in later years.[2]

■   ■   ■

Preparing for the 1976 presidential primaries, his people took care not only to learn the rules this time but to help formulate them; among other things, the Wallace forces saw to it that proportional primaries were effectuated nearly everywhere.[3] By the time Wallace formally announced his candidacy by saying he would enter as many as thirty Democratic primaries, his intention was to use Florida as his launching pad, much as he had four years earlier, and spend his time and money there. But the polls showed him so far ahead in Florida that he was lured into the fatal political mistake of overconfidence. In September 1975, more than half of Florida's voters said they would vote for Wallace, while his nearest challenger, Jimmy Carter, attracted under 30 percent. Most other Democrats (with Scoop Jackson the principal exception) decided to shun Florida so as not to draw any votes away from Carter; they hoped that Carter would knock off Wallace in Florida and that they could defeat Carter in subsequent contests. The strategy worked into Carter's hands; he believed, rightly, that if he could follow a win in New Hampshire (where Wallace did not run) with an upset victory over Wallace in Florida, he would be seen as more than a marginal candidate. In January, Wallace's lead over Carter had shrunk to seven points. But Wallace, who had been greeted by overflowing crowds in Massachusetts, mistakenly thought Florida was safe enough to pour a quarter of a million dollars into Massachusetts and spend twenty-two days campaigning there. An unexpected win in Massachusetts, he thought, would be a coup that might provide the momentum for him to go all the way.[4]

But Wallace was disappointed in Massachusetts. He finished in third place, behind Jackson and Rep. Morris Udall of Arizona. The only good news was that he finished a point ahead of Carter, whose fourth-place showing in Massachusetts might hurt him in Florida. But Carter's people had been working Florida for months, building county organizations, canvassing voters door to door. Carter appealed to moderates who previously had backed Wallace by presenting himself as an electable Southerner, someone through whom Southern voters could send Washington a president, not just a message. He painted Jackson as just another Washington insider. And, with no liberal candidates in the race, Carter sought their votes by condemning Jackson's focus in Massachusetts on the volatile busing issue (passions over busing had cooled in Florida since 1972). When Carter was asked why he waited until after the Massachusetts primary to speak out against Jackson's busing position, he did an adroit two-step: he agreed with Jackson's opposition to mandatory busing, he said, but he believed that basing one's campaign on such an emotional issue exploited racism.

Wallace, meanwhile, was pulling good-sized crowds, but not nearly as large or enthusiastic as he had attracted in 1972. Carter's strategy was working; he had the liberals (roughly 10 percent of the electorate) to himself and was pulling moderates from both Jackson and Wallace. Wallace had sorely underestimated Carter's tenacity; worse, he had failed to gauge the extent of the negative impact on voters of his paralysis. He augmented his schedule to demonstrate that he was fit, but just as the tactic seemed to be working, fate intervened. As two Alabama state troopers were carrying Wallace aboard a plane in Pensacola, one of them tripped and fell. Wallace tumbled out of his chair atop the fallen trooper, but the other state patrolman lost his balance and crashed on top of the governor, seriously injuring Wallace's leg. The incident proved to be a turning point. As a Wallace aide, Mickey Griffin, put it later, "When they dropped him down there in the panhandle, it was over for us. That was the day the campaign should have folded up. . . . Wallace started being perceived by the American public as a disabled person." Carter edged Wallace by only three points, 34 percent to 31 percent, with Jackson receiving 24 percent. But Wallace had been beaten in his must-win state. Two of every five voters said they did not think Wallace could physically handle the demands of the presidency. Then Carter finished first and Wallace second in Illinois—and, again, two in five voters, most of whom voted for Carter, said they were troubled by Wallace's health. And when Carter trounced Wallace in North Carolina, it was all over. Wallace hung on grimly, saying he could be a factor at the convention and provide a voice for his supporters. But he was repudiated in primary after primary—fourth place in Pennsylvania with 11 percent; 15 percent in Indiana to Carter's 68 percent; no delegates in Texas. The bitterest pills were Michigan and Maryland, where he had triumphed so spectacularly four years earlier: in both states, he finished far behind the leaders, with percentages in single digits.[5]

In mid-June, a month before the Democratic National Convention, Wallace threw his support to Carter, who went to Montgomery to express his gratitude. Wallace boasted that his efforts over the years had made it possible for a Southerner to be nominated for president, and many observers agreed with him. Wallace attended the convention, but was a figure of no import.[6]

■　■　■

Not long after the convention, Wallace's personal life, along with his national political stature, began to disintegrate. He discovered that Cornelia had been tapping his phones in the Governor's Mansion. He suspected that she wanted to catch him in what she alleged was one of his long and intimate conversations with old girlfriends. If there was to be a divorce, she said later, she wanted evidence to improve her chances for a generous settlement. Wallace's aides found a stack of tapes in a safe in the mansion, bundled them in a weighted plastic bag, and dropped them into the Alabama River. Meanwhile, Wallace's state troopers, who traveled with Cornelia as bodyguards, reported to the governor that his wife was having extramarital sexual liaisons; she denied the stories, but Wallace said he wanted a divorce. Over the next year, the two lived in a state of tension and barely concealed animosity; finally, in June 1977, Cornelia moved out of the mansion. A divorce was granted the following January on the date of what would have been their seventh anniversary. She was given a settlement of seventy thousand dollars, about a third of Wallace's court-certified total personal wealth. Wallace refused to discuss publicly the issues surrounding the divorce, particularly anything to do with conjectured sexual peccadillos. It was Cornelia who kept the gossip columnists busy with statements about her alleged infidelities and Wallace's supposed girlfriends. Her progressively erratic public behavior included numerous utterances about a planned reconciliation with Wallace (which he emphatically denied), frequent unannounced visits to the mansion (he finally ordered her thrown out and barred from future entry), a claim that Wallace had ordered her airbrushed out of photos of the assassination attempt, and a call for public prayer to dissuade Wallace from remarrying a younger woman. In 1981, she was arrested for stealing a pickup truck (the owner did not press charges) and later, her mother committed her to a mental institution. After that, with her occasionally recurring health problems apparently in check, she spent most of her time living with or near her mother in Montgomery.[7]

■   ■   ■

George Wallace's third term (or fourth, counting Lurleen Wallace's tenure) ended a year after the divorce was granted. He had toyed with the idea of running for the U.S. Senate in 1978 to succeed the retiring John Sparkman, but his physical condition, the publicity from the divorce, and mixed polls on his popularity convinced him to drop the idea. Instead, he accepted faculty status at the University of Alabama, Birmingham, where he lectured occasionally. Mostly, he was used effectively in fund-raising drives for the university. He lived on income from the university and from his occasional lectures and articles. In 1981, he remarried. His third wife was Lisa Taylor, who, with her sister, Mona, had been a singing attraction at Wallace's rallies in 1968 and 1972 (see chapter 15). Thirty years younger than Wallace, she was a divorced thirty-two-year-old who had a six-year-old son. She claimed to have loved Wallace since first meeting him when she was nineteen. He said that after his divorce to Cornelia had been finalized, Lisa had telephoned him and proposed marriage. He had tried to put her off, but she had pursued her cause aggressively; and, Wallace said, "I finally gave in." Lisa and her son moved into Wallace's Montgomery home.

Never one for domestic bliss, however, Wallace was soon back on the political trail, seeking yet another term as governor. Fob James, the man who had succeeded Wallace, had sweated out a difficult term in which unemployment had skyrocketed, his legislative programs had gone nowhere, and his aloof manner had alienated voters. But, four years earlier, James had fortuitously ruled out running for a second term, so he was spared embarrassment at the hands of the voters. And, given four years to compare Wallace, wheelchair and all, to James and a field of no-names eager to succeed him, the Alabama electorate started pining for Wallace's familiar face and colorful style; polls showed that Wallace could easily win the Democratic primary, and he decided to seek another term.

As he had in 1974, Wallace took about 25 percent of the black vote. He came close to winning the primary without a runoff, leading his nearest opponent by 130,000 votes. But his runoff opponent, the incumbent lieutenant governor, George McMillan, mounted a vigorous campaign—denouncing Wallace with vague charges of corruption, trotting out the voluminous (but largely unsupported and unproven) allegations of kickbacks that Wallace's political foes had made over the years, and maintaining that Wallace's racist baggage would limit outside investments, and thus economic growth, in Alabama. For his part, Wallace staged his standard rallies but was physically unable to campaign at the pace or with the heat and enthusiasm that had characterized his earlier campaigns. The polls showed the two men closing, with McMillan having the momentum. But Wallace, surprisingly increasing his original share of the black vote to about a third, edged out McMillan by less than twenty-four thousand votes, or just over one percentage point. The narrowness of the victory induced Wallace to augment his courtship of black voters because, for the first time in his career, he now faced a serious Republican challenge in the general election. Fortunately for Wallace, the GOP nominee was Emory Folmar, the millionaire mayor of Montgomery, whose eccentricity (he carried a loaded pistol everywhere) was exceeded by his abrasive, hard-line opposition to every social and economic program advocated by Democrats, white and black, on the city council. As a result, Wallace was endorsed, somewhat reluctantly, by his defeated primary opponents and by black organizations. A leading black political luminary in Alabama, Joe Reed, said of Folmar: "I know of no man in the country worse than this nominee. You can't believe a word he tells you. He's not for blacks. He doesn't support education. And he's not for working folks." Wallace went on to collect 60 percent of a million votes cast, including near unanimous support from blacks.[8]

■   ■   ■

Wallace's final term was marked by substantial increases in education financing, establishment with oil and gas revenues of a unique trust fund to provide regular support for unpopular programs like improving prison facilities and mental hospitals, acquisition of a supercomputer for research among the state's universities, and expansion of a Southern Alabama medical college built in an earlier term.[9] In his previous terms, he had broadened educational opportunity by providing free textbooks to public school children and by establishing a network of junior colleges and technical schools; he lured considerable industry to the state that provided jobs to blue-collar workers of both races; he forced the banks to pay interest on state deposits; he virtually eradicated loan-sharking practices, and limited garnishments and repossessions; he fought, with intermittent success, repeated efforts by the utilities to raise rates; he improved the highways and the economically important farm-to-market roads.

■   ■   ■

As he bade his supporters an emotional farewell in April 1982—announcing, "I have climbed my last political mountain"—he faced yet another personal crisis. His wife, Lisa, and her son, now twelve, had moved out of the Governor's Mansion and, temporarily, into Wallace's private home in Montgomery. Lisa, who had married Wallace before he had mounted his final campaign, detested public life and participated in few official functions; her son was "miserable." Lisa and George Wallace were divorced a year later, in February 1987, shortly after he left office for the last time. Financially secure from mining interests developed by her father, she continued living in Montgomery.[10]

When Wallace returned to private life in 1987, Troy State University offered him a small sinecure as a consultant. His daughters—Bobbi Jo Parsons, Peggy Sue Kennedy, and Lee Dye—had married, had borne children, and appeared to be in secure marriages. George, Jr., whose stormy life had included a brief career as a rock musician, a pattern of dropping in and out of colleges, and three marriages ending in divorce, had been elected the state treasurer. In that office, he succeeded in, among other things, devising an innovative plan to make it easier for parents to finance their children's higher education. And, despite having lost a close race for Congress in 1992, George, Jr., appeared headed for a continued successful career in politics.

Among Wallace's many key staff members over the years, Bill Jones, Joe Azbell, and Charles Snider all established successful businesses but dabbled occasionally in politics—although Snider shifted his allegiance to the GOP. Elvin Stanton stayed with Wallace as an executive assistant and was mentioned frequently as a possible candidate for political office. Seymore Trammell, having been released from prison, tried peddling a spiteful story of Wallace as a drunk and philanderer, but found no takers. Wallace named his loyal longtime bodyguard, E. C. Dothard, who had been wounded in the 1972 assassination attempt, to head the Alabama Department of Public Safety. In 1989, suffering from terminal cancer, Dothard, fifty-eight, took his own life.

John Kohn, who had developed most of Wallace's early racist speeches, lived into old age but refused to speak to Wallace after the governor publicly reached out to black voters. Grover Hall, the urbane editor who had persuaded Wallace to moderate some of Kohn's more extreme views, moved to Virginia and started writing a newspaper column; he was planning to join Wallace's 1972 presidential campaign when he was stricken with brain cancer and died. Wallace's old college chums Ralph Adams and Glenn Curlee lived on quietly in retirement; Curlee tried to effect a reconciliation between Wallace and Judge Frank Johnson in 1976, but Johnson adamantly refused. Johnson, who often made his sweeping anti-Wallace judicial decisions at critical political junctures, had effectively taken control of Alabama's overcrowded, underfinanced prison system just as Wallace was launching his 1976 presidential campaign. Wallace, publicly embarrassed, commented that Johnson had the luxury of not having to raise the taxes to pay for his decisions; the judge, he added, ought to take "a barbed-wire enema," a crudity for which he later apologized. But Curlee said it seemed to be the final straw for Johnson, who was elevated by President Carter to the U.S. Circuit Court of Appeals in 1979. Wallace's brother Jack retired as a circuit court judge and lived on quietly in Clayton. Their brother Gerald, broken in health and in finances, died of cancer in 1993 at age seventy-two.[11]

■   ■   ■

For all the dramatis personae who moved on and off Wallace's personal and political stage over the years, Wallace was essentially a loner. He made his own decisions and did so instinctively rather than intellectually. Family and friends always took a back seat to his relentless compulsion for station and authority. His raw, bottomless reserves of energy never left him in one place long enough for anyone to know or reach him fully. He was like the crackling arcs of electricity snapping between poles—fleeting and depthless, but insistent, compelling, and powerful.

Wallace rarely pondered, weighed, deliberated, or brooded; he sensed, sprang, thrusted, and parried. He was like the dark specks one sees after looking at a bright light, darting, inescapable, but apparitional. Yet, through some intuitive wizardry, Wallace sensed and felt the needs and longings of the faceless multitude—those millions who flocked to his banner as if he were leading a crusade to the Holy Land.

"He knew where to find the itch," Joe Azbell said, "and he scratched it." In his early years, the itch he scratched to obtain office was the fear and uncertainty among Alabama's whites over the crumbling of segregation, and he would be forever stained by his bellicose defense of an inherently evil (though, for nearly two centuries, constitutional) system. Wallace never believed he could hold back the tide of integration, and neither did the vast majority of his followers. In fact, because of George Wallace's strident and visible opposition to it, integration came faster and more thoroughly to Alabama than to any other Deep South state. Wallace sought to endow his supporters with his generation's inheritance from the myths of the Civil War: that despite being overrun by the superior forces of the federal government, spiritual victory could be theirs through obdurate refusal to yield to federal mandates; they could pursue yet another Lost Cause, and so delude themselves that though they had gone down to defeat yet again, they had done so with dignity.

Eventually, Wallace recognized that he was selling a myth and that what he had intended as dignified resistance had become, for the most part, obstreperous pandering. So, in the twilight of his career, he went to Alabama's blacks and, by extension, the blacks of America, to ask their forgiveness. There were three reasons—two self-serving, but one an epiphany. First, with the unabashed brass of which politicians are capable, he needed and wanted black votes in his last run for governor. Second, as he approached the end of his life, he hoped to prevent his past racism from obscuring his messages of social conservatism and economic populism. But his third reason revealed a humanity so often lacking in his actions: alone and crippled, forced to introspection for the first time in his life, he realized that though he had purported to be the champion of the poor and the helpless, he had trampled on the poorest and most helpless of all his constituents—the blacks.

■ ■ ■

In 1982 he appeared before the Southern Christian Leadership Conference and apologized for his past behavior toward blacks. He repeated his apology on statewide television, prompting E. D. Nixon, the driving force behind the Montgomery bus boycott, to praise his honesty: "He was the first one to do that," Nixon said, "and he's provided a lot of jobs for blacks." Tuskegee granted him an honorary degree. He named a black man to be his press secretary. As Wallace's periods of confinement increased, he came to depend most on two black men who saw to his personal needs day and night, and he referred to them simply and fondly as his friends. In his final term of office, he named more than 160 blacks to state governing boards, engineered the appointment of blacks to important committees in the legislature, and backed a plan to double the number of black voter registrars in the state's sixty-seven counties. Ollie Carter, a black woman who worked in Wallace's 1982 campaign, said of him: "He has made some mistakes. But haven't we all? You have to understand, the races are more bold and honest with each other in the South."[12]

Most dramatically, he appeared unannounced at the Dexter Avenue Baptist Church in Montgomery, the church whose pulpit Martin Luther King, Jr., occupied when he kindled the modern civil rights movement. And what made it more meaningful than any of his other acts of contrition was its timing—late in 1979, almost a year after he had left office and nearly two years before he decided to seek the governorship again. The visit was unannounced; there was no press; Wallace, two years from seeking office again, had no immediate political design. The singular symbolism of the moment must have pulsed through the sanctuary. As related by the historian Dan Carter, Wallace told the hushed congregation, "I have learned what suffering means. In a way that was impossible before [the shooting], I think I can understand something of the pain that black people have come to endure. I know I contributed to that pain, and I can only ask your forgiveness." Carter described what happened next:

> As his aide pushed Wallace up the aisle, a member of the . . . choir broke into a chorus of "Amazing Grace" while members of the congregation reached out to touch the [former] Alabama governor.[13]

Carter said that it was "difficult not be moved by that moment of reconciliation," but that sympathy for Wallace had to be balanced by his having "exploited the most brutal passions and hatreds of the American people." Speaking to Carter, Virginia Durr, the enduring civil rights advocate from Montgomery, said of Wallace, a born-again Christian, "[He's] just afraid he's going to hell. He ought to [be]."[14]

Countless others would agree, if in more tempered terms. The historian C. Vann Woodward offered this assessment: "Wallace did not create the reaction to the civil rights movement; it was there. He got on it and rode it. [He] was a barometer of feeling, rather than a cause of it. He was an indicator rather than a stimulator of causes and a dramatic illustration of the political results of the reenfranchisement of blacks."[15]

Pervasive racism is America's greatest shame. Politicians have exploited it for votes—Hubert Humphrey, Jimmy Carter, and George Bush among them. Few did it more visibly, more dramatically, or more insistently than George Wallace. The image of Wallace at the schoolhouse door is branded indelibly on our minds. But had Wallace not reached beyond race, he could not have aroused the tens of millions who either voted for him or who switched only when mainstream candidates adopted many of his positions.

Wallace had tapped into deep pools of public distrust of growing federal intrusion into what many considered local or private matters, and he had given voice to widespread uneasiness about increasing crime and civil disorder that few in authority appeared willing to confront for fear of seeming illiberal. Too, he had strengthened the sense of self-worth among owners of small businesses, shopkeepers, blue-collar workers, clerks, secretaries, police officers, fire-fighters, taxi drivers, beauticians, and all those who felt oppressed or ignored by powerful institutions such as big government and the national media. At the same time, he had articulated the prevalent alarm over the concentration of too much wealth in too few hands, too much dependence on foreign capital and foreign sources of energy, too many "giveaways" to foreign governments while too many Americans "live under bridges (or) lie on grates in the winter to keep warm."[16]

One need not accept any of those views to agree that they had appealed to real concerns of real people, not to mindless, unreasoning fears, racial or otherwise. And though many of those concerns once had been arrogantly or ignorantly dismissed as mere racial "code words," every president from Nixon to Clinton based his successful campaign on some key elements from the Wallace political canon.

Though by no means universally applauded, it is this, rather than the attempted obstruction of integration, that is Wallace's legacy— and this uncomfortable truth may underlie the preference of many political historians and commentators to pigeonhole Wallace as a racist. Over the years, many of Wallace's positions had become politically respectable: among them, shrinking the federal bureaucracy, strengthening local enforcement of crime, allowing parents freedom of choice among schools, and taxing the "super-rich." Toward the end of his life, having tried to atone for the sins of segregation (as if he alone had perpetrated them), he wanted desperately to become *personally* respectable.

The Alabama writer Diane McWhorter, a self-described Wallace adversary, put it succinctly: "George Wallace may have done it for political self-preservation, but he said the three words probably never before uttered consecutively in the Old Confederacy: 'I was wrong.' "[17] She could have added "or in the North" and cited such people as Earl Warren, who never apologized in his lifetime for his role in interning Japanese Americans during World War II.

But Wallace said he had been wrong. He apologized. The injustices he perpetrated in the name of segregation need not be dismissed nor forgotten to be forgiven. But because Wallace admitted his guilt and sought to atone for it, many forgave. Coretta Scott King forgave him. Fred Gray forgave him. E.D. Nixon forgave him. Jesse Jackson forgave him.

It was supremely ironic that as Wallace and the South moved closer to the goal of racial reconciliation, much of America was turning in the other direction—whether bloody confrontations in Crown Heights or East Los Angeles, or whites protesting fair housing laws in Yonkers, or white parents fighting school busing for integration in LaCrosse, Wisconsin, or black students demanding segregated housing and social facilities on college campuses—the latter with the encouragement of Wallace's severest critics, those "pseudo-intellectual" bicycle-riding professors.

■　■　■

But the advantage of history is perspective. For all the social churning that we may see on a given day or over a given year or decade, the fact is that the incredibly improved status of American blacks since World War II constitutes a social revolution that in its scope and speed is unequaled in history. And when Jesse Jackson came to call on the pain-wracked, bed-ridden George Wallace in July 1987, it provided a microcosmic authentication of that colossal change.

The July heat was suffocating, and it exacerbated Wallace's perpetual discomfort. For weeks before Jackson's visit, Wallace had been confined to his king-sized hospital bed in the airy master bedroom of his Montgomery home. The room was sparsely furnished with two chairs, two bookcases, and an oversized color television set equipped with special earphones so the nearly deaf Wallace could hear. Tending him were his "friends," Eddie Holsey (who, at twenty-two, had become Wallace's companion in 1972) and Bernard Adams; the two black men took turns dressing and undressing him, turning him, helping bathe him, and replenishing his supply of Garcia y Vega Gran Premo cigars.

After preparing for Jackson's arrival by dressing Wallace in a suit and tie, they gently lifted him into his wheelchair and rolled him into the living room to greet his guest and participate in a photo opportunity for the two dozen or so reporters and photographers who were following Jackson's early campaign for the 1988 Democratic presidential nomination.

When the house was cleared of reporters, Wallace turned to Jackson and, genuinely touched by the visit, said, "I appreciate you coming to see me. You haven't forgotten me. . . . You be careful.

There's a lot of violent kooks. One of them got me." Jackson promised that he would take care. He said he was trying to broaden his political base by emphasizing an economic message—the need to become more than a service economy.

Jackson said to Wallace, "You had a message about challenging the rich and powerful to be fair. It's a message that's going to have a place in this campaign, too. The extremes of wealth and poverty— the billionaires on one end and the dirt poor on the other—have a real threat to our stability now."

Wallace tried to concentrate, to read Jackson's lips when he could not hear the words. But he was tiring; it was the longest he had sat up for a week. Suddenly, his left leg jerked in an uncontrollable spasm. He grabbed at it, and Jackson gently patted Wallace's arm.

"These bullets begin to take their toll," Wallace said. "There are so many kooks loose in this country."

Jackson rose slowly from his chair, leaned over Wallace, and whispered something in his ear. Wallace looked up and said, "I'd like you to pray for me."

The two men clasped hands and clamped their eyes shut. They were joined in a circle by Wallace's son, two black ministers who had accompanied Jackson, and Wallace's black domestic, Dolores Coleman. Eddie Holsey, Bernard Adams, Wallace's aide Elvin Stanton, and I stood nearby. Jackson spoke:

> Father and our God, we come together to ask you for
> Governor Wallace, asking you to have mercy and for your
> healing power. . . . Help relieve the pain. May he share the
> courage of his convictions and to use every breath to
> encourage people to come together, to study war no more, to
> say no to violence, to fight for that bright day of justice when
> all of God's children—red and yellow, brown, black, and
> white—will come together and be precious in thy sight.

"Yes! Amen! Thank you, Lord!" said the others.

Wallace tightened his grip on Jackson's hand. The moment was energized by the rhythmic baritone cadences of a Southern black preacher, and the sight of that particular white hand enfolded by that particular black hand created an almost palpable sense of history flowing from that astonishing nexus.

> We know you're the God of redemption and the God of mercy.
> In this hour, be with Governor Wallace. . . . The people seek

leadership, and they seek to be led to higher ground. . . . Let us be present on this new day when lions and lambs will lie down together, and none will be afraid, and all of us can realize the joy in each other and the joy in thee.

George Wallace, Jesse Jackson, and the rest of us said, "Amen."[18]

Notes

Between January 1987 and July 1991, George Wallace, at the author's request and in response to a series of queries, dictated his recollections and answers in thirty-five sessions (totalling some sixty hours), each of which was transcribed and numbered. The transcripts, now part of the Wallace papers at the University of Alabama, Birmingham, are referred to numerically throughout these notes.

All interviews were conducted by the author unless otherwise indicated.

Prologue: *The Wallace Evolution*

1. The author was present at the July 20, 1987, meeting between Wallace and Jackson.

2. Interview with Elvin Stanton, Wallace's executive secretary from 1983 to 1987, in July 1987.

3. Ibid.

4. Wallace transcript, no. 18.

5. Interview with George Wallace, July 18, 1987.

6. Stephan Lesher, "Who Knows What Evil Lurks in the Hearts of 'X' Million Americans? George Wallace Knows—and He's Off and Running," *New York Times Magazine,* January 2, 1972, p. 32.

7. "Exit George Wallace," *Washington Post,* April 4, 1986, p. 18A.

8. David S. Broder, "George Wallace, without Solutions," *Washington Post,* April 6, 1986, p. 7C.

9. Howard Fineman, "Poppy the Populist," *Newsweek*, November 7, 1988, p. 58.

10. Broder, "George Wallace."

11. Marshall Frady, *Wallace* (New York: New American Library, 1972), p. 5.

12. William Kennedy, *Legs* (New York: Penguin Books, 1983), pp. 14, 36.

13. Broder, "George Wallace."

14. Interview with George Wallace, July 14, 1987.

15. Interview with George Wallace, March 16, 1986.

16. Jack Bass, "A Prophet of the New Politics," *Philadelphia Inquirer Magazine*, December 25, 1988, p. 28.

17. Roy Reed, "In Memory of Dr. King, If He Were Alive," *New York Times*, January 20, 1986, p. 31A.

18. Ben A. Franklin, "Profligate Nonprofits," *Washington Spectator*, June 1, 1993, pp. 1–3. Franklin quoted extensively from a seven-part investigative series in the *Philadelphia Inquirer* that ran April 18–25, 1993. The series documented widespread abuses among tax-exempt organizations, including hospitals and charities such as United Way of America—inflated salaries for executives, hundred-dollar-a-head "business lunches," huge interest-free loans to allow executives to buy private homes, and directors of charities (lawyers, financiers, business executives) profiting by doing business with the charities they direct. In all, major U.S. nonprofit organizations are valued at $850 billion and growing—yet they give away only about $9 billion a year.

19. Cited by James MacGregor Burns in *The Crosswinds of Freedom* (New York: Knopf, 1989).

1: *"The Good White Families"*

1. Interview with George Wallace, December 15, 1986.

2. A. Bartlett Giamatti, *Exile and Change in Renaissance Literature* (New Haven, Conn.: Yale University Press, 1984), cited by Roger Angell, *New Yorker*, August 22, 1988, p. 50.

3. In 1968, Mrs. Hope Lane of Enterprise, Alabama, sent the Wallace family detailed genealogical material, which Wallace misplaced. The author found the material in a cardboard box among thousands of campaign papers, boxes, and artifacts that were piled willy-nilly, uncatalogued, on a balcony in the library of the University of Alabama, Birmingham (UAB). (Further citations of material from this location will refer to Wallace papers, UAB.)

4. Letter from James G. L. Huey of Magnolia, Alabama, to a distant cousin, George W. Huey of Enterprise, Alabama, June 19, 1884, Wallace papers, UAB.

5. Ibid.; letter from George W. Huey to his son, Walton S. Huey, both of Enterprise, Alabama, May 24, 1924; letter from W. B. Smith of McRae, Georgia, to his distant cousin, Walton S. Huey, September 7, 1945, Wallace papers, UAB.

6. Horace Edwin Hayden, *Virginia Genealogies* (privately published), p. 13; V. H. Huey, *Huey Family History* (privately published, 1963); Page Smith, *The Shaping of America* (New York: McGraw-Hill, 1980), p. 610.

7. Smith, *Shaping of America*, p. 595.

8. Albert James Pickett, *History of Alabama* (Sheffield, Ala.: Randolph, 1896), p. 511.

9. Smith, *Shaping of America*, pp. 645–46.

10. Ibid., pp. 646–47.

11. Ibid., p. 736.

12. Letter from G. W. Huey to W. S. Huey; letter from W. B. Smith to W. S. Huey, Wallace papers, UAB.

13. Federal Writers Project, Works Progress Administration (WPA), Alabama State File—History, 1935.

14. Letter from G. W. Huey to W. S. Huey, Wallace papers, UAB.

15. Federal Writers Project, WPA, *Alabama Archeology*, no. 4454, 1939, p. 1.

16. Smith, *Shaping of America*, pp. 696–97.

17. Ibid., p. 654.

18. WPA, *Alabama Archeology*, pp. 1, 3.

19. WPA, *Alabama Archeology*, pp. 1–4.

20. Alto L. Jackson, *Clio, Alabama—A History* (Clio, Ala.: privately published, 1979), p. 32.

21. Wallace transcript, no. 7, pp. 10–11.

22. Federal Writers Project, WPA, *Alabama History—Barbour County*, no. 2322, 1935.

23. Ibid.

24. James M. McPherson, *Battle Cry of Freedom: The Civil War Era* (New York: Oxford University Press, 1988), p. 97.

25. Ibid., p. 92.

26. Ibid., p. 99.

27. Federal Writers Project, WPA, *Alabama Agriculture*, 1935, pp. 1, 6.

28. McPherson, *Battle Cry*, pp. 40–41.

29. Ibid., p. 40.

30. Ibid., p. 333.

31. Federal Writers Project, WPA, *Political History of Barbour County*, no. 4454, pp. 6–7.

32. Ibid., p. 7.

33. McPherson, *Battle Cry*, pp. 214–15. George Wallace, an alternate delegate from Alabama to the 1948 Democratic National Convention, refused to join the Southerners who bolted from the floor over Harry

Truman's civil rights program. Instead, Wallace, in seconding the presidential nomination of Sen. Richard Russell of Georgia, issued his earliest national condemnation of civil rights legislation.

34. Ibid., p. 234.

35. Shelby Foote, *The Civil War: A Narrative—Fort Sumter to Perryville* (New York: Vintage Books, 1986), p. 17.

36. McPherson, *Battle Cry*, p. 245; pp. 272–73.

37. Ibid., p. 243.

38. Marshall Frady, *Wallace* (New York: New American Library, 1972), p. 53.

39. WPA, *Political History*, p. 7. After the war and the end of federal occupation, Barbour's citizens defiantly chose the very spot on which Lincoln had been hanged in effigy to erect a Confederate memorial.

40. Ibid., pp. 316, 547.

41. Federal Writers Project WPA, *Political History*, p. 5; Barbour County—Clayton, Alabama, p. 1.

42. McPherson, *Battle Cry*, pp. xviii, xix, 854.

43. WPA, *Alabama Agriculture*, pp. 7, 13–14.

44. Foote, *Civil War*, pp. 1011, 1034, 1048–49; Hodding Carter, *The Angry Scar: The Story of Reconstruction* (Garden City, N.Y.: Doubleday, 1959), p. 33.

45. Carter, *Angry Scar*, p. 47.

46. Foote, *Civil War*, p. 1043.

47. Carter, *Angry Scar*, pp. 47–55.

48. Claude G. Bowers, *The Tragic Era: The Revolution after Lincoln* (Cambridge, Mass.: Riverside, 1929), p. 64.

49. Carter, *Angry Scar*, p. 54.

50. W. E. B. DuBois, *Black Reconstruction in America* (New York: Macmillan, 1972).

51. William S. McFeeley, "A Moment of Terrifying Promise," *New York Times Book Review*, May 22, 1988, p. 12.

52. Foote, *Civil War*, pp. 1042–43.

53. Carter, *Angry Scar*, pp. 146, 150.

54. Ibid., p. 157.

55. Ibid., p. 158.

56. Ibid., pp. 154–55.

57. McPherson, *Battle Cry*, pp. 860–61.

58. Foote, *Civil War*, p. 1042.

59. Federal Writers Project, WPA, *Reconstruction in Barbour County*, no. 4454, 1939, pp. 9–11.

60. Wallace transcripts: no. 1, p. 4; no. 20, p. 6.

61. WPA, *Political History*, p. 11.

62. Carter, *Angry Scar*, pp. 157, 162.

63. WPA, *Political History*, pp. 9–10. George Wallace also used Barbour

County's voter registration rolls for political advantage when he was the judge of Alabama's Third Judicial Circuit. In a celebrated act of defiance, as discussed in chapter 5, Wallace impounded the rolls to prevent federal voting rights authorities from examining them to see if there was a pattern of excluding blacks.

64. Ibid.

65. Gertha Couric, of the *Eufaula* (Ala.) *Tribune,* June 14, 1939, quoted in WPA, *Political History*, p. 10; WPA, *Political History*, pp. 11–12.

66. Ibid.

67. Ibid., pp. 12–13.

68. McFeeley, "Terrifying Promise," p. 11. The Redeemers were a loose political coalition formed to reduce the power of state governments and tighten control over blacks, generally undoing changes wrought during Reconstruction.

69. Eric Foner, *Reconstruction: America's Unfinished Revolution 1863–1877* (New York: Harper & Row, 1988), p. 582.

70. Carter, *Angry Scar*, pp. 243, 247.

71. WPA, *Alabama Agriculture*, p. 13.

72. William Greider, "Annals of Finance: The Fed—Part II," *New Yorker*, November 16, 1987, pp. 76–77.

73. Foner, *Reconstruction*, p. 170.

74. William Barnard, the chairman of the history department, University of Alabama, quoted in the *Montgomery Advertiser*, special section, January 11, 1987, p. 7 (hereafter referred to as *Montgomery Advertiser*, special sec.).

75. *Montgomery Advertiser*, special sec., p. 7.

76. Wallace transcript, no. 1, p. 7.

77. Carter, *Angry Scar*, p. 363.

78. Ibid., pp. 351–52.

79. Ibid., p. 365.

80. Ibid., pp. 366–70.

81. Ibid., p. 373.

82. Quoted in Carter, *Angry Scar*, p. 373.

2: *"A True Blue Southerner"*

1. Leon F. Litwack, "The Intellectual History of Jim Crow," *New York Times Book Review*, September 16, 1984, p. 12.

2. Alto L. Jackson, *Clio, Alabama—A History* (Clio, Ala.: privately published, 1979), p. 126.

3. Ibid., pp. 1, 3–4, 24.

4. Ibid., p. 126; letter from George W. Huey to his son, W. S. Huey, Enterprise, Alabama, May 24, 1924, George C. Wallace papers, University of Alabama at Birmingham (UAB) (hereafter referred to as Wallace papers, UAB).

5. Mattie Thomas Thompson, *History of Barbour County, Alabama* (Eufaula, Ala.: privately published, 1939), p. 243; Shelby Foote, *The Civil War: A Narrative—Red River to Appomattox* (New York: Vintage Books, 1974), pp. 1055–57. Davis, stopping in Eufaula en route from Montgomery to Atlanta, reiterated the theme of unrepentance he had first articulated two years earlier in Mississippi's Capitol chamber: "[Despite] all which has been suffered, all which has been lost, [the] disappointed hopes and crushed aspirations . . . if it were to do all over again, I would do again just as I did in 1861" (Foote, *Civil War*, pp. 1055–57).

6. Jackson, *Clio*, pp. 23, 32, 102–3.

7. Ibid., pp. 8, 28–29.

8. E. Culpepper Clark, *A Sense of Place: Survivors on the Land* (Troy, Ala.: Troy State University Press, 1978), p. 40.

9. Sidney Lanier, "The New South" [1880], in *Retrospects and Prospects* (New York: privately published, 1899), pp. 104–5, 110–11.

10. C. Vann Woodward, *Origins of the New South* (Baton Rouge, La.: Louisiana State University [LSU] Press, 1951), p. 175.

11. Jackson, *Clio*, p. 127.

12. Clark, *Sense of Place*, p. 40.

13. William Warren Rogers, *The One-Gallused Rebellion: Agrarianism in Alabama, 1865–1896* (Baton Rouge, La.: LSU Press, 1970).

14. Jackson, *Clio*, p. 127.

15. Ibid.

16. *Clio Free Press*, February 4, 1908; Jackson, *Clio*, p. 13.

17. *Clio Free Press*, February 4, 1908.

18. *Montgomery Advertiser*, special sec., p. 8.

19. Wallace transcript, no. 1, pp. 1–2.

20. Jackson, *Clio*, p. 51.

21. Wallace transcript, no. 1, p. 2.

22. Marshall Frady, *Wallace* (New York: New American Library, 1972), pp. 56, 58.

23. Frady, *Wallace*, p. 57; *Montgomery Advertiser*, special sec., p. 9.

24. Jackson, *Clio*, p. 37; *Montgomery Advertiser*, special sec., p. 9.

25. Frady, *Wallace*, p. 60; Wallace transcript, no. 1, p. 3.

26. Frady, *Wallace*, p. 60.

27. Frady, *Wallace*, pp. 56–61.

28. Wallace transcript, no. 19, pp. 3–4. Until a few months before his death at the age of eighty, Dr. Wallace enjoyed early morning rides. His grandson George recalled that "a lot of people said they could set their clocks from hearing . . . my grandfather riding his horse . . . in the morning around six or six-thirty."

29. Frady, *Wallace*, p. 55; letter to Lurleen and George Wallace from May Wyatt Wallace, c. January, 1963, Wallace papers, UAB.

30. Frady, *Wallace*, p. 55.

31. *Montgomery Advertiser*, special sec., p. 9.

32. Frady, *Wallace*, p. 59.

33. Ibid., pp. 55–56.

34. Wallace transcripts: no. 1, p. 5; no. 11, pp. 2–4; no. 19, p. 5.

35. Wallace transcript, no. 19, p. 3.

36. Wallace transcript, no. 18, pp. 17–18.

37. Wallace transcripts: no. 2, pp. 18–19; no. 3, pp. 1–8; no. 5, p. 10.

38. Wallace transcripts: no. 5, p. 5; no. 21, p. 4.

39. Frady, *Wallace*, p. 65.

40. Wallace transcript, no. 3, pp. 1–8.

41. *Montgomery Advertiser*, special sec., p. 9.

42. Wallace transcript, no. 1, pp. 1, 3.

43. Jackson, *Clio*, p. 52.

44. *Montgomery Advertiser*, special sec., p. 6.

45. James Agee, *Let Us Now Praise Famous Men* (New York: Riverside, 1939).

46. Jack Wallace in *Montgomery Advertiser*, special sec., p. 9.

47. Wallace transcript, no. 6, p. 2.

48. Frady, *Wallace*, pp. 62, 64; "Wallace's Mother Praised," *Mobile Press Register*, October 29, 1988; Wallace transcripts: no. 3, p. 5; no. 10, pp. 12–13.

49. *Montgomery Advertiser*, special sec., p. 10.

50. Ibid.

51. Ibid., pp. 8–9.

52. Wallace transcript, no. 10, p. 19.

53. Ibid.

54. Ibid., pp. 15–16, 18–20.

55. Ibid., p. 17.

56. Ibid.; Wallace transcript, no. 1, pp. 11–12.

57. Wallace transcript, no. 9, pp. 3–4.

58. Wallace transcript, no. 26, p. 4.

59. Wallace transcript, no. 18, pp. 6–7.

60. Wallace transcripts: no. 10, p. 12; no. 14, p. 10.

61. Wallace transcript, no. 18, pp. 6–7.

62. Clark, *Sense of Place*, p. 40.

63. Agee, *Let Us Now*.

64. Wallace transcript, no. 2, p. 23.

65. Wallace transcripts: no. 4, pp. 2–3; no. 9, pp. 2–3; no. 10, p. 10.

66. Wallace transcript, no. 2, pp. 21–22.

67. Wallace transcripts: no. 20, p. 16; no. 3, pp. 2–3.

68. *Montgomery Advertiser*, special sec., p. 10; Wallace transcript, no. 20, pp. 16–17.

69. *Montgomery Advertiser*, special sec., p. 10.

70. Ibid., p. 9.

71. Wallace transcript, no. 6, pp. 2–3.

72. Ibid., p. 4.

73. Wallace transcript, no. 23, p. 25.

74. Wallace transcript, no. 6, pp. 4, 8–9.

75. Wallace transcript, no. 20, p. 29.

76. Wallace transcript, no. 6, p. 10.

77. Wallace transcript, no. 27, pp. 4–5.

78. Ibid., pp. 5–6.

79. Ibid.

80. Wallace transcript, no. 10, p. 3.

81. Ibid.

82. Wallace transcripts: no. 3, pp. 3, 8; no. 14, p. 12; Frady, *Wallace*, p. 74; interview with George Wallace, July 10, 1987.

83. Wallace transcripts: no. 10, p. 8; no. 14, p. 12.

84. Wallace transcripts: no. 3, pp. 3, 8; no. 14, p. 12; Frady, *Wallace*, p. 74; interview with George Wallace, July 10, 1987.

85. Wallace transcript, no. 10, p. 8.

86. Wallace transcript, no. 14, pp. 7–9.

87. Ibid., p. 12.

88. Wallace transcript, no. 10, pp. 6–7; *Montgomery Advertiser*, special sec., p. 11.

89. Wallace transcript, no. 10, pp. 3–4.

90. Wallace transcripts: no. 10, p. 8; no. 14, p. 14.

91. Wallace transcripts: no. 7, pp. 21–22; no. 9, pp. 11–12.

92. Wallace transcript, no. 30, p. 3. Stephens would be a lifelong Wallace supporter; one of his rewards was Governor Wallace's agreement to build an expressway that linked the posh Birmingham suburb of Mountain Brook to an interstate highway, a suggestion that the governor had opposed until Stephens "insisted and talked [him] into it." Appropriately, the completed project was named the Elton B. Stephens Expressway.

93. Wallace transcript, no. 30, p. 3.

94. Wallace transcript, no. 1, pp. 12–15.

95. Wallace transcripts: no. 1, pp. 12–13; no. 5, pp. 16–21; no. 9, pp. 8–11; no. 14, pp. 17–19.

96. Wallace transcripts: no. 3, p. 13; no. 13, p. 10; no. 34, p. 1.

97. Wallace transcripts: no. 1, p. 10; no. 10, p. 3.

98. Wallace transcripts: no. 2, pp. 19–20; no. 10, p. 12; no. 16, pp. 2-4.

99. Frady, *Wallace*, p. 62.

100. Ibid.; Wallace transcript, no. 10, p. 12.

101. Wallace transcript, no. 13; pp. 10–11.

102. Interview with George Wallace, July 1987.

103. Frady, *Wallace*, p. 76.

104. Wallace transcripts: no. 11, p. 20; no. 34, pp. 2–3.

105. Wallace transcripts: no. 6, p. 1; no. 13, pp. 19–21.

106. Ibid.

107. Ibid.

108. Wallace transcripts: no. 4, p. 1; no. 20, pp. 18–19; no. 24, p. 9. In 1967, after he had completed his first term as governor, Wallace was notified by Delta Chi fraternity that records had been found showing he had pledged Delta Chi as a freshman but had dropped out before becoming a member. The fraternity's national governing body voted unanimously to offer him full membership. "I frankly don't recall being a pledge of any fraternity," Wallace said, "but I told them that anybody nationally who would vote for me unanimously, I would join."

109. Wallace transcripts: no. 20, p. 18; no. 24, pp. 9–10. Although Wallace indeed succeeded in defeating organized opposition, he sometimes joined that opposition. For instance, while blacks almost defeated Wallace in the 1970 Democratic gubernatorial primary by voting overwhelmingly for his opponent, Wallace unabashedly—and successfully—sought their support in his final campaign for governor in 1982, as discussed in the Epilogue.

110. Wallace transcript, no. 3, pp. 23–27.

111. Wallace transcript, no. 24, p. 8.

112. Ibid., pp. 3–4.

113. Wallace transcripts: no. 1, pp. 17–18; no. 17, pp. 10–12; no. 24, p. 4.

114. Wallace transcript, no. 1, pp. 18–19.

115. Ibid., pp. 19–20.

116. Ibid., p. 20.

117. Frady, *Wallace*, pp. 84–85.

118. Wallace transcript, no. 1, p. 21.

119. Wallace transcript, no. 4, p. 5.

120. Frady, *Wallace*, p. 84.

121. Wallace transcripts: no. 1, pp. 21–22; no. 8, p. 16; no. 17, pp. 12–13.

122. Ibid.

123. Wallace transcripts: no. 1, p. 21; no. 8, p. 17; no. 17, p. 13.

3: *The Desperate Hours*

1. Wallace transcripts: no. 1, p. 21; no. 8, p. 17; no. 17, p. 13.

2. Wallace transcripts: no. 1, pp. 22–24; no. 8, pp. 17–18.

3. Ibid.

4. Wallace transcripts: no. 1, pp. 24–25; no. 8, p. 18; no. 14, p. 3; Marshall Frady, *Wallace* (New York, New American Library, 1972), p. 85.

5. Frady, *Wallace*, p. 85.

6. Ibid.

7. Wallace transcript, no. 8, pp. 18–19.

8. Wallace transcripts: no. 8, p. 19; no. 9, p. 14; no. 12, pp. 3–4; no. 13, pp. 16–17.

9. Wallace transcript, no. 23, pp. 25–26.

10. Wallace transcripts: no. 8, p. 19; no. 9, p. 14; no. 12, p. 4.

11. Wallace transcript, no. 8, pp. 2–4.

12. Wallace transcripts: no. 8, p. 20; no. 12, pp. 4–5.

13. Wallace transcript, no. 13, p. 21.

14. Ibid., p. 17.

15. Peter Wyden, *Day One: Before Hiroshima and After* (New York: Simon & Schuster, 1984), pp. 203, 236.

16. Wallace transcript, no. 9, p. 15.

17. Ibid.

18. Wallace transcript, no. 14, pp. 2–3.

19. Wallace transcripts: no. 2, p. 2; no. 14, p. 21.

20. *WWII: Time-Life Books History of the Second World War* (New York: Prentice Hall, 1989), pp. 406–7.

21. Wallace transcript, no. 2, pp. 5–6.

22. Ibid.

23. Wallace transcripts: no. 1, pp. 26–27, 29; no. 2, pp. 1–7; no. 8, pp. 22–23; no. 14, pp. 19–21; no. 18, pp. 1–2; no. 27, pp. 9–10; no. 33, p. 1.

24. Wyden, *Day One*, pp. 235–37.

25. Wallace transcripts: no. 1, p. 28; no. 2, pp. 3–4; Wyden, *Day One*, p. 246.

26. Wallace transcripts: no. 1, pp. 28–29; no. 2, pp. 4, 7; no. 33, pp. 2–3.

27. Wallace transcript, no. 12, p. 6.

28. Ibid.

29. Ibid., pp. 6–7.

30. Wallace transcripts: no. 1, pp. 28–30; no. 12, pp. 6–8.

31. Wallace transcripts: no. 1, pp. 29–30, no. 12, p. 8.

32. *Congressional Record*, September 6, 1963.

33. Wallace transcript, no. 12, pp. 8–9.

34. Ibid., p. 10.

35. Marjorie Hunter, "Morse, in New Attack, Cites Wallace War Illness," *New York Times*, September 6, 1963, p. 14.

36. Ibid.

4: *Onto the Playing Field*

1. Wallace transcripts: no. 1, p. 31; no. 12, p. 10.

2. Wallace transcripts: no. 1, p. 31; no. 12, pp. 10–11.

3. Wallace transcripts: no. 1, p. 31; no. 12, p. 11.

4. Wallace transcript, no. 25, p. 2.

5. Interview with Joe Azbell, December 29, 1990.

6. Wallace transcript, no. 6, pp. 3, 7.

7. Wallace transcripts: no. 9, p. 16; no. 12, p. 11.

8. Wallace transcripts: no. 7, p. 8; no. 17, pp. 14–15.

9. Wallace transcripts: no. 12, pp. 11–15; no. 13, p. 21; Marshall Frady, *Wallace* (New York: New American Library, 1972), p. 92.

10. Frady, *Wallace*, pp. 92, 98–100.

11. Wallace transcripts: no. 6, p. 18; no. 12, pp. 12–13.

12. Wallace transcript, no. 12, pp. 11–12.

13. Interview with Joe Azbell, December 29, 1990.

14. On the other hand, there were men like my father-in-law, Phil Eisenberg, the owner of a small business, who, though hardly a revolutionary on the subject of segregation, sharply opposed its excesses. Eisenberg upbraided Weinstein for allowing himself to be named a director of Montgomery's White Citizens Council; when Weinstein explained that he wanted people to see a Jewish name among those of the council's leaders "to deflect criticism from our [Jewish] community," Eisenberg accused him of pandering to a "bunch of foolishness." When he received hate mail and threatening phone calls after the host of a televised sports program he sponsored shook hands on camera with a black player from the Harlem Globetrotters, Eisenberg refused to apologize; perhaps coincidentally, the program was soon pulled off the air.

15. The incident, observed by the author, occurred close to the Jewish festival of Passover in 1956.

16. Interview with Joe Azbell, December 29, 1990.

17. Wallace transcripts: no. 4, p. 13; no. 9, pp. 16–17.

18. Wallace transcripts: no. 4, p. 13; no. 12, p. 16; no. 13, p. 2.

19. Wallace transcript, no. 4, p. 14.

20. Ibid., pp. 13–14.

21. Wallace transcripts: no. 12, pp. 15–16; no. 13, p. 2.

22. Wallace transcripts: no. 11, pp. 3–4; no. 12, pp. 15–16; no. 13, p. 2; George C. Wallace papers, University of Alabama at Birmingham (UAB) (hereafter referred to as Wallace papers, UAB); interview with Joe Azbell, December 29, 1990.

23. The law was designed to discourage possible resale to minors, or selling of whisky on a shot-by-shot basis, or watering down and rebottling of it.

24. *Boy* was the patronizing term that some Southern whites at the time used to describe or address black men.

25. Interview with George Wallace, December 29, 1990; interview with Bill Jones, March 6, 1991.

26. Wallace transcript, no. 16, pp. 10–14; Wallace papers, UAB.

27. Wallace transcript, no. 16, pp. 10–14.

28. Ibid.

29. Wallace transcripts: no. 3, p. 29; no. 6, p. 13; no. 9, pp. 16–17.

30. Wallace transcripts: no. 3, p. 29; no. 9, p. 17; no. 26, pp. 10–11.

31. Ibid.

32. William E. Leuchtenburg, "The Conversion of Harry Truman," *American Heritage,* November 1991, pp. 56–58.

33. William Manchester, *The Glory and the Dream: A Narrative History of America, 1932–1972* (Boston: Little, Brown, 1974), pp. 530–53.

34. Ibid.

35. Wallace papers, UAB.

36. David McCullough, *Truman* (New York: Simon & Schuster, 1992), p. 641.

37. Wallace papers, UAB; Wallace transcripts: no. 8, pp. 4–5; no. 11, pp. 8, 19.

38. The description of Connor is from a July 14, 1948, column by Grover C. Hall, the editor of the *Montgomery Advertiser,* in a clipping preserved in one of Wallace's scrapbooks in the Sterne Library, University of Alabama at Birmingham (Wallace papers, UAB).

39. Manchester, *Glory and the Dream,* pp. 555–56.

40. Grover C. Hall, *Montgomery Advertiser,* July 15, 1948.

41. Wallace papers, UAB.

42. Wallace transcripts: no. 4, p. 14; no. 21, p. 13.

43. Wallace papers, UAB; *Encyclopaedia Britannica Yearbook,* 1946. The law permitted registrars to thwart blacks seeking to vote by asking difficult questions like which amendments guaranteed the right to speedy public trials (the Sixth) and provided for popular election of senators (the Seventeenth).

44. Wallace transcripts: no. 14, p. 2; no. 24, p. 1; no. 25, pp. 14–15.

45. Wallace papers, UAB.

46. Frady, *Wallace,* p. 98.

47. Wallace papers, UAB.

48. Wallace transcript, no. 12, p. 15; Wallace papers, UAB.

49. Wallace papers, UAB.

50. Ibid.; Wallace transcript, no. 4, pp. 15–16.

51. Wallace papers, UAB; Wallace transcript, no. 4, pp. 14–15; Hugh Sparrow, *Birmingham News,* August 8, 1951, p. 8.

52. Wallace transcripts: no. 4, pp. 17–18; no. 11, pp. 4–5; no. 14, p. 16; Wallace papers, UAB.

53. Wallace papers, UAB; *Alabama Local Government Journal,* April 1951.

5: *Here Comes the Judge*

1. George C. Wallace papers, University of Alabama at Birmingham (UAB) (hereafter referred to as Wallace papers, UAB); Marshall Frady, *Wallace* (New York: New American Library, 1972), p. 117.

2. Frady, *Wallace,* p. 118.

3. Wallace papers, UAB.

4. Wallace transcript, no. 6, p. 15.

5. Wallace transcript, no. 7, p. 15.

6. Geoffrey Birt, "George Wallace Begins Career as Third Judicial Circuit Judge," *Columbus* (Ga.) *Ledger*, February 3, 1953 (Wallace papers, UAB).

7. Frady, *Wallace*, p. 120.

8. Wallace transcripts: no. 10, p. 7; no. 16, p. 3.

9. Wallace transcript, no. 25, pp. 12–13.

10. Ibid.

11. Ibid.

12. Frady, *Wallace*, p. 120.

13. *Encyclopaedia Britannica Yearbook*, 1956, p. 283.

14. Ibid.

15. J. L. Chestnut, Jr., and Julia Cass, *Black in Selma: The Uncommon Life of J. L. Chestnut, Jr.* (New York: Farrar, Straus & Giroux, 1990), p. 126.

16. Ibid.

17. Frady, *Wallace*, p. 121.

18. Ibid., p. 122.

19. Wallace papers, UAB; "Grand Jury Backs Wallace Decision on Jail for 'Invaders,' " *Montgomery Advertiser*, February 8, 1956 (Wallace papers, UAB).

20. Ibid.

21. Bill Jones, *The Wallace Story* (Northport, Ala.: American Southern, 1966), p. 7.

22. Ibid., pp. 6–7.

23. Ibid.

24. Wallace papers, UAB; "Southern Judge and Editor Debate Desegregation Issue," *Colorado Springs Sun*, November 21, 1957, p. 1.

25. Wallace papers, UAB; "News Editor, Judge Debate Segregation," *Rocky Mountain News*, November 21, 1957, p. 1.

26. Ibid.; ibid.

27. Wallace transcript, no. 25, pp. 14–15.

28. Ibid., pp. 15–16.

29. Ibid.

30. Ibid, p. 16; Frady, *Wallace*, p. 108.

31. Steve Coates, "Rogues' Gallery: That Good Ole-Time Politics," *Wall Street Journal*, June 5, 1989, p. A12.

32. Frady, *Wallace*, pp. 104–5.

33. Letter to the author from George Wallace, July 11, 1991.

34. Rex Thomas, "Clayton's Judge Wallace Eyed as Key Influence with Folsom," *Montgomery Advertiser*, January, 1955, p. 1 (Wallace papers, UAB).

35. Wallace papers, UAB.

36. Ibid.

37. Frady, *Wallace*, p. 106.

38. Interview with Jim Folsom, March 15, 1956.

39. Folsom Christmas message, 1949, Alabama Archives.

40. Bob Ingram, undated article from the *Montgomery Advertiser*, from Wallace papers, UAB.

41. Frady, *Wallace*, pp. 102, 106.

42. Billy Bowles and Remer Tyson, *They Love a Man in the Country: Saints and Sinners in the South* (Atlanta: Peachtree, 1989).

43. Interview with George Wallace, December 22, 1990.

44. Wallace papers, UAB.

45. Contemporaneous notes of the author, who was present at that meeting in Montgomery.

46. *Montgomery Advertiser*, February 28, 1956; February 25, 1956; *Montgomery Advertiser*, February 18, 1956.

47. *Encyclopaedia Britannica Yearbook*, 1956, p. 284.

48. Undated clipping from the *Birmingham News*, from Wallace papers, UAB.

49. Bob Ingram, *Montgomery Advertiser*, March 1, 1956, p. 1.

50. *Montgomery Advertiser*, February 26, 1956.

51. Ibid; ibid.

52. Ibid.

53. *Montgomery Advertiser*, special section, January 11, 1987, p. 12.

54. Ibid.

55. Frady, *Wallace*, p. 109.

56. Taylor Branch, *Parting the Waters: America in the King Years, 1954–63* (New York: Simon & Schuster, 1988), p. 223.

57. William Manchester, *The Glory and the Dream: A Narrative History of America, 1932–1972* (Boston: Little, Brown, 1974), pp. 978–81.

58. Branch, *Parting the Waters*, p. 223.

59. Manchester, *Glory and the Dream*, pp. 980–81.

60. Ibid., pp. 983–84; Branch, *Parting the Waters*, pp. 223–24.

61. Manchester, *Glory and the Dream*, p. 984.

62. Branch, *Parting the Waters*, p. 224.

63. Manchester, *Glory and the Dream*, p. 989. An indignant Eisenhower responded to Senator Russell's slur by pointing out that Hitler's use of military power was "to further the ambitions of a ruthless dictator," whereas Eisenhower's in Little Rock was "to preserve the institutions of free government."

64. Branch, *Parting the Waters*, p. 224. In fact, Faubus was elected to a third term as governor in 1958 by a margin of more than four to one, and he was reelected to three additional two-year terms.

6: *Striking Out*

1. Letter from Grover C. Hall to Justice Hugo Black, November 9,

1955, from the private papers of Hugo Black, Library of Congress, Washington, D.C. (hereafter referred to as Black papers).

2. Ibid., January 19, 1956, Black papers.

3. Ibid.

4. Ibid. By "painted sticks," Hall was referring to the red, white, and blue stakes that carpetbaggers sold to gullible freed slaves, ostensibly to be used in staking out land that the Freedmen's Bureau was redistributing. Hall is thus saying that carpetbaggers swindled blacks for quick profits.

5. In II Samuel 1:20, David sought to suppress the news of the death in battle of Saul and Jonathan, "lest the daughters of the Philistines rejoice."

6. As a young reporter for the *Montgomery Advertiser*, I wrote three of the articles in the series that won for Hall and the *Advertiser* staff the 1957 National Headliner Award for distinguished editorial writing.

7. Martin Weil, "Grover C. Hall Jr., Ala. Editor, 56, Critic of Northern Press," obituary appearing in the *Washington Post*, [Date NA], 1973.

8. Arthur M. Schlesinger, Jr., *Robert Kennedy and His Times* (Boston: Houghton Mifflin, 1978), p. 137. The other principal contenders were Estes Kefauver (the eventual winner) and Hubert Humphrey, both strongly committed to civil rights legislation.

9. Peter Maas, "Robert Kennedy Speaks Out," *Look*, March 22, 1961.

10. Wallace transcript, no. 8, pp. 5–6.

11. Schlesinger, *Robert Kennedy*, p. 137.

12. Wallace transcript, no. 11, pp. 6–7. Actually, Smith's candidacy resulted in the first break of the solid South since Reconstruction, with the Republicans carrying Virginia, North Carolina, Tennessee, Florida, and Texas. In 1960, Kennedy lost Virginia, Tennessee, and Florida to Richard Nixon, while unpledged electors, who cast their ballots for Sen. Harry Byrd of Virginia, carried Mississippi. Alabamians gave comfortable majorities to both Smith in 1928 and Kennedy in 1960.

13. Wallace transcripts: no. 8, pp. 5–6; no. 11, p. 7.

14. Wallace transcript, no. 8, p. 6.

15. Norman Cousins, *The Improbable Triumvirate* (New York: Norton, 1972), p. 114.

16. Bill Jones, *The Wallace Story* (Northport, Ala.: American Southern, 1966), pp. 7–9.

17. Ibid., pp. 9–11.

18. Wallace transcript, no. 7, p. 15.

19. Wallace transcripts: no. 3, p. 29; no. 9, p. 17.

20. Wallace transcript, no. 23, pp. 5–6.

21. Charles Snider, Wallace's national campaign chairman, told me that Lurleen often complained to women friends (Snider's mother-in-law among them) that Wallace frequently "cheated" on her. Cornelia's suspicions exploded into headlines years later, as discussed in the Epilogue.

22. Wallace transcripts: no. 3, p. 29–30; no. 7, p. 15; no. 9, pp. 17–18.

Few of Wallace's political intimates ever knew that Lurleen felt such despair or that she wanted a divorce.

23. George Wallace, Jr., with James Gregory, *The Wallaces of Alabama: My Family* (Chicago: Follett, 1975), pp. 33–34. As noted earlier, Lurleen did reveal her feelings about the marriage to several friends, although apparently not to her children.

24. Ibid., 39–41.

25. Ibid., p. 43.

26. Ibid., pp. xiii-xiv.

27. *Montgomery Advertiser*, special section, January 11, 1987, p. 16 (hereafter referred to as *Montgomery Advertiser*, special sec.); interview with Joe Azbell, December 20, 1990.

28. Ibid.; ibid.

29. Marshall Frady, *Wallace* (New York: New American Library, 1972), p. 123.

30. *Montgomery Advertiser*, special sec., p. 15.

31. Ibid.; Frady, *Wallace*, p. 124.

32. Jones, *Wallace Story*, pp. 13–16.

33. Taylor Branch, *Parting the Waters: America in the King Years, 1954–63* (New York: Simon & Schuster, 1988), pp. 144, 152, 163, 176, 186.

34. Ibid., pp. 186–87.

35. Jones, *Wallace Story*, pp. 13–15; *Montgomery Advertiser*, special sec., p. 15.

36. Jones, *Wallace Story*, p. 14; *Montgomery Advertiser*, special sec., pp. 15–16.

37. Jones, *Wallace Story*, p. 16.

38. Ibid.

39. *Montgomery Advertiser*, special sec., p. 16.

40. Interview with Joe Azbell, December 29, 1990.

41. Jones, *Wallace Story*, p. 17.

42. Letter from Virginia Durr to Hugo Black, November 23, 1964, from Black papers. John Crommelin, a retired navy admiral, spent most of his retirement in Alabama and ranged throughout the state and the South delivering hate-mongering diatribes against blacks, Catholics, and Jews; a typical assertion, from a speech that I covered as a reporter for the *Montgomery Advertiser* in 1955, was: "Niggers have brains barely half the size of the white man's, so if a nigger like King is able to graduate from a self-respecting college, my name is Finkelstein."

43. Jones, *Wallace Story*, pp. 17–18; interview with Joe Azbell, December 29, 1990; *Montgomery Advertiser*, special sec., pp. 15–16.

44. Letter from Virginia Durr to Hugo Black, June 5, 1958, from Black papers.

45. *Montgomery Advertiser*, special sec., p. 16. Ray Jenkins was, for many years, the editorial page editor of the *Alabama Journal*, Montgomery's after-

noon daily newspaper; in later years, he was an assistant press secretary in the Carter White House and the editorial page editor of the *Baltimore Sun*.

46. Interview with George Wallace, July 14, 1987.

47. *Montgomery Advertiser*, special sec., p. 16.

48. Interview with John Patterson by the author, then representing the *Columbus Ledger*, June 2, 1958.

49. Letter from Virginia Durr to Hugo Black, June 5, 1958, from Black papers.

7: *Stand and Deliver*

1. Interview with Joe Azbell, December 29, 1990.

2. Marshall Frady, *Wallace* (New York: New American Library, 1972), p. 127.

3. Ibid.

4. Wallace transcript, no. 3, p. 19.

5. Recollections of Joseph B. Cumming, of *Newsweek*, September 12, 1963.

6. *Montgomery Advertiser*, special section, January 11, 1987, p. 16.

7. Eric Foner, *Reconstruction: America's Unfinished Revolution, 1863–1877* (New York: Harper & Row, 1988), pp. 13, 300, 553, 612.

8. Tinsley E. Yarbrough, *Judge Frank Johnson and Human Rights in Alabama* (Tuscaloosa, Ala.: University of Alabama Press, 1981), p. 161.

9. Interview with George Wallace, July 14, 1987.

10. Bill Jones, *The Wallace Story* (Northport, Ala.: American Southern, 1966), p. 25.

11. In upholding the majority view in the Montgomery busing case, the Supreme Court cited *Brown* and two subsequent holdings issued without opinions pursuant to the reasoning in *Brown*—rulings that abolished segregation at Baltimore's public beaches and Atlanta's municipal golf courses. Beyond that, the Court gave no hint why it took its action in the Montgomery case or provided any reasoning behind the decision. As one of Earl Warren's law clerks said later, "I thought at the time that it was a pretty casual way for the Court to advance a major proposition of constitutional law—and I still do" (Bernard Schwartz, with Stephan Lesher, *Inside the Warren Court: 1953–1969* [New York: Doubleday, 1983], p. 101).

12. Schwartz, with Lesher, *Inside the Warren Court*, pp. 190–91.

13. Yarbrough, *Judge Frank Johnson*, pp. 62–64.

14. Ibid., p. 64; Jones, *Wallace Story*, pp. 20–21.

15. Jones, *Wallace Story*, pp. 20–21.

16. Yarbrough, *Judge Frank Johnson*, pp. 64–65; Jones, *Wallace Story*, pp. 21–22.

17. Yarbrough, *Judge Frank Johnson*, pp. 65–66.

18. Ibid., pp. 65–67; Jones, *Wallace Story*, p. 23.

19. Interview with Glen Curlee, October 15, 1991.

20. Yarbrough, *Judge Frank Johnson,* pp. 67–68.

21. Wallace transcripts: no. 14, pp. 26–29; no. 20, p. 8; interview with Glen Curlee, November 15, 1991.

22. Yarbrough, *Judge Frank Johnson,* p. 68; Jones, *Wallace Story,* p. 23; interview with Glen Curlee, November 15, 1991.

23. Letter from George Wallace to the author, July 30, 1991; Wallace transcript, no. 14, p. 27; Yarbrough, *Judge Frank Johnson,* pp. 68–69; Jones, *Wallace Story,* p. 24.

24. Don McKee in the *Montgomery Advertiser,* January 13, 1959.

25. Yarbrough, *Judge Frank Johnson,* p. 69.

26. Jones, *Wallace Story,* p. 26.

27. Yarbrough, *Judge Frank Johnson,* p. 69.

28. Ibid., p. 70.

29. Ibid.; Jones, *Wallace Story,* p. 28.

30. Jones, *Wallace Story,* pp. 28–29; Yarbrough, *Judge Frank Johnson,* pp. 70–71.

31. Jones, *Wallace Story,* pp. 30–31; Yarbrough, *Judge Frank Johnson,* p. 71.

32. Jones, *Wallace Story,* pp. 29–30; Yarbrough, *Judge Frank Johnson,* pp. 71–72.

33. Wallace transcript, no. 6, p. 15.

34. *Montgomery Advertiser,* special sec., p. 17.

35. Ibid.

36. Wallace transcript, no. 6, p. 12; interview with Elvin Stanton, December 29, 1990.

37. *Encyclopaedia Britannica Yearbook,* 1959, pp. 165–66; Eric Foner and John A. Garraty, eds., *The Reader's Companion to American History* (Boston: Houghton Mifflin, 1991), p. 899.

38. Yarbrough, *Judge Frank Johnson,* pp. 64–65.

39. Frady, *Wallace,* p. 125.

40. Taylor Branch, *Parting the Waters: America in the King Years, 1954–63* (New York: Simon & Schuster, 1988), pp. 226, 268–69, 277–78, 282, 287–88, 292–97, 300–1.

41. Ibid., pp. 288–89; Schwartz, with Lesher, *Inside the Warren Court,* p. 231.

42. Branch, *Parting the Waters,* pp. 280–82.

43. Ibid., pp. 412–17; Arthur M. Schlesinger, Jr., *Robert Kennedy and His Times* (Boston: Houghton Mifflin, 1978), pp. 306–7; William Manchester, *The Glory and the Dream: A Narrative History of America, 1932–1972* (Boston: Little, Brown, 1974), pp. 1146–48.

44. Branch, *Parting the Waters,* pp. 417–20, 442.

45. Howell Raines, "Grady's Gift," *New York Times Magazine,* December 1, 1991, p. 89.

46. Branch, *Parting the Waters*, pp. 420–21; Manchester, *Glory and the Dream*, pp. 1149–50; Schlesinger, *Robert Kennedy*, p. 307.

47. Schlesinger, *Robert Kennedy*, pp. 307–8.

48. Branch, *Parting the Waters*, pp. 432–42; Schlesinger, *Robert Kennedy*, p. 308.

49. Schlesinger, *Robert Kennedy*, pp. 308–9; Manchester, *Glory and the Dream*, p. 1151; Branch, *Parting the Waters*, pp. 442–44.

50. Manchester, *Glory and the Dream*, p. 1152.

51. Schlesinger, *Robert Kennedy*, p. 309; Branch, *Parting the Waters*, pp. 445–50; Manchester, *Glory and the Dream*, p. 1152.

52. Schlesinger, *Robert Kennedy*, pp. 309–10; Schwartz, with Lesher, *Inside the Warren Court*, p. 205; Branch, *Parting the Waters*, p. 461.

53. Schlesinger, *Robert Kennedy*, p. 311; Branch, *Parting the Waters*, p. 464. The reference to "Kelsey's nuts," which seemed to puzzle King and inhibit further rejoinders, never has been explained beyond probably being "an Irish expression of unknown provenance" (Schlesinger) or "an obscure term Kennedy had heard in Boston politics" (Branch). An Irish friend of mine who was involved in Boston politics for years told me the phrase "clearly refers to a sterile man—probably old, certainly Irish, and most likely a Republican."

54. Branch, *Parting the Waters*, pp. 471, 475; Schwartz, with Lesher, *Inside the Warren Court*, p. 205.

55. Schlesinger, *Robert Kennedy*, pp. 311–12.

56. Interviews with George Wallace, July 14 and 18, 1987; Branch, *Parting the Waters*, pp. 465–66.

57. Interview with Bill Jones, December 18, 1991; *Montgomery Advertiser*, special sec., p. 17; Frady, *Wallace*, p. 132.

58. *Montgomery Advertiser*, special sec., pp. 17–18.

59. Frady, *Wallace*, p. 132; *Montgomery Advertiser*, special sec., p. 18.

60. Interview with Bill Jones, December 18, 1991; Frady, *Wallace*, p. 131.

61. Interview with Bill Jones, December 18, 1991; Jones, *Wallace Story*, pp. 37–41.

62. Jones, *Wallace Story*, pp. 41–42.

63. Ibid., p. 43; *Montgomery Advertiser*, special sec., p. 18.

64. Frady, *Wallace*, pp. 110–11; *Montgomery Advertiser*, special sec., p. 18.

65. Jones, *Wallace Story*, pp. 43, 45; *Montgomery Advertiser*, special sec., p. 18.

66. Jones, *Wallace Story*, p. 45; *Montgomery Advertiser*, special sec., p. 18.

67. *Encyclopaedia Britannica Yearbook*, 1962, pp. 273–77.

68. Recollections of Joseph B. Cumming, of *Newsweek*, May 2, 1962.

69. Ibid.

70. Ibid.

71. Jones, *Wallace Story*, pp. 45–46.

72. Robert E. Baker, "Wallace Wins Try for Governor in Race-Based Alabama Primary," *Washington Post*, May 31, 1962.

73. Jones, *Wallace Story*, pp. 45–46.

74. Cumming recollections, September 12, 1963.

75. *Montgomery Advertiser*, special sec., p. 18.

76. Ibid.

77. Ibid.

78. Interview with Bill Jones, December 18, 1991.

79. Ibid.

80. Frady, *Wallace*, pp. 142–45.

81. Ibid.

82. Ibid.

8: *The Fire This Time*

1. The opponent, Georgia State Sen. Carl Sanders, would win; and though he maintained that Griffin, unlike himself, was "woefully weak on segregation," he would prove to be among the more moderate of Southern governors. Eight years later, however, Sanders's moderation on racial issues and his antipathy toward Wallace would be turned against him in a losing campaign for governor against a more vocal supporter of segregation, Jimmy Carter. During his term as governor, Sanders had barred Wallace from speaking in a state-owned facility. When Carter ran for governor in 1970, one of the stock lines in his stump speech was a vow that, if elected, he would invite Wallace to speak in Georgia.

2. Bill Jones, *The Wallace Story* (Northport, Ala.: American Southern, 1966), pp. 50–51. In apology for Wallace's indiscretion in intruding into the politics of a neighboring state, the *Montgomery Advertiser* editor Grover Hall explained that Wallace had an obligation to repay Griffin for having invited him, toward the end of Griffin's term as governor four years earlier, to address the Georgia legislature.

3. Ibid., p. 52; Arthur M. Schlesinger, Jr., *Robert Kennedy and His Times* (Boston: Houghton Mifflin, 1978), pp. 330–41; William Manchester, *The Glory and the Dream: A Narrative History of America, 1932–1972* (Boston: Little, Brown, 1974), pp. 1158, 1161.

4. Jones, *Wallace Story*, p. 52.

5. Manchester, *Glory and the Dream*, pp. 1160, 1165; Taylor Branch, *Parting the Waters: America in the King Years, 1954–63* (New York: Simon & Schuster, 1988), p. 668.

6. "Chief Alabama Trooper: Albert Jennings Lingo," *New York Times*, May 13, 1963, p. 25.

7. Interview with George Wallace, July 19, 1987.

8. Ibid.

9. Interview with George Wallace, July 14, 1987.

10. Interview with Bill Jones, December 18, 1991; recollections of Joseph B. Cumming, of *Newsweek*, April 26, 1968 (hereafter referred to as Cumming recollections).

11. Wallace transcript, no. 20, pp. 4–5.

12. Marshall Frady, *Wallace* (New York: New American Library, 1972), p. 143.

13. Interview with Bill Jones, March 12, 1991.

14. Cumming recollections.

15. "Chief Alabama Trooper," *New York Times*, p. 25.

16. Cumming recollections.

17. John F. Kennedy, *Profiles in Courage* (New York: HarperCollins, 1956), chap. 6.

18. Schlesinger, *Robert Kennedy*, p. 339.

19. Ibid.

20. Letter from Mrs. Golden Gray Burke, Anniston, November 16, 1962; letter from Mrs. Carleton S. Lentz, Anniston, November 17, 1962; Alabama Archives and History, correspondence on civil rights (hereafter referred to as Archives correspondence).

21. Letter from J. P. West, Jr., Gadsden, October 25, 1962; letter from W. Raymond Berry, Huntsville, undated; letter from Mrs. W. E. Ellis, Fort Payne, October 25, 1962; Archives correspondence.

22. Letter from Newton S. Chamblee, Birmingham, October 28, 1962; letter from Adolphe LeBron, Rockford, October 28, 1962; letter from Lee B. Williams, Grove Hill, October 29, 1962; letter from C. E. Hornsby, Jr., Centreville, October 31, 1962; Archives correspondence.

23. Letter from C. E. Hornsby, Jr., Centreville, October 31, 1962; Archives correspondence. Even many black leaders were less than impressed with the achievement of enrolling Meredith at Ole Miss. In a November 17, 1964, article in *Look*, Martin Luther King, Jr., said that he considered Ole Miss nothing more than a token victory handled with "clumsiness and hesitancy" by the White House in a way that "made Negroes feel like pawns in a white man's political game."

24. Jones, *Wallace Story*, pp. 53–54.

25. Ibid., pp. 54–55.

26. Miscellaneous notes left by Lurleen Wallace for her children, George C. Wallace papers, University of Alabama at Birmingham (UAB) (hereafter referred to as Wallace papers, UAB).

27. Bill to "Mrs. Wallace, Thomas Ave.," January 18, 1963, Wallace papers, UAB.

28. Letter from "Mom" Sanders, December 27, 1962, Wallace papers, UAB.

29. "Press release," January 15, 1963, Wallace papers, UAB.

30. Interview with Joe Azbell, December 29, 1990. The Klansman was a notorious hate-monger named Asa Carter who, among other things, had

organized an attack on the singer, Nat "King" Cole, during a Birmingham concert in 1956. Under the pseudonym Forrest Carter, he wrote popular Western fiction, including the best-seller, *The Education of Little Tree* and *The Rebel Outlaw: Josey Wales,* which the popular actor and director Clint Eastwood turned into a motion picture.

31. Jones, *Wallace Story,* pp. 70–76.

32. In 1966, Flowers himself, speaking of the period of Alabama's racial crises during Wallace's first term, told the journalist Marshall Frady: "The Justice Department kept telling me, 'You're the bright light down there.' " Any hope that Flowers had for a federal sinecure, however, vanished when he was convicted in 1967 of exacting kickbacks from firms doing business in the state.

33. Frady, *Wallace,* p. 140.

34. Wallace transcript, no. 6, p. 18.

35. Frady, *Wallace,* p. 135.

36. Jones, *Wallace Story,* p. 81.

37. Branch, *Parting the Waters,* p. 570.

38. Zellner file, Wallace administration papers, Alabama Archives.

39. Branch, *Parting the Waters,* pp. 513–14, 522, 534, 537, 754.

40. Manchester, *Glory and the Dream,* p. 1195.

41. Vincent Harding, "A Beginning in Birmingham," *Reporter,* June 6, 1963, p. 14.

42. Branch, *Parting the Waters,* pp. 703, 709; *Encyclopaedia Britannica Yearbook,* 1963, p. 250; *New York Times,* April 4, 1963, p. 24; Harding, "Beginning," p. 14.

43. Harding, "Beginning," p. 15.

44. Interview with Bill Jones, December 18, 1991.

45. Ibid.

46. Governor's statement, April 3, 1963, Alabama Archives.

47. Wire from the governor to Lister Hill and John Sparkman, April 4, 1963, Alabama Archives.

48. Near Chattanooga, author Taylor Branch reported, a man ripped up Moore's sign urging equality for "white and black" because he found the word *black* offensive; the correct term (for himself and others), he said, was *colored.*

49. Branch, *Parting the Waters,* pp. 748–49.

50. Harold Curtis Fleming, "Civil Rights," *Encyclopaedia Britannica Yearbook,* 1963; *New York Times,* April 25, 1963, p. 20; *New York Times,* April 27, 1963, p. 9; *New York Times,* April 28, 1963, p. 84; *Facts on File,* September 13, 1963, p. 343.

51. Herblock, "Ah Yes—The Murder of That Hiker Was a Dastardly Act," *Washington Post,* April 28, 1963.

52. "Murder Most Foul," *Chicago Sun-Times,* April 26, 1963.

53. ' "He Was So Kind,' " *Denver Post*, date unavailable (Alabama Archives).

54. Reprint by an unidentified Florida newspaper of an editorial in the *Montgomery Advertiser*. The reprint was received by the governor's office on May 3, 1963, and filed with state papers in the Alabama Archives.

55. Fleming, "Civil Rights," p. 251; "Chief Alabama Trooper," *New York Times*.

56. Branch, *Parting the Waters*, pp. 750–51, 763–64.

57. Rep. Brooks Hays, reporting to President Kennedy on November 30, 1962, on a conversation with Senator Sparkman, Robert F. Kennedy papers (John F. Kennedy Library and Museum, Columbia Point, Mass.) (hereafter referred to as RFK papers).

58. President Kennedy to Robert F. Kennedy, RFK papers.

59. Schlesinger, *Robert Kennedy*, p. 351; Frady, *Wallace*, p. 150.

60. Jones, *Wallace Story*, p. 81; Cumming recollections.

61. Schlesinger, *Robert Kennedy*, pp. 352–53; Frady, *Wallace*, pp. 150–68; transcript of a conversation between Attorney General Robert F. Kennedy and Governor Wallace, Montgomery, Alabama, April 25, 1963, RFK papers.

62. Schlesinger, *Robert Kennedy*, p. 354; Manchester, *Glory and the Dream*, p. 1199; Cumming recollections.

63. Frady, *Wallace*, p. 155.

64. Branch, *Parting the Waters*, pp. 734, 747, 750–54; Harding, "Beginning," p. 15.

65. Martin Luther King, Jr., *Why We Can't Wait* (New York: New American Library, Signet reprint, 1964), p. 97; Schlesinger, *Robert Kennedy*, p. 342; Branch, *Parting the Waters*, p. 759.

66. Branch, *Parting the Waters*, pp. 758–60, 777; Manchester, *Glory and the Dream*, p. 1196.

67. Live report of Elvin Stanton, WSGN Radio, Birmingham, May 3, 1963.

68. Branch, *Parting the Waters*, pp. 758, 760–62; Schlesinger, *Robert Kennedy*, p. 342; Manchester, *Glory and the Dream*, pp. 1196–97. The October 10, 1963, issue of *Jet* reported that Walter Gadsden, the teenager who was photographed being attacked by the police dog, was more an onlooker than a participant in the demonstrations; indeed, Gadsden, a member of a prosperous black Birmingham family, decided the attack occurred principally because he had been "mixing with a bad crowd" and that, in the future, he would stay away from demonstrations.

69. Harding, "Beginning,", p. 16; Branch, *Parting the Waters*, pp. 762, 775.

70. *New York Times*, May 6, 1963, p. 59; *New York Times*, May 7, pp. 1, 33; *New York Times*, May 8, p. 1; Branch, *Parting the Waters*, pp. 775, 779; Harding,

"Beginning," p. 16; Cumming recollections, March 11, 1965; report of Jim Strickland, of the *Montgomery Advertiser*, May 9, 1963.

71. Harding, "Beginning," pp. 16–17; Branch, *Parting the Waters*, pp. 780–81.

72. *New York Times*, May 9, 1963, p. 1; Branch, *Parting the Waters*, pp. 782–83; Cumming recollections, May 9, 1963.

73. Report of Jim Strickland, of the *Montgomery Advertiser*, May 9, 1963.

74. Harding, "Beginning," p. 17; "Explosion in Alabama," *Newsweek*, May 20, 1963, p. 25.

75. *New York Times*, May 9, 1963, p. 17.

76. 1961 Fifty State Report of Advisory Commission on Civil Rights (Washington, D.C.: U.S. Government Printing Office, 1961), pp. 67–84.

77. Don O. Noel, reporting in the *Hartford Courant*, May 9, 1963, p. 17.

78. Letter from William Scalise, Kensington, Connecticut, undated, Archives correspondence.

79. Letter from E. N. Robertson, Whitneyville, Connecticut, undated, Archives correspondence.

80. Letters from Mrs. Albert F. Williams, South Windham, Connecticut; William E. Gemmell, Ansonia, Connecticut; Henry Hottinger, New York City; Constance Dall, New York City; C. D. Buckley, Boonville, New York; Malcolm Craven, San Francisco; others; Archive correspondence.

81. Letters from Mrs. H. F. Ellerbe, Fayetteville, North Carolina; H. M. Miller, San Francisco; Harry Klein, M.D., New Haven, Connecticut; others; Archives correspondence.

82. Harding, "Beginnings"; Branch, *Parting the Waters*, p. 790.

83. Associated Press, "Facets of Strife Emerge in Court," *New York Times*, May 9, 1963, p. 17.

84. Claude Sitton, "Fifty Hurt in Negro Rioting after Birmingham Blasts," *New York Times*, May 13, 1963, pp. 1, 24; "Explosion in Alabama," *Newsweek*, May 20, 1963, pp. 25–26; Schlesinger, *Robert Kennedy*, p. 343.

85. Sitton, "Fifty Hurt."

86. Branch, *Parting the Waters*, pp. 798–800.

87. Anthony Lewis, "U.S. Sends Troops into Alabama after Riots Sweep Birmingham," *New York Times*, May 13, 1963, pp. 1, 13.

88. Interview with George Wallace, July 19, 1987.

89. Donald R. Matthews and James W. Prothro, *Negroes and the New Southern Politics* (New York: Harcourt, Brace and World, 1966), p. 240.

90. Interview with George Wallace, July 19, 1987.

91. Associated Press (AP), "Statements by Wallace and Boutwell," *New York Times*, May 13, 1963, p. 24.

92. Sitton, "Fifty Hurt."

93. AP, "Statements by Wallace."

94. *New York Times*, May 14, 1963, pp. 1, 4, 26.

95. *New York Times*, May 21, 1963, p. 1; *New York Times*, May 23, 1963, p. 1; *New York Times*, May 24, 1963, p. 37.

96. Report of Charles D. Kelly, the head of the Alabama Game and Fish Division, to the Alabama director of conservation, May 28, 1963.

97. Letter to Governor Wallace from J. A. Barclay, manager, Northrop/Huntsville Department, May 23, 1963, Archives correspondence.

98. Letter to Governor Wallace from William J. Rielly, Velva-Sheen Manufacturing Company, Cincinnati, Ohio, May 14, 1963, Archives correspondence.

99. *Encyclopaedia Britannica Yearbook*, 1963, pp. 250–51.

100. Schlesinger, *Robert Kennedy*, p. 353.

101. Pierre Salinger, "Memorandum of Conversation between President Kennedy and Governor George Wallace," May 18, 1963, John F. Kennedy papers (JFK Library, Columbia Point, Mass.).

102. Jones, *Wallace Story*, pp. 83–84.

103. Burke Marshall, "Memorandum to the Members of the Cabinet re: University of Alabama," May 21, 1963, JFK papers.

104. Robert F. Kennedy interview by Anthony Lewis, December 4, 1964, John F. Kennedy Oral History Project, JFK Library.

9: *The Defining Moment*

1. Robert F. Kennedy interview by Anthony Lewis, December 4, 1964, John F. Kennedy Oral History Project, JFK Library.

2. Robert Drew (producer), *Kennedy v. Wallace: A Crisis Up Close* (PBS, June 1963).

3. Recollections of Jim Strickland, of the *Montgomery Advertiser* (hereafter referred to as Strickland recollections), May 29, 1963; Bill Jones, *The Wallace Story* (Northport, Ala.: American Southern, 1966), p. 85.

4. Strickland recollections, May 29, 1963.

5. Strickland recollections, May 31, 1963.

6. Jones, *Wallace Story*, p. 90.

7. Recollections of Joseph B. Cumming, of *Newsweek*, May 30, 1963 (hereafter referred to as Cumming recollections).

8. Marshall Frady, *Wallace* (New York: New American Library, 1972), p. 148.

9. Interview with Bill Jones, March 12, 1991. "Before I left Wallace's employ as press secretary," Jones said, "I could sign Wallace's name and I guarantee you couldn't tell which one of us had signed it. Wallace made the major decisions, of course, but he expected us to get them carried out."

10. Letter from Governor George C. Wallace to Art Wallace, Toronto, Canada, September 13, 1963, Archives correspondence.

11. Ibid.

12. Ibid.

13. Interview with George Wallace, July 18, 1987; excerpts from letters from George C. Wallace to L. F. Cushenbery of Oberlin, Kansas, June 6, 1963, and to Mary Dannelly Hobbs of Selma, Alabama, October 9, 1963, Archives correspondence.

14. Letter from George C. Wallace to Mary Dannelly Hobbs of Selma, Alabama, October 9, 1963, Archives correspondence.

15. Letter from George C. Wallace to Emory K. Crenshaw, the president of the Henry Grady Hotel, Atlanta, August 22, 1963; reply from Crenshaw to Wallace, August 27, 1963, Archives correspondence.

16. Exchange of letters between George C. Wallace and Henry L. Lyon, Jr., October 14, 1963, and October 28, 1963, Archives correspondence.

17. Letter from George C. Wallace to Louise Day Hicks of Boston, November 19, 1963, after receiving a copy of Mrs. Hicks's letter to Robert F. Kennedy, November 12, 1963, Archives correspondence.

18. "Governor Wallace Called 'Absurd,' " editorial in *Richmond* (Va.) *News Leader*, September 25, 1963, Alabama Archives.

19. Ibid.

20. Cumming recollections, May 29, 1963. The comment was an inconsistency typical of Wallace and other bigots who would maintain that Southern blacks were content with the system of segregation, yet were plotting to integrate.

21. Ibid.

22. Jones, *Wallace Story*, p. 85.

23. "Meet the Press," transcript, June 2, 1963.

24. Richard D. Lowe, "Apologies from Kansas—An Open Letter to Governor Wallace of Alabama," *Winona* (Kan.) *Leader*, June 27, 1963.

25. Grover Hall, in the *Montgomery Advertiser*, quoted in Jones, *Wallace Story*, pp. 86–87.

26. "Text of Opinion by U.S. Judge Lynne," *New York Times*, June 6, 1963, pp. 21.

27. Jones, *Wallace Story*, p. 89.

28. Interview with Bill Jones, March 12, 1991.

29. William Manchester, *The Glory and the Dream: A Narrative History of America, 1932–1972* (Boston: Little, Brown, 1974), p. 1200.

30. Jones, *Wallace Story*, p. 91.

31. Interview with Nicholas Katzenbach, July 13, 1992; Booth Gunter, " 'Schoolhouse Stand' Gave Wallace National Attention," *Montgomery Advertiser*, April 3, 1986, p. 1A.

32. Interview with Nicholas Katzenbach, July 13, 1992; Gunter, "'Schoolhouse Stand,'" p. 11A.

33. Jones, *Wallace Story*, pp. 91–94.

34. Interview with George Wallace, December 28, 1990.

35. Arthur M. Schlesinger, Jr., *Robert Kennedy and His Times* (Boston: Houghton Mifflin, 1978), p. 356.

36. Ibid.

37. Jones, *Wallace Story*, p. 96; interview with Bill Jones, December 18, 1991; Frady, *Wallace*, p. 169; Gunter, " 'Schoolhouse Stand.' "

38. "The Next Stand," *Time*, June 7, 1963, p. 19; "An End and a Beginning," *Newsweek*, June 24, 1963, pp. 30–31.

39. Ibid.; Jones, *Wallace Story*, p. 95.

40. Drew, *Kennedy v. Wallace*; recollections of Marshall Frady, June 4, 1965; "An End," *Newsweek*, p. 32.

41. Ibid.

42. Drew, *Kennedy v. Wallace*.

43. Ibid.

44. Graham, a brigadier general during the Freedom Riders crisis, had been promoted.

45. Drew, *Kennedy v. Wallace*.

46. Interview with Bill Jones, May 12, 1991; Jones, *Wallace Story*, p. 95; interview with George Wallace, December 28, 1990.

47. Interview with George Wallace, December 28, 1990.

48. Drew, *Kennedy v. Wallace*.

49. Ibid.

50. Schlesinger, *Robert Kennedy*, pp. 344–48. Kennedy's difficulty in understanding the depth of black anger was mirrored nearly thirty years later in public exchanges among the Democratic presidential candidate Bill Clinton, the Rainbow Coalition leader Jesse Jackson, and the rap singer Sister Souljah. In the spring of 1992, following race riots in Los Angeles, Souljah was quoted in the *Washington Post* as saying, "If black people kill black people every day, why not have a week and kill white people?" Clinton, speaking at a Rainbow Coalition forum the day after Souljah had appeared there, chided the group for having invited someone who made such racially divisive remarks. The *New York Times* reported that Jackson was offended at what he called "a very well planned sneak attack" on himself. And, reacting to the criticism of Souljah in much the same way that Clark, Horne, and Hansberry had defended Jerome Smith three decades earlier, Jackson said that Souljah "represents the feelings and hopes of a whole generation of [black] people."

51. As Katzenbach told me in an interview on July 13, 1992: "Kennedy was so determined not to use troops because he felt that Eisenhower had used troops at Little Rock and that nothing had ever happened after that. That's why Bobby trained all these marshals and wanted to do it all with civilian enforcement, which we're not well equipped to do in the federal government."

52. Drew, *Kennedy v. Wallace*.

53. Ibid.

54. Ibid.

55. Interview with Nicholas Katzenbach, July 13, 1992; Drew, *Kennedy v. Wallace*.

56. Ibid. Katzenbach, in an interview with the author, said he knew from experience that, despite the taciturnity, Kennedy was feeling deep emotion: "He never said much and he never changed from a flat voice. That was his management style. When he wanted to tell you that you had done something really stupid, he'd say very quietly, 'Now that's not very satisfactory, is it?' When you heard that, you knew it was time to consider moving on."

57. Ibid.; interview with Bill Jones, December 18, 1991; Bob Ingram, "Handled Role with Dignity; Received Plaudits," *Montgomery Advertiser*, June 12, 1963; Manchester, *Glory and the Dream*, p. 1200.

58. Drew, *Kennedy v. Wallace*; interview with Nicholas Katzenbach, July 13, 1992; Manchester, *Glory and the Dream*, p. 1200; Jones, *Wallace Story*, pp. 97–98; Gunter, " 'Schoolhouse Stand,' " p. 11A; Frady recollections; "An End," *Newsweek*, p. 31.

59. Drew, *Kennedy v. Wallace*; interview with Nicholas Katzenbach, July 13, 1992.

60. "Text of Proclamation by Gov. Wallace," *New York Times*, June 12, 1963, p. 20.

61. Ibid.; interview with Nicholas Katzenbach, July 13, 1992.

62. Drew, *Kennedy v. Wallace*; Jones, *Wallace Story*, p. 100.

63. Interview with Nicholas Katzenbach, July 13, 1992.

64. Gunter, " 'Schoolhouse Stand,' " p. 11A; Frady recollections.

65. Interview with Nicholas Katzenbach, July 13, 1992.

66. Drew, *Kennedy v. Wallace*.

67. Interview with Nicholas Katzenbach, July 13, 1992.

68. Drew, *Kennedy v. Wallace*; Ingram, "Handled Role"; interview with Nicholas Katzenbach, July 13, 1992; "An End," *Newsweek*; Jones, *Wallace Story*.

69. Drew, *Kennedy v. Wallace*.

70. Doris Flora, "UA's Hood Wouldn't Repeat His Lonely Role," *Tuscaloosa News*, September 13, 1989, pp. 5A, 6A; "What Ever Happened to . . . Vivian Malone," *Ebony*, December, 1978, p. 65; Drew, *Kennedy v. Wallace*.

71. Drew, *Kennedy v. Wallace*; Schlesinger, *Robert Kennedy*, p. 358.

72. Drew, *Kennedy v. Wallace*; Manchester, *Glory and the Dream*, p. 1201; Schlesinger, *Robert Kennedy*, p. 356; Frady, *Wallace*, p. 177.

10: *The Turning Point*

1. Wallace transcripts: no. 2, p. 25; no. 20, pp. 1–4.

2. Interview with George Wallace, March 16, 1986.

3. Dan Carter, "George Wallace and the Politics of Rage," unpublished essay, June 1990, p. 1.

4. Bill Jones, *Wallace* (Northport, Ala.: American Southern, 1966), p. 105.

5. "Wallace Abandons Bill to Allow Him 2d Term," *New York Times*, September 7, 1963, p. 9.

6. Article from unidentified newspaper, datelined Hanover, New Hampshire, November 6, 1963, George C. Wallace papers, University of Alabama at Birmingham (UAB) (hereafter referred to as Wallace papers, UAB).

7. William Manchester, *The Glory and the Dream: A Narrative History of America, 1932–1972* (Boston: Little, Brown, 1974), p. 1201.

8. Manchester, *Glory and the Dream*, p. 1202; Arthur M. Schlesinger, Jr., *Robert Kennedy and His Times* (Boston: Houghton Mifflin, 1978), p. 358; Taylor Branch, *Parting the Waters: America and the King Years, 1954–63* (New York: Simon & Schuster, 1988), pp. 824–25.

9. *Encyclopaedia Britannica Yearbook*, 1963, pp. 251–52; Branch, *Parting the Waters*, pp. 824–27; "Role in Murder of Evers Laid to Southern Officials," *New York Times*, June 16, 1963, p. 1. A forty-two-year-old Mississippi fertilizer salesman and self-professed white supremacist, Byron de la Beckwith, was charged with Evers's murder. In both of Beckwith's trials in 1964, all-white juries were unable to reach verdicts, and the charges were dropped in 1969. In 1990, a grand jury in Jackson indicted him again after new evidence, which included eyewitnesses' accounts of Beckwith near the murder scene, was introduced. In December 1992, more than a year after Beckwith was extradited from Tennessee and held without bond in Mississippi, the Mississippi Supreme Court ruled in a 4–3 vote that Beckwith could be retried.

10. *Encyclopaedia Britannica Yearbook*, 1963, pp. 252, 256–57, 259.

11. Ibid., p. 258.

12. Ibid., p. 252; Manchester, *Glory and the Dream*, pp. 1202–3.

13. Pat Watters, *The South and the Nation* (New York: Pantheon Books, 1969), pp. 239–40.

14. *Encyclopaedia Britannica Yearbook*, 1963, p. 257.

15. Robert Drew (producer), *Kennedy v. Wallace: A Crisis Up Close* (PBS, June 1963); Schlesinger, *Robert Kennedy*, p. 360.

16. Schlesinger, *Robert Kennedy*, p. 363.

17. Ibid., pp. 380–82; E. W. Kenworthy, "Wallace Asserts Air Force Offers Aid to Race Riots," *New York Times*, July 16, 1963, p. 1; E. W. Kenworthy, "Robert Kennedy Says Bill Is Just," *New York Times*, July 19, 1963, p. 1; interview with Bill Jones, December 18, 1991.

18. Statement by George C. Wallace before the Senate Committee on Commerce in Opposition to Senate Bill 1732, July 15, 1963, pp. 2–3, 11–12, 14–15, 17, Alabama Archives.

19. *Newsweek*, July 29, 1963, p. 36, from Wallace papers, UAB.

20. Interview with Bill Jones, December 18, 1991.

21. Tinsley E. Yarbrough, *Judge Frank Johnson and Human Rights in Alabama* (Tuscaloosa, Ala.: University of Alabama Press, 1981), p. 91. Under the placement law, students were not assigned to schools on the basis of race,

but, in making assignments, school officials were permitted to consider factors such as "psychological qualifications," "the maintenance or sever-ance of established social and psychological relationships with other pupils and teachers," and the threat of disorder or economic retaliation. The judicial panel of Richard Rives of the U.S. Court of Appeals for the Fifth Circuit and U.S. district court judges Hobart Grooms and Seybourn Lynne said the law's application would bear scrutiny, but they were reluctant to prejudge the motive behind the statute.

22. Ibid.

23. Ibid.; interview with George Wallace, July 14, 1987.

24. Yarbrough, *Judge Frank Johnson,* p. 92; Claude Sitton, "Alabama Police Prevent Opening of Tuskegee High," *New York Times,* September 3, 1963, p. 1; "Boomerang," *Newsweek,* September 16, 1963, p. 26.

25. Claude Sitton, "Test Looms in Birmingham," *New York Times,* September 4, 1963, p. 26.

26. Claude Sitton, "Birmingham Shuts Schools Scheduled for Integra-tion," *New York Times,* September 6, 1963, p. 1; "Boomerang," *Newsweek;* Wallace papers, UAB. Among Wallace's papers was a sheet from a yellow legal pad containing the names and telephone numbers of the principals of the three Birmingham schools to be integrated, as well as the names and grade levels of the five black students scheduled to attend the three all-white schools, two of them high schools. A notation next to the names of fifth-grader Dwight Armstrong and his sixth-grade brother, Floyd, said that they lived "next to school," presumably negating any point Wallace might make about blacks being bused out of their neighborhoods to make a social statement. The page of names and numbers does not appear to be in Wallace's handwriting, and he does not recall why he had it in his possession other than that it probably "helped" him in tracking "developments."

27. "Boomerang," *Newsweek,* p. 27; interview with Elvin Stanton, De-cember 27, 1990; Sitton, "Birmingham Shuts Schools."

28. Ibid.

29. John Herbers, "Wallace Urges Racial 'Reality'; Scorns the Advice of 'Theorists,' " *New York Times,* September 6, 1963, p. 14.

30. "Boomerang," *Newsweek.*

31. *Time,* September 20, 1963, from Wallace papers, UAB.

32. Ibid.; Yarbrough, *Judge Frank Johnson,* p. 93.

33. Claude Sitton, "Wallace to Let Schools Reopen in Four Cities Today," *New York Times,* September 9, 1963, p. 1.

34. Interview with George Wallace, December 27, 1991. An indication of the contempt for Wallace's actions in Huntsville was the unusually force-ful comment by the city's chief of police, Chris Spurlock, quoted in the September 16, 1963, issue of *Newsweek:* "This is a shameful thing. If it isn't clear to the world that our executive head is a sick man, then, by God, none of us is discerning enough to read the facts."

35. Claude Sitton, "Wallace Orders Guard Units Out for School Duty," *New York Times*, September 10, 1963, p. 1; "Text of Wallace Order," United Press International, September 9, 1963.

36. Sitton, "Wallace Orders Guard"; "Kennedy's Alabama Text," Associated Press, September 9, 1963; Yarbrough, *Judge Frank Johnson*, p. 93; "Letting George Do It," *Newsweek*, September 23, 1963, p. 33; Wallace transcript, no. 15, p. 5.

37. Yarbrough, *Judge Frank Johnson*, pp. 94–99.

38. Bob Ingram, article with headline and page number missing, *Montgomery Advertiser*, September 11, 1963, in a scrapbook from Wallace papers, UAB.

39. "Letting George," *Newsweek*, p. 34; *Time*, September 20, 1963, from Wallace papers, UAB.

40. Branch, *Parting the Waters*, p. 889; "The Sunday School Bombing," *Time*, September 27, 1963, p. 17.

41. Recollections of Karl Fleming, of *Newsweek*, September 30, 1963; Howell Raines, "The Birmingham Bombing," *New York Times Magazine*, p. 22; "Birmingham: 'My God, You're Not Even Safe in Church,' " *Newsweek*, September 30, 1963, p. 21.

42. Raines, "Birmingham Bombing," pp. 14, 23, 26; "Farce in Birmingham," *Time*, October 18, 1963, p. 27.

43. Interview with Bill Jones, December 18, 1991.

44. There was a legal question whether the Alabama National Guard, having been federalized the week before in connection with Wallace's attempt to flout school desegregation orders, remained under Washington's control or had reverted to direction from Montgomery. The guard was not used in the crisis surrounding the church bombing, so the question remained moot.

45. Claude Sitton, "Birmingham Bomb Kills Four Negro Girls in Church," *New York Times*, September 16, 1963, pp. 1, 26.

46. Branch, *Parting the Waters*, p. 891; "Case History of a Sick City," *Newsweek*, September 30, 1963, p. 24. Morgan would later become the national counsel for the American Civil Liberties Union.

47. Tom Wicker, "Kennedy Decries Racial Bombings; Impugns Wallace," *New York Times*, September 17, 1963, pp. 1, 25.

48. Wallace transcript, no. 2, p. 24.

49. Raines, "Birmingham Bombing," pp. 23–26; "Half-Cocked," *Newsweek*, October 14, 1963, p. 35; "Farce in Birmingham," *Time*, October 18, 1963, pp. 27–28; live report of Elvin Stanton, WSGN Radio, Birmingham, September 29, 1963.

50. Letter from Governor Wallace to Lawton Ford of Oakdale, Louisiana, January 6, 1964, Alabama Archives. As often was the case in letters signed by Wallace, this one contained misspellings and typographical errors, indicating it was prepared and sent in haste and may neither have been

personally reviewed nor signed by the governor. That was accepted procedure at the time because of the avalanche of mail directed to the Alabama Capitol; indeed, the reply to the Ford letter was made more than three months after its receipt, and it began, as did all of Wallace's correspondence at the time, with an apology for the delay. Nonetheless, all of Wallace's aides from that time insist that Wallace approved in advance the tone and essential messages conveyed in all correspondence.

51. Claude Sitton, "Alabama Compiling Files on Civil Rights Advocates," *New York Times*, February 15, 1964, pp. 1, 16.

52. Curt Gentry, *J. Edgar Hoover: The Man and His Secrets* (New York: Norton, 1991), p. 501.

53. Memorandum to Maj. W. R. Jones, the commander of the Investigative and Identification Division of the Alabama Department of Public Safety, from Capt. R. W. Godwin, October 16, 1963; letter from George C. Wallace to U.S. Attorney Ben Hardeman, October 23, 1963; statement of the Department of Justice, November 6, 1963; all from Alabama Archives.

54. Letter from George C. Wallace to James F. Harrison of Birmingham, November 12, 1963, Alabama Archives; "A Lesson on Truth," editorial in the *Dothan* (Ala.) *Eagle*, November 7, 1963.

55. "Where the Stars Fall," *Time*, September 27, 1963, p. 17; letter from Governor Wallace to Pamela Mayo of Santa Maria, California, February 20, 1964, Alabama Archives.

56. Raines, "Birmingham Bombing," pp. 23–25, 28–29; Gentry, *J. Edgar Hoover*, pp. 484, 585.

57. Letter from Grover C. Hall, Jr., to Justice Hugo L. Black, October 21, 1963, from the Hugo Black papers at the Library of Congress, Washington, D.C. (hereafter referred to as Black papers).

58. Ibid., November 7, 1963.

59. Jones, *Wallace Story*, pp. 107–11; Governor Wallace's itinerary, November 3–8, 1963, Wallace papers, UAB.

60. Ibid.

61. Martin Arnold, "Alabama Lawyer Hits Moderates," *New York Times*, September 24, 1963, p. 32. After protests by student groups and complaints from civil libertarians, Brewster reversed his stand. By then, however, Wallace had made other arrangements.

62. Wallace transcript, no. 20, pp. 21–22; letter from Hall to Black, November 7, 1963, Black papers.

63. Text of Wallace's speech at Harvard, November 4, 1963, Wallace papers, UAB.

64. Ibid.; "An Alabamian in Harvard Yard," editorial in the *Montgomery Advertiser*, November 6, 1963.

65. Wallace itinerary, Wallace papers, UAB; article from unidentified Boston newspaper, datelined Hanover, New Hampshire, November 6, 1963, Wallace papers, UAB.

66. "Alabamian in Harvard Yard," *Montgomery Advertiser*.

67. Bob Ingram, *Montgomery Advertiser*, November 5, 1963, p. 1 from Wallace papers, UAB.

68. "Tributes Cite Loss to U.S. and World," *New York Times*, November 23, 1963, p. 8.

69. Jones, *Wallace Story*, p. 120; interview with George Wallace, December 28, 1990.

70. Interview with George Wallace, December 28, 1990.

11: *Shaking Their Eyeteeth*

1. In 1992, presidential candidates borrowed from Wallace by making numerous campaign appearances on interview programs with relaxed settings and listener/viewer call-in questions. These were the so-called infotainment shows that had proliferated with the growth of cable television and "talk" radio. It was the first national campaign in which all the candidates appeared regularly on talk shows and interview shows with structures that departed from the rigid reporter/subject question-and-answer format.

2. Recollections of Paul Wells, of the Associated Press, January 15, 1964 (hereafter referred to as Wells recollections); Bill Jones, *The Wallace Story* (Northport, Ala.: American Southern, 1966), p. 122.

3. Jody Carlson, *George C. Wallace and the Politics of Powerlessness* (New Brunswick: Transaction Books, 1981), p. 64.

4. Jones, *Wallace Story*, p. 126.

5. So did the voters of California the following November when, by a two-to-one margin, they repealed the state's fair-housing law, despite vigorous efforts of religious, labor and civil rights organizations (*Encyclopaedia Britannica Yearbook*, 1964, p. 246).

6. Jones, *Wallace Story*, p. 126.

7. Ibid., p. 122; Wells recollections; Richard N. Current, "Lincoln," *New Encyclopaedia Britannica*, vol. 23 (Chicago: Encyclopaedia Britannica, 1987), p. 47; James M. McPherson, *Battle Cry of Freedom: The Civil War Era* (New York: Oxford University Press, 1988), p. 186.

8. Wells recollections; Jones, *Wallace Story*, pp. 130–31.

9. Jones, *Wallace Story*, p. 132. On March 10, 1964, Seattle voters rejected an open-housing law (*Facts on File*, 1961–1965 index, p. 416).

10. Wells recollections.

11. Editorial in the *Birmingham News*, January 20, 1964, in George C. Wallace papers, University of Alabama at Birmingham (UAB).

12. Just two weeks earlier, no less an authority than J. Edgar Hoover had asserted that world communism was exploiting the civil rights movement (*Facts on File*, 1961–1965 index, p. 413).

13. Jones, *Wallace Story*, pp. 143–45.

14. Ibid., pp. 139, 145, 174.

15. Although Wallace's statement implied that people in Cleveland were injured in race-related incidents, none were; he was referring to urban violence in general—from domestic brawls to muggings to murder—recorded in Cleveland on a single day.

16. Jones, *Wallace Story*, pp. 142–49, 156–57.

17. Ibid., pp. 152–55; recollections of Marshall Frady, February 14, 1964.

18. Wallace transcript, no. 26, p. 6.

19. Letter from Grover C. Hall to Justice Hugo Black, October 21, 1963, Hugo Black papers, Library of Congress, Washington, D.C. (hereafter referred to as Black papers).

20. Wallace transcript, no. 11, p. 14.

21. Wallace transcript, no. 33, p. 1.

22. Jones, *Wallace Story*, pp. 171–72, 174–75; Carlson, *Politics of Powerlessness*, p. 28; "Wallace Victory Guided by Woman," *New York Times*, April 12, 1964, p. 76.

23. "Wallace Victory," *New York Times*; Claude Sitton, "Wallace Asserts Popular Response Calls for a Serious Bid in Wisconsin," *New York Times*, March 18, 1964, p. 28.

24. Carlson, *Politics of Powerlessness*, p. 28; Jones, *Wallace Story*, pp. 184–85.

25. Carlson, *Politics of Powerlessness*, pp. 28–31; Jones, *Wallace Story*, pp. 194–95; recollections of Bob Ingram, of the *Montgomery Advertiser*, March 20, 1964 (hereafter referred to as Ingram recollections); "How Accurate Are Polls in '64 Elections?" *U.S. News & World Report*, June 1, 1964, p. 30.

26. Jones, *Wallace Story*, pp. 176–77, 185, 212; Ingram recollections.

27. Ingram recollections; Jones, *Wallace Story*, pp. 184, 212.

28. Harold H. Martin, "The Meaning of Governor Wallace's 'Victory,' " *Saturday Evening Post*, May 9, 1964, p. 86.

29. George C. Wallace, speech at Whitewater State College, Wisconsin, March 23, 1964, Alabama Archives (hereafter referred to as Whitewater speech).

30. Ibid.

31. Martin, "Governor Wallace's 'Victory,' " p. 87.

32. Whitewater speech. Although the unwieldiness (or "gridlock") of Congress was a target of public and political scorn in the 1992 presidential campaign, Wallace's concept of Congress's role appeared closer to the intent of the founding fathers than that of either President Bush, who blamed national problems on an adversarial Congress, or independent candidate Ross Perot, who implied that, if elected, he would force Congress to do the bidding of the executive, who, in turn, would receive his instructions through a nationwide electronic "town hall." But, as explained by

Justice Louis D. Brandeis in a 1926 opinion, *Myers v. United States,* "The doctrine of the separation of powers was adopted by the Convention of 1787 not to promote efficiency, but to preclude the exercise of arbitrary power. The purpose was not to avoid friction but, by means of the inevitable friction incident to the distribution of the governmental powers among three departments, to save the people from autocracy."

33. Jones, *Wallace Story,* p. 182.

34. Martin, "Governor Wallace's 'Victory,' " p. 87.

35. George C. Wallace, *Hear Me Out* (Anderson, S.C.: Droke House, 1968), pp. 5–6; Jones, *Wallace Story,* pp. 129, 159.

36. Ingram recollections; Martin, "Governor Wallace's 'Victory,' " p. 86. In fact, Sen. Abraham Ribicoff of Connecticut later castigated Wallace for "sheer hypocrisy" because, he said, for every fifty-seven cents paid by Alabamians in federal taxes, the state received one dollar in federal assistance for roads, hospitals, education, airports, and urban renewal.

37. Whitewater speech.

38. Martin, "Governor Wallace's 'Victory,' " pp. 86–87.

39. Jones, *Wallace Story,* pp. 180–83; Ingram recollections; Carlson, *Politics of Powerlessness,* pp. 30–31; "Elections: What Wisconsin Meant," *Time,* April 17, 1964; Austin C. Wehrwein, "Wallace's Vote Exceeds 200,000 in Wisconsin Test," *New York Times,* April 8, 1964, p. 18.

40. Wallace, *Hear Me Out,* pp. 19, 22, 26; Martin, "Governor Wallace's 'Victory,' " p. 87; Jones, *Wallace Story,* pp. 188–89.

41. Jones, *Wallace Story,* pp. 189, 217–20; Carlson, *Politics of Powerlessness,* p. 31.

42. "Wisconsin's Vote a Test for Rights," *New York Times,* April 5, 1964, p. 80; "Wisconsin Governor Praised by Johnson," *New York Times,* April 6, 1964, p. 44; Austin C. Wehrwein, "Heavy Vote Today Seen in Wisconsin," *New York Times,* April 7, 1964, p. 21.

43. Claude Sitton, "Wisconsin Vote Hailed in South by Rights Foes," *New York Times,* April 9, 1964, p. 1; Claude Sitton, "Wallace: South's Mood," *New York Times,* April 12, 1964, sec. 4, p. 5; "CORE Leader Sees Lessons," *New York Times,* April 9, 1964, p. 19; Austin C. Wehrwein, "Midwest Jolted by Wallace Vote," *New York Times,* April 9, 1964, p. 19; Earl Mazo, "Wisconsin's Meanings," *New York Times,* April 9, 1964, p. 19; letters to the *New York Times,* p. 30 on April 10, 1964, p. 34 on April 14, 1964, p. 36 on April 20, 1964; "Opinion of the Week," *New York Times,* April 12, 1964, sec. 4, p. 9; "What Wisconsin Meant," *Time,* April 17, 1964; Martin, "Governor Wallace's 'Victory,' " p. 87; Wallace transcript, no. 11, p. 12.

44. Mazo, "Wisconsin's Meanings."

45. Robert G. Sherrill, "Wallace and the Future of Dixie," *Nation,* October 26, 1964, p. 267; Martin, "Governor Wallace's 'Victory,' " p. 85.

46. Associated Press, "Indiana Scanning Wallace Petition," *New York Times,* March 28, 1964, p. 9; Austin C. Wehrwein, "Indiana Governor Strives

to Hold State for Johnson in Face of Wallace Bid," *New York Times*, April 1, 1964, p. 24; "Who's Wallace?" *Time*, April 24, 1964, p. 22; recollections of Joseph B. Cumming, of *Newsweek*, April 22, 1964 (hereafter referred to as Cumming recollections).

47. Jones, *Wallace Story*, pp. 229–30; Claude Sitton, "Johnson Prestige on Line in Indiana," *New York Times*, April 19, 1964, p. 83.

48. Jones, *Wallace Story*, pp. 239–41; Wallace, *Hear Me Out*, p. 7; Claude Sitton, "Wallace Pleased by Indiana Drive," *New York Times*, April 16, 1964, p. 30.

49. Cumming recollections.

50. "Who's Wallace?" *Time*; Austin C. Wehrwein, "Indiana Publicity Drive Aimed against Wallace," *New York Times*, April 25, 1964, p. 14; Cumming recollections. Welsh's allegations concerning Wallace's responsibility for the church bombings and the response to the Birmingham protesters were clearly arguable, but his charges about the billboards and subordination of the American flag were not entirely true. As to the billboards, *Newsweek*'s Joseph Cumming said, "Nobody in Alabama ever saw such." And, technically, the Alabama legislature, not the governor, maintains jurisdiction over the flags atop the statehouse; nonetheless, the American flag flies from a flagpole erected in 1918 on the Alabama capitol grounds especially to display the national banner.

51. Carlson, *Politics of Powerlessness*, p. 32; Wehrwein, "Indiana Publicity"; Jones, *Wallace Story*, pp. 230–31, 235; Cumming recollections. At the time, as the press secretary to Sen. Birch Bayh of Indiana, I participated in the formulation of anti-Wallace strategy and so had firsthand knowledge of the tactics used in trying to minimize his vote.

52. UPI, "Wallace Predicts Victory in Indiana," *New York Times*, April 21, 1964, p. 25; Austin C. Wehrwein, "Indiana Democrats Push Drive to Cut Wallace Primary Votes," *New York Times*, May 3, 1964, p. 73.

53. Cumming recollections; UPI, "Alabama Scored by Wallace's Foe," *New York Times*, April 22, 1964, p. 35; "Who's Wallace?" *Time*.

54. Cumming recollections.

55. UPI, "Alabama Scored"; Austin C. Wehrwein, "Indiana Students Jeer at Wallace," *New York Times*, April 24, 1964, p. 22; "Wallace Is Jeered at Notre Dame Talk," *New York Times*, April 30, 1964, p. 21; Jones, *Wallace Story*, pp. 251–53.

56. Richard L. Lyons, "Sheen, Wallace Urge Amendment on Prayer," *Washington Post*, May 1, 1964, p. 1. When photographers posed Wallace, Sheen, and Celler prior to the hearing, Sheen looked at the Protestant conservative Wallace and the Jewish liberal Celler and commented, "This is a strange kind of trinity."

57. Wehrwein, "Indiana Publicity Drive"; "Senator Kennedy Talks in Indiana," *New York Times*, April 26, 1964, p. 77; "Indiana Democrats Push Drive to Cut Wallace Primary Votes," *New York Times*, May 3, 1964, p. 73;

"Wallace Ending Drive in Indiana," *New York Times*, May 4, 1964, p. 17; Jones, *Wallace Story*, pp. 248–49.

58. Wallace, *Hear Me Out*, pp. 18–20.

59. Ibid., p. 25.

60. Ibid., p. 42.

61. Ibid., p. 58; Jones, *Wallace Story*, p. 248.

62. Claude Sitton, "Goldwater Finds North Is Uneasy," *New York Times*, May 2, 1964, p. 22.

63. Austin C. Wehrwein, "Big Wallace Vote Likely in Indiana," *New York Times*, May 5, 1964, p. 35.

64. Wallace transcript, no. 23, p. 20; "More of the Backlash," *Time*, May 15, 1964.

65. John D. Morris, "Johnson Doubts Gain by Wallace," *New York Times*, May 7, 1964, p. 19; Austin C. Wehrwein, "Democrats Hail Welsh's Victory," *New York Times*, May 7, 1964, p. 20; Carlson, *Politics of Powerlessness*, p. 33; Ingram recollections, May 7, 1964.

66. Jones, *Wallace Story*, pp. 257, 263; Carlson, *Politics of Powerlessness*, p. 34.

67. Jones, *Wallace Story*, p. 264; Ben A. Franklin, "Maryland Democrats Alarmed by Wallace Campaign," *New York Times*, April 5, 1964, p. 41; Ben A. Franklin, "Democrats Move to Stop Wallace," *New York Times*, April 26, 1964, p. 76.

68. Ben A. Franklin, "Brewster Attack, Johnson Visit Bolster Drive against Wallace," *New York Times*, May 8, 1964, p. 18.

69. "Truman Hailed in Capitol at Eighty; Gets Standing Ovation in Senate," *New York Times*, May 9, 1964, p. 14. Ironically, despite Truman's powerful commitment as president to civil rights and equality before the law, he long had shared Wallace's elemental views of the civil rights movement. As David McCullough relates in *Truman* (New York: Simon & Schuster, 1992), "Truman strongly disapproved of the methods of the civil rights movement, the sit-ins and marches. The leaders of the movement, it seemed to him, were flouting the law, resorting to mob rule, which was not his idea of the right way to bring about progress. He also appeared to take seriously the view of J. Edgar Hoover that much of the movement was communist-inspired" (p. 971).

70. Ben A. Franklin, "Collegians Treat Wallace Kindly," *New York Times*, May 10, 1964, p. 69; Jones, *Wallace Story*, pp. 263–64.

71. Franklin, "Collegians Treat."

72. Ben A. Franklin, "Wallace Keying Maryland Campaign to Prayer and Anecdotes," *New York Times*, May 11, 1964, p. 23.

73. AP, "Cambridge Negroes Protest on Wallace," *New York Times*, May 11, 1964, p. 25; Ben A. Franklin, "Cambridge, Md., Negroes Routed by Tear Gas after Wallace Talk," *New York Times*, May 12, 1964, p. 1; Jones, *Wallace Story*, pp. 278–80.

74. Franklin, "Cambridge, Md., Negroes"; UPI, "Autopsy Finds Gas Did Not Kill Baby," *New York Times*, May 13, 1964, p. 21; Jones, *Wallace Story*, pp. 280–81, 285; interview with George Wallace, July 18, 1987.

75. Ben A. Franklin, "Eight in House Back Wallace's Drive," *New York Times*, May 13, 1964, p. 21; Carlson, *Politics of Powerlessness*, p. 35.

76. Ben A. Franklin, "Wallace Impugns Negroes' Motives," *New York Times*, May 16, 1964, p. 10; Ben A. Franklin, "Wallace Foes Bid for Union Votes," *New York Times*, May 18, 1964, p. 16; Carlson, *Politics of Powerlessness*, p. 34.

77. Ben A. Franklin, " 'Hate' Groups Back Wallace Bid," *New York Times*, May 14, 1964, p. 27.

78. Wallace campaign film, May 1964; Greg MacGregor, "Reaction Divided on Wallace Vote, *New York Times*, May 20, 1964, p. 26; Carlson, *Politics of Powerlessness*, p. 34.

79. Franklin, "Wallace Impugns"; Wallace Maryland campaign film, May 1964.

80. Jones, *Wallace Story*, pp. 292, 295–98.

81. "Record Vote Seen in Maryland Today," *New York Times*, May 19, 1964, p. 31; Jones, *Wallace Story*, p. 302.

82. Ben A. Franklin, "Brewster Victor, Wallace Has 43% in Maryland Vote," *New York Times*, May 20, 1964, p. 1; "A Reluctant Contender," *New York Times*, May 20, 1964, p. 26; Jones, *Wallace Story*, pp. 292, 294.

83. Franklin, "Brewster Victor"; Ben A. Franklin, "Maryland's Vote Held Anti-Negro," *New York Times*, May 21, 1964, p. 1; E. W. Kenworthy, "Senators Doubt Wallace Impact on Rights Action," *New York Times*, May 21, 1964, p. 1; Jones, *Wallace Story*, pp. 303–6; Carlson, *Politics of Powerlessness*, pp. 36–37; *Encyclopaedia Britannica Yearbook*, 1964, p. 242.

84. Kenworthy, "Senators Doubt."

85. Carlson, *Politics of Powerlessness*, p. 37.

86. Jones, *Wallace Story*, pp. 311–21, 328–31; Earl Mazo, "Wallace to Push Presidency Race," *New York Times*, June 8, 1964, p. 1.

87. Mazo, "Wallace to Push"; Peter Kihss, "South's Leaders Are Split on Enforcing Rights Law," *New York Times*, June 22, 1964, p. 1; UPI, "Wallace in Dallas; Scores Prayer Ban and Civil Rights Bill, *New York Times*, June 24, 1964, p. 15.

88. Maddox became a hero of sorts to segregationist hard-liners when he vowed to go to jail rather than comply with the civil rights law and allow blacks in his establishment; only the night before the rally, Maddox had brandished a pistol when three black people had tried to enter his restaurant. Maddox, in an extraordinary comment on the times, became his state's governor in 1966.

89. Kihss, "South's Leaders Are Split"; recollections of Reg Murphy, of the *Washington Post*, July 6, 1964; UPI, "Negroes Beaten in Georgia Rally," *New York Times*, July 5, 1964, p. 37.

90. Canadian Press, "Liberals Peril U.S. Democracy, Wallace Asserts in Toronto Talk," *New York Times,* July 10, 1964, p. 13.

91. Charles Mohr, "Arizonan Presses Wallace to Yield," *New York Times,* July 13, 1964, p. 18; Wallace Turner, "Nixon Supports GOP Platform," *New York Times,* July 15, 1964, p. 22; Carlson, *Politics of Powerlessness,* pp. 39–40; Jones, *Wallace Story,* pp. 325–26, 336.

92. Jones, *Wallace Story,* p. 340; "Wallace Drops Presidency Bid," *New York Times,* July 20, 1964, p. 1.

93. "What Wallace Proved in the North," *U.S. News & World Report,* June 1, 1964, p. 29.

94. "*Playboy* Interview: Governor George Wallace," November 1964, p. 63.

95. "The Wallace Vote: The Candidate's Own Story," *U.S. News & World Report,* June 1, 1964, p. 63.

12: *Crossing the Bridge*

1. Jefferson Morley, "Bush and the Blacks: An Unknown Story," *New York Review of Books,* January 16, 1992, p. 20. Wallace and other critics of the civil rights bill attacked its provision for administrative, rather than judicial, enforcement of discrimination complaints. The bill later was amended to require jury trials, should administrative penalties exceed fines of three hundred dollars or thirty days in jail.

2. Ibid.

3. Tom Wicker, "Reagan Shuns Image of Goldwater in Coast Race," *New York Times,* June 1, 1966, p. 38; recollections of the journalist Andrew Glass of Ronald Reagan's address to the National Press Club, June 16, 1966.

4. Howard Fineman, "Poppy the Populist," *Newsweek,* November 7, 1988, p. 58. Fineman quoted the conservative theoretician Kevin Phillips as saying, "[Bush], the nation's leading preppy [is] winning as a barefoot populist. . . . It's the ultimate triumph of the populist revolution in Republican politics."

5. Interview with George Wallace, December 27, 1990.

6. Ibid.

7. Robert C. McMath, Jr., *American Populism: A Social History, 1877–1898* (New York: Farrar, Straus & Giroux, Hill & Wang, 1992).

8. Garry Wills, "Clinton's Hell-Raiser," *New Yorker,* October 12, 1992, p. 94; interview with George Wallace, December 27, 1990.

9. *Encyclopaedia Britannica Yearbook,* 1964, pp. 243–45.

10. William Manchester, *The Glory and the Dream: A Narrative History of America, 1932–1972* (Boston: Little, Brown, 1974), pp. 1252–54.

11. Mary King, *Freedom Song: A Personal Story of the 1960s Civil Rights Movement* (New York: Morrow, 1987), pp. 390–91.

12. Manchester, *Glory and the Dream,* pp. 1254–55.

13. King, *Freedom Song*, pp. 27–28.

14. Gay Talese, "Selma: Bitter City in the Eye of a Storm," *New York Times*, March 14, 1965, p. 1.

15. Ralph David Abernathy, *And the Walls Came Tumbling Down* (New York: Harper & Row, 1989), p. 297.

16. John Herbers, "The Change in Selma," *New York Times*, March 18, 1965, p. 28.

17. Bill Jones, *The Wallace Story* (Northport, Ala.: American Southern, 1966), p. 351.

18. Abernathy, *Walls Came Tumbling*, pp. 298, 307–8, 312–20; recollections of William Cook, of *Newsweek*, February 4, 1965 (hereafter referred to as Cook recollections).

19. Abernathy, *Walls Came Tumbling*, pp. 321–23.

20. Doris Kearns, *Lyndon Johnson and the American Dream* (New York: Harper & Row, 1976), p. 228.

21. Taylor Branch, *Parting the Waters: America in the King Years, 1954–63* (New York: Simon & Schuster, 1988), pp. 892–93.

22. Cook recollections.

23. Ibid.

24. Abernathy, *Walls Came Tumbling*, p. 324; John Herbers, "Negroes Beaten in Alabama Riot," *New York Times*, February 19, 1965, p. 1; "The Freedom Fever," *Time*, February 26, 1965.

25. Herbers, "Negroes Beaten"; John Herbers, "Two Inquiries Open on Racial Clash in Alabama Town," *New York Times*, February 20, 1965, p. 1.

26. Herbers, "Negroes Beaten"; Herbers, "Two Inquiries Open"; Roy Reed, "Alabama Victim Called a Martyr," *New York Times*, March 4, 1965, p. 23.

27. Abernathy, *Walls Came Tumbling*, p. 325.

28. Jones, *Wallace Story*, pp. 355–57; recollections of Michael Hirsley, of the *Chicago Tribune*, March 3, 1985.

29. Recollections of Bob Ingram, of the *Montgomery Advertiser*, March 7, 1965 (hereafter referred to as Ingram recollections).

30. Interview with Bill Jones, December 18, 1991.

31. Interview with George Wallace, December 28, 1990.

32. Abernathy, *Walls Came Tumbling*, pp. 325–27.

33. Cook recollections, March 8, 1965.

34. Ibid.

35. Abernathy, *Walls Came Tumbling*, p. 327.

36. Cook recollections, March 8, 1965.

37. Ibid.

38. Abernathy, *Walls Came Tumbling*, pp. 327–29.

39. Cook recollections, March 8, 1965.

40. Jones, *Wallace Story*, p. 361; J. L. Chestnut, Jr., and Julia Cass, *Black in*

Selma: The Uncommon Life of J. L. Chestnut, Jr. (New York: Farrar, Straus & Giroux, 1990), p. 206.

41. Cook recollections, March 8, 1965.

42. Ibid.

43. Wallace transcript, no. 3, p. 19.

44. Jones, *Wallace Story*, pp. 368–70. After a "decent interval" of a few months, Wallace quietly allowed Lingo to resign.

45. Abernathy, *Walls Came Tumbling*, p. 335.

46. Chestnut and Cass, *Black in Selma*, pp. 205–6.

47. Jones, *Wallace Story*, p. 370.

48. Abernathy, *Walls Came Tumbling*, p. 334; Jones, *Wallace Story*, p. 371.

49. "The Central Point," *Time*, March 19, 1965, pp. 24–25.

50. Tinsley E. Yarbrough, *Judge Frank Johnson and Human Rights in Alabama* (Tuscaloosa, Ala.: University of Alabama, 1981), pp. 115–16.

51. John D. Pomfret, "U.S. Sues to Void Ban of Marches; Accuses Wallace," *New York Times*, March 11, 1965, p. 1.

52. Richard N. Goodwin, *Remembering America: A Voice from the Sixties* (Boston: Little, Brown, 1988), pp. 319–20.

53. Jones, *Wallace Story*, p. 375.

54. Abernathy, *Walls Came Tumbling*, pp. 337–39.

55. Interview with Nicholas Katzenbach, July 13, 1992; Pomfret, "U.S. Sues."

56. Jones, *Wallace Story*, p. 373.

57. Ibid., pp. 373–74; Abernathy, *Walls Came Tumbling*, pp. 344–45; Manchester, *Glory and the Dream*, p. 1298; "Central Point," *Time*, pp. 25–26; "An American Tragedy," *Newsweek*, March 22, 1965, p. 20; John Herbers, "Clergyman Dies of Selma Beating," *New York Times*, March 12, 1965, p. 1.

58. "Central Point," *Time*.

59. Yarbrough, *Judge Frank Johnson*, pp. 117–19; "Central Point," *Time*, pp. 27–28; Ben A. Franklin, "Official in Alabama Says Trooper Shot Negro Who Died," *New York Times*, March 14, 1965, p. 1.

60. David Grubin, producer/director of "LBJ," documentary telecast on *The American Experience*, PBS, October 1, 1991, quoting Katzenbach; Jones, *Wallace Story*, p. 379.

61. Goodwin, *Remembering America*, p. 321; Lyndon Baines Johnson Library, University of Texas Oral History Project, transcript of Wallace interview, May 15, 1969, p. 23 (hereafter referred to as Johnson Library).

62. Goodwin, *Remembering America*, p. 321.

63. Johnson Library, pp. 11–14.

64. Ibid., p. 17.

65. Goodwin, *Remembering America*, pp. 322–23; Grubin, "LBJ," interviews with Goodwin and Katzenbach; interview with Bill Jones, January 3, 1993.

66. Johnson Library, p. 21; interview with George Wallace, July 21, 1986. Wallace was extremely reluctant to allow me to report that the president had frequently used the term *nigger* in their conversation. He agreed only after he read portions of Richard Goodwin's account of the meeting; Wallace was particularly incensed by Goodwin's contention that Johnson and Wallace had agreed at the meeting to a subterfuge: Wallace would ask for federal help to prevent violence in a Selma-to-Montgomery march, and Johnson would comply to "save [Wallace's] political ass." Wallace contended that the use of federal troops, which Johnson desperately wanted to avert, never was discussed.

67. "Central Point," *Time*, p. 28.

68. Ibid.

69. "Face the Nation," CBS, transcript, March 14, 1965.

70. Joseph A. Califano, *The Triumph and Tragedy and Lyndon Johnson* (New York: Simon & Schuster, 1991).

71. Kearns, *Lyndon Johnson*, p. 229.

72. Goodwin, *Remembering America*, pp. 331–34.

73. Ibid., p. 334.

74. Ibid.; Jones, *Wallace Story*, p. 399.

75. Chestnut and Cass, *Black in Selma*, p. 212.

76. Yarbrough, *Judge Frank Johnson*, pp. 118–19.

77. Recollections of Ward Just, of *Newsweek*, March 18–19, 1965.

78. Jones, *Wallace Story*, pp. 400, 404, 406–10.

79. Abernathy, *Walls Came Tumbling*, p. 350.

80. Chestnut and Cass, *Black in Selma*, p. 213.

81. Abernathy, *Walls Came Tumbling*, p. 349; "Road from Selma: Hope—and Death," *Newsweek*, April 5, 1965, pp. 23–25.

82. "Road from Selma," *Newsweek*, p. 25.

83. Abernathy, *Walls Came Tumbling*, p. 355; Jones, *Wallace Story*, p. 428.

84. Jones, *Wallace Story*, pp. 429, 431.

85. Yarbrough, *Judge Frank Johnson*, pp. 121–22.

86. Abernathy, *Walls Came Tumbling*, pp. 357–59.

87. Jones, *Wallace Story*, pp. 430, 434.

88. Goodwin, *Remembering America*, p. 320; Jones, *Wallace Story*, p. 407; Wallace transcript, no. 15, pp. 2–3.

89. Yarbrough, *Judge Frank Johnson*, p. 125.

90. "The Trial," *Time*, May 14, 1965, p. 27; "Hung Jury," *Newsweek*, May 17, 1965, pp. 40–41; Yarbrough, *Judge Frank Johnson*, pp. 125–33; Manchester, *Glory and the Dream*, p. 1299; Norman Sinclair, "Selma Victim's Husband Sees Progress," *Washington Post*, March 10, 1975.

91. "Juries and Justice in Alabama," *Time*, October 29, 1965. A year later, Eugene Thomas would be acquitted by another Lowndes County jury; William Orville Eaton would die of a heart attack before a state trial was conducted.

92. In 1978, a state grand jury in Alabama indicted Gary Thomas Rowe on a charge of first-degree murder in the killing of Liuzzo. Additionally, Sen. Edward M. Kennedy of Massachusetts, citing reports that Rowe had acted as an *agent provocateur* in the very civil rights violence he had been paid by the FBI to monitor, requested a Justice Department investigation of Rowe and the FBI's actions in running him. In late 1980, a federal judge enjoined Rowe's prosecution on the ground that Rowe's undercover work gave him immunity. In December of that year, the Justice Department report, issued by Attorney General Benjamin Civiletti, cleared Rowe of responsibility in the Liuzzo shooting, although the report indicated that the FBI had known about and covered up Rowe's involvement in several violent attacks on black citizens, civil rights activists, and journalists. And in May 1983, a federal judge, in a civil case brought by the Liuzzo family, found that Rowe neither killed Viola Liuzzo nor prompted the others to do so. At the trial, Eugene Thomas's former wife testified that Thomas had confided in her that Wilkins had, indeed, fired the fatal shots (Howell Raines, "FBI Cover-up Seen in '60s Klan Attack," *New York Times*, February 17, 1980, pp. 1, 16; "Inquiry Clears Rowe in Slaying of Civil Rights Worker," *New York Times*, December 16, 1980, p. 16A; George Lardner, "FBI Is Cleared of Responsibility in 1965 Slaying of Mrs. Liuzzo," *Washington Post*, May 28, 1983, p. 3A; "Woman Says Klansman Killed Rights Worker," UPI, March 31, 1983).

93. Yarbrough, *Judge Frank Johnson*, pp. 130–35; Raines, "FBI Cover-up," p. 16; Jones, *Wallace Story*, p. 437.

94. Yarbrough, *Judge Frank Johnson*, p. 135.

95. Recollections of Joseph Cumming, of *Newsweek*, March 11, 1965.

96. Jones, *Wallace Story*, pp. 435–37; transcript, "Today," NBC, March 26, 1965.

97. Jones, *Wallace Story*, pp. 437–38.

98. Ibid., pp. 410, 438–44; Ingram recollections, March 31, 1965.

99. Interview with George Wallace, December 28, 1990.

100. Ingram recollections, March 31, 1965.

101. William E. Schmidt, "Twenty Years after the Rights March," *New York Times*, March 1, 1985, p. 1; Roy Reed, "Five Years after, Selma Cannot Forget Historic Rights March," *New York Times*, March 22, 1970, p. 44; "Selma Revisited," *Newsweek*, April 25, 1966, pp. 25–26; Yarbrough, *Judge Frank Johnson*, pp. 124, 137.

102. William E. Schmidt, "March for Rights Resounds after Twenty Years," *New York Times*, March 8, 1985, p. 16A.

103. Kearns, *Lyndon Johnson*, pp. 249–50.

104. Ibid., pp. 304–5; Manchester, *Glory and the Dream*, pp. 1301–4; *Encyclopaedia Britannica Yearbook*, 1965, pp. 650–51.

105. Kearns, *Lyndon Johnson*, p. 304; Manchester, *Glory and the Dream*, pp. 1296–97; Chestnut and Cass, *Black in Selma*, p. 180.

13: *Lady in Waiting*

1. *Montgomery Advertiser,* special section, January 11, 1987, p. 22 (hereafter referred to as *Montgomery Advertiser,* special sec.).

2. Ibid., p. 20.

3. Letter from Virginia Durr to Elizabeth and Hugo Black, September 23, 1965, Hugo Black papers, Library of Congress, Washington, D.C. (hereafter referred to as Black papers); Ray Jenkins, "Mr. and Mrs. Wallace Run for Governor of Alabama," *New York Times Magazine,* April 24, 1966, p. 89. Just two years later, Flowers would receive a jail term for accepting kickbacks on state contracts his office had awarded or influenced.

4. Wallace transcript, no. 7, p. 4; Marshall Frady, *Wallace* (New York: New American Library, 1972), pp. 179–80.

5. Frady, *Wallace,* pp. 180–82; *Montgomery Advertiser,* special sec., p. 20.

6. Wallace transcript, no. 6, pp. 19–20; Frady, *Wallace,* pp. 184–86; Jenkins, "Mr. and Mrs. Wallace," p. 84; *Montgomery Advertiser,* special sec., pp. 20–21.

7. *Montgomery Advertiser,* special sec., pp. 20–21; Jenkins, "Mr. and Mrs. Wallace," p. 84; John Corry, "Wallace Ponders a New Strategy for Retaining His Power in Alabama," *New York Times,* October 31, 1965; Bill Whitworth, "Mrs. Wallace for Governor?" *New York Herald Tribune,* December 12, 1965; interview with George C. Wallace, Jr., March 4, 1993.

8. Interview with Bill Jones, February 15, 1993.

9. *Montgomery Advertiser,* special sec., p. 20; Wallace transcript, no. 6, pp. 20–21; George C. Wallace, Jr., with James Gregory, *The Wallaces of Alabama: My Family* (Chicago: Follett, 1975), pp. 85–86, 100.

10. *Montgomery Advertiser,* special sec., pp. 21–22; Frady, *Wallace,* pp. 190–91.

11. "Alabama's New Era: The Negro Votes," *Newsweek,* May 16, 1966, p. 25; Theo Lippman, "Ma and Pa Wallace?" *Baltimore Sun,* September 22, 1965.

12. Lyndon Baines Johnson Library, University of Texas Oral History Project, transcript of Wallace interview, May 15, 1969, pp. 10–11 (hereafter referred to as Johnson Library); Lippman, "Ma and Pa Wallace?"; Jenkins, "Mr. and Mrs. Wallace," p. 79.

13. *Montgomery Advertiser,* special sec., pp. 22–23; Frady, *Wallace,* p. 111.

14. Wallace transcripts: no. 7, p. 6; no. 14, p. 11; American Liberty Records, *The Wallaces: Governors of the State of Alabama* (Montgomery: privately issued, 1967); Jenkins, "Mr. and Mrs. Wallace," pp. 29, 74, 77.

15. Wallace, with Gregory, *Wallaces of Alabama,* p. 90; Frady, *Wallace,* p. 193; Jenkins, "Mr. and Mrs. Wallace," pp. 77, 79.

16. Roy Reed, "Flowers Joins Alabama Race for Governorship Nomination," *New York Times,* February 26, 1966; Jenkins, "Mr. and Mrs. Wallace," p. 86.

17. Associated Press (AP), "Wallace Orders All Teachers Shifted to Schools of Their Race," Montgomery, September 9, 1966; United Press International (UPI), "Lawmakers Back Wallace's Program Rebuffing U.S. Aid," Montgomery, August 23, 1966; UPI, "Wallace Will Seek State School Funds," Montgomery, August 15, 1966; UPI, "Wallace's Son Enters Desegregated School," Montgomery, September 6, 1966; Gene Roberts, "Wallace Orders New Segregation," *New York Times*, April 28, 1966, p. 24; Gene Roberts, "Alabama Negroes Key to Vote Today," *New York Times*, May 3, 1966, p. 1.

18. American Liberty Records, *Wallaces*; "Alabama's New Era," *Newsweek*, p. 27.

19. *Montgomery Advertiser*, special sec., p. 26; Louis Harris, "Analyzing the Vote—And Its Lessons," *Newsweek*, May 16, 1966, p. 27; "Alabama's New Era," *Newsweek*, p. 25.

20. Gene Roberts, "Alabama Chiefs Bid South Fight," *New York Times*, May 14, 1966, p. 28.

21. American Liberty Records, *Wallaces*.

22. Nicholas von Hoffman, "Mississippians Accept the 'Magic' of Wallace," *Washington Post*, October 15, 1966, p. 1.

23. Recollections of Ray Jenkins, of the *Alabama Journal*, September 6, 1966; Roy Reed, "Wallace Doubts Reagan's Beliefs," *New York Times*, November 10, 1966, p. 30; Von Hoffman, "Mississippians Accept."

24. Reed, "Wallace Doubts."

25. "Report to the Alabama Legislature by Governor George C. Wallace," January 10, 1967, Alabama Archives.

26. Ibid.

27. Ibid.; Bernard Schwartz, with Stephan Lesher, *Inside the Warren Court, 1953–1969* (New York: Doubleday, 1983), pp. 170, 175.

28. Interview with Bill Jones, February 15, 1993.

29. Wallace transcript, no. 2, pp. 10–11, 30.

30. James J. Kilpatrick, "What Makes Wallace Run?" *National Review*, April 18, 1967, p. 402.

31. Wallace transcript, no. 2, pp. 30–31; *Montgomery Advertiser*, special sec., p. 22; interview with George C. Wallace, Jr., March 4, 1993; David Margolick, "In Death, as in Life, Still in Shadows," *New York Times*, June 19, 1991, p. 16A.

32. Tinsley E. Yarbrough, *Judge Frank Johnson and Human Rights in Alabama* (Tuscaloosa, Ala.: University of Alabama Press, 1981), p. 165.

33. Ibid., pp. 155–58.

34. Ibid., pp. 139–40.

35. Recollections of Gerald Lubenow, of *Newsweek*, March 31, 1967.

36. Ibid.

37. "Speech by Governor Lurleen B. Wallace to the Alabama Legislature," March 30, 1967, Alabama Archives.

38. Yarbrough, *Judge Frank Johnson*, pp. 139–40.

39. Ibid., pp. 140–42.

40. Ibid., pp. 141–42.

41. Interview with George Wallace, December 27, 1990.

42. Catherine Steineker, quoted in *Montgomery Advertiser*, special sec., p. 22.

43. Letter from Bill Jones to the City Club Forum, Alabama Archives. The date on the letter was obliterated, but its language indicates it was late January 1967, after Lurleen had taken office but before the move into the Hall Street headquarters was completed.

44. Recollections of James Naughton, of the *Cleveland Plain Dealer*, March 23, 1967; recollections of Bos Nitsche in Reno, Nevada, March 12, 1968; recollections of Tom Taylor in Omaha, Nebraska, March 13, 1968.

45. Recollections of Leroy Natanson, of the *Syracuse Post-Standard*, April 27, 1967.

46. Recollections of Bryan Artis, of the *Pittsburgh Press*, April 28, 1967.

47. Johnson Library, pp. 13–14.

48. Wallace, with Gregory, *Wallaces of Alabama*, p. 94; Bill Hewitt, with Ron Ridenhour, "Another Wallace in Alabama," *People*, June 29, 1992, p. 65.

49. Wallace transcripts: no. 2, pp. 9–12, 14; no. 7, p. 2; *Montgomery Advertiser*, special sec., pp. 23, 26; Wallace, with Gregory, *Wallaces of Alabama*, p. 104.

50. Wallace transcripts: no. 3, p. 16; no. 4, p. 9; no. 7, p. 2.

51. Wallace transcripts: no. 3, p. 17; no. 4, pp. 9–10; Wallace, with Gregory, *Wallaces of Alabama*, pp. 115–17.

52. Wallace transcripts: no. 4, pp. 10–11; no. 14, p. 1; Wallace, with Gregory, *Wallaces of Alabama*, pp. 117–19.

53. Wallace transcripts: no. 4, pp. 7, 11–12; no. 7, p. 2; no. 14, p. 1.

54. Wallace transcript, no. 7, p. 6; Margolick, "In Death as in Life"; interview with George C. Wallace, Jr., March 4, 1993; Wallace, with Gregory, *Wallaces of Alabama*, pp. 100, 122–28.

55. Wallace, with Gregory, *Wallaces of Alabama*, pp. 100, 122.

14: *Waking a Sleeping Giant*

1. Interview with Bill Jones, February 15, 1993.

2. Ibid.; Jody Carlson, *George C. Wallace and the Politics of Powerlessness* (New Brunswick: Transaction Books, 1981), p. 72; recollections of Gerald Lubenow, of *Newsweek* (hereafter referred to as Lubenow recollections), November 1, 1968.

3. Interview with Bill Jones; Carlson, *Politics of Powerlessness*, pp. 72–76.

4. "Meet the Press," NBC, transcript, April 23, 1967.

5. Recollections of Bill Cook, of *Newsweek*, March 12, 1968.

6. Tom Wicker, "George Wallace: A Gross and Simple Heart," *Harper's Magazine*, April, 1967, pp. 42, 45, 49.

7. Wallace invited reporters to dine with him even though several had angered him over the years by depicting his inelegant table manners. In 1971, when I was asked to join him and Mrs. Wallace for lunch at the governor's mansion, he told her, "You watch. He's gonna have me wipin' off my mouth with the back of my hand and makin' suckin' sounds with my teeth." As he was speaking, he had a fleck of rice on his cheek, a smudge of gravy on his chin, had just spit loudly into his linen napkin, and was busily picking at his teeth with his fingernails. Later, he tossed a stack of mail onto the stewed tomatoes on his plate and, not noticing, transferred the letters to the inside pocket of his suit coat. Wallace's eating habits were illustrative of his compulsive nature; eating was a chore to be gotten through as quickly as possible so he could get back to the business of politics.

8. Wicker, "A Gross and Simple Heart," p. 43.

9. James J. Kilpatrick, "What Makes Wallace Run?" *National Review*, April 18, 1967, p. 402.

10. Lubenow recollections, April 28, 1967.

11. Kilpatrick, "Wallace Run?" p. 409.

12. Lubenow recollections, April 28, 1967.

13. Ibid.; "The Spoiler," *Newsweek*, May 8, 1967, p. 39.

14. George Gallup, "Wallace Hurts GOP in South," *Washington Post*, April 23, 1967, p. 1G.

15. Warren Weaver, Jr., "Romney Cautions South on Wallace," *New York Times*, May 2, 1967, p. 31; "Johnson Strategists Bank on South in '68," *New York Times*, May 11, 1967, pp. 1, 33.

16. Kilpatrick, "Wallace Run?" p. 408.

17. Kilpatrick, "Wallace Run?"; Donald Janson, "Wallace Is Pleased by Receptions in Wisconsin and Michigan," *New York Times*, June 19, 1967, p. 20.

18. Recollections of Jane Brumley, of *Newsweek*, May 5, 1967.

19. George Gallup, *The Gallup Report*, June 7, 1967.

20. Carlson, *Politics of Powerlessness*, p. 80.

21. Kenneth Crawford, "What George Is Doing," *Newsweek*, May 22, 1967, p. 45.

22. Tom Wicker, "In the Nation: Minor Parties, Major Problem," *New York Times*, June 1, 1967, p. 42.

23. Carlson, *Politics of Powerlessness*, p. 77.

24. Gene Roberts, "Wallace Developing an Informal Campaign Style," *New York Times*, September 24, 1967, p. 66; "Wallace Refuses to Pass Pickets in San Francisco," *New York Times*, October 28, 1967, p. 32; James R. Dickenson, "George Wallace Is the Cicero of the Cab Driver," *National Observer*,

December 4, 1967, p. 1; Ward Just, "Discontent Is the Mood of Wallace Audiences," *Washington Post*, November 12, 1967, p. 1B; Carlson, *Politics of Powerlessness*, p. 78.

25. Carlson, *Politics of Powerlessness*, pp. 78–79.

26. "The Big Issue: Five Positions on Vietnam," *Newsweek*, July 10, 1967.

27. Interviews with Bill Jones on March 12, 1992, and February 15, 1993.

28. Wallace never disputed the court's assertion, but rather argued that "if that number of people wanted an individual like George Wallace on the ballot in Ohio, then the law that kept him off the ballot was unconstitutional" (Wallace transcript, no. 2, p. 15). By election day in 1968, the American Independent party was called by six different names, including the Conservative party in Kansas and the Courage party in New York. The campaign was well under way before a party platform was issued, and a vice-presidential nominee was not selected until a month before the election.

29. Wallace transcripts: no. 2, p. 15; no. 26, p. 5; "Stand Up for George," *Newsweek*, December 4, 1967, p. 31; recollections of Bob Giles (journalist; Akron, Ohio), September 12, 1968.

30. Interview with Bill Jones, February 15, 1993.

31. Neil Maxwell, "Wallace Commandeers Officials in Alabama for His Campaign Bid," *Wall Street Journal*, December 7, 1967.

32. Ibid.

33. Tom Wicker, "In the Nation: Wallace's Powerful Medicine," *New York Times*, December 12, 1967, p. 46; "California Countdown," *Newsweek*, January 1, 1968, p. 13.

34. Wallace transcript, no. 13, p. 12; Carlson, *Politics of Powerlessness*, p. 73.

35. Carlson, *Politics of Powerlessness*, p. 73; "California Countdown," *Newsweek*; "A New Look at Wallace—What He May Do to the Election," *U.S. News & World Report*, January 29, 1968, p. 57.

36. "Stand Up for George," *Newsweek*.

37. Russell Baker, "Observer: George in Gooseland," *New York Times*, January 2, 1968, p. 36.

38. "Wallace Is Termed a 'Flaming Liberal' by Kirk of Florida," *New York Times*, December 8, 1967, p. 28.

39. Recollections of Phil Carter, of *Newsweek*, February 8, 1968 (hereafter referred to as P. Carter recollections).

40. Ben A. Franklin, "Wallace in Race; Will 'Run to Win,' " *New York Times*, February 9, 1968, p. 21.

41. P. Carter recollections.

42. Richard L. Strout, "Does Wallace Candidacy Signal Split of Democratic Coalition?" *Christian Science Monitor*, February 10, 1968, p. 10.

43. Ben A. Franklin, "As a 'Spoiler,' Wallace Could Produce a National Crisis," *New York Times*, February 11, 1968, p. 4E.

44. United Press International (UPI), "Bingham Proposes a Runoff Ballot," February 14, 1968.

45. "Threat of Wallace," Letter to the *New York Times* from Professor Walter S. G. Kohn, Normal, Illinois, February 22, 1968, p. 30.

46. UPI, "Scott Says That Wallace Is 'Menace' to Everybody," February 18, 1968.

47. Ben A. Franklin, "Wallace Backed in Pennsylvania," *New York Times*, February 20, 1968, p. 29. Actually, before Wallace arrived in Pennsylvania, his supporters had gathered a thousand more signatures than required to put him on the state's ballot.

48. "Coast Leaders Split," *New York Times*, February 9, 1968, p. 21; "Wallace Groups in Widening Split," *New York Times*, February 16, 1968.

49. Doris Kearns, *Lyndon Johnson and the American Dream* (New York: Harper & Row, 1976), p. 338.

50. U.S. Senator Birch Bayh of Indiana, for whom I was press secretary at the time, passed the White House strategy along to me shortly after he had met with several Johnson aides concerning the 1968 elections.

51. *Encyclopaedia Britannica Yearbook*, 1968, p. 642.

52. *Facts on File 1968 Yearbook* (New York: Facts on File, 1968), listings under March 6, March 7, September 12, September 17, October 13, and November 2.

53. Kearns, *Lyndon Johnson*; Stephan Lesher, *Media Unbound: The Impact of Television Journalism on the Public* (Boston: Houghton Mifflin, 1982), p. 95.

54. Kearns, *Lyndon Johnson*, pp. 4, 348–50; interview with Bill Jones, February 15, 1993.

55. Recollections of Drake Mabry, of the *Des Moines Register*, March 6, 1968; *Montgomery Advertiser*, special sec., p. 27.

56. Wallace transcripts: no. 2, p. 32; no. 22, pp. 14–16.

57. Ben A. Franklin, "Double Loss for Wallace," *New York Times*, May 12, 1968, p. 3E.

58. Ibid.

59. Neil Maxwell, "Death of Lurleen May Portend Closer Ties between Alabama, Rest of U.S.," *Wall Street Journal*, May 8, 1968.

60. "Kickbacks Laid to Wallace Ally," *New York Times*, April 6, 1968, p. 15; "Suit against a Wallace Aide Settled out of Court," *New York Times*, May 24, 1968, p. 15.

61. *Facts on File 1968 Yearbook*, p. 221.

62. Lubenow recollections; interview with Bill Jones, February 15, 1993.

63. Recollections of Joseph B. Cumming, of *Newsweek*, June 14, 1968 (hereafter referred to as Cumming recollections).

64. Because a number of rabbis in the South (most of them Reform

Jews) were among the region's most outspoken critics of segregation—and their synagogues frequent targets of midnight bombings—it is often assumed that prominent Southern Jews shunned, if not actively opposed, Wallace. Many, in fact, visibly supported him—some, like his long-time chum Dave Silverman, because they genuinely liked him; others because they, like most other white Southerners, supported segregation as their "traditional way of life"; and, I suspect, most out of fear. In the mid-1950s, when I wrote an article for *Look* about a Protestant minister in Georgia who opposed segregation, many Jews—including my stepmother-in-law—said flatly that a Jew had no business writing such a piece; my name on such an article would expose *all* Jews to community ostracism. And, at the height of the Montgomery bus boycott, one Jewish merchant—a gentle, thoughtful man named Yale Friedlander—told me with heartfelt remorse, "If not for them [blacks], they'd come after us."

65. Wallace transcript, no. 31, pp. 11–12.

66. Cumming recollections; Carter, pp. 8–10; interviews with George Wallace, Joe Azbell, and Charles Snider, December 27 and 28, 1990; interview with Bill Jones, February 15, 1993; recollections of Walt Thatcher, of the *Jacksonville Journal*, June 20, 1968.

67. Cumming recollections.

68. Louis Harris, "The Harris Survey," *Los Angeles Times Syndicate*, July 15, 1968.

69. Recollections of Warren Koon (journalist; Charleston, South Carolina), June 20, 1968.

70. Recollections of Charles Whiteford, of the *Baltimore Sun*, June 20, 1968.

71. Recollections of Frank Morgan, of *Newsweek*, July 25, 1968.

72. Cumming recollections, September 5, 1968.

73. Robert G. Spivack, *The Spivack Report* 3 (July 15, 1968).

74. Ibid.

75. "Worrying about the Wallace Impact," *Business Week*, August 17, 1968, p. 98.

76. Jules Witcover, "George Wallace's Potential for Mischief," *Progressive*, July, 1968, p. 18.

77. Susanna McBee, "The Wallace Clout," *Life*, August 2, 1968, pp. 17–21.

78. Ibid.; recollections of *Newsweek* correspondents: Frank Morgan, July 26, 1968; Samuel Shaffer, August 14, 1968; and Jon Lowell, September 5, 1968 (hereafter referred to, respectively, as Morgan, Shaffer, or Lowell recollections).

79. Lowell recollections; recollections of Don Holt, of *Newsweek*, September 6, 1968; recollections of Steve Ball, of the *Atlanta Constitution*, September 5, 1968.

80. In my view, a correct assessment.

81. Recollections of Marshall Frady, September 5, 1968 (hereafter referred to as Frady recollections).

82. Cumming recollections, September 5, 1968 (quoting Robert Sherrill from the May 8, 1967, issue of *Nation*).

83. Nathan Glazer, "The Negro's Stake in America's Future," *New York Times Magazine*, September 22, 1968, pp. 30, 31, 90, 92, 94, 96, 99, 100, 102, 104.

84. Cumming recollections, September 5, 1968.

85. Ibid., September 6, 1968; Holt recollections, September 13, 1968.

86. Lubenow recollections, October 11, 1968.

87. Val Adams, "ABC Charges Wallace Aide Seized Film of Shelton Greeting," *New York Times*, June 28, 1968, p. 83.

88. Recollections of Andrew Jaffe, of *Newsweek*, September 27, 1968 (hereafter referred to as Jaffe recollections); Wallace transcript, no. 31, pp. 9–11.

89. The performers often included The Taylor Sisters, Mona and Lisa, the latter sister a nineteen-year-old blonde who would become the third Mrs. George Wallace fifteen years later.

90. Lubenow recollections, September 5 and 19, 1968; interview with Charles Snider, December 27, 1990; Jim Hampton, "Suddenly, Mr. Wallace Figures He's a Winner," *National Observer*, September 23, 1968.

91. Jaffe and Lubenow recollections, September 26, 1993.

92. Lesher, *Media Unbound*, pp. 99–100.

93. Jaffe and Lubenow recollections, September 26, 1993.

94. George Lardner, Jr., "The Governor Drives a One-Man Bandwagon," *Washington Post*, September 22, 1968, p. 5B; Hampton, "Suddenly, Mr. Wallace," p. 9.

95. Hampton, "Suddenly, Mr. Wallace."

96. Lubenow recollections, October 17, 1968.

97. "The Public Record of George C. Wallace," *Congressional Quarterly*, September 27, 1968, p. 2564.

98. Ibid., p. 2565.

99. Lubenow recollections, October 17, 1968; Stanley Karnow, *Vietnam: A History* (New York: Viking Press, 1983), p. 581.

100. *Facts on File 1968 Yearbook*, p. 422.

101. Samuel Lubell, "North Carolina Leaning toward Wallace Despite Its Prosperity," United Feature Syndicate, October 3, 1968.

102. Norman C. Miller, "Why Wallace?" *Wall Street Journal*, September 27, 1968.

103. Jaffe recollections, October 25, 1968.

104. Douglas Kiker, "Red Neck New York: Is This Wallace Country?" *New York*, October 1, 1968, p. 27.

105. Lubenow recollections, September 5, 1968.

106. Joseph A. Loftus, "Chandler Suggests a 'Mr. Big' Decides for Wallace," *New York Times*, September 18, 1968, pp. 1, 28; Wallace transcript, no. 26, pp. 13–14.

107. Alfonso A. Narvaez, "Gen. Curtis E. LeMay Dies at Eighty-three; Architect of Strategic Air Power," *New York Times*, October 2, 1990, p. 6B; Karnow, *Vietnam*, pp. 41, 325, 399–400. Karnow reported that LeMay advocated massive bombing despite his participation in secret war games in 1963 and 1964, which indicated that even half a million U.S. combat troops supported by saturation bombing of North Vietnam would not exhaust the Communists' will to fight and die for their cause.

108. Wallace transcript, no. 14, pp. 21–22.

109. *Facts on File 1968 Yearbook*, p. 422.

110. Interview with Charles Snider, December 27, 1990; Jules Wicover, *Marathon: The Pursuit of the Presidency, 1972–1976* (New York: Viking, 1977), p. 266.

111. Lubenow recollections, October 11, 1968.

112. "Gallup Poll Shows a Humphrey Gain; Nixon Leads, 43–31," *New York Times*, October 22, 1968, p. 1.

113. "Harris Poll Gives Nixon 40–37 Lead," *New York Times*, November 2, 1968, p. 22.

114. Interview with Bill Jones, February 15, 1993.

115. Wallace transcript, no. 21, p. 10.

116. Interview with Bill Jones, February 15, 1993; interview with Charles Snider; recollections of Stephan Lesher, of *Newsweek*, November 16, 1971 (hereafter referred to as Lesher recollections).

117. *Facts on File 1968 Yearbook*, p. 423.

118. Wallace transcript, no. 23, pp. 14–15.

119. Wallace transcript, no. 11, p. 11; Lawrence J. Goodrich, "Third-Party Candidates Aren't Rare," *Christian Science Monitor*, June 2, 1992, p. 8.

120. Walter Rugaber, "Wallace Is Left with Nostalgia," *New York Times*, December 8, 1968, p. 1.

121. "Wallace in Defeat," *Newsweek*, November 18, 1968.

122. Ibid.; Rugaber, "Wallace Is Left."

123. Interview with Charles Snider; interview with Joe Azbell, December 27, 1990; Homer Bigart, "Wallace Has No 'Political Plans,' but His Staff in Alabama Is Larger Than That of National Democrats," *New York Times*, June 2, 1969, p. 34.

124. Wallace transcripts: no. 4, p. 20; no. 7, p. 3.

125. Richard Scammon, "Wallace Will Keep on Trying," *Washington Post*, September 22, 1968, pp. 1B, 5B.

126. Lesher recollections, September 15, 1969.

127. Ibid.

128. Wallace transcript, no. 21, p. 10.

15: *Triumph and Tragedy*

1. Recollections of Stephan Lesher, of *Newsweek* (hereafter referred to as Lesher recollections), June 4, 1970.

2. *Montgomery Advertiser*, special section, January 11, 1987, pp. 27–28 (hereafter referred to as *Montgomery Advertiser*, special sec.).

3. Ibid., p. 28.

4. Interview with Charles Snider, December 27, 1990.

5. Lesher recollections, September 15, 1969; Richard Spong, "The Wallace Party Meets," *Editorial Research Reports*, July 11, 1969.

6. General Abrams, ironically, had been the Justice Department's military adviser in Tuscaloosa during Wallace's 1963 "stand" at the University of Alabama; during their meeting in Saigon six and a half years later, neither mentioned the incident (Wallace transcript, no. 25, p. 5).

7. Recollections of Paul Brinkley-Rogers, of *Newsweek*, November 13, 1969 (hereafter referred to as Brinkley-Rogers recollections).

8. Ibid.

9. "Meet the Press," NBC, transcript, November 30, 1969; Stanley Karnow, *Vietnam: A History* (New York: Viking, 1983), pp. 589–92. The clandestine bombing of Cambodia was officially acknowledged in 1973 and fueled the growing congressional clamor for President Nixon's impeachment.

10. Wallace transcript, no. 23, p. 3.

11. *Montgomery Advertiser*, special sec., p. 28.

12. Ray Jenkins, "Is Wallace Running Uphill?" *Christian Science Monitor*, March 18, 1970.

13. William Greider, "George Wallace: Portrait of a Candidate Running Scared," *Washington Post*, April 20, 1970.

14. Greider, "George Wallace"; Jenkins, "Is Wallace."

15. Lesher recollections, June 4, 1970.

16. David E. Rosenbaum, "Kalmbach Says Strangers Got $400,000 From Him," *New York Times*, July 18, 1973, pp. 1, 22.

17. Lesher recollections; interview with Charles Snider, December 27, 1990; Greider, "George Wallace"; Jenkins, "Is Wallace."

18. Lesher recollections; *Encyclopaedia Britannica Yearbook*, 1969, pp. 653–54.

19. *Montgomery Advertiser*, special sec., pp. 22–23, 26, 28; Mark Pazniokas, "Candidates Find Bid for Mainstream to Be Swim against Tide," *Hartford Courant*, March 30, 1992, p. 1A; "Two Rivals Woo Alabama Loser," *New York Times*, May 17, 1970, p. 71. In 1974, Woods ran for lieutenant governor and led the first Democratic primary but lost the runoff. He later moved to Lake Tahoe, Nevada, and in 1992, at the age of seventy, entered several Democratic presidential primaries, campaigning principally by buying television time to show a twenty-eight-minute documentary of his life. At

the time, he owned ten television stations and three radio stations across the country.

20. Lesher recollections; Greider, "George Wallace."

21. Lesher recollections.

22. Ibid.

23. United Press International (UPI), "Brochure Backs Wallace," *New York Times*, May 22, 1970, p. 46.

24. *Montgomery Advertiser*, special sec., p. 28.

25. Dan Carter, "The Nixon Cover-Up Goes On," *New York Times*, July 25, 1988, p. 17A; "George's Brother, Gerald, a Regular on State Scene," *Birmingham News*, January 11, 1987, p. 11A. The disclosure that Wallace was the first target of the Justice Department's government corruption unit came from Ira DeMent, the U.S. attorney in Montgomery from 1969 to 1977 who, in 1993, became a U.S. circuit court judge for Alabama's middle district.

26. In 1987, President Reagan named Sessions director of the Federal Bureau of Investigation.

27. Interview with D. Broward Segrest (assistant U.S. attorney; Montgomery, Alabama), April 12, 1993; Lesher recollections, March 17, 1972; Bruce Oudes, ed., *From: The President—Richard Nixon's Secret Files* (New York: Harper & Row, 1988), pp. 118–19.

28. Lesher recollections.

29. "Wallace Brother Assails Newsman," *New York Times*, April 16, 1970; Oudes, *From: The President*, pp. 119, 121.

30. "George's Brother," *Birmingham News*.

31. Reuters, "George Wallace's Brother Fined $100,000 for Tax Evasion," March 10, 1990; interview with Jim Wilson (U.S. attorney; Montgomery, Alabama), July 28, 1993.

32. From the moment the investigation of Gerald Wallace was suspended, there was widespread speculation that George had entered into a "deal" with President Nixon: if the White House called its dogs off Gerald, George would run in 1972 as a Democrat rather than on a third-party ticket. As discussed in this chapter, however, no one connected with the investigation, including William Sessions, lends credence to the rumors; in addition, as is discussed, Wallace was persuaded by his campaign director to run in the Democratic primaries for reasons wholly unconnected to Gerald. And, until he was shot, he regularly held out the threat of running on a third-party ticket unless he was "treated with respect" at the 1972 Democratic National Convention.

33. D. Broward Segrest, the assistant U.S. attorney in Montgomery, who was among the lead investigators into possible corruption in the Wallace administrations, told the author on April 12, 1993, that the probe focused on "loyal Wallacites [who] did a helluva lot of business with the state." The alleged payoffs to Wallace, he said, were believed to be disguised

by indirect buying of political ads or by placement of Wallace campaign workers on their payrolls. But, except for nabbing Trammell, the investigators came up empty. "One thing's for sure," Segrest said, "we never got sufficient direct evidence of anything on George."

34. Segrest interview; Wallace transcript, no. 24, pp. 5–6; "Ex-Aide to Wallace Is Guilty of Evading U.S. Tax on Bribes," *New York Times*, September 16, 1972, p. 13; "Parole Unit Denies Plea by Gallagher," *New York Times*, January 29, 1974, p. 38. Soon after the Trammell indictment, Nixon rewarded Sessions, then forty-one, by naming him the U.S. attorney for the western district of Texas. Late in 1974, President Ford put Sessions on the federal bench, and in 1987, President Reagan selected him to head the FBI. After being elevated by three successive Republican administrations, a fourth, that of George Bush, concluded that Sessions had been guilty of serious ethical (and possibly legal) lapses, including having enjoyed numerous personal and family trips at government expense. Almost six years to the day after being named FBI director, Sessions was fired by President Clinton, who concluded Sessions could no longer effectively lead the agency.

35. Wallace transcript, no. 24, p. 6.

36. Ibid.; Lesher recollections, March 17, 1972.

37. Lesher recollections, June 4, 1970.

38. *Montgomery Advertiser*, special sec., p. 29.

39. Interview with Charles Snider, December 27, 1990.

40. Lesher recollections.

41. Ibid.

42. Ibid.

43. *Encyclopaedia Britannica Yearbook*, 1970, p. 631.

44. Lesher recollections, March 17, 1972.

45. Ibid., June 4, 1970.

46. Ibid., March 17, 1970.

47. Ibid.

48. Ibid.

49. Stewart Alsop, "Wallace and the Shape of Politics," *Newsweek*, May 4, 1970, p. 108.

50. Lesher recollections, June 4 and June 8, 1970.

51. Lesher recollections, June 4, 1970.

52. Ibid.

53. *Montgomery Advertiser*, special sec., p. 29.

54. Lesher recollections, June 4, 1970.

55. "Primaries: Leaning Toward the Right," *Time*, June 15, 1970, p. 14.

56. R. W. Apple, Jr., "Elections: Wallace Victory May Affect '72 Race," *New York Times*, June 7, 1970, IV, p. 1.

57. Confidential memorandum from Tom Turnipseed to Governor Wallace and General Hardin, December 1969 (hereafter referred to as

Turnipseed memorandum), George C. Wallace papers, University of Alabama at Birmingham (UAB) (hereafter referred to as Wallace papers, UAB).

58. Interview with George Wallace, December 27, 1990.

59. Ibid., December 29, 1990; Jay Horning, "Cornelia Has Slowed Down a Bit, but Keeps Writing," *St. Petersburg Times*, January 18, 1987, p. 13A; Joy Billington, "Getting in Gear for '72," *Washington Star*, December 5, 1971, p. 1F; author's conversations with Cornelia Wallace, November and December 1971 (hereafter referred to as Cornelia Wallace conversations).

60. Stephan Lesher, "Who Knows What Evil Lurks in the Hearts of 'X' Million Americans? George Wallace Knows—and He's Off and Running," *New York Times Magazine*, January 2, 1972, pp. 9, 32, 33, 35.

61. Ibid.; interview with George Wallace, December 27, 1990; Cornelia Wallace conversations; author's conversations with Ruby Folsom Ellis Austin, November and December 1971, and May 1972 (hereafter referred to as Ruby Austin conversations); PR Newswire, "John A. Snively Elementary School Receives $750,000 Grant," April 16, 1991.

62. Interview with George Wallace, December 27, 1990; Cornelia Wallace conversations; Ruby Austin conversations.

63. Interview with George Wallace, December 27, 1990; Cornelia Wallace conversations; Ruby Austin conversations; Myra McPherson, "Drying Out with Big Ruby," *Washington Post*, April 15, 1979, p. 1B. Variations of Ruby's condescending remark about Wallace's height have appeared in newspaper accounts by both Myra McPherson and Sally Quinn in the *Washington Post*; the version appearing here is the one Ruby used in telling me the story in December 1971.

64. Billington, "Getting in Gear"; Lesher, "Who Knows What"; David Davidson, "Who Said That? Other Wild and Wacky Kin," *Atlanta Constitution*, March 29, 1992, p. 1M.

65. Billington, "Getting in Gear,"; James C. Clark, "The First Tourist Attraction Came in 1936," *Orlando Sentinel Tribune*, April 5, 1992, p. 5; Cornelia Wallace conversations; Ruby Austin conversations.

66. Draft of a letter from Cornelia Ellis Snively to "Mary and John" of Key West, July 6, 1970, Wallace papers, UAB; letter to Cornelia Ellis Snively from "Erlyn" of Daphne, Alabama, August 3, 1970, Wallace papers, UAB; Cornelia Wallace conversations.

67. Interview with George Wallace, December 27, 1990; Cornelia Wallace conversations; Horning, "Cornelia Has Slowed Down"; "Wallace Weds Divorcee in Alabama," *New York Times*, January 5, 1971, p. 32.

68. Lesher, "Who Knows What"; Lesher recollections, January 21, 1971.

69. Lesher recollections, January 21, 1971.

70. Lesher, "Who Knows What."

71. Interview with Charles Snider, December 27, 1990.

72. Turnipseed memorandum.

73. Interview with George Wallace, December 28, 1990.

74. Author's conversations with Tom Turnipseed, July 1971 (hereafter referred to as Turnipseed conversations); interview with Charles Snider, December 27, 1990.

75. Turnipseed memorandum.

76. Interview with Charles Snider, December 27, 1990.

77. Ibid.

78. Interview with William Sessions, July 29, 1993.

79. Lesher, "Who Knows What"; interview with George Wallace, December 10, 1971.

80. Wallace transcript, no. 5, p. 3; *Montgomery Advertiser*, special sec., p. 30.

81. Interview with Charles Snider, December 27, 1990.

82. Ibid.; "New York Seeks to Ban Wallace's Fund-Raiser," *New York Times*, December 22, 1975, p. 17; "Carswell Backers Ask Campaign Aid," *New York Times*, May 29, 1970, p. 59; William Greider, "That Season Again," *Washington Post*, August 30, 1971.

83. Lesher, "Who Knows What."

84. Ibid.

85. Interview with Charles Snider, December 27, 1990.

86. Lesher, "Who Knows What."

87. Lesher recollections, November 16, 1971.

88. AP, "Wallace and Humphrey to Discuss Rural U.S.," *New York Times*, July 8, 1971, p. 25.

89. "Richard Nixon on the Cuff-Link Trail," *Newsweek*, June 7, 1971, p. 26.

90. *Encyclopaedia Britannica Yearbook*, 1971, p. 597.

91. Lesher recollections, August 13, 1971; Greider, "That Season Again."

92. James T. Wooten, "Either Way, Mr. Wallace Gets What He Wants," *New York Times*, August 22, 1971, p. 3E.

93. "Meet the Press," NBC transcript, August 22, 1971.

94. Ibid.

95. William Greider, "Gov. Wallace Urges Parents to Fight Busing," *Washington Post*, August 27, 1971, p. 2A.

96. Lesher, "Who Knows What."

97. Lesher recollections, November 9, 1971.

98. Lesher recollections, November 16, 1971.

99. Lesher recollections, November 22 and 26, 1971.

100. Lesher, "Who Knows What."

101. Ibid.

102. Lesher recollections, March 14, 1972.

103. Ibid.

104. Kenneth Auchincloss and Stephan Lesher, "They Have to Listen Now," *Newsweek*, March 27, 1972.

105. Lesher recollections, March 14, 1972.

106. Wallace interview, July 17, 1987.

107. Wallace transcript, no. 7, p. 17; Eleanor Clift, "The Better Half," *Newsweek*, May 15, 1972, p. 34.

108. Lesher recollections, March 14, 1972.

109. Auchincloss and Lesher, "Listen Now," p. 24.

110. Lesher recollections, March 14, 1972.

111. Auchincloss and Lesher, "Listen Now," p. 23.

112. Lesher recollections, March 14, 1972.

113. Auchincloss and Lesher, "Listen Now," p. 24.

114. Ibid.

115. James T. Wooten, "Humphrey's Busing View Linked to Wallace Stand," *New York Times*, February 25, 1972, p. 22.

116. Lesher recollections, January 6 and March 14, 1972; "A Jarring Message from George," *Time*, March 27, 1972, p. 22.

117. Lesher recollections, March 16 and 17, 1972.

118. Lesher recollections, March 16, 1972.

119. "Retreat from Integration," *Time*, March 27, 1972, p. 21.

120. Lesher recollections, March 17, 1972.

121. Frank Trippett, "'Lordy, Ain't It Sweet!'" *Life*, March 31, 1972.

122. "The Lessons of Florida," *Time*, March 27, 1972.

123. Lesher recollections, April 20, 1972; Jody Carlson, *George C. Wallace and the Politics of Powerlessness* (New Brunswick: Transaction Books, 1981), pp. 144–45; George Lardner, "Wallace Aims Protest Drive at Taxes," *Washington Post*, pp. 1A-2A.

124. Carlson, *Politics of Powerlessness*, p. 146.

125. Ibid., p. 149.

126. Ibid., pp. 147–48; Lesher recollections, April 20, 1972; recollections of Hugh Aynesworth, of *Newsweek*, May 3, 1972 (hereafter referred to as Aynesworth recollections).

127. Wallace transcript, no. 26, pp. 12–13; Lesher recollections, April 20, 1972.

128. Ibid.; "Jarring Message," *Time*, pp. 24–25.

129. Quoted in Lesher, "Who Knows What."

130. Lesher recollections, May 18, 1972.

131. Quoted by James Jones, of *Newsweek*, Michael F. Wendland, *Detroit News*, May 16, 1972.

132. "George Wallace's Appointment in Laurel," *Time*, May 29, 1972, p. 18; recollections of *Newsweek* correspondents Nicholas Horrock, Robert Shogan, Evert Clark, Nancy Ball, Tom DeFrank, Diane Camper, Tom Joyce,

and Stephan Lesher, May 16–18, 1972 (hereafter referred to as recollections of Horrock et al.).

133. Recollections of Horrock et al.

134. Lesher recollections, May 18, 1972; Warren Weaver, Jr., "Shooting Suspect Shouted: 'Hey George! Over Here!' " *New York Times*, May 16, 1972, p. 34.

135. "George Wallace's Appointment," *Time*, p. 19.

136. Recollections of Horrock et al.

137. Ibid.

138. "George Wallace's Appointment," *Time.*

139. Interview with George Wallace, July 17, 1987.

140. Lesher recollections, May 18, 1972.

141. Charles Snider and William Neely, "George Wallace," unpublished essay, p. 15.

142. Recollections of Horrock et al.

143. Garry Wills, "Wallace Agonistes," *New York*, July 10, 1972, pp. 48–51.

144. "George Wallace's Appointment," *Time*; "One Sick Assassin," *Time*, August 14, 1972, p. 22; Carl Bernstein and Bob Woodward, *All the President's Men* (New York: Simon & Schuster, 1974), p. 326.

145. Seymour M. Hersh, "Nixon's Last Cover-Up: The Tapes He Wants the Archives to Suppress," *New Yorker*, December 14, 1992, p. 76; Bernstein and Woodward, *All the President's Men*, pp. 326–28; recollections of Horrock et al. In June 1973, Hunt, then in jail for his part in the Watergate break-in a year earlier, disclosed to a Senate attorney Colson's directive to break into Bremer's apartment. Colson flatly denied it to the *Washington Post* reporter Bob Woodward, who included the denial in a subsequent story. The reporter Seymour Hersh learned of Nixon's personal involvement by discovering the contents of some White House tapes still being withheld from the public. Colson, twenty years after denying the story to Woodward, admitted its validity to Hersh: "Nixon said, 'It'd be great to get [Hunt] out there and put some things in [Bremer's apartment].' But I don't know which one of us actually said, 'Too bad we can't plant McGovern literature.' "

146. AP, "Wallace's Son Wants New Inquiry into 1972 Assassination Attempt," *New York Times*, December 14, 1992, p. 14A.

147. Hersh, "The Pardon: Nixon, Ford, Haig, and the Transfer of Power," *Atlantic*, August, 1983, p. 55.

148. To me, the heart-stopping aspect of Hersh's revelation is that it unequivocally brands Nixon as the reprehensible crook he claimed not to be. Nixon had been forced out of office because of his role in covering up the break-in at Democratic party headquarters; there is no evidence that he ordered the break-in or even knew about it in advance. But a month before the Watergate break-in, the president ordered his subordinates to enter the apartment of the man who had just shot a presidential candidate, plant

phony evidence, possibly affect the outcome of the nominating and electoral processes, and perhaps skew the conclusions that investigators might reach concerning the safety of all future campaigners. The episode brands Nixon as a morally bankrupt felon who made it clear that any act, regardless of its illegality, would be condoned and protected if it served the president's ambitions.

149. Homer Bigart, "Bremer Guilty in Shooting of Wallace, Gets Sixty-three Years," *New York Times*, August 5, 1972, p. 1.

150. "George Wallace's Appointment," *Time*, p. 20.

151. Carlson, *Politics of Powerlessness*, p. 148.

152. Ibid., pp. 148–49; "Credentials Committee Votes, 72–66, to Reapportion California Votes," *New York Times*, June 30, 1972, p. 1.

153. "Credentials Committee," *New York Times*.

154. According to the July 11, 1972, issue of the *New York Times*, the composition of the Democratic National Convention was "the most unusual in many decades." Ninety percent of the participants were first-timers in a national convention; 40 percent were women; 25 percent were under age thirty; 14 percent were blacks; only 10 percent were union members; and only sixty members of Congress obtained delegate seats.

155. Ibid.

156. Letter from Jimmy Faulkner, Bay Minette, Alabama, to Paul Harvey, Chicago, November 8, 1979, Wallace papers, UAB.

157. Ibid.

158. Interview with Charles Snider, December 27, 1990.

159. Ibid.

160. Max Frankel, "McGovern Wins by Big Margin on Disputed California Seats," *New York Times*, July 11, 1972, p. 1.

161. Interview with Charles Snider, December 27, 1990.

162. Faulkner letter.

163. Ibid.; R. W. Apple, Jr., "Convention Notes: Irate Leader of Ohio Bloc Says It's His 'Last Go at This,'" *New York Times*, July 12, 1972, p. 20; Frankel, "McGovern Wins."

164. Frankel, "McGovern Wins."

165. Wallace transcripts: no. 11, pp. 18–19; no. 14, p. 4.

166. Interview with Norman Sherman, July 29, 1993.

167. Wallace transcript, no. 14, pp. 4–6.

168. James T. Wooten, "Wallace Tells Convention He Wants to Help Party," *New York Times*, July 12, 1972, p. 1.

169. Kevin Phillips, *The Politics of Rich and Poor: Wealth and the American Electorate in the Reagan Aftermath* (New York: Random House, 1990), p. 64n.

170. Thomas Byrne Edsall, with Mary D. Edsall, "The Real Subject Is Race," *Atlantic*, May 1991, pp. 62–63.

171. Interview with Norman Sherman, July 29, 1993.

Epilogue: *The Last Political Mountain*

1. Jody Carlson, *George C. Wallace and the Politics of Powerlessness* (New Brunswick: Transaction Books, 1981), pp. 183–84; Jon Nordheimer, "Wallace Rebounds from Despair," *New York Times,* May 14, 1973, p. 1; "Wallace Raises $1.3 Million, Widening Fund Lead," *New York Times,* July 15, 1975, p. 17.

2. Carlson, *Politics of Powerlessness,* pp. 188–89, 194; *Montgomery Advertiser,* special section, January 11, 1987, p. 31 (hereafter referred to as *Montgomery Advertiser,* special sec.).

3. Carlson, *Politics of Powerlessness,* pp. 184–85, 192–93.

4. Carlson, *Politics of Powerlessness,* pp. 209–10; Jules Witcover, *Marathon: The Pursuit of the Presidency, 1972–1976* (New York: Viking, 1977), pp. 237, 254.

5. Witcover, *Marathon,* pp. 334–38; Carlson, *Politics of Powerlessness,* pp. 212–18.

6. Carlson, *Politics of Powerlessness,* pp. 214, 218–19.

7. Interviews with George Wallace, George Snider, and Elvin Stanton, July 1987 and December 1990.

8. *Montgomery Advertiser,* special sec., pp. 32–33; interviews with George Wallace, July 17, 1987, and December 27, 1990.

9. *Montgomery Advertiser,* special sec., p. 39.

10. William E. Schmidt, "Ending an Era, Wallace Announces He Will Retire," *New York Times,* April 3, 1986, p. 1A; Associated Press (AP), "George Wallace Divorced from Third Wife," February 3, 1987.

11. Bessie Ford, "Lee Wallace to Marry," United Press International (UPI), March 6, 1983; UPI, "Alabama Judges Appointed," March 18, 1983; Gregory Gordon, "Wallace Son-in-Law Linked to Waste Firm," UPI, March 23, 1983; Associated Press (AP), "Wallaces Divorce," February 3, 1987; "E. C. Dothard, State Trooper," *New York Times,* December 17, 1989, p. 60; Bill Hewitt and Ron Ridenhour, "Another Wallace in Alabama," *Time,* June 29, 1992, p. 65; Yemi Toure, "Newsmakers," *Los Angeles Times,* January 7, 1992, p. 1E; "Gerald O. Wallace," *Washington Post,* August 6, 1993, p. 32.

12. Lance Morrow, "I Spoke . . . As a Brother," *Time,* January 9, 1984, p. 27; Lance Morrow, "George Wallace Overcomes," *Time,* October 11, 1982, p. 15; Michael Hirsley, "Alabama Voters Reluctantly Give Up Wallace," *Chicago Tribune,* June 6, 1986, p. 5; Schmidt, "Ending an Era."

13. Dan Carter, "George Wallace and the Politics of Rage," unpublished essay, June 1990, p. 12.

14. Ibid.

15. *Montgomery Advertiser,* special sec., p. 41.

16. Interview with George Wallace, January 7, 1991.

17. Diane McWhorter, "Maybe We Needed George Wallace," *Wall Street Journal,* June 27, 1986, p. 16.

18. The author was present during the July 20, 1987, meeting.

Index

Acknowledgments

The act of writing a book is a lonely pursuit, but its development involves hundreds of people whose time and talents—and their willingness to share them—turn ideas into tangible reality.

Research into a person's life and times by a nonacademic holding down a full-time job requires the support of people who help open doors and provide guidance to the mountains of documents and books that shed illuminating, accurate glimpses into the past. My former colleagues at *Newsweek* offered me access to their rich collection of newspapers, magazines, reference books, and other materials, and allowed me to read and work in their library whenever I pleased. Of special help to me were *Newsweek*'s contributing editor, Peter Goldman, the best news magazine writer of his generation, and *Newsweek*'s research director, Ted Slate, and his staff, who not only responded to my every request fully and warmly but also often anticipated my needs and helped me fulfill them.

In Washington, U.S. Rep. Bill Nichols of Alabama obtained on my behalf the use of a small office in the Library of Congress that I shared with Neil Sheehan, who then was nearing the end of his long effort to produce *A Bright and Shining Lie*. The perquisite of a Library of Congress research office meant that the books and materials one requested were delivered to the office and could be retained there as long as one liked, and a copying machine and telephones, though not free, were close at hand. To a researcher, it was pig heaven. Dr.

Marvin Kranz, an American history specialist at the library (and an old friend), compiled a list of the hundreds of books, manuscripts, and collections in the library that furnished insight into my subject. As important, he directed me away from the hundreds of other books that experience had taught him would prove of little help. Through Marvin's good offices, Mary Wolfskill and David Wigdor in the library's manuscript room helped me sort through thousands of documents and private papers that added vivid, contemporaneous details to the events I was examining. Equally essential was the hospitality provided by my dear friend Virginia Martino, who saw to it that during my weeks in Washington I was well-housed and well-fed.

In Montgomery, Alabama, Mrs. Janet Sowter, librarian at the Archives of Alabama, provided similar direction and support as I pored through the stacks of official papers, letters, memoranda, and reports of the five administrations of George and Lurleen Wallace. In Birmingham, Jerry Stephens and Steve Laughlin offered access to the private papers and memorabilia of George and Lurleen Wallace stored on the balcony of the closed-shelves area of the library at the University of Alabama, Birmingham. Because funds were unavailable to properly catalogue the papers, the materials were piled helter-skelter amid overturned metal shelves, discarded and torn cartons, water-stained rugs, a broken wheelchair (the good ones had been donated to the university's medical clinics), boxes stuffed with photos, scrapbooks, video and audio tapes, and other mementos of a lifetime. Ploughing (a word I use advisedly) through this material was a physical as well as intellectual adventure, but I often found treasure at the end of the hunt. Al Morrison, the now-retired Montgomery branch manager of IBM, supplied indispensable use of an IBM PC during my trips to Alabama; Al and his lovely wife, Shirley, also supplied indispensable friendship. Milt Livingston, an advertising executive of the *Montgomery Advertiser* and a transplanted Northerner, not only shared his comfortable townhouse with me but also his insights into the sense of victimization that continues to plague many Southerners. Fred Burger of the *Anniston Star* provided a wealth of background material.

Many people were generous with their time—George Wallace's former aides, family, friends, and enemies; journalists who witnessed the events that Wallace confronted or, in some cases, wrought; public officials, civil rights activists, and others who played a role, willingly or otherwise, in Wallace's career. Their views and observations give fullness and perspective to Wallace's story. But no one was more magnanimous with his time than Elvin Stanton, Wallace's long-time executive assistant. His knowledge of Alabama politics, his help in encouraging the cooperation of sometimes recalcitrant individuals and institutions, his provision of a continuous conduit between me and Wallace, and his own keen recollections of Wallace's career were essential to the book's preparation. Wallace himself provided more than sixty hours of interviews, remembrances, and dictated responses to written questions—this despite his continuing serious infirmities. My old friend and former colleague, the award-winning photographer Joe Holloway, volunteered some of his brilliant pictures of Wallace, one of which graces the jacket of this book.

Writers traditionally tell horror stories of their publishers, but I have nothing but praise and gratitude for the people of Addison-Wesley—the wise and incisive editing of William Patrick; the gentle prodding and unflagging support of his colleague, Sharon Broll; the thorough professionalism and encouragement of the production editor, Beth Burleigh; the meticulous and perceptive copy editing of Sharon Sharp; Karen Savary's handsome text design; and the enthusiasm of the marketing team. They all cared about this book, and it shows.

Finally, there are always those special few without whom the book would not have seen the light of day. In this case, there were four: my agent, neighbor, and friend, Gerard McCauley, who saw to it that the book was placed in the hands of publishers who believed in it; my good pals, Irv Rosen of Chicago and the late Jack McDonald of South Salem, New York, who believed in me and who consistently cheered the project on; and most of all my wife, Nancy, whose commentaries, criticisms, ideas, patience, and, especially, love saw me through.

Stephan Lesher
Katonah, New York
October 1993